The Complete Works
of
Lewis Carroll

BARNES
& NOBLE
CLASSICS

The Complete Works
Of
Lewis Carroll

Lewis Carroll

Illustrations by Sir John Tenniel

BARNES
&NOBLE
BOOKS
NEW YORK

This edition published by Barnes & Noble, Inc.

2001 Barnes & Noble Books

ISBN 0-7607-3001-6 *paperback*

Printed and bound in the United States of America

01 02 03 04 MP 9 8 7 6 5 4 3 2 1

RRD-H

CONTENTS

INTRODUCTION
BY LEONARD S. MARCUS   I

I. ALICE'S ADVENTURES IN WONDER-LAND

1. Down the Rabbit-Hole   15
2. The Pool of Tears   23
3. A Caucus-Race and a Long Tale   31
4. The Rabbit Sends in a Little Bill   38
5. Advice from a Caterpillar   48
6. Pig and Pepper   57
7. A Mad Tea-Party   68
8. The Queen's Croquet Ground   76
9. The Mock Turtle's Story   86
10. The Lobster-Quadrille   95
11. Who Stole the Tarts?   104
12. Alice's Evidence   111

II. THROUGH THE LOOKING-GLASS

PREFACE TO 1896 EDITION   126
1. Looking-Glass House   129
2. The Garden of Live Flowers   143
3. Looking-Glass Insects   154
4. Tweedledum and Tweedledee   165
5. Wool and Water   179
6. Humpty Dumpty   191
7. The Lion and the Unicorn   203
8. "It's My Own Invention"   214
9. Queen Alice   229
10. Shaking   246
11. Waking   246
12. Which Dreamed It?   247

III. SYLVIE AND BRUNO

PREFACE 255
1. Less Bread! More Taxes! 264
2. L'Amie Inconnue 271
3. Birthday-Presents 277
4. A Cunning Conspiracy 284
5. A Beggar's Palace 290
6. The Magic Locket 298
7. The Baron's Embassy 305
8. A Ride on a Lion 311
9. A Jester and a Bear 317
10. The Other Professor 324
11. Peter and Paul 331
12. A Musical Gardener 337
13. A Visit to Dogland 345
14. Fairy-Sylvie 352
15. Bruno's Revenge 363
16. A Changed Crocodile 370
17. The Three Badgers 376
18. Queer Street, Number Forty 386
19. How to Make a Phlizz 394
20. Light Come, Light Go 402
21. Through the Ivory Door 410
22. Crossing the Line 421
23. An Outlandish Watch 431
24. The Frogs' Birthday-Treat 439
25. Looking Eastward 450

IV. SYLVIE AND BRUNO CONCLUDED

PREFACE 461
1. Bruno's Lessons 473
2. Love's Curfew 482
3. Streaks of Dawn 490
4. The Dog-King 498
5. Matilda Jane 505
6. Willie's Wife 513
7. Mein Herr 519
8. In a Shady Place 527
9. The Farewell-Party 535
10. Jabbering and Jam 545
11. The Man in the Moon 553

12. Fairy-Music 560
13. What Tottles Meant 569
14. Bruno's Picnic 578
15. The Little Foxes 589
16. Beyond These Voices 596
17. To the Rescue! 603
18. A Newspaper-Cutting 613
19. A Fairy-Duet 615
20. Gammon and Spinach 627
21. The Professor's Lecture 636
22. The Banquet 644
23. The Pig-Tale 652
24. The Beggar's Return 661
25. Life Out of Death 670

V. VERSE

THE HUNTING OF THE SNARK

PREFACE 677
Fit the First 680
   (The Landing)
Fit the Second 683
   (The Bellman's Speech)
Fit the Third 686
   (The Baker's Tale)
Fit the Fourth 688
   (The Hunting)
Fit the Fifth 690
   (The Beaver's Lesson)
Fit the Sixth 694
   (The Barrister's Dream)
Fit the Seventh 696
   (The Banker's Fate)
Fit the Eighth 698
   (The Vanishing)

EARLY VERSE

My Fairy 700
Punctuality 701
Melodies 702
Brother and Sister 702
Facts 703

Rules and Regulations   704
Horrors   705
Misunderstandings   706
As It fell upon a Day   707
Ye Fattale Cheyse   707
Lays of Sorrow, No. 1   709
Lays of Sorrow, No. 2   712
The Two Brothers   716
The Lady of the Ladle   721
Coronach   722
She's All my Fancy painted Him   723
Photography Extraordinary   724
Lays of Mystery, Imagination, and Humour, No. 1: 725
    The Palace of Humbug
The Mock Turtle's Song (Early version)   727
Upon the Lonely Moor   727
Miss Jones   730

PUZZLES FROM WONDERLAND

Puzzles   733
Solutions   735

PROLOGUES TO PLAYS

Prologue to "La Guida di Bragia"   737
Prologue   737
Prologue   739

PHANTASMAGORIA

Phantasmagoria
    Canto   I: The Trysting   741
    Canto   II: Hys Fyve Rules   745
    Canto   III: Scarmoges   748
    Canto   IV: Hys Nouryture   752
    Canto   V: Byckerment   756
    Canto   VI: Discomfyture   760
    Canto VII: Sad Souvenaunce   764
Echoes   765
A Sea Dirge   766
Ye Carpette Knyghte   768
Hiawatha's Photographing   768
Melancholetta   772
A Valentine   775

The Three Voices 776
Theme with Variations 788
A Game of Fives 789
Poeta Fit, non Nascitur 790
Size and Tears 793
Atalanta in Camden-Town 795
The Lang Coortin' 797
Four Riddles 802
Fame's Penny-Trumpet 807

COLLEGE RHYMES AND NOTES
BY AN OXFORD CHIEL

Ode to Damon 809
Those Horrid Hurdy-Gurdies! 811
My Fancy 811
The Majesty of Justice 812
The Elections to the Hebdomadal Council 815
The Deserted Parks 823
Examination Statute 826

ACROSTICS, INSCRIPTIONS,
AND OTHER VERSE

Acrostic: Little maidens, when you look 827
To three puzzled little Girls, from the Author 828
Double Acrostic: I sing a place wherein agree 828
Three Little Maids 830
Puzzle 830
Three Children 831
Two Thieves 832
Two Acrostics: Round the wondrous globe 832
                 Maidens, if a maid you meet 833
Double Acrostic: Two little girls near London dwell 833
Acrostic: "Are you deaf, Father William?" 834
Acrostic: Maidens! if you love the tale 834
Acrostic: Love-lighted eyes, that will not start 835
To M. A. B. 836
Acrostic: Maiden, though thy heart may quail 836
Madrigal 837
Love among the Roses 837
Two Poems to Rachel Daniel 838
The Lyceum 839
Acrostic: Around my lonely hearth to-night 840

Dreamland 841
To my Child-Friend 842
A Riddle 842
A Limerick 843
Rhyme? and Reason? 843
A Nursery Darling 843
Maggie's Visit to Oxford 844
Maggie B—— 848

THREE SUNSETS AND OTHER POEMS

Three Sunsets 849
The Path of Roses 852
The Valley of the Shadow of Death 856
Solitude 860
Beatrice 861
Stolen Waters 863
The Willow-Tree 867
Only a Woman's Hair 868
The Sailor's Wife 870
After Three Days 872
Faces in the Fire 875
A Lesson in Latin 876
Puck Lost and Found 877

VI. STORIES

A Tangled Tale 883
Novelty and Romancement 970
A Photographer's Day Out 979
Wilhelm von Schmitz 986
The Legend of Scotland 999

VII. A MISCELLANY

The Offer of the Clarendon Trustees 1009
The New Method of Evaluation 1011
The Dynamics of a Parti-cle 1016
The New Belfry of Christ Church, Oxford 1026
The Vision of the Three T's 1036
The Blank Cheque 1054
Twelve Months in a Curatorship 1060
Three Years in a Curatorship 1064
Resident Women-Students 1068

Some Popular Fallacies about Vivisection 1071
Lawn Tennis Tournaments 1082
Eight or Nine Wise Words about Letter Writing 1091
What the Tortoise said to Achilles 1104
The Two Clocks 1108
Photography Extraordinary 1109
Hints for Etiquette; or, Dining Out made Easy 1113
A Hemispherical Problem 1115
A Selection from Symbolic Logic 1116
Rules for Court Circular 1140
Croquet Castles 1143
Mischmasch 1146
Doublets 1147
A Postal Problem 1153
The Alphabet-Cipher 1156
Introduction to *The Lost Plum Cake* 1158

INDEX OF FIRST LINES OF VERSE 1161

—————————————————————————————

As far as can be ascertained, the following pieces have never appeared in print except in their original editions. We are grateful to Mr. Morris L. Parrish for his courtesy in allowing us to copy them from the originals in his collection.

> "Resident Women-Students"
> "Some Popular Fallacies about Vivisection"
> "Lawn Tennis Tournaments"
> "Rules for Court Circular"
> "Croquet Castles"
> "Mischmasch"
> "Doublets"
> "A Postal Problem"
> "The Alphabet-Cipher"
> "Introduction to *The Lost Plum Cake*"

CHRONOLOGICAL TABLE

1845	My Fairy
1845	Punctuality
1845	Melodies
1845	Brother and Sister
1845	Facts
1845	Rules and Regulations
1849	Hints for Etiquette; or, Dining Out made Easy
1849	A Hemispherical Problem
1850	Horrors
1850	Misunderstandings
1850	As It fell upon a Day
1850–1853	Ye Fattale Cheyse
1850–1853	Lays of Sorrow, No. 1
1850–1853	Lays of Sorrow, No. 2
1853	The Two Brothers
1853	Solitude
1854	Wilhelm von Schmitz
1854	The Lady of the Ladle
1854	Coronach
1855	She's All my Fancy painted Him
1855	Photography Extraordinary
1855	Lays of Mystery, Imagination, and Humour, No. 1: The Palace of Humbug
1856	Upon the Lonely Moor
1856	Ye Carpette Knyghte
1856	The Three Voices
1856	The Path of Roses
1856	Novelty and Romancement
1856–1860	The Legend of Scotland
1857	Hiawatha's Photographing
1857	The Sailor's Wife
1859	The Willow-Tree
1860	Faces in the Fire
1860	A Photographer's Day Out
1860	Rules for Court Circular
1860	A Valentine
1860–1863	Poeta Fit, non Nascitur
1861	A Sea Dirge

1861	Ode to Damon
1861	Those Horrid Hurdy-Gurdies!
1861	Acrostic: Little maidens, when you look
1861	Three Sunsets
1861	After Three Days
1862	My Fancy
1862	Beatrice
1862	Stolen Waters
1862	Only a Woman's Hair
1862	The Mock Turtle's Song (Early version)
1863	Croquet Castles
1863	Size and Tears
1863	The Majesty of Justice
1864	Examination Statute
1865	The New Method of Evaluation
1865	The Dynamics of a Parti-cle
1865	Alice's Adventures in Wonderland
1866	The Elections to the Hebdomadal Council
1867	The Deserted Parks
1868	The Valley of the Shadow of Death
1868	The Offer of the Clarendon Trustees
1868	The Alphabet-Cipher
1869	Phantasmagoria
1869	Melancholetta
1869	Theme with Variations
1869	Atalanta in Camden Town
1869	The Lang Coortin'
1869	To three puzzled little Girls, from the Author
1869	Double Acrostic: I sing a place wherein agree
1869	Three Little Maids
1870	Puzzles from Wonderland
1871	Prologue (p. 737)
1871	Prologue to "La Guida di Bragia"
1871	Three Children
1872	Two Thieves
1872	The New Belfry of Christ Church, Oxford
1872	Through the Looking-Glass
1873	Prologue (p. 740)
1873	The Vision of the Three T's
1874	The Blank Cheque
1875	Some Popular Fallacies about Vivisection
1876	The Hunting of the Snark

1876	Fame's Penny-Trumpet
1876	Acrostic: "Are you deaf, Father William?"
1876	Acrostic: Maidens! if you love the tale
1876	Acrostic: Love-lighted eyes, that will not start
1876	Acrostic: Maiden, though thy heart may quail
1877	Madrigal
1878	Love among the Roses
1879	Doublets
1880	A Tangled Tale
1880, 1881	Two Poems to Rachel Daniel
1881	The Lyceum
1882	Dreamland
1882	Mischmasch
1883	Echoes
1883	A Game of Fives
1883	Rhyme? and Reason?
1883	Lawn Tennis Tournaments
1884	Twelve Months in a Curatorship
1886	To my Child-Friend
1886	Three Years in a Curatorship
1888	A Lesson in Latin
1889	Sylvie and Bruno
1889	A Nursery Darling
1889	Maggie's Visit to Oxford
1890	Eight or Nine Wise Words about Letter Writing
1891	Maggie B——
1891	Puck Lost and Found
1891	A Postal Problem
1893	Sylvie and Bruno Concluded
1894	What the Tortoise said to Achilles
1895	A Selection from Symbolic Logic
1896	Resident Women-Students
1897	Introduction to *The Lost Plum Cake*
N.D.	Miss Jones
N.D.	Four Riddles (p. 802)
N.D.	Puzzle (p. 830)
N.D.	Acrostics : Round the wondrous globe
	Maidens, if a maid you meet
	Around my lonely hearth to-night
N.D.	A Riddle (p. 842)
N.D.	A Limerick (p. 843)
N.D.	To M. A. B.

INTRODUCTION

CHARLES LUTWIDGE DODGSON (1832–1898), the man whom the world knows as Lewis Carroll, is most often recalled in caricature, as a perfect specimen of the prudish bachelor and eccentric Oxford don, a sort of Victorian nutty professor with a predilection (innocent or otherwise) for the companionship of young girls. "Lewd Carroll," as James Joyce remarked, summarizing a body of suspicion that gathered force in the overheated atmosphere of the 1920s and 30s surrounding Freud's oracular pronouncements on sex, repression, the unconscious, and our dreams. Critics of those years tended either to eye Carroll's best known literary fantasies as "products of the author's subconscious mind," as A. M. E. Goldschmidt ventured to do in 1933; or, contrariwise, as Edmund Wilson observed, to "revel" nostalgically in the Wonderland creator's "delightfulness and cuteness but [without giving] him any serious attention."

The 1932 centenary of Carroll's birth, Wilson reported at the time, had failed to inspire even one significant reappraisal of that "most interesting man"'s varied literary output, a large proportion of which had by then been allowed to go out of print. Yet, said Wilson, "The truth is that, if Dodgson and his work were shown as an organic whole, his 'nonsense' would not seem the anomaly which it is usually represented as being." From his magisterial high perch at the *New Republic*, Wilson proceeded to call for England's Nonesuch Press to publish a Carroll omnibus on the plan of the firm's Blake and Donne compilations. In 1936, the press obliged by issuing an edition with an introduction by Alexander Woollcott in which, strikingly under the circumstances, Woollcott chose to

I

confine his breezy remarks almost entirely to Carroll as author of the Alice books. Casting his lot with the nostalgia buffs over the Freudians (and ignoring altogether the third possibility signalled by Wilson), Woollcott concluded: "Those of us whose own memories of childhood are inextricably interwoven with all the gay tapestry of *Alice* ... would rather leave unexplored the shy, retreating man who left so much bubbling laughter in his legacy to the world."

Yet *Alice's Adventures in Wonderland* (1865) and its "Looking-Glass" sequel (1872) are themselves among the most defiantly unsentimental, least nostalgic books ever written for children or about childhood. And while critics have long since taken note of this fact (see, for instance, the essays collected in *Aspects of Alice*, edited by Robert Phillips), most Carrollians probably have yet to look much beyond the author's two most famous comic provocations to see where the Alices belong within the larger context of Lewis Carroll's many-sided creativity. The present volume (which does not include *The Russian Journal*, Carroll's one travel book, or the bulk of Carroll's scientific writings) is herewith offered as remedy to readers curious to do so.

Carroll was a conscious experimenter in the fields of children's literature, photography, and, as has only recently come to be appreciated, in mathematics and logic, the two disciplines he taught. His first book for young readers, as has often been told, had its origins in a story improvised during a summer's outing for the entertainment of three small children, the daughters of the Dean of Christ Church, Oxford, where the thirty-year-old Dodgson was then Mathematical Lecturer. That was in 1862; and when later that year he yielded to the middle sister Alice Liddell's request that he write the story down, he produced a homemade book for her (handwritten, self-illustrated) in time for Christmas. One of the best known children's books till then, Heinrich Hoffmann's *Struwwelpeter* (or, *Slovenly Peter*; 1845) had had similar beginnings, as a

Frankfurt pediatrician's present for his son. Hoffmann had gone shopping for a suitable gift book and, having found all the selections either saccharine or moralistic, had returned home with a blank notebook and set himself to work in a highstrung spirit of parody. In the first of the Alice books (which literary friends persuaded Dodgson to publish, and which he chose to do under a pseudonym), Carroll likewise reserved some of his most pointed satire for the didactic tradition of children's literature, with its battery of scare tactics and penchant for deceptively clear-cut pronouncements on good and bad behavior. In Wonderland, Alice searches her memory in vain for lessons learned from such books that might now serve her:

> *for she had read several nice little histories about children who had got burnt, and eaten by wild beasts, and many other unpleasant things, all because they* would *not remember the simple rules their friends had taught them: such as, that a red-hot poker will burn you if you hold it too long; and that, if you cut your finger* very *deeply with a knife, it usually bleeds. . . .*

Slouching through Wonderland, Alice never gets her wish for an all-purpose "book of rules," but she does learn not to put undue faith in sham books like those often offered her contemporaries.

Carroll was just as contemptuous of the sentimental strain of children's literature that Hoffmann before him had found inadequate. Hardly the fey nature sprite of such books, Alice considers "in her own mind . . . whether the pleasure of making a daisy-chain [is] worth the trouble of getting up and picking the daisies." She clearly has a good head on her shoulders (though the changing relationship of that head to its young mistress's body proves a source not just of some of *Wonderland*'s most hilarious set pieces but of its most powerful representations of the complex rhythms of growing up).

Alice is most remarkable however for the fact that for

much of the narrative she is made to seem such an utterly disagreeable character. Alice is demanding, petty, snobbish, domineering, selfish, rude—not someone the reader would likely wish to know, much less *be*. In this, the Alice books make a striking departure from traditional types of narrative centered on the exploits of a conventionally worthy hero or heroine. Carroll's game is rather the more extravagant one of entangling readers in a sort of Wonderland/Looking-Glass predicament of their own, a challenging maze of puzzling images, logical conundrums, and ambiguous characters and remarks, a world of shifting contexts and elastic intentions, in which virtually nothing can be taken for granted. Like Alice, readers are thrown back on their wits to grapple as best they can with the ludicrous spectacle of pot-tossing parents, cardboard soldiers, ineffectual kings and queens, and other equally unworthy authority figures. The Alice books comprise a bracing, as well as outrageously funny guide to what not to believe. Writers as varied as Franz Kafka, André Breton, Vladimir Nabokov, W. H. Auden, and Groucho Marx have found them instructive.

In his photographs of children, Carroll captured something very like the Alices' spirit of clear-eyed skepticism and intelligent curiosity. That Carroll in his mid-twenties took up photography as a serious avocation, less than twenty years after the camera's invention, is itself a reflection of his own curiosity and predisposition to experiment. And in "Photography Extraordinary," an early squib, he makes a sly case for photography as an art form by conjuring up the absurdity of a camera-like device capable of producing memorable novels by strictly mechanical means. Carroll's point was that if a viewer is genuinely moved by a photograph, something more than a technological trick must be responsible. When his own best images of child subjects are placed beside those of his most celebrated contemporary, Julia Margaret Cameron, one sees too that Carroll lifted Romanticism's often-hazy veil for a harder-edged, more psychologically acute type of portraiture.

His portraits of young girls in the nude—for obvious reasons the subject of much of the malicious speculation about the man—were in fact, with one known exception, among his more conventional photographic images. The elaborate hand-tinting that Carroll commissioned for three of the four extant photographs of this kind effectively clothed them in layers of idealized innocence. (James Joyce notwithstanding, the evidence bearing on the making of the photographs tends to confirm Carroll's own innocence in the enterprise.) But the fourth surviving nude photograph is unmistakably erotic in tenor. That portrait, like passages in the Alice books in which the heroine chucks her good manners for a romp in the fast lane of her more primitive drives, more likely marks Carroll as a precursor of Freud, however, than as a would-be patient.

The word games Carroll invented are still good fun for people who like that sort of thing. "Doublets"—a game involving a series of letter substitutions by means of which a starting word (black, for example) is changed into an antonym of the same number of letters (white)—can also be read as a playful gloss on the Wonderland insight that language has a life of its own quite apart from that which we intend for it. The letter-by-letter transformations of Doublets—cat-cot-cog-dog—recall, on the literal plane, Alice's freefall descent down the Rabbit-hole, during the course of which words she thought she knew run together in her mind and become interchangeable once she realizes they lack the power to save her: "And here Alice . . . went on saying to herself, . . . 'Do cats eat bats? Do cats eat bats?' and sometimes, 'Do bats eat cats?' for, you see, as she couldn't answer either question, it didn't much matter which way she put it." And in Looking-Glass Land, Humpty Dumpty sounds less than convincing when he boasts: "When *I* use a word . . . it means just what I choose it to mean—neither more or less. . . . The question is . . . which is to be master—that's all." Which indeed. As Carroll demonstrates time and again, words rarely stand in perfect alignment with the meanings we assign to them. When held up to close inspection, "opposites" generally are found to rest on arbitrary assumptions that cloud, not clarify our thoughts.

Carroll, the son of a High Church cleric and himself a Church deacon, was a devoutly religious man. Perhaps no detail of his biography has proven more bothersome for some of his admirers (those who have wanted to imagine him *only* as an iconoclast). Detractors in turn have cited his piety as evidence in itself of a fundamentally repressed or divided nature. It is also possible however to see Carroll's authorship of the Alice books, and of his other major nonsense work, "The Hunting of the Snark," as wholly consistent with his religious convictions, especially as the latter impinged on his belief in the spiritual purity of children. Nonsense writing suited Carroll in part because he took it for granted that the young were too knowing to mistake the genre's wild characters and plots for real world signs and reflections. Children were capable both of smiling over the Alices and of seriously contemplating God's word. As he sensibly proposed in the preface to *Sylvie and Bruno* (1889), a skillfully abridged, well-illustrated Bible might have a better chance of holding young readers' interest than the ponderous standard editions then being offered them for study. And in his introduction to E. G. Wilcox's "The Lost Plum Cake," he proposed that children in church be permitted to read for pleasure rather than be forced to attend to long, potentially interest-deadening sermons. Alice among the hymnals sounds so improbable at first, but Carroll's sympathetic concern for children's needs supplies the common thread.

Sylvie and Bruno and its sequel *Sylvie and Bruno Concluded* (1893) together constitute Carroll's most ambitious literary experiment. Meandering, polyphonic fantasies for advanced Carrollians, they met with a cool reception in the author's lifetime, and were thereafter all but forgotten until quite recently. In the Carroll centenary exhibition held at Columbia University in the spring of 1932, the two books were relegated to the section devoted to "minor works." By the time of the next important Carroll celebration a half century later, however, scholars had begun to offer more positive appraisals of books that the author himself had counted among his major achievements. This elevation in critical standing has, it seems clear, resulted only in part from the perennial need for new grist for the publish-or-perish academic mill (or, publish-*and*-perish, as Carroll himself would doubtless have thought more precise). The "Sylvie and Bruno" books can be read for all the pleasures and insights that an extraordinary artist's sketchbooks might be expected to yield: memorable aphorisms; brilliant comic set pieces, like the one (in the chapter in *Sylvie and Bruno* called "An Outlandish Watch") in which everything happens in reverse action; and asides that shed light on the author's creative process. There is less of moralizing, and a good deal more of highspirited virtuosity in the two books than one might ever have guessed from their old, still-lingering reputation. Moreover, the element of melodramatic romance and the supposedly sentimentalized portrayal of the story's child protagonists—both of which have often been cited as flaws— seem now, for post-modern readers, to have acquired a beguiling, strangely cartoonish aspect. It is as though in his search for connecting links between the spiritual dimension of human experience and the purely intellectual dimension (which had been the focus of his earlier writings *on* logic and *in* the nonsense vein), Carroll deliberately appropriated, and collaged together, a range of the most conventional narrative forms and types available to him, as a means to the visionary end of looking past all artifice.

Carroll's search for essentials took many forms. In a letter written in July 1885 to a child friend's mother, Carroll, who was then 53, took the occasion to reflect on the varieties of religious faith. "My dear father," he wrote, had been a " 'High Church' man . . .

and I have seen little cause to modify the views I learned from him, though perhaps I regard the holding of different views as a less important matter than he did. As life draws nearer to its end, I feel more and more clearly that it will not matter *in the least* [Carroll's emphasis], at the last day, what *form* of religion a man has professed."

Time and again, the legendary donnishness proves to have amounted to little more than the gentlemanly outward dress of this unfettered, extraordinarily open mind.

—Leonard S. Marcus

I
Alice's Adventures
in
Wonderland

All in the golden afternoon
   Full leisurely we glide;
For both our oars, with little skill,
   By little arms are plied,
While little hands make vain pretence
   Our wanderings to guide.

Ah, cruel Three! In such an hour,
   Beneath such dreamy weather,
To beg a tale of breath too weak
   To stir the tiniest feather!
Yet what can one poor voice avail
   Against three tongues together?

Imperious Prima flashes forth
   Her edict "to begin it":
In gentler tones Secunda hopes
   "There will be nonsense in it!"
While Tertia interrupts the tale
   Not *more* than once a minute.

Anon, to sudden silence won,
   In fancy they pursue
The dream-child moving through a land
   Of wonders wild and new,
In friendly chat with bird or beast—
   And half believe it true.

And ever, as the story drained
   The wells of fancy dry,
And faintly strove that weary one
   To put the subject by,
"The rest next time—" "It *is* next time!"
   The happy voices cry.

Thus grew the tale of Wonderland:
    Thus slowly, one by one,
Its quaint events were hammered out—
    And now the tale is done,
And home we steer, a merry crew,
    Beneath the setting sun.

Alice! A childish story take,
    And, with a gentle hand,
Lay it where Childhood's dreams are twined
    In Memory's mystic band.
Like pilgrim's wither'd wreath of flowers
    Pluck'd in a far-off land.

CHRISTMAS-GREETINGS

[FROM A FAIRY TO A CHILD]

LADY dear, if Fairies may
    For a moment lay aside
Cunning tricks and elfish play,
    'Tis at happy Christmas-tide.

We have heard the children say—
    Gentle children, whom we love—
Long ago, on Christmas-Day,
    Came a message from above.

Still, as Christmas-tide comes round,
    They remember it again—
Echo still the joyful sound
    "Peace on earth, good-will to men!"

Yet the hearts must child-like be
    Where such heavenly guests abide;
Unto children, in their glee,
    All the year is Christmas-tide.

Thus, forgetting tricks and play
    For a moment, Lady dear,
We would wish you, if we may,
    Merry Christmas, glad New Year!

Christmas, 1867.

CHAPTER I

Down the Rabbit-Hole

ALICE was beginning to get very tired of sitting by her sister on the bank and of having nothing to do: once or twice she had peeped into the book her sister was reading, but it had no pictures or conversations in it, "and what is the use of a book", thought Alice, "without pictures or conversations?"

So she was considering, in her own mind (as well as she could, for the hot day made her feel very sleepy and stupid), whether the pleasure of making a daisy-chain would be worth the trouble of getting up and picking the daisies, when suddenly a White Rabbit with pink eyes ran close by her.

15

There was nothing so *very* remarkable in that; nor did Alice think it so *very* much out of the way to hear the Rabbit say to itself "Oh dear! Oh dear! I shall be too late!" (when she thought it over afterwards it occurred to her that she ought to have wondered at this, but at the time it all seemed quite natural); but, when the Rabbit actually *took a watch out of its waistcoat-pocket*, and looked at it, and then hurried on, Alice started to her feet, for it flashed across her mind that she had never before seen a rabbit with either a waistcoat-pocket, or a watch to take out of it, and burning with curiosity, she ran across the field after it, and was just in time to see it pop down a large rabbit-hole under the hedge.

In another moment down went Alice after it, never once considering how in the world she was to get out again.

The rabbit-hole went straight on like a tunnel for some way, and then dipped suddenly down, so suddenly that Alice had not a moment to think about stopping herself before she found herself falling down what seemed to be a very deep well.

Either the well was very deep, or she fell very slowly, for she had plenty of time as she went down to look about her, and to wonder what was going to happen next. First, she tried to look down and make out what she was coming to, but it was too dark to see anything: then she looked at the sides of the well, and noticed that they were filled with cupboards and book-shelves: here and there she saw maps and pictures hung upon pegs. She took down a jar from one of the shelves as she passed: it was labelled "ORANGE MARMALADE" but to her great disappointment it was empty: she did not like to drop the jar, for fear of killing somebody underneath, so managed to put it into one of the cupboards as she fell past it.

"Well!" thought Alice to herself. "After such a fall as this, I shall think nothing of tumbling down-stairs! How brave they'll all think me at home! Why, I wouldn't say

anything about it, even if I fell off the top of the house!"
(Which was very likely true.)

Down, down, down. Would the fall *never* come to
an end? "I wonder how many miles I've fallen by this
time?" she said aloud. "I must be getting somewhere near
the centre of the earth. Let me see: that would be four
thousand miles down, I think——" (for, you see, Alice had
learnt several things of this sort in her lessons in the
school-room, and though this was not a *very* good opportunity for showing off her knowledge, as there was no
one to listen to her, still it was good practice to say it over)
"——yes, that's about the right distance—but then I wonder what Latitude or Longitude I've got to?" (Alice had
not the slightest idea what Latitude was, or Longitude
either, but she thought they were nice grand words to say.)

Presently she began again. "I wonder if I shall fall right
through the earth! How funny it'll seem to come out
among the people that walk with their heads downwards!
The antipathies, I think——" (she was rather glad there
was no one listening, this time, as it didn't sound at all
the right word) "——but I shall have to ask them what the
name of the country is, you know. Please, Ma'am, is this
New Zealand? Or Australia?" (and she tried to curtsey
as she spoke—fancy, *curtseying* as you're falling through
the air! Do you think you could manage it?) "And what
an ignorant little girl she'll think me for asking! No, it'll
never do to ask: perhaps I shall see it written up somewhere."

Down, down, down. There was nothing else to do, so
Alice soon began talking again. "Dinah'll miss me very
much to-night, I should think!" (Dinah was the cat.) "I
hope they'll remember her saucer of milk at tea-time.
Dinah, my dear! I wish you were down here with me!
There are no mice in the air, I'm afraid, but you might
catch a bat, and that's very like a mouse, you know. But
do cats eat bats, I wonder?" And here Alice began to get
rather sleepy, and went on saying to herself, in a dreamy
sort of way, "Do cats eat bats? Do cats eat bats?" and

sometimes "Do bats eat cats?" for, you see, as she couldn't
answer either question, it didn't much matter which
way she put it. She felt that she was dozing off, and had
just begun to dream that she was walking hand in hand
with Dinah, and was saying to her, very earnestly, "Now,
Dinah, tell me the truth: did you ever eat a bat?" when
suddenly, thump! thump! down she came upon a heap of
sticks and dry leaves, and the fall was over.

Alice was not a bit hurt, and she jumped up on to her
feet in a moment: she looked up, but it was all dark overhead: before her was another long passage, and the White
Rabbit was still in sight, hurrying down it. There was not
a moment to be lost: away went Alice like the wind, and
was just in time to hear it say, as it turned a corner, "Oh
my ears and whiskers, how late it's getting!" She was
close behind it when she turned the corner, but the
Rabbit was no longer to be seen: she found herself in a
long, low hall, which was lit up by a row of lamps hanging
from the roof.

There were doors all round the hall, but they were all
locked; and when Alice had been all the way down one

side and up the other, trying every door, she walked sadly down the middle, wondering how she was ever to get out again.

Suddenly she came upon a little three-legged table, all made of solid glass: there was nothing on it but a tiny golden key, and Alice's first idea was that this might belong to one of the doors of the hall; but, alas! either the locks were too large, or the key was too small, but at any rate it would not open any of them. However, on the second time round, she came upon a low curtain she had not noticed before, and behind it was a little door about fifteen inches high: she tried the little golden key in the lock, and to her great delight it fitted!

Alice opened the door and found that it led into a small passage, not much larger than a rat-hole: she knelt down and looked along the passage into the loveliest garden you ever saw. How she longed to get out of that dark hall, and wander about among those beds of bright flowers and those cool fountains, but she could not even get her head through the doorway; "and even if my head *would* go through", thought poor Alice, "it would be of very little use without my shoulders. Oh, how I wish I could shut up like a telescope! I think I could, if I only knew how to begin." For, you see, so many out-of-the-way things had happened lately, that Alice had begun to think that very few things indeed were really impossible.

There seemed to be no use in waiting by the little door, so she went back to the table, half hoping she might find another key on it, or at any rate a book of rules for shutting people up like telescopes: this time she found a little bottle on it ("which certainly was not here before", said Alice), and tied around the neck of the bottle was a paper label, with the words "DRINK ME" beautifully printed on it in large letters.

It was all very well to say "Drink me", but the wise little Alice was not going to do *that* in a hurry. "No, I'll look first", she said, "and see whether it's marked '*poison*' or not"; for she had read several nice little stories about children who had got burnt, and eaten up by wild beasts, and other unpleasant things, all because they *would* not remember the simple rules their friends had taught them: such as, that a red-hot poker will burn you if you hold it too long; and that, if you cut your finger *very* deeply with a knife, it usually bleeds; and she had never forgotten

that, if you drink much from a bottle marked "poison", it is almost certain to disagree with you, sooner or later.

However, this bottle was *not* marked "poison", so Alice ventured to taste it, and, finding it very nice (it had, in fact, a sort of mixed flavour of cherry-tart, custard, pineapple, roast turkey, toffee, and hot buttered toast), she very soon finished it off.

*   *   *   *

   *   *   *

  *   *   *   *

"What a curious feeling!" said Alice. "I must be shutting up like a telescope!"

And so it was indeed: she was now only ten inches high, and her face brightened up at the thought that she was now the right size for going through the little door into that lovely garden. First, however, she waited for a few minutes to see if she was going to shrink any further: she felt a little nervous about this; "for it might end, you know", said Alice to herself, "in my going out altogether, like a candle. I wonder what I should be like then?" And she tried to fancy what the flame of a candle looks like after the candle is blown out, for she could not remember ever having seen such a thing.

After a while, finding that nothing more happened, she decided on going into the garden at once; but, alas for poor Alice! when she got to the door, she found she had forgotten the little golden key, and when she went back to the table for it, she found she could not possibly reach it: she could see it quite plainly through the glass, and she tried her best to climb up one of the legs of the table, but it was too slippery; and when she had tired herself out with trying, the poor little thing sat down and cried.

"Come, there's no use in crying like that!" said Alice to herself rather sharply. "I advise you to leave off this minute!" She generally gave herself very good advice (though she very seldom followed it), and sometimes she scolded herself so severely as to bring tears into her eyes; and once she remembered trying to box her own ears for having cheated herself in a game of croquet she was playing against herself, for this curious child was very fond of pretending to be two people. "But it's no use now", thought poor Alice, "to pretend to be two people! Why, there's hardly enough of me left to make *one* respectable person!"

Soon her eye fell on a little glass box that was lying under the table: she opened it, and found in it a very small cake, on which the words "EAT ME" were beautifully marked in currants. "Well, I'll eat it," said Alice, "and if it makes me grow larger, I can reach the key; and if it makes me grow smaller, I can creep under the door: so either way I'll get into the garden, and I don't care which happens!"

She ate a little bit, and said anxiously to herself "Which way? Which way?", holding her hand on the top of her head to feel which way it was growing; and she was quite surprised to find that she remained the same size. To be sure, this is what generally happens when one eats cake; but Alice had got so much into the way of expecting nothing but out-of-the-way things to happen, that it seemed quite dull and stupid for life to go on in the common way.

So she set to work, and very soon finished off the cake.

     *   *   *   *
        *   *   *
     *   *   *   *

Chapter II

The Pool of Tears

"CURIOUSER and curiouser!" cried Alice (she was so much surprised, that for the moment she quite forgot how to speak good English). "Now, I'm opening out like the largest telescope that ever was! Good-bye, feet!" (for when she looked down at her feet, they seemed to be almost out of sight, they were getting so far off). "Oh, my poor little feet, I wonder who will put on your shoes and stockings for you now, dears? I'm sure *I* sha'n't be able! I shall be a great deal too far off to trouble myself about you: you must manage the best way you can—but I must be kind to them", thought Alice, "or perhaps they wo'n't walk the way I want to go! Let me see, I'll give them a new pair of boots every Christmas."

And she went on planning to herself how she would manage it. "They must go by the carrier," she thought; "and how funny it'll seem, sending presents to one's own feet! And how odd the directions will look!

> *Alice's Right Foot, Esq.*
> *Hearthrug,*
> *near the Fender,*
> *(with Alice's love).*

Oh dear, what nonsense I'm talking!"

23

Just at this moment her head struck against the roof of the hall: in fact she was now rather more than nine feet high, and she at once took up the little golden key and hurried off to the garden door.

Poor Alice! It was as much as she could do, lying down on one side, to look through into the garden with one eye; but to get through was more hopeless than ever: she sat down and began to cry again.

"You ought to be ashamed of yourself," said Alice, "a great girl like you", (she might well say this), "to go on crying in this way! Stop this moment, I tell you!" But she went on all the same, shedding gallons of tears, until there was a large pool around her, about four inches deep, and reaching half down the hall.

After a time she heard a little pattering of feet in the distance, and she hastily dried her eyes to see what was coming. It was the White Rabbit returning splendidly dressed, with a pair of white kid-gloves in one hand and a large fan in the other: he came trotting along in a great hurry, muttering to himself, as he came, "Oh! The Duchess, the Duchess! Oh! *Wo'n't* she be savage if I've kept her waiting!" Alice felt so desperate that she was ready to ask help of any one: so, when the Rabbit came near her, she began, in a low, timid voice, "If you please, Sir——" The Rabbit started violently, dropped the white kid-gloves and the fan, and scurried away into the darkness as hard as he could go.

Alice took up the fan and gloves and, as the hall was very hot, she kept fanning herself all the time she went on talking. "Dear, dear! How queer everything is to-day! And yesterday things went on just as usual, I wonder if I've changed in the night? Let me think: *was* I the same when I got up this morning? I almost think I can remember feeling a little different. But if I'm not the same, the next question is 'Who in the world am I?' Ah, *that's* the great puzzle!" And she began thinking over all the children she knew that were of the same age as herself, to see if she could have been changed for any of them.

"I'm sure I'm not Ada," she said, "for her hair goes in such long ringlets, and mine doesn't go in ringlets at all; and I'm sure I ca'n't be Mabel, for I know all sorts of things, and she, oh, she knows such a very little! Besides, *she's* she, and *I'm* I, and—oh dear, how puzzling it all is! I'll try if I know all the things I used to know. Let me see: four times five is twelve, and four times six is thirteen, and four times seven is—oh dear! I shall never get to twenty at that rate! However, the Multiplication-Table doesn't signify: let's try Geography. London is the capital of Paris, and Paris is the capital of Rome, and Rome—no, *that's* all wrong, I'm certain! I must have been changed for Mabel! I'll try and say '*How doth the little*——'," and she crossed her hands on her lap as if she were saying lessons, and began to repeat it, but her voice sounded hoarse and strange, and the words did not come the same as they used to do:

> "*How doth the little crocodile*
> *Improve his shining tail,*
> *And pour the waters of the Nile*
> *On every golden scale!*
>
> "*How cheerfully he seems to grin,*
> *How neatly spreads his claws,*
> *And welcomes little fishes in,*
> *With gently smiling jaws!*

"I'm sure those are not the right words," said poor Alice, and her eyes filled with tears again as she went on, "I must be Mabel after all, and I shall have to go and live in that poky little house, and have next to no toys to play with, and oh, ever so many lessons to learn! No, I've made up my mind about it: if I'm Mabel, I'll stay down here! It'll be no use their putting their heads down and saying 'Come up again, dear!' I shall only look up and say 'Who am I, then? Tell me that first, and then, if I like being that person, I'll come up: if not, I'll stay down here till I'm somebody else'—but, oh dear!" cried Alice, with a sudden burst of tears, "I do wish they *would* put their heads down! I am so *very* tired of being all alone here!"

As she said this she looked down at her hands, and was surprised to see that she had put on one of the Rabbit's little white kid-gloves while she was talking. "How *can* I have done that?" she thought. "I must be growing small again." She got up and went to the table to measure herself by it, and found that, as nearly as she could guess, she was now about two feet high, and was going on shrinking rapidly: she soon found out that the cause of this was the fan she was holding, and she dropped it hastily, just in time to save herself from shrinking away altogether.

"That *was* a narrow escape!" said Alice, a good deal frightened at the sudden change, but very glad to find herself still in existence. "And now for the garden!" And she ran with all speed back to the little door; but, alas! the little door was shut again, and the little golden key was lying on the glass table as before, "and things are

worse than ever," thought the poor child, "for I never was so small as this before, never! And I declare it's too bad, that it is!"

As she said these words her foot slipped, and in another moment, splash! she was up to her chin in salt-water. Her first idea was that she had somehow fallen into the sea, "and in that case I can go back by railway," she said to herself. (Alice had been to the seaside once in her life, and had come to the general conclusion that wherever you go to on the English coast, you find a number of bathing-machines in the sea, some children digging in the sand with wooden spades, then a row of lodging-houses, and behind them a railway station.) However, she soon made out that she was in the pool of tears which she had wept when she was nine feet high.

"I wish I hadn't cried so much!" said Alice, as she swam about, trying to find her way out. "I shall be punished for it now, I suppose, by being drowned in my own tears! That *will* be a queer thing, to be sure! However, everything is queer to-day."

Just then she heard something splashing about in the pool a little way off, and she swam nearer to make out what it was: at first she thought it must be a walrus or

hippopotamus, but then she remembered how small she was now, and she soon made out that it was only a mouse, that had slipped in like herself.

"Would it be of any use, now," thought Alice, "to speak to this mouse? Everything is so out-of-the-way down here, that I should think very likely it can talk: at any rate, there's no harm in trying." So she began: "O Mouse, do you know the way out of this pool? I am very tired of swimming about here, O Mouse!" (Alice thought this must be the right way of speaking to a mouse: she had never done such a thing before, but she remembered having seen, in her brother's Latin Grammar, "A mouse —of a mouse—to a mouse—a mouse—O mouse!") The mouse looked at her rather inquisitively, and seemed to her to wink with one of its little eyes, but it said nothing.

"Perhaps it doesn't understand English," thought Alice. "I daresay it's a French mouse, come over with William the Conqueror." (For, with all her knowledge of history, Alice had no very clear notion how long ago anything had happened.) So she began again: "Où est ma chatte?" which was the first sentence in her French lesson-book. The Mouse gave a sudden leap out of the water, and seemed to quiver all over with fright. "Oh, I beg your pardon!" cried Alice hastily, afraid that she had hurt the poor animal's feelings. "I quite forgot you didn't like cats."

"Not like cats!" cried the Mouse in a shrill passionate voice. "Would *you* like cats, if you were me?"

"Well, perhaps not," said Alice in a soothing tone: "don't be angry about it. And yet I wish I could show you our cat Dinah. I think you'd take a fancy to cats, if you could only see her. She is such a dear quiet thing", Alice went on, half to herself, as she swam lazily about in the pool, "and she sits purring so nicely by the fire, licking her paws and washing her face—and she is such a nice soft thing to nurse—and she's such a capital one for catching mice—oh, I beg your pardon!" cried Alice again, for this time the Mouse was bristling all over, and she felt certain it must be really offended. "We won't talk about her any more if you'd rather not."

"We, indeed!" cried the Mouse, who was trembling down to the end of its tail. "As if *I* would talk on such a subject! Our family always *hated* cats: nasty, low, vulgar things! Don't let me hear the name again!"

"I wo'n't indeed!" said Alice, in a great hurry to change the subject of conversation. "Are you—are you fond—of —of dogs?" The Mouse did not answer, so Alice went on eagerly: "There is such a nice little dog, near our house, I should like to show you! A little bright-eyed terrier, you know, with oh, such long curly brown hair! And it'll fetch things when you throw them, and it'll sit up and beg for its dinner, and all sorts of things—I ca'n't remember half of them—and it belongs to a farmer, you know, and he says it's so useful, it's worth a hundred pounds! He says it kills all the rats and—oh dear!" cried Alice in a sorrowful tone. "I'm afraid I've offended it again!" For the Mouse was swimming away from her as hard as it could go, and making quite a commotion in the pool as it went.

So she called softly after it, "Mouse dear! Do come back again, and we wo'n't talk about cats, or dogs either, if you don't like them!" When the Mouse heard this, it turned round and swam slowly back to her: its face was quite pale (with passion, Alice thought), and it said, in a low trembling voice, "Let us get to the shore, and then I'll tell you my history, and you'll understand why it is I hate cats and dogs."

It was high time to go, for the pool was getting quite crowded with the birds and animals that had fallen into it: there was a Duck and a Dodo, a Lory and an Eaglet, and several other curious creatures. Alice led the way, and the whole party swam to the shore.

Chapter III

A Caucus-Race and a Long Tale

THEY were indeed a queer-looking party that assembled on the bank—the birds with draggled feathers, the animals with their fur clinging close to them, and all dripping wet, cross, and uncomfortable.

The first question of course was, how to get dry again: they had a consultation about this, and after a few minutes it seemed quite natural to Alice to find herself talking familiarly with them, as if she had known them all her life. Indeed, she had quite a long argument with the Lory, who at last turned sulky, and would only say, "I'm older than you, and must know better." And this Alice would not allow, without knowing how old it was, and as the Lory positively refused to tell its age, there **was no** more to be said.

At last the Mouse, who seemed to be a person of some authority among them, called out "Sit down, all of you, and listen to me! *I'll* soon make you dry enough!" They all sat down at once, in a large ring, with the Mouse in the middle. Alice kept her eyes anxiously fixed on it, for she felt sure she would catch a bad cold if she did not get dry very soon.

"Ahem!" said the Mouse with an important air. "Are you all ready? This is the driest thing I know. Silence all round, if you please! 'William the Conqueror, whose cause was favoured by the pope, was soon submitted to by the English, who wanted leaders, and had been of late much accustomed to usurpation and conquest. Edwin and Morcar, the earls of Mercia and Northumbria——' "

"Ugh!" said the Lory, with a shiver.

"I beg your pardon!" said the Mouse, frowning, but very politely. "Did you speak?"

"Not I!" said the Lory, hastily.

"I thought you did," said the Mouse. "I proceed. 'Edwin and Morcar, the earls of Mercia and Northumbria, declared for him; and even Stigand, the patriotic archbishop of Canterbury, found it advisable——' "

"Found *what*?" said the Duck.

"Found *it*," the Mouse replied rather crossly: "of course you know what 'it' means."

"I know what 'it' means well enough, when *I* find a thing," said the Duck: "it's generally a frog, or a worm. The question is, what did the archbishop find?"

The Mouse did not notice this question, but hurriedly went on, " '—found it advisable to go with Edgar Atheling to meet William and offer him the crown. William's conduct at first was moderate. But the insolence of his Normans——' How are you getting on now, my dear?" it continued, turning to Alice as it spoke.

"As wet as ever," said Alice in a melancholy tone: "it doesn't seem to dry me at all."

"In that case," said the Dodo solemnly, rising to its

feet, "I move that the meeting adjourn, for the immediate adoption of more energetic remedies———"

"Speak English!" said the Eaglet. "I don't know the meaning of half those long words, and, what's more, I don't believe you do either!" And the Eaglet bent down its head to hide a smile: some of the other birds tittered audibly.

"What I was going to say", said the Dodo in an offended tone, "was, that the best thing to get us dry would be a Caucus-race."

"What *is* a Caucus-race?" said Alice; not that she much wanted to know, but the Dodo had paused as if it thought that *somebody* ought to speak, and no one else seemed inclined to say anything.

"Why," said the Dodo, "the best way to explain it is to do it." (And, as you might like to try the thing yourself some winter-day, I will tell you how the Dodo managed it.)

First it marked out a race-course, in a sort of circle, ("the exact shape doesn't matter," it said,) and then all the party were placed along the course, here and there. There was no "One, two, three, and away!" but they began running when they liked, and left off when they liked, so that it was not easy to know when the race was over. However, when they had been running half an hour or so, and were quite dry again, the Dodo suddenly called out "The race is over!" and they all crowded round it, panting, and asking "But who has won?"

This question the Dodo could not answer without a great deal of thought, and it stood for a long time with one finger pressed upon its forehead (the position in which you usually see Shakespeare, in the pictures of him), while the rest waited in silence. At last the Dodo said "*Everybody* has won, and *all* must have prizes."

"But who is to give the prizes?" quite a chorus of voices asked.

"Why, *she*, of course," said the Dodo, pointing to Alice

with one finger; and the whole party at once crowded round her, calling out, in a confused way, "Prizes! Prizes!"

Alice had no idea what to do, and in despair she put her hand in her pocket, and pulled out a box of comfits (luckily the salt-water had not got into it), and handed them round as prizes. There was exactly one a-piece, all round.

"But she must have a prize herself, you know," said the Mouse.

"Of course," the Dodo replied very gravely. "What else have you got in your pocket?" it went on, turning to Alice.

"Only a thimble," said Alice sadly.

"Hand it over here," said the Dodo.

Then they all crowded round her once more, while the Dodo solemnly presented the thimble, saying "We beg your acceptance of this elegant thimble"; and, when it had finished this short speech, they all cheered.

Alice thought the whole thing very absurd, but they all looked so grave that she did not dare to laugh; and, as she could not think of anything to say, she simply bowed, and took the thimble, looking as solemn as she could.

The next thing was to eat the comfits: this caused some noise and confusion, as the large birds complained that they could not taste theirs, and the small ones choked and had to be patted on the back. However, it was over at last, and they sat down again in a ring, and begged the Mouse to tell them something more.

"You promised to tell me your history, you know," said Alice, "and why it is you hate—C and D," she added in a whisper, half afraid that it would be offended again.

"Mine is a long and a sad tale!" said the Mouse, turning to Alice, and sighing.

"It *is* a long tail, certainly," said Alice, looking down with wonder at the Mouse's tail; "but why do you call it sad?" And she kept on puzzling about it while the Mouse was speaking, so that her idea of the tale was something like this:

"Fury said to
a mouse, That
he met in the
house, 'Let
us both go
to law: *I*
will prose-
cute *you*.
Come, I'll
take no de-
nial; We
must have
a trial:
For really
this morn-
ing I've
nothing
to do.'
Said the
mouse to
the cur,
'Such a
trial, dear
Sir, With
no jury
or judge,
w o u l d
be wast-
ing our
breath.'
'I'll be
judge,
I'll be
jury,'
Said
cun-
ning
old
Fury:
'I'll
t r y
the
whole
cause,
a n d
con-
demn
you to
death.' "

"You are not attending!" said the Mouse to Alice, severely. "What are you thinking of?"

"I beg your pardon," said Alice very humbly: "you had got to the fifth bend, I think?"

"I had *not*!" cried the Mouse, sharply and very angrily.

"A knot!" said Alice, always ready to make herself useful, and looking anxiously about her. "Oh, do let me help to undo it!"

"I shall do nothing of the sort," said the Mouse, getting up and walking away. "You insult me by talking such nonsense!"

"I didn't mean it!" pleaded poor Alice. "But you're so easily offended, you know!"

The Mouse only growled in reply.

"Please come back, and finish your story!" Alice called after it. And the others all joined in chorus "Yes, please do!" But the Mouse only shook its head impatiently, and walked a little quicker.

"What a pity it wouldn't stay!" sighed the Lory, as soon as it was quite out of sight. And an old Crab took the opportunity of saying to her daughter "Ah, my dear! Let this be a lesson to you never to lose *your* temper!" "Hold your tongue, Ma!" said the young Crab, a little snappishly. "You're enough to try the patience of an oyster!"

"I wish I had our Dinah here, I know I do!" said Alice aloud, addressing nobody in particular. "*She'd* soon fetch it back!"

"And who is Dinah, if I might venture to ask the question?" said the Lory.

Alice replied eagerly, for she was always ready to talk about her pet: "Dinah's our cat. And she's such a capital one for catching mice, you ca'n't think! And oh, I wish you could see her after the birds! Why, she'll eat a little bird as soon as look at it!"

This speech caused a remarkable sensation among the party. Some of the birds hurried off at once: one old Magpie began wrapping itself up very carefully, remarking "I really must be getting home: the night-air doesn't suit my throat!" And a Canary called out in a trembling voice, to its children, "Come away, my dears! It's high time you were all in bed!" On various pretexts they all moved off, and Alice was soon left alone.

"I wish I hadn't mentioned Dinah!" she said to herself in a melancholy tone. "Nobody seems to like her, down here, and I'm sure she's the best cat in the world! Oh, my dear Dinah! I wonder if I shall ever see you any more!" And here poor Alice began to cry again, for she felt very lonely and low-spirited. In a little while, however, she again heard a little pattering of footsteps in the distance, and she looked up eagerly, half hoping that the Mouse had changed his mind, and was coming back to finish his story.

CHAPTER IV

The Rabbit Sends in a Little Bill

IT was the White Rabbit, trotting slowly back again, and looking anxiously about as it went, as if it had lost something; and she heard it muttering to itself, "The Duchess! The Duchess! Oh my dear paws! Oh my fur and whiskers! She'll get me executed, as sure as ferrets are ferrets! Where *can* I have dropped them, I wonder?" Alice guessed in a moment that it was looking for the fan and the pair of white kid-gloves, and she very good-naturedly began hunting about for them, but they were nowhere to be seen—everything seemed to have changed since her swim in the pool; and the great hall, with the glass table and the little door, had vanished completely.

Very soon the Rabbit noticed Alice, as she went hunting about, and called out to her, in an angry tone, "Why, Mary Ann, what *are* you doing out here? Run home this moment, and fetch me a pair of gloves and a fan! Quick, now!" And Alice was so much frightened that she ran off at once in the direction it pointed to, without trying to explain the mistake that it had made.

"He took me for his housemaid," she said to herself as she ran. "How surprised he'll be when he finds out who I am! But I'd better take him his fan and gloves—that is, if I can find them." As she said this, she came upon a neat little house, on the door of which was a bright brass plate with the name "W. RABBIT" engraved upon it. She went in without knocking, and hurried upstairs, in great fear lest she should meet the real Mary Ann, and be turned out of the house before she had found the fan and gloves.

"How queer it seems", Alice said to herself, "to be going messages for a rabbit! I suppose Dinah'll be sending me on messages next!" and she began fancying the sort of thing that would happen: " 'Miss Alice! Come here directly, and get ready for your walk!' 'Coming in a minute, nurse! But I've got to watch this mouse-hole till Dinah comes back, and see that the mouse doesn't get out.' Only I don't think", Alice went on, "that they'd let Dinah stop in the house if it began ordering people about like that!"

By this time she had found her way into a tidy little room with a table in the window, and on it (as she had hoped) a fan and two or three pairs of tiny white kid-gloves: she took up the fan and a pair of the gloves, and was just going to leave the room, when her eye fell upon a little bottle that stood near the looking-glass. There was no label this time with the words "DRINK ME", but nevertheless she uncorked it and put it to her lips. "I know *something* interesting is sure to happen", she said to herself, "whenever I eat or drink anything: so I'll just see what this bottle does. I do hope it'll make me grow large again, for really I'm quite tired of being such a tiny little thing!"

It did so indeed, and much sooner than she had expected: before she had drunk half the bottle, she found her head pressing against the ceiling, and had to stoop to save her neck from being broken. She hastily put down the bottle, saying to herself "That's quite enough —I hope I sha'n't grow any more—As it is, I ca'n't get out at the door—I do wish I hadn't drunk quite so much!"

Alas! It was too late to wish that! She went on growing, and growing, and very soon had to kneel down on the floor: in another minute there was not even room for this, and she tried the effect of lying down with one elbow against the door, and the other arm curled round her head. Still she went on growing, and, as a last resource, she put one arm out of the window, and one foot up the chimney, and said to herself "Now I can do no more, whatever happens. What *will* become of me?"

Luckily for Alice, the little magic bottle had now had its full effect, and she grew no larger: still it was very uncomfortable, and, as there seemed to be no sort of chance of her ever getting out of the room again, no wonder she felt unhappy.

"It was much pleasanter at home", thought poor Alice, "when one wasn't always growing larger and smaller, and being ordered about by mice and rabbits. I almost wish I hadn't gone down that rabbit-hole—and yet—and yet— it's rather curious, you know, this sort of life! I do wonder

what *can* have happened to me! When I used to read fairy tales, I fancied that kind of thing never happened, and now here I am in the middle of one! There ought to be a book written about me, that there ought! And when I grow up, I'll write one—but I'm grown up now," she added in a sorrowful tone: "at least there's no room to grow up any more *here*."

"But then", thought Alice, "shall I *never* get any older than I am now? That'll be a comfort, one way—never to be an old woman—but then—always to have lessons to learn! Oh, I shouldn't like *that*!"

"Oh, you foolish Alice!" she answered herself. "How

can you learn lessons in here? Why, there's hardly room for *you*, and no room at all for any lesson-books!"

And so she went on, taking first one side and then the other, and making quite a conversation of it altogether;

but after a few minutes she heard a voice outside, and stopped to listen.

"Mary Ann! Mary Ann!" said the voice. "Fetch me my gloves this moment!" Then came a little pattering of feet on the stairs. Alice knew it was the Rabbit coming to look for her, and she trembled till she shook the house, quite forgetting that she was now about a thousand times as large as the Rabbit, and had no reason to be afraid of it.

Presently the Rabbit came up to the door, and tried to open it; but, as the door opened inwards, and Alice's elbow was pressed hard against it, that attempt proved a failure. Alice heard it say to itself "Then I'll go round and get in at the window."

"*That* you wo'n't!" thought Alice, and, after waiting till she fancied she heard the Rabbit just under the window, she suddenly spread out her hand, and made a snatch in the air. She did not get hold of anything, but she heard a little shriek and a fall, and a crash of broken glass, from which she concluded that it was just possible it had fallen into a cucumber-frame, or something of the sort.

Next came an angry voice—the Rabbit's—"Pat! Pat! Where are you?" And then a voice she had never heard before, "Sure then I'm here! Digging for apples, yer honour!"

"Digging for apples, indeed!" said the Rabbit angrily. "Here! Come help me out of *this*!" (Sounds of more broken glass.)

"Now tell me, Pat, what's that in the window?"

"Sure, it's an arm, yer honour!" (He pronounced it "arrum".)

"An arm, you goose! Who ever saw one that size? Why, it fills the whole window!"

"Sure, it does, yer honour: but it's an arm for all that."

"Well, it's got no business there, at any rate: go and take it away!"

There was a long silence after this, and Alice could only hear whispers now and then; such as "Sure, I don't like it, yer honour, at all, at all!" "Do as I tell you, you coward!" and at last she spread out her hand again, and made another snatch in the air. This time there were *two* little shrieks, and more sounds of broken glass. "What a number of cucumber-frames there must be!" thought Alice. "I wonder what they'll do next! As for pulling me out of the window, I only wish *they could*! I'm sure *I* don't want to stay in here any longer!"

She waited for some time without hearing anything more: at last came a rumbling of little cart-wheels, and the sound of a good many voices all talking together: she made out the words: "Where's the other ladder?—Why,

I hadn't to bring but one.
Bill's got the other—Bill! Fetch
it here, lad!—Here, put 'em up
at this corner—No, tie 'em together first—they don't reach
half high enough yet—Oh,
they'll do well enough. Don't
be particular—Here, Bill! Catch
hold of this rope—Will the roof
bear?—Mind that loose slate—
Oh, it's coming down! Heads
below!'' (a loud crash)—
''Now, who did that?—It was
Bill, I fancy—Who's to go
down the chimney?—Nay, *I*
sha'n't! *You* do it!—*That* I
wo'n't, then!—Bill's got to go
down—Here, Bill! The master
says you've got to go down
the chimney!''

"Oh! So Bill's got to come
down the chimney, has he?''
said Alice to herself. ''Why,
they seem to put everything
upon Bill! I wouldn't be in
Bill's place for a good deal; this
fireplace is narrow, to be sure;
but I *think* I can kick a little!''

She drew her foot as far down the chimney as she could,
and waited till she heard a little animal (she couldn't
guess of what sort it was) scratching and scrambling
about in the chimney close above her: then, saying to
herself "This is Bill," she gave one sharp kick, and waited
to see what would happen next.

The first thing she heard was a general chorus of
"There goes Bill!" then the Rabbit's voice alone—"Catch
him, you by the hedge!" then silence, and then another
confusion of voices—"Hold up his head—Brandy now—

Don't choke him—How was it, old fellow? What happened to you? Tell us all about it!"

Last came a little feeble, squeaking voice. ("That's Bill," thought Alice.) "Well, I hardly know—No more, thank ye; I'm better now—but I'm a deal too flustered to tell you—all I know is, something comes at me like a Jack-in-the-box, and up I goes like a sky-rocket!"

"So you did, old fellow!" said the others.

"We must burn the house down!" said the Rabbit's voice. And Alice called out, as loud as she could, "If you do, I'll set Dinah at you!"

There was a dead silence instantly, and Alice thought to herself "I wonder what they *will* do next! If they had any sense, they'd take the roof off." After a minute or two they began moving about again, and Alice heard the Rabbit say "A barrowful will do, to begin with."

"A barrowful of *what*?" thought Alice. But she had not long to doubt, for the next moment a shower of little pebbles came rattling in at the window, and some of them hit her in the face. "I'll put a stop to this," she said to herself, and shouted out "You'd better not do that again!" which produced another dead silence.

Alice noticed, with some surprise, that the pebbles were all turning into little cakes as they lay on the floor, and a bright idea came into her head. "If I eat one of these cakes", she thought, "it's sure to make *some* change in my size; and, as it ca'n't possibly make me larger, it must make me smaller, I suppose."

So she swallowed one of the cakes, and was delighted to find that she began shrinking directly. As soon as she was small enough to get through the door, she ran out of the house, and found quite a crowd of little animals and birds waiting outside. The poor little Lizard, Bill, was in the middle, being held up by two guinea-pigs, who were giving it something out of a bottle. They all made a rush at Alice the moment she appeared; but she ran off as hard as she could, and soon found herself safe in a thick wood.

"The first thing I've got to do", said Alice to herself, as

she wandered about in the wood, "is to grow to my right size again; and the second thing is to find my way into that lovely garden. I think that will be the best plan."

It sounded an excellent plan, no doubt, and very neatly and simply arranged: the only difficulty was, that she had not the smallest idea how to set about it; and, while she was peering about anxiously among the trees, a little sharp bark just over her head made her look up in a great hurry.

An enormous puppy was looking down at her with large round eyes, and feebly stretching out one paw, trying to touch her. "Poor little thing!" said Alice, in a coaxing tone, and she tried hard to whistle to it; but she was terribly frightened all the time at the thought that it might be hungry, in which case it would be very likely to eat her up in spite of all her coaxing.

Hardly knowing what she did, she picked up a little bit of stick, and held it out to the puppy: whereupon the puppy jumped into the air off all its feet at once, with a yelp of delight, and rushed at the stick, and made believe to worry it: then Alice dodged behind a great thistle, to keep herself from being run over; and, the moment she appeared on the other side, the puppy made another rush at the stick, and tumbled head over heels in its hurry to get hold of it: then Alice, thinking it was very like having a game of play with a cart-horse, and expecting every moment to be trampled under its feet, ran round the thistle again: then the puppy began a series of short charges at the stick, running a very little way forwards each time and a long way back, and barking hoarsely all the while, till at last it sat down a good way off, panting, with its tongue hanging out of its mouth, and its great eyes half shut.

This seemed to Alice a good opportunity for making her escape: so she set off at once, and ran till she was quite tired and out of breath, and till the puppy's bark sounded quite faint in the distance.

"And yet what a dear little puppy it was!" said Alice, as she leant against a buttercup to rest herself, and fanned herself with one of the leaves. "I should have liked teaching it tricks very much, if—if I'd only been the right size to do it! Oh dear! I'd nearly forgotten that I've got to grow up again! Let me see—how *is* it to be managed? I suppose I ought to eat or drink something or other; but the great question is 'What?' "

The great question certainly was "What?" Alice looked all round her at the flowers and the blades of grass, but she could not see anything that looked like the right thing to eat or drink under the circumstances. There was a large mushroom growing near her, about the same height as herself; and, when she had looked under it, and on both sides of it, and behind it, it occurred to her that she might as well look and see what was on top of it.

She stretched herself up on tiptoe, and peeped over the edge of the mushroom, and her eyes immediately met those of a large blue caterpillar, that was sitting on the top, with its arms folded, quietly smoking a long hookah, and taking not the smallest notice of her or of anything else.

CHAPTER V

Advice from a Caterpillar.

THE Caterpillar and Alice looked at each other for some time in silence: at last the Caterpillar took the hookah out of its mouth, and addressed her in a languid, sleepy voice.

"Who are *you*?" said the Caterpillar.

This was not an encouraging opening for a conversation. Alice replied, rather shyly, "I—I hardly know, Sir, just at present—at least I know who I *was* when I got up this morning, but I think I must have been changed several times since then."

"What do you mean by that?" said the Caterpillar, sternly. "Explain yourself!"

"I ca'n't explain *myself*, I'm afraid, Sir," said Alice, "because I'm not myself, you see."

"I don't see," said the Caterpillar.

"I'm afraid I ca'n't put it more clearly," Alice replied, very politely, "for I ca'n't understand it myself, to begin with; and being so many different sizes in a day is very confusing."

"It isn't," said the Caterpillar.

"Well, perhaps you haven't found it so yet," said Alice; "but when you have to turn into a chrysalis—you will some day, you know—and then after that into a butterfly, I should think you'll feel it a little queer, wo'n't you?"

"Not a bit," said the Caterpillar.

"Well, perhaps *your* feelings may be different," said Alice: "all I know is, it would feel very queer to *me*."

"You!" said the Caterpillar contemptuously. "Who are *you*?"

Which brought them back again to the beginning of the conversation. Alice felt a little irritated at the Caterpillar's making such *very* short remarks, and she drew herself up and said, very gravely, "I think you ought to tell me who *you* are, first."

"Why?" said the Caterpillar.

Here was another puzzling question; and, as Alice could not think of any good reason, and the Caterpillar seemed to be in a *very* unpleasant state of mind, she turned away.

"Come back!" the Caterpillar called after her. "I've something important to say!"

This sounded promising, certainly. Alice turned and came back again.

"Keep your temper," said the Caterpillar.

"Is that all?" said Alice, swallowing down her anger as well as she could.

"No," said the Caterpillar.

Alice thought she might as well wait, as she had nothing else to do, and perhaps after all it might tell her something worth hearing. For some minutes it puffed away without speaking; but at last it unfolded its arms, took the hookah out of its mouth again, and said "So you think you're changed, do you?"

"I'm afraid I am, Sir," said Alice. "I ca'n't remember things as I used—and I don't keep the same size for ten minutes together!"

"Ca'n't remember *what* things?" said the Caterpillar.

"Well, I've tried to say '*How doth the little busy bee*', but it all came different!" Alice replied in a very melancholy voice.

"Repeat '*You are old, Father William*'," said the Caterpillar.

Alice folded her hands, and began:

"You are old, Father William," the young man said
  "And your hair has become very white;
And yet you incessantly stand on your head—
  Do you think, at your age, it is right?"

"In my youth", Father William replied to his son,
  "I feared it might injure the brain;
But, now that I'm perfectly sure I have none,
  Why, I do it again and again."

"You are old," said the youth, "as I mentioned before.
  And have grown most uncommonly fat;
Yet you turned a back-somersault in at the door—
  Pray, what is the reason of that?"

"In my youth", said the sage, as he shook his grey locks,
  "I kept all my limbs very supple
By the use of this ointment—one shilling the box—
  Allow me to sell you a couple?"

"You are old", said the youth, "and your jaws are too weak
  For anything tougher than suet;
Yet you finished the goose, with the bones and the beak—
  Pray, how did you manage to do it?"

"In my youth", said his father, "I took to the law,
  And argued each case with my wife;
And the muscular strength, which it gave to my jaw
  Has lasted the rest of my life."

"*You are old,*" *said the youth,* "*one would hardly suppose*
  That your eye was as steady as ever;
Yet you balanced an eel on the end of your nose—
  What made you so awfully clever?"

"*I have answered three questions, and that is enough,*"
  Said his father, "*Don't give yourself airs!*
Do you think I can listen all day to such stuff?
  Be off, or I'll kick you down-stairs!"

"That is not said right," said the Caterpillar.

"Not *quite* right, I'm afraid," said Alice, timidly: "some of the words have got altered."

"It is wrong from beginning to end," said the Caterpillar, decidedly; and there was silence for some minutes.

The Caterpillar was the first to speak.

"What size do you want to be?" it asked.

"Oh, I'm not particular as to size," Alice hastily replied; "only one doesn't like changing so often, you know."

"I *don't* know," said the Caterpillar.

Alice said nothing: she had never been so much contra-

dicted in all her life before, and she felt that she was losing her temper.

"Are you content now!" said the Caterpillar.

"Well, I should like to be a *little* larger, Sir, if you wouldn't mind," said Alice: "three inches is such a wretched height to be."

"It is a very good height indeed!" said the Caterpillar angrily, rearing itself upright as it spoke (it was exactly three inches high).

"But I'm not used to it!" pleaded poor Alice in a piteous tone. And she thought to herself "I wish the creatures wouldn't be so easily offended!"

"You'll get used to it in time," said the Caterpillar; and it put the hookah into its mouth, and began smoking again.

This time Alice waited patiently until it chose to speak again. In a minute or two the Caterpillar took the hookah out of its mouth, and yawned once or twice, and shook itself. Then it got down off the mushroom, and crawled away into the grass, merely remarking, as it went, "One side will make you grow taller, and the other side will make you grow shorter."

"One side of *what*? The other side of *what*?" thought Alice to herself.

"Of the mushroom," said the Caterpillar, just as if she had asked it aloud; and in another moment it was out of sight.

Alice remained looking thoughtfully at the mushroom for a minute, trying to make out which were the two sides of it; and, as it was perfectly round, she found this a very difficult question. However, at last she stretched her arms round it as far as they would go, and broke off a bit of the edge with each hand.

"And now which is which?" she said to herself, and nibbled a little of the right-hand bit to try the effect. The next moment she felt a violent blow underneath her chin: it had struck her foot!

She was a good deal frightened by this very sudden change, but she felt that there was no time to be lost, as she was shrinking rapidly: so she set to work at once to eat some of the other bit. Her chin was pressed so closely against her foot, that there was hardly room to open her mouth; but she did it at last, and managed to swallow a morsel of the left-hand bit.

*   *   *   *   *

   *   *   *   *

*   *   *   *   *

"Come, my head's free at last!" said Alice in a tone of delight, which changed into alarm in another moment, when she found that her shoulders were nowhere to be found: all she could see, when she looked down, was an immense length of neck, which seemed to rise like a stalk out of a sea of green leaves that lay far below her.

"What *can* all that green stuff be?" said Alice. "And where *have* my shoulders got to? And oh, my poor hands, how is it I ca'n't see you?" She was moving them about, as she spoke, but no result seemed to follow, except a little shaking among the distant green leaves.

As there seemed to be no chance of getting her hands up to her head, she tried to get her head down to *them*, and was delighted to find that her neck would bend about easily in any direction, like a serpent. She had just succeeded in curving it down into a graceful zigzag, and was going to dive in among the leaves, which she found to be nothing but the tops of the trees under which she had been wandering, when a sharp hiss made her draw back in a hurry: a large pigeon had flown into her face, and was beating her violently with its wings.

"Serpent!" screamed the Pigeon.

"I'm *not* a serpent!" said Alice indignantly. "Let me alone!"

"Serpent, I say again!" repeated the Pigeon, but in a more subdued tone, and added, with a kind of sob, "I've tried every way, but nothing seems to suit them!"

"I haven't the least idea what you're talking about," said Alice.

"I've tried the roots of trees, and I've tried banks, and I've tried hedges," the Pigeon went on, without attending to her; "but those serpents! There's no pleasing them!"

Alice was more and more puzzled, but she thought there was no use in saying anything more till the Pigeon had finished.

"As if it wasn't trouble enough hatching the eggs," said the Pigeon; "but I must be on the look-out for serpents, night and day! Why, I haven't had a wink of sleep these three weeks!"

"I'm very sorry you've been annoyed," said Alice, who was beginning to see its meaning.

"And just as I'd taken the highest tree in the wood," continued the Pigeon, raising its voice to a shriek, "and just as I was thinking I should be free of them at last, they must needs come wriggling down from the sky! Ugh, Serpent!"

"But I'm *not* a serpent, I tell you!" said Alice. "I'm a—
I'm a——"

"Well! *What* are you?" said the Pigeon. "I can see
you're trying to invent something!"

"I—I'm a little girl," said Alice, rather doubtfully, as
she remembered the number of changes she had gone
through, that day.

"A likely story indeed!" said the Pigeon, in a tone of the
deepest contempt. "I've seen a good many little girls in
my time, but never *one* with such a neck as that! No, no!
You're a serpent; and there's no use denying it. I suppose
you'll be telling me next that you never tasted an egg!"

"I *have* tasted eggs, certainly," said Alice, who was a
very truthful child; "but little girls eat eggs quite as much
as serpents do, you know."

"I don't believe it," said the Pigeon; "but if they do,
then they're a kind of serpent: that's all I can say."

This was such a new idea to Alice, that she was quite
silent for a minute or two, which gave the Pigeon the opportunity of adding "You're looking for eggs, I know *that*
well enough; and what does it matter to me whether
you're a little girl or a serpent?"

"It matters a good deal to *me*," said Alice hastily; "but
I'm not looking for eggs, as it happens; and, if I was, I
shouldn't want *yours*: I don't like them raw."

"Well, be off, then!" said the Pigeon in a sulky tone, as
it settled down again into its nest. Alice crouched down
among the trees as well as she could, for her neck kept
getting entangled among the branches, and every now and
then she had to stop and untwist it. After a while she remembered that she still held the pieces of mushroom in
her hands, and she set to work very carefully, nibbling
first at one and then at the other, and growing sometimes
taller, and sometimes shorter, until she had succeeded in
bringing herself down to her usual height.

It was so long since she had been anything near the
right size, that it felt quite strange at first; but she got
used to it in a few minutes, and began talking to herself,

as usual, "Come, there's half my plan done now! How puzzling all these changes are! I'm never sure what I'm going to be, from one minute to another! However, I've got back to my right size: the next thing is, to get into that beautiful garden—how *is* that to be done, I wonder?" As she said this, she came suddenly upon an open place, with a little house in it about four feet high. "Whoever lives there," thought Alice, "it'll never do to come upon them *this* size: why, I should frighten them out of their wits!" So she began nibbling at the right-hand bit again, and did not venture to go near the house till she had brought herself down to nine inches high.

Chapter VI

Pig and Pepper

F OR a minute or two she stood looking at the house, and wondering what to do next, when suddenly a footman in livery came running out of the wood—(she considered him to be a footman because he was in livery: otherwise, judging by his face only, she would have called him a fish)—and rapped loudly at the door with his knuckles. It was opened by another footman in livery, with a round face, and large eyes like a frog; and both footmen, Alice noticed, had powdered hair that curled all over their heads. She felt very curious to know what it was all about, and crept a little way out of the wood to listen.

The Fish-Footman began by producing from under his arm a great letter, nearly as large as himself, and this he handed over to the other, saying, in a solemn tone, "For the Duchess. An invitation from the Queen to play croquet." The Frog-Footman repeated, in the same solemn tone, only changing the order of the words a little, "From the Queen. An invitation for the Duchess to play croquet."

Then they both bowed, and their curls got entangled together.

Alice laughed so much at this, that she had to run back into the wood for fear of their hearing her; and, when she next peeped out, the Fish-Footman was gone, and the other was sitting on the ground near the door, staring stupidly up into the sky.

Alice went timidly up to the door, and knocked.

"There's no sort of use in knocking," said the Footman, "and that for two reasons. First, because I'm on the same side of the door as you are: secondly, because they're making such a noise inside, no one could possibly hear you." And certainly there *was* a most extraordinary noise going on within—a constant howling and sneezing, and every now and then a great crash, as if a dish or kettle had been broken to pieces.

"Please, then," said Alice, "how am I to get in?"

"There might be some sense in your knocking", the Footman went on, without attending to her, "if we had the door between us. For instance, if you were *inside*, you might knock, and I could let you out, you know." He was looking up into the sky all the time he was speaking, and this Alice thought decidedly uncivil. "But perhaps he ca'n't help it," she said to herself; "his eyes are so *very* nearly at the top of his head. But at any rate he might answer questions.—How am I to get in?" she repeated, aloud.

"I shall sit here", the Footman remarked, "till to-mor-row——"

At this moment the door of the house opened, and a large plate came skimming out, straight at the Footman's head: it just grazed his nose, and broke to pieces against one of the trees behind him.

"——or next day, maybe," the Footman continued in the same tone, exactly as if nothing had happened.

"How am I to get in?" asked Alice again, in a louder tone.

"*Are* you to get in at all?" said the Footman. "That's the first question, you know."

It was, no doubt: only Alice did not like to be told so. "It's really dreadful", she muttered to herself, "the way all the creatures argue. It's enough to drive one crazy!"

The Footman seemed to think this a good opportunity for repeating his remark, with variations. "I shall sit here," he said, "on and off, for days and days."

"But what am *I* to do?" said Alice.

"Anything you like," said the Footman, and began whistling.

"Oh, there's no use in talking to him," said Alice desperately: "he's perfectly idiotic!" And she opened the door and went in.

The door led right into a large kitchen, which was full

of smoke from one end to the other: the Duchess was sitting on a three-legged stool in the middle, nursing a baby: the cook was leaning over the fire, stirring a large cauldron which seemed to be full of soup.

"There's certainly too much pepper in that soup!" Alice said to herself, as well as she could for sneezing.

There was certainly too much of it in the *air*. Even the Duchess sneezed occasionally; and as for the baby, it was sneezing and howling alternately without a moment's pause. The only two creatures in the kitchen, that did *not* sneeze, were the cook, and a large cat, which was lying on the hearth and grinning from ear to ear.

"Please would you tell me", said Alice, a little timidly, for she was not quite sure whether it was good manners for her to speak first, "why your cat grins like that?"

"It's a Cheshire-Cat", said the Duchess, "and that's why. Pig!"

She said the last word with such sudden violence that Alice quite jumped; but she saw in another moment that it was addressed to the baby, and not to her, so she took courage, and went on again:

"I didn't know that Cheshire-Cats always grinned; in fact, I didn't know that cats *could* grin."

"They all can," said the Duchess; "and most of 'em do."

"I don't know of any that do," Alice said very politely, feeling quite pleased to have got into a conversation.

"You don't know much," said the Duchess; "and that's a fact."

Alice did not at all like the tone of this remark, and thought it would be as well to introduce some other subject of conversation. While she was trying to fix on one, the cook took the cauldron of soup off the fire, and at once set to work throwing everything within her reach at the Duchess and the baby—the fire-irons came first; then followed a shower of sauce-pans, plates, and dishes. The Duchess took no notice of them even when they hit her; and the baby was howling so much already, that it was quite impossible to say whether the blows hurt it or not.

"Oh, *please* mind what you're doing!" cried Alice, jumping up and down in an agony of terror. "Oh, there goes his *precious* nose!" as an unusually large saucepan flew close by it, and very nearly carried it off.

"If everybody minded their own business", the Duchess said, in a hoarse growl, "the world would go round a deal faster than it does."

"Which would *not* be an advantage," said Alice, who felt very glad to get an opportunity of showing off a little of her knowledge. "Just think what work it would make with the day and night! You see the earth takes twenty-four hours to turn round on its axis——"

"Talking of axes," said the Duchess, "chop off her head!"

Alice glanced rather anxiously at the cook, to see if she meant to take the hint; but the cook was busily stirring the soup, and seemed not to be listening, so she went on again: "Twenty-four hours, I *think*; or is it twelve? I——"

"Oh, don't bother *me*!" said the Duchess. "I never could abide figures!" And with that she began nursing her child again, singing a sort of lullaby to it as she did so, and giving it a violent shake at the end of every line:

> *"Speak roughly to your little boy,*
> *And beat him when he sneezes:*
> *He only does it to annoy,*
> *Because he knows it teases."*

CHORUS

(in which the cook and the baby joined):
"Wow! wow! wow!"

While the Duchess sang the second verse of the song, she kept tossing the baby violently up and down, and the poor little thing howled so, that Alice could hardly hear the words:

> *"I speak severely to my boy,*
> *I beat him when he sneezes;*
> *For he can thoroughly enjoy*
> *The pepper when he pleases!"*

CHORUS

"Wow! wow! wow!"

"Here! You may nurse it a bit, if you like!" the Duchess said to Alice, flinging the baby at her as she spoke. "I must go and get ready to play croquet with the Queen," and she hurried out of the room. The cook threw a frying-pan after her as she went, but it just missed her.

Alice caught the baby with some difficulty, as it was a queer-shaped little creature, and held out its arms and legs in all directions, "just like a star-fish", thought Alice. The poor little thing was snorting like a steam-engine when she caught it, and kept doubling itself up and straightening itself out again, so that altogether, for the first minute or two, it was as much as she could do to hold it.

As soon as she had made out the proper way of nursing it (which was to twist it up into a sort of knot, and then keep tight hold of its right ear and left foot, so as to prevent its undoing itself), she carried it out into the open air. "If I don't take this child away with me," thought Alice, "they're sure to kill it in a day or two. Wouldn't

it be murder to leave it behind?" She said the last words out loud, and the little thing grunted in reply (it had left off sneezing by this time). "Don't grunt," said Alice; "that's not at all a proper way of expressing yourself."

The baby grunted again, and Alice looked very anxiously into its face to see what was the matter with it. There could be no doubt that it had a *very* turn-up nose, much more like a snout than a real nose: also its eyes were getting extremely small for a baby: altogether Alice did not like the look of the thing at all. "But perhaps it was only sobbing," she thought, and looked into its eyes again, to see if there were any tears.

No, there were no tears. "If you're going to turn into a pig, my dear," said Alice, seriously, "I'll have nothing more to do with you. Mind now!" The poor little thing sobbed again (or grunted, it was impossible to say which), and they went on for some while in silence.

Alice was just beginning to think to herself, "Now, what am I to do with this creature, when I get it home?" when it grunted again, so violently, that she looked down into its face in some alarm. This time there could be *no* mistake about it: it was neither more nor less than a pig, and she felt that it would be quite absurd for her to carry it any further.

So she set the little creature down, and felt quite relieved to see it trot away quietly into the wood. "If it had grown up", she said to herself, "it would have made a dreadfully ugly child: but it makes rather a handsome pig, I think." And she began thinking over other children she knew, who might do very well as pigs, and was just saying to herself "if one only knew the right way to change them——" when she was a little startled by seeing the Cheshire-Cat sitting on a bough of a tree a few yards off.

The Cat only grinned when it saw Alice. It looked good-natured, she thought: still it had *very* long claws and a great many teeth, so she felt that it ought to be treated with respect.

"Cheshire-Puss," she began, rather timidly, as she did not at all know whether it would like the name: however, it only grinned a little wider. "Come, it's pleased so far," thought Alice, and she went on. "Would you tell me, please, which way I ought to go from here?"

"That depends a good deal on where you want to get to," said the Cat.

"I don't much care where——" said Alice.

"Then it doesn't matter which way you go," said the Cat.

"——so long as I get *somewhere*," Alice added as an explanation.

"Oh, you're sure to do that", said the Cat, "if you only walk long enough."

Alice felt that this could not be denied, so she tried another question. "What sort of people live about here?"

"In *that* direction", the Cat said, waving its right paw round, "lives a Hatter: and in *that* direction", waving the other paw, "lives a March Hare. Visit either you like: they're both mad."

"But I don't want to go among mad people," Alice remarked.

"Oh, you ca'n't help that," said the Cat: "we're all mad here. I'm mad. You're mad."

"How do you know I'm mad?" said Alice.

"You must be", said the Cat, "or you wouldn't have come here."

Alice didn't think that proved it at all: however, she went on: "And how do you know that you're mad?"

"To begin with," said the Cat, "a dog's not mad. You grant that?"

"I suppose so," said Alice.

"Well, then," the Cat went on, "you see a dog growls when it's angry, and wags its tail when it's pleased. Now *I* growl when I'm pleased, and wag my tail when I'm angry. Therefore I'm mad."

"*I* call it purring, not growling," said Alice.

"Call it what you like," said the Cat. "Do you play croquet with the Queen to-day?"

"I should like it very much," said Alice, "but I haven't been invited yet."

"You'll see me there," said the Cat, and vanished.

Alice was not much surprised at this, she was getting so well used to queer things happening. While she was still looking at the place where it had been, it suddenly appeared again.

"By-the-bye, what became of the baby?" said the Cat. "I'd nearly forgotten to ask."

"It turned into a pig," Alice answered very quietly, just as if the Cat had come back in a natural way.

"I thought it would," said the Cat, and vanished again.

Alice waited a little, half expecting to see it again, but it did not appear, and after a minute or two she walked on in the direction in which the March Hare was said to live. "I've seen hatters before," she said to herself: "the March Hare will be much the most interesting, and perhaps, as this is May, it wo'n't be raving mad—at least not so mad as it was in March." As she said this, she looked up, and there was the Cat again, sitting on a branch of a tree.

"Did you say 'pig', or 'fig'?" said the Cat.

"I said 'pig'," replied Alice; "and I wish you wouldn't keep appearing and vanishing so suddenly: you make one quite giddy!"

"All right," said the Cat; and this time it vanished quite slowly, beginning with the end of the tail, and ending with the grin, which remained some time after the rest of it had gone.

"Well! I've often seen a cat without a grin," thought Alice; "but a grin without a cat! It's the most curious thing I ever saw in all my life!"

She had not gone much farther before she came in sight of the house of the March Hare: she thought it must be the right house, because the chimneys were shaped like ears and the roof was thatched with fur. It was so large a house, that she did not like to go nearer till she had nibbled some more of the left-hand bit of mushroom, and raised herself to about two feet high: even then she walked up towards it rather timidly, saying to herself "Suppose it should be raving mad after all! I almost wish I'd gone to see the Hatter instead!"

CHAPTER VII

A Mad Tea-Party

THERE was a table set out under a tree in front of the house, and the March Hare and the Hatter were having tea at it: a Dormouse was sitting between them, fast asleep, and the other two were using it as a cushion, resting their elbows on it, and talking over its head. "Very uncomfortable for the Dormouse," thought Alice; "only as it's asleep, I suppose it doesn't mind."

The table was a large one, but the three were all crowded together at one corner of it. "No room! No room!" they cried out when they saw Alice coming. "There's *plenty* of room!" said Alice indignantly, and she sat down in a large arm-chair at one end of the table.

"Have some wine," the March Hare said in an encouraging tone.

Alice looked all round the table, but there was nothing on it but tea. "I don't see any wine," she remarked.

"There isn't any," said the March Hare.

"Then it wasn't very civil of you to offer it," said Alice angrily.

"It wasn't very civil of you to sit down without being invited," said the March Hare.

"I didn't know it was *your* table," said Alice: "it's laid for a great many more than three."

"Your hair wants cutting," said the Hatter. He had been looking at Alice for some time with great curiosity, and this was his first speech.

"You should learn not to make personal remarks," Alice said with some severity: "It's very rude."

The Hatter opened his eyes very wide on hearing this; but all he *said* was "Why is a raven like a writing-desk?"

"Come, we shall have some fun now!" thought Alice.

"I'm glad they've begun asking riddles—I believe I can guess that," she added aloud.

"Do you mean that you think you can find out the answer to it?" said the March Hare.

"Exactly so," said Alice.

"Then you should say what you mean," the March Hare went on.

"I do," Alice hastily replied; "at least—at least I mean what I say—that's the same thing, you know."

"Not the same thing a bit!" said the Hatter. "Why, you might just as well say that 'I see what I eat' is the same thing as 'I eat what I see'!"

"You might just as well say", added the March Hare, "that 'I like what I get' is the same thing as 'I get what I like'!"

"You might just as well say", added the Dormouse, which seemed to be talking in its sleep, "that 'I breathe when I sleep' is the same thing as 'I sleep when I breathe'!"

"It *is* the same thing with you," said the Hatter, and

here the conversation dropped, and the party sat silent for a minute, while Alice thought over all she could remember about ravens and writing-desks, which wasn't much.

The Hatter was the first to break the silence. "What day of the month is it?" he said, turning to Alice: he had taken his watch out of his pocket, and was looking at it uneasily, shaking it every now and then, and holding it to his ear.

Alice considered a little, and then said "The fourth".

"Two days wrong!" sighed the Hatter. "I told you butter wouldn't suit the works!" he added, looking angrily at the March Hare.

"It was the *best* butter," the March Hare meekly replied.

"Yes, but some crumbs must have got in as well," the Hatter grumbled: "you shouldn't have put it in with the bread-knife."

The March Hare took the watch and looked at it gloomily: then he dipped it into his cup of tea, and looked at it again: but he could think of nothing better to say than his first remark, "It was the *best* butter, you know."

Alice had been looking over his shoulder with some curiosity. "What a funny watch!" she remarked. "It tells the day of the month, and doesn't tell what o'clock it is!"

"Why should it?" muttered the Hatter. "Does *your* watch tell you what year it is?"

"Of course not," Alice replied very readily: "but that's because it stays the same year for such a long time together."

"Which is just the case with *mine*," said the Hatter.

Alice felt dreadfully puzzled. The Hatter's remark seemed to her to have no sort of meaning in it, and yet it was certainly English. "I don't quite understand you," she said, as politely as she could.

"The Dormouse is asleep again," said the Hatter, and he poured a little hot tea upon its nose.

The Dormouse shook its head impatiently, and said,

without opening its eyes. "Of course, of course: just what I was going to remark myself."

"Have you guessed the riddle yet?" the Hatter said, turning to Alice again.

"No, I give it up," Alice replied. "What's the answer?"

"I haven't the slightest idea," said the Hatter.

"Nor I," said the March Hare.

Alice sighed wearily. "I think you might do something better with the time", she said, "than wasting it in asking riddles that have no answers."

"If you knew Time as well as I do," said the Hatter, "you wouldn't talk about wasting *it*. It's *him*."

"I don't know what you mean," said Alice.

"Of course you don't!" the Hatter said, tossing his head contemptuously. "I dare say you never even spoke to Time!"

"Perhaps not," Alice cautiously replied; "but I know I have to beat time when I learn music."

"Ah! That accounts for it," said the Hatter. "He wo'n't stand beating. Now, if you only kept on good terms with him, he'd do almost anything you liked with the clock. For instance, suppose it were nine o'clock in the morning, just time to begin lessons: you'd only have to whisper a hint to Time, and round goes the clock in a twinkling! Half-past one, time for dinner!"

("I only wish it was," the March Hare said to itself in a whisper.)

"That would be grand, certainly," said Alice thoughtfully; "but then—I shouldn't be hungry for it, you know."

"Not at first, perhaps," said the Hatter: "but you could keep it to half-past one as long as you liked."

"Is that the way *you* manage?" Alice asked.

The Hatter shook his head mournfully. "Not I!" he replied. "We quarreled last March——just before *he* went mad, you know——" (pointing with his teaspoon at the March Hare,) "——it was at the great concert given by the Queen of Hearts, and I had to sing

> '*Twinkle, twinkle, little bat!*
> *How I wonder what you're at!*'

You know the song, perhaps?"

"I've heard something like it," said Alice.

"It goes on, you know," the Hatter continued, "in this way:

> '*Up above the world you fly,*
> *Like a tea-tray in the sky.*
> *Twinkle, twinkle—*' "

Here the Dormouse shook itself, and began singing in its sleep "*Twinkle, twinkle, twinkle, twinkle——*" and went on so long that they had to pinch it to make it stop.

"Well, I'd hardly finished the first verse", said the Hatter, "when the Queen bawled out 'He's murdering the time! Off with his head!' "

"How dreadfully savage!" exclaimed Alice.

"And ever since that", the Hatter went on in a mournful tone, "he wo'n't do a thing I ask! It's always six o'clock now."

A bright idea came into Alice's head. "Is that the reason so many tea-things are put out here?" she asked.

"Yes, that's it," said the Hatter with a sigh: "it's always tea-time, and we've no time to wash the things between whiles."

"Then you keep moving round, I suppose?" said Alice.

"Exactly so," said the Hatter: "as the things get used up."

"But what happens when you come to the beginning again?" Alice ventured to ask.

"Suppose we change the subject," the March Hare interrupted, yawning. "I'm getting tired of this. I vote the young lady tells us a story."

"I'm afraid I don't know one," said Alice, rather alarmed at the proposal.

"Then the Dormouse shall!" they both cried. "Wake up, Dormouse!" And they pinched it on both sides at once.

The Dormouse slowly opened its eyes. "I wasn't asleep," it said in a hoarse, feeble voice, "I heard every word you fellows were saying."

"Tell us a story!" said the March Hare.

"Yes, please do!" pleaded Alice.

"And be quick about it", added the Hatter, "or you'll be asleep again before it's done."

"Once upon a time there were three little sisters," the Dormouse began in a great hurry; "and their names were Elsie, Lacie, and Tillie; and they lived at the bottom of a well——"

"What did they live on?" said Alice, who always took a great interest in questions of eating and drinking.

"They lived on treacle," said the Dormouse, after thinking a minute or two.

"They couldn't have done that, you know," Alice gently remarked. "They'd have been ill."

"So they were," said the Dormouse; "*very* ill."

Alice tried a little to fancy to herself what such an extraordinary way of living would be like, but it puzzled her too much: so she went on: "But why did they live at the bottom of a well?"

"Take some more tea," the March Hare said to Alice, very earnestly.

"I've had nothing yet," Alice replied in an offended tone: "so I ca'n't take more."

"You mean you ca'n't take *less*," said the Hatter: "it's very easy to take *more* than nothing."

"Nobody asked *your* opinion," said Alice.

"Who's making personal remarks now?" the Hatter asked triumphantly.

Alice did not quite know what to say to this: so she helped herself to some tea and bread-and-butter, and then turned to the Dormouse, and repeated her question. "Why did they live at the bottom of a well?"

The Dormouse again took a minute or two to think about it, and then said "It was a treacle-well."

"There's no such thing!" Alice was beginning very angrily, but the Hatter and the March Hare went "Sh! Sh!" and the Dormouse sulkily remarked "If you ca'n't be civil, you'd better finish the story for yourself."

"No, please go on!" Alice said very humbly. "I wo'n't interrupt you again. I dare say there may be *one*."

"One, indeed!" said the Dormouse indignantly. However, he consented to go on. "And so these three little sisters—they were learning to draw, you know——"

"What did they draw?" said Alice, quite forgetting her promise.

"Treacle," said the Dormouse, without considering at all, this time.

"I want a clean cup," interrupted the Hatter: "let's all move one place on."

He moved on as he spoke, and the Dormouse followed him: the March Hare moved into the Dormouse's place, and Alice rather unwillingly took the place of the March Hare. The Hatter was the only one who got any advantage from the change; and Alice was a good deal worse off than before, as the March Hare had just upset the milk-jug into his plate.

Alice did not wish to offend the Dormouse again, so she

began very cautiously: "But I don't understand. Where did they draw the treacle from?"

"You can draw water out of a water-well," said the Hatter; "so I should think you could draw treacle out of a treacle-well—eh, stupid?"

"But they were *in* the well," Alice said to the Dormouse, not choosing to notice this last remark.

"Of course they were," said the Dormouse: "well in."

This answer so confused poor Alice, that she let the Dormouse go on for some time without interrupting it.

"They were learning to draw," the Dormouse went on, yawning and rubbing its eyes, for it was getting very sleepy; "and they drew all manner of things—everything that begins with an M——"

"Why with an M?" said Alice.

"Why not?" said the March Hare.

Alice was silent.

The Dormouse had closed its eyes by this time, and was going off into a doze; but, on being pinched by the Hatter, it woke up again with a little shriek, and went on: "——that begins with an M, such as mouse-traps, and the moon, and memory, and muchness—you know you say things are 'much of a muchness'—did you ever see such a thing as a drawing of a muchness!''

"Really, now you ask me," said Alice, very much confused, "I don't think——''

"Then you shouldn't talk," said the Hatter.

This piece of rudeness was more than Alice could bear: she got up in great disgust, and walked off: the Dormouse fell asleep instantly, and neither of the others took the least notice of her going, though she looked back once or twice, half hoping that they would call after her: the last time she saw them, they were trying to put the Dormouse into the teapot.

"At any rate I'll never go *there* again!" said Alice, as she picked her way through the wood. "It's the stupidest tea-party I ever was at in all my life!"

Just as she said this, she noticed that one of the trees had a door leading right into it. "That's very curious!" she thought. "But everything's curious to-day. I think I may as well go in at once." And in she went.

Once more she found herself in the long hall, and close to the little glass table. "Now, I'll manage better this time," she said to herself, and began by taking the little golden key, and unlocking the door that led into the garden. Then she set to work nibbling at the mushroom (she had kept a piece of it in her pocket) till she was about a foot high: then she walked down the little passage; and *then*—she found herself at last in the beautiful garden, among the bright flower-beds and the cool fountains.

Chapter VIII

The Queen's Croquet Ground

A LARGE rose-tree stood near the entrace of the garden: the roses growing on it were white, but there were three

gardeners at it, busily painting them red. Alice thought this a very curious thing, and she went nearer to watch them, and, just as she came up to them, she heard one of them say "Look out now, Five! Don't go splashing paint over me like that!"

"I couldn't help it," said Five, in a sulky tone. "Seven jogged my elbow."

On which Seven looked up and said "That's right, Five! Always lay the blame on others!"

"*You'd* better not talk!" said Five. "I heard the Queen say only yesterday you deserved to be beheaded."

"What for?" said the one who had spoken first.

"That's none of *your* business, Two!" said Seven.

"Yes, it *is* his business!" said Five. "And I'll tell him— it was for bringing the cook tulip-roots instead of onions."

Seven flung down his brush, and had just begun "Well,

of all the unjust things———" when his eye chanced to fall upon Alice, as she stood watching them, and he checked himself suddenly: the others looked round also, and all of them bowed low.

"Would you tell me, please," said Alice, a little timidly, "why you are painting those roses?"

Five and Seven said nothing, but looked at Two. Two began, in a low voice, "Why, the fact is, you see, Miss, this here ought to have been a *red* rose-tree, and we put a white one in by mistake; and, if the Queen was to find it out, we should all have our heads cut off, you know. So you see, Miss, we're doing our best, afore she comes, to———" At this moment, Five, who had been anxiously looking across the garden, called out "The Queen! The Queen!" and the three gardeners instantly threw themselves flat upon their faces. There was a sound of many footsteps, and Alice looked round, eager to see the Queen.

First came ten soldiers carrying clubs: these were all shaped like the three gardeners, oblong and flat, with their hands and feet at the corners: next the ten courtiers: these were ornamented all over with diamonds, and walked two and two, as the soldiers did. After these came the royal children: there were ten of them, and the little dears came jumping merrily along, hand in hand, in couples: they were all ornamented with hearts. Next came the guests, mostly Kings and Queens, and among them Alice recognized the White Rabbit: it was talking in a hurried nervous manner, smiling at everything that was said, and went by without noticing her. Then followed the Knave of Hearts, carrying the King's crown on a crimson velvet cushion; and, last of all this grand procession, came THE KING AND THE QUEEN OF HEARTS.

Alice was rather doubtful whether she ought not to lie down on her face like the three gardeners, but she could not remember ever having heard of such a rule at processions; "and besides, what would be the use of a procession", thought she, "if people had all to lie down on

their faces, so that they couldn't see it?" So she stood where she was, and waited.

When the procession came opposite to Alice, they all stopped and looked at her, and the Queen said, severely, "Who is this?" She said it to the Knave of Hearts, who only bowed and smiled in reply.

"Idiot!" said the Queen, tossing her head impatiently; and, turning to Alice, she went on: "What's your name, child?"

"My name is Alice, so please your Majesty," said Alice very politely; but she added, to herself, "Why, they're only a pack of cards, after all. I needn't be afraid of them!"

"And who are *these*?" said the Queen, pointing to the three gardeners who were lying round the rose-tree; for, you see, as they were lying on their faces, and the pattern on their backs was the same as the rest of the pack, she could not tell whether they were gardeners, or soldiers, or courtiers, or three of her own children.

"How should *I* know?" said Alice, suprised at her own courage. "It's no business of *mine*."

The Queen turned crimson with fury, and, after glaring at her for a moment like a wild beast, began screaming "Off with her head! Off with——"

"Nonsense!" said Alice, very loudly and decidedly, and the Queen was silent.

The King laid his hand upon her arm, and timidly said "Consider, my dear: she is only a child!"

The Queen turned angrily away from him, and said to the Knave "Turn them over!"

The Knave did so, very carefully, with one foot.

"Get up!" said the Queen in a shrill, loud voice, and the three gardeners instantly jumped up, and began bowing to the King, the Queen, the royal children, and everybody else.

"Leave off that!" screamed the Queen. "You make me giddy." And then, turning to the rose-tree, she went on "What *have* you been doing here?"

"May it please your Majesty," said Two, in a very humble tone, going down on one knee as he spoke, "we were trying——"

"*I* see!" said the Queen, who had meanwhile been examining the roses. "Off with their heads!" and the procession moved on, three of the soldiers remaining behind to execute the unfortunate gardeners, who ran to Alice for protection.

"You sha'n't be beheaded!" said Alice, and she put them into a large flower-pot that stood near. The three soldiers wandered about for a minute or two, looking for them, and then quietly marched off after the others.

"Are their heads off?" shouted the Queen.

"Their heads are gone, if it please your Majesty!" the soldiers shouted in reply.

"That's right!" shouted the Queen. "Can you play croquet?"

The soldiers were silent, and looked at Alice, as the question was evidently meant for her.

"Yes!" shouted Alice.

"Come on, then!" roared the Queen, and Alice joined the procession, wondering very much what would happen next.

"It's—it's a very fine day!" said a timid voice at her side. She was walking by the White Rabbit, who was peeping anxiously into her face.

"Very," said Alice. "Where's the Duchess?"

"Hush! Hush!" said the Rabbit in a low hurried tone. He looked anxiously over his shoulder as he spoke, and then raised himself upon tiptoe, put his mouth close to her ear, and whispered "She's under sentence of execution."

"What for?" said Alice.

"Did you say 'What a pity!'?" the Rabbit asked.

"No, I didn't," said Alice. "I don't think it's at all a pity. I said 'What for?'"

"She boxed the Queen's ears——" the Rabbit began. Alice gave a little scream of laughter. "Oh, hush!" the Rabbit whispered in a frightened tone. "The Queen will hear you! You see she came rather late, and the Queen said——"

"Get to your places!" shouted the Queen in a voice of thunder, and people began running about in all directions, tumbling up against each other: however, they got settled down in a minute or two, and the game began.

Alice thought she had never seen such a curious croquet ground in her life: it was all ridges and furrows: the croquet balls were live hedgehogs, and the mallets live flamingoes, and the soldiers had to double themselves up and stand on their hands and feet, to make the arches.

The chief difficulty Alice found at first was in managing her flamingo: she succeeded in getting its body tucked away, comfortably enough, under her arm, with its legs hanging down, but generally, just as she had got its neck

nicely straightened out, and was going to give the hedge-hog a blow with its head, it *would* twist itself round and look up in her face, with such a puzzled expression that she could not help bursting out laughing; and, when she had got its head down, and was going to begin again, it was very provoking to find that the hedgehog had un-rolled itself, and was in the act of crawling away: besides all this, there was generally a ridge or a furrow in the way wherever she wanted to send the hedgehog to, and, as the doubled-up soldiers were always getting up and walking off to other parts of the ground, Alice soon came to the conclusion that it was a very difficult game indeed.

The players all played at once, without waiting for

turns, quarreling all the while, and fighting for the hedgehogs; and in a very short time the Queen was in a furious
passion, and went stamping about, and shouting "Off
with his head!" or "Off with her head!" about once in a
minute.

Alice began to feel very uneasy: to be sure, she had not
as yet had any dispute with the Queen, but she knew that
it might happen any minute, "and then", thought she,
"what would become of me? They're dreadfully fond of
beheading people here: the great wonder is, that there's
any one left alive!"

She was looking about for some way of escape, and
wondering whether she could get away without being
seen, when she noticed a curious appearance in the air: it
puzzled her very much at first, but after watching it a
minute or two she made it out to be a grin, and she said
to herself "It's the Cheshire-Cat: now I shall have somebody to talk to."

"How are you getting on?" said the Cat, as soon as
there was mouth enough for it to speak with.

Alice waited till the eyes appeared, and then nodded.
"It's no use speaking to it", she thought, "till its ears have
come, or at least one of them." In another minute the
whole head appeared, and then Alice put down her flamingo, and began an account of the game, feeling very glad
she had some one to listen to her. The Cat seemed to
think that there was enough of it now in sight, and no
more of it appeared.

"I don't think they play at all fairly," Alice began, in
rather a complaining tone, "and they all quarrel so dreadfully one ca'n't hear oneself speak—and they don't seem
to have any rules in particular: at least, if there are, nobody attends to them—and you've no idea how confusing
it is all the things being alive: for instance, there's the
arch I've got to go through next walking about at the
other end of the ground—and I should have croqueted
the Queen's hedgehog just now, only it ran away when
it saw mine coming!"

"How do you like the Queen?" said the Cat in a low voice.

"Not at all," said Alice: "she's so extremely——" Just then she noticed that the Queen was close behind her, listening: so she went on "——likely to win, that it's hardly worth while finishing the game."

The Queen smiled and passed on.

"Who *are* you talking to?" said the King, coming up to Alice, and looking at the Cat's head with great curiosity.

"It's a friend of mine—a Cheshire-Cat," said Alice: "allow me to introduce it."

"I don't like the look of it at all," said the King: "however, it may kiss my hand, if it likes."

"I'd rather not," the Cat remarked.

"Don't be impertinent," said the King, "and don't look at me like that!" He got behind Alice as he spoke.

"A cat may look at a king," said Alice. "I've read that in some book, but I don't remember where."

"Well, it must be removed," said the King very decidedly: and he called to the Queen, who was passing at the moment, "My dear! I wish you would have this cat removed!"

The Queen had only one way of settling all difficulties, great or small. "Off with his head!" she said without even looking around.

"I'll fetch the executioner myself," said the King eagerly, and he hurried off.

Alice thought she might as well go back and see how the game was going on, as she heard the Queen's voice in the distance, screaming with passion. She had already heard her sentence three of the players to be executed for having missed their turns, and she did not like the look of things at all, as the game was in such confusion that she never knew whether it was her turn or not. So she went off in search of her hedgehog.

The hedgehog was engaged in a fight with another hedgehog, which seemed to Alice an excellent opportunity for croqueting one of them with the other: the only

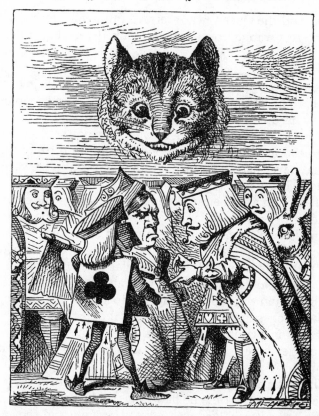

difficulty was, that her flamingo was gone across the
other side of the garden, where Alice could see it trying
in a helpless sort of way to fly up into a tree.

By the time she had caught the flamingo and brought
it back, the fight was over, and both the hedgehogs were
out of sight: "but it doesn't matter much", thought
Alice, "as all the arches are gone from this side of the
ground." So she tucked it away under her arm, that it
might not escape again, and went back to have a little
more conversation with her friend.

When she got back to the Cheshire-Cat, she was surprised to find quite a large crowd collected round it: there
was a dispute going on between the executioner, the

King, and the Queen, who were all talking at once, while all the rest were quite silent, and looked very uncomfortable.

The moment Alice appeared, she was appealed to by all three to settle the question, and they repeated their arguments to her, though, as they all spoke at once, she found it very hard to make out exactly what they said.

The executioner's argument was, that you couldn't cut off a head unless there was a body to cut it off from: that he had never had to do such a thing before, and he wasn't going to begin at *his* time of life.

The King's argument was that anything that had a head could be beheaded, and that you weren't to talk nonsense.

The Queen's argument was that, if something wasn't done about it in less than no time, she'd have everybody executed, all round. (It was this last remark that had made the whole party look so grave and anxious.)

Alice could think of nothing else to say but "It belongs to the Duchess: you'd better ask *her* about it."

"She's in prison," the Queen said to the executioner: "fetch her here." And the executioner went off like an arrow.

The Cat's head began fading away the moment he was gone, and, by the time he had come back with the Duchess, it had entirely disappeared: so the King and the executioner ran wildly up and down, looking for it, while the rest of the party went back to the game.

CHAPTER IX

The Mock Turtle's Story

"You ca'n't think how glad I am to see you again, you dear old thing!" said the Duchess, as she tucked her arm affectionately into Alice's, and they walked off together.

Alice was very glad to find her in such a pleasant temper, and thought to herself that perhaps it was only the pepper that had made her so savage when they met in the kitchen.

"When *I'm* a Duchess", she said to herself (not in a very hopeful tone, though), "I won't have any pepper in

my kitchen *at all*. Soup does very well without—Maybe it's always pepper that makes people hot-tempered," she went on, very much pleased at having found out a new kind of rule, "and vinegar that makes them sour—and camomile that makes them bitter—and—and barley-sugar and such things that make children sweet-tempered. I only wish people knew *that*: then they wouldn't be so stingy about it, you know——"

She had quite forgotten the Duchess by this time, and was a little startled when she heard her voice close to her ear. "You're thinking about something, my dear, and that makes you forget to talk. I ca'n't tell you just now what the moral of that is, but I shall remember it in a bit."

"Perhaps it hasn't one," Alice ventured to remark.

"Tut, tut, child!" said the Duchess. "Everything's got a moral, if only you can find it." And she squeezed herself up closer to Alice's side as she spoke.

Alice did not much like her keeping so close to her: first because the Duchess was *very* ugly; and secondly, because she was exactly the right height to rest her chin on Alice's shoulder, and it was an uncomfortably sharp chin. However, she did not like to be rude: so she bore it as well as she could.

"The game's going on rather better now," she said, by way of keeping up the conversation a little.

" 'Tis so," said the Duchess: "and the moral of that is —'Oh, 'tis love, 'tis love, that makes the world go round!' "

"Somebody said", Alice whispered, "that it's done by everybody minding their own business!"

"Ah well! It means much the same thing," said the Duchess, digging her sharp little chin into Alice's shoulder as she added "and the moral of *that* is—'Take care of the sense and the sounds will take care of themselves.' "

"How fond she is of finding morals in things!" Alice thought to herself.

"I dare say you're wondering why I don't put my arm round your waist," the Duchess said, after a pause: "the reason is, that I'm doubtful about the temper of your flamingo. Shall I try the experiment?"

"He might bite," Alice cautiously replied, not feeling at all anxious to have the experiment tried.

"Very true," said the Duchess: "flamingoes and mustard both bite. And the moral of that is—'Birds of a feather flock together.' "

"Only mustard isn't a bird," Alice remarked.

"Right, as usual," said the Duchess: "what a clear way you have of putting things!"

"It's a mineral, I *think*," said Alice.

"Of course it is," said the Duchess, who seemed ready to agree to everything that Alice said: "there's a large mustard-machine near here. And the moral of that is—'The more there is of mine, the less there is of yours.' "

"Oh, I know!" exclaimed Alice, who had not attended to this last remark. "It's a vegetable. It doesn't look like one, but it is."

"I quite agree with you," said the Duchess; "and the moral of that is—'Be what you would seem to be'—or, if you'd like it put more simply—'Never imagine yourself not to be otherwise than what it might appear to others that what you were or might have been was not otherwise than what you had been would have appeared to them to be otherwise.' "

"I think I should understand that better", Alice said very politely, "if I had it written down: but I ca'n't quite follow it as you say it."

"That's nothing to what I could say if I chose," the Duchess replied, in a pleased tone.

"Pray don't trouble yourself to say it any longer than that," said Alice.

"Oh, don't talk about trouble!" said the Duchess. "I make you a present of everything I've said as yet."

"A cheap sort of present!" thought Alice. "I'm glad people don't give birthday-presents like that!" But she did not venture to say it out loud.

"Thinking again?" the Duchess asked, with another dig of her sharp little chin.

"I've a right to think," said Alice sharply, for she was beginning to feel a little worried.

"Just about as much right", said the Duchess, "as pigs have to fly; and the m——"

But here, to Alice's great surprise, the Duchess's voice died away, even in the middle of her favourite word "moral", and the arm that was linked into hers began to tremble. Alice looked up, and there stood the Queen in front of them, with her arms folded, frowning like a thunder-storm.

"A fine day, your Majesty!" the Duchess began in a low, weak voice.

"Now, I give you fair warning," shouted the Queen, stamping on the ground as she spoke; "either you or your head must be off, and that in about half no time! Take your choice!"

The Duchess took her choice, and was gone in a moment.

"Let's go on with the game," the Queen said to Alice; and Alice was too much frightened to say a word, but slowly followed her back to the croquet ground.

The other guests had taken advantage of the Queen's absence, and were resting in the shade: however, the moment they saw her, they hurried back to the game, the Queen merely remarking that a moment's delay would cost them their lives.

All the time they were playing the Queen never left off quarreling with the other players and shouting "Off with his head!" or "Off with her head!" Those whom she sentenced were taken into custody by the soldiers, who of course had to leave off being arches to do this, so that, by the end of half an hour or so, there were no arches left, and all the players, except the King, the Queen, and Alice, were in custody and under sentence of execution.

Then the Queen left off, quite out of breath, and said to Alice, "Have you seen the Mock Turtle yet?"

"No," said Alice. "I don't even know what a Mock Turtle is."

"It's the thing Mock Turtle Soup is made from," said the Queen.

"I never saw one, or heard of one," said Alice.

"Come on, then," said the Queen, "and he shall tell you his history."

As they walked off together, Alice heard the King say in a low voice, to the company, generally, "You are all

pardoned." "Come, *that's* a good thing!" she said to herself, for she had felt quite unhappy at the number of
executions the Queen had ordered.

They very soon came upon a Gryphon, lying fast
asleep in the sun. (If you don't know what a Gryphon is,
look at the picture.) "Up, lazy thing!" said the Queen,
"and take this young lady to see the Mock Turtle, and to

hear his history. I must go back and see after some executions I have ordered"; and she walked off, leaving Alice
alone with the Gryphon. Alice did not quite like the look
of the creature, but on the whole she thought it would be
quite as safe to stay with it as to go after that savage
Queen: so she waited.

The Gryphon sat up and rubbed its eyes: then it
watched the Queen till she was out of sight then it
chuckled. "What fun!" said the Gryphon, half to itself,
half to Alice.

"What *is* the fun?" said Alice.

"Why, *she*," said the Gryphon. "It's all her fancy that:
they never executes nobody, you know. Come on!"

"Everybody says 'come on!' here," thought Alice, as she went slowly after it: "I never was so ordered about before, in all my life, never!"

They had not gone far before they saw the Mock Turtle in the distance, sitting sad and lonely on a little ledge of rock, and, as they came nearer, Alice could hear him sighing as if his heart would break. She pitied him deeply. "What is his sorrow?" she asked the Gryphon. And the Gryphon answered, very nearly in the same words as before, "It's all his fancy, that: he hasn't got no sorrow, you know. Come on!"

So they went up to the Mock Turtle, who looked at them with large eyes full of tears, but said nothing.

"This here young lady," said the Gryphon, "she wants for to know your history, she do."

"I'll tell it her," said the Mock Turtle in a deep, hollow tone. "Sit down, both of you, and don't speak a word till I've finished."

So they sat down, and nobody spoke for some minutes. Alice thought to herself "I don't see how he can *ever* finish, if he doesn't begin." But she waited patiently.

"Once", said the Mock Turtle at last, with a deep sigh, "I was a real Turtle."

These words were followed by a very long silence, broken only by an occasional exclamation of "Hjckrrh!" from the Gryphon, and the constant heavy sobbing of the Mock Turtle. Alice was very nearly getting up and saying, "Thank you, Sir, for your interesting story," but she could not help thinking there *must* be more to come, so she sat still and said nothing.

"When we were little", the Mock Turtle went on at last, more calmly, though still sobbing a little now and then, "we went to school in the sea. The master was an old Turtle—we used to call him Tortoise——"

"Why did you call him Tortoise, if he wasn't one?" Alice asked.

"We called him Tortoise because he taught us," said the Mock Turtle angrily. "Really you are very dull!"

"You ought to be ashamed of yourself for asking such a simple question," added the Gryphon; and then they both sat silent and looked at poor Alice, who felt ready to sink into the earth. At last the Gryphon said to the Mock Turtle "Drive on, old fellow! Don't be all day about it!" and he went on in these words:

"Yes, we went to school in the sea, though you mayn't believe it——"

"I never said I didn't!" interrupted Alice.

"You did," said the Mock Turtle.

"Hold your tongue!" added the Gryphon, before Alice

could speak again. The Mock Turtle went on.

"We had the best of educations—in fact, we went to school every day——"

"*I've* been to a day-school, too," said Alice. "You needn't be so proud as all that."

"With extras?" asked the Mock Turtle, a little anxiously.

"Yes," said Alice: "we learned French and music."

"And washing?" said the Mock Turtle.

"Certainly not!" said Alice, indignantly.

"Ah! Then yours wasn't a really good school," said the Mock Turtle in a tone of great relief. "Now, at *ours*, they had, at the end of the bill, 'French, music *and* washing—extra'."

"You couldn't have wanted it much," said Alice; "living at the bottom of the sea."

"I couldn't afford to learn it," said the Mock Turtle with a sigh. "I only took the regular course."

"What was that?" inquired Alice.

"Reeling and Writhing, of course, to begin with," the Mock Turtle replied; "and then the different branches of Arithmetic—Ambition, Distraction, Uglification, and Derision."

"I never heard of 'Uglification'," Alice ventured to say. "What is it?"

The Gryphon lifted up both its paws in surprise. "Never heard of uglifying!" it exclaimed. "You know what to beautify is, I suppose?"

"Yes," said Alice doubtfully: "it means—to—make—anything—prettier."

"Well, then," the Gryphon went on, "if you don't know what to uglify is, you *are* a simpleton."

Alice did not feel encouraged to ask any more questions about it: so she turned to the Mock Turtle, and said "What else had you to learn?"

"Well, there was Mystery," the Mock Turtle replied, counting off the subjects on his flappers—"Mystery, ancient and modern, with Seaography: then Drawling—

the Drawling-master was an old conger-eel, that used to come once a week: *he* taught us Drawling, Stretching, and Fainting in Coils."

"What was *that* like?" said Alice.

"Well, I ca'n't show it you, myself," the Mock Turtle said "I'm too stiff. And the Gryphon never learnt it."

"Hadn't time," said the Gryphon: "I went to the Classical master, though. He was an old crab, *he* was."

"I never went to him," the Mock Turtle said with a sigh. "He taught Laughing and Grief, they used to say."

"So he did, so he did," said the Gryphon, sighing in his turn; and both creatures hid their faces in their paws.

"And how many hours a day did you do lessons?" said Alice, in a hurry to change the subject.

"Ten hours the first day," said the Mock Turtle: "nine the next, and so on."

"What a curious plan!" exclaimed Alice.

"That's the reason they're called lessons," the Gryphon remarked: "because they lessen from day to day."

This was quite a new idea to Alice, and she thought it over a little before she made her next remark. "Then the eleventh day must have been a holiday?"

"Of course it was," said the Mock Turtle.

"And how did you manage on the twelfth?" Alice went on eagerly.

"That's enough about lessons," the Gryphon interrupted in a very decided tone. "Tell her something about the games now."

Chapter X

The Lobster-Quadrille

THE Mock Turtle sighed deeply, and drew the back of one flapper across his eyes. He looked at Alice and tried to speak, but, for a minute or two, sobs choked his voice.

"Same as if he had a bone in his throat," said the Gryphon; and it set to work shaking him and punching him in the back. At last the Mock Turtle recovered his voice, and, with tears running down his cheeks, he went on again:

"You may not have lived much under the sea—" ("I haven't," said Alice)—"and perhaps you were never even introduced to a lobster—" (Alice began to say "I once tasted——" but checked herself hastily and said "No never") "—so you can have no idea what a delightful thing a Lobster-Quadrille is!"

"No, indeed," said Alice. "What sort of a dance is it?"

"Why," said the Gryphon, "you first form into a line along the sea-shore——"

"Two lines!" cried the Mock Turtle. "Seals, turtles, salmon, and so on: then, when you've cleared all the jelly-fish out of the way——"

"*That* generally takes some time," interrupted the Gryphon.

"—you advance twice——"

"Each with a lobster as a partner!" cried the Gryphon.

"Of course," the Mock Turtle said: "advance twice, set to partners——"

"—change lobsters, and retire in same order," continued the Gryphon.

"Then, you know," the Mock Turtle went on, "you throw the——"

"The lobsters!" shouted the Gryphon with a bound into the air.

"—as far out to sea as you can——"

"Swim after them!" screamed the Gryphon.

"Turn a somersault in the sea!" cried the Mock Turtle, capering wildly about.

"Change lobsters again!" yelled the Gryphon at the top of its voice.

"Back to land again, and—that's all the first figure," said the Mock Turtle, suddenly dropping his voice; and the two creatures, who had been jumping about like mad

things all this time, sat down again very sadly and quietly and looked at Alice.

"It must be a very pretty dance," said Alice timidly.

"Would you like to see a little of it?" said the Mock Turtle.

"Very much indeed," said Alice.

"Come, let's try the first figure!" said the Mock Turtle to the Gryphon. "We can do it without lobsters, you know. Which shall sing?"

"Oh, *you* sing," said the Gryphon. "I've forgotten the words."

So they began solemnly dancing round and round Alice, every now and then treading on her toes when they passed too close, and waving their fore-paws to mark the time, when the Mock Turtle sang this, very slowly and sadly:

"Will you walk a little faster?" said a whiting to a snail,
"There's a porpoise close behind us, and he's treading on my tail.
See how eagerly the lobsters and the turtles all advance!
They are waiting on the shingle—will you come and join the dance?
   Will you, wo'n't you, will you, wo'n't you, will you join the dance?
   Will you, wo'n't you, will you, wo'n't you, wo'n't you join the dance?

"You can really have no notion how delightful it will be
"When they take us up and throw us, with the lobsters, out to sea!"
But the snail replied "Too far, too far!" and gave a look askance—
Said he thanked the whiting kindly, but he would not join the dance.
   Would not, could not, would not, could not, would not join the dance.
   Would not, could not, would not, could not, could not join the dance.

"What matters it how far we go?" his scaly friend replied.
"There is another shore, you know, upon the other side.
The further off from England the nearer is to France—
Then turn not pale, beloved snail, but come and join the dance.
   Will you, wo'n't you, will you, wo'n't you, will you join the dance?
   Will you, wo'n't you, will you, wo'n't you, wo'n't you join the dance?"

"Thank you, it's a very interesting dance to watch," said Alice, feeling very glad that it was over at last: "and I do so like that curious song about the whiting!"

"Oh, as to the whiting," said the Mock Turtle, "they— you've seen them, of course?"

"Yes," said Alice, "I've often seen them at dinn——" she checked herself hastily.

"I don't know where Dinn may be," said the Mock Turtle; "but, if you've seen them so often, of course you know what they're like?"

"I believe so," Alice replied thoughtfully. "They have their tails in their mouths—and they're all over crumbs."

"You're wrong about the crumbs," said the Mock Turtle: "crumbs would all wash off in the sea. But they *have* their tails in their mouths; and the reason is——" here the Mock Turtle yawned and shut his eyes. "Tell her about the reason and all that," he said to the Gryphon.

"The reason is", said the Gryphon, "that they *would* go with the lobsters to the dance. So they got thrown out to sea. So they had to fall a long way. So they got their tails fast in their mouths. So they couldn't get them out again. That's all."

"Thank you," said Alice, "it's very interesting. I never knew so much about a whiting before."

"I can tell you more than that, if you like," said the Gryphon. "Do you know why it's called a whiting?"

"I never thought about it," said Alice. "Why?"

"*It does the boots and shoes*," the Gryphon replied very solemnly.

Alice was thoroughly puzzled. "Does the boots and shoes!" she repeated in a wondering tone.

"Why, what are *your* shoes done with?" said the Gryphon. "I mean, what makes them so shiny?"

Alice looked down at them, and considered a little before she gave her answer. "They're done with blacking, I believe."

"Boots and shoes under the sea", the Gryphon went on in a deep voice, "are done with whiting. Now you know."

"And what are they made of?" Alice asked in a tone of great curiosity.

"Soles and eels, of course," the Gryphon replied, rather impatiently: "any shrimp could have told you that."

"If I'd been the whiting", said Alice, whose thoughts were still running on the song, "I'd have said to the porpoise 'Keep back, please! We don't want *you* with us!' "

"They were obliged to have him with them," the Mock Turtle said. "No wise fish would go anywhere without a porpoise."

"Wouldn't it, really?" said Alice, in a tone of great surprise.

"Of course not," said the Mock Turtle. "Why, if a fish came to *me*, and told me he was going a journey, I should say 'With what porpoise?'"

"Don't you mean 'purpose'?" said Alice.

"I mean what I say," the Mock Turtle replied, in an offended tone. And the Gryphon added "Come, let's hear some of *your* adventures."

"I could tell you my adventures—beginning from this morning," said Alice a little timidly; "but it's no use going back to yesterday, because I was a different person then."

"Explain all that," said the Mock Turtle.

"No, no! The adventures first," said the Gryphon in an impatient tone: "explanations take such a dreadful time."

So Alice began telling them her adventures from the time when she first saw the White Rabbit. She was a little nervous about it, just at first, the two creatures got so close to her, one on each side, and opened their eyes and mouths so *very* wide; but she gained courage as she went on. Her listeners were perfectly quiet till she got to the part about her repeating "*You are old, Father William*," to the Caterpillar, and the words all coming different, and then the Mock Turtle drew a long breath, and said "That's very curious!"

"It's all about as curious as it can be," said the Gryphon.

"It all came different!" the Mock Turtle repeated thoughtfully. "I should like to hear her try and repeat something now. Tell her to begin." He looked at the Gryphon as if he thought it had some kind of authority over Alice.

"Stand up and repeat ''*Tis the voice of the sluggard*'," said the Gryphon.

"How the creatures order one about, and make one repeat lessons!" thought Alice. "I might just as well be at
school at once." However, she got up, and began to repeat it, but her head was so full of the Lobster-Quadrille,
that she hardly knew what she was saying; and the words
came very queer indeed:

> "'*Tis the voice of the Lobster: I heard him declare*
> '*You have baked me too brown, I must sugar my hair.*'
> *As a duck with his eyelids, so he with his nose*
> *Trims his belt and his buttons, and turns out his toes.*
> *When the sands are all dry, he is gay as a lark,*
> *And will talk in contemptuous tones of the Shark:*
> *But, when the tide rises and sharks are around,*
> *His voice has a timid and tremulous sound.*"

"That's different from what *I* used to say when I was a child," said the Gryphon.

"Well, *I* never heard it before," said the Mock Turtle; "but it sounds uncommon nonsense."

Alice said nothing: she had sat down with her face in her hands, wondering if anything would *ever* happen in a natural way again.

"I should like to have it explained," said the Mock Turtle.

"She ca'n't explain it," said the Gryphon hastily. "Go on with the next verse."

"But about his toes?" the Mock Turtle persisted. "How *could* he turn them out with his nose, you know?"

"It's the first position in dancing," Alice said; but she was dreadfully puzzled by the whole thing, and longed to change the subject.

"Go on with the next verse," the Gryphon repeated: "it begins '*I passed by his garden*'."

Alice did not dare to disobey, though she felt sure it would all come wrong, and she went on in a trembling voice:

> "*I passed by his garden, and marked, with one eye,*
> *How the Owl and the Panther were sharing a pie:*
> *The Panther took pie-crust, and gravy, and meat,*
> *While the Owl had the dish as its share of the treat.*
> *When the pie was all finished, the Owl, as a boon,*
> *Was kindly permitted to pocket the spoon:*
> *While the Panther received knife and fork with a growl,*
> *And concluded the banquet by —— "*

"What *is* the use of repeating all that stuff?" the Mock Turtle interrupted, "if you don't explain it as you go on? It's by far the most confusing thing that *I* ever heard!"

"Yes, I think you'd better leave off," said the Gryphon, and Alice was only too glad to do so.

"Shall we try another figure of the Lobster-Quadrille?" the Gryphon went on. "Or would you like the Mock Turtle to sing you another song?"

"Oh, a song, please, if the Mock Turtle would be so kind," Alice replied, so eagerly that the Gryphon said, in a rather offended tone, "Hm! No accounting for tastes! Sing her *'Turtle Soup'*, will you, old fellow?"

The Mock Turtle sighed deeply, and began in a voice choked with sobs, to sing this:

"Beautiful Soup, so rich and green,
Waiting in a hot tureen!
Who for such dainties would not stoop?
Soup of the evening, beautiful Soup!
Soup of the evening, beautiful Soup!
Beau—ootiful Soo—oop!
Beau—ootiful Soo—oop!
Soo—oop of the e—e—evening,
Beautiful, beautiful Soup!

"Beautiful Soup! Who cares for fish,
Game, or any other dish?
Who would not give all else for two p
ennyworth only of beautiful Soup?
Pennyworth only of beautiful Soup?
Beau—ootiful Soo—oop!
Beau—ootiful Soo—oop!
Soo—oop of the e—e—evening,
Beautiful beauti—FUL SOUP!"

"Chorus again!" cried the Gryphon, and the Mock Turtle had just begun to repeat it, when a cry of "The trial's beginning!" was heard in the distance.

"Come on!" cried the Gryphon, and, taking Alice by the hand, it hurried off, without waiting for the end of the song.

"What trial is it?" Alice panted as she ran: but the Gryphon only answered "Come on!" and ran the faster, while more and more faintly came, carried on the breeze that followed them, the melancholy words:

"Soo—oop of the e—e—evening,
Beautiful, beautiful Soup!"

Chapter XI

Who Stole the Tarts?

THE King and Queen of Hearts were seated on their throne when they arrived, with a great crowd assembled about them—all sorts of little birds and beasts, as well as the whole pack of cards: the Knave was standing before them, in chains, with a soldier on each side to guard him; and near the King was the White Rabbit, with a trumpet in one hand, and a scroll of parchment in the other. In the very middle of the court was a table, with a large dish of tarts upon it: they looked so good, that it made Alice quite hungry to look at them—"I wish they'd get the trial done," she thought, "and hand round the refreshments!" But there seemed to be no chance of this; so she began looking at everything about her to pass away the time.

Alice had never been in a court of justice before, but she had read about them in books, and she was quite pleased to find that she knew the name of nearly everything there. "That's the judge," she said to herself, "because of his great wig."

The judge, by the way, was the King; and, as he wore his crown over the wig (look at the frontispiece if you want to see how he did it), he did not look at all comfortable, and it was certainly not becoming.

"And that's the jury-box," thought Alice; "and those twelve creatures," (she was obliged to say "creatures," you see, because some of them were animals, and some were birds,) "I suppose they are the jurors." She said this last word two or three times over to herself, being rather proud of it: for she thought, and rightly too, that very few little girls of her age knew the meaning of it at all. However, "jurymen" would have done just as well.

The twelve jurors were all writing very busily on slates. "What are they doing?" Alice whispered to the Gryphon.

"They ca'n't have anything to put down yet, before the trial's begun."

"They're putting down their names", the Gryphon whispered in reply, "for fear they should forget them before the end of the trial."

"Stupid things!" Alice began in a loud indignant voice; but she stopped herself hastily, for the White Rabbit cried

out "Silence in the court!" and the King put on his spectacles and looked anxiously round, to make out who was talking.

Alice could see, as well as if she were looking over their shoulders, that all the jurors were writing down "Stupid things!" on their slates, and she could even make out that one of them didn't know how to spell "stupid", and that he had to ask his neighbour to tell him. "A nice muddle their slates'll be in, before the trial's over!" thought Alice.

One of the jurors had a pencil that squeaked. This, of

course, Alice could *not* stand, and she went round the court and got behind him, and very soon found an opportunity of taking it away. She did it so quickly that the poor little juror (it was Bill, the Lizard) could not make out at all what had become of it; so, after hunting all about for it, he was obliged to write with one finger for the rest of the day; and this was of very little use, as it left no mark on the slate.

"Herald, read the accusation!" said the King.

On this the White Rabbit blew three blasts on the trumpet, and then unrolled the parchment-scroll, and read as follows:

> *"The Queen of Hearts, she made some tarts,*
> *All on a summer day:*
> *The Knave of Hearts, he stole those tarts*
> *And took them quite away!"*

"Consider your verdict," the King said to the jury.

"Not yet, not yet!" the Rabbit hastily interrupted. "There's a great deal to come before that!"

"Call the first witness," said the King; and the White Rabbit blew three blasts on the trumpet, and called out "First witness!"

The first witness was the Hatter. He came in with a teacup in one hand and a piece of bread-and-butter in the other. "I beg pardon, your Majesty," he began, "for bringing these in; but I hadn't quite finished my tea when I was sent for."

"You ought to have finished," said the King. "When did you begin?"

The Hatter looked at the March Hare, who had followed him into the court, arm-in-arm with the Dormouse. "Fourteenth of March, I *think* it was," he said.

"Fifteenth," said the March Hare.

"Sixteenth," said the Dormouse.

"Write that down," the King said to the jury; and the jury eagerly wrote down all three dates on their slates, and then added them up, and reduced the answer to shillings and pence.

"Take off your hat," the King said to the Hatter.

"It isn't mine," said the Hatter.

"*Stolen!*" the King exclaimed, turning to the jury, who instantly made a memorandum of the fact.

"I keep them to sell," the Hatter added as an explanation. "I've none of my own. I'm a hatter."

Here the Queen put on her spectacles, and began staring hard at the Hatter, who turned pale and fidgeted.

"Give your evidence," said the King; "and don't be nervous, or I'll have you executed on the spot."

This did not seem to encourage the witness at all: he kept shifting from one foot to the other, looking uneasily at the Queen, and in his confusion he bit a large piece out of his teacup instead of the bread-and-butter.

Just at this moment Alice felt a very curious sensation, which puzzled her a great deal until she made out what it was: she was beginning to grow larger again, and she thought at first she would get up and leave the court; but on second thoughts she decided to remain where she was as long as there was room for her.

"I wish you wouldn't squeeze so," said the Dormouse, who was sitting next to her. "I can hardly breathe."

"I ca'n't help it," said Alice very meekly: "I'm growing."

"You've no right to grow *here*," said the Dormouse.

"Don't talk nonsense," said Alice more boldly: "you know you're growing too."

"Yes, but *I* grow at a reasonable pace," said the Dormouse: "not in that ridiculous fashion." And he got up very sulkily and crossed over to the other side of the court.

All this time the Queen had never left off staring at the Hatter, and, just as the Dormouse crossed the court, she said, to one of the officers of the court, "Bring me the list of the singers in the last concert!" on which the wretched Hatter trembled so, that he shook off both his shoes.

"Give your evidence", the King repeated angrily, "or I'll have you executed, whether you are nervous or not."

"I'm a poor man, your Majesty," the Hatter began, in a trembling voice, "and I hadn't begun my tea—not above a week or so—and what with the bread-and-butter getting so thin—and the twinkling of the tea——"

"The twinkling of *what*?" said the King.

"It *began* with the tea," the Hatter replied.

"Of course twinkling *begins* with a T!" said the King sharply. "Do you take me for a dunce? Go on!"

"I'm a poor man," the Hatter went on, "and most things twinkled after that—only the March Hare said——"

"I didn't!" the March Hare interrupted in a great hurry.

"You did!" said the Hatter.

"I deny it!" said the March Hare.

"He denies it," said the King: "leave out that part."

"Well, at any rate, the Dormouse said——" the Hatter went on, looking anxiously round to see if he would deny it too; but the Dormouse denied nothing, being fast asleep.

"After that", continued the Hatter, "I cut some more bread-and-butter——"

"But what did the Dormouse say?" one of the jury asked.

"That I ca'n't remember", said the Hatter.

"You *must* remember", remarked the King, "or I'll have you executed."

The miserable Hatter dropped his teacup and bread-and-butter, and went down on one knee. "I'm a poor man, your Majesty," he began.

"You're a *very* poor *speaker*," said the King.

Here one of the guinea-pigs cheered, and was immediately suppressed by the officers of the court. (As that is rather a hard word, I will just explain to you how it was done. They had a large canvas bag, which tied up at the mouth with strings: into this they slipped the guinea-pig, head first, and then sat upon it.)

"I'm glad I've seen that done," thought Alice. "I've so often read in the newspapers, at the end of trials, 'There was some attempt at applause, which was immediately suppressed by the officers of the court,' and I never understood what it meant till now."

"If that's all you know about it, you may stand down," continued the King.

"I ca'n't go no lower," said the Hatter: "I'm on the floor, as it is."

"Then you may *sit* down," the King replied.

Here the other guinea-pig cheered, and was suppressed.

"Come, that finishes the guinea-pigs!" thought Alice. "Now we shall get on better."

"I'd rather finish my tea," said the Hatter, with an anxious look at the Queen, who was reading the list of singers.

"You may go," said the King, and the Hatter hurriedly left the court, without even waiting to put his shoes on.

"——and just take his head off outside," the Queen added to one of the officers; but the Hatter was out of sight before the officer could get to the door.

"Call the next witness!" said the King.

The next witness was the Duchess's cook. She carried the pepper-box in her hand, and Alice guessed who it was, even before she got into the court, by the way the people near the door began sneezing all at once.

"Give your evidence," said the King.

"Sha'n't," said the cook.

The King looked anxiously at the White Rabbit, who said, in a low voice, "Your Majesty must cross-examine *this* witness."

"Well, if I must, I must," the King said with a melancholy air, and, after folding his arms and frowning at the cook till his eyes were nearly out of sight, he said, in a deep voice, "What are tarts made of?"

"Pepper, mostly," said the cook.

"Treacle," said a sleepy voice behind her.

"Collar that Dormouse!" the Queen shrieked out. "Behead that Dormouse! Turn that Dormouse out of court! Suppress him! Pinch him! Off with his whiskers!"

For some minutes the whole court was in confusion, getting the Dormouse turned out, and, by the time they had settled down again, the cook had disappeared.

"Never mind!" said the King, with an air of great relief. "Call the next witness." And he added, in an undertone to the Queen, "Really, my dear, *you* must cross-examine the next witness. It quite makes my forehead ache!"

Alice watched the White Rabbit as he fumbled over the list, feeling very curious to see what the next witness would be like, "—for they haven't got much evidence *yet*," she said to herself. Imagine her surprise, when the White Rabbit read out, at the top of his shrill little voice, the name "Alice!"

Chapter XII

Alice's Evidence

"Here!" cried Alice, quite forgetting in the flurry of the moment how large she had grown in the last few minutes, and she jumped up in such a hurry that she tipped over the jury-box with the edge of her skirt, upsetting all the jurymen on to the heads of the crowd below and there they lay sprawling about, reminding her very much of a globe of gold-fish she had accidentally upset the week before.

"Oh, I *beg* your pardon!" she exclaimed in a tone of great dismay, and began picking them up again as quickly as she could, for the accident of the gold-fish kept running in her head, and she had a vague sort of idea that they must be collected at once and put back into the jury-box, or they would die.

"The trial cannot proceed", said the King, in a very grave voice, "until all the jurymen are back in their proper places—*all*," he repeated with great emphasis, looking hard at Alice as he said so.

Alice looked at the jury-box, and saw that, in her haste, she had put the Lizard in head downwards, and the poor

little thing was waving its tail about in a melancholy way, being quite unable to move. She soon got it out again, and put it right; "not that it signifies much," she said to herself; "I should think it would be *quite* as much use in the trial one way up as the other."

As soon as the jury had a little recovered from the shock of being upset, and their slates and pencils had been found and handed back to them, they set to work very diligently to write out a history of the accident, all except the Lizard, who seemed too much overcome to do anything but sit with its mouth open, gazing up into the roof of the court.

"What do you know about this business?" the King said to Alice.

"Nothing," said Alice.

"Nothing *whatever*?" persisted the King.

"Nothing whatever," said Alice.

"That's very important," the King said, turning to the jury. They were just beginning to write this down on their slates, when the White Rabbit interrupted: "*Un*important, your Majesty means, of course," he said, in a very respectful tone, but frowning and making faces at him as he spoke.

"*Un*important, of course, I meant," the King hastily said, and went on to himself in an undertone, "important —unimportant—unimportant—important——" as if he were trying which word sounded best.

Some of the jury wrote it down "important", and some "unimportant". Alice could see this, as she was near enough to look over their slates; "but it doesn't matter a bit," she thought to herself.

At this moment the King, who had been for some time busily writing in his note-book, called out "Silence!" and read out from his book "Rule Forty-two. *All persons more than a mile high to leave the court.*"

Everybody looked at Alice.

"*I'm* not a mile high," said Alice.

"You are," said the King.

"Nearly two miles high," added the Queen.

"Well, I sha'n't go, at any rate," said Alice; "besides, that's not a regular rule: you invented it just now."

"It's the oldest rule in the book," said the King.

"Then it ought to be Number One," said Alice.

The King turned pale, and shut his note-book hastily. "Consider your verdict," he said to the jury, in a low trembling voice.

"There's more evidence to come yet, please your Majesty," said the White Rabbit, jumping up in a great hurry: "this paper has just been picked up."

"What's in it?" said the Queen.

"I haven't opened it yet," said the White Rabbit; "but it seems to be a letter, written by the prisoner to—to somebody."

"It must have been that," said the King, "unless it was written to nobody, which isn't usual, you know."

"Who is it directed to?" said one of the jurymen.

"It isn't directed at all," said the White Rabbit: "in fact, there's nothing written on the *outside*." He unfolded the paper as he spoke, and added "It isn't a letter, after all: it's a set of verses."

"Are they in the prisoner's handwriting?" asked another of the jurymen.

"No, they're not," said the White Rabbit, "and that's the queerest thing about it." (The jury all looked puzzled.)

"He must have imitated somebody else's hand," said the King. (The jury all brightened up again.)

"Please, your Majesty," said the Knave, "I didn't write it, and they ca'n't prove that I did: there's no name signed at the end."

"If you didn't sign it", said the King, "that only makes the matter worse. You *must* have meant some mischief, or else you'd have signed your name like an honest man."

There was a general clapping of hands at this: it was the first really clever thing the King had said that day.

"That *proves* his guilt, of course," said the Queen: "so, off with——"

"It doesn't prove anything of the sort!" said Alice. "Why, you don't even know what they're about!"

"Read them," said the King.

The White Rabbit put on his spectacles. "Where shall I begin, please your Majesty?" he asked.

"Begin at the beginning", the King said, very gravely, "and go on till you come to the end: then stop."

There was dead silence in the court, whilst the White Rabbit read out these verses:

"They told me you had been to her,
And mentioned me to him:
She gave me a good character,
But said I could not swim.

He sent them word I had not gone
(We know it to be true):
If she should push the matter on,
What would become of you?

I gave her one, they gave him two,
You gave us three or more;
They all returned from him to you,
Though they were mine before.

If I or she should chance to be
Involved in this affair,
He trusts to you to set them free,
Exactly as we were.

My notion was that you had been
(Before she had this fit)
An obstacle that came between
Him, and ourselves, and it.

Don't let him know she liked them best,
For this must ever be
A secret, kept from all the rest,
Between yourself and me."

"That's the most important piece of evidence we've heard yet," said the King, rubbing his hands; "so now let the jury——"

"If any one of them can explain it", said Alice, (she had grown so large in the last few minutes that she wasn't a bit afraid of interrupting him), "I'll give him sixpence. *I* don't believe there's an atom of meaning in it."

The jury all wrote down, on their slates, "*She* doesn't believe there's an atom of meaning in it," but none of them attempted to explain the paper.

"If there's no meaning in it," said the King, "that saves a world of trouble, you know, as we needn't try to find any. And yet I don't know," he went on, spreading out the verses on his knee, and looking at them with one eye; "I seem to see some meaning in them, after all.

'—*said I could not swim* —' you ca'n't swim, can you?" he added, turning to the Knave.

The Knave shook his head sadly. "Do I look like it?" he said. (Which he certainly did *not*, being made entirely of cardboard.)

"All right, so far," said the King; and he went on muttering over the verses to himself: " '*We know it to be true*'—that's the jury, of course—'*If she should push the matter on*' —that must be the Queen —'*What would become of you?*'—What, indeed!—'*I gave her one, they gave him two*'—why, that must be what he did with the tarts, you know——"

"But it goes on '*they all returned from him to you,*' " said Alice.

"Why, there they are!" said the King triumphantly, pointing to the tarts on the table. "Nothing can be clearer than *that*. Then again—'*before she had this fit*'—you never had *fits*, my dear, I think?" he said to the Queen.

"Never!" said the Queen, furiously, throwing an inkstand at the Lizard as she spoke. (The unfortunate little Bill had left off writing on his slate with one finger, as he found it made no mark; but he now hastily began again, using the ink, that was trickling down his face, as long as it lasted.)

"Then the words don't *fit* you," said the King looking round the court with a smile. There was a dead silence.

"It's a pun!" the King added in an angry tone, and everybody laughed. "Let the jury consider their verdict," the King said, for about the twentieth time that day.

"No, no!" said the Queen. "Sentence first—verdict afterwards."

"Stuff and nonsense!" said Alice loudly. "The idea of having the sentence first!"

"Hold your tongue!" said the Queen, turning purple.

"I wo'n't!" said Alice.

"Off with her head!" the Queen shouted at the top of her voice. Nobody moved.

"Who cares for *you*?" said Alice (she had grown to her full size by this time). "You're nothing but a pack of cards!"

At this the whole pack rose up into the air, and came flying down upon her; she gave a little scream, half of fright and half of anger, and tried to beat them off, and found herself lying on the bank, with her head in the lap of her sister, who was gently brushing away some dead leaves that had fluttered down from the trees upon her face.

"Wake up, Alice dear!" said her sister. "Why, what a long sleep you've had!"

"Oh, I've had such a curious dream!" said Alice. And she told her sister, as well as she could remember them, all these strange Adventures of hers that you have just

been reading about; and, when she had finished, her sister kissed her, and said "It *was* a curious dream, dear, certainly; but now run in to your tea: it's getting late." So Alice got up and ran off, thinking while she ran, as well she might, what a wonderful dream it had been.

But her sister sat still just as she left her, leaning her head on her hand, watching the setting sun, and thinking of little Alice and all her wonderful Adventures, till she too began dreaming after a fashion, and this was her dream:—

First, she dreamed about little Alice herself: once again the tiny hands were clasped upon her knee, and the bright eager eyes were looking up into hers—she could hear the very tones of her voice, and see that queer little toss of her head to keep back the wandering hair that *would* always get into her eyes—and still as she listened, or seemed to listen, the whole place around her became alive with the strange creatures of her little sister's dream.

The long grass rustled at her feet as the White Rabbit hurried by—the frightened Mouse splashed his way through the neighbouring pool—she could hear the rattle of the teacups as the March Hare and his friends shared their never-ending meal, and the shrill voice of the Queen ordering off her unfortunate guests to execution—once more the pig-baby was sneezing on the Duchess's knee, while plates and dishes crashed around it—once more the shriek of the Gryphon, the squeaking of the 'Lizard's slate-pencil, and the choking of the suppressed guinea-pigs, filled the air, mixed up with the distant sob of the miserable Mock Turtle.

So she sat on, with closed eyes, and half believed herself in Wonderland, though she knew she had but to open them again, and all would change to dull reality—the grass would be only rustling in the wind, and the pool rippling to the waving of the reeds—the rattling teacups would change to tinkling sheep-bells, and the Queen's shrill cries to the voice of the shepherd-boy—and the sneeze of the baby, the shriek of the Gryphon, and all the other queer noises, would change (she knew) to the confused clamour of the busy farm-yard—while the lowing of the cattle in the distance would take the place of the Mock Turtle's heavy sobs.

Lastly, she pictured to herself how this same little sister of hers would, in the after-time, be herself a grown woman; and how she would keep, through all her riper years, the simple and loving heart of her childhood; and how she would gather about her other little children, and make *their* eyes bright and eager with many a strange tale, perhaps even with the dream of Wonderland of long ago; and how she would feel with all their simple sorrows, and find a pleasure in all their simple joys, remembering her own child-life, and the happy summer days.

II
Through the
Looking-Glass
and what Alice found there

Child of the pure unclouded brow
  And dreaming eyes of wonder!
Though time be fleet, and I and thou
  Are half a life asunder,
Thy loving smile will surely hail
The love-gift of a fairy-tale.

I have not seen thy sunny face,
  Nor heard thy silver laughter:
No thought of me shall find a place
  In thy young life's hereafter—
Enough that now thou wilt not fail
To listen to my fairy-tale.

A tale begun in other days,
  When summer suns were glowing—
A simple chime, that served to time
  The rhythm of our rowing—
Whose echoes live in memory yet,
Though envious years would say "forget".

Come, hearken then, ere voice of dread,
  With bitter tidings laden,
Shall summon to unwelcome bed
  A melancholy maiden!
We are but older children, dear,
Who fret to find our bedtime near.

Without, the frost, the blinding snow,
  The storm-wind's moody madness—
Within, the firelight's ruddy glow,
  And childhood's nest of gladness.
The magic words shall hold thee fast:
Thou shalt not heed the raving blast.

And, though the shadow of a sigh
May tremble through the story,
For "happy summer days" gone by,
And vanish'd summer glory—
It shall not touch with breath of bale,
The pleasance of our fairy-tale.

White Pawn (Alice) to play, and win in eleven moves.

	PAGE		PAGE
1. Alice meets R. Q.	148	1. R. Q. to K. R's 4th	153
2. Alice through Q's 3d (*by railway*) .	153	2. W. Q. to Q. B's 4th (*after shawl*) . .	179
to Q's 4th (*Tweedledum and Tweedledee*) . .	155		
3. Alice meets W. Q. (*with shawl*) . .	178	3. W. Q. to Q. B's 5th (*becomes sheep*) .	185
4. Alice to Q's 5th (*shop, river, shop*)	185	4. W. Q. to K. B's 8th (*leaves egg on shelf*)	190
5. Alice to Q's 6th (*Humpty Dumpty*)	191	5. W. Q. to Q. B's 8th (*flying from R.Kt.*)	210
6. Alice to Q's 7th (*forest*) . . .	205	6. R. Kt. to K's 2nd (ch.)	216
7. W. Kt. takes R. Kt.	215	7. W. Kt. to K. B's 5th	229
8. Alice to Q's 8th (*coronation*) . .	229	8. R. Q. to K's sq. (*examination*) .	232
9. Alice becomes Queen	229	9. Queens castle . .	237
10. Alice castles (*feast*)	232	10. W. Q. to Q. R's 6th (*soup*) . . .	240
11. Alice takes R. Q. & wins . . .	244		

PREFACE TO 1896 EDITION

As the chess-problem, given on the previous page, has puzzled some of my readers, it may be well to explain that it is correctly worked out, so far as the *moves* are concerned. The *alternation* of Red and White is perhaps not so strictly observed as it might be, and the "castling" of the three Queens is merely a way of saying that they entered the palace; but the "check" of the White King at move 6, the capture of the Red Knight at move 7, and the final "checkmate" of the Red King, will be found, by any one who will take the trouble to set the pieces and play the moves as directed, to be strictly in accordance with the laws of the game.

The new words, in the poem "Jabberwocky" (see p. 140), have given rise to some differences of opinion as to their pronunciation: so it may be well to give instructions on *that* point also. Pronounce "slithy" as if it were the two words "sly, the": make the "g" *hard* in "gyre" and "gimble": and pronounce "rath" to rhyme with "bath".

For this sixty-first thousand, fresh electrotypes have been taken from the wood-blocks (which, never having been used for printing from, are in as good condition as when first cut in 1871), and the whole book has been set up afresh with new type. If the artistic qualities of this reissue fall short, in any particular, of those possessed by the original issue, it will not be for want of painstaking on the part of author, publisher, or printer.

I take this opportunity of announcing that the Nursery "Alice", hitherto priced at four shillings, net, is now to be had on the same terms as the ordinary shilling picturebooks—although I feel sure that it is, in every quality (except the *text* itself, in which I am not qualified to pronounce), greatly superior to them. Four shillings was a perfectly reasonable price to charge, considering the very heavy initial outlay I had incurred: still, as the Public have practically said, "We will *not* give more than a shilling for a picture-book, however artistically got-up," I am content to reckon my outlay on the book as so much dead loss, and, rather than let the little ones, for whom it was written, go without it, I am selling it at a price which is, to me, much the same thing as *giving* it away.

Christmas, 1896

Chapter I

Looking-Glass House

ONE thing was certain, that the *white* kitten had had nothing to do with it—it was the black kitten's fault entirely. For the white kitten had been having its face washed by the old cat for the last quarter of an hour (and bearing it pretty well, considering): so you see that it *couldn't* have had any hand in the mischief.

The way Dinah washed her children's faces was this: first she held the poor thing down by its ear with one paw, and then with the other paw she rubbed its face all over, the wrong way, beginning at the nose: and just now, as I said, she was hard at work on the white kitten, which was lying quite still and trying to purr—no doubt feeling that it was all meant for its good.

But the black kitten had been finished with earlier in the afternoon, and so, while Alice was sitting curled up in a corner of the great armchair, half talking to herself and half asleep, the kitten had been having a grand game of romps with the ball of worsted Alice had been trying to wind up, and had been rolling it up and down till it had all come undone again; and there it was, spread over the

hearth-rug, all knots and tangles, with the kitten running
after its own tail in the middle.

"Oh, you wicked, wicked little thing!" cried Alice,
catching up the kitten, and giving it a little kiss to make

it understand that it was in disgrace. "Really, Dinah
ought to have taught you better manners! You *ought*,
Dinah, you know you ought!" she added, looking reproachfully at the old cat, and speaking in as cross a voice
as she could manage—and then she scrambled back into
the arm-chair, taking the kitten and the worsted with

her, and began winding up the ball again. But she didn't get on very fast, as she was talking all the time, sometimes to the kitten, and sometimes to herself. Kitty sat very demurely on her knee, pretending to watch the progress of the winding, and now and then putting out one paw and gently touching the ball, as if it would be glad to help if it might.

"Do you know what to-morrow is, Kitty?" Alice began. "You'd have guessed if you'd been up in the window with me—only Dinah was making you tidy, so you couldn't. I was watching the boys getting in sticks for the bonfire—and it wants plenty of sticks, Kitty! Only it got so cold, and it snowed so, they had to leave off. Never mind, we'll go and see the bonfire to-morrow." Here Alice wound two or three turns of the worsted round the kitten's neck, just to see how it would look: this led to a scramble, in which the ball rolled down upon the floor, and yards and yards of it got unwound again.

"Do you know, I was so angry, Kitty," Alice went on, as soon as they were comfortably settled again, "when I saw all the mischief you had been doing, I was very nearly opening the window, and putting you out into the snow! And you'd have deserved it, you little mischievous darling! What have you got to say for yourself? Now don't interrupt me!" she went on, holding up one finger. "I'm going to tell you all your faults. Number one: you squeaked twice while Dinah was washing your face this morning. Now you ca'n't deny it, Kitty: I heard you! What's that you say?" (pretending that the kitten was speaking). "Her paw went into your eye? Well, that's *your* fault, for keeping your eyes open—if you'd shut them tight up, it wouldn't have happened. Now don't make any more excuses, but listen! Number two: you pulled Snowdrop away by the tail just as I had put down the saucer of milk before her! What, you were thirsty, were you? How do you know she wasn't thirsty too? Now for number three: you unwound every bit of the worsted while I wasn't looking!

"That's three faults, Kitty, and you've not been punished for any of them yet. You know I'm saving up all your punishments for Wednesday week—Suppose they had saved up all *my* punishments?" she went on, talking more to herself than the kitten. "What *would* they do at the end of a year? I should be sent to prison, I suppose, when the day came. Or—let me see—suppose each punishment was to be going without a dinner: then, when the miserable day came, I should have to go without fifty dinners at once! Well, I shouldn't mind *that* much! I'd far rather go without them than eat them!

"Do you hear the snow against the window-panes, Kitty? How nice and soft it sounds! Just as if some one was kissing the window all over outside. I wonder if the snow *loves* the trees and fields, that it kisses them so gently? And then it covers them up snug, you know, with a white quilt; and perhaps it says 'Go to sleep, darlings, till the summer comes again.' And when they wake up in the summer, Kitty, they dress themselves all in green, and dance about—whenever the wind blows—oh, that's very pretty!" cried Alice, dropping the ball of worsted to clap her hands. "And I do so *wish* it was true! I'm sure the woods look sleepy in the autumn, when the leaves are getting brown.

"Kitty, can you play chess? Now, don't smile, my dear, I'm asking it seriously. Because, when we were playing just now, you watched just as if you understood it: and when I said 'Check!' you purred! Well, it *was* a nice check, Kitty, and really I might have won, if it hadn't been for that nasty Knight, that came wriggling down among my pieces. Kitty, dear, let's pretend——" And here I wish I could tell you half the things Alice used to say, beginning with her favourite phrase "Let's pretend". She had had quite a long argument with her sister only the day before—all because Alice had begun with "Let's pretend we're kings and queens"; and her sister, who liked being very exact, had argued that they couldn't, because there were only two of them, and Alice had been reduced at last to say "Well, *you* can be one of them, then, and *I'll* be all the rest." And once she had really frightened her old nurse by shouting suddenly in her ear, "Nurse! Do let's pretend that I'm a hungry hyæna, and you're a bone!"

But this is taking us away from Alice's speech to the kitten. "Let's pretend that you're the Red Queen, Kitty! Do you know, I think if you sat up and folded your arms, you'd look exactly like her. Now do try, there's a dear!" And Alice got the Red Queen off the table, and set it up before the kitten as a model for it to imitate: however, the thing didn't succeed, principally, Alice said, because the kitten wouldn't fold its arms properly. So, to punish it, she held it up to the Looking-glass, that it might see how sulky it was, "—and if you're not good directly," she added, "I'll put you through into Looking-glass House. How would you like *that*?

"Now, if you'll only attend, Kitty, and not talk so much, I'll tell you all my ideas about Looking-glass House. First, there's the room you can see through the glass—that's just the same as our drawing-room, only the things go the other way. I can see all of it when I get upon a chair—all but the bit just behind the fireplace. Oh! I do so wish I could see *that* bit! I want so much to know whether they've a fire in the winter: you never *can* tell, you know, unless our fire smokes, and then smoke comes up in that room too—but that may be only pretence, just to make it look as if they had a fire. Well then, the books are something like our books, only the words go the wrong way: I know *that*, because I've held up one of our books to the glass, and then they hold up one in the other room.

"How would you like to live in Looking-glass House, Kitty? I wonder if they'd give you milk in there? Perhaps Looking-glass milk isn't good to drink—but oh, Kitty, now we come to the passage. You can just see a little *peep* of the passage in Looking-glass House, if you leave the door of our drawing-room wide open: and it's very like

our passage as far as you can see, only you know it may
be quite different on beyond. Oh, Kitty, how nice it
would be if we could only get through into Looking-glass
House! I'm sure it's got, oh! such beautiful things in it!
Let's pretend there's a way of getting through into it,
somehow, Kitty. Let's pretend the glass has got all soft
like gauze, so that we can get through. Why, it's turning
into a sort of mist now, I declare! It'll be easy enough to
get through——'' She was up on the chimney-piece while
she said this, though she hardly knew how she had got

there. And certainly the glass *was* beginning to melt away, just like a bright silvery mist.

In another moment Alice was through the glass, and had jumped lightly down into the Looking-glass room. The very first thing she did was to look whether there was a fire in the fireplace, and she was quite pleased to find that there was a real one, blazing away as brightly as the one she had left behind. "So I shall be as warm here as I was in the old room," thought Alice: "warmer, in fact, because there'll be no one here to scold me away from the fire. Oh, what fun it'll be, when they see me through the glass in here, and ca'n't get at me!"

Then she began looking about, and noticed that what could be seen from the old room was quite common and uninteresting, but that all the rest was as different as possible. For instance, the pictures on the wall next the fire seemed to be all alive, and the very clock on the chimney-piece (you know you can only see the back of it in the Looking-glass) had got the face of a little old man, and grinned at her.

"They don't keep this room so tidy as the other," Alice thought to herself, as she noticed several of the chessmen down in the hearth among the cinders; but in another moment, with a little "Oh!" of surprise, she was down on her hands and knees watching them. The chessmen were walking about, two and two!

"Here are the Red King and the Red Queen," Alice said (in a whisper, for fear of frightening them), "and there are the White King and the White Queen sitting on the edge of the shovel—and here are two Castles walking arm in arm—I don't think they can hear me," she went on, as she put her head closer down, "and I'm nearly sure they ca'n't see me, I feel somehow as if I was getting invisible——"

Here something began squeaking on the table behind Alice, and made her turn her head just in time to see one of the White Pawns roll over and begin kicking: she watched it with great curiosity to see what would happen next.

"It is the voice of my child!" the White Queen cried out, as she rushed past the King, so violently that she knocked him over among the cinders. "My precious Lily! My imperial kitten!" and she began scrambling wildly up the side of the fender.

"Imperial fiddlestick!" said the King, rubbing his nose, which had been hurt by the fall. He had a right to be a *little* annoyed with the Queen, for he was covered with ashes from head to foot.

Alice was very anxious to be of use, and, as the poor

little Lily was nearly screaming herself into a fit, she hastily picked up the Queen and set her on the table by the side of her noisy little daughter.

The Queen gasped, and sat down: the rapid journey through the air had quite taken away her breath, and for a minute or two she could do nothing but hug the little Lily in silence. As soon as she had recovered her breath

a little, she called out to the White King, who was sitting sulkily among the ashes, "Mind the volcano!"

"What volcano?" said the King, looking up anxiously into the fire, as if he thought that was the most likely place to find one.

"Blew—me—up," panted the Queen, who was still a little out of breath. "Mind you come up—the regular way —don't get blown up!"

Alice watched the White King as he slowly struggled up from bar to bar, till at last she said "Why, you'll be hours and hours getting to the table, at that rate. I'd far better help you, hadn't I?" But the King took no notice of the question: it was quite clear that he could neither hear her nor see her.

So Alice picked him up very gently, and lifted him across more slowly than she had lifted the Queen, that she mightn't take his breath away; but, before she put him on the table, she thought she might as well dust him a little, he was so covered with ashes.

She said afterwards that she had never seen in all her life such a face as the King made, when he found himself held in the air by an invisible hand, and being dusted: he was far too much astonished to cry out, but his eyes and his mouth went on getting larger and larger, and rounder and rounder, till her hand shook so with laughing that she nearly let him drop upon the floor.

"Oh! *please* don't make such faces, my dear!" she cried out, quite forgetting that the King couldn't hear her. "You make me laugh so that I can hardly hold you! And don't keep your mouth so wide open! All the ashes will get into it—there, now I think you're tidy enough!'' she added, as she smoothed his hair, and set him upon the table near the Queen.

The King immediately fell flat on his back, and lay perfectly still; and Alice was a little alarmed at what she had done, and went round the room to see if she could

find any water to throw over him. However, she could find nothing but a bottle of ink, and when she got back with it she found he had recovered, and he and the Queen were talking together in a frightened whisper—so low, that Alice could hardly hear what they said.

The King was saying ''I assure you, my dear, I turned cold to the very ends of my whiskers!''

To which the Queen replied ''You haven't got any whiskers.''

''The horror of that moment'', the King went on, ''I shall never, *never* forget!''

''You will, though,'' the Queen said, ''if you don't make a memorandum of it.''

Alice looked on with great interest as the King took an enormous memorandum book out of his pocket, and began writing. A sudden thought struck her, and she took hold of the end of the pencil, which came some way over his shoulder, and began writing for him.

The poor King looked puzzled and unhappy, and struggled with the pencil for some time without saying anything; but Alice was too strong for him, and at last he panted out "My dear! I really *must* get a thinner pencil. I ca'n't manage this one a bit: it writes all manner of things that I don't intend——"

"What manner of things?" said the Queen, looking over the book (in which Alice had put '*The White Knight is sliding down the poker. He balances very badly*'). "That's not a memorandum of *your* feelings!"

There was a book lying near Alice on the table, and while she sat watching the White King (for she was still a little anxious about him, and had the ink all ready to throw over him, in case he fainted again), she turned over the leaves, to find some part that she could read, "—for it's all in some language I don't know," she said to herself.

It was like this.

ʎʞↃOϺᴚƎᗺᗺⱯſ

'Ⓣⱳⱥƨ ⰱⱤⰱⰼⰼⰹⱪ, ⱥⱧⰬ ⱧⱨⰬ ⱨⰼⰹⱨⱨⱨ ⱨⱦⱶⰬⱨ;
ⰃⰱⰬ ⱪⱨⰬⱨ ⱥⱧⰬ ⱪⱨⰱⰱⰼⰬ ⰹⱧ ⱨⱨⱨ ⱳⱥⰱⱨ:
Ⱥⰼⰼ ⰱⰱⰱⱨ ⱳⱨⰱⱨ ⱨⱨⰬ ⰱⱨⱨⱨⱨⱨⱨ,
ȺⱧⰬ ⱨⱨⱨ ⱨⱨⰱⱨ ⱨⱨⱨⱨ ⱨⱨⱨⱨⱨⱥⰱⱨ.

She puzzled over this for some time, but at last a bright thought struck her. "Why, it's a Looking-glass book, of course! And, if I hold it up to a glass, the words will all go the right way again."

This was the poem that Alice read

JABBERWOCKY

> *'Twas brillig, and the slithy toves*
> *Did gyre and gimble in the wabe:*
> *All mimsy were the borogoves,*
> *And the mome raths outgrabe.*

"*Beware the Jabberwock, my son!*
The jaws that bite, the claws that catch!
Beware the Jubjub bird, and shun
The frumious Bandersnatch!"

He took his vorpal sword in hand:
  Long time the manxome foe he sought—
So rested he by the Tumtum tree,
  And stood awhile in thought.

And, as in uffish thought he stood,
  The Jabberwock, with eyes of flame,
Came whiffling through the tulgey wood,
  And burbled as it came!

One, two! One, two! And through and through
  The vorpal blade went snicker-snack!
He left it dead, and with its head
  He went galumphing back.

"And hast thou slain the Jabberwock?
  Come to my arms, my beamish boy!
O frabjous day! Callooh! Callay!"
  He chortled in his joy.

'Twas brillig, and the slithy toves
  Did gyre and gimble in the wabe:
All mimsy were the borogoves,
  And the mome raths outgrabe.

"It seems very pretty," she said when she had finished it, "but it's *rather* hard to understand!" (You see she didn't like to confess, even to herself, that she couldn't make it out at all.) "Somehow it seems to fill my head with ideas—only I don't exactly know what they are! However, *somebody* killed *something*: that's clear, at any rate——"

"But oh!" thought Alice, suddenly jumping up, "if I don't make haste, I shall have to go back through the Looking-glass, before I've seen what the rest of the house is like! Let's have a look at the garden first!" She was out of the room in a moment, and ran down stairs—or, at least, it wasn't exactly running, but a new invention for getting down stairs quickly and easily, as Alice said to herself. She just kept the tips of her fingers on the hand-rail, and floated gently down without even touching the stairs with her feet: then she floated on through the hall, and would have gone straight out at the door in the same way, if she hadn't caught hold of the door-post. She was getting a little giddy with so much floating in the air, and was rather glad to find herself walking again in the natural way.

CHAPTER II

The Garden of Live Flowers

"I should see the garden far better", said Alice to herself, "if I could get to the top of that hill; and here's a path that leads straight to it—at least, no, it doesn't do *that*——" (after going a few yards along the path, and turning several sharp corners), "but I suppose it will at last. But how curiously it twists! It's more like a corkscrew than a path! Well *this* turn goes to the hill, I suppose—no, it doesn't! This goes straight back to the house! Well then, I'll try it the other way."

And so she did: wandering up and down, and trying turn after turn, but always coming back to the house, do what she would. Indeed, once, when she turned a corner rather more quickly than usual, she ran against it before she could stop herself.

"It's no use talking about it," Alice said, looking up at the house and pretending it was arguing with her. "I'm *not* going in again yet. I know I should have to get through the Looking-glass again—back into the old room —and there'd be an end of all my adventures!"

So, resolutely turning her back upon the house, she set out once more down the path, determined to keep straight on till she got to the hill. For a few minutes all went on well, and she was just saying "I really *shall* do it this time

———" when the path gave a sudden twist and shook itself (as she described it afterwards), and the next moment she found herself actually walking in at the door.

"Oh, it's too bad!" she cried. "I never saw such a house for getting in the way! Never!"

However, there was the hill full in sight, so there was nothing to be done but start again. This time she came upon a large flower-bed, with a border of daisies, and a willow-tree growing in the middle.

"O Tiger-lily!" said Alice, addressing herself to one that

was waving gracefully about in the wind, "I *wish* you could talk!"

"We *can* talk", said the Tiger-lily, "when there's anybody worth talking to."

Alice was so astonished that she couldn't speak for a minute: it quite seemed to take her breath away. At length, as the Tiger-lily only went on waving about, she spoke again, in a timid voice—almost in a whisper. "And can *all* the flowers talk?"

"As well as *you* can," said the Tiger-lily. "And a great deal louder."

"It isn't manners for us to begin, you know," said the Rose, "and I really was wondering when you'd speak! Said I to myself, 'Her face has got *some* sense in it, though it's not a clever one!' Still, you're the right colour, and that goes a long way."

"I don't care about the colour," the Tiger-lily remarked. "If only her petals curled up a little more, she'd be all right."

Alice didn't like being criticised, so she began asking questions. "Aren't you sometimes frightened at being planted out here, with nobody to take care of you?"

"There's the tree in the middle," said the Rose. "What else is it good for?"

"But what could it do, if any danger came?" Alice asked.

"It could bark," said the Rose.

"It says 'Boughwough!' " cried a Daisy. "That's why its branches are called boughs!"

"Didn't you know *that*?" cried another Daisy. And here they all began shouting together, till the air seemed quite full of little shrill voices. "Silence, every one of you!" cried the Tiger-lily, waving itself passionately from side to side, and trembling with excitement. "They know I ca'n't get at them!" it panted, bending its quivering head towards Alice, "or they wouldn't dare to do it!"

"Never mind!" Alice said in a soothing tone, and, stooping down to the daisies, who were just beginning again, she whispered "If you don't hold your tongues, I'll pick you!"

There was silence in a moment, and several of the pink daisies turned white.

"That's right!" said the Tiger-lily. "The daisies are worst of all. When one speaks, they all begin together, and it's enough to make one wither to hear the way they go on!"

"How is it you can all talk so nicely?" Alice said, hoping to get it into a better temper by a compliment. "I've been in many gardens before, but none of the flowers could talk."

"Put your hand down, and feel the ground," said the Tiger-lily. "Then you'll know why."

Alice did so. "It's very hard," she said; "but I don't see what that has to do with it."

"In most gardens", the Tiger-lily said, "they make the beds too soft—so that the flowers are always asleep."

This sounded a very good reason, and Alice was quite pleased to know it. "I never thought of that before!" she said.

"It's *my* opinion that you never think *at all*," the Rose said, in a rather severe tone.

"I never saw anybody that looked stupider," a Violet said, so suddenly, that Alice quite jumped; for it hadn't spoken before.

"Hold *your* tongue!" cried the Tiger-lily. "As if *you* ever saw anybody! You keep your head under the leaves, and snore away there, till you know no more what's going on in the world, than if you were a bud!"

"Are there any more people in the garden besides me?" Alice said, not choosing to notice the Rose's last remark.

"There's one other flower in the garden that can move about like you," said the Rose. "I wonder how you do it ——" ("You're always wondering," said the Tiger-lily), "but she's more bushy than you are."

"Is she like me?" Alice asked eagerly, for the thought crossed her mind, "There's another little girl in the garden, somewhere!"

"Well, she has the same awkward shape as you," the Rose said; "but she's redder—and her petals are shorter, I think."

"They're done up close, like a dahlia," said the Tiger-lily: "not tumbled about, like yours."

"But that's not *your* fault," the Rose added kindly. "You're beginning to fade, you know—and then one ca'n't help one's petals getting a little untidy."

Alice didn't like this idea at all: so, to change the subject, she asked "Does she ever come out here?"

"I daresay you'll see her soon," said the Rose. "She's one of the kind that has nine spikes, you know."

"Where does she wear them?" Alice asked with some curiosity.

"Why, all round her head, of course," the Rose replied. "I was wondering *you* hadn't got some too. I thought it was the regular rule."

"She's coming!" cried the Larkspur. "I hear her foot-step, thump, thump, along the gravel-walk!"

Alice looked round eagerly and found that it was the Red Queen. "She's grown a good deal!" was her first remark. She had indeed: when Alice first found her in the ashes, she had been only three inches high—and here she was, half a head taller than Alice herself!

"It's the fresh air that does it," said the Rose: "wonderfully fine air it is, out here."

"I think I'll go and meet her," said Alice, for, though the flowers were interesting enough, she felt that it would be far grander to have a talk with a real Queen.

"You ca'n't possibly do that," said the Rose: "*I* should advise you to walk the other way."

This sounded nonsense to Alice, so she said nothing, but set off at once towards the Red Queen. To her surprise she lost sight of her in a moment, and found herself walking in at the front-door again.

A little provoked, she drew back, and, after looking everywhere for the Queen (whom she spied out at last, a long way off), she thought she would try the plan, this time, of walking in the opposite direction.

It succeeded beautifully. She had not been walking a minute before she found herself face to face with the Red Queen, and full in sight of the hill she had been so long aiming at.

"Where do you come from?" said the Red Queen. "And where are you going? Look up, speak nicely, and don't twiddle your fingers all the time."

Alice attended to all these directions, and explained, as well as she could, that she had lost her way.

"I don't know what you mean by *your* way," said the Queen: "all the ways about here belong to *me*—but why did you come out here at all?" she added in a kinder tone. "Curtsey while you're thinking what to say. It saves time."

Alice wondered a little at this, but she was too much in awe of the Queen to disbelieve it. "I'll try it when I go home," she thought to herself, "the next time I'm a little late for dinner."

"It's time for you to answer now," the Queen said looking at her watch: "open your mouth a *little* wider when you speak, and always say 'your Majesty'."

"I only wanted to see what the garden was like, your Majesty——"

"That's right," said the Queen, patting her on the head, which Alice didn't like at all: "though, when you say 'garden'—*I've* seen gardens, compared with which this would be a wilderness."

Alice didn't dare to argue the point, but went on: "—and I thought I'd try and find my way to the top of that hill——"

"When you say 'hill'," the Queen interrupted, "*I* could show you hills, in comparison with which you'd call that a valley."

"No, I shouldn't," said Alice, surprised into contradicting her at last: "a hill *ca'n't* be a valley, you know. That would be nonsense——"

The Red Queen shook her head. "You may call it 'nonsense' if you like," she said, "but *I've* heard nonsense, compared with which that would be as sensible as a dictionary!"

Alice curtseyed again, as she was afraid from the Queen's tone that she was a *little* offended: and they walked on in silence till they got to the top of the little hill.

For some minutes Alice stood without speaking, looking out in all directions over the country—and a most curious country it was. There were a number of tiny little brooks running straight across it from side to side, and the ground between was divided up into squares by a number of little green hedges, that reached from brook to brook.

"I declare it's marked out just like a large chess-board!" Alice said at last. "There ought to be some men moving about somewhere—and so there are!" she added in a tone of delight, and her heart began to beat quick with excitement as she went on. "It's a great huge game of chess that's being played—all over the world—if this *is* the world at all, you know. Oh, what fun it is! How I *wish* I was one of them! I wouldn't mind being a Pawn, if only I might join—though of course I should *like* to be a Queen, best."

She glanced rather shyly at the real Queen as she said this, but her companion only smiled pleasantly, and said "That's easily managed. You can be the White Queen's Pawn, if you like, as Lily's too young to play: and you're in the Second Square to begin with: when you get to the Eighth Square you'll be a Queen——" Just at this moment, somehow or other, they began to run.

Alice never could quite make out, in thinking it over afterwards, how it was that they began: all she remembers is, that they were running hand in hand, and the Queen went so fast that it was all she could do to keep up with her: and still the Queen kept crying "Faster! Faster!" but Alice felt she *could not* go faster, though she had no breath left to say so.

The most curious part of the thing was, that the trees and the other things round them never changed their places at all: however fast they went, they never seemed to pass anything. "I wonder if all the things move along with us?" thought poor puzzled Alice. And the Queen seemed to guess her thoughts, for she cried "Faster! Don't try to talk!"

Not that Alice had any idea of doing *that*. She felt as if she would never be able to talk again, she was getting so much out of breath: and still the Queen cried "Faster! Faster!" and dragged her along. "Are we nearly there?" Alice managed to pant out at last.

"Nearly there!" the Queen repeated. "Why, we passed it ten minutes ago! Faster!" And they ran on for a time in silence, with the wind whistling in Alice's ears, and almost blowing her hair off her head, she fancied.

"Now! Now!" cried the Queen. "Faster! Faster!" And they went so fast that at last they seemed to skim through the air, hardly touching the ground with their feet, till suddenly, just as Alice was getting quite exhausted, they stopped, and she found herself sitting on the ground, breathless and giddy.

The Queen propped her up against a tree, and said kindly, "You may rest a little, now."

Alice looked round her in great surprise. "Why, I do believe we've been under this tree the whole time! Everything's just as it was!"

"Of course it is," said the Queen. "What would you have it?"

"Well, in *our* country", said Alice, still panting a little, "you'd generally get to somewhere else—if you ran very fast for a long time as we've been doing."

"A slow sort of country!" said the Queen. "Now, *here*, you see, it takes all the running *you* can do, to keep in the same place. If you want to get somewhere else, you must run at least twice as fast as that!"

"I'd rather not try, please!" said Alice. "I'm quite content to stay here—only I *am* so hot and thirsty!"

"I know what *you'd* like!" the Queen said good-naturedly, taking a little box out of her pocket. "Have a biscuit?"

Alice thought it would not be civil to say "No", though it wasn't at all what she wanted. She took it, and ate it as well as she could: and it was *very* dry: and she thought she had never been so nearly choked in all her life.

"While you're refreshing yourself", said the Queen, "I'll just take the measurements." And she took a ribbon out of her pocket, marked in inches, and began measuring the ground, and sticking little pegs in here and there.

"At the end of two yards", she said, putting in a peg to mark the distance, "I shall give you your directions—have another biscuit?"

"No, thank you," said Alice: "one's *quite* enough!"

"Thirst quenched, I hope?" said the Queen.

Alice did not know what to say to this, but luckily the Queen did not wait for an answer, but went on. "At the end of *three* yards I shall repeat them—for fear of your forgetting them. At the end of *four*, I shall say good-bye. And at the end of *five*, I shall go!"

She had got all the pegs put in by this time, and Alice

looked on with great interest as she returned to the tree, and then began slowly walking down the row.

At the two-yard peg she faced round, and said "A pawn goes two squares in its first move, you know. So you'll go *very* quickly through the Third Square—by railway, I should think—and you'll find yourself in the Fourth Square in no time. Well, *that* square belongs to Tweedledum and Tweedledee—the Fifth is mostly water —the Sixth belongs to Humpty Dumpty—But you make no remark?"

"I—I didn't know I had to make one—just then," Alice faltered out.

"You *should* have said," the Queen went on in a tone of grave reproof, " 'It's extremely kind of you to tell me all this'—however, we'll suppose it said—the Seventh Square is all forest—however, one of the Knights will show you the way—and in the Eighth Square we shall be Queens together, and it's all feasting and fun!" Alice got up and curtseyed, and sat down again.

At the next peg the Queen turned again, and this time she said "Speak in French when you ca'n't think of the English for a thing—turn out your toes as you walk—and remember who you are!" She did not wait for Alice to curtsey, this time, but walked on quickly to the next peg, where she turned for a moment to say "Good-bye", and then hurried on to the last.

How it happened, Alice never knew, but exactly as she came to the last peg, she was gone. Whether she vanished into the air, or whether she ran quickly into the wood ("and she *can* run very fast!" thought Alice), there was no way of guessing, but she was gone, and Alice began to remember that she was a Pawn, and that it would soon be time for her to move.

CHAPTER III

Looking-Glass Insects

OF course the first thing to do was to make a grand survey of the country she was going to travel through. "It's something very like learning geography," thought Alice, as she stood on tiptoe in hopes of being able to see a little further. "Principal rivers—there *are* none. Principal mountains—I'm on the only one, but I don't think it's got any name. Principal towns—why, what *are* those creatures, making honey down there? They ca'n't be bees—nobody ever saw bees a mile off, you know——" and for some time she stood silent, watching one of them that was bustling about among the flowers, poking its proboscis into them, "just as if it was a regular bee," thought Alice.

However, this was anything but a regular bee: in fact, it was an elephant—as Alice soon found out, though the idea quite took her breath away at first. "And what enormous flowers they must be!" was her next idea. "Something like cottages with the roofs taken off, and stalks put to them—and what quantities of honey they must make! I think I'll go down and—no, I wo'n't go *just* yet," she went on, checking herself just as she was beginning to run down the hill, and trying to find some excuse for turning shy so suddenly. "It'll never do to go down among them without a good long branch to brush them away—and what fun it'll be when they ask me how I liked my walk. I shall say 'Oh, I liked it well enough——' (here came the favourite little toss of the head), 'only it *was* so dusty and hot, and the elephants *did* tease so!' "

"I think I'll go down the other way," she said after a pause; "and perhaps I may visit the elephants later on. Besides, I *do* so want to get into the Third Square!"

154

So, with this excuse, she ran down the hill, and jumped over the first of the six little brooks.

```
    *       *       *       *       *
        *       *       *       *
    *       *       *       *       *
```

"Tickets, please!" said the Guard, putting his head in at the window. In a moment everybody was holding out a ticket: they were about the same size as the people, and quite seemed to fill the carriage.

"Now then! Show your ticket, child!" the Guard went on, looking angrily at Alice. And a great many voices all said together ("like the chorus of a song," thought Alice) "Don't keep him waiting, child! Why, his time is worth a thousand pounds a minute!"

"I'm afraid I haven't got one," Alice said in a frightened tone: "there wasn't a ticket-office where I came from." And again the chorus of voices went on. "There wasn't room for one where she came from. The land there is worth a thousand pounds an inch!"

"Don't make excuses," said the Guard: "you should have bought one from the engine-driver." And once more the chorus of voices went on with "The man that drives the engine. Why, the smoke alone is worth a thousand pounds a puff!"

Alice thought to herself "Then there's no use in speaking." The voices didn't join in, *this* time, as she hadn't spoken, but, to her great surprise, they all *thought* in chorus (I hope you understand what *thinking in chorus* means—for I must confess that *I* don't), "Better say nothing at all. Language is worth a thousand pounds a word!"

"I shall dream about a thousand pounds to-night, I know I shall!" thought Alice.

All this time the Guard was looking at her, first through a telescope, then through a microscope, and then through an opera-glass. At last he said "You're travelling the wrong way," and shut up the window, and went away.

"So young a child", said the gentleman sitting opposite to her, (he was dressed in white paper), "ought to know which way she's going, even if she doesn't know her own name!"

A Goat that was sitting next to the gentleman in white, shut his eyes and said in a loud voice, "She ought to know

her way to the ticket-office, even if she doesn't know her alphabet!"

There was a Beetle sitting next the Goat (it was a very queer carriage-full of passengers altogether), and, as the rule seemed to be that they should all speak in turn, *he* went on with "She'll have to go back from here as luggage!"

Alice couldn't see who was sitting beyond the Beetle, but a hoarse voice spoke next. "Change engines——" it said, and there it choked and was obliged to leave off.

"It sounds like a horse," Alice thought to herself. And

an extremely small voice, close to her ear, said "You might make a joke on that—something about 'horse' and 'hoarse', you know."

Then a very gentle voice in the distance said, "She must be labelled 'Lass, with care', you know——"

And after that other voices went on ("What a number of people there are in the carriage!" thought Alice), saying "She must go by post, as she's got a head on her——" "She must be sent as a message by the telegraph——" "She must draw the train herself the rest of the way——", and so on.

But the gentleman dressed in white paper leaned forwards and whispered in her ear, "Never mind what they all say, my dear, but take a return-ticket every time the train stops."

"Indeed I sha'n't!" Alice said rather impatiently. "I don't belong to this railway journey at all—I was in a wood just now—and I wish I could get back there!"

"You might make a joke on *that*," said the little voice close to her ear: "something about 'you *would* if you could', you know."

"Don't tease so," said Alice, looking about in vain to see where the voice came from. "If you're so anxious to have a joke made, why don't you make one yourself?"

The little voice sighed deeply. It was *very* unhappy, evidently, and Alice would have said something pitying to comfort it, "if it would only sigh like other people!" she thought. But this was such a wonderfully small sigh, that she wouldn't have heard it at all, if it hadn't come *quite* close to her ear. The consequence of this was that it tickled her ear very much, and quite took off her thoughts from the unhappiness of the poor little creature.

"I know you are a friend," the little voice went on: "a dear friend, and an old friend. And you wo'n't hurt me, though I *am* an insect."

"What kind of insect?" Alice inquired, a little anxiously. What she really wanted to know was, whether it could sting or not, but she thought this wouldn't be quite a civil question to ask.

"What, then you don't——" the little voice began, when it was drowned by a shrill scream from the engine, and every-body jumped up in alarm, Alice among the rest.

The Horse, who had put his head out of the window, quietly drew it in and said "It's only a brook we have to jump over." Everybody seemed satisfied with this, though Alice felt a little nervous at the idea of trains jumping at all. "However, it'll take us into the Fourth Square, that's some comfort!" she said to herself. In another moment she felt the carriage rise straight up into the air, and in her fright she caught at the thing nearest to her hand, which happened to be the Goat's beard.

    *   *   *   *   *

        *   *   *   *

    *   *   *   *   *

But the beard seemed to melt away as she touched it, and she found herself sitting quietly under a tree—while the Gnat (for that was the insect she had been talking to) was balancing itself on a twig just over her head, and fanning her with its wings.

It certainly was a *very* large Gnat: "about the size of a chicken," Alice thought. Still, she couldn't feel nervous with it, after they had been talking together so long.

"—then you don't like *all* insects?" the Gnat went on, as quietly as if nothing had happened.

"I like them when they can talk," Alice said. "None of them ever talk, where *I* come from."

"What sort of insects do you rejoice in, where *you* come from?" the Gnat inquired.

"I don't *rejoice* in insects at all," Alice explained, "because I'm rather afraid of them—at least the large kinds. But I can tell you the names of some of them."

"Of course they answer to their names?" the Gnat remarked carelessly.

"I never knew them do it."

"What's the use of their having names", the Gnat said, "if they wo'n't answer to them?"

"No use to *them*," said Alice; "but it's useful to the

people that name them, I suppose. If not, why do things
have names at all?"

"I ca'n't say," the Gnat replied. "Further on, in the
wood down there, they've got no names—however, go on
with your list of insects: you're wasting time."

"Well, there's the Horse-fly," Alice began, counting off
the names on her fingers.

"All right," said the Gnat. "Half way up that bush,
you'll see a Rocking-horse-fly, if you look. It's made
entirely of wood, and gets about by swinging itself from
branch to branch."

"What does it live on?" Alice asked, with great curiosity.

"Sap and sawdust," said the Gnat. "Go on with the
list."

Alice looked at the Rocking-horse-fly with great
interest, and made up her mind that it must have been
just repainted, it looked so bright and sticky; and then
she went on.

"And there's the Dragon-fly."

"Look on the branch above your head", said the Gnat,
"and there you'll find a Snap-dragon-fly. Its body is

made of plum-pudding, its wings of holly-leaves, and its
head is a raisin burning in brandy."

"And what does it live on?" Alice asked, as before.

"Frumenty and mince-pie," the Gnat replied; "and it
makes its nest in a Christmas-box."

"And then there's the Butterfly," Alice went on, after
she had taken a good look at the insect with its head on

fire, and had thought to herself, "I wonder if that's the
reason insects are so fond of flying into candles—because
they want to turn into Snap-dragon-flies!"

"Crawling at your feet", said the Gnat (Alice drew her
feet back in some alarm), "you may observe a Bread-
and-butter-fly. Its wings are thin slices of bread-and-
butter, its body is a crust, and its head is a lump of
sugar."

"And what does *it* live on?"

"Weak tea with cream in it."

A new difficulty came into Alice's head. "Supposing it
couldn't find any?" she suggested.

"Then it would die, of course."

"But that must happen very often," Alice remarked
thoughtfully.

"It always happens," said the Gnat.

After this, Alice was silent for a minute or two pondering. The Gnat amused itself meanwhile by humming round and round her head: at last it settled again and remarked "I suppose you don't want to lose your name?"

"No, indeed," Alice said, a little anxiously.

"And yet I don't know," the Gnat went on in a careless

tone: "only think how convenient it would be if you could manage to go home without it! For instance, if the governess wanted to call you to your lessons, she would call out 'Come here——', and there she would have to leave off, because there wouldn't be any name for her to call, and of course you wouldn't have to go, you know."

"That would never do, I'm sure," said Alice: "the governess would never think of excusing me lessons for that. If she couldn't remember my name, she'd call me 'Miss', as the servants do."

"Well, if she said 'Miss', and didn't say anything more," the Gnat remarked, "of course you'd miss your lessons. That's a joke. I wish *you* had made it."

"Why do you wish *I* had made it?" Alice asked. "It's a very bad one."

But the Gnat only sighed deeply while two large tears come rolling down its cheeks.

"You shouldn't make jokes", Alice said, "if it makes you so unhappy."

Then came another of those melancholy little sighs, and this time the poor Gnat really seemed to have sighed itself away, for, when Alice looked up, there was nothing whatever to be seen on the twig, and, as she was getting quite chilly with sitting still so long, she got up and walked on.

She very soon came to an open field, with a wood on the other side of it: it looked much darker than the last wood, and Alice felt a little timid about going into it. However, on second thoughts, she made up her mind to go on: "for I certainly won't go *back*," she thought to herself, and this was the only way to the Eighth Square.

"This must be the wood", she said thoughtfully to herself, "where things have no names. I wonder what'll become of *my* name when I go in? I shouldn't like to lose it at all—because they'd have to give me another, and it would be almost certain to be an ugly one. But then the fun would be, trying to find the creature that had got my old name! That's just like the advertisements, you know, when people lose dogs—'*answers to the name of "Dash": had on a brass collar*'—just fancy calling everything you met 'Alice', till one of them answered! Only they wouldn't answer at all, if they were wise."

She was rambling on in this way when she reached the wood: it looked very cool and shady. "Well, at any rate it's a great comfort," she said as she stepped under the trees, "after being so hot, to get into the—into the—into *what*?" she went on, rather surprised at not being able to think of the word. "I mean to get under the—under the—under *this*, you know!" putting her hand on the trunk of the tree. "What *does* it call itself, I wonder? I do believe it's got no name—why, to be sure it hasn't!"

She stood silent for a minute, thinking: then she suddenly began again. "Then it really *has* happened, after all! And now, who am I? I *will* remember, if I can! I'm determined to do it!" But being determined didn't help her much, and all she could say, after a great deal of puzzling, was "L, I *know* it begins with L!"

Just then a Fawn came wandering by: it looked at Alice with its large gentle eyes, but didn't seem at all frightened. "Here then! Here then!" Alice said, as she

held out her hand and tried to stroke it; but it only started back a little, and then stood looking at her again.

"What do you call yourself?" the Fawn said at last. Such a soft sweet voice it had!

"I wish I knew!" thought poor Alice. She answered, rather sadly, "Nothing just now."

"Think again," it said: "that wo'n't do."

Alice thought, but nothing came of it. "Please, would

you tell me what *you* call yourself?" she said timidly. "I think that might help a little."

"I'll tell you, if you'll come a little further on," the Fawn said. "I ca'n't remember *here*."

So they walked on together through the wood, Alice with her arms clasped lovingly round the soft neck of the Fawn, till they came out into another open field, and here the Fawn gave a sudden bound into the air, and shook itself free from Alice's arm. "I'm a Fawn!" it cried out in a voice of delight. "And, dear me! you're a human child!" A sudden look of alarm came into its beautiful brown eyes, and in another moment it had darted away at full speed.

Alice stood looking after it, almost ready to cry with vexation at having lost her dear little fellow-traveler so suddenly. "However, I know my name now," she said: "that's *some* comfort. Alice—Alice—I won't forget it again. And now which of these finger-posts ought I to follow, I wonder?"

It was not a very difficult question to answer, as there was only one road through the wood, and the two finger-posts both pointed along it. "I'll settle it", Alice said to herself, "when the road divides and they point different ways."

But this did not seem likely to happen. She went on and on, a long way, but wherever the road divided, there were sure to be two finger-posts pointing the same way, one marked "TO TWEEDLEDUM'S HOUSE", and the other "TO THE HOUSE OF TWEEDLEDEE".

"I do believe", said Alice at last, "that they live in the *same* house! I wonder I never thought of that before— But I ca'n't stay there long. I'll just call and say 'How d'ye do?' and ask them the way out of the wood. If I could only get to the Eighth Square before it gets dark!" So she wandered on, talking to herself as she went, till, on turning a sharp corner, she came upon two fat little men, so suddenly that she could not help starting back, but in another moment she recovered herself, feeling sure that they must be

Chapter IV

Tweedledum and Tweedledee

THEY were standing under a tree, each with an arm round the other's neck, and Alice knew which was which in a moment, because one of them had 'DUM' embroidered on his collar, and the other 'DEE'. "I suppose

they've each got 'TWEEDLE' round at the back of the collar," she said to herself.

They stood so still that she quite forgot they were alive, and she was just going round to see if the word 'TWEEDLE' was written at the back of each collar, when she was startled by a voice coming from the one marked 'DUM'.

"If you think we're wax-works," he said, "you ought to pay, you know. Wax-works weren't made to be looked at for nothing. Nohow!"

"Contrariwise," added the one marked 'DEE', "if you think we're alive, you ought to speak."

"I'm sure I'm very sorry," was all Alice could say; for the words of the old song kept ringing through her head like the ticking of a clock, and she could hardly help saying them out loud:

> "*Tweedledum and Tweedledee*
> *Agreed to have a battle;*
> *For Tweedledum said Tweedledee*
> *Had spoiled his nice new rattle.*
>
> *Just then flew down a monstrous crow,*
> *As black as a tar-barrel;*
> *Which frightened both the heroes so,*
> *They quite forgot their quarrel.*"

"I know what you're thinking about," said Tweedledum; "but it isn't so, nohow."

"Contrariwise," continued Tweedledee, "if it was so, it might be; and if it were so, it would be; but as it isn't, it ain't. That's logic."

"I was thinking," Alice said politely, "which is the best way out of this wood: it's getting so dark. Would you tell me, please?"

But the fat little men only looked at each other and grinned.

They looked so exactly like a couple of great schoolboys, that Alice couldn't help pointing her finger at Tweedledum, and saying "First Boy!"

"Nohow!" Tweedledum cried out briskly, and shut his mouth up again with a snap.

"Next Boy!" said Alice, passing on to Tweedledee, though she felt quite certain he would only shout out "Contrariwise!" and so he did.

"You've begun wrong!" cried Tweedledum. "The first thing in a visit is to say 'How d'ye do?' and shake hands!" And here the two brothers gave each other a hug, and then they held out the two hands that were free, to shake hands with her.

Alice did not like shaking hands with either of them first, for fear of hurting the other one's feelings; so, as the best way out of the difficulty, she took hold of both hands at once: the next moment they were dancing round in a ring. This seemed quite natural (she remembered afterwards), and she was not even surprised to hear music playing: it seemed to come from the tree under which they were dancing, and it was done (as well as she could make it out) by the branches rubbing one across the other, like fiddles and fiddle-sticks.

"But it certainly *was* funny", (Alice said afterwards, when she was telling her sister the history of all this), "to find myself singing '*Here we go round the mulberry bush*'. I don't know when I began it, but somehow I felt as if I'd been singing it a long long time!"

The other two dancers were fat, and very soon out of breath. "Four times round is enough for one dance," Tweedledum panted out, and they left off dancing as suddenly as they had begun: the music stopped at the same moment.

Then they let go of Alice's hands, and stood looking at her for a minute: there was a rather awkward pause, as Alice didn't know how to begin a conversation with people she had just been dancing with. "It would never do to say 'How d'ye do?' *now*," she said to herself: "we seem to have got beyond that, somehow!"

"I hope you're not much tired?" she said at last.

"Nohow. And thank you *very* much for asking," said Tweedledum.

"So *much* obliged!" added Tweedledee. "You like poetry?"

"Ye-es, pretty well—*some* poetry," Alice said doubtfully. "Would you tell me which road leads out of the wood?"

"What shall I repeat to her?" said Tweedledee, looking round at Tweedledum with great solemn eyes, and not noticing Alice's question.

" '*The Walrus and the Carpenter*' is the longest,"

Tweedledum replied, giving his brother an affectionate hug.

Tweedledee began instantly:

> *"The sun was shining——"*

Here Alice ventured to interrupt him. "If it's *very* long," she said, as politely as she could, "would you please tell me first which road——"

Tweedledee smiled gently, and began again:

> *"The sun was shining on the sea,*
> *Shining with all his might:*
> *He did his very best to make*
> *The billows smooth and bright—*
> *And this was odd, because it was*
> *The middle of the night.*
>
> *The moon was shining sulkily,*
> *Because she thought the sun*
> *Had got no business to be there*
> *After the day was done—*
> *'It's very rude of him', she said,*
> *'To come and spoil the fun!'*
>
> *The sea was wet as wet could be,*
> *The sands were dry as dry.*
> *You could not see a cloud, because*
> *No cloud was in the sky:*
> *No birds were flying overhead—*
> *There were no birds to fly.*
>
> *The Walrus and the Carpenter*
> *Were walking close at hand:*
> *They wept like anything to see*
> *Such quantities of sand:*
> *'If this were only cleared away,'*
> *They said, 'it would be grand!'*
>
> *'If seven maids with seven mops*
> *Swept it for half a year,*

Do you suppose', the Walrus said,
  'That they could get it clear?'
'I doubt it,' said the Carpenter,
  And shed a bitter tear.

'O Oysters, come and walk with us!'
  The Walrus did beseech.
'A pleasant walk, a pleasant talk,
  Along the briny beach:
We cannot do with more than four,
  To give a hand to each.'

The eldest Oyster looked at him,
  But never a word he said:
The eldest Oyster winked his eye,
  And shook his heavy head—
Meaning to say he did not choose
  To leave the oyster-bed.

But four young Oysters hurried up,
  All eager for the treat:
Their coats were brushed, their faces washed,
  Their shoes were clean and neat—
And this was odd, because, you know,
  They hadn't any feet.

Four other Oysters followed them,
And yet another four;
And thick and fast they came at last,
And more, and more, and more—
All hopping through the frothy waves,
And scrambling to the shore.

The Walrus and the Carpenter
Walked on a mile or so,
And then they rested on a rock
Conveniently low:
And all the little Oysters stood
And waited in a row.

'The time has come', the Walrus said,
'To talk of many things:
Of shoes—and ships—and sealing wax—
Of cabbages—and kings—
And why the sea is boiling hot—
And whether pigs have wings.'

'But wait a bit,' the Oysters cried,
'Before we have our chat;

For some of us are out of breath,
    And all of us are fat!'
'No hurry!' said the Carpenter.
    They thanked him much for that.

'A loaf of bread', the Walrus said,
    'Is what we chiefly need:
Pepper and vinegar besides
    Are very good indeed—
Now, if you're ready, Oysters dear,
    We can begin to feed.'

'But not on us!' the Oysters cried,
    Turning a little blue.
'After such kindness, that would be
    A dismal thing to do!'
'The night is fine,' the Walrus said.
    'Do you admire the view?

'It was so kind of you to come!
    And you are very nice!'
The Carpenter said nothing but
    'Cut us another slice.

I wish you were not quite so deaf—
I've had to ask you twice!'

'*It seems a shame*', *the Walrus said*,
'To play them such a trick.
After we've brought them out so far,
And made them trot so quick!'
The Carpenter said nothing but
'The butter's spread too thick!'

'*I weep for you,' the Walrus said:*
'*I deeply sympathize.'*
With sobs and tears he sorted out
Those of the largest size,
Holding his pocket-handkerchief
Before his streaming eyes.

'*O Oysters,' said the Carpenter,*
'*You've had a pleasant run!*
Shall we be trotting home again?'
But answer came there none—
And this was scarcely odd, because
They'd eaten every one.''

"I like the Walrus best," said Alice: "because he was a *little* sorry for the poor oysters."

"He ate more than the Carpenter, though," said Tweedledee. "You see he held his handkerchief in front, so that the Carpenter couldn't count how many he took: contrariwise."

"That was mean!" Alice said indignantly. "Then I like the Carpenter best—if he didn't eat so many as the Walrus."

"But he ate as many as he could get," said Tweedledum.

This was a puzzler. After a pause, Alice began, "Well! They were *both* very unpleasant characters——" Here she checked herself in some alarm, at hearing something that sounded to her like the puffing of a large steam-engine in the wood near them, though she feared it was more likely to be a wild beast. "Are there any lions or tigers about here?" she asked timidly.

"It's only the Red King snoring," said Tweedledee.

"Come and look at him!" the brothers cried, and they each took one of Alice's hands, and led her up to where the King was sleeping.

"Isn't he a *lovely* sight?" said Tweedledum.

Alice couldn't say honestly that he was. He had a tall red night-cap on, with a tassel, and he was lying crumpled up into a sort of untidy heap, and snoring loud——"fit to snore his head off!" as Tweedledum remarked.

"I'm afraid he'll catch cold with lying on the damp grass," said Alice, who was a very thoughtful little girl.

"He's dreaming now," said Tweedledee: "and what do you think he's dreaming about?"

Alice said "Nobody can guess that."

"Why, about *you*!" Tweedledee exclaimed, clapping his hands triumphantly. "And if he left off dreaming about you, where do you suppose you'd be?"

"Where I am now, of course," said Alice.

"Not you!" Tweedledee retorted contemptuously. "You'd be nowhere. Why, you're only a sort of thing in his dream!"

"If that there King was to wake", added Tweedledum, "you'd go out—bang!—just like a candle!"

"I shouldn't!" Alice exclaimed indignantly. "Besides, if *I'm* only a sort of thing in his dream, what are *you*, I should like to know?"

"Ditto," said Tweedledum.

"Ditto, ditto!" cried Tweedledee.

He shouted this so loud that Alice couldn't help saying "Hush! You'll be waking him, I'm afraid, if you make so much noise."

"Well, it's no use *your* talking about waking him," said Tweedledum, "when you're only one of the things in his dream. You know very well you're not real."

"I *am* real!" said Alice, and began to cry.

"You wo'n't make yourself a bit realler by crying," Tweedledee remarked: "there's nothing to cry about."

"If I wasn't real", Alice said—half laughing through her tears, it all seemed so ridiculous—"I shouldn't be able to cry."

"I hope you don't suppose those are *real* tears?" Tweedledum interrupted in a tone of great contempt.

"I know they're talking nonsense," Alice thought to herself: "and it's foolish to cry about it." So she brushed away her tears, and went on, as cheerfully as she could, "At any rate, I'd better be getting out of the wood, for really it's coming on very dark. Do you think it's going to rain?"

Tweedledum spread a large umbrella over himself and his brother, and looked up into it. "No, I don't think it is," he said: "at least—not under *here*. Nohow."

"But it may rain *outside*?"

"It may—if it chooses," said Tweedledee: "we've no objection. Contrariwise."

"Selfish things!" thought Alice, and she was just going to say "Good-night" and leave them, when Tweedledum sprang out from under the umbrella, and seized her by the wrist.

"Do you see *that*?" he said, in a voice choking with passion, and his eyes grew large and yellow all in a moment, as he pointed with a trembling finger at a small white thing lying under the tree.

"It's only a rattle," Alice said, after a careful examina-

tion of the little white thing. "Not a rattle-*snake*, you know," she added hastily, thinking that he was frightened: "only an old rattle—quite old and broken."

"I know it was!" cried Tweedledum, beginning to stamp about wildly and tear his hair. "It's spoilt, of course!" Here he looked at Tweedledee, who immediately sat down on the ground, and tried to hide himself under the umbrella.

Alice laid her hand upon his arm and said, in a soothing tone, "You needn't be so angry about an old rattle."

"But it *isn't* old!" Tweedledum cried, in a greater fury than ever. "It's *new*, I tell you—I bought it yesterday—

my nice NEW RATTLE!" and his voice rose to a perfect scream.

All this time Tweedledee was trying his best to fold up the umbrella, with himself in it: which was such an extraordinary thing to do, that it quite took off Alice's attention from the angry brother. But he couldn't quite succeed, and it ended in his rolling over, bundling up in the umbrella, with only his head out: and there he lay, opening and shutting his mouth and his large eyes ——"looking more like a fish than anything else," Alice thought.

"Of course you agree to have a battle?" Tweedledum said in a calmer tone.

"I suppose so," the other sulkily replied, as he crawled out of the umbrella: "only *she* must help us to dress up, you know."

So the two brothers went off hand-in-hand into the wood, and returned in a minute with their arms full of things—such as bolsters, blankets, hearth-rugs, table-cloths, dish-covers, and coal-scuttles. "I hope you're a good hand at pinning and tying strings?" Tweedledum remarked. "Every one of these things has got to go on, somehow or other."

Alice said afterwards she had never seen such a fuss made about anything in all her life—the way those two bustled about—and the quantity of things they put on— and the trouble they gave her in tying strings and fastening buttons—"Really they'll be more like bundles of old clothes than anything else, by the time they're ready!" she said to herself, as she arranged a bolster round the neck of Tweedledee, "to keep his head from being cut off," as he said.

"You know," he added very gravely, "it's one of the most serious things that can possibly happen to one in a battle—to get one's head cut off."

Alice laughed loud: but she managed to turn it into a cough, for fear of hurting his feelings.

"Do I look very pale?" said Tweedledum, coming up to

have his helmet tied on. (He *called* it a helmet, though it certainly looked much more like a saucepan.)

"Well—yes—a *little*," Alice replied gently.

"I'm very brave, generally," he went on in a low voice: "only to-day I happen to have a headache."

"And *I've* got a toothache!" said Tweedledee, who had overheard the remark. "I'm far worse than you!"

"Then you'd better not fight to-day," said Alice, thinking it a good opportunity to make peace.

"We *must* have a bit of a fight, but I don't care about going on long," said Tweedledum. "What's the time now?"

Tweedledee looked at his watch, and said "Half-past four."

"Let's fight till six, and then have dinner," said Tweedledum.

"Very well," the other said, rather sadly: "and *she* can watch us—only you'd better not come *very* close," he added; "I generally hit every thing I can see—when I get really excited."

"And *I* hit every thing within reach," cried Tweedledum, "whether I can see it or not!"

Alice laughed. "You must hit the *trees* pretty often, I should think," she said.

Tweedledum looked round him with a satisfied smile. "I don't suppose", he said, "there'll be a tree left standing, for ever so far round, by the time we've finished!"

"And all about a rattle!" said Alice, still hoping to make them a *little* ashamed of fighting for such a trifle.

"I shouldn't have minded it so much", said Tweedledum, "if it hadn't been a new one."

"I wish the monstrous crow would come!" thought Alice.

"There's only one sword, you know," Tweedledum said to his brother: "but *you* can have the umbrella—it's quite as sharp. Only we must begin quick. It's getting as dark as it can."

"And darker," said Tweedledee.

It was getting dark so suddenly that Alice thought there must be a thunderstorm coming on. "What a thick black cloud that is!" she said. "And how fast it comes! Why, I do believe it's got wings!"

"It's the crow!" Tweedledum cried out in a shrill voice of alarm; and the two brothers took to their heels and were out of sight in a moment.

Alice ran a little way into the wood, and stopped under a large tree. "It can never get at me *here*," she thought: "it's far too large to squeeze itself in among the trees. But I wish it wouldn't flap its wings so—it makes quite a hurricane in the wood—here's somebody's shawl being blown away!"

CHAPTER V

Wool and Water

SHE caught the shawl as she spoke, and looked about for the owner: in another moment the White Queen came running wildly through the wood, with both arms stretched out wide, as if she were flying, and Alice very civilly went to meet her with the shawl.

"I'm very glad I happened to be in the way," Alice said, as she helped her to put on her shawl again.

The White Queen only looked at her in a helpless frightened sort of way, and kept repeating something in a whisper to herself that sounded like "Bread-and-butter, bread-and-butter", and Alice felt that if there was to be any conversation at all, she must manage it herself. So she began rather timidly: "Am I addressing the White Queen?"

"Well, yes, if you call that a-dressing," the Queen said. "It isn't *my* notion of the thing, at all."

Alice thought it would never do to have an argument at the very beginning of their conversation, so she smiled and said "If your Majesty will only tell me the right way to begin, I'll do it as well as I can."

"But I don't want it done at all!" groaned the poor Queen. "I've been a-dressing myself for the last two hours."

It would have been all the better, as it seemed to Alice, if she had got some one else to dress her, she was so dreadfully untidy. "Every single thing's crooked," Alice thought to herself, "and she's all over pins!——May I put your shawl straight for you?" she added aloud.

"I don't know what's the matter with it!" the Queen said, in a melancholy voice. "It's out of temper, I think. I've pinned it here, and I've pinned it there, but there's no pleasing it!"

"It *ca'n't* go straight, you know, if you pin it all on one side," Alice said, as she gently put it right for her; "and dear me, what a state your hair is in!"

"The brush has got entangled in it!" the Queen said with a sigh. "And I lost the comb yesterday."

Alice carefully released the brush, and did her best to get the hair into order. "Come, you look rather better

now!" she said, after altering most of the pins. "But really you should have a lady's-maid!"

"I'm sure I'll take *you* with pleasure!" the Queen said. "Two pence a week and jam every other day."

Alice couldn't help laughing, as she said "I don't want you to hire *me*—and I don't care for jam."

"It's very good jam," said the Queen.

"Well, I don't want any *to-day*, at any rate."

"You couldn't have it if you *did* want it," the Queen said. "The rule is, jam to-morrow and jam yesterday—but never jam *to-day*."

"It *must* come sometimes to 'jam to-day'," Alice objected.

"No, it ca'n't," said the Queen. "It's jam every *other* day: to-day isn't any other day, you know."

"I don't understand you," said Alice. "It's dreadfully confusing!"

"That's the effect of living backwards," the Queen said kindly: "it always makes one a little giddy at first——"

"Living backwards!" Alice repeated in great astonishment. "I never heard of such a thing!"

"——but there's one great advantage in it, that one's memory works both ways."

"I'm sure *mine* only works one way," Alice remarked. "I ca'n't remember things before they happen."

"It's a poor sort of memory that only works backwards," the Queen remarked.

"What sort of things do *you* remember best?" Alice ventured to ask.

"Oh, things that happened the week after next," the Queen replied in a careless tone. "For instance, now," she went on, sticking a large piece of plaster on her finger as she spoke, "there's the King's Messenger. He's in prison now, being punished: and the trial doesn't even begin till next Wednesday: and of course the crime comes last of all."

"Suppose he never commits the crime?" said Alice.

"That would be all the better, wouldn't it?" the Queen said, as she bound the plaster round her finger with a bit of ribbon.

Alice felt there was no denying *that*. "Of course it would be all the better," she said: "but it wouldn't be all the better his being punished."

"You're wrong *there*, at any rate," said the Queen. "Were *you* ever punished?"

"Only for faults," said Alice.

"And you were all the better for it, I know!" the Queen said triumphantly.

"Yes, but then I *had* done the things I was punished for," said Alice: "that makes all the difference."

"But if you *hadn't* done them", the Queen said, "that would have been better still; better, and better, and bet-

ter!" Her voice went higher with each "better", till it got quite to a squeak at last.

Alice was just beginning to say "There's a mistake somewhere——," when the Queen began screaming, so loud that she had to leave the sentence unfinished. "Oh, oh, oh!" shouted the Queen, shaking her hand about as if she wanted to shake it off. "My finger's bleeding! Oh, oh, oh, oh!"

Her screams were so exactly like the whistle of a steam-engine, that Alice had to hold both her hands over her ears.

"What *is* the matter?" she said, as soon as there was a chance of making herself heard. "Have you pricked your finger?"

"I haven't pricked it *yet*," the Queen said, "but I soon shall—oh, oh, oh!"

"When do you expect to do it?" Alice said, feeling very much inclined to laugh.

"When I fasten my shawl again," the poor Queen groaned out: "the brooch will come undone directly. Oh, oh!" As she said the words the brooch flew open, and the Queen clutched wildly at it, and tried to clasp it again.

"Take care!" cried Alice. "You're holding it all crooked!" And she caught at the brooch; but it was too late: the pin had slipped, and the Queen had pricked her finger.

"That accounts for the bleeding, you see," she said to Alice with a smile. "Now you understand the way things happen here."

"But why don't you scream *now*?" Alice asked, holding her hands ready to put over her ears again.

"Why, I've done all the screaming already," said the Queen. "What would be the good of having it all over again?"

By this time it was getting light. "The crow must have flown away, I think," said Alice: "I'm so glad it's gone. I thought it was the night coming on."

"I wish *I* could manage to be glad!" the Queen said. "Only I never can remember the rule. You must be very happy, living in this wood, and being glad whenever you like!"

"Only it is so *very* lonely here!" Alice said in a melancholy voice; and, at the thought of her loneliness, two large tears came rolling down her cheeks.

"Oh, don't go on like that!" cried the poor Queen, wringing her hands in despair. "Consider what a great girl you are. Consider what a long way you've come to-day. Consider what o'clock it is. Consider anything, only don't cry!"

Alice could not help laughing at this, even in the midst of her tears. "Can *you* keep from crying by considering things?" she asked.

"That's the way it's done," the Queen said with great decision: "nobody can do two things at once, you know. Let's consider your age to begin with—how old are you?"

"I'm seven and a half, exactly."

"You needn't say 'exactly'," the Queen remarked. "I can believe it without that. Now I'll give *you* something to believe. I'm just one hundred and one, five months and a day."

"I ca'n't believe *that*!" said Alice.

"Ca'n't you?" the Queen said in a pitying tone. "Try again: draw a long breath, and shut your eyes."

Alice laughed. "There's no use trying," she said "one *ca'n't* believe impossible things."

"I daresay you haven't had much practice," said the Queen. "When I was your age, I always did it for half-an-hour a day. Why, sometimes I've believed as many as six impossible things before breakfast. There goes the shawl again!"

The brooch had come undone as she spoke, and a sudden gust of wind blew the Queen's shawl across a little brook. The Queen spread out her arms again and went flying after it, and this time she succeeded in catching it herself. "I've got it!" she cried in triumphant tone. "Now you shall see me pin it on again, all by myself!"

"Then I hope your finger is better now?" Alice said very politely, as she crossed the little brook after the Queen.

*   *   *   *   *

*   *   *   *

*   *   *   *   *

"Oh, much better!" cried the Queen, her voice rising into a squeak as she went on. "Much be-etter! Be-etter! Be-e-e-etter! Be-e-ehh!" The last word ended in a long bleat, so like a sheep that Alice quite started.

She looked at the Queen, who seemed to have suddenly wrapped herself up in wool. Alice rubbed her eyes, and looked again. She couldn't make out what had happened at all. Was she in a shop? And was that really—was it really a *sheep* that was sitting on the other side of the counter? Rub as she would, she could make nothing more of it: she was in a little dark shop, leaning with her elbows on the counter, and opposite to her was an old Sheep, sitting in an arm-chair, knitting, and every now and then leaving off to look at her through a great pair of spectacles.

"What is it you want to buy?" the Sheep said at last, looking up for a moment from her knitting.

"I don't *quite* know yet," Alice said very gently. "I should like to look all round me first, if I might."

"You may look in front of you, and on both sides, if you like," said the Sheep; "but you ca'n't look *all* round you—unless you've got eyes at the back of your head."

But these, as it happened, Alice had *not* got: so she contented herself with turning round, looking at the shelves as she came to them.

The shop seemed to be full of all manner of curious things—but the oddest part of it all was that, whenever she looked hard at any shelf, to make out exactly what it had on it, that particular shelf was always quite empty, though the others round it were crowded as full as they could hold.

"Things flow about so here!" she said at last in a plaintive tone, after she had spent a minute or so in vainly pursuing a large bright thing that looked sometimes like a doll and sometimes like a work-box, and was always in the shelf next above the one she was looking at. "And this one is the most provoking of all—but I'll tell you what——" she added, as a sudden thought struck her.

"I'll follow it up to the very top shelf of all. It'll puzzle it to go through the ceiling, I expect!"

But even this plan failed: the "thing" went through the ceiling as quietly as possible, as if it were quite used to it.

"Are you a child or a teetotum?" the Sheep said, as she took up another pair of needles. "You'll make me giddy soon, if you go on turning round like that." She was now working with fourteen pairs at once, and Alice couldn't help looking at her in great astonishment.

"How *can* she knit with so many?" the puzzled child thought to herself. "She gets more and more like a porcupine every minute!"

"Can you row?" the Sheep asked, handing her a pair of knitting-needles as she spoke.

"Yes, a little—but not on land—and not with needles ——" Alice was beginning to say, when suddenly the needles turned into oars in her hands, and she found they were in a little boat, gliding along between banks: so there was nothing for it but to do her best.

"Feather!" cried the Sheep, as she took up another pair of needles.

This didn't sound like a remark that needed any answer: so Alice said nothing, but pulled away. There was something very queer about the water, she thought, as every now and then the oars got fast in it, and would hardly come out again.

"Feather! Feather!" the Sheep cried again, taking more needles. "You'll be catching a crab directly."

"A dear little crab!" thought Alice. "I should like that."

"Didn't you hear me say 'Feather'?" the Sheep cried angrily, taking up quite a bunch of needles.

"Indeed I did," said Alice: "you've said it very often—and very loud. Please where *are* the crabs?"

"In the water, of course!" said the Sheep, sticking some of the needles into her hair, as her hands were full. "Feather, I say!"

"*Why* do you say 'Feather' so often?" Alice asked at last, rather vexed. "I'm not a bird!"

"You are," said the Sheep: "you're a little goose."

This offended Alice a little, so there was no more conversation for a minute or two, while the boat glided gently on, sometimes among beds of weeds (which made the oars stick fast in the water, worse than ever), and sometimes under trees, but always with the same tall riverbanks frowning over their heads.

"Oh, please! There are some scented rushes!" Alice cried in a sudden transport of delight. "There really are— and *such* beauties!"

"You needn't say 'please' to *me* about 'em," the Sheep said, without looking up from her knitting: "I didn't put 'em there, and I'm not going to take 'em away."

"No, but I meant—please, may we wait and pick

some?" Alice pleaded. "If you don't mind stopping the boat for a minute."

"How am *I* to stop it?" said the Sheep. "If you leave off rowing, it'll stop of itself."

So the boat was left to drift down the stream as it would, till it glided gently in among the waving rushes. And then the little sleeves were carefully rolled up, and the little arms were plunged in elbow-deep, to get hold of the rushes a good long way down before breaking them off—and for a while Alice forgot all about the Sheep and the knitting, as she bent over the side of the boat, with just the ends of her tangled hair dipping into the water— while with bright eager eyes she caught at one bunch after another of the darling scented rushes.

"I only hope the boat wo'n't tipple over!" she said to herself. "Oh, *what* a lovely one! Only I couldn't quite reach it." And it certainly *did* seem a little provoking ("almost as if it happened on purpose," she thought) that, though she managed to pick plenty of beautiful rushes as the boat glided by, there was always a more lovely one that she couldn't reach.

"The prettiest are always further!" she said at last with a sigh at the obstinacy of the rushes in growing so far off, as, with flushed cheeks and dripping hair and hands, she scrambled back into her place, and began to arrange her new-found treasures.

What mattered it to her just then that the rushes had begun to fade, and to lose all their scent and beauty, from the very moment that she picked them? Even real scented rushes, you know, last only a very little while—and these, being dream-rushes, melted away almost like snow, as they lay in heaps at her feet—but Alice hardly noticed this, there were so many other curious things to think about.

They hadn't gone much farther before the blade of one of the oars got fast in the water and *wouldn't* come out again (so Alice explained it afterwards), and the consequence was that the handle of it caught her under the chin, and, in spite of a series of little shrieks of "Oh, oh,

oh!" from poor Alice, it swept her straight off the seat,
and down among the heap of rushes.

However, she wasn't a bit hurt, and was soon up again:
the Sheep went on with her knitting all the while, just as
if nothing had happened. "That was a nice crab you
caught!" she remarked, as Alice got back into her place,
very much relieved to find herself still in the boat.

"Was it! I didn't see it," said Alice, peeping cautiously
over the side of the boat into the dark water. "I wish it
hadn't let go—I should so like a little crab to take home

with me!" But the Sheep only laughed scornfully, and went on with her knitting.

"Are there many crabs here?" said Alice.

"Crabs, and all sorts of things," said the Sheep: "plenty of choice, only make up your mind. Now, what *do* you want to buy?"

"To buy!" Alice echoed in a tone that was half astonished and half frightened—for the oars, and the boat, and the river, had vanished all in a moment, and she was back again in the little dark shop.

"I should like to buy an egg, please," she said timidly. "How do you sell them?"

"Fivepence farthing for one—twopence for two," the Sheep replied.

"Then two are cheaper than one?" Alice said in a surprised tone, taking out her purse.

"Only you *must* eat them both, if you buy two," said the Sheep.

"Then I'll have *one*, please," said Alice, as she put the money down on the counter. For she thought to herself, "They mightn't be at all nice, you know."

The Sheep took the money, and put it away in a box: then she said "I never put things into people's hands— that would never do—you must get it for yourself." And so saying, she went off to the other end of the shop, and set the egg upright on a shelf.

"I wonder *why* it wouldn't do?" thought Alice, as she groped her way among the tables and chairs, for the shop was very dark towards the end. "The egg seems to get further away the more I walk towards it. Let me see, is this a chair? Why, it's got branches, I declare! How very odd to find trees growing here! And actually here's a little brook! Well, this is the very queerest shop I ever saw!"

*   *   *   *   *

*   *   *   *

*   *   *   *   *

So she went on, wondering more and more at every step, as everything turned into a tree the moment she came up to it, and she quite expected the egg to do the same.

CHAPTER VI

Humpty Dumpty

HOWEVER, the egg only got larger and larger, and more and more human: when she had come within a few yards of it, she saw that it had eyes and a nose and mouth; and, when she had come close to it, she saw clearly that it was HUMPTY DUMPTY himself. "It ca'n't be anybody else!" she said to herself. "I'm as certain of it, as if his name were written all over his face!"

It might have been written a hundred times, easily, on that enormous face. Humpty Dumpty was sitting, with his legs crossed like a Turk, on the top of a high wall— such a narrow one that Alice quite wondered how he could keep his balance—and, as his eyes were steadily fixed in the opposite direction, and he didn't take the least notice of her, she thought he must be a stuffed figure, after all.

"And how exactly like an egg he is!" she said aloud, standing with her hands ready to catch him, for she was every moment expecting him to fall.

"It's *very* provoking", Humpty Dumpty said after a long silence, looking away from Alice as he spoke, "to be called an egg—*very*!"

"I said you *looked* like an egg, Sir," Alice gently explained. "And some eggs are very pretty, you know," she added, hoping to turn her remark into a sort of compliment.

"Some people", said Humpty Dumpty, looking away from her as usual, "have no more sense than a baby!"

Alice didn't know what to say to this: it wasn't at all like conversation, she thought, as he never said anything to *her*; in fact, his last remark was evidently addressed to a tree—so she stood and softly repeated to herself:

> *"Humpty Dumpty sat on a wall:*
> *Humpty Dumpty had a great fall.*
> *All the King's horses and all the King's men*
> *Couldn't put Humpty Dumpty in his place again.*

"That last line is much too long for the poetry," she added, almost out loud, forgetting that Humpty Dumpty would hear her.

"Don't stand chattering to yourself like that," Humpty Dumpty said, looking at her for the first time, "but tell me your name and your business."

"My *name* is Alice, but——"

"It's a stupid name enough!" Humpty Dumpty interrupted impatiently. "What does it mean?"

"*Must* a name mean something?" Alice asked doubtfully.

"Of course it must," Humpty Dumpty said with a short laugh: "*my* name means the shape I am—and a good handsome shape it is, too. With a name like yours, you might be any shape, almost."

"Why do you sit out here all alone?" said Alice, not wishing to begin an argument.

"Why, because there's nobody with me!" cried Humpty Dumpty. "Did you think I didn't know the answer to *that*? Ask another."

"Don't you think you'd be safer down on the ground?" Alice went on, not with any idea of making another riddle, but simply in her good-natured anxiety for the queer creature. "That wall is so *very* narrow!"

"What tremendously easy riddles you ask!" Humpty Dumpty growled out. "Of course I don't think so! Why, if ever I *did* fall off—which there's no chance of—but *if* I did——" Here he pursed up his lips, and looked so solemn and grand that Alice could hardly help laughing.

"*If* I *did* fall," he went on, "*the King has promised me—*ah, you may turn pale, if you like! You didn't think I was going to say that, did you? *The King has promised me—with his very own mouth*—to—to——"

"To send all his horses and all his men," Alice interrupted, rather unwisely.

"Now I declare that's too bad!" Humpty Dumpty cried, breaking into a sudden passion. "You've been listening at doors—and behind trees—and down chimneys—or you couldn't have known it!"

"I haven't indeed!" Alice said very gently. "It's in a book."

"Ah, well! They may write such things in a *book*," Humpty Dumpty said in a calmer tone. "That's what you call a History of England, that is. Now, take a good look at me! I'm one that has spoken to a King, *I* am: mayhap you'll never see such another: and, to show you I'm not proud, you may shake hands with me!" And he grinned almost from ear to ear, as he leant forwards (and as nearly as possible fell off the wall in doing so) and offered Alice his hand. She watched him a little anxiously as she took it. "If he smiled much more the ends of his mouth might meet behind," she thought: "And then I don't know *what* would happen to his head! I'm afraid it would come off!"

"Yes, all his horses and all his men," Humpty Dumpty went on. "They'd pick me up again in a minute, *they* would! However, this conversation is going on a little too fast: let's go back to the last remark but one."

"I'm afraid I ca'n't quite remember it," Alice said, very politely.

"In that case we start afresh," said Humpty Dumpty, "and it's my turn to choose a subject——" ("He talks about it just as if it was a game!" thought Alice.) "So here's a question for you. How old did you say you were?"

Alice made a short calculation, and said "Seven years and six months."

"Wrong!" Humpty Dumpty exclaimed triumphantly. "You never said a word like it!"

"I thought you meant 'How old *are* you?' " Alice explained.

"If I'd meant that, I'd have said it," said Humpty Dumpty.

Alice didn't want to begin another argument, so she said nothing.

"Seven years and six months!" Humpty Dumpty repeated thoughtfully. "An uncomfortable sort of age. Now if you'd asked *my* advice, I'd have said 'Leave off at seven'——but it's too late now."

"I never ask advice about growing," Alice said indignantly.

"Too proud?" the other enquired.

Alice felt even more indignant at this suggestion. "I mean", she said, "that one ca'n't help growing older."

"*One* ca'n't, perhaps," said Humpty Dumpty; "but *two*

can. With proper assistance, you might have left off at seven."

"What a beautiful belt you've got on!" Alice suddenly remarked. (They had had quite enough of the subject of age, she thought: and, if they really were to take turns in choosing subjects, it was *her* turn now.) "At least," she corrected herself on second thoughts, "a beautiful cravat, I should have said—no, a belt, I mean—I beg your pardon!" she added in dismay, for Humpty Dumpty looked thoroughly offended, and she began to wish she hadn't chosen that subject. "If only I knew", she thought to herself, "which was neck and which was waist!"

Evidently Humpty Dumpty was very angry, though he said nothing for a minute or two. When he *did* speak again, it was in a deep growl.

"It is a—*most—provoking*—thing", he said at last, "when a person doesn't know a cravat from a belt!"

"I know it's very ignorant of me," Alice said, in so humble a tone that Humpty Dumpty relented.

"It's a cravat, child, and a beautiful one, as you say. It's a present from the White King and Queen. There now!"

"Is it really?" said Alice, quite pleased to find that she *had* chosen a good subject after all.

"They gave it me," Humpty Dumpty continued thoughtfully as he crossed one knee over the other and clasped his hands round it, "they gave it me—for an un-birthday present."

"I beg your pardon?" Alice said with a puzzled air.

"I'm not offended," said Humpty Dumpty.

"I mean, what *is* an un-birthday present?"

"A present given when it isn't your birthday, of course."

Alice considered a little. "I like birthday presents best," she said at last.

"You don't know what you're talking about!" cried Humpty Dumpty. "How many days are there in a year?"

"Three hundred and sixty-five," said Alice.

"And how many birthdays have you?"

"One."

"And if you take one from three hundred and sixty-five what remains?"

"Three hundred and sixty-four, of course."

Humpty Dumpty looked doubtful. "I'd rather see that done on paper," he said.

Alice couldn't help smiling as she took out her memorandum book, and worked the sum for him:

$$3\,6\,5$$
$$1$$
$$\overline{}$$
$$3\,6\,4$$
$$\overline{}$$

Humpty Dumpty took the book and looked at it carefully. "That seems to be done right——" he began.

"You're holding it upside down!" Alice interrupted.

"To be sure I was!" Humpty Dumpty said gaily as she turned it round for him. "I thought it looked a little queer. As I was saying, that *seems* to be done right—though I haven't time to look it over thoroughly just now—and that shows that there are three hundred and sixty-four days when you might get un-birthday presents——"

"Certainly," said Alice.

"And only *one* for birthday presents, you know. There's glory for you!"

"I don't know what you mean by 'glory'," Alice said.

Humpty Dumpty smiled contemptuously. "Of course you don't—till I tell you. I meant 'there's a nice knock-down argument for you!'"

"But 'glory' doesn't mean 'a nice knock-down argument', " Alice objected.

"When *I* use a word", Humpty Dumpty said, in rather a scornful tone, "it means just what I choose it to mean—neither more nor less."

"The question is", said Alice, "whether you *can* make words mean so many different things."

"The question is", said Humpty Dumpty, "which is to be master——that's all."

Alice was too much puzzled to say anything; so after a minute Humpty Dumpty began again. "They've a temper, some of them—particularly verbs: they're the proudest—adjectives you can do anything with, but not verbs—however, *I* can manage the whole lot of them! Impenetrability! That's what *I* say!"

"Would you tell me please," said Alice, "what that means?"

"Now you talk like a reasonable child," said Humpty Dumpty, looking very much pleased. "I meant by 'impenetrability' that we've had enough of that subject, and it would be just as well if you'd mention what you mean to do next, as I suppose you don't mean to stop here all the rest of your life."

"That's a great deal to make one word mean," Alice said in a thoughtful tone.

"When I make a word do a lot of work like that," said Humpty Dumpty, "I always pay it extra."

"Oh!" said Alice. She was too much puzzled to make any other remark.

"Ah, you should see 'em come round me of a Saturday night", Humpty Dumpty went on, wagging his head gravely from side to side, "for to get their wages, you know."

(Alice didn't venture to ask what he paid them with; and so you see I ca'n't tell *you*.)

"You seem very clever at explaining words, Sir," said Alice. "Would you kindly tell me the meaning of the poem called 'Jabberwocky'?"

"Let's hear it," said Humpty Dumpty. "I can explain all the poems that ever were invented—and a good many that haven't been invented just yet."

This sounded very hopeful, so Alice repeated the first verse:

> " *'Twas brillig, and the slithy toves*
> *Did gyre and gimble in the wabe:*
> *All mimsy were the borogoves,*
> *And the mome raths outgrabe.*"

"That's enough to begin with," Humpty Dumpty interrupted: "there are plenty of hard words there. '*Brillig*'
means four o'clock in the afternoon—the time when you
begin *broiling* things for dinner."

"That'll do very well," said Alice: "and '*slithy*'?"

"Well, '*slithy*' means 'lithe and slimy'. 'Lithe' is the
same as 'active'. You see it's like a portmanteau—there
are two meanings packed up into one word."

"I see it now," Alice remarked thoughtfully: "and
what are '*toves*'?"

"Well, 'toves' are something like badgers—they're something like lizards—and they're something like cork-screws."

"They must be very curious-looking creatures."

"They are that," said Humpty Dumpty; "also they make. their nests under sun-dials—also they live on cheese."

"And what's to 'gyre' and to 'gimble'?"

"To 'gyre' is to go round and round like a gyroscope. To 'gimble' is to make holes like a gimlet."

"And 'the wabe' is the grass-plot round a sun-dial, I suppose?" said Alice, surprised at her own ingenuity.

"Of course it is. It's called 'wabe' you know, because it goes a long way before it, and a long way behind it——"

"And a long way beyond it on each side," Alice added.

"Exactly so. Well then, 'mimsy' is 'flimsy and miser-able' (there's another portmanteau for you). And a 'boro-gove' is a thin shabby-looking bird with its feathers stick-ing out all round—something like a live mop."

"And then 'mome raths'?" said Alice. "I'm afraid I'm giving you a great deal of trouble."

"Well, a 'rath' is a sort of green pig: but 'mome' I'm not certain about. I think it's short for 'from home'—meaning that they'd lost their way, you know."

"And what does 'outgrabe' mean?"

"Well, 'outgribing' is something between bellowing and whistling, with a kind of sneeze in the middle: however, you'll hear it done, maybe—down in the wood yonder—and, when you've once heard it, you'll be quite content. Who's been repeating all that hard stuff to you?"

"I read it in a book," said Alice. "But I had some poetry repeated to me much easier than that, by—Tweedledee, I think it was."

"As to poetry, you know," said Humpty Dumpty, stretching out one of his great hands, "I can repeat poetry as well as other folk, if it comes to that——"

"Oh, it needn't come to that!" Alice hastily said, hoping to keep him from beginning.

"The piece I'm going to repeat", he went on without noticing her remark, "was written entirely for your amusement."

Alice felt that in that case she really *ought* to listen to it; so she sat down, and said "Thank you" rather sadly,

> *"In winter, when the fields are white,*
> *I sing this song for your delight ——*

only I don't sing it," he added, as an explanation.

"I see you don't," said Alice.

"If you can *see* whether I'm singing or not, you've sharper eyes than most," Humpty Dumpty remarked severely. Alice was silent.

> *"In spring, when woods are getting green,*
> *I'll try and tell you what I mean:"*

"Thank you very much," said Alice.

> *"In summer, when the days are long,*
> *Perhaps you'll understand the song:*
>
> *In autumn, when the leaves are brown,*
> *Take pen and ink, and write it down."*

"I will, if I can remember it so long," said Alice.

"You needn't go on making remarks like that," Humpty Dumpty said: "they're not sensible, and they put me out."

> *"I sent a message to the fish:*
> *I told them 'This is what I wish.'*
>
> *The little fishes of the sea,*
> *They sent an answer back to me.*
>
> *The little fishes' answer was*
> *'We cannot do it, Sir, because ——' "*

"I'm afraid I don't quite understand," said Alice.

"It gets easier further on," Humpty Dumpty replied.

"I sent to them again to say
'It will be better to obey'.

The fishes answered, with a grin,
'Why, what a temper you are in!'

I told them once, I told them twice:
They would not listen to advice.

I took a kettle large and new,
Fit for the deed I had to do.

My heart went hop, my heart went thump:
I filled the kettle at the pump.

Then some one came to me and said
'The little fishes are in bed.'

I said to him, I said it plain,
'Then you must wake them up again.'

I said it very loud and clear:
I went and shouted in his ear."

Humpty Dumpty raised his voice almost to a scream as
he repeated this verse, and Alice thought, with a shudder,
"I wouldn't have been the messenger for *anything!*"

"But he was very stiff and proud:
He said, 'You needn't shout so loud!'

And he was very proud and stiff:
He said 'I'd go and wake them, if ——'

I took a corkscrew from the shelf:
I went to wake them up myself.

And when I found the door was locked,
I pulled and pushed and kicked and knocked.

And when I found the door was shut,
I tried to turn the handle, but ——"

There was a long pause.

"Is that all?" Alice timidly asked.

"That's all," said Humpty Dumpty. "Good-bye."

This was rather sudden, Alice thought: but, after such a
very strong hint that she ought to be going, she felt that it
would hardly be civil to stay. So she got up, and held out
her hand. "Good-bye, till we meet again!" she said as
cheerfully as she could.

"I shouldn't know you again if we *did* meet," Humpty
Dumpty replied in a discontented tone, giving her one of
his fingers to shake: "you're so exactly like other people."

"The face is what one goes by, generally," Alice remarked in a thoughtful tone.

"That's just what I complain of," said Humpty
Dumpty. "Your face is the same as everybody has—the
two eyes, so——" (marking their places in the air with
his thumb) "nose in the middle, mouth under. It's always
the same. Now if you had the two eyes on the same side
of the nose, for instance—or the mouth at the top—that
would be *some* help."

"It wouldn't look nice," Alice objected. But Humpty Dumpty only shut his eyes, and said "Wait till you've tried."

Alice waited a minute to see if he would speak again, but, as he never opened his eyes or took any further notice of her, she said "Good-bye!" once more, and, getting no answer to this, she quietly walked away: but she couldn't help saying to herself, as she went, "of all the unsatisfactory——" (she repeated this aloud, as it was a great comfort to have such a long word to say) "of all the unsatisfactory people I *ever* met——" She never finished the sentence, for at this moment a heavy crash shook the forest from end to end.

Chapter VII

The Lion and the Unicorn

THE next moment soldiers came running through the wood, at first in twos and threes, then ten or twenty together, and at last in such crowds that they seemed to fill the whole forest. Alice got behind a tree, for fear of being run over, and watched them go by.

She thought that in all her life she had never seen soldiers so uncertain on their feet: they were always tripping over something or other, and whenever one went down, several more always fell over him, so that the ground was soon covered with little heaps of men.

Then came the horses. Having four feet, these managed rather better than the foot-soldiers; but even *they* stumbled now and then; and it seemed to be a regular rule that, whenever a horse stumbled, the rider fell off instantly. The confusion got worse every moment, and Alice was very glad to get out of the wood into an open place, where she found the White King seated on the ground, busily writing in his memorandum-book.

"I've sent them all!" the King cried in a tone of delight, on seeing Alice. "Did you happen to meet any soldiers, my dear, as you came through the wood?"

"Yes, I did," said Alice: "several thousand, I should think."

"Four thousand two hundred and seven, that's the exact number," the King said, referring to his book. "I couldn't send all the horses, you know, because two of them are wanted in the game. And I haven't sent the two

Messengers, either. They're both gone to the town. Just look along the road, and tell me if you can see either of them."

"I see nobody on the road," said Alice.

"I only wish *I* had such eyes," the King remarked in a fretful tone. "To be able to see Nobody! And at that distance too! Why, it's as much as *I* can do to see real people, by this light!"

All this was lost on Alice, who was still looking intently along the road, shading her eyes with one hand. "I see somebody now!" she exclaimed at last. "But he's coming very slowly—and what curious attitudes he goes into!" (For the Messenger kept skipping up and down, and wriggling like an eel, as he came along, with his great hands spread out like fans on each side.)

"Not at all," said the King. "He's an Anglo-Saxon Messenger—and those are Anglo-Saxon attitudes. He only does them when he's happy. His name is Haigha." (He pronounced it so as to rhyme with 'mayor'.)

"I love my love with an H," Alice couldn't help beginning, "because he is Happy. I hate him with an H, because he is Hideous. I fed him with—with—with Ham-sandwiches and Hay. His name is Haigha, and he lives ——"

"He lives on the Hill," the King remarked simply, without the least idea that he was joining in the game, while Alice was still hesitating for the name of a town beginning with H. "The other Messenger's called Hatta. I must have *two*, you know—to come and go. One to come, and one to go."

"I beg your pardon?" said Alice.

"It isn't respectable to beg," said the King.

"I only meant that I didn't understand," said Alice. "Why one to come and one to go?"

"Don't I tell you?" the King repeated impatiently. "I must have *two*—to fetch and carry. One to fetch, and one to carry."

At this moment the Messenger arrived: he was far too

much out of breath to say a word, and could only wave his hands about, and make the most fearful faces at the poor King.

"This young lady loves you with an H," the King said, introducing Alice in the hope of turning off the Messenger's attention from himself—but it was of no use—the Anglo-Saxon attitudes only got more extraordinary every moment, while the great eyes rolled wildly from side to side.

"You alarm me!" said the King. "I feel faint—Give me a ham-sandwich!"

On which the Messenger, to Alice's great amusement, opened a bag that hung round his neck, and handed a sandwich to the King, who devoured it greedily.

"Another sandwich!" said the King.

"There's nothing but hay left now," the Messenger said, peeping into the bag.

"Hay, then," the King murmured in a faint whisper.

Alice was glad to see that it revived him a good deal. "There's nothing like eating hay when you're faint," he remarked to her, as he munched away.

"I should think throwing cold water over you would be better," Alice suggested: "—or some sal-volatile."

"I didn't say there was nothing *better*," the King replied. "I said there was nothing *like* it." Which Alice did not venture to deny.

"Who did you pass on the road?" the King went on, holding out his hand to the Messenger for some hay.

"Nobody," said the Messenger.

"Quite right," said the King: "this young lady saw him too. So of course Nobody walks slower than you."

"I do my best," the Messenger said in a sullen tone. "I'm sure nobody walks much faster than I do!"

"He ca'n't do that," said the King, "or else he'd have been here first. However, now you've got your breath, you may tell us what's happened in the town."

"I'll whisper it," said the Messenger, putting his hands to his mouth in the shape of a trumpet and stooping so as to get close to the King's ear. Alice was sorry for this, as she wanted to hear the news too. However, instead of whispering, he simply shouted, at the top of his voice, "They're at it again!"

"Do you call *that* a whisper?" cried the poor King, jumping up and shaking himself. "If you do such a thing again I'll have you buttered! It went through and through my head like an earthquake!"

"It would have to be a very tiny earthquake!" thought Alice. "Who are at it again?" she ventured to ask.

"Why the Lion and the Unicorn, of course," said the King.

"Fighting for the crown?"

"Yes, to be sure," said the King: "and the best of the joke is, that it's *my* crown all the while! Let's run and see them." And they trotted off, Alice repeating to herself, as she ran, the words of the old song:

"The Lion and the Unicorn were fighting for the crown:
The Lion beat the Unicorn all round the town.
Some gave them white bread, some gave them brown:
Some gave them plum-cake and drummed them out of town."

"Does——the one——that wins——get the crown?"
she asked, as well as she could, for the run was putting
her quite out of breath.

"Dear me, no!" said the King. "What an idea!"

"Would you——be good enough——" Alice panted
out, after running a little further, "to stop a minute—just
to get—one's breath again?"

"I'm *good* enough," the King said, "only I'm not *strong*
enough. You see, a minute goes by so fearfully quick.
You might as well try to stop a Bandersnatch!"

Alice had no more breath for talking; so they trotted on
in silence, till they came into sight of a great crowd, in the
middle of which the Lion and Unicorn were fighting.
They were in such a cloud of dust, that at first Alice could
not make out which was which; but she soon managed to
distinguish the Unicorn by his horn.

They placed themselves close to where Hatta, the other
Messenger, was standing watching the fight, with a cup
of tea in one hand and a piece of bread-and-butter in the
other.

"He's only just out of prison, and he hadn't finished his
tea when he was sent in," Haigha whispered to Alice:
"and they only give them oyster-shells in there—so you
see he's very hungry and thirsty. How are you, dear
child?" he went on, putting his arm affectionately round
Hatta's neck.

Hatta looked round and nodded, and went on with his
bread-and-butter.

"Were you happy in prison, dear child?" said Haigha.

Hatta looked round once more, and this time a tear or
two trickled down his cheek; but not a word would he say.

"Speak, ca'n't you!" Haigha cried impatiently. But
Hatta only munched away, and drank some more tea.

"Speak, wo'n't you!" cried the King. "How are they getting on with the fight?"

Hatta made a desperate effort, and swallowed a large piece of bread-and-butter. "They're getting on very well," he said in a choking voice: "each of them has been down about eighty-seven times."

"Then I suppose they'll soon bring the white bread and the brown?" Alice ventured to remark.

"It's waiting for 'em now," said Hatta; "this is a bit of it as I'm eating."

There was a pause in the fight just then, and the Lion and the Unicorn sat down, panting, while the King called out "Ten minutes allowed for refreshments!" Haigha and Hatta set to work at once, carrying round trays of white and brown bread. Alice took a piece to taste, but it was *very* dry.

"I don't think they'll fight any more to-day," the King said to Hatta: "go and order the drums to begin." And Hatta went bounding away like a grasshopper.

For a minute or two Alice stood silent, watching him. Suddenly she brightened up. "Look, look!" she cried, pointing eagerly. "There's the White Queen running across the country! She came flying out of the wood over yonder—— How fast those Queens *can* run!"

"There's some enemy after her, no doubt," the King said, without even looking round. "That wood's full of them."

"But aren't you going to run and help her?" Alice asked, very much surprised at his taking it so quietly.

"No use, no use!" said the King. "She runs so fearfully quick. You might as well try to catch a Bandersnatch! But I'll make a memorandum about her, if you like—— She's a dear good creature," he repeated softly to himself, as he opened his memorandum-book. "Do you spell 'creature' with a double 'e'?"

At this moment the Unicorn sauntered by them, with his hands in his pockets. "I had the best of it this time?" he said to the King, just glancing at him as he passed.

"A little—a little," the King replied, rather nervously. "You shouldn't have run him through with your horn, you know."

"It didn't hurt him," the Unicorn said carelessly, and he was going on, when his eye happened to fall upon Alice: he turned round instantly, and stood for some time looking at her with an air of the deepest disgust.

"What—is—this?" he said at last.

"This is a child!" Haigha replied eagerly, coming in front of Alice to introduce her, and spreading out both his hands towards her in an Anglo-Saxon attitude. "We only found it to-day. It's as large as life, and twice as natural!"

"I always thought they were fabulous monsters!" said the Unicorn. "Is it alive?"

"It can talk," said Haigha solemnly.

The Unicorn looked dreamily at Alice, and said "Talk, child."

Alice could not help her lips curling up into a smile as

she began: "Do you know, I always thought Unicorns were fabulous monsters, too? I never saw one alive before!"

"Well, now that we *have* seen each other," said the Unicorn, "if you'll believe in me, I'll believe in you. Is that a bargain?"

"Yes, if you like," said Alice.

"Come, fetch out the plum-cake, old man!" the Unicorn went on, turning from her to the King. "None of your brown bread for me!"

"Certainly—certainly!" the King muttered, and beckoned to Haigha. "Open the bag!" he whispered. "Quick! Not that one—that's full of hay!"

Haigha took a large cake out of the bag, and gave it to Alice to hold, while he got out a dish and carving-knife. How they all came out of it Alice couldn't guess. It was just like a conjuring trick, she thought.

The Lion had joined them while this was going on: he looked very tired and sleepy, and his eyes were half shut.

"What's this!" he said, blinking lazily at Alice, and speaking in a deep hollow tone that sounded like the tolling of a great bell.

"Ah, what *is* it, now?" the Unicorn cried eagerly. "You'll never guess! *I* couldn't."

The Lion looked at Alice wearily. "Are you animal—or vegetable—or mineral?" he said, yawning at every other word.

"It's a fabulous monster!" the Unicorn cried out, before Alice could reply.

"Then hand round the plum-cake, Monster," the Lion said, lying down and putting his chin on his paws. "And sit down, both of you," (to the King and the Unicorn): "fair play with the cake, you know!"

The King was evidently very uncomfortable at having to sit down between the two great creatures; but there was no other place for him.

"What a fight we might have for the crown, *now*!" the Unicorn said, looking slyly up at the crown, which the poor King was nearly shaking off his head, he trembled so much.

"I should win easy," said the Lion.

"I'm not so sure of that," said the Unicorn.

"Why, I beat you all round the town, you chicken!" the Lion replied angrily, half getting up as he spoke.

Here the King interrupted, to prevent the quarrel going on: he was very nervous, and his voice quite quivered. "All round the town?" he said. "That's a good long way. Did you go by the old bridge, or the market-place? You get the best view by the old bridge."

"I'm sure I don't know," the Lion growled out as he lay down again. "There was too much dust to see anything. What a time the Monster is, cutting up that cake!"

Alice had seated herself on the bank of a little brook, with the great dish on her knees, and was sawing away diligently with the knife. "It's very provoking!" she said, in reply to the Lion (she was getting quite used to being called 'the Monster'). "I've cut several slices already, but they always join on again!"

"You don't know how to manage Looking-glass cakes," the Unicorn remarked. "Hand it round first, and cut it afterwards."

This sounded nonsense, but Alice very obediently got up, and carried the dish round, and the cake divided itself

into three pieces as she did so. "*Now* cut it up," said the Lion, as she returned to her place with the empty dish.

"I say, this isn't fair!" cried the Unicorn, as Alice sat with the knife in her hand, very much puzzled how to begin. "The Monster has given the Lion twice as much as me!"

"She's kept none for herself, anyhow," said the Lion. "Do you like plum-cake, Monster?"

But before Alice could answer him, the drums began.

Where the noise came from, she couldn't make out: the air seemed full of it, and it rang through and through her head till she felt quite deafened. She started to her feet and sprang across the little brook in her terror, and had just time to see the Lion and the Unicorn rise to their

*　　　*　　　*　　　*　　　*
*　　　*　　　*　　　*
*　　　*　　　*　　　*　　　*

feet, with angry looks at being interrupted in their feast, before she dropped to her knees, and put her hands over her ears, vainly trying to shut out the dreadful uproar.

"If *that* doesn't 'drum them out of town'," she thought to herself, "nothing ever will!"

Chapter VIII

"It's My Own Invention"

AFTER a while the noise seemed gradually to die away, till all was dead silence, and Alice lifted up her head in some alarm. There was no one to be seen, and her first thought was that she must have been dreaming about the Lion and the Unicorn and those queer Anglo-Saxon Messengers. However, there was the great dish still lying at her feet, on which she had tried to cut the plum-cake, "So I wasn't dreaming, after all," she said to herself, "unless—unless we're all part of the same dream. Only I do hope it's *my* dream, and not the Red King's! I don't like belonging to another person's dream," she went on in a rather complaining tone: "I've a great mind to go and wake him, and see what happens!"

At this moment her thoughts were interrupted by a

loud shouting of "Ahoy! Ahoy! Check!" and a Knight, dressed in crimson armour, came galloping down upon her, brandishing a great club. Just as he reached her, the horse stopped suddenly: "You're my prisoner!" the Knight cried, as he tumbled off his horse.

Startled as she was, Alice was more frightened for him than for herself at the moment, and watched him with some anxiety as he mounted again. As soon as he was comfortably in the saddle, he began once more "You're my——" but here another voice broke in "Ahoy! Ahoy! Check!" and Alice looked round in some surprise for the new enemy.

This time it was a White Knight. He drew up at Alice's side, and tumbled off his horse just as the Red Knight had done: then he got on again, and the two Knights sat and looked at each other for some time without speaking. Alice looked from one to the other in some bewilderment.

"She's *my* prisoner, you know!" the Red Knight said at last.

"Yes, but then *I* came and rescued her!" the White Knight replied.

"Well, we must fight for her, then," said the Red Knight, as he took up his helmet (which hung from the saddle, and was something the shape of a horse's head) and put it on.

"You will observe the Rules of Battle, of course?" the White Knight remarked, putting on his helmet too.

"I always do," said the Red Knight, and they began banging away at each other with such fury that Alice got behind a tree to be out of the way of the blows.

"I wonder, now, what the Rules of Battle are," she said to herself, as she watched the fight, timidly peeping out from her hiding-place. "One Rule seems to be, that if one Knight hits the other, he knocks him off his horse; and, if he misses, he tumbles off himself—and another Rule seems to be that they hold their clubs with their arms, as if they were Punch and Judy—— What a noise they make when they tumble! Just like a whole set of fire-irons falling into the fender! And how quiet the horses are! They let them get on and off them just as if they were tables!"

Another Rule of Battle, that Alice had not noticed, seemed to be that they always fell on their heads; and the battle ended with their both falling off in this way, side by side. When they got up again, they shook hands, and then the Red Knight mounted and galloped off.

"It was a glorious victory, wasn't it?" said the White Knight, as he came up panting.

"I don't know," Alice said doubtfully. "I don't want to be anybody's prisoner. I want to be a Queen."

"So you will, when you've crossed the next brook," said the White Knight. "I'll see you safe to the end of the wood—and then I must go back, you know. That's the end of my move."

"Thank you very much," said Alice. "May I help you off with your helmet?" It was evidently more than he could manage by himself: however she managed to shake him out of it at last.

"Now one can breathe more easily," said the Knight, putting back his shaggy hair with both hands, and turning his gentle face and large mild eyes to Alice. She thought she had never seen such a strange-looking soldier in all her life.

He was dressed in tin armour, which seemed to fit him very badly, and he had a queer-shaped little deal box fastened across his shoulders, upside-down, and with the lid hanging open. Alice looked at it with great curiosity.

"I see you're admiring my little box," the Knight said in a friendly tone. "It's my own invention—to keep clothes and sandwiches in. You see I carry it upside-down, so that the rain ca'n't get in."

"But the things can get *out*," Alice gently remarked. "Do you know the lid's open?"

"I didn't know it," the Knight said, a shade of vexation passing over his face. "Then all the things must have fallen out! And the box is no use without them." He unfastened it as he spoke, and was just going to throw it into the bushes, when a sudden thought seemed to strike him, and he hung it carefully on a tree. "Can you guess why I did that?" he said to Alice.

Alice shook her head.

"In hopes some bees may make a nest in it—then I should get the honey."

"But you've got a bee-hive—or something like one—fastened to the saddle," said Alice.

"Yes, it's a very good bee-hive," the Knight said in a discontented tone, "one of the best kind. But not a single bee has come near it yet. And the other thing is a mouse-trap. I suppose the mice keep the bees out—or the bees keep the mice out, I don't know which."

"I was wondering what the mouse-trap was for," said Alice. "It isn't very likely there would be any mice on the horse's back."

"Not very likely, perhaps," said the Knight; "but, if they *do* come, I don't choose to have them running all about."

"You see," he went on after a pause, "it's as well to be provided for *everything*. That's the reason the horse has all those anklets round his feet."

"But what are they for?" Alice asked in a tone of great curiosity.

"To guard against the bites of sharks," the Knight replied. "It's an invention of my own. And now help me on. I'll go with you to the end of the wood—What's that dish for?"

"It's meant for plum-cake," said Alice.

"We'd better take it with us," the Knight said. "It'll come in handy if we find any plum-cake. Help me to get it into this bag."

This took a long time to manage, though Alice held the bag open very carefully, because the knight was so *very* awkward in putting in the dish: the first two or three times that he tried he fell in himself instead. "It's rather a tight fit, you see," he said, as they got it in at last; "there are so many candlesticks in the bag." And he hung it to the saddle, which was already loaded with bunches of carrots, and fire-irons, and many other things.

"I hope you've got your hair well fastened on?" he continued, as they set off.

"Only in the usual way," Alice said, smiling.

"That's hardly enough," he said, anxiously. "You see the wind is so *very* strong here. It's as strong as soup."

"Have you invented a plan for keeping the hair from being blown off?" Alice enquired.

"Not yet," said the Knight. "But I've got a plan for keeping it from *falling* off."

"I should like to hear it, very much."

"First you take an upright stick," said the Knight.

"Then you make your hair creep up it, like a fruit-tree. Now the reason hair falls off is because it hangs *down*— things never fall *upwards*, you know. It's a plan of my own invention. You may try it if you like."

It didn't sound a comfortable plan, Alice thought, and for a few minutes she walked on in silence, puzzling over

the idea, and every now and then stopping to help the poor Knight, who certainly was *not* a good rider.

Whenever the horse stopped (which it did very often), he fell off in front; and, whenever it went on again (which it generally did rather suddenly), he fell off behind. Otherwise he kept on pretty well, except that he had a habit of now and then falling off sideways; and, as he generally did this on the side on which Alice was walking, she soon found that it was the best plan not to walk *quite* close to the horse.

"I'm afraid you've not had much practice in riding," she ventured to say, as she was helping him up from his fifth tumble.

The Knight looked very much surprised, and a little offended at the remark. "What makes you say that?" he asked, as he scrambled back into the saddle, keeping hold of Alice's hair with one hand, to save himself from falling over on the other side.

"Because people don't fall off quite so often, when they've had much practice."

"I've had plenty of practice," the Knight said very gravely: "plenty of practice!"

Alice could think of nothing better to say than "Indeed?" but she said it as heartily as she could. They went on a little way in silence after this, the Knight with his eyes shut, muttering to himself, and Alice watching anxiously for the next tumble.

"The great art of riding", the Knight suddenly began in a loud voice, waving his right arm as he spoke, "is to keep——" Here the sentence ended as suddenly as it had begun, as the Knight fell heavily on the top of his head exactly in the path where Alice was walking. She was quite frightened this time, and said in an anxious tone, as she picked him up, "I hope no bones are broken?"

"None to speak of," the Knight said, as if he didn't mind breaking two or three of them. "The great art of riding, as I was saying, is—to keep your balance properly. Like this, you know——"

He let go the bridle, and stretched out both his arms to show Alice what he meant, and this time he fell flat on his back, right under the horse's feet.

"Plenty of practice!" he went on repeating, all the time that Alice was getting him on his feet again. "Plenty of practice!"

"It's too ridiculous!" cried Alice, losing all her patience this time. "You ought to have a wooden horse on wheels, that you ought!"

"Does that kind go smoothly?" the Knight asked in a

tone of great interest, clasping his arms round the horse's neck as he spoke, just in time to save himself from tumbling off again.

"Much more smoothly than a live horse," Alice said, with a little scream of laughter, in spite of all she could do to prevent it.

"I'll get one," the Knight said thoughtfully to himself. "One or two—several."

There was a short silence after this, and then the Knight went on again. "I'm a great hand at inventing things. Now, I daresay you noticed, the last time you picked me up, that I was looking rather thoughtful?"

"You *were* a little grave," said Alice.

"Well, just then I was inventing a new way of getting over a gate—would you like to hear it?"

"Very much indeed," Alice said politely.

"I'll tell you how I came to think of it," said the Knight. "You see, I said to myself 'The only difficulty is with the feet: the *head* is high enough already.' Now, first I put my head on the top of the gate—then the head's high enough—then I stand on my head—then the feet are high enough, you see—then I'm over, you see."

"Yes, I suppose you'd be over when that was done," Alice said thoughtfully: "but don't you think it would be rather hard?"

"I haven't tried it yet," the Knight said, gravely; "so I ca'n't tell for certain—but I'm afraid it *would* be a little hard."

He looked so vexed at the idea, that Alice changed the subject hastily. "What a curious helmet you've got!" she said cheerfully. "Is that your invention too?"

The Knight looked down proudly at his helmet, which hung from the saddle. "Yes," he said; "but I've invented a better one than that—like a sugar-loaf. When I used to wear it, if I fell off the horse, it always touched the ground directly. So I had a *very* little way to fall, you see —But there *was* the danger of falling *into* it, to be sure. That happened to me once—and the worst of it was, be-

fore I could get out again, the other White Knight came
and put it on. He thought it was his own helmet."

The Knight looked so solemn about it that Alice did
not dare to laugh. "I'm afraid you must have hurt him,"
she said in a trembling voice, "being on the top of his
head."

"I had to kick him, of course," the Knight said, very
seriously. "And then he took the helmet off again—but it
took hours and hours to get me out. I was as fast as—as
lightning, you know."

"But that's a different kind of fastness," Alice objected.

The Knight shook his head. "It was all kinds of fastness with me, I can assure you!" he said. He raised his
hands in some excitement as he said this, and instantly
rolled out of the saddle, and fell headlong into a deep
ditch.

Alice ran to the side of the ditch to look for him. She
was rather startled by the fall, as for some time he had
kept on very well, and she was afraid that he really *was*
hurt this time. However, though she could see nothing
but the soles of his feet, she was much relieved to hear
that he was talking on in his usual tone. "All kinds of

fastness," he repeated: "but it was careless of him to put another man's helmet on—with the man in it, too."

"How *can* you go on talking so quietly, head downwards?" Alice asked, as she dragged him out by the feet, and laid him in a heap on the bank.

The Knight looked surprised at the question. "What does it matter where my body happens to be?" he said. "My mind goes on working all the same. In fact, the more head-downwards I am, the more I keep inventing new things."

"Now the cleverest thing of the sort that I ever did," he went on after a pause, "was inventing a new pudding during the meat-course."

"In time to have it cooked for the next course?" said Alice. "Well, that *was* quick work, certainly!"

"Well, not the *next* course," the Knight said in a slow thoughtful tone: "no, certainly not the next *course*."

"Then it would have to be the next day. I suppose you wouldn't have two pudding-courses in one dinner?"

"Well, not the *next* day," the Knight repeated as before: "not the next *day*. In fact," he went on, holding his head down, and his voice getting lower and lower, "I don't believe that pudding ever *was* cooked! In fact, I don't believe that pudding ever *will* be cooked! And yet it was a very clever pudding to invent."

"What did you mean it to be made of?" Alice asked, hoping to cheer him up, for the poor Knight seemed quite low-spirited about it.

"It began with blotting-paper," the Knight answered with a groan.

"That wouldn't be very nice, I'm afraid——"

"Not very nice *alone*," he interrupted, quite eagerly: "but you've no idea what a difference it makes, mixing it with other things—such as gunpowder and sealing-wax. And here I must leave you." They had just come to the end of the wood.

Alice could only look puzzled: she was thinking of the pudding.

"You are sad," the Knight said in an anxious tone: "let me sing you a song to comfort you."

"Is it very long?" Alice asked, for she had heard a good deal of poetry that day.

"It's long," said the Knight, "but it's very, *very* beautiful. Everybody that hears me sing it—either it brings the *tears* into their eyes, or else——"

"Or else what?" said Alice, for the Knight had made a sudden pause.

"Or else it doesn't, you know. The name of the song is called '*Haddocks' Eyes*'."

"Oh, that's the name of the song, is it?" Alice said, trying to feel interested.

"No, you don't understand," the Knight said, looking a little vexed. "That's what the name is *called*. The name really *is* '*The Aged Aged Man*'."

"Then I ought to have said 'That's what the *song* is called'?" Alice corrected herself.

"No, you oughtn't: that's quite another thing! The *song* is called '*Ways and Means*': but that's only what it's *called*, you know!"

"Well, what *is* the song, then?" said Alice, who was by this time completely bewildered.

"I was coming to that," the Knight said. "The song really *is* '*A-sitting On A Gate*': and the tune's my own invention."

So saying, he stopped his horse and let the reins fall on its neck: then, slowly beating time with one hand, and with a faint smile lighting up his gentle foolish face, as if he enjoyed the music of his song, he began.

Of all the strange things that Alice saw in her journey Through The Looking-Glass, this was the one that she always remembered most clearly. Years afterwards she could bring the whole scene back again, as if it had been only yesterday—the mild blue eyes and kindly smile of the Knight—the setting sun gleaming through his hair, and shining on his armour in a blaze of light that quite dazzled her—the horse quietly moving about, with the reins hanging loose on his neck, cropping the grass at her feet—and the black shadows of the forest behind—all this she took in like a picture, as, with one hand shading her eyes, she leant against a tree, watching the strange pair, and listening, in a half-dream, to the melancholy music of the song.

"But the tune *isn't* his own invention," she said to herself: "it's '*I give thee all, I can no more*'." She stood and listened very attentively, but no tears came into her eyes.

> "*I'll tell thee everything I can:*
> *There's little to relate.*
> *I saw an aged aged man,*
> *A-sitting on a gate.*
> '*Who are you, aged man?*' *I said.*
> '*And how is it you live?*'
> *And his answer trickled through my head,*
> *Like water through a sieve.*
>
> *He said* '*I look for butterflies*
> *That sleep among the wheat:*
> *I make them into mutton-pies,*
> *And sell them in the street.*
> *I sell them unto men*', *he said,*
> '*Who sail on stormy seas;*
> *And that's the way I get my bread—*
> *A trifle, if you please.*'
>
> *But I was thinking of a plan*
> *To dye one's whiskers green,*
> *And always use so large a fan*
> *That they could not be seen.*
> *So, having no reply to give*
> *To what the old man said,*
> *I cried* '*Come, tell me how you live!*'
> *And thumped him on the head.*
>
> *His accents mild took up the tale:*
> *He said* '*I go my ways,*
> *And when I find a mountain-rill,*
> *I set it in a blaze;*

And thence they make a stuff they call
  Rowland's Macassar-Oil—
Yet twopence-halfpenny is all
  They give me for my toil.'

But I was thinking of a way
  To feed oneself on batter,
And so go on from day to day
  Getting a little fatter.
I shook him well from side to side,
  Until his face was blue:
'Come, tell me how you live,' I cried,
  'And what it is you do!'

He said 'I hunt for haddocks' eyes
  Among the heather bright,
And work them into waistcoat-buttons
  In the silent night.
And these I do not sell for gold
  Or coin of silvery shine,
But for a copper halfpenny,
  And that will purchase nine.

'I sometimes dig for buttered rolls,
 Or set limed twigs for crabs:
I sometimes search the grassy knolls
 For wheels of Hansom-cabs.
And that's the way' (he gave a wink)
 'By which I get my wealth—
And very gladly will I drink
 Your Honour's noble health.'

I heard him then, for I had just
 Completed my design
To keep the Menai bridge from rust
 By boiling it in wine.
I thanked him much for telling me
 The way he got his wealth,
But chiefly for his wish that he
 Might drink my noble health.

And now, if e'er by chance I put
 My fingers into glue,
Or madly squeeze a right-hand foot
 Into a left-hand shoe,
Or if I drop upon my toe
 A very heavy weight,
I weep, for it reminds me so
Of that old man I used to know—
Whose look was mild, whose speech was slow
Whose hair was whiter than the snow,
Whose face was very like a crow,
With eyes, like cinders, all aglow,
Who seemed distracted with his woe,
Who rocked his body to and fro,
And muttered mumblingly and low,
As if his mouth were full of dough,
Who snorted like a buffalo——
That summer evening long ago,
 A-sitting on a gate."

As the Knight sang the last words of the ballad, he gathered up the reins, and turned his horse's head along the road by which they had come. "You've only a few yards to go," he said, "down the hill and over that little

brook, and then you'll be a Queen——But you'll stay and
see me off first?" he added as Alice turned with an eager
look in the direction to which he pointed. "I sha'n't be
long. You'll wait and wave your handkerchief when I get
to that turn in the road! I think it'll encourage me, you
see."

"Of course I'll wait," said Alice: "and thank you very

much for coming so far—and for the song—I liked it very
much."

"I hope so," the Knight said doubtfully: "but you
didn't cry so much as I thought you would."

So they shook hands, and then the Knight rode slowly
away into the forest. "It wo'n't take long to see him *off*,
I expect," Alice said to herself, as she stood watching him.
"There he goes! Right on his head as usual! However,
he gets on again pretty easily—that comes of having so

many things hung round the horse——" So she went on talking to herself, as she watched the horse walking leisurely along the road, and the Knight tumbling off, first on one side and then on the other. After the fourth or fifth tumble he reached the turn, and then she waved her handkerchief to him, and waited till he was out of sight.

"I hope it encouraged him," she said, as she turned to run down the hill: "and now for the last brook, and to be a Queen! How grand it sounds!" A very few steps brought her to the edge of the brook. "The Eighth Square at last!" she cried as she bounded across,

*   *   *   *   *

   *   *   *   *

*   *   *   *   *

and threw herself down to rest on a lawn as soft as moss, with little flowerbeds dotted about it here and there. "Oh, how glad I am to get here! And what *is* this on my head?" she exclaimed in a tone of dismay, as she put her hands up to something very heavy, that fitted tight all around her head.

"But how *can* it have got there without my knowing it?" she said to herself, as she lifted it off, and set it on her lap to make out what it could possibly be.

It was a golden crown.

Chapter IX

Queen Alice

"WELL, this *is* grand!" said Alice. "I never expected I should be a Queen so soon—and I'll tell you what it is, your Majesty," she went on, in a severe tone (she was always rather fond of scolding herself), "It'll never do for you to be lolling about on the grass like that! Queens have to be dignified, you know!"

So she got up and walked about—rather stiffly just at first, as she was afraid that the crown might come off: but she comforted herself with the thought that there was nobody to see her, "and if I really am a Queen", she said as she sat down again, "I shall be able to manage it quite well in time."

Everything was happening so oddly that she didn't feel a bit surprised at finding the Red Queen and the White Queen sitting close to her, one on each side: she would have liked very much to ask them how they came there, but she feared it would not be quite civil. However, there would be no harm, she thought, in asking if the game was over. "Please, would you tell me——" she began, looking timidly at the Red Queen.

"Speak when you're spoken to!" the Queen sharply interrupted her.

"But if everybody obeyed that rule," said Alice, who was always ready for a little argument, "and if you only spoke when you were spoken to, and the other person always waited for *you* to begin, you see nobody would ever say anything, so that——"

"Ridiculous!" cried the Queen. "Why, don't you see, child——" here she broke off with a frown, and, after thinking for a minute, suddenly changed the subject of the conversation. "What do you mean by 'If you really are a Queen'? What right have you to call yourself so? You ca'n't be a Queen, you know, till you've passed the proper examination. And the sooner we begin it, the better."

"I only said 'if'!" poor Alice pleaded in a piteous tone.

The two Queens looked at each other, and the Red Queen remarked, with a little shudder, "She *says* she only said 'if'——"

"But she said a great deal more than that!" the White Queen moaned, wringing her hands. "Oh, ever so much more than that!"

"So you did, you know," the Red Queen said to Alice.

"Always speak the truth—think before you speak—and write it down afterwards."

"I'm sure I didn't mean——" Alice was beginning, but the Red Queen interrupted her impatiently.

"That's just what I complain of! You *should* have meant! What do you suppose is the use of a child without any meaning? Even a joke should have some meaning—

and a child's more important than a joke, I hope. You couldn't deny that, even if you tried with both hands."

"I don't deny things with my *hands*," Alice objected.

"Nobody said you did," said the Red Queen. "I said you couldn't if you tried."

"She's in that state of mind", said the White Queen, "that she wants to deny *something*—only she doesn't know what to deny!"

"A nasty, vicious temper," the Red Queen remarked; and then there was an uncomfortable silence for a minute or two.

The Red Queen broke the silence by saying, to the White Queen, "I invite you to Alice's dinner-party this afternoon."

The White Queen smiled feebly, and said "And I invite *you*."

"I didn't know I was to have a party at all," said Alice; "but, if there *is* to be one, I think *I* ought to invite the guests."

"We gave you the opportunity of doing it," the Red Queen remarked: "but I daresay you've not had many lessons in manners yet."

"Manners are not taught in lessons," said Alice. "Lessons teach you to do sums, and things of that sort."

"Can you do Addition?" the White Queen asked. "What's one and one and one and one and one and one and one and one and one and one?"

"I don't know," said Alice. "I lost count."

"She ca'n't do Addition," the Red Queen interrupted. "Can you do Subtraction? Take nine from eight."

"Nine from eight I ca'n't, you know," Alice replied very readily: "but——"

"She ca'n't do Subtraction," said the White Queen. "Can you do Division? Divide a loaf by a knife—what's the answer to *that*?"

"I suppose——" Alice was beginning, but the Red Queen answered for her. "Bread-and-butter, of course. Try another Subtraction sum. Take a bone from a dog: what remains?"

Alice considered. "The bone wouldn't remain, of course, if I took it—and the dog wouldn't remain: it would come to bite me—and I'm sure *I* shouldn't remain!"

"Then you think nothing would remain?" said the Red Queen.

"I think that's the answer."

"Wrong, as usual," said the Red Queen: "the dog's temper would remain."

"But I don't see how——"

"Why, look here!" the Red Queen cried. "The dog would lose its temper, wouldn't it?"

"Perhaps it would," Alice replied cautiously.

"Then if the dog went away, its temper would remain!" the Queen exclaimed triumphantly.

Alice said, as gravely as she could, "They might go different ways." But she couldn't help thinking to herself "What dreadful nonsense we *are* talking!"

"She ca'n't do sums a *bit*!" the Queens said together, with great emphasis.

"Can *you* do sums?" Alice said, turning suddenly on the White Queen, for she didn't like being found fault with so much.

The Queen gasped and shut her eyes. "I can do Addition", she said, "if you give me time—but I ca'n't do Subtraction under *any* circumstances!"

"Of course you know your ABC?" said the Red Queen.

"To be sure I do," said Alice.

"So do I," the White Queen whispered: "we'll often say it over together, dear. And I'll tell you a secret—I can read words of one letter! Isn't *that* grand? However, don't be discouraged. You'll come to it in time."

Here the Red Queen began again. "Can you answer useful questions?" she said. "How is bread made?"

"I know *that*!" Alice cried eagerly. "You take some flour——"

"Where do you pick the flower?" the White Queen asked: "In a garden or in the hedges?"

"Well, it isn't *picked* at all," Alice explained: "it's *ground*——"

"How many acres of ground?" said the White Queen. "You mustn't leave out so many things."

"Fan her head!" the Red Queen anxiously interrupted. "She'll be feverish after so much thinking." So they set to work and fanned her with bunches of leaves, till she had to beg them to leave off, it blew her hair about so.

"She's all right again now," said the Red Queen. "Do you know Languages? What's the French for fiddle-de-dee?"

"Fiddle-de-dee's not English," Alice replied gravely.

"Who ever said it was?" said the Red Queen.

Alice thought she saw a way out of the difficulty, this time. "If you'll tell me what language 'fiddle-de-dee' is, I'll tell you the French for it!" she exclaimed triumphantly.

But the Red Queen drew herself up rather stiffly, and said, "Queens never make bargains."

"I wish Queens never asked questions," Alice thought to herself.

"Don't let us quarrel," the White Queen said in an anxious tone. "What is the cause of lightning?"

"The cause of lightning", Alice said very decidedly, for she felt quite certain about this, "is the thunder—no, no!" she hastily corrected herself. "I meant the other way."

"It's too late to correct it," said the Red Queen: "when you've once said a thing, that fixes it, and you must take the consequences."

"Which reminds me——" the White Queen said, looking down and nervously clasping and unclasping her hands, "we had *such* a thunderstorm last Tuesday—I mean one of the last set of Tuesdays, you know."

Alice was puzzled. "In *our* country", she remarked, "there's only one day at a time."

The Red Queen said "That's a poor thin way of doing things. Now *here*, we mostly have days and nights two or three at a time, and sometimes in the winter we take as many as five nights together—for warmth, you know."

"Are five nights warmer than one night, then?" Alice ventured to ask.

"Five times as warm, of course."

"But they should be five times as *cold*, by the same rule——"

"Just so!" cried the Red Queen. "Five times as warm, *and* five times as cold—just as I'm five times as rich as you are, *and* five times as clever!"

Alice sighed and gave it up. "It's exactly like a riddle with no answer!" she thought.

"Humpty Dumpty saw it too," the White Queen went

on in a low voice, more as if she were talking to herself. "He came to the door with a corkscrew in his hand——"

"What did he want?" said the Red Queen.

"He said he *would* come in," the White Queen went on, "because he was looking for a hippopotamus. Now, as it happened, there wasn't such a thing in the house, that morning."

"Is there generally?" Alice asked in an astonished tone.

"Well, only on Thursdays," said the Queen.

"I know what he came for," said Alice: "he wanted to punish the fish, because——"

Here the White Queen began again. "It was *such* a thunderstorm, you ca'n't think!" ("She *never* could, you know," said the Red Queen.) "And part of the roof came off, and ever so much thunder got in—and it went rolling round the room in great lumps—and knocking over the tables and things—till I was so frightened, I couldn't remember my own name!"

Alice thought to herself "I never should *try* to remember my name in the middle of an accident! Where would be the use of it?" but she did not say this aloud, for fear of hurting the poor Queen's feelings.

"Your Majesty must excuse her," the Red Queen said to Alice, taking one of the White Queen's hands in her own, and gently stroking it: "she means well, but she ca'n't help saying foolish things as a general rule."

The White Queen looked timidly at Alice, who felt she *ought* to say something kind, but really couldn't think of anything at the moment.

"She never was really well brought up," the Red Queen went on: "but it's amazing how good-tempered she is! Pat her on the head, and see how pleased she'll be!" But this was more than Alice had courage to do.

"A little kindness—and putting her hair in papers— would do wonders with her——"

The White Queen gave a deep sigh, and laid her head on Alice's shoulder. "I *am* so sleepy!" she moaned.

"She's tired, poor thing!" said the Red Queen. "Smooth

her hair—lend her your nightcap—and sing her a soothing lullaby."

"I haven't got a nightcap with me," said Alice, as she
tried to obey the first direction: "and I don't know any
soothing lullabies."

"I must do it myself, then," said the Red Queen, and
she began:

"Hush-a-by lady, in Alice's lap!
Till the feast's ready, we've time for a nap.
When the feast's over, we'll go to the ball—
Red Queen, and White Queen, and Alice, and all!

"And now you know the words," she added, as she put
her head down on Alice's other shoulder, "just sing it
through to *me*. I'm getting sleepy, too." In another moment both Queens were fast asleep, and snoring loud.

"What *am* I to do?" exclaimed Alice, looking about in
great perplexity, as first one round head, and then the
other, rolled down from her shoulder, and lay like a heavy
lump in her lap. "I don't think it *ever* happened before,
that any one had to take care of two Queens asleep at
once! No, not in all the History of England—it couldn't,

you know, because there never was more than one Queen
at a time. Do wake up, you heavy things!'' she went on in
an impatient tone; but there was no answer but a gentle
snoring.

The snoring got more distinct every minute, and sounded more like a tune: at last she could even make out

words, and she listened so eagerly that, when the two
great heads suddenly vanished from her lap, she hardly
missed them.

She was standing before an arched doorway, over which
were the words "QUEEN ALICE" in large letters, and
on each side of the arch there was a bell-handle; one was

marked "Visitors' Bell", and the other "Servants' Bell".

"I'll wait till the song's over," thought Alice, "and then I'll ring the—the—*which* bell must I ring?" she went on, very much puzzled by the names. "I'm not a visitor, and I'm not a servant. There *ought* to be one marked 'Queen', you know——"

Just then the door opened a little way, and a creature with a long beak put its head out for a moment and said "No admittance till the week after next!" and shut the door again with a bang.

Alice knocked and rang in vain for a long time; but at last a very old Frog, who was sitting under a tree, got up and hobbled slowly towards her: he was dressed in bright yellow, and had enormous boots on.

"What is it, now?" the Frog said in a deep hoarse whisper.

Alice turned round, ready to find fault with anybody. "Where's the servant whose business it is to answer the door?" she began angrily.

"Which door?" said the Frog.

Alice almost stamped with irritation at the slow drawl in which he spoke. "*This* door, of course!"

The Frog looked at the door with his large dull eyes for a minute: then he went nearer and rubbed it with his thumb, as if he were trying whether the paint would come off: then he looked at Alice.

"To answer the door?" he said. "What's it been asking of?" He was so hoarse that Alice could scarcely hear him.

"I don't know what you mean," she said.

"I speaks English, doesn't I?" the Frog went on. "Or are you deaf? What did it ask you?"

"Nothing!" Alice said impatiently. "I've been knocking at it!"

"Shouldn't do that—shouldn't do that——" the Frog muttered. "Wexes it, you know." Then he went up and gave the door a kick with one of his great feet. "You let *it* alone," he panted out, as he hobbled back to his tree, "and it'll let *you* alone, you know."

At this moment the door was flung open, and a shrill voice was heard singing:

"To the Looking-Glass world it was Alice that said
'I've a sceptre in hand, I've a crown on my head.
Let the Looking-Glass creatures, whatever they be
Come and dine with the Red Queen, the White Queen, and
me!' "

And hundreds of voices joined in the chorus:

"Then fill up the glasses as quick as you can,
And sprinkle the table with buttons and bran:
Put cats in the coffee, and mice in the tea—
And welcome Queen Alice with thirty-times-three!"

Then followed a confused noise of cheering, and Alice thought to herself "Thirty times three makes ninety. I wonder if any one's counting?" In a minute there was silence again, and the same shrill voice sang another verse:

" 'O Looking-Glass creatures', quoth Alice, 'draw near!
'Tis an honour to see me, a favour to hear:
'Tis a privilege high to have dinner and tea
Along with the Red Queen, the White Queen, and me!' "

Then came the chorus again:

"Then fill up the glasses with treacle and ink,
Or anything else that is pleasant to drink:
Mix sand with the cider, and wool with the wine—
And welcome Queen Alice with ninety-times-nine!"

"Ninety times nine!" Alice repeated in despair. "Oh, that'll never be done! I'd better go in at once——" and in she went, and there was a dead silence the moment she appeared.

Alice glanced nervously along the table, as she walked up the large hall, and noticed that there were about fifty guests, of all kinds: some were animals, some birds, and there were even a few flowers among them. "I'm glad they've come without waiting to be asked," she thought:

"I should never have known who were the right people to invite!"

There were three chairs at the head of the table: the Red and White Queens had already taken two of them, but the middle one was empty. Alice sat down in it, rather uncomfortable at the silence, and longing for some one to speak.

At last the Red Queen began. "You've missed the soup and fish," she said. "Put on the joint!" And the waiters set a leg of mutton before Alice, who looked at it rather anxiously, as she had never had to carve a joint before.

"You look a little shy: let me introduce you to that leg of mutton," said the Red Queen. "Alice——Mutton: Mutton——Alice." The leg of mutton got up in the dish and made a little bow to Alice! and Alice returned the bow, not knowing whether to be frightened or amused.

"May I give you a slice?" she said, taking up the knife and fork, and looking from one Queen to the other.

"Certainly not," the Red Queen said very, decidedly: "it isn't etiquette to cut anyone you've been introduced to. Remove the joint!" And the waiters carried it off, and brought a large plum-pudding in its place.

"I won't be introduced to the pudding, please," Alice said rather hastily, "or we shall get no dinner at all. May I give you some?"

But the Red Queen looked sulky, and growled "Pudding——Alice: Alice——Pudding. Remove the pudding!" and the waiters took it away so quickly that Alice couldn't return its bow.

However, she didn't see why the Red Queen should be the only one to give orders; so, as an experiment, she called out "Waiter! Bring back the pudding!" and there it was again in a moment, like a conjuring trick. It was so large that she couldn't help feeling a *little* shy with it, as she had been with the mutton; however, she conquered her shyness by a great effort, and cut a slice and handed it to the Red Queen.

"What impertinence!" said the Pudding. "I wonder

how you'd like it, if I were to cut a slice out of *you*, you
creature!''

It spoke in a thick, suety sort of voice, and Alice hadn't
a word to say in reply: she could only sit and look at it
and gasp.

"Make a remark," said the Red Queen: "it's ridiculous
to leave all the conversation to the pudding!"

"Do you know, I've had such a quantity of poetry repeated to me to-day," Alice began, a little frightened at
finding that, the moment she opened her lips, there was
dead silence, and all eyes were fixed upon her; "and it's a
very curious thing, I think—every poem was about fishes
in some way. Do you know why they're so fond of fishes,
all about here?"

She spoke to the Red Queen, whose answer was a little
wide of the mark. "As to fishes," she said, very slowly and
solemnly, putting her mouth close to Alice's ear, "her

White Majesty knows a lovely riddle—all in poetry—all about fishes. Shall she repeat it?"

"Her Red Majesty's very kind to mention it," the White Queen murmured into Alice's other ear, in a voice like the cooing of a pigeon. "It would be *such* a treat! May I?"

"Please do," Alice said very politely.

The White Queen laughed with delight, and stroked Alice's cheek. Then she began:

> " '*First, the fish must be caught.*'
> *That is easy: a baby, I think, could have caught it.*
> '*Next, the fish must be bought.*'
> *That is easy: a penny, I think, would have bought it.*
>
> '*Now cook me the fish!*'
> *That is easy, and will not take more than a minute.*
> '*Let it lie in a dish!*'
> *That is easy, because it already is in it.*
>
> '*Bring it here! Let me sup!*'
> *It is easy to set such a dish on the table.*
> '*Take the dish-cover up!*'
> *Ah, that is so hard that I fear I'm unable!*
>
> *For it holds it like glue—*
> *Holds the lid to the dish, while it lies in the middle:*
> *Which is easiest to do,*
> *Un-dish-cover the fish, or dishcover the riddle?*"

"Take a minute to think about it, and then guess," said the Red Queen. "Meanwhile, we'll drink your health— Queen Alice's health!" she screamed at the top of her voice, and all the guests began drinking it directly, and very queerly they managed it: some of them put their glasses upon their heads like extinguishers, and drank all that trickled down their faces—others upset the decanters, and drank the wine as it ran off the edges of the table—and three of them (who looked like kangaroos) scrambled into the dish of roast mutton, and began eagerly lapping up the gravy, "just like pigs in a trough!" thought Alice.

"You ought to return thanks in a neat speech," the Red Queen said, frowning at Alice as she spoke.

"We must support you, you know," the White Queen whispered, as Alice got up to do it, very obediently, but a little frightened.

"Thank you very much," she whispered in

reply, "but I can do quite well without."

"That wouldn't be at all the thing," the Red Queen said very decidedly: so Alice tried to submit to it with a good grace.

("And they *did* push so!" she said afterwards, when she

was telling her sister the history of the feast. "You would have thought they wanted to squeeze me flat!")

In fact it was rather difficult for her to keep in her place while she made her speech: the two Queens pushed her so, one on each side, that they nearly lifted her up into the air. "I rise to return thanks——" Alice began: and she really *did* rise as she spoke, several inches; but she got hold of the edge of the table, and managed to pull herself down again.

"Take care of yourself!" screamed the White Queen, seizing Alice's hair with both her hands. "Something's going to happen!"

And then (as Alice afterwards described it) all sorts of things happened in a moment. The candles all grew up to the ceiling, looking something like a bed of rushes with fireworks at the top. As to the bottles, they each took a pair of plates, which they hastily fitted on as wings, and so, with forks for legs, went fluttering about in all directions: "and very like birds they look," Alice thought to herself, as well as she could in the dreadful confusion that was beginning.

At this moment she heard a hoarse laugh at her side, and turned to see what was the matter with the White Queen; but, instead of the Queen, there was the leg of mutton sitting in the chair. "Here I am!" cried a voice from the soup-tureen, and Alice turned again, just in time to see the Queen's broad good-natured face grinning at her for a moment over the edge of the tureen, before she disappeared into the soup.

There was not a moment to be lost. Already several of the guests were lying down in the dishes, and the soup-ladle was walking up the table towards Alice's chair, and beckoning to her impatiently to get out of its way.

"I ca'n't stand this any longer!" she cried, as she jumped up and seized the tablecloth with both hands: one good pull, and plates, dishes, guests, and candles came crashing down together in a heap on the floor.

"And as for *you*," she went on, turning fiercely upon

the Red Queen, whom she considered as the cause of all
the mischief—but the Queen was no longer at her side—
she had suddenly dwindled down to the size of a little
doll, and was now on the table, merrily running round
and round after her own shawl, which was trailing behind her.

At any other time, Alice would have felt surprised at
this, but she was far too much excited to be surprised at
anything *now*. "As for *you*," she repeated, catching hold
of the little creature in the very act of jumping over a
bottle which had just lighted upon the table, "I'll shake
you into a kitten, that I will!"

Chapter X

Shaking

She took her off the table as she spoke, and shook her backwards and forwards with all her might.

The Red Queen made no resistance whatever: only her face grew very small, and her eyes got large and green: and still, as Alice went on shaking her, she kept on growing shorter—and fatter—and softer—and rounder—and——

Chapter XI

Waking

——and it really *was* a kitten, after all.

Chapter XII

Which Dreamed It?

"Your Red Majesty shouldn't purr so loud," Alice said, rubbing her eyes, and addressing the kitten, respectfully, yet with some severity. "You woke me out of oh! such a nice dream! And you've been along with me, Kitty— all through the Looking-glass world. Did you know it, dear?"

It is a very inconvenient habit of kittens (Alice had once made the remark) that, whatever you say to them, they *always* purr. "If they would only purr for 'yes', and mew for 'no', or any rule of that sort," she had said, "so that one could keep up a conversation! But how *can* you talk with a person if they *always* say the same thing?"

On this occasion the kitten only purred: and it was impossible to guess whether it meant "yes" or "no".

So Alice hunted among the chessmen on the table till she had found the Red Queen: then she went down on her knees on the hearth-rug, and put the kitten and the Queen to look at each other. "Now, Kitty!" she cried, clapping her hands triumphantly. "Confess that was what you turned into!"

("But it wouldn't look at it," she said, when she was explaining the thing afterwards to her sister: "it turned away its head, and pretended not to see it: but it looked a *little* ashamed of itself, so I think it *must* have been the Red Queen.")

"Sit up a little more stiffly, dear!" Alice cried with a merry laugh. "And curtsey while you're thinking what to—what to purr. It saves time, remember!" And she caught it up and gave it one little kiss, "just in honour of its having been a Red Queen".

"Snowdrop, my pet!" she went on, looking over her shoulder at the White Kitten, which was still patiently undergoing its toilet, "when *will* Dinah have finished

with your White Majesty, I wonder? That must be the
reason you were so untidy in my dream.——Dinah! Do
you know that you're scrubbing a White Queen? Really,
it's most disrespectful of you!"

"And what did *Dinah* turn to, I wonder?" she prattled
on, as she settled comfortably down, with one elbow on
the rug, and her chin in her hand, to watch the kittens.

"Tell me, Dinah, did you turn to Humpty Dumpty? I
think you did—however, you'd better not mention it to
your friends just yet, for I'm not sure.

"By the way, Kitty, if only you'd been really with me
in my dream, there was one thing you *would* have enjoyed
——I had such a quantity of poetry said to me, all about
fishes! To-morrow morning you shall have a real treat.
All the time you're eating your breakfast, I'll repeat 'The
Walrus and the Carpenter' to you; and then you can
make believe it's oysters, dear!

"Now, Kitty, let's consider who it was that dreamed it all. This is a serious question, my dear, and you should *not* go on licking your paw like that—as if Dinah hadn't washed you this morning! You see, Kitty, it *must* have been either me or the Red King. He was part of my dream, of course—but then I was part of his dream, too! *Was* it the Red King, Kitty? You were his wife, my dear, so you ought to know——Oh, Kitty, *do* help to settle it! I'm sure your paw can wait!" But the provoking kitten only began on the other paw, and pretended it hadn't heard the question.

Which do *you* think it was?

A BOAT, beneath a sunny sky
Lingering onward dreamily
In an evening of July—

Children three that nestle near,
Eager eye and willing ear,
Pleased a simple tale to hear—

Long has paled that sunny sky:
Echoes fade and memories die:
Autumn frosts have slain July.

Still she haunts me, phantomwise.
Alice moving under skies
Never seen by waking eyes.

Children yet, the tale to hear,
Eager eye and willing ear,
Lovingly shall nestle near.

In a Wonderland they lie,
Dreaming as the days go by,
Dreaming as the summers die:

Ever drifting down the stream—
Lingering in the golden gleam—
Life, what is it but a dream?

Editor's note: The initial letters of this poem
  when read downward give the full name of
  the original Alice—Alice Pleasance Liddell.

III
Sylvie and Bruno

Is all our Life, then, but a dream
Seen faintly in the golden gleam
Athwart Time's dark resistless stream?

Bowed to the earth with bitter woe,
Or laughing at some raree-show,
We flutter idly to and fro.

Man's little Day in haste we spend,
And, from its merry noontide, send
No glance to meet the silent end.

PREFACE

THE descriptions, at pp. 452, 453, of Sunday as spent by children of the last generation, are quoted *verbatim* from a speech made to me by a child-friend and a letter written to me by a lady-friend.

The Chapters, headed "Fairy Sylvie" and "Bruno's Revenge", are a reprint, with a few alterations, of a little fairy-tale which I wrote in the year 1867, at the request of the late Mrs. Gatty, for "Aunt Judy's Magazine", which she was then editing.

It was in 1874, I believe, that the idea first occurred to me of making it the nucleus of a longer story. As the years went on, I jotted down, at odd moments, all sorts of odd ideas, and fragments of dialogue, that occurred to me—who knows how?—with a transitory suddenness that left me no choice but either to record them then and there, or to abandon them to oblivion. Sometimes one could trace to their source these random flashes of thought—as being suggested by the book one was reading, or struck out from the "flint" of one's own mind by the "steel" of a friend's chance remark—but they had also a way of their own, of occurring, *à propos* of nothing—specimens of that hopelessly illogical phenomenon, "an effect without a cause". Such, for example, was the last line of "The Hunting of the Snark", which came into my head (as I have already related in "The Theatre" for April, 1887) quite suddenly, during a solitary walk; and such, again, have been passages which occurred in *dreams*, and which I cannot trace to any antecedent cause whatever. There are at least *two* instances of such dream-suggestions in this book—one, my Lady's remark, "it often runs in families, just as a love for pastry does", at p. 306; the other, Eric Lindon's *badinage* about having been in domestic service, at p. 425.

And thus it came to pass that I found myself at last in possession of a huge unwieldy mass of litterature—if the reader will kindly excuse the spelling—which only needed stringing together, upon the thread of a consecutive story, to constitute the book I hoped to write. Only! The task, at first, seemed absolutely hopeless, and gave me a far clearer idea, than I ever had before, of the meaning of the word "chaos": and I think it must have been ten years, or more, before I had succeeded in classifying these odds-and-ends sufficiently to see what sort of a story they indicated: for the story had to grow out of the incidents, not the incidents out of the story.

I am telling all this, in no spirit of egoism, but because I really believe that some of my readers will be interested in these details of the "genesis" of a book, which looks so simple and straight-forward a matter, when completed, that they might suppose it to have been written straight off, page by page, as one would write a letter, beginning at the beginning and ending at the end.

It is, no doubt, *possible* to write a story in that way: and, if it be not vanity to say so, I believe that I could, myself,—if I were in the unfortunate position (for I do hold it to be a real misfortune) of being obliged to produce a given amount of fiction in a given time that I could "fulfil my task", and produce my "tale of bricks", as other slaves have done. One thing, at any rate I could guarantee as to the story so produced—that it should be utterly commonplace, should contain no new ideas whatever, and should be very very weary reading!

This species of literature has received the very appropriate name of "padding"—which might fitly be defined as "that which all can write and none can read". That the present volume contains *no* such writing I dare not avow: sometimes, in order to bring a picture into its proper place, it has been necessary to eke out a page with two or three extra lines: but I can honestly say I have put in no more than I was absolutely compelled to do.

My readers may perhaps like to amuse themselves by

trying to detect, in a given passage, the one piece of "padding" it contains. While arranging the "slips" into pages, I found that the passage, which now extends from the top of p. 280 to the middle of p. 282, was 3 lines too short. I supplied the deficiency, not by interpolating a word here and a word there, but by writing in 3 consecutive lines. Now can my readers guess *which* they are?

A harder puzzle—if a harder be desired—would be to determine, as to the Gardener's Song, in *which* cases (if any) the stanza was adapted to the surrounding text, and in *which* (if any) the text was adapted to the stanza.

Perhaps the hardest thing in all literature—at least *I* have found it so: by no voluntary effort can I accomplish it: I have to take it as it comes—is to write anything *original*. And perhaps the easiest is, when once an original line has been struck out, to follow it up, and to write any amount more to the same tune. I do not know if "Alice in Wonderland" was an *original* story—I was, at least, no *conscious* imitator in writing it—but I do know that, since it came out, something like a dozen story-books have appeared, on identically the same pattern. The path I timidly explored—believing myself to be "the first that ever burst into that silent sea"—is now a beaten highroad: all the way-side flowers have long ago been trampled into the dust: and it would be courting disaster for me to attempt that style again.

Hence it is that, in "Sylvie and Bruno", I have striven —with I know not what success—to strike out yet another new path: be it bad or good, it is the best I can do. It is written, not for money, and not for fame, but in the hope of supplying, for the children whom I love, some thoughts that may suit those hours of innocent merriment which are the very life of Childhood: and also, in the hope of suggesting, to them and to others, some thoughts that may prove, I would fain hope, not wholly out of harmony with the graver cadences of Life.

If I have not already exhausted the patience of my readers, I would like to seize this opportunity—perhaps the last I shall have of addressing so many friends at once —of putting on record some ideas that have occurred to me, as to books desirable to be written—which I should much like to *attempt*, but may not ever have the time or power to carry through—in the hope that, if *I* should fail (and the years are gliding away *very* fast) to finish the task I have set myself, other hands may take it up.

First, a Child's Bible. The only real *essentials* of this would be, carefully selected passages, suitable for a child's reading, and pictures. One principle of selection, which I would adopt, would be that Religion should be put before a child as a revelation of *love*—no need to pain and puzzle the young mind with the history of crime and punishment. (On such a principle I should, for example, omit the history of the Flood.) The supplying of the pictures would involve no great difficulty: no new ones would be needed: hundreds of excellent pictures already exist, the copyright of which has long ago expired, and which simply need photo-zincography, or some similar process, for their successful reproduction. The book should be handy in size—with a pretty attractive-looking cover—in a clear legible type—and, above all, with abundance of pictures, pictures, pictures!

Secondly, a book of pieces selected from the Bible—not single texts, but passages of from 10 to 20 verses each—to be committed to memory. Such passages would be found useful, to repeat to one's self and to ponder over, on many occasions when reading is difficult, if not impossible: for instance, when lying awake at night—on a railway-journey—when taking a solitary walk—in old age, when eye-sight is failing or wholly lost—and, best of all, when illness, while incapacitating us for reading or any other occupation, condemns us to lie awake through many weary silent hours: at such a time how keenly one may realize the truth of David's rapturous cry *"O how sweet*

*are thy words unto my throat: yea, sweeter than honey unto
my mouth!"*

I have said "passages", rather than single texts, because we have no means of *recalling* single texts: memory
needs *links,* and here are none: one may have a hundred
texts stored in the memory, and not be able to recall, at
will, more than half-a-dozen—and those by mere chance:
whereas, once get hold of any portion of a *chapter* that has
been committed to memory, and the whole can be
recovered: all hangs together.

Thirdly, a collection of passages, both prose and verse,
from books other than the Bible. There is not perhaps
much, in what is called "un-inspired" literature (a misnomer, I hold: if Shakespeare was not inspired, one may
well doubt if any man ever was), that will bear the process of being pondered over, a hundred times: still there
are such passages—enough, I think, to make a goodly
store for the memory.

These two books—of sacred, and secular, passages for
memory—will serve other good purposes besides merely
occupying vacant hours: they will help to keep at bay
many anxious thoughts, worrying thoughts, uncharitable
thoughts, unholy thoughts. Let me say this, in better
words than my own, by copying a passage from that most
interesting book, Robertson's Lectures on the Epistles to
the Corinthians, Lecture XLIX. "If a man finds himself
haunted by evil desires and unholy images, which will
generally be at periodical hours, let him commit to memory passages of Scripture, or passages from the best
writers in verse or prose. Let him store his mind with
these, as safeguards to repeat when he lies awake in some
restless night, or when despairing imaginations, or gloomy,
suicidal thoughts, beset him. Let these be to him the
sword, turning everywhere to keep the way of the Garden
of Life from the intrusion of profaner footsteps."

Fourthly, a "Shakespeare" for girls: that is, an edition
in which everything, not suitable for the perusal of girls
of (say) from 10 to 17, should be omitted. Few children

under 10 would be likely to understand or enjoy the greatest of poets: and those, who have passed out of girlhood, may safely be left to read Shakespeare, in any edition, "expurgated" or not, that they may prefer; but it seems a pity that so many children, in the intermediate stage, should be debarred from a great pleasure for want of an edition suitable to them. Neither Bowdler's, Chambers's, Brandram's, nor Cundell's "Boudoir" Shakespeare, seems to me to meet the want: they are not sufficiently "expurgated". Bowdler's is the most extraordinary of all: looking through it, I am filled with a deep sense of wonder, considering what he has left in, that he should have cut *anything* out! Besides relentlessly erasing all that is unsuitable on the score of reverence or decency, I should be inclined to omit also all that seems too difficult, or not likely to interest young readers. The resulting book might be slightly fragmentary: but it would be a real treasure to all British maidens who have any taste for poetry.

If it be needful to apologize to any one for the new departure I have taken in this story—by introducing, along with what will, I hope, prove to be acceptable nonsense for children, some of the graver thoughts of human life—it must be to one who has learned the Art of keeping such thoughts wholly at a distance in hours of mirth and careless ease. To him such a mixture will seem, no doubt, illjudged and repulsive. And that such an Art *exists* I do not dispute: with youth, good health, and sufficient money, it seems quite possible to lead, for years together, a life of unmixed gaiety—with the exception of one solemn fact, with which we are liable to be confronted at *any* moment, even in the midst of the most brilliant company or the most sparkling entertainment. A man may fix his own times for admitting serious thought, for attending public worship, for prayer, for reading the Bible: all such matters he can defer to that "convenient season", which is so apt never to occur at all: but he cannot defer, for one single moment, the necessity of attending to a message, which may come before he has finished reading this page, *"this night shall thy soul be required of thee."*

The ever-present sense of this grim possibility has been, in all ages,[1] an incubus that men have striven to shake off. Few more interesting subjects of enquiry could be found, by a student of history, than the various weapons that have been used against this shadowy foe. Saddest of all must have been the thoughts of those who saw indeed an *existence* beyond the grave, but an existence far more terrible than annihilation—an existence as filmy, impalpable, all but invisible spectres, drifting about, through endless ages, in a world of shadows, with nothing to do, nothing to hope for, nothing to love! In the midst of the gay verses of that genial "bon vivant" Horace, there stands one dreary word whose utter sadness goes to one's heart. It is the word *"exilium"* in the well-known passage

> *Omnes eodem cogimur, omnium*
> *Versatur urnâ serius ocius*
> *Sors exitura et nos in æternum*
> *Exilium impositura cymbæ.*

Yes, to him this present life—spite of all its weariness and all its sorrow—was the only life worth having: all else was "exile"! Does it not seem almost incredible that one, holding such a creed, should ever have smiled?

And many in this day, I fear, even though believing in an existence beyond the grave far more real than Horace ever dreamed of, yet regard it as a sort of "exile" from all the joys of life, and so adopt Horace's theory, and say "let us eat and drink, for to-morrow we die".

We go to entertainments, such as the theatre—I say "we", for *I* also go to the play, whenever I get a chance of seeing a really good one—and keep at arm's length, if possible, the thought that we may not return alive. Yet how do you know—dear friend, whose patience has

---

[1] At the moment, when I had written these words, there was a knock at the door, and a telegram was brought me, announcing the sudden death of a dear friend.

carried you through this garrulous preface—that it may not be *your* lot, when mirth is fastest and most furious, to feel the sharp pang, or the deadly faintness, which heralds the final crisis—to see, with vague wonder, anxious friends bending over you—to hear their troubled whispers —perhaps yourself to shape the question, with trembling lips, "Is it serious?" and to be told "Yes: the end is near" (and oh, how different all Life will look when those words are said!)—how do you know, I say, that all this may not happen to *you*, this night?

And *dare* you, knowing this, say to yourself "Well, perhaps it *is* an immoral play: perhaps the situations *are* a little too 'risky', the dialogue a little too strong, the 'business' a little too suggestive. I don't say that conscience is *quite* easy: but the piece is so clever, I must see it this once! I'll begin a stricter life to-morrow." *To-morrow, and to-morrow, and to-morrow!*

> *"Who sins in hope, who, sinning, says,*
> *'Sorrow for sin God's judgement stays!'*
> *Against God's Spirit he lies; quite stops*
> *Mercy with insult; dares, and drops,*
> *Like a scorch'd fly, that spins in vain*
> *Upon the axis of its pain,*
> *Then takes its doom, to limp and crawl,*
> *Blind and forgot, from fall to fall."*

Let me pause for a moment to say that I believe this thought, of the possibility of death—if calmly realized, and steadily faced—would be one of the best possible tests as to our going to any scene of amusement being right or wrong. If the thought of sudden death acquires, for *you*, a special horror when imagined as happening in a *theatre*, then be very sure the theatre is harmful for *you*, however harmless it may be for others; and that *you* are incurring a deadly peril in going. Be sure the safest rule is that we should not dare to *live* in any scene in which we dare not *die*.

But, once realize what the true object *is* in life—that it

is *not* pleasure, *not* knowledge, *not* even fame itself, "that last infirmity of noble minds"—but that it *is* the development of *character*, the rising to a higher, nobler, purer standard, the building-up of the perfect *Man*—and then, so long as we feel that this is going on, and will (we trust) go on for evermore, death has for us no terror; it is not a shadow, but a light; not an end, but a beginning!

One other matter may perhaps seem to call for apology —that I should have treated with such entire want of sympathy the British passion for "Sport", which no doubt has been in by-gone days, and is still, in some forms of it, an excellent school for hardihood and for coolness in moments of danger. But I am not entirely without sympathy for *genuine* "Sport": I can heartily admire the courage of the man who, with severe bodily toil, and at the risk of his life, hunts down some "man-eating" tiger: and I can heartily sympathize with him when he exults in the glorious excitement of the chase and the hand-to-hand struggle with the monster brought to bay. But I can but look with deep wonder and sorrow on the hunter who, at his ease and in safety, can find pleasure in what involves, for some defenceless creature, wild terror and a death of agony: deeper, if the hunter be one who has pledged himself to preach to men the Religion of universal Love: deepest of all, if it be one of those *"tender and delicate"* beings, whose very name serves as a symbol of Love —*"thy love to me was wonderful, passing the love of women"* —whose mission here is surely to help and comfort all that are in pain or sorrow!

> *"Farewell, farewell! but this I tell*
> *To thee, thou Wedding-Guest!*
> *He prayeth well, who loveth well*
> *Both man and bird and beast.*
>
> *He prayeth best, who loveth best*
> *All things both great and small;*
> *For the dear God who loveth us,*
> *He made and loveth all."*

CHAPTER I

Less Bread! More Taxes!

—AND then all the people cheered again, and one man, who was more excited than the rest, flung his hat high into the air, and shouted (as well as I could make out) "Who roar for the Sub-Warden?" *Everybody* roared, but whether it was for the Sub-Warden, or not, did not clearly appear: some were shouting "Bread!" and some "Taxes!", but no one seemed to know what it was they really wanted.

All this I saw from the open window of the Warden's breakfast-saloon, looking across the shoulder of the Lord Chancellor, who had sprung to his feet the moment the shouting began, almost as if he had been expecting it, and had rushed to the window which commanded the best view of the market-place.

"What *can* it all mean?" he kept repeating to himself, as, with his hands clasped behind him, and his gown floating in the air, he paced rapidly up and down the room. "I never heard such shouting before—and at this time of the morning, too! And with such unanimity! Doesn't it strike *you* as very remarkable?"

I represented, modestly, that to *my* ears it appeared that they were shouting for different things, but the Chancellor would not listen to my suggestion for a moment. "They all shout the same words, I assure you!" he said: then, leaning well out of the window, he whispered to a man who was standing close underneath, "Keep 'em together, ca'n't you? The Warden will be here directly. Give 'em the signal for the march up!" All this was evidently not meant for *my* ears, but I could scarcely help hearing it, considering that my chin was almost on the Chancellor's shoulder.

The "march up" was a very curious sight: a straggling procession of men, marching two and two, began from the other side of the market-place, and advanced in an irregular zig-zag fashion towards the Palace, wildly tacking from side to side, like a sailing vessel making way against an unfavourable wind—so that the head of the procession was often further from us at the end of one tack than it had been at the end of the previous one.

Yet it was evident that all was being done under orders, for I noticed that all eyes were fixed on the man who stood just under the window, and to whom the Chancellor was continually whispering. This man held his hat in one hand and a little green flag in the other: whenever he waved the flag the procession advanced a little nearer, when he dipped it they sidled a little farther off, and whenever he waved his hat they all raised a hoarse cheer. "Hoo-roah!" they cried, carefully keeping time with the hat as it bobbed up and down. "Hoo-roah! Noo! Consti! Tooshun! Less! Bread! More! Taxes!"

"That'll do, that'll do!" the Chancellor whispered. "Let 'em rest a bit till I give you the word. He's not here yet!" But at this moment the great folding-doors of the saloon were flung open, and he turned with a guilty start to receive His High Excellency. However it was only Bruno, and the Chancellor gave a little gasp of relieved anxiety.

"Morning!" said the little fellow, addressing the remark, in a general sort of way, to the Chancellor and the waiters. "Doos oo know where Sylvie is? I's looking for Sylvie!"

"She's with the Warden, I believe, y'reince!" the Chancellor replied with a low bow. There was, no doubt, a certain amount of absurdity in applying this title (which, as of course you see without my telling you, was nothing but "your Royal Highness" condensed into one syllable) to a small creature whose father was merely the Warden of Outland: still, large excuse must be made for a man who had passed several years at the Court of Fairyland,

and had there acquired the almost impossible art of pronouncing five syllables as one.

But the bow was lost upon Bruno, who had run out of the room, even while the great feat of The Unpronounceable Monosyllable was being triumphantly performed.

Just then, a single voice in the distance was understood to shout "A speech from the Chancellor!" "Certainly, my friends!" the Chancellor replied with extraordinary promptitude. "You shall have a speech!" Here one of the waiters, who had been for some minutes busy making a queer-looking mixture of egg and sherry, respectfully presented it on a large silver salver. The Chancellor took it haughtily, drank it off thoughtfully, smiled benevolently on the happy waiter as he set down the empty glass, and began. To the best of my recollection this is what he said.

"Ahem! Ahem! Ahem! Fellow-sufferers, or rather suffering fellows——" ("Don't call 'em names!" muttered the man under the window. "I didn't say *felons*!" the Chancellor explained.) "You may be sure that I always sympa——" (" 'Ear, 'ear!" shouted the crowd, so loudly as quite to drown the orator's thin squeaky voice) "——that I always sympa——" he repeated. ("Don't simper quite so much!" said the man under the window. "It makes yer look a hidiot!" And, all this time, " 'Ear, 'ear!" went rumbling round the market-place, like a peal of thunder.) "That I always *sympathize!*" yelled the Chancellor, the first moment there was silence. "But your *true* friend is the *Sub-Warden!* Day and night he is brooding on your wrongs—I should say your *rights*—that is to say your *wrongs*—no, I mean your *rights*——" ("Don't talk no more!" growled the man under the window. "You're making a mess of it!") At this moment the Sub-Warden entered the saloon. He was a thin man, with a mean and crafty face, and a greenish-yellow complexion; and he crossed the room very slowly, looking suspiciously about him as if he thought there might be a savage dog hidden somewhere. "Bravo!" he cried, patting the Chancellor on the back. "You did that speech very well indeed. Why, you're a born orator, man!"

"Oh, that's nothing!" the Chancellor replied, modestly, with downcast eyes. "Most orators are *born*, you know." The Sub-Warden thoughtfully rubbed his chin. "Why, so they are!" he admitted. "I never considered it in that light. Still, you did it very well. A word in your ear!"

The rest of their conversation was all in whispers: so, as I could hear no more, I thought I would go and find Bruno.

I found the little fellow standing in the passage, and being addressed by one of the men in livery, who stood before him, nearly bent double from extreme respectfulness, with his hands hanging in front of him like the fins of a fish. "His High Excellency", this respectful man was saying, "is in his Study, y'reince!" (He didn't pronounce this quite so well as the Chancellor.) Thither Bruno trotted, and I thought it well to follow him.

The Warden, a tall dignified man with a grave but very pleasant face, was seated before a writing-table, which was covered with papers, and holding on his knee one of the sweetest and loveliest little maidens it has ever been my lot to see. She looked four or five years older than Bruno, but she had the same rosy cheeks and sparkling eyes, and the same wealth of curly brown hair. Her eager smiling face was turned upwards towards her father's, and it was a pretty sight to see the mutual love with which the two faces—one in the Spring of Life, the other in its late Autumn—were gazing on each other.

"No, you've never seen him," the old man was saying: "you couldn't, you know, he's been away so long—traveling from land to land, and seeking for health, more years than you've been alive, little Sylvie!"

Here Bruno climbed upon his other knee, and a good deal of kissing, on a rather complicated system, was the result.

"He only came back last night," said the Warden, when the kissing was over: "he's been traveling post-haste, for the last thousand miles or so, in order to be here on Sylvie's birthday. But he's a very early riser, and I dare say he's in the Library already. Come with me and see him. He's always kind to children. You'll be sure to like him."

"Has the Other Professor come too?" Bruno asked in an awe-struck voice.

"Yes, they arrived together. The Other Professor is—well, you wo'n't like him quite so much, perhaps. He's a little more *dreamy*, you know."

"I wiss *Sylvie* was a little more dreamy," said Bruno.

"What *do* you mean, Bruno?" said Sylvie.

Bruno went on addressing his father. "She says she *ca'n't*, oo know. But I thinks it isn't *ca'n't*, it's *wo'n't*."

"Says she *ca'n't* dream!" the puzzled Warden repeated.

"She *do* say it," Bruno persisted. "When I says to her 'Let's stop lessons!', she says 'Oh, I ca'n't *dream* of letting oo stop yet!' "

"He always wants to stop lessons", Sylvie explained, "five minutes after we begin!"

"Five minutes' lessons a day!" said the Warden. "You wo'n't learn much at *that* rate, little man!"

"That's just what Sylvie says," Bruno rejoined. "She says I *wo'n't* learn my lessons. And I tells her, over and over, I *ca'n't* learn 'em. And what does oo think she says? She says 'It isn't *ca'n't*, it's *wo'n't*!' "

"Let's go and see the Professor," the Warden said, wisely avoiding further discussion. The children got down off his knees, each secured a hand, and the happy trio set off for the Library—followed by me. I had come to the conclusion by this time that none of the party (except, for a few moments, the Lord Chancellor) was in the least able to see me.

"What's the matter with him?" Sylvie asked, walking with a little extra sedateness, by way of example to Bruno at the other side, who never ceased jumping up and down.

"What *was* the matter—but I hope he's all right now—was lumbago, and rheumatism, and that kind of thing. He's been curing *himself*, you know: he's a very learned doctor. Why, he's actually *invented* three new diseases, besides a new way of breaking your collar-bone!"

"Is it a nice way?" said Bruno.

"Well, hum, not *very*," the Warden said, as we entered the Library. "And here *is* the Professor. Good morning, Professor! Hope you're quite rested after your journey!"

A jolly-looking, fat little man, in a flowery dressing-gown, with a large book under each arm, came trotting in at the other end of the room, and was going straight across without taking any notice of the children. "I'm looking for Vol. Three," he said. "Do you happen to have seen it?"

"You don't see my *children*, Professor!" the Warden exclaimed, taking him by the shoulders and turning him round to face them.

The Professor laughed violently: then he gazed at them through his great spectacles, for a minute or two, without speaking.

At last he addressed Bruno. "I hope you have had a good night, my child?"

Bruno looked puzzled. "I's had the same night *oo've* had," he replied. "There's only been *one* night since yesterday!"

It was the Professor's turn to look puzzled now. He took off his spectacles, and rubbed them with his handkerchief. Then he gazed at them again. Then he turned to the Warden. "Are they bound?" he enquired.

"No, we aren't," said Bruno, who thought himself quite able to answer *this* question.

The Professor shook his head sadly. "Not even half-bound?"

"Why *would* we be half-bound?" said Bruno. "We're not prisoners!"

But the Professor had forgotten all about them by this time, and was speaking to the Warden again. "You'll be glad to hear", he was saying, "that the Barometer's beginning to move——"

"Well, which way?" said the Warden—adding to the

children, "Not that *I* care, you know. Only *he* thinks it affects the weather. He's a wonderfully clever man, you know. Sometimes he says things that only the Other Professor can understand. Sometimes he says things that *nobody* can understand! Which way is it, Professor? Up or down?"

"Neither!" said the Professor, gently clapping his hands. "It's going sideways—if I may so express myself."

"And what kind of weather does *that* produce?" said the Warden. "Listen children! Now you'll hear something worth knowing!"

"Horizontal weather," said the Professor, and made straight for the door, very nearly trampling on Bruno, who had only just time to get out of his way.

"*Isn't* he learned?" the Warden said, looking after him with admiring eyes. "Positively he runs over with learning!"

"But he needn't run over *me*!" said Bruno.

The Professor was back in a moment: he had changed his dressing-gown for a frock-coat, and had put on a pair of very strange-looking boots, the tops of which were open umbrellas. "I thought you'd like to see them," he said. "*These* are the boots for horizontal weather!"

"But what's the use of wearing umbrellas round one's knees?"

"In *ordinary* rain," the Professor admitted, "they would *not* be of much use. But if ever it rained *horizontally*, you know, they would be invaluable—simply invaluable!"

"Take the Professor to the breakfast-saloon, children," said the Warden. "And tell them not to wait for me. I had breakfast early, as I've some business to attend to." The children seized the Professor's hands, as familiarly as if they had known him for years, and hurried him away. I followed respectfully behind.

CHAPTER II

L'Amie Inconnue

As we entered the breakfast saloon, the Professor was saying "—and he had breakfast by himself, early: so he begged you wouldn't wait for him, my Lady. This way, my Lady," he added, "this way!" And then, with (as it seemed to me) most superfluous politeness, he flung open the door of my compartment, and ushered in "—a young and lovely lady!" I muttered to myself with some bitterness. "And this is, of course, the opening scene of Vol. I. *She* is the Heroine. And *I* am one of those subordinate characters that only turn up when needed for the development of her destiny, and whose final appearance is outside the church, waiting to greet the Happy Pair!"

"Yes, my lady, change at Fayfield," were the next words I heard (oh that too obsequious Guard!), "next station but one." And the door closed, and the lady settled down into her corner, and the monotonous throb of the engine (making one feel as if the train were some gigantic monster, whose very circulation we could feel) proclaimed that we were once more speeding on our way. "The lady had a perfectly formed nose," I caught myself saying to myself, "hazel eyes, and lips——" and here it occurred to me that to see, for myself, what "the lady" was really like, would be more satisfactory than much speculation.

I looked round cautiously, and—was entirely disappointed of my hope. The veil, which shrouded her whole face, was too thick for me to see more than the glitter of bright eyes and the hazy outline of what *might* be a lovely oval face, but might also, unfortunately, be an equally *un*lovely one. I closed my eyes again, saying to myself "—couldn't have a better chance for an experiment in Telepathy! I'll *think out* her face and afterwards test the portrait with the original."

At first, no result at all crowned my efforts, though I

271

"divided my swift mind", now hither, now thither, in a way that I felt sure would have made Æneas green with envy: but the dimly-seen oval remained as provokingly blank as ever—a mere Ellipse, as if in some mathematical diagram, without even the Foci that might be made to do duty as a nose and a mouth. Gradually, however, the conviction came upon me that I could, by a certain concentration of thought, *think the veil away*, and so get a glimpse of the mysterious face—as to which the two questions, "is she pretty?" and "is she plain?", still hung suspended, in my mind, in beautiful equipoise.

Success was partial—and fitful—still there *was* a result: ever and anon, the veil seemed to vanish, in a sudden flash of light: but, before I could fully realize the face, all was dark again. In each such glimpse, the face seemed to grow more childish and more innocent: and, when I had at last *thought* the veil entirely away, it was, unmistakeably, the sweet face of little Sylvie!

"So, either I've been dreaming about Sylvie," I said to myself, "and this is the reality. Or else I've really been with Sylvie, and this is a dream! Is Life itself a dream, I wonder?"

To occupy the time, I got out the letter which had caused me to take this sudden railway-journey from my London home down to a strange fishing-town on the North coast, and read it over again:

"Dear old Friend,

"*I'm sure it will be as great a pleasure to me, as it can possibly be to you, to meet once more after so many years: and of course I shall be ready to give you all the benefit of such medical skill as I have: only, you know, one mustn't violate professional etiquette! And you are already in the hands of a first-rate London doctor, with whom it would be utter affectation for me to pretend to compete. (I make no doubt he is right in saying the heart is affected: all your symptoms point that way.) One thing, at any rate, I have already done in my doctorial capacity— secured you a bedroom on the ground-floor, so that you will not need to ascend the stairs at all.*

"I shall expect you by last train on Friday, in accordance with your letter: and, till then, I shall say, in the words of the old song, 'Oh for Friday nicht! Friday's lang a-coming!'

"Yours always,

"ARTHUR FORESTER

"P.S. Do you believe in Fate?"

This Postscript puzzled me sorely. "He is far too sensible a man", I thought, "to have become a Fatalist. And yet what else can he mean by it?" And, as I folded up the letter and put it away, I inadvertently repeated the words aloud. "Do you believe in Fate?"

The fair "Incognita" turned her head quickly at the sudden question. "No, I don't!" she said with a smile. "Do you?"

"I—I didn't mean to ask the question!" I stammered, a little taken aback at having begun a conversation in so unconventional a fashion.

The lady's smile became a laugh—not a mocking laugh, but the laugh of a happy child who is perfectly at her ease. "Didn't you?" she said. "Then it was a case of what you Doctors call 'unconscious cerebration'?"

"I am no Doctor," I replied. "Do I look so like one? Or what makes you think it?"

She pointed to the book I had been reading, which was so lying that its title, "Diseases of the Heart", was plainly visible.

"One needn't be a *Doctor*", I said, "to take an interest in medical books. There's another class of readers, who are yet more deeply interested——"

"You mean the *Patients*?" she interrupted, while a look of tender pity gave new sweetness to her face. "But", with an evident wish to avoid a possibly painful topic, "one needn't be *either*, to take an interest in books of *Science*. Which contain the greatest amount of Science, do you think, the books, or the minds?"

"Rather a profound question for a lady!" I said to myself, holding, with the conceit so natural to Man, that Woman's intellect is essentially shallow. And I considered a minute before replying. "If you mean *living* minds, I don't think it's possible to decide. There is so much *written* Science that no living person has ever *read*: and there is so much *thought-out* Science that hasn't yet been *written*. But, if you mean the whole human race, then I think the *minds* have it: everything, recorded in *books*, must have once been in some *mind*, you know."

"Isn't that rather like one of the Rules in Algebra?" my Lady enquired. ("*Algebra* too!" I thought with increasing wonder.) "I mean, if we consider thoughts as *factors*, may we not say that the Least Common Multiple of all the *minds* contains that of all the books; but not the other way?"

"Certainly we may!" I replied, delighted with the illustration. "And what a grand thing it would be", I went on dreamily, thinking aloud rather than talking, "if we could only *apply* that Rule to books! You know, in finding the Least Common Multiple, we strike out a quantity wherever it occurs, except in the term where it is raised to its highest power. So we should have to erase every recorded thought, except in the sentence where it is expressed with the greatest intensity."

My Lady laughed merrily. "*Some* books would be reduced to blank paper, I'm afraid!" she said.

"They would. Most libraries would be terribly diminished in *bulk*. But just think what they would gain in *quality*!"

"When will it be done?" she eagerly asked. "If there's any chance of it in *my* time, I think I'll leave off reading, and wait for it!"

"Well, perhaps in another thousand years or so——"

"Then there's no use waiting!" said my Lady. "Let's sit down. Uggug, my pet, come and sit by me!"

"Anywhere but by *me*!" growled the Sub-Warden. "The little wretch always manages to upset his coffee!"

I guessed at once (as perhaps the reader will also have

guessed, if, like myself, he is *very* clever at drawing conclusions) that my Lady was the Sub-Warden's wife, and
that Uggug (a hideous fat boy, about the same age as
Sylvie, with the expression of a prize-pig) was their son.
Sylvie and Bruno, with the Lord Chancellor, made up a
party of seven.

"And you actually got a plunge-bath every morning?"
said the Sub-Warden, seemingly in continuation of a
conversation with the Professor. "Even at the little
roadside-inns?"

"Oh, certainly, certainly!" the Professor replied with a
smile on his jolly face. "Allow me to explain. It is, in fact,
a very simple problem in Hydrodynamics. (That means a
combination of Water and Strength.) If we take a plunge-
bath, and a man of great strength (such as myself) about
to plunge into it, we have a perfect example of this
science. I am bound to admit", the Professor continued,
in a lower tone and with downcast eyes, "that we need a
man of *remarkable* strength. He must be able to spring
from the floor to about twice his own height, gradually
turning over as he rises, so as to come down again head
first."

"Why, you need a *flea*, not a *man!*" exclaimed the Sub-
Warden.

"Pardon me," said the Professor. "This particular kind
of bath is *not* adapted for a flea. Let us suppose", he continued, folding his table-napkin into a graceful festoon,
"that this represents what is perhaps *the* necessity of this
Age—the Active Tourist's Portable Bath. You may describe it briefly, if you like," looking at the Chancellor,
"by the letters A. T. P. B."

The Chancellor, much disconcerted at finding everybody looking at him, could only murmur, in a shy
whisper, "Precisely so!"

"One great advantage of this plunge-bath", continued
the Professor, "is that it requires only half-a-gallon of
water——"

"I don't call it a *plunge*-bath", His Sub-Excellency

remarked, "unless your Active Tourist goes *right under!*"

"But he *does* go right under," the old man gently replied. "The A. T. hangs up the P. B. on a nail—*thus.* He then empties the water-jug into it—places the empty jug below the bag—leaps into the air—descends head-first into the bag—the water rises round him to the top of the bag—and there you are!" he triumphantly concluded. "The A. T. is as much under water as if he'd gone a mile or two down into the Atlantic!"

"And he's drowned, let us say, in about four minutes——"

"By no means!" the Professor answered with a proud smile. "After about a minute, he quietly turns a tap at the lower end of the P. B.—all the water runs back into the jug—and there you are again!"

"But how in the world is he to get *out* of the bag again?"

"*That*, I take it," said the Professor, "is the most beautiful part of the whole invention. All the way up the P. B. inside, are loops for the thumbs; so it's something like going up-stairs, only perhaps less comfortable; and, by the time the A. T. has risen out of the bag, all but his head, he's sure to topple over, one way or the other—the Law of Gravity secures *that.* And there he is on the floor again!"

"A little bruised, perhaps?"

"Well, yes, a little bruised; but *having had his plunge-bath:* that's the great thing."

"Wonderful! It's almost beyond belief!" murmured the Sub-Warden. The Professor took it as a compliment, and bowed with a gratified smile.

"*Quite* beyond belief!" my Lady added—meaning, no doubt, to be more complimentary still. The Professor bowed, but he didn't smile *this* time.

"I can assure you", he said earnestly, "that, *provided the bath was made*, I used it every morning. I certainly *ordered* it—*that* I am clear about—my only doubt is, whether the man ever finished making it. It's difficult to remember, after so many years——"

At this moment the door, very slowly and creakingly, began to open, and Sylvie and Bruno jumped up, and ran to meet the well-known footstep.

CHAPTER III

Birthday-Presents

"IT'S my brother!" the Sub-Warden exclaimed, in a warning whisper. "Speak out and be quick about it!"

The appeal was evidently addressed to the Lord Chancellor, who instantly replied, in a shrill monotone, like a little boy repeating the alphabet, "As I was remarking, your Sub-Excellency, this portentous movement——"

"You began too soon!" the other interrupted, scarcely able to restrain himself to a whisper, so great was his excitement. "He couldn't have heard you. Begin again!"

"As I was remarking," chanted the obedient Lord Chancellor, "this portentous movement has already assumed the dimensions of a Revolution!"

"And what *are* the dimensions of a Revolution?" The voice was genial and mellow, and the face of the tall dignified old man, who had just entered the room, leading Sylvie by the hand, and with Bruno riding triumphantly on his shoulder, was too noble and gentle to have scared a less guilty man: but the Lord Chancellor turned pale instantly, and could hardly articulate the words "The dimensions—your—your High Excellency? I—I—scarcely comprehend!"

"Well, the length, breadth, and thickness, if you like it better!" And the old man smiled, half-contemptuously.

The Lord Chancellor recovered himself with a great effort, and pointed to the open window. "If your High Excellency will listen for a moment to the shouts of the

exasperated populace—" ("of the exasperated populace!" the Sub-Warden repeated in a louder tone, as the
Lord Chancellor, being in a state of abject terror, had
dropped almost into a whisper) "—you will understand
what it is they want."

And at that moment there surged into the room a
hoarse confused cry, in which the only clearly audible
words were "Less—bread—More—taxes!" The old man
laughed heartily. "What in the world——" he was beginning: but the Chancellor heard him not. "Some mistake!"
he muttered, hurrying to the window, from which he
shortly returned with an air of relief. "*Now* listen!" he
exclaimed, holding up his hand impressively. And now
the words came quite distinctly, and with the regularity
of the ticking of a clock, "More—bread—Less—taxes!"

"More bread!" the Warden repeated in astonishment.
"Why, the new Government Bakery was opened only last
week, and I gave orders to sell the bread at cost-price
during the present scarcity! What *can* they expect more?"

"The Bakery's closed, y'reince!" the Chancellor said,
more loudly and clearly than he had spoken yet. He was
emboldened by the consciousness that *here*, at least, he
had evidence to produce: and he placed in the Warden's
hands a few printed notices, that were lying ready, with
some open ledgers, on a side-table.

"Yes, yes, *I* see!" the Warden muttered, glancing carelessly through them. "Order countermanded by my
brother, and supposed to be *my* doing! Rather sharp practice! It's all right!" he added in a louder tone. "My name
is signed to it: so I take it on myself. But what do you
mean by 'Less Taxes'? How *can* they be less? I abolished
the last of them a month ago!"

"It's been put on again, y'reince, and by y'reince's
own orders!" and other printed notices were submitted
for inspection.

The Warden, whilst looking them over, glanced once
or twice at the Sub-Warden, who had seated himself before one of the open ledgers, and was quite absorbed in

adding it up; but he merely repeated "It's all right. I accept it as my doing."

"And they do say", the Chancellor went on sheepishly —looking much more like a convicted thief than an Officer of State, "that a change of Government, by the abolition of the Sub-Warden—I mean," he hastily added, on seeing the Warden's look of astonishment, "the abolition of the *office* of Sub-Warden, and giving the present holder the right to act as *Vice*-Warden whenever the Warden is absent—would appease all this seedling discontent. I mean," he added, glancing at a paper he held in his hand, "all this *seething* discontent!"

"For fifteen years", put in a deep but very harsh voice, "my husband has been acting as Sub-Warden. It is too long! It is much too long!" My Lady was a vast creature at all times: but, when she frowned and folded her arms, as now, she looked more gigantic than ever, and made one try to fancy what a haystack would look like, if out of temper.

"He would distinguish himself as a Vice!" my Lady proceeded, being far too stupid to see the double meaning of her words. "There has been no such Vice in Outland for many a long year, as he would be!"

"What course would *you* suggest, Sister?" the Warden mildly enquired.

My Lady stamped, which was undignified: and snorted, which was ungraceful. "This is no *jesting* matter!" she bellowed.

"I will consult my brother," said the Warden. "Brother!"

"——and seven makes a hundred and ninety-four, which is sixteen and twopence," the Sub-Warden replied. "Put down two and carry sixteen."

The Chancellor raised his hands and eyebrows, lost in admiration. "*Such* a man of business!" he murmured.

"Brother, could I have a word with you in my Study?" the Warden said in a louder tone. The Sub-Warden rose with alacrity, and the two left the room together.

My Lady turned to the Professor, who had uncovered the urn, and was taking its temperature with his pocket-thermometer. "Professor!" she began, so loudly and suddenly that even Uggug, who had gone to sleep in his chair, left off snoring and opened one eye. The Professor pocketed his thermometer in a moment, clasped his hands, and put his head on one side with a meek smile.

"You were teaching my son before breakfast, I believe?" my Lady loftily remarked. "I hope he strikes you as having talent?"

"Oh, very much so indeed, my Lady!" the Professor hastily replied, unconsciously rubbing his ear, while some painful recollection seemed to cross his mind. "I was very forcibly struck by His Magnificence, I assure you!"

"He is a charming boy!" my Lady exclaimed. "Even his snores are more musical than those of other boys!"

If that *were* so, the Professor seemed to think, the snores of *other* boys must be something too awful to be endured: but he was a cautious man, and he said nothing.

"And he's so clever!" my Lady continued "No one will enjoy your Lecture more—by the way, have you fixed the time for it yet? You've never given one, you know: and it was promised years ago, before you——"

"Yes, yes, my Lady, *I* know! Perhaps next Tuesday—or Tuesday week——"

"That will do very well," said my Lady, graciously. "Of course you will let the Other Professor lecture as well?"

"I think *not*, my Lady," the Professor said with some hesitation. "You see, he always stands with his back to the audience. It does very well for *reciting;* but for *lecturing*——"

"You are quite right," said my Lady. "And, now I come to think of it, there would hardly be time for more than *one* Lecture. And it will go off all the better, if we begin with a Banquet, and a Fancy-dress Ball——"

"It will indeed!" the Professor cried, with enthusiasm.

"I shall come as a Grass-hopper," my Lady calmly proceeded. "What shall *you* come as, Professor?"

The Professor smiled feebly. "I shall come as—as early as I can, my Lady!"

"You mustn't come in before the doors are opened," said my Lady.

"I ca'n't," said the Professor. "Excuse me a moment. As this is Lady Sylvie's birthday, I would like to——" and he rushed away.

Bruno began feeling in his pockets, looking more and more melancholy as he did so: then he put his thumb in his mouth, and considered for a minute: then he quietly left the room.

He had hardly done so before the Professor was back again, quite out of breath. "Wishing you many happy returns of the day, my dear child!" he went on, addressing the smiling little girl, who had run to meet him. "Allow me to give you a birthday-present. It's a second-hand pin-cushion, my dear. And it only cost fourpence-halfpenny!"

"Thank you, it's *very* pretty!" And Sylvie rewarded the old man with a hearty kiss.

"And the *pins* they gave me for nothing!" the Professor added in high glee. "Fifteen of em, and only *one* bent!"

"I'll make the bent one into a *hook!*" said Sylvie. "To catch Bruno with, when he runs away from his lessons!"

"You ca'n't guess what *my* present is!" said Uggug, who had taken the butter-dish from the table, and was standing behind her, with a wicked leer on his face.

"No, I ca'n't guess," Sylvie said without looking up. She was still examining the Professor's pincushion.

"It's *this!*" cried the bad boy, exultingly, as he emptied the dish over her, and then, with a grin of delight at his own cleverness, looked round for applause.

Sylvie coloured crimson, as she shook off the butter from her frock: but she kept her lips tight shut, and walked away to the window, where she stood looking out and trying to recover her temper.

Uggug's triumph was a very short one: the Sub-Warden had returned, just in time to be a witness of his dear child's playfulness, and in another moment a skilfully applied box on the ear had changed his grin of delight into a howl of pain.

"My darling!" cried his mother, enfolding him in her fat arms. "Did they box his ears for nothing? A precious pet!"

"It's not for *nothing*!" growled the angry father. "Are you aware, Madam, that *I* pay the house-bills, out of a fixed annual sum? The loss of all that wasted butter falls on *me*! Do you hear, Madam!"

"Hold your tongue, Sir!" My Lady spoke very quietly —almost in a whisper. But there was something in her *look* which silenced him. "Don't you see it was only a *joke*? And a very clever one, too! He only meant that he loved nobody *but* her! And, instead of being pleased with the compliment, the spiteful little thing has gone away in a huff!"

The Sub-Warden was a very good hand at changing a subject. He walked across to the window. "My dear," he said, "is that a *pig* that I see down below, rooting about among your flower-beds?"

"A *pig*!" shrieked my Lady, rushing madly to the window, and almost pushing her husband out, in her anxiety to see for herself. "Whose pig is it? How did it get in? Where's that crazy Gardener gone?"

At this moment Bruno re-entered the room, and passing Uggug (who was blubbering his loudest, in the hope of attracting notice) as if he was quite used to that sort of thing, he ran up to Sylvie and threw his arms round her. "I went to my toy-cupboard", he said with a very sorrowful face, "to see if there were *somefin* fit for a present for oo! And there isn't *nuffin*! They's *all* broken, every one! And I haven't got *no* money left, to buy oo a birthday-present! And I ca'n't give oo nuffin but *this*!" ("*This*" was a very earnest hug and a kiss.)

"Oh, thank you, darling!" cried Sylvie. "I like *your* present best of all!" (But if so, why did she give it back so quickly?)

His Sub-Excellency turned and patted the two children on the head with his long lean hands. "Go away, dears!" he said. "There's business to talk over."

Sylvie and Bruno went away hand in hand: but, on reaching the door, Sylvie came back again and went up to Uggug timidly. "I don't mind about the butter," she said, "and I—I'm sorry he hurt you!" And she tried to shake hands with the little ruffian: but Uggug only blubbered louder, and wouldn't make friends. Sylvie left the room with a sigh.

The Sub-Warden glared angrily at his weeping son. "Leave the room, Sirrah!" he said, as loud as he dared. His wife was still leaning out of the window, and kept repeating "I *ca'n't* see that pig! Where *is* it?"

"It's moved to the right—now it's gone a little to the left," said the Sub-Warden: but he had his back to the window, and was making signals to the Lord Chancellor, pointing to Uggug and the door, with many a cunning nod and wink.

The Chancellor caught his meaning at last, and crossing the room, took that interesting child by the ear—the next moment he and Uggug were out of the room, and the door shut behind them: but not before one piercing yell had rung through the room, and reached the ears of the fond mother.

"What *is* that hideous noise?" she fiercely asked, turning upon her startled husband.

"It's some hyæna—or other," replied the Sub-Warden, looking vaguely up to the ceiling, as if that was where they usually were to be found. "Let us to business, my dear. Here comes the Warden." And he picked up from the floor a wandering scrap of manuscript, on which I just caught the words "after which Election duly holden the said Sibimet and Tabikat his wife may at their pleasure assume Imperial——" before, with a guilty look, he crumpled it up in his hand.

CHAPTER IV

A Cunning Conspiracy

THE Warden entered at this moment: and close behind him came the Lord Chancellor, a little flushed and out of breath, and adjusting his wig, which appeared to have been dragged partly off his head.

"But where is my precious child?" my Lady enquired, as the four took their seats at the small side-table devoted to ledgers and bundles and bills.

"He left the room a few minutes ago—with the Lord Chancellor," the Sub-Warden briefly explained.

"Ah!" said my Lady, graciously smiling on that high official. "Your Lordship has a very *taking* way with children! I doubt if any one could *gain the ear* of my darling Uggug so quickly as *you* can!" For an entirely stupid woman, my Lady's remarks were curiously full of meaning, of which she herself was wholly unconscious.

The Chancellor bowed, but with a very uneasy air. "I think the Warden was about to speak," he remarked, evidently anxious to change the subject.

But my Lady would not be checked. "He is a clever boy," she continued with enthusiasm, "but he needs a man like your Lordship to *draw him out!*"

The Chancellor bit his lip, and was silent. He evidently feared that, stupid as she looked, she understood what she said *this* time, and was having a joke at his expense. He might have spared himself all anxiety: whatever accidental meaning her *words* might have, she *herself* never meant anything at all.

"It is all settled!" the Warden announced, wasting no time over preliminaries. "The Sub-Wardenship is abolished, and my brother is appointed to act as Vice-Warden whenever I am absent. So, as I am going abroad for a while, he will enter on his new duties at once."

"And there will really be a Vice after all?" my Lady enquired.

"I hope so!" the Warden smilingly replied.

My Lady looked much pleased, and tried to clap her hands: but you might as well have knocked two feather-beds together, for any noise it made. "When my husband is Vice", she said, "it will be the same as if we had a *hundred* Vices!"

"Hear, hear!" cried the Sub-Warden.

"You seem to think it very remarkable", my Lady remarked with some severity, "that your wife should speak the truth!"

"No, not *remarkable* at all!" her husband anxiously explained. "*Nothing* is remarkable that *you* say, sweet one!"

My Lady smiled approval of the sentiment, and went on. "And am I Vice-Wardeness?"

"If you choose to use that title," said the Warden: "but 'Your Excellency' will be the proper style of address. And I trust that both '*His* Excellency' and '*Her* Excellency' will observe the Agreement I have drawn up. The provision I am *most* anxious about is this." He unrolled a large parchment scroll, and read aloud the words " '*item*, that we will be kind to the poor'. The Chancellor worded it for me," he added, glancing at that great Functionary. "I suppose, now, that word '*item*' has some deep legal meaning?"

"Undoubtedly!" replied the Chancellor, as articulately as he could with a pen between his lips. He was nervously rolling and unrolling several other scrolls, and making room among them for the one the Warden had just handed to him. "These are merely the rough copies," he explained: "and, as soon as I have put in the final corrections—" making a great commotion among the different parchments, "—a semi-colon or two that I have accidentally omitted—" here he darted about, pen in hand, from one part of the scroll to another, spreading sheets of blotting-paper over his corrections, "all will be ready for signing."

"Should it not be read out, first?" my Lady enquired.

"No need, no need!" the Sub-Warden and the Chancellor exclaimed at the same moment, with feverish eagerness.

"No need at all," the Warden gently assented. "Your husband and I have gone through it together. It provides that he shall exercise the full authority of Warden, and shall have the disposal of the annual revenue attached to the office, until my return, or, failing that, until Bruno comes of age: and that he shall then hand over, to myself or to Bruno as the case may be, the Wardenship, the unspent revenue, and the contents of the Treasury, which are to be preserved, intact, under his guardianship."

All this time the Sub-Warden was busy, with the Chancellor's help, shifting the papers from side to side, and pointing out to the Warden the place where he was to sign. He then signed it himself, and my Lady and the Chancellor added their names as witnesses.

"Short partings are best," said the Warden. "All is ready for my journey. My children are waiting below to see me off." He gravely kissed my Lady, shook hands with his brother and the Chancellor, and left the room.

The three waited in silence till the sound of wheels announced that the Warden was out of hearing: then, to my surprise, they broke into peals of uncontrollable laughter.

"What a game, oh, what a game!" cried the Chancellor. And he and the Vice-Warden joined hands, and skipped wildly about the room. My Lady was too dignified to skip, but she laughed like the neighing of a horse, and waved her handkerchief above her head: it was clear to her very limited understanding that *something* very clever had been done, but what it *was* she had yet to learn.

"You said I should hear all about it when the Warden had gone," she remarked, as soon as she could make herself heard.

"And so you shall, Tabby!" her husband graciously replied, as he removed the blotting paper, and showed the two parchments lying side by side. "This is the one he read but didn't sign: and this is the one he signed but didn't read! You see it was all covered up, except the place for signing the names——"

"Yes, yes!" my Lady interrupted eagerly, and began comparing the two Agreements. " '*Item*, that he shall exercise the authority of Warden, in the Warden's absence.' Why, that's been changed into 'shall be absolute governor for life, with the title of Emperor, if elected to that office by the people.' What! Are you *Emperor*, darling?"

"Not yet, dear," the Vice-Warden replied. "It wo'n't do to let this paper be seen, just at present. All in good time."

My Lady nodded, and read on. " '*Item*, that we will be kind to the poor.' Why, that's omitted altogether!"

"Course it is!" said her husband. "*We're* not going to bother about the wretches!"

"*Good*," said my Lady, with emphasis, and read on again. " '*Item*, that the contents of the Treasury be preserved intact.' Why, that's altered into 'shall be at the absolute disposal of the Vice-Warden'! Well, Sibby, that *was* a clever trick! *All* the Jewels, only think! May I go and put them on directly?"

"Well, not *just* yet, Lovey," her husband uneasily replied "You see the public mind isn't quite ripe for it yet. We must feel our way. Of course we'll have the coach-and-four out, at once. And I'll take the title of Emperor, as soon as we can safely hold an Election. But they'll hardly stand our using the *Jewels*, as long as they know the Warden's alive. We must spread a report of his death. A little Conspiracy——"

"A Conspiracy!" cried the delighted lady, clapping her hands. "Of all things, I *do* like a Conspiracy! It's so interesting!"

The Vice-Warden and the Chancellor interchanged a wink or two. "Let her conspire to her heart's content!" the cunning Chancellor whispered. "It'll do no harm!"

"And when will the Conspiracy——"

"Hist!" her husband hastily interrupted her, as the door opened, and Sylvie and Bruno came in, with their arms twined lovingly round each other—Bruno sobbing convulsively, with his face hidden on his sister's shoulder, and Sylvie more grave and quiet, but with tears streaming down her cheeks.

"Mustn't cry like that!" the Vice-Warden said sharply, but without any effect on the weeping children. "Cheer 'em up a bit!" he hinted to my Lady.

"*Cake!*" my Lady muttered to herself with great decision, crossing the room and opening a cupboard, from which she presently returned with two slices of plum-cake. "Eat, and don't cry!" were her short and simple orders: and the poor children sat down side by side, but seemed in no mood for eating.

For the second time the door opened—or rather was *burst* open, this time, as Uggug rushed violently into the room, shouting "that old Beggar's come again!"

"He's not to have any food——" the Vice-Warden was beginning, but the Chancellor interrupted him. "It's all right," he said, in a low voice: "the servants have their orders."

"He's just under here," said Uggug, who had gone to the window, and was looking down into the court-yard.

"Where, my darling?" said his fond mother, flinging her arms round the neck of the little monster. All of us (except Sylvie and Bruno, who took no notice of what was going on) followed her to the window. The old Beggar looked up at us with hungry eyes. "Only a crust of bread, your Highness!" he pleaded. He was a fine old man, but looked sadly ill and worn. "A crust of bread is what I crave!" he repeated. "A single crust and a little water!"

"Here's some water, drink this!" Uggug bellowed, emptying a jug of water over his head.

"Well done, my boy!" cried the Vice-Warden. "That's the way to settle such folk!"

"Clever boy!" the Wardeness chimed in. "*Hasn't* he good spirits?"

"Take a stick to him!" shouted the Vice-Warden, as

the old Beggar shook the water from his ragged cloak, and again gazed meekly upwards.

"Take a red-hot poker to him!" my Lady again chimed in.

Possibly there was no red-hot poker handy: but some *sticks* were forthcoming in a moment, and threatening faces surrounded the poor old wanderer, who waved them back with quiet dignity. "No need to break my old bones," he said. "I am going. Not even a crust!"

"Poor, *poor* old man!" exclaimed a little voice at my side, half choked with sobs. Bruno was at the window, trying to throw out his slice of plum-cake, but Sylvie held him back.

"He *shall* have my cake!" Bruno cried, passionately struggling out of Sylvie's arms.

"Yes, yes, darling!" Sylvie gently pleaded. "But don't *throw* it out! He's gone away, don't you see? Let's go after him." And she led him out of the room, unnoticed by the rest of the party, who were wholly absorbed in watching the old Beggar.

The Conspirators returned to their seats, and continued their conversation in an undertone, so as not to be heard by Uggug, who was still standing at the window.

"By the way, there was something about Bruno succeeding to the Wardenship," said my Lady. "How does *that* stand in the new Agreement?"

The Chancellor chuckled. "Just the same, word for word," he said, "with *one* exception, my Lady. Instead of 'Bruno', I've taken the liberty to put in—" he dropped his voice to a whisper, "—to put in 'Uggug', you know!"

"Uggug, indeed!" I exclaimed, in a burst of indignation I could no longer control. To bring out even that one word seemed a gigantic effort: but, the cry once uttered, all effort ceased at once: a sudden gust swept away the whole scene, and I found myself sitting up, staring at the young lady in the opposite corner of the carriage, who had now thrown back her veil, and was looking at me with an expression of amused surprise.

CHAPTER V

A Beggar's Palace

THAT I had said *something*, in the act of waking, I felt sure: the hoarse stifled cry was still ringing in my ears, even if the startled look of my fellow-traveler had not been evidence enough: but what could I possibly say by way of apology?

"I hope I didn't frighten you?" I stammered out at last. "I have no idea what I said. I was dreaming."

"You said '*Uggug indeed!*'" the young lady replied, with quivering lips that *would* curve themselves into a smile, in spite of all her efforts to look grave. "At least—you didn't *say* it—you *shouted* it!"

"I'm very sorry," was all I could say, feeling very penitent and helpless. "She *has* Sylvie's eyes!" I thought to myself, half-doubting whether, even now, I were fairly awake. "And that sweet look of innocent wonder is all Sylvie's, too. But Sylvie *hasn't* got that calm resolute mouth—nor that far-away look of dreamy sadness, like one that has had some deep sorrow, very long ago——" And the thick-coming fancies almost prevented my hearing the lady's next words.

"If you had had a 'Shilling Dreadful' in your hand," she proceeded, "something about Ghosts—or Dynamite—or Midnight Murder—one could understand it: those things aren't worth the shilling, unless they give one a Nightmare. But really—with only a *medical treatise*, you know——" and she glanced, with a pretty shrug of contempt, at the book over which I had fallen asleep.

Her friendliness, and utter unreserve, took me aback for a moment; yet there was no touch of forwardness, or boldness, about the child—for child, almost, she seemed to be: I guessed her at scarcely over twenty—all was the innocent frankness of some angelic visitant, new to the ways of earth and the conventionalisms—or, if you will, the barbarisms—of Society. "Even so", I mused, "will *Sylvie* look and speak, in another ten years."

"You don't care for Ghosts, then," I ventured to suggest, "unless they are really terrifying?"

"Quite so," the lady assented. "The regular Railway-Ghosts—I mean the Ghosts of ordinary Railway-literature—are very poor affairs. I feel inclined to say, with Alexander Selkirk, 'Their tameness is shocking to me'! And they never do any Midnight Murders. They couldn't 'welter in gore', to save their lives!"

" 'Weltering in gore' is a very expressive phrase, certainly. Can it be done in *any* fluid, I wonder?"

"I think *not*," the lady readily replied—quite as if she had thought it out, long ago. "It has to be something *thick*. For instance, you might welter in bread-sauce. That, being *white*, would be more suitable for a Ghost, supposing it wished to welter!"

"You have a real good *terrifying* Ghost in that book?" I hinted.

"How *could* you guess?" she exclaimed with the most engaging frankness, and placed the volume in my hands. I opened it eagerly, with a not unpleasant thrill (like what a good ghost-story gives one) at the "uncanny" coincidence of my having so unexpectedly divined the subject of her studies.

It was a book of Domestic Cookery, open at the article "Bread Sauce".

I returned the book, looking, I suppose, a little blank, as the lady laughed merrily at my discomfiture. "It's far more exciting than some of the modern ghosts, I assure you! Now there was a Ghost last month—I don't mean a *real* Ghost in—in Supernature—but in a Magazine. It was a perfectly *flavourless* Ghost. It wouldn't have frightened a mouse! It wasn't a Ghost that one would even offer a chair to!"

"Three score years and ten, baldness, and spectacles, have their advantages after all!" I said to myself. "Instead of a bashful youth and maiden, gasping out monosyllables at awful intervals, here we have an old man and a child, quite at their ease, talking as if they had known each other for years! Then you think", I continued aloud, "that we ought *sometimes* to ask a Ghost to sit down? But have we any authority for it? In Shakespeare, for instance—there are plenty of ghosts *there*—does Shakespeare ever give the stage-direction '*hands chair to Ghost*'?"

The lady looked puzzled and thoughtful for a moment: then she *almost* clapped her hands. "Yes, yes, he *does*!" she cried. "He makes Hamlet say '*Rest, rest, perturbed Spirit!*'"

"And that, I suppose, means an easy-chair?"

"An American rocking-chair, I *think*——"

"Fayfield Junction, my Lady, change for Elveston!" the guard announced, flinging open the door of the carriage: and we soon found ourselves, with all our portable property around us, on the platform.

The accommodation, provided for passengers waiting at this Junction, was distinctly inadequate—a single wooden bench, apparently intended for three sitters only: and even this was already partially occupied by a very old man, in a smock frock, who sat, with rounded shoulders and drooping head, and with hands clasped on the top of his stick so as to make a sort of pillow for that wrinkled face with its look of patient weariness.

"Come, you be off!" the Station-master roughly accosted the poor old man. "You be off, and make way for your betters! This way, my Lady!" he added in a perfectly different tone. "If your Ladyship will take a seat, the train will be up in a few minutes." The cringing servility of his manner was due, no doubt, to the address legible on the pile of luggage, which announced their owner to be "Lady Muriel Orme, passenger to Elveston, *via* Fayfield Junction".

As I watched the old man slowly rise to his feet, and hobble a few paces down the platform, the lines came to my lips:

"From sackcloth couch the Monk arose,
  With toil his stiffen'd limbs he rear'd;
A hundred years had flung their snows
  On his thin locks and floating beard."

But the lady scarcely noticed the little incident. After one glance at the "banished man" who stood tremulously leaning on his stick, she turned to me. "This is *not* an American rocking-chair, by any means! Yet may I say," slightly changing her place, so as to make room for me beside her, "may I say, in Hamlet's words, 'Rest, rest ——' " she broke off with a silvery laugh.

" '—perturbed Spirit!' " I finished the sentence for her. "Yes, that describes a railway-traveler *exactly*! And here is an instance of it," I added, as the tiny local train drew up alongside the platform, and the porters bustled about, opening carriage-doors—one of them helping the poor old man to hoist himself into a third-class carriage, while another of them obsequiously conducted the lady and myself into a first-class.

She paused, before following him, to watch the progress of the other passenger. "Poor old man!" she said. "How weak and ill he looks! It was a shame to let him be turned away like that. I'm very sorry——" At this moment it dawned on me that these words were not addressed to *me*, but that she was unconsciously thinking aloud. I moved away a few steps, and waited to follow her into the carriage, where I resumed the conversation.

"Shakespeare *must* have traveled by rail, if only in a dream: 'perturbed Spirit' is such a happy phrase."

" 'Perturbed' referring, no doubt," she rejoined, "to the sensational booklets, peculiar to the Rail. If Steam has done nothing else, it has at least added a whole new Species of English Literature!"

"No doubt of it," I echoed. "The true origin of all our medical books—and all our cookery-books——"

"No, no!" she broke in merrily. "I didn't mean *our* Literature! *We* are quite abnormal. But the booklets— the little thrilling romances, where the Murder comes at page fifteen, and the Wedding at page forty—surely *they* are due to Steam?"

"And when we travel by Electricity—if I may venture to develop your theory—we shall have leaflets instead of booklets, and the Murder and the Wedding will come on the same page."

"A development worthy of Darwin!" the lady exclaimed enthusiastically. "Only *you* reverse his theory. Instead of developing a mouse into an elephant, you would develop an elephant into a mouse!" But here we plunged into a tunnel, and I leaned back and closed my eyes for a moment, trying to recall a few of the incidents of my recent dream.

"I thought I saw——" I murmured sleepily: and then the phrase insisted on conjugating itself, and ran into "you thought you saw—he thought he saw——" and then it suddenly went off into a song:

> "*He thought he saw an Elephant,*
> *That practised on a fife:*
> *He looked again, and found it was*
> *A letter from his wife.*
> *'At length I realise', he said,*
> *'The bitterness of Life!'*"

And what a wild being it was who sang these wild words! A Gardener he seemed to be—yet surely a mad one, by the way he brandished his rake—madder, by the way he broke, ever and anon, into a frantic jig—maddest of all, by the shriek in which he brought out the last words of the stanza!

It was so far a description of himself that he had the *feet* of an Elephant: but the rest of him was skin and bone: and the wisps of loose straw, that bristled all about him, suggested that he had been originally stuffed with it, and that nearly all the stuffing had come out.

Sylvie and Bruno waited patiently till the end of the first verse. Then Sylvie advanced alone (Bruno having suddenly turned shy) and timidly introduced herself with the words "Please, I'm Sylvie!"

"And who's that other thing?" said the Gardener.

"What thing?" said Sylvie, looking round. "Oh, that's Bruno. He's my brother."

"Was he your brother yesterday?" the Gardener anxiously enquired.

"Course I were!" cried Bruno, who had gradually crept nearer, and didn't at all like being talked about without having his share in the conversation.

"Ah, well!" the Gardener said with a kind of groan. "Things change so, here. Whenever I look again it's sure to be something different! Yet I does my duty! I gets up wriggle-early at five——"

"If I was *oo*," said Bruno, "I wouldn't wriggle so early. It's as bad as being a worm!" he added, in an undertone to Sylvie.

"But you shouldn't be lazy in the morning, Bruno," said Sylvie. "Remember, it's the *early* bird that picks up the worm!"

"It may, if it likes!" Bruno said with a slight yawn. "I don't like eating worms, one bit. I always stop in bed till the early bird has picked them up!"

"I wonder you've the face to tell me such fibs!" cried the Gardener.

To which Bruno wisely replied, "Oo don't want a *face* to tell fibs wiz—only a *mouf*."

Sylvie discreetly changed the subject. "And did you plant all these flowers?" she said. "What a lovely garden you've made! Do you know, I'd like to live here *always*!"

"In the winter-nights——" the Gardener was beginning.

"But I'd nearly forgotten what we came about!" Sylvie interrupted. "Would you please let us through into the road? There's a poor old beggar just gone out—and he's very hungry—and Bruno wants to give him his cake, you know!"

"It's as much as my place is worth!" the Gardener

muttered, taking a key from his pocket, and beginning to unlock a door in the garden-wall.

"How much *are* it wurf?" Bruno innocently enquired.

But the Gardener only grinned. "That's a secret!" he said. "Mind you come back quick!" he called after the children, as they passed out into the road. I had just time to follow them, before he shut the door again.

We hurried down the road, and very soon caught sight of the old Beggar, about a quarter of a mile ahead of us, and the children at once set off running to overtake him. Lightly and swiftly they skimmed over the ground, and I could not in the least understand how it was I kept up with them so easily. But the unsolved problem did not worry me so much as at another time it might have done, there were so many other things to attend to.

The old Beggar must have been very deaf, as he paid no attention whatever to Bruno's eager shouting, but trudged wearily on, never pausing until the child got in front of him and held up the slice of cake. The poor little fellow was quite out of breath, and could only utter the one word "Cake!"—not with the gloomy decision with which Her Excellency had so lately pronounced it, but with a sweet childish timidity, looking up into the old man's face with eyes that loved "all things both great and small".

The old man snatched it from him, and devoured it greedily, as some hungry wild beast might have done, but never a word of thanks did he give his little bene-factor—only growled "More, more!" and glared at the half-frightened children.

"There *is* no more!" Sylvie said with tears in her eyes. "I'd eaten mine. It was a shame to let you be turned away like that. I'm very sorry——"

I lost the rest of the sentence, for my mind had re-curred, with a great shock of surprise, to Lady Muriel Orme, who had so lately uttered these very words of Sylvie's—yes, and in Sylvie's own voice, and with Sylvie's gentle pleading eyes!

"Follow me!" were the next words I heard, as the old man waved his hand, with a dignified grace that ill suited his ragged dress, over a bush, that stood by the road side, which began instantly to sink into the earth. At another time I might have doubted the evidence of my eyes, or at least have felt some astonishment: but, in *this* strange scene, my whole being seemed absorbed in strong curiosity as to what would happen next.

When the bush had sunk quite out of our sight, marble steps were seen, leading downwards into darkness. The old man led the way, and we eagerly followed.

The staircase was so dark, at first, that I could only just see the forms of the children as, hand-in-hand, they groped their way down after their guide: but it got lighter every moment, with a strange silvery brightness, that seemed to exist in the air, as there were no lamps visible; and, when at last we reached a level floor, the room, we found ourselves in, was almost as light as day.

It was eight-sided, having in each angle a slender pillar, round which silken draperies were twined. The wall between the pillars was entirely covered, to the height of six or seven feet, with creepers, from which hung quantities of ripe fruit and of brilliant flowers, that almost hid the leaves. In another place, perchance, I might have wondered to see fruit and flowers growing together: here, my chief wonder was that neither fruit nor flowers were such as I had ever seen before. Higher up, each wall contained a circular window of coloured glass; and over all was an arched roof, that seemed to be spangled all over with jewels.

With hardly less wonder, I turned this way and that, trying to make out how in the world we had come in: for there was no door: and all the walls were thickly covered with the lovely creepers.

"We are safe here, my darlings!" said the old man, laying a hand on Sylvie's shoulder, and bending down to kiss her. Sylvie drew back hastily, with an offended air:

but in another moment, with a glad cry of "Why, it's *Father*!", she had run into his arms.

"Father! Father!" Bruno repeated: and, while the happy children were being hugged and kissed, I could but rub my eyes and say "Where, then, are the rags gone to?"; for the old man was now dressed in royal robes that glittered with jewels and gold embroidery, and wore a circlet of gold around his head.

CHAPTER VI

The Magic Locket

"WHERE are we, father?" Sylvie whispered, with her arms twined closely around the old man's neck, and with her rosy cheek lovingly pressed to his.

"In Elfland, darling. It's one of the provinces of Fairyland."

"But I thought Elfland was *ever* so far from Outland: and we've come such a *tiny* little way!"

"You came by the Royal Road, sweet one. Only those of royal blood can travel along it: but *you've* been royal ever since I was made King of Elfland—that's nearly a month ago. They sent *two* ambassadors, to make sure that their invitation to me, to be their new King, should reach me. One was a Prince; so *he* was able to come by the Royal Road, and to come invisibly to all but me: the other was a Baron; so *he* had to come by the common road, and I dare say he hasn't even *arrived* yet."

"Then how far have we come?" Sylvie enquired.

"Just a thousand miles, sweet one, since the Gardener unlocked that door for you."

"A thousand miles!" Bruno repeated. "And may I eat one?"

"Eat a *mile*, little rogue?"

"No," said Bruno. "I mean may I eat one of that fruits?"

"Yes, child," said the father: "and then you'll find out what *Pleasure* is like—the Pleasure we all seek so madly, and enjoy so mournfully!"

Bruno ran eagerly to the wall, and picked a fruit that was *shaped* something like a banana, but had the *colour* of a strawberry.

He ate it with beaming looks, that became gradually more gloomy, and were very blank indeed by the time he had finished.

"It hasn't got no taste at all!" he complained. "I couldn't feel nuffin in my mouf! It's a—what's that hard word, Sylvie?"

"It was a *Phlizz*," Sylvie gravely replied. "Are they *all* like that, father?"

"They're all like that to *you*, darling, because you don't belong to Elfland—yet. But to *me* they are real."

Bruno looked puzzled. "I'll try anuvver kind of fruits!" he said, and jumped down off the King's knee. "There's some lovely striped ones, just like a rainbow!" And off he ran.

Meanwhile the Fairy-King and Sylvie were talking together, but in such low tones that I could not catch the words: so I followed Bruno, who was picking and eating other kinds of fruit, in the vain hope of finding *some* that had a taste. I tried to pick some myself—but it was like grasping air, and I soon gave up the attempt and returned to Sylvie.

"Look well at it, my darling," the old man was saying, "and tell me how you like it."

"It's just *lovely*," cried Sylvie delightedly. "Bruno, come and look!" And she held up, so that he might see the light through it, a heart-shaped Locket, apparently cut out of a single jewel, of a rich blue colour, with a slender gold chain attached to it.

"It are welly pretty," Bruno more soberly remarked: and he began spelling out some words inscribed on it.

"All—will—love—Sylvie," he made them out at last.
"And so they doos!" he cried, clasping his arms round
her neck. "*Everybody* loves Sylvie!"

"But *we* love her best, don't we, Bruno?" said the old
King, as he took possession of the Locket. "Now, Sylvie,
look at *this*." And he showed her, lying on the palm of
his hand, a Locket of a deep crimson colour, the same
shape as the blue one, and, like it, attached to a slender
golden chain.

"Lovelier and lovelier!" exclaimed Sylvie, clasping her
hands in ecstasy. "Look, Bruno!"

"And there's words on this one, too," said Bruno.
"Sylvie—will—love—all."

"Now you see the difference," said the old man: "different colours and different words. Choose one of them,
darling. I'll give you whichever you like best."

Sylvie whispered the words, several times over, with a
thoughtful smile, and then made her decision. "It's *very*
nice to be loved," she said: "but it's nicer to love other
people! May I have the red one, Father?"

The old man said nothing: but I could see his eyes fill
with tears, as he bent his head and pressed his lips to her
forehead in a long loving kiss. Then he undid the chain,
and showed her how to fasten it round her neck, and to
hide it away under the edge of her frock. "It's for you to
keep, you know," he said in a low voice, "not for other
people to *see*. You'll remember how to use it?"

"Yes, I'll remember," said Sylvie.

"And now, darlings, it's time for you to go back, or
they'll be missing you, and then that poor Gardener will
get into trouble!"

Once more a feeling of wonder rose in my mind as to
how in the world we were to *get* back again—since I
took it for granted that wherever the children went, *I*
was to go—but no shadow of doubt seemed to cross *their*
minds, as they hugged and kissed him, murmuring, over
and over again, "Good-bye, darling Father!" And then,
suddenly and swiftly, the darkness of midnight seemed

to close in upon us, and through the darkness harshly
rang a strange wild song:

> "*He thought he saw a Buffalo*
> *Upon the chimney-piece:*
> *He looked again, and found it was*
> *His Sister's Husband's Niece.*
> *'Unless you leave this house', he said,*
> *'I'll send for the Police!'* "

"That was *me!*" he added, looking out at us, through
the half-opened door, as we stood waiting in the road.
"And that's what I'd have done—as sure as potatoes
aren't radishes—if she hadn't have tooken herself off!
But I always loves my *pay-rints* like anything."

"Who *are* oor *pay-rints*?" said Bruno.

"Them as pay *rint* for me, of course!" the Gardener
replied. "You can come in now, if you like."

He flung the door open as he spoke, and we got out,
a little dazzled and stupefied (at least *I* felt so) at the
sudden transition from the half-darkness of the railway-
carriage to the brilliantly-lighted platform of Elveston
Station.

A footman, in a handsome livery, came forward and
respectfully touched his hat. "The carriage is here, my
Lady," he said, taking from her the wraps and small
articles she was carrying: and Lady Muriel, after shaking
hands and bidding me "Good-night!" with a pleasant
smile, followed him.

It was with a somewhat blank and lonely feeling that
I betook myself to the van from which the luggage was
being taken out: and, after giving directions to have my
boxes sent after me, I made my way on foot to Arthur's
lodgings, and soon lost my lonely feeling in the hearty
welcome my old friend gave me, and the cosy warmth
and cheerful light of the little sitting-room into which
he led me.

"Little, as you see, but quite enough for us two. Now,
take the easy-chair, old fellow, and let's have another

look at you! Well, you *do* look a bit pulled down!" and he put on a solemn professional air. "I prescribe Ozone, *quant. suff.* Social dissipation, *fiant pilulæ quam plurimæ:* to be taken, feasting, three times a day!"

"But, Doctor!" I remonstrated. "Society doesn't 'receive' three times a day!"

"That's all *you* know about it!" the young Doctor gaily replied. "At home, lawn-tennis, 3 P.M. At home, kettledrum, 5 P.M. At home, music (Elveston doesn't give dinners), 8 P.M. Carriages at 10. There you are!"

It sounded very pleasant, I was obliged to admit. "And I know some of the *lady*-society already," I added. "One of them came in the same carriage with me."

"What was she like? Then perhaps I can identify her."

"The *name* was Lady Muriel Orme. As to what she was *like*—well, *I* thought her very beautiful. Do you know her?"

"Yes—I do know her." And the grave Doctor coloured slightly as he added "Yes, I agree with you. She *is* beautiful."

"*I* quite lost my heart to her!" I went on mischievously. "We talked——"

"Have some supper!" Arthur interrupted with an air of relief, as the maid entered with the tray. And he steadily resisted all my attempts to return to the subject of Lady Muriel until the evening had almost worn itself away. Then, as we sat gazing into the fire, and conversation was lapsing into silence, he made a hurried confession.

"I hadn't meant to tell you anything about her", he said (naming no names, as if there were only one "she" in the world!) "till you had seen more of her, and formed your own judgment of her: but somehow you surprised it out of me. And I've not breathed a word of it to any one else. But I can trust *you* with a secret, old friend! Yes! It's true of *me*, what I suppose *you* said in jest."

"In the merest jest, believe me!" I said earnestly. "Why, man, I'm three times her age! But if she's

your choice, then I'm sure she's all that is good and—"
"—and sweet," Arthur went on, "and pure, and self-
denying, and true-hearted, and——" he broke off hastily,
as if he could not trust himself to say more on a subject
so sacred and so precious. Silence followed: and I leaned
back drowsily in my easy-chair, filled with bright and
beautiful imaginings of Arthur and his lady-love, and of
all the peace and happiness in store for them.

I pictured them to myself walking together, lingeringly
and lovingly, under arching trees, in a sweet garden of
their own, and welcomed back by their faithful gardener,
on their return from some brief excursion.

It seemed natural enough that the gardener should be
filled with exuberant delight at the return of so gracious
a master and mistress—and how strangely childlike they
looked! I could have taken them for Sylvie and Bruno
—less natural that he should show it by such wild dances,
such crazy songs!

> *"He thought he saw a Rattlesnake*
> *That questioned him in Greek:*
> *He looked again, and found it was*
> *The Middle of Next Week.*
> *'The one thing I regret', he said,*
> *'Is that it cannot speak!'"*

—least natural of all that the Vice-Warden and "my
Lady" should be standing close beside me, discussing an
open letter, which had just been handed to him by the
Professor, who stood, meekly waiting, a few yards off.

"If it were not for those two brats", I heard him mut-
ter, glancing savagely at Sylvie and Bruno, who were
courteously listening to the Gardener's song, "there
would be no difficulty whatever."

"Let's hear that bit of the letter again," said my Lady.
And the Vice-Warden read aloud:

"—and we therefore entreat you graciously to accept
the Kingship, to which you have been unanimously elected by the Council of Elfland: and that you will allow

your son Bruno—of whose goodness, cleverness, and beauty, reports have reached us—to be regarded as Heir-Apparent."

"But what's the difficulty?" said my Lady.

"Why, don't you see? The Ambassador, that brought this, is waiting in the house: and he's sure to see Sylvie and Bruno: and then, when he sees Uggug, and remembers all that about 'goodness, cleverness, and beauty,' why, he's sure to——"

"And *where* will you find a better boy than *Uggug*?" my Lady indignantly interrupted. "Or a wittier, or a lovelier?"

To all of which the Vice-Warden simply replied "Don't you be a great blethering goose! Our only chance is to keep those two brats out of sight. If *you* can manage *that*, you may leave the rest to *me. I'll* make him believe Uggug to be a model of cleverness and all that."

"We must change his name to Bruno, of course?" said my Lady.

The Vice-Warden rubbed his chin. "Humph! No!" he said musingly. "Wouldn't do. The boy's such an utter idiot, he'd never learn to answer to it."

"*Idiot*, indeed!" cried my Lady. "He's no more an idiot than *I* am!"

"You're right, my dear," the Vice-Warden soothingly replied. "He isn't, indeed!"

My Lady was appeased. "Let's go in and receive the Ambassador," she said, and beckoned to the Professor. "Which room is he waiting in?" she inquired.

"In the Library, Madam."

"And *what* did you say his name was?" said the Vice-Warden.

The Professor referred to a card he held in his hand. "His Adiposity the Baron Doppelgeist."

"Why does he come with such a funny name?" said my Lady.

"He couldn't well change it on the journey," the Professor meekly replied, "because of the luggage."

"*You* go and receive him", my Lady said to the Vice-Warden, "and *I'll* attend to the children."

Chapter VII

The Baron's Embassy

I WAS following the Vice-Warden, but, on second thoughts, went after my Lady, being curious to see how she would manage to keep the children out of sight.

I found her holding Sylvie's hand, and with her other hand stroking Bruno's hair in a most tender and motherly fashion: both children were looking bewildered and half-frightened.

"My own darlings," she was saying, "I've been planning a little treat for you! The Professor shall take you a long walk into the woods this beautiful evening: and you shall take a basket of food with you, and have a little picnic down by the river!"

Bruno jumped, and clapped his hands. "That *are* nice!" he cried. "Aren't it, Sylvie?"

Sylvie, who hadn't quite lost her surprised look, put up her mouth for a kiss. "Thank you *very* much," she said earnestly.

My Lady turned her head away to conceal the broad grin of triumph that spread over her vast face, like a ripple on a lake. "Little simpletons!" she muttered to herself, as she marched up to the house. I followed her in.

"Quite so, your Excellency," the Baron was saying as we entered the Library. "All the infantry were under *my* command." He turned, and was duly presented to my Lady.

"A *military* hero?" said my Lady. The fat little man simpered. "Well, yes," he replied, modestly casting down his eyes. "My ancestors were all famous for military genius."

My Lady smiled graciously. "It often runs in families," she remarked: "just as a love for pastry does."

The Baron looked slightly offended, and the Vice-Warden discreetly changed the subject. "Dinner will soon be ready," he said. "May I have the honour of conducting your Adiposity to the guest-chamber?"

"Certainly, certainly!" the Baron eagerly assented. "It would never do to keep *dinner* waiting!" And he almost trotted out of the room after the Vice-Warden.

He was back again so speedily that the Vice-Warden had barely time to explain to my Lady that her remark about "a love for pastry" was "unfortunate. You might have seen, with half an eye," he added, "that that's *his* line. Military genius, indeed! Pooh!"

"Dinner ready yet?" the Baron enquired, as he hurried into the room.

"Will be in a few minutes," the Vice-Warden replied. "Meanwhile, let's take a turn in the garden. You were telling me," he continued, as the trio left the house, "something about a great battle in which you had the command of the infantry——"

"True," said the Baron. "The enemy, as I was saying, far outnumbered us: but I marched my men right into the middle of—what's that?" the Military Hero exclaimed in agitated tones, drawing back behind the Vice-Warden, as a strange creature rushed wildly upon them, brandishing a spade.

"It's only the Gardener!" the Vice-Warden replied in an encouraging tone. "Quite harmless, I assure you. Hark, he's singing! It's his favourite amusement."

And once more those shrill discordant tones rang out:

> *"He thought he saw a Banker's Clerk*
> *Descending from the bus:*
> *He looked again, and found it was*
> *A Hippopotamus:*
> *'If this should stay to dine', he said,*
> *'There wo'n't be much for us!'"*

Throwing away the spade, he broke into a frantic jig, snapping his fingers, and repeating, again and again

"There wo'n't be much for us!
There wo'n't be much for us!"

Once more the Baron looked slightly offended, but the Vice-Warden hastily explained that the song had no allusion to *him*, and in fact had no meaning at all. "You didn't mean anything by it, now *did* you?" He appealed to the Gardener, who had finished his song, and stood, balancing himself on one leg, and looking at them, with his mouth open.

"I never means nothing," said the Gardener: and Uggug luckily came up at the moment, and gave the conversation a new turn.

"Allow me to present my son," said the Vice-Warden; adding, in a whisper, "one of the best and cleverest boys that ever lived! I'll contrive for you to see some of his cleverness. He knows everything that other boys *don't* know; and in archery, in fishing, in painting, and in music, his skill is—but you shall judge for yourself. You see that target over there? He shall shoot an arrow at it. Dear boy," he went on aloud, "his Adiposity would like to see you shoot. Bring his Highness' bow and arrows!"

Uggug looked very sulky as he received the bow and arrow, and prepared to shoot. Just as the arrow left the bow, the Vice-Warden trod heavily on the toe of the Baron, who yelled with the pain.

"Ten thousand pardons!" he exclaimed. "I stepped back in my excitement. See! It is a bull's-eye!"

The Baron gazed in astonishment. "He held the bow so awkwardly, it seemed impossible!" he muttered. But there was no room for doubt: there was the arrow, right in the centre of the bull's-eye!

"The lake is close by," continued the Vice-Warden. "Bring his Highness' fishing-rod!" And Uggug most unwillingly held the rod, and dangled the fly over the water.

"A beetle on your arm!" cried my Lady, pinching the

poor Baron's arm worse than if ten lobsters had seized it at once. "*That* kind is poisonous," she explained. "But *what* a pity! You missed seeing the fish pulled out!"

An enormous dead cod-fish was lying on the bank, with the hook in its mouth.

"I had always fancied", the Baron faltered, "that cod were *salt*-water fish?"

"Not in *this* country," said the Vice-Warden. "Shall we go in? Ask my son some question on the way—*any* subject you like!" And the sulky boy was violently shoved forwards to walk at the Baron's side.

"Could your Highness tell me", the Baron cautiously began, "how much seven times nine would come to?"

"Turn to the left!" cried the Vice-Warden, hastily stepping forwards to show the way—so hastily, that he ran against his unfortunate guest, who fell heavily on his face.

"*So* sorry!" my Lady exclaimed, as she and her husband helped him to his feet again. "My son was in the act of saying 'sixty-three' as you fell!"

The Baron said nothing: he was covered with dust, and seemed much hurt, both in body and mind. However, when they had got him into the house, and given him a good brushing, matters looked a little better.

Dinner was served in due course, and every fresh dish seemed to increase the good-humour of the Baron: but all efforts, to get him to express his opinion as to Uggug's cleverness, were in vain, until that interesting youth had left the room, and was seen from the open window, prowling about the lawn with a little basket, which he was filling with frogs.

"So fond of Natural History as he is, dear boy!" said the doting mother. "Now *do* tell us, Baron, what you think of him!"

"To be perfectly candid," said the cautious Baron, "I would like a *little* more evidence. I think you mentioned his skill in—"

"Music?" said the Vice-Warden. "Why, he's simply a prodigy! You shall hear him play the piano." And he walked to the window. "Ug—I mean my boy! Come in for a minute, *and bring the music-master with you*! To turn over the music for him," he added as an explanation.

Uggug, having filled his basket with frogs, had no objection to obey, and soon appeared in the room, followed by a fierce-looking little man, who asked the Vice-Warden "Vot music vill you haf?"

"The Sonata that His Highness plays so charmingly," said the Vice-Warden.

"His Highness haf not—" the music-master began, but was sharply stopped by the Vice-Warden.

"Silence, Sir! Go and turn over the music for His Highness. My dear," (to the Wardeness) "will you show him what to do? And meanwhile, Baron, I'll just show you a most interesting map we have—of Outland, and Fairyland, and that sort of thing."

By the time my Lady had returned from explaining things to the music-master, the map had been hung up, and the Baron was already much bewildered by the Vice-Warden's habit of pointing to one place while he shouted out the name of another.

My Lady joining in, pointing out other places, and shouting other names, only made matters worse; and at last the Baron, in despair, took to pointing out places for himself, and feebly asked "Is that great yellow splotch *Fairyland*?"

"Yes, that's Fairyland," said the Vice-Warden: "and you might as well give him a hint," he muttered to my Lady, "about going back to-morrow. He eats like a shark! It would hardly do for *me* to mention it."

His wife caught the idea, and at once began giving hints of the most subtle and delicate kind. "Just see what a short way it is back to Fairyland! Why, if you started to-morrow morning, you'd get there in very little more than a week!"

The Baron looked incredulous. "It took me a full month to *come*," he said.

"But it's ever so much shorter, going *back*, you know!"

The Baron looked appealingly to the Vice-Warden, who chimed in readily. "You can go back *five* times, in the time it took you to come here *once*—if you start to-morrow morning!"

All this time the Sonata was pealing through the room. The Baron could not help admitting to himself that it was being magnificently played: but he tried in vain to get a glimpse of the youthful performer. Every time he had nearly succeeded in catching sight of him, either the Vice-Warden or his wife was sure to get in the way, pointing out some new place on the map, and deafening him with some new name.

He gave in at last, wished a hasty good-night, and left the room, while his host and hostess interchanged looks of triumph.

"Deftly done!" cried the Vice-Warden. "Craftily con-trived! But what means all that tramping on the stairs?" He half-opened the door, looked out, and added in a tone of dismay, "The Baron's boxes·are being carried down!"

"And what means all that rumbling of wheels?" cried my Lady. She peeped through the window curtains. "The Baron's carriage has come round!" she groaned.

At this moment the door opened: a fat, furious face looked in: a voice, hoarse with passion, thundered out the words "My room is full of frogs—I leave you!" and the door closed again.

And still the noble Sonata went pealing through the room: but it was *Arthur's* masterly touch that roused the echoes, and thrilled my very soul with the tender music of the immortal "Sonata Pathetique": and it was not till the last note had died away that the tired but happy traveler could bring himself to utter the words "good-night!" and to seek his much-needed pillow.

Chapter VIII

A Ride on a Lion

THE next day glided away, pleasantly enough, partly in settling myself in my new quarters, and partly in strolling round the neighbourhood, under Arthur's guidance, and trying to form a general idea of Elveston and its inhabitants. When five o'clock arrived, Arthur proposed—without any embarrassment this time—to take me with him up to "the Hall", in order that I might make acquaintance with the Earl of Ainslie, who had taken it for the season, and renew acquaintance with his daughter Lady Muriel.

My first impressions of the gentle, dignified, and yet genial old man were entirely favourable: and the *real* satisfaction that showed itself on his daughter's face, as she met me with the words "this is indeed an unlooked-for pleasure!", was very soothing for whatever remains of personal vanity the failures and disappointments of many long years, and much buffeting with a rough world, had left in me.

Yet I noted, and was glad to note, evidence of a far deeper feeling than mere friendly regard, in her meeting with Arthur—though this was, as I gathered, an almost daily occurrence—and the conversation between them, in which the Earl and I were only occasional sharers, had an ease and a spontaneity rarely met with except between *very* old friends: and, as I knew that they had not known each other for a longer period than the summer which was now rounding into autumn, I felt certain that "Love", and Love alone, could explain the phenomenon.

"How convenient it would be", Lady Muriel laughingly remarked, *à propos* of my having insisted on saving her the trouble of carrying a cup of tea across the room to the Earl, "if cups of tea had no weight at all! Then perhaps ladies would *sometimes* be permitted to carry them for short distances!"

"One can easily imagine a situation", said Arthur, "where things would *necessarily* have no weight, relatively to each other, though each would have its usual weight, looked at by itself."

"Some desperate paradox!" said the Earl. "Tell us how it could be. We shall never guess it."

"Well, suppose this house, just as it is, placed a few billion miles above a planet, and with nothing else near enough to disturb it: of course it falls *to* the planet?"

The Earl nodded. "Of course—though it might take some centuries to do it."

"And is five-o'clock-tea to be going on all the while?" said Lady Muriel.

"That, and other things," said Arthur. "The inhabitants would live their lives, grow up and die, and still the house would be falling, falling, falling! But now as to the relative weight of things. Nothing can be *heavy*, you know, except by *trying* to fall, and being prevented from doing so. You all grant that?"

We all granted that.

"Well, now, if I take this book, and hold it out at arm's length, of course I feel its *weight*. It is trying to fall, and I prevent it. And, if I let go, it falls to the floor. But, if we were all falling together, it couldn't be *trying* to fall any quicker, you know: for, if I let go, what more could it do than fall? And, as my hand would be falling too— at the same rate—it would never leave it, for that would be to get ahead of it in the race. And it could never overtake the falling floor!"

"I see it clearly," said Lady Muriel. "But it makes one dizzy to think of such things! How *can* you make us do it?"

"There is a more curious idea yet," I ventured to say. "Suppose a cord fastened to the house, from below, and pulled down by some one on the planet. Then of course the *house* goes faster than its natural rate of falling: but the furniture—with our noble selves—would go on falling at their old pace, and would therefore be left behind."

"Practically, we should rise to the ceiling," said the Earl. "The inevitable result of which would be concussion of brain."

"To avoid that," said Arthur, "let us have the furniture fixed to the floor, and ourselves tied down to the furniture. Then the five-o'clock-tea could go on in peace."

"With one little drawback!" Lady Muriel gaily interrupted. "We should take the *cups* down with us: but what about the *tea*?"

"I had forgotten the *tea*," Arthur confessed. "*That*, no doubt, would rise to the ceiling—unless you chose to drink it on the way!"

"Which, I think, is *quite* nonsense enough for one while!" said the Earl. "What news does this gentleman bring us from the great world of London?"

This drew *me* into the conversation, which now took a more conventional tone. After a while, Arthur gave the signal for our departure, and in the cool of the evening we strolled down to the beach, enjoying the silence, broken only by the murmur of the sea and the far-away music of some fishermen's song, almost as much as our late pleasant talk.

We sat down among the rocks, by a little pool, so rich in animal, vegetable, and zoöphytic—or whatever is the right word—life, that I became entranced in the study of it, and, when Arthur proposed returning to our lodgings, I begged to be left there for a while, to watch and muse alone.

The fishermen's song grew ever nearer and clearer, as their boat stood in for the beach; and I would have gone down to see them land their cargo of fish, had not the microcosm at my feet stirred my curiosity yet more keenly.

One ancient crab, that was for ever shuffling frantically from side to side of the pool, had particularly fascinated me: there was a vacancy in its stare, and an aimless violence in its behaviour, that irresistibly recalled the Gardener who had befriended Sylvie and Bruno: and, as I gazed, I caught the concluding notes of the tune of his crazy song.

The silence that followed was broken by the sweet voice of Sylvie. "Would you please let us out into the road?"

"What! After that old beggar again?" the Gardener yelled, and began singing:

> *"He thought he saw a Kangaroo*
> *That worked a coffee-mill:*
> *He looked again, and found it was*
> *A Vegetable-Pill.*
> *'Were I to swallow this', he said,*
> *'I should be very ill!'"*

"We don't want him to swallow *anything*," Sylvie explained. "He's not hungry. But we want to see him. So will you please——"

"Certainly!" the Gardener promptly replied. "I *always* please. Never displeases nobody. There you are!" And he flung the door open, and let us out upon the dusty high-road.

We soon found our way to the bush, which had so mysteriously sunk into the ground: and here Sylvie drew the Magic Locket from its hiding-place, turned it over with a thoughtful air, and at last appealed to Bruno in a rather helpless way. "What *was* it we had to do with it, Bruno? It's all gone out of my head!"

"Kiss it!" was Bruno's invariable recipe in cases of doubt and difficulty. Sylvie kissed it, but no result followed.

"Rub it the wrong way," was Bruno's next suggestion.

"Which *is* the wrong way?" Sylvie most reasonably enquired. The obvious plan was to try *both* ways.

Rubbing from left to right had no visible effect whatever.

From right to left—"Oh, stop, Sylvie!" Bruno cried in sudden alarm. "Whatever *is* going to happen?"

For a number of trees, on the neighbouring hillside, were moving slowly upwards, in solemn procession: while a mild little brook, that had been rippling at our feet a moment before, began to swell, and foam, and hiss, and bubble, in a truly alarming fashion.

"Rub it some other way!" cried Bruno. "Try up-and-down! Quick!"

It was a happy thought. Up-and-down did it: and the landscape, which had been showing signs of mental aberration in various directions, returned to its normal condition of sobriety—with the exception of a small yellowish-brown mouse, which continued to run wildly up and down the road, lashing its tail like a little lion.

"Let's follow it," said Sylvie: and this also turned out a happy thought. The mouse at once settled down into a business-like jog-trot, with which we could easily keep pace. The only phenomenon, that gave me any uneasiness, was the rapid increase in the *size* of the little creature we were following, which became every moment more and more like a real lion.

Soon the transformation was complete: and a noble lion stood patiently waiting for us to come up with it. No thought of fear seemed to occur to the children, who patted and stroked it as if it had been a Shetland-pony.

"Help me up!" cried Bruno. And in another moment Sylvie had lifted him upon the broad back of the gentle beast, and seated herself behind him, pillion-fashion. Bruno took a good handful of mane in each hand, and made believe to guide this new kind of steed. "Gee-up!" seemed quite sufficient by way of *verbal* direction: the lion at once broke into an easy canter, and we soon found ourselves in the depths of the forest. I say "*we*", for I am certain that *I* accompanied them—though *how* I managed to keep up with a cantering lion I am wholly unable to explain. But I was certainly one of the party when we came upon an old beggar-man cutting sticks, at whose feet the lion made a profound obeisance, Sylvie and Bruno at the same moment dismounting, and leaping into the arms of their father.

"From bad to worse!" the old man said to himself,

dreamily, when the children had finished their rather confused account of the Ambassador's visit, gathered no
doubt from general report, as they had not seen him
themselves. "From bad to worse! That is their destiny. I
see it, but I cannot alter it. The selfishness of a mean and
crafty man—the selfishness of an ambitious and silly
woman—the selfishness of a spiteful and loveless child—
all tend one way, from bad to worse! And you, my darlings, must suffer it awhile, I fear. Yet, when things are
at their worst, you can come to me. I can do but little
as yet——"

Gathering up a handful of dust and scattering it in the
air, he slowly and solemnly pronounced some words that
sounded like a charm, the children looking on in awe-
struck silence:

> "*Let craft, ambition, spite,*
> *Be quenched in Reason's night,*
> *Till weakness turn to might,*
> *Till what is dark be light,*
> *Till what is wrong be right!*"

The cloud of dust spread itself out through the air, as
if it were alive, forming curious shapes that were for ever
changing into others.

"It makes letters! It makes words!" Bruno whispered,
as he clung, half-frightened, to Sylvie. "Only I *ca'n't* make
them out! Read them, Sylvie!"

"I'll try," Sylvie gravely replied. "Wait a minute—if
only I could see that word——"

"I should be very ill!" a discordant voice yelled in our
ears.

> "*'Were I to swallow this', he said,*
> *'I should be very ill!'*"

CHAPTER IX

A Jester and a Bear

YES, we were in the garden once more: and, to escape that horrid discordant voice, we hurried indoors, and found ourselves in the library—Uggug blubbering, the Professor standing by with a bewildered air, and my Lady, with her arms clasped round her son's neck, repeating, over and over again, "and *did* they give him nasty lessons to learn? My own pretty pet!"

"What's all this noise about?" the Vice-Warden angrily enquired, as he strode into the room. "And who put the hat-stand here?" And he hung his hat up on Bruno, who was standing in the middle of the room, too much astonished by the sudden change of scene to make any attempt at removing it, though it came down to his shoulders, making him look something like a small candle with a large extinguisher over it.

The Professor mildly explained that His Highness had been graciously pleased to say he wouldn't do his lessons.

"Do your lessons this instant, you young cub!" thundered the Vice-Warden. "And take *this*!" and a resounding box on the ear made the unfortunate Professor reel across the room.

"Save me!" faltered the poor old man, as he sank, half-fainting, at my Lady's feet.

"Shave you? Of course I will!" my Lady replied, as she lifted him into a chair, and pinned an anti-macassar round his neck. "Where's the razor?"

The Vice-Warden meanwhile had got hold of Uggug, and was belabouring him with his umbrella. "Who left this loose nail in the floor?" he shouted. "Hammer it in, I say! Hammer it in!" Blow after blow fell on the writhing Uggug, till he dropped howling to the floor.

Then his father turned to the "shaving" scene which was being enacted, and roared with laughter. "Excuse

317

me, dear, I ca'n't help it!" he said as soon as he could speak. "You *are* such an utter donkey! Kiss me, Tabby!"

And he flung his arms round the neck of the terrified Professor, who raised a wild shriek, but whether he received the threatened kiss or not I was unable to see, as Bruno, who had by this time released himself from his extinguisher, rushed headlong out of the room, followed by Sylvie; and I was so fearful of being left alone among all these crazy creatures that I hurried after them.

"We must go to Father!" Sylvie panted, as they ran down the garden. "I'm *sure* things are at their worst! I'll ask the Gardener to let us out again."

"But we ca'n't *walk* all the way!" Bruno whimpered. "How I *wiss* we had a coach-and-four, like Uncle!"

And, shrill and wild, rang through the air the familiar voice:

> "*He thought he saw a Coach-and-Four*
> *That stood beside his bed:*
> *He looked again, and found it was*
> *A Bear without a Head.*
> *'Poor thing,' he said, 'poor silly thing!*
> *It's waiting to be fed!'*"

"No, I ca'n't let you out again!" he said, before the children could speak. "The Vice-Warden gave it me, he did, for letting you out last time! So be off with you!" And, turning away from them, he began digging frantically in the middle of a gravel-walk, singing, over and over again,

> " '*Poor thing,' he said, 'poor silly thing!*
> *It's waiting to be fed!'*"

but in a more musical tone than the shrill screech in which he had begun.

The music grew fuller and richer at every moment: other manly voices joined in the refrain: and soon I heard the heavy thud that told me the boat had touched the beach, and the harsh grating of the shingle as the men dragged it up. I roused myself, and, after lending them a hand in hauling up their boat, I lingered yet awhile to watch them disembark a goodly assortment of the hard-won "treasures of the deep".

When at last I reached our lodgings I was tired and sleepy, and glad enough to settle down again into the easy-chair, while Arthur hospitably went to his cupboard, to get me out some cake and wine, without which, he declared, he could not, as a doctor, permit my going to bed.

And how that cupboard-door *did* creak! It surely could not be *Arthur*, who was opening and shutting it so often, moving so restlessly about, and muttering like the soliloquy of a tragedy-queen!

No, it was a *female* voice. Also the figure—half-hidden by the cupboard-door—was a *female* figure, massive, and in flowing robes. Could it be the landlady? The door opened, and a strange man entered the room.

"What *is* that donkey doing?" he said to himself, pausing, aghast, on the threshold.

The lady, thus rudely referred to, was his wife. She had got one of the cupboards open, and stood with her back to him, smoothing down a sheet of brown paper on one of the shelves, and whispering to herself "So, so! Deftly done! Craftily contrived!"

Her loving husband stole behind her on tip-toe, and tapped her on the head. "Boh!" he playfully shouted at her ear. "Never tell me again I ca'n't say 'boh' to a goose!"

My Lady wrung her hands. "Discovered!" she groaned. "Yet no—he is one of us! Reveal it not, oh Man! Let it bide its time!"

"Reveal *what* not?" her husband testily replied, dragging out the sheet of brown paper. "What are you hiding here, my Lady? I insist upon knowing!"

My Lady cast down her eyes, and spoke in the littlest of little voices. "Don't make fun of it, Benjamin!" she pleaded. "It's—it's—don't you understand? It's a DAGGER!"

"And what's *that* for?" sneered His Excellency. "We've only got to make people *think* he's dead! We haven't got to *kill* him! And made of tin, too!" he snarled, contemptuously bending the blade round his thumb. Now, Madam, you'll be good enough to explain. First, what do you call me *Benjamin* for?"

"It's part of the Conspiracy, Love! One *must* have an alias, you know——"

"Oh, an *alias*, is it? Well! And next, what did you get this dagger for? Come, no evasions? You ca'n't deceive *me*!"

"I got it for—for—for——" the detected Conspirator stammered, trying her best to put on the assassin-expression that she had been practising at the looking-glass. "For——"

"For *what*, Madam!"

"Well, for eighteenpence, if you *must* know, dearest! That's what I got it for, on my——"

"Now *don't* say your Word and Honour!" groaned the other Conspirator. "Why, they aren't worth half the money, put together!"

"On my *birthday*," my Lady concluded in a meek whisper. "One *must* have a dagger, you know. It's part of the——"

"Oh, don't talk of Conspiracies!" her husband savagely interrupted, as he tossed the dagger into the cupboard. "You know about as much how to manage a Conspiracy as if you were a chicken. Why, the first thing is to get a disguise. Now, just look at this!"

And with pardonable pride he fitted on the cap and bells, and the rest of the Fool's dress, and winked at her, and put his tongue in his cheek. "Is *that* the sort of thing, now?" he demanded.

My Lady's eyes flashed with all a Conspirator's enthusiasm. "The very thing!" she exclaimed, clapping her hands. "You do look, oh, such a *perfect* Fool!"

The Fool smiled a doubtful smile. He was not quite clear whether it was a compliment or not, to express it

so plainly. "You mean a Jester? Yes, that's what I intended. And what do you think *your* disguise is to be?"
And he proceeded to unfold the parcel, the lady watching
him in rapture.

"Oh, how lovely!" she cried, when at last the dress was
unfolded. "What a *splendid* disguise! An Esquimaux
peasant-woman!"

"An Esquimaux peasant, indeed!" growled the other.
"Here, put it on, and look at yourself in the glass. Why,
it's a *Bear*, ca'n't you use your eyes?" He checked himself
suddenly, as a harsh voice yelled through the room

> *"He looked again, and found it was*
> *A Bear without a Head!"*

But it was only the Gardener, singing under the open
window. The Vice-Warden stole on tip-toe to the window,
and closed it noiselessly, before he ventured to go on.
"Yes, Lovey, a *Bear*: but not without a *head*, I hope!
You're the Bear, and me the Keeper. And if·any one
knows us, they'll have sharp eyes, that's all!"

"I shall have to practise the steps a bit," my Lady said,
looking out through the Bear's mouth: "one ca'n't help
being rather human just at first, you know. And of course
you'll say, 'Come up, Bruin!', won't you?"

"Yes, of course," replied the Keeper, laying hold of the
chain, that hung from the Bear's collar, with one hand,
while with the other he cracked a little whip. "Now go
round the room in a sort of a dancing attitude. Very
good, my dear, very good. Come up, Bruin! Come up,
I say!"

He roared out the last words for the benefit of Uggug,
who had just come into the room, and was now standing,
with his hands spread out, and eyes and mouth wide
open, the very picture of stupid amazement. "Oh, my!"
was all he could gasp out.

The Keeper pretended to be adjusting the bear's collar,
which gave him an opportunity of whispering, unheard
by Uggug, "*my* fault, I'm afraid! Quite forgot to fasten

the door. Plot's ruined if *he* finds it out! Keep it up a minute or two longer. Be savage!" Then, while seeming to pull it back with all his strength, he let it advance upon the scared boy: my Lady, with admirable presence of mind, kept up what she no doubt intended for a savage growl, though it was more like the purring of a cat: and Uggug backed out of the room with such haste that he tripped over the mat, and was heard to fall heavily out-side—an accident to which even his doting mother paid no heed, in the excitement of the moment.

The Vice-Warden shut and bolted the door. "Off with the disguises!" he panted. "There's not a moment to lose. He's sure to fetch the Professor, and we couldn't take *him* in, you know!" And in another minute the disguises were stowed away in the cupboard, the door unbolted, and the two Conspirators seated lovingly side-by-side on the sofa, earnestly discussing a book the Vice-Warden had hastily snatched off the table, which proved to be the City-Directory of the capital of Outland.

The door opened, very slowly and cautiously, and the Professor peeped in, Uggug's stupid face being just visible behind him.

"It is a beautiful arrangement!" the Vice-Warden was saying with enthusiasm. "You see, my precious one, that there are fifteen houses in Green Street, *before* you turn into West Street."

"*Fifteen* houses! Is it *possible?*" my Lady replied. "I thought it was fourteen!" And, so intent were they on this interesting question, that neither of them even looked up till the Professor, leading Uggug by the hand, stood close before them.

My Lady was the first to notice their approach. "Why, here's the Professor!" she exclaimed in her blandest tones. "And my precious child too! Are lessons over?"

"A strange thing has happened!" the Professor began in a trembling tone. "His Exalted Fatness" (this was one of Uggug's many titles) "tells me he has just seen, in this very room, a Dancing-Bear and a Court-Jester!"

The Vice-Warden and his wife shook with well-acted merriment.

"Not in *this* room, darling!" said the fond mother. "We've been sitting here this hour or more, reading——," here she referred to the book lying on her lap, "——reading the—the City-Directory."

"Let me feel your pulse, my boy!" said the anxious father. "Now put out your tongue. Ah, I thought so! He's a little feverish, Professor, and has had a bad dream. Put him to bed at once, and give him a cooling draught."

"I ain't been dreaming!" his Exalted Fatness remonstrated, as the Professor led him away.

"Bad grammar, Sir!" his father remarked with some sternness. "Kindly attend to *that* little matter, Professor, as soon as you have corrected the feverishness. And, by the way, Professor!" (The Professor left his distinguished pupil standing at the door, and meekly returned.) "There is a rumour afloat, that the people wish to elect an—in point of fact, an—you understand that I mean an——"

"Not *another Professor*!" the poor old man exclaimed in horror.

"No! Certainly not!" the Vice-Warden eagerly explained. "Merely an *Emperor*, you understand."

"An *Emperor*!" cried the astonished Professor, holding his head between his hands, as if he expected it to come to pieces with the shock. "What will the Warden——"

"Why, the *Warden* will most likely *be* the new Emperor!" my Lady explained. "Where could we find a better? Unless, perhaps——" she glanced at her husband.

"Where, indeed!" the Professor fervently responded, quite failing to take the hint.

The Vice-Warden resumed the thread of his discourse. "The reason I mentioned it, Professor, was to ask *you* to be so kind as to preside at the Election. You see it would make the thing *respectable*—no suspicion of anything underhand——"

"I fear I ca'n't, your Excellency!" the old man faltered. "What will the Warden——"

"True, true!" the Vice-Warden interrupted. "Your position, as Court-Professor, makes it awkward, I admit. Well, well! Then the Election shall be held without you."

"Better so, than if it were held *within* me!" the Professor murmured with a bewildered air, as if he hardly knew what he was saying. "Bed, I think your Highness said, and a cooling-draught?" And he wandered dreamily back to where Uggug sulkily awaited him.

I followed them out of the room, and down the passage, the Professor murmuring to himself, all the time, as a kind of aid to his feeble memory, "C, C, C; Couch, Cooling-Draught, Correct-Grammar", till, in turning a corner, he met Sylvie and Bruno, so suddenly that the startled Professor let go of his fat pupil, who instantly took to his heels.

Chapter X

The Other Professor

"We were looking for you!" cried Sylvie, in a tone of great relief. "We *do* want you so much, you ca'n't think!"

"What is it, dear children?" the Professor asked, beaming on them with a very different look from what Uggug ever got from him.

"We want you to speak to the Gardener for us," Sylvie said, as she and Bruno took the old man's hands and led him into the hall.

"He's ever so unkind!" Bruno mournfully added. "They's *all* unkind to us, now that Father's gone. The Lion were *much* nicer!"

"But you must explain to me, please," the Professor said with an anxious look, "*which* is the Lion, and *which* is the Gardener. It's *most* important not to get two such

animals confused together. And one's very liable to do it
in their case—both having mouths, you know——"

"Doos oo *always* confuses two animals together?"
Bruno asked.

"Pretty often, I'm afraid," the Professor candidly confessed. "Now, for instance, there's the rabbit-hutch and
the hall-clock." The Professor pointed them out. "One
gets a little confused with *them*—both having doors, you
know. Now, only yesterday—would you believe it?—I
put some lettuces into the clock, and tried to wind up the
rabbit!"

"Did the rabbit *go*, after oo wounded it up?" said
Bruno.

The Professor clasped his hands on the top of his head,
and groaned. "Go? I should think it *did* go! Why, it's
gone! And where ever it's gone to—that's what I ca'n't
find out! I've done my best—I've read all the article
'Rabbit' in the great dictionary—Come in!"

"Only the tailor, Sir, with your little bill," said a meek
voice outside the door.

"Ah, well, I can soon settle *his* business," the Professor
said to the children, "if you'll just wait a minute. How
much is it, this year, my man?" The tailor had come in
while he was speaking.

"Well, it's been a doubling so many years, you see,"
the tailor replied, a little gruffly, "and I think I'd like the
money now. It's two thousand pound, it is!"

"Oh, that's nothing!" the Professor carelessly remarked, feeling in his pocket, as if he always carried at
least *that* amount about with him. "But wouldn't you like
to wait just another year, and make it *four* thousand?
Just think how rich you'd be! Why, you might be a *King*,
if you liked!"

"I don't know as I'd care about being a *King*," the man
said thoughtfully. "But it *dew* sound a powerful sight o'
money! Well, I think I'll wait——"

"Of course you will!" said the Professor. "There's good
sense in *you*, I see. Good-day to you, my man!"

"Will you ever have to pay him that four thousand pounds?" Sylvie asked as the door closed on the departing creditor.

"*Never*, my child!" the Professor replied emphatically. "He'll go on doubling it, till he dies. You see it's *always* worth while waiting another year, to get twice as much money! And now what would you like to do, my little friends? Shall I take you to see the Other Professor? This would be an excellent opportunity for a visit," he said to himself, glancing at his watch: "he generally takes a short rest—of fourteen minutes and a half—about this time."

Bruno hastily went round to Sylvie, who was standing at the other side of the Professor, and put his hand into hers. "I *thinks* we'd like to go," he said doubtfully: "only please let's go all together. It's best to be on the safe side, oo know!"

"Why, you talk as if you were *Sylvie!*" exclaimed the Professor.

"I know I did," Bruno replied very humbly. "I quite forgotted I wasn't Sylvie. Only I fought he might be rarver fierce!"

The Professor laughed a jolly laugh. "Oh, he's quite tame!" he said. "He never bites. He's only a little—a little *dreamy*, you know." He took hold of Bruno's other hand, and led the children down a long passage I had never noticed before—not that there was anything remarkable in *that*: I was constantly coming on new rooms and passages in that mysterious Palace, and very seldom succeeded in finding the old ones again.

Near the end of the passage the Professor stopped. "This is his room," he said, pointing to the solid wall.

"We ca'n't get in through *there!*" Bruno exclaimed.

Sylvie said nothing, till she had carefully examined whether the wall opened anywhere. Then she laughed merrily. "You're playing us a trick, you dear old thing!" she said. "There's no *door* here!"

"There isn't any door to the room," said the Professor. "We shall have to climb in at the window."

So we went into the garden, and soon found the window of the Other Professor's room. It was a ground-floor window, and stood invitingly open: the Professor first lifted the two children in, and then he and I climbed in after them.

The Other Professor was seated at a table, with a large book open before him, on which his forehead was resting: he had clasped his arms round the book, and was snoring heavily. "He usually reads like that", the Professor remarked, "when the book's very interesting: and then sometimes it's very difficult to get him to attend!"

This seemed to be one of the difficult times: the Professor lifted him up, once or twice, and shook him violently: but he always returned to his book the moment he was let go of, and showed by his heavy breathing that the book was as interesting as ever.

"How dreamy he is!" the Professor exclaimed. "He must have got to a *very* interesting part of the book!" And he rained quite a shower of thumps on the Other Professor's back, shouting "Hoy! Hoy!" all the time. "Isn't it *wonderful* that he should be so dreamy?" he said to Bruno.

"If he's always as *sleepy* as that," Bruno remarked, "a *course* he's dreamy!"

"But what are we to *do*?" said the Professor. "You see he's quite wrapped up in the book!"

"Suppose oo *shuts* the book?" Bruno suggested.

"That's it!" cried the delighted Professor. "Of course that'll do it!" And he shut up the book so quickly that he caught the Other Professor's nose between the leaves, and gave it a severe pinch.

The Other Professor instantly rose to his feet, and carried the book away to the end of the room, where he put it back in its place in the book-case. "I've been reading for eighteen hours and three-quarters," he said, "and now I shall rest for fourteen minutes and a half. Is the Lecture all ready?"

"Very nearly," the Professor humbly replied. "I shall

ask you to give me a hint or two—there will be a few little difficulties——"

"And a Banquet, I think you said?"

"Oh, yes! The Banquet comes *first*, of course. People never enjoy Abstract Science, you know, when they're ravenous with hunger. And then there's the Fancy-Dress-Ball. Oh, there'll be lots of entertainment!"

"Where will the Ball come in?" said the Other Professor.

"I *think* it had better come at the beginning of the Banquet—it brings people together so nicely, you know."

"Yes, that's the right order. First the Meeting: then the Eating: then the Treating—for I'm sure any Lecture *you* give us will be a treat!" said the Other Professor, who had been standing with his back to us all this time, occupying himself in taking the books out, one by one, and turning them upside-down. An easel, with a blackboard on it, stood near him: and, every time that he turned a book upside-down, he made a mark on the board with a piece of chalk.

"And as to the 'Pig-Tale'—which *you* have so kindly promised to give us——" the Professor went on, thoughtfully rubbing his chin. "I think that had better come at the *end* of the Banquet: then people can listen to it quietly."

"Shall I *sing* it?" the Other Professor asked, with a smile of delight.

"If you *can*," the Professor replied, cautiously.

"Let me try," said the Other Professor, seating himself at the pianoforte. "For the sake of argument, let us assume that it begins on A flat." And he struck the note in question. "La, la, la! I think that's within an octave of it." He struck the note again, and appealed to Bruno, who was standing at his side. "Did I sing it like *that*, my child?"

"No, oo didn't," Bruno replied with great decision. "It were more like a duck."

"Single notes are apt to have that effect," the Other Professor said with a sigh. "Let me try a whole verse.

> *There was a Pig, that sat alone,*
> *Beside a ruined Pump.*
> *By day and night he made his moan:*
> *It would have stirred a heart of stone*
> *To see him wring his hoofs and groan,*
> *Because he could not jump.*

Would you call that a tune, Professor?" he asked, when he had finished.

The Professor considered a little. "Well," he said at last, "some of the notes are the same as others—and some are different—but I should hardly call it a *tune*."

"Let me try it a bit by myself," said the Other Professor. And he began touching the notes here and there, and humming to himself like an angry bluebottle.

"How do you like his singing?" the Professor asked the children in a low voice.

"It isn't very *beautiful*," Sylvie said, hesitatingly.

"It's very extremely *ugly*!" Bruno said, without any hesitation at all.

"All extremes are bad," the Professor said, very gravely. "For instance, Sobriety is a very good thing, when practised *in moderation*: but even Sobriety, when carried to an *extreme*, has its disadvantages."

"What are its disadvantages?" was the question that rose in my mind—and, as usual, Bruno asked it for me. "What *are* its lizard bandages?"

"Well, this is *one* of them," said the Professor. "When a man's tipsy (that's one extreme, you know), he sees one thing or two. But, when he's *extremely* sober (that's the other extreme), he sees two things as one. It's equally inconvenient, whichever happens."

"What does 'illconvenient' mean?" Bruno whispered to Sylvie.

"The difference between 'convenient' and 'inconvenient' is best explained by an example," said the Other

Professor, who had overheard the question. "If you'll just think over any Poem that contains the two words—such as——"

The Professor put his hands over his ears, with a look of dismay. "If you once let him begin a *Poem*," he said to Sylvie, "he'll never leave off again! He never does!"

"Did he ever begin a Poem and not leave off again?" Sylvie enquired.

"Three times," said the Professor.

Bruno raised himself on tiptoe, till his lips were on a level with Sylvie's ear. "What became of them three Poems?" he whispered. "Is he saying them all now?"

"Hush!" said Sylvie. "The Other Professor is speaking!"

"I'll say it very quick," murmured the Other Professor, with downcast eyes, and melancholy voice, which contrasted oddly with his face, as he had forgotten to leave off smiling. ("At least it wasn't exactly a *smile*," as Sylvie said afterwards: "it looked as if his mouth was made that shape.")

"Go on then," said the Professor. "*What must be must be.*"

"Remember that!" Sylvie whispered to Bruno. "It's a very good rule for whenever you hurt yourself."

"And it's a very good rule for whenever I make a noise," said the saucy little fellow. "So *you* remember it too, Miss!"

"Whatever *do* you mean?" said Sylvie, trying to frown, a thing she never managed particularly well.

"Oftens and oftens," said Bruno, "haven't oo told me 'There mustn't be so much noise, Bruno!' when I've tolded oo 'There *must*!' Why, there isn't no rules at all about 'There mustn't'! But oo never believes *me*!"

"As if any one *could* believe *you*, you wicked wicked boy!" said Sylvie. The *words* were severe enough, but I am of opinion that, when you are really *anxious* to impress a criminal with a sense of his guilt, you ought not to pronounce the sentence with your lips *quite* close to his cheek—since a kiss at the end of it, however accidental, weakens the effect terribly.

Chapter XI

Peter and Paul

"As I was saying," the Other Professor resumed, "if you'll just think over any Poem, that contains the words —such as

> *'Peter is poor,' said noble Paul,*
> *'And I have always been his friend:*
> *And, though my means to give are small,*
> *At least I can afford to lend.*
> *How few, in this cold age of greed,*
> *Do good, except on selfish grounds!*
> *But I can feel for Peter's need,*
> *And I WILL LEND HIM FIFTY POUNDS!'*
>
> *How great was Peter's joy to find*
> *His friend in such a genial vein!*
> *How cheerfully the bond he signed,*
> *To pay the money back again!*
> *'We ca'n't', said Paul, 'be too precise:*
> *'Tis best to fix the very day:*
> *So, by a learned friend's advice,*
> *I've made it Noon, the Fourth of May.'*
>
> *'But this is April!' Peter said.*
> *'The First of April, as I think.*
> *Five little weeks will soon be fled:*
> *One scarcely will have time to wink!*
> *Give me a year to speculate—*
> *To buy and sell—to drive a trade—'*
> *Said Paul 'I cannot change the date.*
> *On May the Fourth it must be paid.'*

'*Well, well!*' *said Peter, with a sigh.*
  '*Hand me the cash, and I will go.*
I'll form a Joint-Stock Company,
  And turn an honest pound or so.'
'*I'm grieved*', *said Paul*, '*to seem unkind:*
  The money shall of course be lent:
But, for a week or two, I find
  It will not be convenient.'

So, week by week, poor Peter came
  And turned in heaviness away;
For still the answer was the same,
  '*I cannot manage it to-day.*'
And now the April showers were dry—
  The five short weeks were nearly spent—
Yet still he got the old reply,
  '*It is not quite convenient!*'

The Fourth arrived, and punctual Paul
  Came, with his legal friend, at noon.
'*I thought it best*', *said he*, '*to call:*
  One cannot settle things too soon.'
Poor Peter shuddered in despair:
  His flowing locks he wildly tore:
And very soon his yellow hair
  Was lying all about the floor.

The legal friend was standing by,
  With sudden pity half unmanned:
The tear-drop trembled in his eye,
  The signed agreement in his hand:
But when at length the legal soul
  Resumed its customary force,
'*The Law*', *he said*, '*we can't control:*
  Pay, or the Law must take its course!'

Said Paul '*How bitterly I rue*
  That fatal morning when I called!
Consider, Peter, what you do!
  You wo'n't be richer when you're bald!

Think you, by rending curls away,
To make your difficulties less?
Forbear this violence, I pray:
You do but add to my distress!'

'Not willingly would I inflict',
Said Peter, 'on that noble heart
One needless pang. Yet why so strict?
Is this to act a friendly part?
However legal it may be
To pay what never has been lent,
This style of business seems to me
Extremely inconvenient!

'No Nobleness of soul have I,
Like some that in this Age are found!'
(Paul blushed in sheer humility,
And cast his eyes upon the ground.)
'This debt will simply swallow all,
And make my life a life of woe!'
'Nay, nay, my Peter!' answered Paul.
'You must not rail on Fortune so!

'You have enough to eat and drink:
You are respected in the world:
And at the barber's, as I think,
You often get your whiskers curled.
Though Nobleness you ca'n't attain—
To any very great extent—
The path of Honesty is plain,
However inconvenient!'

' 'Tis true', said Peter, 'I'm alive:
I keep my station in the world:
Once in the week I just contrive
To get my whiskers oiled and curled.
But my assets are very low:
My little income's overspent:
To trench on capital, you know,
Is always inconvenient!'

'But pay your debts!' cried honest Paul.
    'My gentle Peter, pay your debts!
What matter if it swallows all
    That you describe as your "assets"?
Already you're an hour behind:
    Yet Generosity is best.
It pinches me—but never mind!
    I WILL NOT CHARGE YOU INTEREST!'

'How good! How great!' poor Peter cried.
    'Yet I must sell my Sunday wig—
The scarf-pin that has been my pride—
    My grand piano—and my pig!'
Full soon his property took wings:
    And daily, as each treasure went,
He sighed to find the state of things
    Grow less and less convenient.

Weeks grew to months, and months to years:
    Peter was worn to skin and bone:
And once he even said, with tears,
    'Remember, Paul, that promised Loan!'
Said Paul 'I'll lend you, when I can,
    All the spare money I have got—
Ah, Peter, you're a happy man!
    Yours is an enviable lot!

'I'm getting stout, as you may see:
    It is but seldom I am well:
I cannot feel my ancient glee
    In listening to the dinner-bell:
But you, you gambol like a boy,
    Your figure is so spare and light:
The dinner-bell's a note of joy
    To such a healthy appetite!'

Said Peter 'I am well aware
    Mine is a state of happiness:
And yet how gladly could I spare
    Some of the comforts I possess!

What you *call healthy appetite*
    I feel as Hunger's savage tooth:
And, when no dinner is in sight,
    The dinner-bell's a sound of ruth!

'*No scare-crow would accept this coat:*
    Such boots as these you seldom see,
Ah, Paul, a single five-pound note
    Would make another man of me!'
Said Paul 'It fills me with surprise
    To hear you talk in such a tone:
I fear you scarcely realize
    The blessings that are all your own!

'*You're safe from being overfed:*
    You're sweetly picturesque in rags:
You never know the aching head
    That comes along with money-bags:
And you have time to cultivate
    That best of qualities, Content—
For which you'll find your present state
    Remarkably convenient!'

Said Peter 'Though I cannot sound
    The depths of such a man as you,
Yet in your character I've found
    An inconsistency or two.
You seem to have long years to spare
    When there's a promise to fulfil:
And yet how punctual you were
    In calling with that little bill!'

'*One ca'n't be too deliberate*',
    Said Paul, 'in parting with one's pelf.
With bills, as you correctly state,
    I'm punctuality itself.
A man may surely claim his dues:
    But, when there's money to be lent,
A man must be allowed to choose
    Such times as are convenient!'

It chanced one day, as Peter sat
  Gnawing a crust—his usual meal—
Paul bustled in to have a chat,
  And grasped his hand with friendly zeal.
'I knew', said he, 'your frugal ways:
  So, that I might not wound your pride
By bringing strangers in to gaze,
  I've left my legal friend outside!

'You well remember, I am sure,
  When first your wealth began to go,
And people sneered at one so poor,
  I never used my Peter so!
And when you'd lost your little all,
  And found yourself a thing despised,
I need not ask you to recall
  How tenderly I sympathized!

'Then the advice I've poured on you,
  So full of wisdom and of wit:
All given gratis, though 'tis true
  I might have fairly charged for it!
But I refrain from mentioning
  Full many a deed I might relate—
For boasting is a kind of thing
  That I particularly hate.

'How vast the total sum appears
  Of all the kindnesses I've done,
From Childhood's half-forgotten years
  Down to that Loan of April One!
That Fifty Pounds! You little guessed
  How deep it drained my slender store:
But there's a heart within this breast,
  And I WILL LEND YOU FIFTY MORE!'

'Not so,' was Peter's mild reply,
  His cheeks all wet with grateful tears:
'No man recalls, so well as I,
  Your services in bygone years:

And this new offer, I admit,
  Is very very kindly meant—
Still, to avail myself of it
  Would not be quite convenient!'

"You'll see in a moment what the difference is between 'convenient' and 'inconvenient'. You quite understand it now, don't you?" he added, looking kindly at Bruno, who was sitting, at Sylvie's side, on the floor.

"Yes," said Bruno, very quietly. Such a short speech was very unusual, for him: but just then he seemed, I fancied, a little exhausted. In fact, he climbed up into Sylvie's lap as he spoke, and rested his head against her shoulder. "What a many verses it was!" he whispered.

CHAPTER XII

A Musical Gardener

THE Other Professor regarded him with some anxiety. "The smaller animal ought to go to bed *at once*," he said with an air of authority.

"Why *at once?*" said the Professor.

"Because he ca'n't go at twice," said the Other Professor.

The Professor gently clapped his hands. "Isn't he *wonderful!*" he said to Sylvie. "Nobody else could have thought of the reason, so quick. Why, *of course* he ca'n't go at twice! It would hurt him to be divided."

This remark woke up Bruno, suddenly and completely. "I don't want to be *divided*," he said decisively.

"It does very well on a *diagram*," said the Other Professor. "I could show it you in a minute, only the chalk's a little blunt."

"Take care!" Sylvie anxiously exclaimed, as he began, rather clumsily, to point it. "You'll cut your finger off, if you hold the knife so!"

"If oo cuts it off, will oo give it to *me*, please?" Bruno thoughtfully added.

"It's like this," said the Other Professor, hastily drawing a long line upon the black board, and marking the letters "*A*", "*B*", at the two ends, and "*C*" in the middle: "let me explain it to you. If *AB* were to be divided into two parts at *C*——"

"It would be drownded," Bruno pronounced confidently.

The Other Professor gasped. "*What* would be drownded?"

"Why the bumble-bee, of course!" said Bruno. "And the two bits would sink down in the sea!"

Here the Professor interfered, as the Other Professor was evidently too much puzzled to go on with his diagram.

"When I said it would *hurt* him, I was merely referring to the action of the nerves——"

The Other Professor brightened up in a moment. "The action of the nerves", he began eagerly, "is curiously slow in some people. I had a friend, once, that if you burnt him with a red-hot poker, it would take years and years before he felt it!"

"And if you only *pinched* him?" queried Sylvie.

"Then it would take ever so much longer, of course. In fact, I doubt if the man *himself* would ever feel it, at all. His grandchildren might."

"I wouldn't like to be the grandchild of a pinched grandfather, would *you*, Mister Sir?" Bruno whispered. "It might come just when you wanted to be happy!"

That would be awkward, I admitted, taking it quite as a matter of course that he had so suddenly caught sight of me. "But don't you *always* want to be happy, Bruno?"

"Not *always*," Bruno said thoughtfully. "Sometimes, when I's *too* happy, I wants to be a little miserable. Then I just tell Sylvie about it, oo know, and Sylvie sets me some lessons. Then it's all right."

"I'm sorry you don't like lessons," I said. "You should copy Sylvie. *She's* always as busy as the day is long!"

"Well, so am *I!*" said Bruno.

"No, no!" Sylvie corrected him. "*You're* as busy as the day is *short!*"

"Well, what's the difference?" Bruno asked. "Mister Sir, isn't the day as short as it's long? I mean, isn't it the *same* length?"

Never having considered the question in this light, I suggested that they had better ask the Professor; and they ran off in a moment to appeal to their old friend. The Professor left off polishing his spectacles to consider. "My dears," he said after a minute, "the day is the same length as anything that is the same length as *it*." And he resumed his never-ending task of polishing.

The children returned, slowly and thoughtfully, to report his answer. "*Isn't* he wise?" Sylvie asked in an awe-struck whisper. "If *I* was as wise as *that*, I should have a headache all day long, I *know* I should!"

"You appear to be talking to somebody—that isn't here," the Professor said, turning round to the children. "Who is it?"

Bruno looked puzzled. "I never talks to nobody when he isn't here!" he replied. "It isn't good manners. Oo should always wait till he comes, before oo talks to him!"

The Professor looked anxiously in my direction, and seemed to look through and through me without seeing me. "Then who are you talking to?" he said. "There isn't anybody here, you know, except the Other Professor—and *he* isn't here!" he added wildly, turning round and round like a teetotum. "Children! Help to look for him! Quick! He's got lost again!"

The children were on their feet in a moment.

"Where shall we look?" said Sylvie.

"Anywhere!" shouted the excited Professor. "Only be quick about it!" And he began trotting round and round the room, lifting up the chairs, and shaking them.

Bruno took a very small book out of the bookcase, opened it, and shook it in imitation of the Professor. "He isn't *here*," he said.

"He *ca'n't* be there, Bruno!" Sylvie said indignantly.

"Course he ca'n't!" said Bruno. "I should have shooked him out, if he'd been in there!"

"Has he ever been lost before?" Sylvie enquired, turning up a corner of the hearth-rug, and peeping under it.

"Once before," said the Professor: "he once lost himself in a wood——"

"And couldn't he find his-self again?" said Bruno. "Why didn't he shout? He'd be sure to hear his-self, 'cause he couldn't be far off, oo know."

"Let's try shouting," said the Professor.

"What shall we shout?" said Sylvie.

"On second thoughts, *don't* shout," the Professor replied. "The Vice-Warden might hear you. He's getting awfully strict!"

This reminded the poor children of all the troubles, about which they had come to their old friend. Bruno sat down on the floor and began crying. "He *is* so cruel!" he sobbed. "And he lets Uggug take away *all* my toys! And such horrid meals!"

"What did you have for dinner to-day?" said the Professor.

"A little piece of a dead crow," was Bruno's mournful reply.

"He means rook-pie," Sylvie explained.

"It *were* a dead crow," Bruno persisted. "And there were a apple-pudding—and Uggug ate it all—and I got nuffin but a crust! And I asked for a orange—and—didn't get it!" And the poor little fellow buried his face in Sylvie's lap, who kept gently stroking his hair, as she went on. "It's all true, Professor dear! They *do* treat my darling Bruno very badly! And they're not kind to *me* either," she added in a lower tone, as if *that* were a thing of much less importance.

The Professor got out a large red silk handkerchief, and

wiped his eyes. "I wish I could help you, dear children!" he said. "But what *can* I do?"

"We know the way to Fairyland—where Father's gone —quite well," said Sylvie: "if only the Gardener would let us out."

"Wo'n't he open the door for you?" said the Professor.

"Not for *us*," said Sylvie: "but I'm sure he would for *you*. Do come and ask him, Professor dear!"

"I'll come this minute!" said the Professor.

Bruno sat up and dried his eyes. "*Isn't* he kind, Mister Sir?"

"He is *indeed*," said I. But the Professor took no notice of my remark. He had put on a beautiful cap with a long tassel, and was selecting one of the Other Professor's walking sticks, from a stand in the corner of the room. "A thick stick in one's hand makes people respectful," he was saying to himself. "Come along, dear children!" And we all went out into the garden together.

"I shall address him, first of all," the Professor explained as we went along, "with a few playful remarks on the weather. I shall then question him about the Other Professor. This will have a double advantage. First, it will open the conversation (you ca'n't even drink a bottle of wine without opening it first): and secondly, if he's seen the Other Professor, we shall find him that way: and, if he hasn't, we sha'n't."

On our way, we passed the target, at which Uggug had been made to shoot during the Ambassador's visit.

"See!" said the Professor, pointing out a hole in the middle of the bull's-eye. "His Imperial Fatness had only *one* shot at it; and he went in just *here!*"

Bruno carefully examined the hole. "Couldn't go in *there*," he whispered to me. "He are too *fat!*"

We had no sort of difficulty in *finding* the Gardener. Though he was hidden from us by some trees, that harsh voice of his served to direct us; and, as we drew nearer, the words of his song became more and more plainly audible:

"He thought he saw an Albatross
That fluttered round the lamp:
He looked again, and found it was
A Penny-Postage-Stamp.
'You'd best be getting home,' he said:
'The nights are very damp!' "

"Would it be afraid of catching cold?" said Bruno.

"If it got *very* damp", Sylvie suggested, "it might stick to something, you know."

"And *that* somefin would have to go by the post, whatever it was!" Bruno eagerly exclaimed. "Suppose it was a cow! Wouldn't it be *dreadful* for the other things!"

"And all these things happened to *him*," said the Professor. "That's what makes the song so interesting."

"He must have had a very curious life," said Sylvie.

"You may say that!" the Professor heartily rejoined.

"Of course she may!" cried Bruno.

By this time we had come up to the Gardener, who was standing on one leg, as usual, and busily employed in watering a bed of flowers with an empty watering-can.

"It hasn't got no water in it!" Bruno explained to him, pulling his sleeve to attract his attention.

"It's lighter to hold," said the Gardener. "A lot of water in it makes one's arms ache." And he went on with his work, singing softly to himself

"The nights are very damp!"

"In digging things out of the ground—which you probably do now and then," the Professor began in a loud voice; "in making things into heaps—which no doubt you often do; and in kicking things about with one heel—which you seem never to leave off doing; have you ever happened to notice another Professor, something like me, but different?"

"Never!" shouted the Gardener, so loudly and violently that we all drew back in alarm. "There ain't such a thing!"

"We will try a less exciting topic," the Professor mildly remarked to the children. "You were asking——"

"We asked him to let us through the garden-door," said Sylvie: "but he wouldn't: but perhaps he would for *you!*"

The Professor put the request, very humbly and courteously.

"I wouldn't mind letting *you* out," said the Gardener. "But I mustn't open the door for *children*. D'you think I'd disobey the *Rules?* Not for one-and-sixpence!"

The Professor cautiously produced a couple of shillings.

"That'll do it!" the Gardener shouted, as he hurled the watering-can across the flower-bed, and produced a handful of keys—one large one, and a number of small ones.

"But look here, Professor dear!" whispered Sylvie. "He needn't open the door for *us*, at all. We can go out with *you.*"

"True, dear child!" the Professor thankfully replied, as he replaced the coins in his pocket. "That saves two shillings!" And he took the children's hands, that they might all go out together when the door was opened. This, however, did not seem a very likely event, though the Gardener patiently tried all the small keys, over and over again.

At last the Professor ventured on a gentle suggestion. "Why not try the *large* one? I have often observed that a door unlocks *much* more nicely with its *own* key."

The very first trial of the large key proved a success: the Gardener opened the door, and held out his hand for the money.

The Professor shook his head. "You are acting by *Rule*", he explained, "in opening the door for *me*. And now it's open, we are going out by *Rule*—the Rule of *Three*."

The Gardener looked puzzled, and let us go out; but, as he locked the door behind us, we heard him singing thoughtfully to himself:

*"He thought he saw a Garden-Door
That opened with a key:
He looked again, and found it was
A Double Rule of Three:
'And all its mystery', he said,
'Is clear as day to me!'"*

"I shall now return," said the Professor, when we had walked a few yards: "you see, it's impossible to read *here*, for all my books are in the house."

But the children still kept fast hold of his hands. *"Do come with us!"* Sylvie entreated with tears in her eyes.

"Well, well!" said the good-natured old man. "Perhaps I'll come after you, some day soon. But I *must* go back, *now*. You see I left off at a comma, and it's so awkward not knowing how the sentence finishes! Besides, you've got to go through Dogland first, and I'm always a little nervous about dogs. But it'll be quite easy to come, as soon as I've completed my new invention—for carrying one's-*self*, you know. It wants just a *little* more working out."

"Won't that be very tiring, to carry *yourself?*" Sylvie enquired.

"Well, no, my child. You see, whatever fatigue one incurs by *carrying*, one saves by *being carried!* Good-bye, dears! Good-bye, Sir!" he added to my intense surprise, giving my hand an affectionate squeeze.

"Good-bye, Professor!" I replied, but my voice sounded strange and far away, and the children took not the slightest notice of our farewell. Evidently they neither saw me nor heard me, as, with their arms lovingly twined round each other, they marched boldly on.

CHAPTER XIII

A Visit to Dogland

"THERE'S a house, away there to the left," said Sylvie after we had walked what seemed to me about fifty miles. "Let's go and ask for a night's lodging."

"It looks a very comfable house," Bruno said, as we turned into the road leading up to it. 'I doos hope the Dogs will be kind to us, I *is* so tired and hungry!"

A Mastiff, dressed in a scarlet collar, and carrying a musket, was pacing up and down, like a sentinel, in front of the entrance. He started, on catching sight of the children, and came forwards to meet them, keeping his musket pointed straight at Bruno, who stood quite still, though he turned pale and kept tight hold of Sylvie's hand, while the Sentinel walked solemnly round and round them, and looked at them from all points of view.

"Oobooh, hooh boohooyah!" he growled at last. "Woobah yahwah oobooh! Bow wahbah woobooyah? Bow wow?" he asked Bruno, severely.

Of course *Bruno* understood all this, easily enough. All Fairies understand Doggee—that is, Dog-language. But, as *you* may find it a little difficult, just at first, I had better put it into English for you. "Humans, I verily believe! A couple of stray Humans! What Dog do you belong to? What do you want?"

"We don't belong to a *Dog*!" Bruno began, in Doggee. ("Peoples *never* belongs to Dogs!" he whispered to Sylvie.)

But Sylvie hastily checked him, for fear of hurting the Mastiff's feelings. "Please, we want a little food, and a night's lodging—if there's room in the house," she added timidly. Sylvie spoke Doggee very prettily: but I think it's almost better, for *you*, to give the conversation in English.

"The *house*, indeed!" growled the Sentinel. "Have you never seen a *Palace* in your life? Come along with me! His Majesty must settle what's to be done with you."

345

They followed him through the entrance-hall, down a long passage, and into a magnificent Saloon, around which were grouped dogs of all sorts and sizes. Two splendid Blood-hounds were solemnly sitting up, one on each side of the crown-bearer. Two or three Bull-dogs—whom I guessed to be the Body-Guard of the King—were waiting in grim silence: in fact the only voices at all plainly audible were those of two little dogs, who had mounted a settee, and were holding a lively discussion that looked very like a quarrel.

"Lords and Ladies in Waiting, and various Court Officials," our guide gruffly remarked, as he led us in. Of *me* the Courtiers took no notice whatever: but Sylvie and Bruno were the subject of many inquisitive looks, and many whispered remarks, of which I only distinctly caught *one*—made by a sly-looking Dachshund to his friend—"Bah wooh wahyah hoobah Oobooh, *hah* bah?" ("She's not such a bad-looking Human, *is* she?")

Leaving the new arrivals in the centre of the Saloon, the Sentinel advanced to a door, at the further end of it, which bore an inscription, painted on it in Doggee, "Royal Kennel—Scratch and Yell."

Before doing this, the Sentinel turned to the children, and said "Give me your names."

"We'd rather not!" Bruno exclaimed, pulling Sylvie away from the door. "We want them ourselves. Come back, Sylvie! Come quick!"

"Nonsense!" said Sylvie very decidedly: and gave their names in Doggee.

Then the Sentinel scratched violently at the door, and gave a yell that made Bruno shiver from head to foot.

"Hooyah wah!" said a deep voice inside. (That's Doggee for "Come in!")

"It's the King himself!" the Mastiff whispered in an awestruck tone. "Take off your wigs, and lay them humbly at his paws." (What *we* should call "at his *feet*".)

Sylvie was just going to explain, very politely, that really they *couldn't* perform *that* ceremony, because their wigs wouldn't come off, when the door of the Royal Kennel opened, and an enormous Newfoundland Dog put his head out. "Bow wow?" was his first question.

"When His Majesty speaks to you", the Sentinel hastily whispered to Bruno, "you should prick up your ears!"

Bruno looked doubtfully at Sylvie. "I'd rather not, please," he said. "It would hurt."

"It doesn't hurt a bit!" the Sentinel said with some indignation. "Look! It's like this!" And he pricked up his ears like two railway signals.

Sylvie gently explained matters. "I'm afraid we ca'n't manage it," she said in a low voice. "I'm very sorry: but our ears haven't got the right——" she wanted to say "machinery" in Doggee: but she had forgotten the word, and could only think of "steam-engine".

The Sentinel repeated Sylvie's explanation to the King.

"Ca'n't prick up their ears without a steam-engine!" His Majesty exclaimed. "They *must* be curious creatures! I must have a look at them!" And he came out of his Kennel, and walked solemnly up to the children.

What was the amazement—not to say the horror—of the whole assembly, when Sylvie actually *patted His Majesty on the head*, while Bruno seized his long ears and pretended to tie them together under his chin!

The Sentinel groaned aloud: a beautiful Greyhound— who appeared to be one of the Ladies in Waiting—fainted away: and all the other Courtiers hastily drew back, and left plenty of room for the huge Newfoundland to spring upon the audacious strangers, and tear them limb from limb.

Only—he didn't. On the contrary His Majesty actually *smiled*—so far as a Dog *can* smile—and (the other Dogs couldn't believe their eyes, but it was true, all the same) His Majesty *wagged his tail!*

"Yah! Hooh hahwooh!" (that is "Well! I never!") was the universal cry.

His Majesty looked round him severely, and gave a slight growl, which produced instant silence. "Conduct

my friends to the banqueting-hall!" he said, laying such
an emphasis on *"my friends"* that several of the dogs
rolled over helplessly on their backs and began to lick
Bruno's feet.

A procession was formed, but I only ventured to follow
as far as the *door* of the banqueting-hall, so furious was
the uproar of barking dogs within. So I sat down by the
King, who seemed to have gone to sleep, and waited till
the children returned to say good-night, when His
Majesty got up and shook himself.

"Time for bed!" he said with a sleepy yawn. "The
attendants will show you your room," he added, aside, to
Sylvie and Bruno. "Bring lights!" And, with a dignified
air, he held out his paw for them to kiss.

But the children were evidently not well practised in
Court-manners. Sylvie simply stroked the great paw:
Bruno hugged it: the Master of Ceremonies looked
shocked.

All this time Dog-waiters, in splendid livery, were running up with lighted candles: but, as fast as they put them
upon the table, other waiters ran away with them, so that
there never seemed to be one for *me*, though the Master
kept nudging me with his elbow, and repeating "I ca'n't
let you sleep *here!* You're not in *bed*, you know!"

I made a great effort, and just succeeded in getting out
the words "I know I'm not. I'm in an arm-chair."

"Well, forty winks will do you no harm," the Master
said, and left me. I could scarcely hear his words: and no
wonder: he was leaning over the side of a ship, that was
miles away from the pier on which I stood. The ship
passed over the horizon, and I sank back into the arm-
chair.

The next thing I remember is that it was morning:
breakfast was just over: Sylvie was lifting Bruno down
from a high chair, and saying to a Spaniel, who was
regarding them with a most benevolent smile, "Yes, thank
you, we've had a *very* nice breakfast. Haven't we,
Bruno?"

"There was too many bones in the——" Bruno began, but Sylvie frowned at him, and laid her finger on her lips, for, at this moment, the travelers were waited on by a very dignified officer, the Head-Growler, whose duty it was, first to conduct them to the King to bid him fare-well, and then to escort them to the boundary of Dogland. The great Newfoundland received them most affably, but, instead of saying "good-bye", he startled the Head-Growler into giving three savage growls, by announcing that he would escort them himself.

"It is a most unusual proceeding, your Majesty!" the Head-Growler exclaimed, almost choking with vexation at being set aside, for he had put on his best Court-suit, made entirely of cat-skins, for the occasion.

"I shall escort them myself," His Majesty repeated, gently but firmly, laying aside the Royal robes, and changing his crown for a small coronet, "and you may stay at home."

"I *are* glad!" Bruno whispered to Sylvie, when they had got well out of hearing. "He were so *welly* cross!" And he not only patted their Royal escort, but even hugged him round the neck in the exuberance of his delight.

His Majesty calmly wagged the Royal tail. "It's quite a relief", he said, "getting away from that Palace now and then! Royal Dogs have a dull life of it, I can tell you! Would you mind" (this to Sylvie, in a low voice, and looking a little shy and embarrassed) "would you mind the trouble of just throwing that stick for me to fetch?"

Sylvie was too much astonished to do anything for a moment: it sounded such a monstrous impossibility that a *King* should wish to run after a stick. But *Bruno* was equal to the occasion, and with a glad shout of "Hi then! Fetch it, good Doggie!" he hurled it over a clump of bushes. The next moment the Monarch of Dogland had bounded over the bushes, and picked up the stick, and came galloping back to the children with it in his mouth. Bruno took it from him with great decision. "Beg for it"!

he insisted; and His Majesty begged. "Paw!" commanded Sylvie; and His Majesty gave his paw. In short, the solemn ceremony of escorting the travelers to the boundaries of Dogland became one long uproarious game of play!

"But business is business!" the Dog-King said at last. "And I must go back to mine. I couldn't come any further," he added, consulting a dog-watch, which hung on a chain round his neck, "not even if there were a *Cat* in sight!"

They took an affectionate farewell of His Majesty, and trudged on.

"That *were* a dear dog!" Bruno exclaimed. "Has we to go far, Sylvie? I's tired!"

"Not much further, darling!" Sylvie gently replied. "Do you see that shining, just beyond those trees? I'm almost *sure* it's the gate of Fairyland! I know it's all golden—Father told me so—and so bright, so bright!" she went on dreamily.

"It dazzles!" said Bruno, shading his eyes with one little hand, while the other clung tightly to Sylvie's hand, as if he were half-alarmed at her strange manner.

For the child moved on as if walking in her sleep, her large eyes gazing into the far distance, and her breath coming and going in quick pantings of eager delight. I knew, by some mysterious mental light, that a great change was taking place in my sweet little friend (for such I loved to think her) and that she was passing from the condition of a mere Outland Sprite into the true Fairy-nature.

Upon Bruno the change came later: but it was completed in both before they reached the golden gate, through which I knew it would be impossible for *me* to follow. I could but stand outside, and take a last look at the two sweet children, ere they disappeared within, and the golden gate closed with a bang.

And with *such* a bang! "It never *will* shut like any other cupboard-door," Arthur explained. "There's something wrong with the hinge. However, here's the cake and wine. And you've had your forty winks. So you really *must* get off to bed, old man! You're fit for nothing else. Witness my hand, Arthur Forester, M.D."

By this time I was wide-awake again. "Not *quite* yet!" I pleaded. "Really I'm not sleepy now. And it isn't midnight yet."

"Well, I did want to say another word to you," Arthur replied in a relenting tone, as he supplied me with the supper he had prescribed. "Only I thought you were too sleepy for it to-night."

We took our midnight meal almost in silence; for an unusual nervousness seemed to have seized on my old friend.

"What kind of a night is it?" he asked, rising and undrawing the window-curtains, apparently to change the subject for a minute. I followed him to the window, and we stood together, looking out, in silence.

"When I first spoke to you about——" Arthur began, after a long and embarrassing silence, "that is, when we first talked about her—for I think it was *you* that introduced the subject—my own position in life forbade me to do more than worship her from a distance: and I was turning over plans for leaving this place finally, and settling somewhere out of all chance of meeting her again. That seemed to be my only chance of usefulness in life."

"Would that have been wise?" I said. "To leave yourself no hope at all?"

"There *was* no hope to leave," Arthur firmly replied, though his eyes glittered with tears as he gazed upwards into the midnight sky, from which one solitary star, the glorious "Vega", blazed out in fitful splendour through the driving clouds. "She was like that star to me—bright, beautiful, and pure, but out of reach, out of reach!"

He drew the curtains again, and we returned to our places by the fireside.

"What I wanted to tell you was this," he resumed. "I heard this evening from my solicitor. I can't go into the details of the business, but the upshot is that my worldly wealth is much more than I thought, and I am (or shall soon be) in a position to offer marriage, without imprudence, to any lady, even if she brought nothing, I doubt if there would be anything on *her* side: the Earl is poor, I believe. But I should have enough for both, even if health failed.''

"I wish you all happiness in your married life!" I cried. "Shall you speak to the Earl to-morrow?"

"Not yet awhile," said Arthur. "He is very friendly, but I dare not think he means more than that, as yet. And as for—as for Lady Muriel, try as I may, I *cannot* read her feelings towards me. If there *is* love, she is hiding it! No, I must wait, I must wait!"

I did not like to press any further advice on my friend, whose judgment, I felt, was so much more sober and thoughtful than my own; and we parted without more words on the subject that had now absorbed his thoughts, nay, his very life.

The next morning a letter from *my* solicitor arrived, summoning me to town on important business.

CHAPTER XIV

Fairy-Sylvie

FOR a full month the business, for which I had returned to London, detained me there: and even then it was only the urgent advice of my physician that induced me to leave it unfinished and pay another visit to Elveston.

Arthur had written once or twice during the month; but in none of his letters was there any mention of Lady Muriel. Still, I did not augur ill from his silence: to me it looked like the natural action of a lover, who, even while his heart was singing "She is mine", would fear to paint his happiness in the cold phrases of a written letter, but would wait to tell it by word of mouth. "Yes," I thought, "I am to hear his song of triumph from his own lips!"

The night I arrived we had much to say on other matters: and, tired with the journey, I went to bed early, leaving the happy secret still untold. Next day, however, as we chatted on over the remains of luncheon, I ventured to put the momentous question. "Well, old friend, you have told me nothing of Lady Muriel—nor when the happy day is to be?"

"The happy day", Arthur said, looking unexpectedly grave, "is yet in the dim future. We need to know—or, rather, *she* needs to know *me* better. I know *her* sweet nature, thoroughly, by this time. But I dare not speak till I am sure that my love is returned."

"Don't wait too long!" I said gaily. "Faint heart never won fair lady!"

"It *is* 'faint heart' perhaps. But really I *dare* not speak just yet."

"But meanwhile", I pleaded, "you are running a risk that perhaps you have not thought of. Some other man——"

"No," said Arthur firmly. "She is heart-whole: I am sure of that. Yet, if she loves another better than me, so be it! I will not spoil her happiness. The secret shall die with me. But she is my first—and my *only* love!"

"That is all very beautiful *sentiment*," I said, "but it is not *practical*. It is not like *you*.

> *He either fears his fate too much*
> *Or his desert is small,*
> *Who dares not put it to the touch,*
> *To win or lose it all."*

"I *dare* not ask the question whether there is another!" he said passionately. "It would break my heart to know it!"

"Yet is it wise to leave it unasked? You must not waste your life upon an 'if'!"

"I tell you I *dare* not!"

"May *I* find it out for you?" I asked, with the freedom of an old friend.

"No, no!" he replied with a pained look. "I entreat you to say nothing. Let it wait."

"As you please," I said: and judged it best to say no more just then. "But this evening", I thought, "I will call on the Earl. I may be able to *see* how the land lies, without so much as saying a word!"

It was a very hot afternoon—too hot to go for a walk or do anything—or else it wouldn't have happened, I believe.

In the first place, I want to know—dear Child who reads this!—why Fairies should always be teaching *us* to do our duty, and lecturing *us* when we go wrong, and we should never teach them anything? You can't mean to say that Fairies are never greedy, or selfish, or cross, or deceitful, because that would be nonsense, you know. Well then, don't you think they might be all the better for a little lecturing and punishing now and then?

I really don't see why it shouldn't be tried, and I'm almost sure that, if you could only catch a Fairy, and put it in the corner, and give it nothing but bread and water for a day or two, you'd find it quite an improved character —it would take down its conceit a little, at all events.

The next question is, what is the best time for seeing Fairies? I believe I can tell you all about that.

The first rule is, that it must be a *very* hot day—that we may consider as settled: and you must be just a *little* sleepy—but not too sleepy to keep your eyes open, mind. Well, and you ought to feel a little—what one may call "fairyish"—the Scotch call it "eerie", and perhaps that's a prettier word; if you don't know what it means, I'm afraid I can hardly explain it; you must wait till you meet a Fairy, and then you'll know.

And the last rule is, that the crickets should not be chirping. I can't stop to explain that: you must take it on trust for the present.

So, if all these things happen together, you have a good chance of seeing a Fairy—or at least a much better chance than if they didn't.

The first thing I noticed, as I went lazily along through an open place in the wood, was a large Beetle lying struggling on its back, and I went down upon one knee to help the poor thing to its feet again. In some things, you know, you ca'n't be quite sure what an insect would like: for instance, I never could quite settle, supposing I were a moth, whether I would rather be kept out of the candle, or be allowed to fly straight in and get burnt—or again, supposing I were a spider, I'm not sure if I should be *quite* pleased to have my web torn down, and the fly let loose— but I feel quite certain that, if I were a beetle and had rolled over on my back, I should always be glad to be helped up again.

So, as I was saying, I had gone down upon one knee and was just reaching out a little stick to turn the Beetle over, when I saw a sight that made me draw back hastily and hold my breath, for fear of making any noise and frightening the little creature away.

Not that she looked as if she would be easily frightened: she seemed so good and gentle that I'm sure she would never expect that any one could wish to hurt her. She was only a few inches high, and was dressed in green, so that you really would hardly have noticed her among the long grass; and she was so delicate and graceful that she quite seemed to belong to the place, almost as if she were one of the flowers. I may tell you, besides, that she had no wings (I don't believe in Fairies with wings), and that she had quantities of long brown hair and large earnest brown eyes, and then I shall have done all I can to give you an idea of her.

Sylvie (I found out her name afterwards) had knelt down, just as I was doing, to help the Beetle; but it needed more than a little stick for *her* to get it on its legs again; it was as much as she could do, with both arms, to roll the heavy thing over; and all the while she was talking to it, half scolding and half comforting, as a nurse might do with a child that had fallen down.

"There, there! You needn't cry so much about it. You're not killed yet—though if you were, you couldn't cry, you know, and so it's a general rule against crying, my dear! And how did you come to tumble over? But I can see well enough how it was—I needn't ask you that—walking over sand-pits with your chin in the air, as usual. Of course if you go among sand-pits like that, you must expect to tumble. You should look."

The Beetle murmured something that sounded like "I *did* look," and Sylvie went on again.

"But I know you didn't! You never do! You always walk with your chin up—you're so dreadfully conceited. Well, let's see how many legs are broken this time. Why, none of them, I declare! And what's the good of having six legs, my dear, if you can only kick them all about in the air when you tumble? Legs are meant to walk with, you know. Now don't begin putting out your wings yet; I've more to say. Go to the frog that lives behind that buttercup—give him my compliments—Sylvie's compliments—can you say 'compliments'?"

The Beetle tried, and, I suppose, succeeded.

"Yes, that's right. And tell him he's to give you some of that salve I left with him yesterday. And you'd better get him to rub it in for you. He's got rather cold hands, but you mustn't mind that."

I think the Beetle must have shuddered at this idea, for Sylvie went on in a graver tone. "Now you needn't pretend to be so particular as all that, as if you were too grand to be rubbed by a frog. The fact is, you ought to be very much obliged to him. Suppose you could get nobody but a toad to do it, how would you like *that?*"

There was a little pause, and then Sylvie added "Now you may go. Be a good beetle, and don't keep your chin in the air." And then began one of those performances of humming, and whizzing, and restless banging about, such as a beetle indulges in when it has decided on flying, but hasn't quite made up its mind which way to go. At last, in one of its awkward zig-zags, it managed to fly right into my face, and, by the time I had recovered from the shock, the little Fairy was gone.

I looked about in all directions for the little creature, but there was no trace of her—and my "eerie" feeling was quite gone off, and the crickets were chirping again merrily—so I knew she was really gone.

And now I've got time to tell you the rule about the crickets. They always leave off chirping when a Fairy goes by—because a Fairy's a kind of queen over them, I suppose—at all events it's a much grander thing than a cricket—so whenever you're walking out, and the crickets suddenly leave off chirping, you may be sure that they see a Fairy.

I walked on sadly enough, you may be sure. However, I comforted myself with thinking "It's been a very wonderful afternoon, so far. I'll just go quietly on and look about me, and I shouldn't wonder if I were to come across another Fairy somewhere."

Peering about in this way, I happened to notice a plant with rounded leaves, and with queer little holes cut in the middle of several of them. "Ah, the leafcutter bee!" I carelessly remarked—you know I am very learned in Natural History (for instance, I can always tell kittens from chickens at one glance)—and I was passing on, when a sudden thought made me stoop down and examine the leaves.

Then a little thrill of delight ran through me—for I noticed that the holes were all arranged so as to form letters; there were three leaves side by side, with "B", "R", and "U" marked on them, and after some search I found two more, which contained an "N" and an "O".

And then, all in a moment, a flash of inner light seemed to illumine a part of my life that had all but faded into oblivion—the strange visions I had experienced during my journey to Elveston: and with a thrill of delight I thought "Those visions are destined to be linked with my waking life!"

By this time the "eerie" feeling had come back again, and I suddenly observed that no crickets were chirping, so I felt quite sure that "Bruno" was somewhere very near.

And so indeed he was—so near that I had very nearly walked over him without seeing him; which would have been dreadful, always supposing that Fairies *can* be walked over—my own belief is that they are something of the nature of Will-o'-the-Wisps: and there's no walking over *them*.

Think of any pretty little boy you know, with rosy cheeks, large dark eyes, and tangled brown hair, and then fancy him made small enough to go comfortably into a coffee-cup, and you'll have a very fair idea of him.

"What's you name, little one?" I began, in as soft a voice as I could manage. And, by the way, why is it we always begin by asking little children their names? Is it because we fancy a name will help to make them a little bigger? You never thought of asking a real large man his name, now, did you? But, however that may be, I felt it quite necessary to know *his* name; so, as he didn't answer my question, I asked it again a little louder. "What's your name, my little man?"

"What's oors?" he said, without looking up.

I told him my name quite gently, for he was much too small to be angry with.

"Duke of Anything?" he asked, just looking at me for a moment, and then going on with his work.

"Not Duke at all," I said, a little ashamed of having to confess it.

"Oo're big enough to be two Dukes," said the little creature. "I suppose oo're Sir Something, then?"

"No," I said, feeling more and more ashamed. "I haven't got any title."

The Fairy seemed to think that in that case I really wasn't worth the trouble of talking to, for he quietly went on digging, and tearing the flowers to pieces.

After a few minutes I tried again. "*Please* tell me what your name is."

"Bruno," the little fellow answered, very readily. "Why didn't oo say 'please' before?"

"That's something like what we used to be taught in the nursery," I thought to myself, looking back through the long years (about a hundred of them, since you ask the question), to the time when I was a little child. And here an idea came into my head, and I asked him "Aren't you one of the Fairies that teach children to be good?"

"Well, we have to do that sometimes," said Bruno, "and a dreadful bother it is." As he said this, he savagely tore a heartsease in two, and trampled on the pieces.

"What *are* you doing there, Bruno?" I said.

"Spoiling Sylvie's garden," was all the answer Bruno would give at first. But, as he went on tearing up the flowers, he muttered to himself "The nasty cross thing—wouldn't let me go and play this morning—said I must finish my lessons first—lessons, indeed! I'll vex her finely, though!"

"Oh, Bruno, you shouldn't do that!" I cried. "Don't you know that's revenge? And revenge is a wicked, cruel, dangerous thing!"

"River-edge?" said Bruno. "What a funny word! I suppose oo call it cruel and dangerous 'cause, if oo wented too far and tumbleded in, oo'd get drownded."

"No, not river-edge," I explained: "revenge" (saying the word very slowly). But I couldn't help thinking that Bruno's explanation did very well for either word.

"Oh!" said Bruno, opening his eyes very wide, but without trying to repeat the word.

"Come! Try to pronounce it, Bruno!" I said, cheerfully. "Re-venge, re-venge."

But Bruno only tossed his little head, and said he couldn't; that his mouth wasn't the right shape for words of that kind. And the more I laughed, the more sulky the little fellow got about it.

"Well, never mind, my little man!" I said. "Shall I help you with that job?"

"Yes, please," Bruno said, quite pacified. "Only I wiss I could think of somefin to vex her more than this. Oo don't know how hard it is to make her angry!"

"Now listen to me, Bruno, and I'll teach you quite a splendid kind of revenge!"

"Somefin that'll vex her finely?" he asked with gleaming eyes.

"Something that will vex her finely. First, we'll get up all the weeds in her garden. See, there are a good many at this end—quite hiding the flowers."

"But *that* won't vex her!" said Bruno.

"After that", I said, without noticing the remark, "we'll water this highest bed—up here. You see it's getting quite dry and dusty."

Bruno looked at me inquisitively, but he said nothing this time.

"Then after that," I went on, "the walks want sweeping a bit; and I think you might cut down that tall nettle—it's so close to the garden that it's quite in the way——"

"What *is* oo talking about?" Bruno impatiently interrupted me. "All that won't vex her a bit!"

"Won't it?" I said, innocently. "Then, after that, suppose we put in some of those coloured pebbles—just to mark the divisions between the different kinds of flowers, you know. That'll have a very pretty effect."

Bruno turned round and had another good stare at me. At last there came an odd little twinkle into his eyes, and he said, with quite a new meaning in his voice, "That'll do nicely. Let's put 'em in rows—all the red together, and all the blue together."

"That'll do capitally," I said; "and then—what kind of flowers does Sylvie like best?"

Bruno had to put his thumb in his mouth and consider a little before he could answer. "Violets," he said, at last.

"There's a beautiful bed of violets down by the brook——"

"Oh, let's fetch 'em!" cried Bruno, giving a little skip into the air. "Here! Catch hold of my hand, and I'll help oo along. The grass is rather thick down that way."

I couldn't help laughing at his having so entirely forgotten what a big creature he was talking to. "No, not yet, Bruno," I said: "we must consider what's the right thing to do first. You see we've got quite a business before us."

"Yes, let's consider," said Bruno, putting his thumb into his mouth again, and sitting down upon a dead mouse.

"What do you keep that mouse for?" I said. "You should either bury it, or else throw it into the brook."

"Why, it's to measure with!" cried Bruno. "How ever would oo do a garden without one? We make each bed three mouses and a half long, and two mouses wide."

I stopped him, as he was dragging it off by the tail to show me how it was used, for I was half afraid the "eerie" feeling might go off before we had finished the garden, and in that case I should see no more of him or Sylvie. "I think the best way will be for *you* to weed the beds, while *I* sort out these pebbles, ready to mark the walks with."

"That's it!" cried Bruno. "And I'll tell oo about the caterpillars while we work."

"Ah, let's hear about the caterpillars," I said as I drew the pebbles together into a heap and began dividing them into colours.

And Bruno went on in a low, rapid tone, more as if he were talking to himself. "Yesterday I saw two little caterpillars, when I was sitting by the brook, just where oo go into the wood. They were quite green, and they had yellow eyes, and they didn't see *me*. And one of them had got a moth's wing to carry—a great brown moth's wing, oo know, all dry, with feathers. So he couldn't want it to eat, I should think—perhaps he meant to make a cloak for the winter?"

"Perhaps," I said, for Bruno had twisted up the last word into a sort of question, and was looking at me for an answer.

One word was quite enough for the little fellow, and he went on merrily. "Well, and so he didn't want the other caterpillar to see the moth's wing, oo know—so what must he do but try to carry it with all his left legs, and he tried to walk on the other set. Of course he toppled over after that."

"After what?" I said, catching at the last word, for, to tell the truth, I hadn't been attending much.

"He toppled over," Bruno repeated, very gravely, "and if *oo* ever saw a caterpillar topple over, oo'd know it's a welly serious thing, and not sit grinning like that—and I sha'n't tell oo no more!"

"Indeed and indeed, Bruno, I didn't mean to grin. See, I'm quite grave again now."

But Bruno only folded his arms, and said "Don't tell *me*. I see a little twinkle in one of oor eyes—just like the moon."

"Why do you think I'm like the moon, Bruno?" I asked.

"Oor face is large and round like the moon," Bruno answered, looking at me thoughtfully. "It doesn't shine quite so bright—but it's more cleaner."

I couldn't help smiling at this. "You know I sometimes wash *my* face, Bruno. The moon never does that."

"Oh, doosn't she though!" cried Bruno; and he leant forwards and added in a solemn whisper, "The moon's face gets dirtier and dirtier every night, till it's black all across. And then, when it's dirty all over—*so*—" (he passed his hand across his own rosy cheeks as he spoke) "then she washes it."

"Then it's all clean again, isn't it?"

"Not all in a moment," said Bruno. "What a deal of teaching oo wants! She washes it little by little—only she begins at the other edge, oo know.

By this time he was sitting quietly on the dead mouse with his arms folded, and the weeding wasn't getting on a bit: so I had to say "Work first, pleasure afterwards: no more talking till that bed's finished."

CHAPTER XV

Bruno's Revenge

AFTER that we had a few minutes of silence, while I sorted out the pebbles, and amused myself with watching Bruno's plan of gardening. It was quite a new plan to me: he always measured each bed before he weeded it, as if he was afraid the weeding would make it shrink; and once, when it came out longer than he wished, he set to work to thump the mouse with his little fist, crying out "There now! It's all gone wrong again! Why don't oo keep oor tail straight when I tell oo!"

"I'll tell oo what I'll do," Bruno said in a half-whisper, as we worked. "Oo like Fairies, don't oo?"

"Yes," I said: "of course I do, or I shouldn't have come here. I should have gone to some place where there are no Fairies."

Bruno laughed contemptuously. "Why, oo might as well say oo'd go to some place where there wasn't any air—supposing oo didn't like air!"

This was a rather difficult idea to grasp. I tried a change of subject. "You're nearly the first Fairy I ever saw. Have *you* ever seen any people besides me?"

"Plenty!" said Bruno. "We see 'em when we walk in the road."

"But they ca'n't see *you*. How is it they never tread on you?"

"Ca'n't *tread* on us," said Bruno, looking amused at my ignorance. "Why, suppose oo're walking, here—so—" (making little marks on the ground) "and suppose there's a Fairy—that's me—walking *here*. Very well then, oo put one foot here, and one foot here, and so oo doesn't tread on the Fairy."

This was all very well as an explanation, but it didn't convince me. "Why shouldn't I put one foot *on* the Fairy?" I asked.

"I don't know *why*," the little fellow said in a thoughtful tone. "But I know oo *wouldn't*. Nobody never walked on the top of a Fairy. Now I'll tell oo what I'll do, as oo're so fond of Fairies. I'll get oo an invitation to the Fairy-King's dinner-party. I know one of the head-waiters."

I couldn't help laughing at this idea. "Do the waiters invite the guests?" I asked.

"Oh, not *to sit down!*" Bruno said. "But to wait at table. Oo'd like that, wouldn't oo? To hand about plates, and so on."

"Well, but that's not so nice as sitting at the table, is it?"

"Of course it isn't," Bruno said, in a tone as if he rather pitied my ignorance; "but if oo're not even Sir Anything, oo ca'n't expect to be allowed to sit at the table, oo know."

I said, as meekly as I could, that I didn't expect it, but it was the only way of going to a dinner-party that I really enjoyed. And Bruno tossed his head, and said, in a rather offended tone, that I might do as I pleased—there were many he knew that would give their ears to go.

"Have you ever been yourself, Bruno?"

"They invited me once, last week," Bruno said, very gravely. "It was to wash up the soup-plates—no, the cheese-plates I mean—that was grand enough. And I waited at table. And I didn't hardly make only *one* mistake."

"What was it?" I said. "You needn't mind telling *me*."

"Only bringing scissors to cut the beef with," Bruno said carelessly. "But the grandest thing of all was, *I* fetched the King a glass of cider!"

"That *was* grand!" I said, biting my lip to keep myself from laughing.

"Wasn't it?" said Bruno, very earnestly. "Oo know it isn't every one that's had such an honour as *that!*"

This set me thinking of the various queer things we call "an honour" in this world, but which, after all, haven't a bit more honour in them than what Bruno enjoyed, when he took the King a glass of cider.

I don't know how long I might not have dreamed on in this way, if Bruno hadn't suddenly roused me. "Oh, come here quick!" he cried, in a state of the wildest excitement. "Catch hold of his other horn! I ca'n't hold him more than a minute!"

He was struggling desperately with a great snail, clinging to one of its horns, and nearly breaking his poor little back in his efforts to drag it over a blade of grass.

I saw we should have no more gardening if I let this sort of thing go on, so I quietly took the snail away, and put it on a bank where he couldn't reach it. "We'll hunt it afterwards, Bruno," I said, "if you really want to catch it. But what's the use of it when you've got it?"

"What's the use of a fox when oo've got it?" said Bruno. "I know oo big things hunt foxes."

I tried to think of some good reason why "big things" should hunt foxes, and he should not hunt snails, but none came into my head: so I said at last, "Well, I suppose one's as good as the other. I'll go snail-hunting myself some day."

"I should think oo wouldn't be so silly", said Bruno, "as to go snail-hunting by oorself. Why, oo'd never get the snail along, if oo hadn't somebody to hold on to his other horn!"

"Of course I sha'n't go *alone*," I said, quite gravely. "By the way, is that the best kind to hunt, or do you recommend the ones without shells?"

"Oh, no, we never hunt the ones without shells," Bruno said, with a little shudder at the thought of it. "They're always so cross about it; and then, if oo tumbles over them, they're ever so sticky!"

By this time we had nearly finished the garden. I had fetched some violets, and Bruno was just helping me to put in the last, when he suddenly stopped and said "I'm tired."

"Rest then," I said: "I can go on without you, quite well."

Bruno needed no second invitation: he at once began

arranging the dead mouse as a kind of sofa. "And I'll sing oo a little song," he said, as he rolled it about.

"Do," said I: "I like songs very much."

"Which song will oo choose?" Bruno said, as he dragged the mouse into a place where he could get a good view of me. " 'Ting, ting, ting' is the nicest."

There was no resisting such a strong hint as this: however, I pretended to think about it for a moment, and then said "Well, I like 'Ting, ting, ting' best of all."

"That shows oo're a good judge of music," Bruno said, with a pleased look. "How many hare-bells would oo like?" And he put his thumb into his mouth to help me to consider.

As there was only one cluster of hare-bells within easy reach, I said very gravely that I thought one would do *this* time, and I picked it and gave it to him. Bruno ran his hand once or twice up and down the flowers, like a musician trying an instrument, producing a most delicious delicate tinkling as he did so. I had never heard flower-music before—I don't think one can, unless one's in the "eerie" state—and I don't know quite how to give you an idea of what it was like, except by saying that it sounded like a peal of bells a thousand miles off. When he had satisfied himself that the flowers were in tune, he seated himself on the dead mouse (he never seemed really comfortable anywhere else), and, looking up at me with a merry twinkle in his eyes, he began. By the way, the tune was rather a curious one, and you might like to try it yourself, so here are the notes.

"Rise, oh, rise! The daylight dies:
The owls are hooting, ting, ting, ting!
Wake, oh, wake! Beside the lake
The elves are fluting, ting, ting, ting!
Welcoming our Fairy King,
We sing, sing, sing."

He sang the first four lines briskly and merrily, making the hare-bells chime in time with the music; but the last two he sang quite slowly and gently, and merely waved the flowers backwards and forwards. Then he left off to explain. "The Fairy-King is Oberon, and he lives across the lake—and sometimes he comes in a little boat—and we go and meet him—and then we sing this song, you know."

"And then you go and dine with him?" I said, mischievously.

"Oo shouldn't talk," Bruno hastily said: "it interrupts the song so."

I said I wouldn't do it again.

"I never talk myself when I'm singing," he went on very gravely: "so *oo* shouldn't either." Then he tuned the hare-bells once more, and sang:

"Hear, oh, hear! From far and near
The music stealing, ting, ting, ting!
Fairy bells adown the dells
Are merrily pealing, ting, ting, ting!
Welcoming our Fairy King,
We ring, ring, ring.

"See, oh, see! On every tree
What lamps are shining, ting, ting, ting!
They are eyes of fiery flies
To light our dining, ting, ting, ting!
Welcoming our Fairy King
They swing, swing, swing.

"Haste, oh, haste, to take and taste
The dainties waiting, ting, ting, ting!
Honey-dew is stored ——"

"Hush, Bruno!" I interrupted in a warning whisper. "She's coming!"

Bruno checked his song, and, as she slowly made her way through the long grass, he suddenly rushed out head-long at her like a little bull, shouting "Look the other way! Look the other way!"

"Which way?" Sylvie asked, in rather a frightened tone, as she looked round in all directions to see where the danger could be.

"*That* way!" said Bruno, carefully turning her round with her face to the wood. "Now, walk backwards—walk gently—don't be frightened: oo sha'n't trip!"

But Sylvie *did* trip notwithstanding: in fact he led her, in his hurry, across so many little sticks and stones, that it was really a wonder the poor child could keep on her feet at all. But he was far too much excited to think of what he was doing.

I silently pointed out to Bruno the best place to lead her to, so as to get a view of the whole garden at once: it was a little rising ground, about the height of a potato; and, when they had mounted it, I drew back into the shade, that Sylvie mightn't see me.

I heard Bruno cry out triumphantly "*Now* oo may look!" and then followed a clapping of hands, but it was all done by Bruno himself. Sylvie was silent—she only stood and gazed with her hands clasped together, and I was half afraid she didn't like it after all.

Bruno too was watching her anxiously, and when she jumped down off the mound, and began wandering up and down the little walks, he cautiously followed her about, evidently anxious that she should form her own opinion of it all, without any hint from him. And when at last she drew a long breath, and gave her verdict—in a hurried whisper, and without the slightest regard to grammar—"It's the loveliest thing as I never saw in all my life before!" the little fellow looked as well pleased as if it had been given by all the judges and juries in England put together.

"And did you really do it all by yourself, Bruno?" said Sylvie. "And all for me?"

"I was helped a bit," Bruno began, with a merry little laugh at her surprise. "We've been at it all the afternoon —I thought oo'd like——" and here the poor little fellow's lip began to quiver, and all in a moment he burst out crying, and running up to Sylvie he flung his arms passionately round her neck, and hid his face on her shoulder.

There was a little quiver in Sylvie's voice too, as she whispered "Why, what's the matter, darling?" and tried to lift up his head and kiss him.

But Bruno only clung to her, sobbing, and wouldn't be comforted till he had confessed. "I tried—to spoil oor garden—first—but I'll never—never——" and then came another burst of tears, which drowned the rest of the sentence. At last he got out the words "I liked—putting in the flowers—for *oo*, Sylvie—and I never was so happy before." And the rosy little face came up at last to be kissed, all wet with tears as it was.

Sylvie was crying too by this time, and she said nothing but "Bruno, dear!" and "*I* never was so happy before," though why these two children who had never been so happy before should both be crying was a mystery to *me*.

I felt very happy too, but of course I didn't cry: "big things" never do, you know—we leave all that to the Fairies. Only I think it must have been raining a little just then, for I found a drop or two on my cheeks.

After that they went through the whole garden again, flower by flower, as if it were a long sentence they were spelling out, with kisses for commas, and a great hug by way of a full-stop when they got to the end.

"Doos oo know, that was my river-edge, Sylvie?" Bruno solemnly began.

Sylvie laughed merrily. "What *do* you mean?" she said. And she pushed back her heavy brown hair with both hands, and looked at him with dancing eyes in which the big tear-drops were still glittering.

Bruno drew in a long breath, and made up his mouth for

a great effort. "I mean re—venge," he said: "now oo under'tand." And he looked so happy and proud at having
said the word right at last, that I quite envied him. I rather think Sylvie didn't "under'tand" at all; but she gave
him a little kiss on each cheek, which seemed to do just as
well.

So they wandered off lovingly together, in among the
buttercups, each with an arm twined round the other,
whispering and laughing as they went, and never so much
as once looked back at poor me. Yes, once, just before I
quite lost sight of them, Bruno half turned his head, and
nodded me a saucy little good-bye over one shoulder. And
that was all the thanks I got for *my* trouble. The very last
thing I saw of them was this—Sylvie was stooping down
with her arms round Bruno's neck, and saying coaxingly
in his ear, "Do you know, Bruno, I've quite forgotten that
hard word. Do say it once more. Come! Only this once,
dear!"

But Bruno wouldn't try it again.

Chapter XVI

A Changed Crocodile

The Marvellous—the Mysterious—had quite passed out
of my life for the moment: and the Common-place reigned
supreme. I turned in the direction of the Earl's house,
as it was now "the witching hour" of five, and I knew I
should find them ready for a cup of tea and a quiet chat.

Lady Muriel and her father gave me a delightfully
warm welcome. They were not of the folk we meet in
fashionable drawing-rooms—who conceal all such feelings as they may chance to possess beneath the impenetrable mask of a conventional placidity. "The Man with
the Iron Mask" was, no doubt, a rarity and a marvel in his
own age: in modern London no one would turn his head
to give him a second look! No, these were *real* people.

When they *looked* pleased, it meant that they *were* pleased: and when Lady Muriel said, with a bright smile, "I'm *very* glad to see you again!" I knew that it was *true*.

Still I did not venture to disobey the injunctions—crazy as I felt them to be—of the love-sick young Doctor, by so much as alluding to his existence: and it was only after they had given me full details of a projected Picnic, to which they invited me, that Lady Muriel exclaimed, almost as an after-thought, "and *do*, if you can, bring Doctor Forester with you! I'm sure a day in the country would do him good. I'm afraid he studies too much——"

It was "on the tip of my tongue" to quote the words "His only books are woman's looks!" but I checked myself just in time—with something of the feeling of one who has crossed a street, and has been all but run over by a passing "Hansom".

"—and I think he has too lonely a life," she went on, with a gentle earnestness that left no room whatever to suspect a double meaning. "*Do* get him to come! And don't forget the day, Tuesday week. We can drive you over. It would be a pity to go by rail—there is so much pretty scenery on the road. And our open carriage just holds four."

"Oh, *I'll* persuade him to come!" I said with confidence —thinking "it would take all *my* powers of persuasion to keep him away!"

The Picnic was to take place in ten days: and though Arthur readily accepted the invitation I brought him, nothing that I could say would induce him to call—either with me or without me—on the Earl and his daughter in the meanwhile. No: he feared to "wear out his welcome", he said: they had "seen enough of him for one while": and, when at last the day for the expedition arrived, he was so childishly nervous and uneasy that I thought it best so to arrange our plans that we should go separately to the house—my intention being to arrive some time after him, so as to give him time to get over a meeting.

With this object I purposely made a considerable circuit

on my way to the Hall (as we called the Earl's house):
"and if I could only manage to lose my way a bit," I
thought to myself, "that would suit me capitally!"

In this I succeeded better, and sooner, than I had ventured to hope for. The path through the wood had been
made familiar to me, by many a solitary stroll, in my former visit to Elveston; and how I could have so suddenly
and so entirely lost it—even though I *was* so engrossed in
thinking of Arthur and his lady-love that I heeded little
else—was a mystery to me. "And this open place", I said
to myself, "seems to have some memory about it I cannot
distinctly recall—surely it is the very spot where I saw
those Fairy-Children! But I hope there are no snakes
about!" I mused aloud, taking my seat on a fallen tree. "I
certainly do *not* like snakes—and I don't suppose *Bruno*
likes them, either!"

"No, he *doesn't* like them!" said a demure little voice at
my side. "He's not *afraid* of them, you know. But he does-
n't *like* them. He says they're too waggly!"

Words fail me to describe the beauty of the little group
—couched on a patch of moss, on the trunk of the fallen
tree, that met my eager gaze: Sylvie reclining with her elbow buried in the moss, and her rosy cheek resting in the
palm of her hand, and Bruno stretched at her feet with his
head in her lap.

"Too waggly?" was all I could say in so sudden an
emergency.

"I'm not particular," Bruno said carelessly: "but I *do*
like straight animals best——"

"But you like a dog when it wags its tail," Sylvie interrupted. "You *know* you do, Bruno!"

"But there's more of a dog, isn't there, Mister Sir?"
Bruno appealed to me. "*You* wouldn't like to have a dog
if it hadn't got nuffin but a head and a tail?"

I admitted that a dog of that kind would be uninteresting.

"There *isn't* such a dog as that," Sylvie thoughtfully remarked.

"But there *would* be," cried Bruno, "if the Professor shortened it up for us!"

"Shortened it up?" I said. "That's something new. How does he do it?"

"He's got a curious machine——" Sylvie was beginning to explain.

"A *welly* curious machine," Bruno broke in, not at all willing to have the story thus taken out of his mouth, "and if oo puts in—somefinoruvver—at *one* end, oo know —and he turns the handle—and it comes out at the uvver end, oh, ever so short!"

"As short as short!" Sylvie echoed.

"And one day—when we was in Outland, oo know— before we came to Fairyland—me and Sylvie took him a big Crocodile. And he shortened it up for us. And it *did* look so funny! And it kept looking round, and saying 'wherever *is* the rest of me got to?' And then its eyes looked unhappy——"

"Not *both* its eyes," Sylvie interrupted.

"Course not!" said the little fellow. "Only the eye that *couldn't* see wherever the rest of it had got to. But the eye that *could* see wherever——"

"How short *was* the Crocodile?" I asked, as the story was getting a little complicated.

"Half as short again as when we caught it—*so* long," said Bruno, spreading out his arms to their full stretch.

I tried to calculate what this would come to, but it was too hard for me. Please make it out for me, dear Child who reads this!

"But you didn't leave the poor thing so short as that, did you?"

"Well, no. Sylvie and me took it back again and we got it stretched to—to—how much was it, Sylvie?"

"Two times and a half, and a little bit more," said Sylvie.

"It wouldn't like that better than the other way, I'm afraid?"

"Oh, but it did though!" Bruno put in eagerly. "It *were*

proud of its new tail! Oo never saw a Crocodile so proud!
Why it could go round and walk on the top of its tail,
and along its back, all the way to its head!"

"Not *quite* all the way," said Sylvie. "It couldn't, you
know."

"Ah, but it *did*, once!" Bruno cried triumphantly. "Oo
weren't looking—but *I* watched it. And it walked on
tipplety-toe, so as it wouldn't wake itself, 'cause it thought
it were asleep. And it got both its paws on its tail. And it
walked and it walked all the way along its back. And it
walked and it walked on its forehead. And it walked a
tiny little way down its nose! There now!"

This was a good deal worse than the last puzzle. Please,
dear Child, help again!

"I don't believe no Crocodile never walked along its
own forehead!" Sylvie cried, too much excited by the controversy to limit the number of her negatives.

"Oo don't know the *reason* why it did it!" Bruno scornfully retorted. "It had a welly good reason. I *heard* it say
'Why *shouldn't* I walk on my own forehead?' So a course
it *did*, oo know!"

"If *that's* a good reason, Bruno," I said, "why shouldn't
you get up that tree?"

"*Shall*, in a minute," said Bruno: "soon as we've done
talking. Only two peoples *ca'n't* talk comfably togevver,
when one's getting up a tree, and the other isn't!"

It appeared to me that a conversation would scarcely
be "comfable" while trees were being climbed, even if
both the "peoples" were doing it: but it was evidently
dangerous to oppose any theory of Bruno's; so I thought
it best to let the question drop, and to ask for an account
of the machine that made things *longer*.

This time Bruno was at a loss, and left it to Sylvie. "It's
like a mangle," she said: "if things are put in, they get
squoze——"

"Squeezeled!" Bruno interrupted.

"Yes." Sylvie accepted the correction, but did not attempt to pronounce the word, which was evidently new

to her. "They get—like that—and they come out, oh, ever so long!"

"Once," Bruno began again, "Sylvie and me writed——"

"Wrote!" Sylvie whispered.

"Well, we *wroted* a Nursery-Song, and the Professor mangled it longer for us. It were '*There was a little Man, And he had a little gun, And the bullets*——' "

"I know the rest," I interrupted. "But would you say it *long*—I mean the way that it came out of the mangle?"

"We'll get the Professor to *sing* it for you," said Sylvie. "It would spoil it to *say* it."

"I would like to meet the Professor," I said. "And I would like to take you all with me, to see some friends of mine, that live near here. Would you like to come?"

"I don't think the *Professor* would like to come," said Sylvie. "He's *very* shy. But *we'd* like it very much. Only we'd better not come *this* size, you know."

The difficulty had occurred to me already: and I had felt that perhaps there *would* be a slight awkwardness in introducing two such tiny friends into Society. "What size will you be?" I enquired.

"We'd better come as—common *children*," Sylvie thoughtfully replied. "That's the easiest size to manage."

"Could you come to-day?" I said, thinking "then we could have you at the Picnic!"

Sylvie considered a little. "Not *to-day*," she replied. "We haven't got the things ready. We'll come on—Tuesday next, if you like. And now, *really*, Bruno, you must come and do your lessons."

"I *wiss* oo wouldn't say '*really* Bruno!' " the little fellow pleaded, with pouting lips that made him look prettier than ever. "It *always* shows there's something horrid coming! And I wo'n't kiss you, if you're so unkind."

"Ah, but you *have* kissed me!" Sylvie exclaimed in merry triumph.

"Well then, I'll *un*kiss you!" And he threw his arms round her neck for this novel, but apparently not *very* painful, operation.

"It's *very* like *kissing!*" Sylvie remarked, as soon as her lips were again free for speech.

"Oo don't know *nuffin* about it! It were just the *conkery!*" Bruno replied with much severity, as he marched away.

Sylvie turned her laughing face to me. "Shall we come on Tuesday?" she said.

"Very well," I said: "let it be Tuesday next. But where *is* the Professor? Did he come with you to Fairyland?"

"No," said Sylvie. "But he promised he'd come and see us, *some* day. He's getting his Lecture ready. So he has to stay at home."

"At home?" I said dreamily, not feeling quite sure what she had said.

"Yes, Sir. His Lordship and Lady Muriel *are* at home. Please to walk this way."

CHAPTER XVII

The Three Badgers

STILL more dreamily I found myself following this imperious voice into a room where the Earl, his daughter, and Arthur, were seated. "So you're come *at last!*" said Lady Muriel, in a tone of playful reproach.

"I was delayed," I stammered. Though *what* it was that had delayed me I should have been puzzled to explain! Luckily no questions were asked.

The carriage was ordered round, the hamper, containing our contribution to the Picnic, was duly stowed away, and we set forth.

There was no need for *me* to maintain the conversation. Lady Muriel and Arthur were evidently on those most delightful of terms, where one has no need to check thought after thought, as it rises to the lips, with the fear "*this* will not be appreciated—*this* will give offence—*this* will sound too serious—this will sound flippant": like very old friends, in fullest sympathy, their talk rippled on.

"Why shouldn't we desert the Picnic and go in some other direction?" she suddenly suggested. "A party of four is surely self-sufficing? And as for *food*, our hamper——"

"Why *shouldn't* we? What a genuine *lady's* argument!" laughed Arthur. "A lady never knows on which side the *onus probandi*—the burden of proving—lies!"

"Do *men* always know?" she asked with a pretty assumption of meek docility.

"With *one* exception—the only one I can think of—Dr. Watts, who has asked the senseless question

> *'Why should I deprive my neighbour*
> *Of his goods against his will?'*

Fancy *that* as an argument for Honesty! His position seems to be 'I'm only honest because I see no reason to steal.' And the *thief's* answer is of course complete and crushing. 'I deprive my neighbour of his goods because I want them myself. And I do it against his will because there's no chance of getting him to consent to it!' "

"I can give you one other exception," I said: "an argument I heard only to-day—and *not* by a lady. 'Why shouldn't I walk on my own forehead?' "

"What a curious subject for speculation!" said Lady Muriel, turning to me, with eyes brimming over with laughter. "May we know who propounded the question? And *did* he walk on his own forehead?"

"I ca'n't remember *who* it was that said it!" I faltered. "Nor *where* I heard it!"

"Whoever it was, I hope we shall meet him at the Picnic!" said Lady Muriel. "It's a *far* more interesting question than '*Isn't* this a picturesque ruin?' '*Aren't* those autumn-tints lovely?' I shall have to answer those two questions *ten* times, at least, this afternoon!"

"That's one of the miseries of Society!" said Arthur. "Why ca'n't people let one enjoy the beauties of Nature without having to *say* so every minute? Why should Life be one long Catechism?"

"It's just as bad at a picture-gallery," the Earl remarked. "I went to the R.A. last May, with a conceited young artist: and he *did* torment me! I wouldn't have minded his criticizing the pictures *himself*: but *I* had to agree with him—or else to argue the point, which would have been worse!"

"It was *depreciatory* criticism, of course?" said Arthur.

"I don't see the 'of course' at all."

"Why, did you ever know a conceited man dare to *praise* a picture? The one thing he dreads (next to not being noticed) is *to be proved fallible!* If you once *praise* a picture, your character for *infallibility* hangs by a thread. Suppose it's a figure-picture, and you venture to say 'draws well'. Somebody measures it, and finds one of the proportions an eighth of an inch wrong. *You* are disposed of as a critic! 'Did you say he draws *well*?' your friends enquire sarcastically, while you hang your head and blush. No. The only *safe* course, if any one says 'draws well', is to shrug your shoulders. '*Draws* well?' you repeat thoughtfully. 'Draws *well*? Humph!' That's the way to become a great critic!"

Thus airily chatting, after a pleasant drive through a few miles of beautiful scenery, we reached the *rendezvous* —a ruined castle—where the rest of the picnic-party were already assembled. We spent an hour or two in sauntering about the ruins: gathering at last, by common consent, into a few random groups, seated on the side of a mound, which commanded a good view of the old castle and its surroundings.

The momentary silence, that ensued, was promptly taken possession of—or, more correctly, taken into custody—by a Voice; a voice so smooth, so monotonous, so sonorous, that one felt, with a shudder, that any other conversation was precluded, and that, unless some desperate remedy were adopted, we were fated to listen to a Lecture, of which no man could foresee the end!

The Speaker was a broadly-built man, whose large, flat, pale face was bounded on the North by a fringe of hair, on the East and West by a fringe of whisker, and on the South by a fringe of beard—the whole constituting a uniform halo of stubbly whitey-brown bristles. His features were so entirely destitute of expression that I could not help saying to myself—helplessly, as if in the clutches of a night-mare—"they are only penciled in: no final touches as yet!" And he had a way of ending every sentence with a sudden smile, which spread like a ripple over that vast blank surface, and was gone in a moment, leaving behind it such absolute solemnity that I felt impelled to murmur "it was not *he*: it was somebody else that smiled!"

"Do you observe?" (such was the phrase with which the wretch began each sentence) "Do you observe the way in which that broken arch, at the very top of the ruin, stands out against the clear sky? It is placed *exactly* right: and there is *exactly* enough of it. A little more, or a little less, and all would be utterly spoiled!"

"Oh gifted architect!" murmured Arthur, inaudibly to all but Lady Muriel and myself. "Foreseeing the exact effect his work would have, when in ruins, centuries after his death!"

"And do you observe, where those trees slope down the hill," (indicating them with a sweep of the hand, and with all the patronising air of the man who has himself arranged the landscape), "how the mists rising from the river fill up *exactly* those intervals where we *need* indistinctness, for artistic effect? Here, in the foreground, a few clear touches are not amiss: but a *back*-ground without mist, you know! It is simply barbarous! Yes, we *need* indistinctness!"

The orator looked so pointedly at *me* as he uttered these words, that I felt bound to reply, by murmuring something to the effect that I hardly felt the need *myself*—and that I enjoyed looking at a thing, better, when I could *see* it.

"Quite so!" the great man sharply took me up. "From

your point of view, that is correctly put. But for any one who has a soul for *Art*, such a view is preposterous. *Nature* is one thing. *Art* is another. *Nature* shows us the world as it *is*. But *Art*—as a Latin author tells us—*Art*, you know—the words have escaped my memory——"

"*Ars est celare Naturam*," Arthur interposed with a delightful promptitude.

"Quite so!" the orator replied with an air of relief. "I thank you! *Ars est celare Naturam*—but that isn't it." And, for a few peaceful moments, the orator brooded, frowningly, over the quotation. The welcome opportunity was seized, and *another* voice struck into the silence.

"What a *lovely* old ruin it is!" cried a young lady in spectacles, the very embodiment of the March of Mind, looking at Lady Muriel, as the proper recipient of all really *original* remarks. "And *don't* you admire those autumn-tints on the trees? *I* do, *intensely!*"

Lady Muriel shot a meaning glance at me; but replied with admirable gravity. "Oh yes indeed, indeed! *So* true!"

"And isn't it strange", said the young lady, passing with startling suddenness from Sentiment to Science, "that the mere impact of certain coloured rays upon the Retina should give us such exquisite pleasure?"

"You have studied Physiology, then?" a certain young Doctor courteously enquired.

"Oh, *yes*! Isn't it a *sweet* Science?"

Arthur slightly smiled. "It seems a paradox, does it not," he went on, "that the image formed on the Retina should be inverted?"

"It *is* puzzling," she candidly admitted. "Why is it we do not *see* things upside-down?"

"You have never heard the Theory, then, that the *Brain* also is inverted?"

"No *indeed*! What a *beautiful* fact! But how is it *proved?*"

"*Thus*," replied Arthur, with all the gravity of ten Professors rolled into one. "What we call the *vertex* of the Brain is really its *base*: and what we call its *base* is really its *vertex*: it is simply a question of *nomenclature*."

This last polysyllable settled the matter. "How truly delightful!" the fair Scientist exclaimed with enthusiasm. "I shall ask our Physiological Lecturer why he never gave us that *exquisite* Theory!"

"I'd give something to be present when the question is asked!" Arthur whispered to me, as, at a signal from Lady Muriel, we moved on to where the hampers had been collected, and devoted ourselves to the more *substantial* business of the day.

We "waited" on ourselves, as the modern barbarism (combining two good things in such a way as to secure the discomforts of both and the advantages of neither) of having a picnic with servants to wait upon you, had not yet reached this out-of-the-way region—and of course the gentlemen did not even take their places until the ladies had been duly provided with all imaginable creature-comforts. Then I supplied myself with a plate of something solid and a glass of something fluid, and found a place next to Lady Muriel.

It had been left vacant—apparently, for Arthur, as a distinguished stranger: but he had turned shy, and had placed himself next to the young lady in spectacles, whose high rasping voice had already cast loose upon Society such ominous phrases as "Man is a bundle of Qualities!", "the Objective is only attainable through the Subjective!". Arthur was bearing it bravely: but several faces wore a look of alarm, and I thought it high time to start some less metaphysical topic.

"In my nursery days," I began, "when the weather didn't suit for an out-of-doors picnic, we were allowed to have a peculiar kind, that we enjoyed hugely. The table cloth was laid *under* the table, instead of upon it: we sat round it on the floor: and I believe we really enjoyed that extremely uncomfortable kind of dinner more than we ever did the orthodox arrangement!"

"I've no doubt of it," Lady Muriel replied. "There's nothing a well-regulated child hates so much as regularity. I believe a really healthy boy would thoroughly enjoy Greek Grammar—if only he might stand on his head to learn it! And your carpet-dinner certainly spared you *one* feature of a picnic, which is to me its chief drawback."

"The chance of a shower?" I suggested.

"No, the chance—or rather the certainty—of *live* things occurring in combination with one's food! *Spiders* are *my* bugbear. Now my father has *no* sympathy with that sentiment—*have* you, dear?" For the Earl had caught the word and turned to listen.

"To each his sufferings, all are men," he replied in the sweet sad tones that seemed natural to him: "each has his pet aversion."

"But you'll never guess *his*!" Lady Muriel said, with that delicate silvery laugh that was music to my ears.

I declined to attempt the impossible.

"He doesn't like *snakes*!" she said, in a stage whisper. "Now, isn't *that* an unreasonable aversion? Fancy not liking such a dear, coaxingly, *clingingly* affectionate creature as a snake!"

"Not like *snakes*!" I exclaimed. "Is such a thing possible?"

"No, he *doesn't* like them," she repeated with a pretty mock-gravity. "He's not *afraid* of them, you know. But he doesn't *like* them. He says they're too waggly!"

I was more startled than I liked to show. There was something so *uncanny* in this echo of the very words I had so lately heard from that little forest-sprite, that it was only by a great effort I succeeded in saying, carelessly, "Let us banish so unpleasant a topic. Wo'n't you sing us something, Lady Muriel? I know you *do* sing without music."

"The only songs I know—without music—are *desperately* sentimental, I'm afraid! Are your tears all ready?"

"Quite ready! Quite ready!" came from all sides, and Lady Muriel—not being one of those lady-singers who think it *de rigueur* to decline to sing till they have been petitioned three or four times, and have pleaded failure of memory, loss of voice, and other conclusive reasons for silence—began at once:

> "*There be three Badgers on a mossy stone,*
> *Beside a dark and covered way:*
> *Each dreams himself a monarch on his throne,*
> *And so they stay and stay—*
> *Though their old Father languishes alone,*
> *They stay, and stay, and stay.*
>
> "*There be three Herrings loitering around,*
> *Longing to share that mossy seat:*
> *Each Herring tries to sing what she has found*
> *That makes Life seem so sweet.*
> *Thus, with a grating and uncertain sound,*
> *They bleat, and bleat, and bleat.*
>
> "*The Mother-Herring, on the salt sea-wave,*
> *Sought vainly for her absent ones:*
> *The Father-Badger, writhing in a cave,*
> *Shrieked out 'Return, my sons!*
> *You shall have buns', he shrieked, 'if you'll behave!*
> *Yea, buns, and buns, and buns!'*
>
> " '*I fear', said she, 'your sons have gone astray?*
> *My daughters left me while I slept.'*
> '*Yes'm,' the Badger said: 'it's as you say.'*
> '*They should be better kept.'*
> *Thus the poor parents talked the time away,*
> *And wept, and wept, and wept.*"

Here Bruno broke off suddenly. "The Herrings' Song wants anuvver tune, Sylvie," he said. "And I ca'n't sing it —not wizout oo plays it for me!"

Instantly Sylvie seated herself upon a tiny mushroom, that happened to grow in front of a daisy, as if it were the most ordinary musical instrument in the world, and played on the petals as if they were the notes of an organ. And such delicious *tiny* music it was! Such teeny-tiny music!

Bruno held his head on one side, and listened very gravely for a few moments until he had caught the melody. Then the sweet childish voice rang out once more:

> *"Oh, dear beyond our dearest dreams,*
> *Fairer than all that fairest seems!*
> *To feast the rosy hours away,*
> *To revel in a roundelay!*
>   *How blest would be*
>   *A life so free—*
> *Ipwergis-Pudding to consume,*
> *And drink the subtle Azzigoom!*
>
> *"And if, in other days and hours,*
> *Mid other fluffs and other flowers,*
> *The choice were given me how to dine—*
> *'Name what thou wilt: it shall be thine!'*
>   *Oh, then I see*
>   *The life for me—*
> *Ipwergis-Pudding to consume,*
> *And drink the subtle Azzigoom!"*

"Oo may leave off playing *now*, Sylvie. I can do the uvver tune much better wizout a compliment."

"He means 'without *accompaniment*,'" Sylvie whispered, smiling at my puzzled look: and she pretended to shut up the stops of the organ.

> *"The Badgers did not care to talk to Fish:*
> *They did not dote on Herrings' songs:*
> *They never had experienced the dish*
> *To which that name belongs:*
> *'And oh, to pinch their tails', (this was their wish),*
> *'With tongs, yea, tongs, and tongs!'"*

I ought to mention that he marked the parenthesis, in the air, with his finger. It seemed to me a very good plan. You know there's no *sound* to represent it—any more than there is for a question.

Suppose you have said to your friend "You are better to-day," and that you want him to understand that you

are asking him a *question*, what can be simpler than just
to make a "?" in the air with your finger? He would
understand you in a moment!

> " '*And are not these the Fish,*' *the Eldest sighed,*
> '*Whose Mother dwells beneath the foam?*'
> '*They* are *the Fish!*' *the Second one replied.*
> '*And they have left their home!*'
> '*Oh wicked Fish,*' *the Youngest Badger cried,*
> '*To roam, yea, roam, and roam!*'

> "*Gently the Badgers trotted to the shore—*
> *The sandy shore that fringed the bay:*
> *Each in his mouth a living Herring bore—*
> *Those aged ones waxed gay:*
> *Clear rang their voices through the ocean's roar,*
> '*Hooray, hooray, hooray!*' "

"So they all got safe home again," Bruno said, after
waiting a minute to see if *I* had anything to say: he evidently felt that *some* remark ought to be made. And I
couldn't help wishing there were some such rule in Society, at the conclusion of a song—that the singer *herself*
should say the right thing, and not leave it to the audience. Suppose a young lady has just been warbling ("with
a grating and uncertain sound") Shelley's exquisite lyric
"*I arise from dreams of thee*": how much nicer it would
be, instead of *your* having to say "Oh, *thank* you, *thank*
you!" for the young lady herself to remark, as she draws
on her gloves, while the impassioned words "*Oh, press
it to thine own, or it will break at last!*" are still ringing
in your ears, "—but she wouldn't do it, you know. So it
did break at last."

"And I *knew* it would!" she added quietly, as I started
at the sudden crash of broken glass. "You've been holding
it sideways for the last minute, and letting all the champagne run out! Were you asleep, I wonder? I'm *so* sorry
my singing has such a narcotic effect!"

Chapter XVIII

Queer Street, Number Forty

LADY MURIEL was the speaker. And, for the moment, that was the only fact I could clearly realize. But how she came to be there—and how *I* came to be there—and how the glass of champagne came to be there—all these were questions which I felt it better to think out in silence, and not commit myself to any statement till I understood things a little more clearly.

"First accumulate a mass of Facts: and *then* construct a Theory." *That*, I believe, is the true Scientic Method. I sat up, rubbed my eyes, and began to accumulate Facts.

A smooth grassy slope, bounded, at the upper end, by venerable ruins half buried in ivy, at the lower, by a stream seen through arching trees—a dozen gaily-dressed people, seated in little groups here and there—some open hampers—the *débris* of a picnic—such were the *Facts* accumulated by the Scientific Researcher. And now, what deep, far-reaching *Theory* was he to construct from them? The Researcher found himself at fault. Yet stay! One Fact had escaped his notice. While all the rest were grouped in twos and in threes, *Arthur* was alone: while all tongues were talking, *his* was silent: while all faces were gay, *his* was gloomy and despondent. Here was a *Fact* indeed! The Researcher felt that a *Theory* must be constructed without delay.

Lady Muriel had just risen and left the party. Could *that* be the cause of his despondency? The Theory hardly rose to the dignity of a Working Hypothesis. Clearly more Facts were needed.

The Researcher looked round him once more: and now the Facts accumulated in such bewildering profusion, that the Theory was lost among them. For Lady Muriel had gone to meet a strange gentleman, just visible in the distance: and now she was returning with him, both of them talking eagerly and joyfully, like old friends who have been long parted: and now she was moving from group to group, introducing the new hero of the hour: and he, young, tall, and handsome, moved gracefully at her side, with the erect bearing and firm tread of a soldier. Verily, the Theory looked gloomy for Arthur! His eye caught mine, and he crossed to me.

"He is very handsome," I said.

"Abominably handsome!" muttered Arthur: then smiled at his own bitter words. "Lucky no one heard me but you!"

"Doctor Forester," said Lady Muriel, who had just joined us, "let me introduce to you my cousin Eric Lindon—*Captain* Lindon, I should say."

Arthur shook off his ill-temper instantly and completely, as he rose and gave the young soldier his hand. "I have heard of you," he said. "I'm very glad to make the acquaintance of Lady Muriel's cousin."

"Yes, that's all I'm distinguished for, *as yet*!" said Eric (so we soon got to call him) with a winning smile. "And I doubt", glancing at Lady Muriel, "if it even amounts to a good-conduct-badge! But it's something to begin with."

"You must come to my father, Eric," said Lady Muriel. "I think he's wandering among the ruins." And the pair moved on.

The gloomy look returned to Arthur's face: and I could see it was only to distract his thoughts that he took his place at the side of the metaphysical young lady, and resumed their interrupted discussion.

"Talking of Herbert Spencer," he began, "do you really find no *logical* difficulty in regarding Nature as a process of involution, passing from definite coherent homogeneity to indefinite incoherent heterogeneity?"

Amused as I was at the ingenious jumble he had made of Spencer's words, I kept as grave a face as I could.

"No *physical* difficulty," she confidently replied: "but I haven't studied *Logic* much. Would you *state* the difficulty?"

"Well," said Arthur, "do you accept it as self-evident?

Is it as obvious, for instance, as that 'things that are greater than the same are greater than one another'?"

"To *my* mind," she modestly replied, "it seems *quite* as obvious. I grasp *both* truths by intuition. But *other* minds may need some logical—I forget the technical terms."

"For a *complete* logical argument", Arthur began with admirable solemnity, "we need two prim Misses——"

"Of course!" she interrupted. "I remember that word now. And they produce——?"

"A Delusion," said Arthur.

"Ye—es?" she said dubiously. "I don't seem to remember that so well. But what is the *whole* argument called?"

"A Sillygism."

"Ah, yes! I remember now. But I don't need a Sillygism, you know, to prove that mathematical axiom you mentioned."

"Nor to prove that 'all angles are equal', I suppose?"

"Why, of course not! One takes such a simple truth as that for granted!"

Here I ventured to interpose, and to offer her a plate of strawberries and cream. I felt really uneasy at the thought that she *might* detect the trick: and I contrived, unperceived by her, to shake my head reprovingly at the pseudo-philosopher. Equally unperceived by her, Arthur slightly raised his shoulders, and spread his hands abroad, as who should say "What else can I say to her?" and moved away leaving her to discuss her strawberries by "involution", or any other way she preferred.

By this time the carriages, that were to convey the revelers to their respective homes, had begun to assemble outside the Castle-grounds: and it became evident—now that Lady Muriel's cousin had joined our party—that the problem, how to convey five people to Elveston, with a carriage that would only hold four, must somehow be solved.

The Honourable Eric Lindon, who was at this moment walking up and down with Lady Muriel, might have solved it at once, no doubt, by announcing his intention of returning on foot. Of *this* solution there did not seem to be the very smallest probability.

The next best solution, it seemed to me, was that *I* should walk home: and this I at once proposed.

"You're sure you don't mind?" said the Earl. "I'm afraid the carriage wo'n't take us all, and I don't like to suggest to Eric to desert his cousin so soon."

"So far from minding it," I said, "I should prefer it. It will give me time to sketch this beautiful old ruin."

"I'll keep you company," Arthur suddenly said. And, in answer to what I suppose was a look of surprise on my face, he said in a low voice, "I *really* would rather. I shall be quite *de trop* in the carriage!"

"I think I'll walk too," said the Earl. "You'll have to be content with *Eric* as your escort," he added, to Lady Muriel, who had joined us while he was speaking.

"You must be as entertaining as Cerberus—'three gentlemen rolled into one'—" Lady Muriel said to her companion. "It will be a grand military exploit!"

"A sort of Forlorn Hope?" the Captain modestly suggested.

"You *do* pay pretty compliments!" laughed his fair cousin. "Good day to you, gentlemen three—or rather deserters three!" And the two young folk entered the carriage and were driven away.

"How long will your sketch take?" said Arthur.

"Well," I said, "I should like an hour for it. Don't you think you had better go without me? I'll return by train. I know there's one in about an hour's time."

"Perhaps that *would* be best," said the Earl. "The Station is quite close."

So I was left to my own devices, and soon found a comfortable seat, at the foot of a tree, from which I had a good view of the ruins.

"It is a very drowsy day," I said to myself, idly turning over the leaves of the sketch-book to find a blank page. "Why, I thought you were a mile off by this time!" For, to my surprise, the two walkers were back again.

"I came back to remind you", Arthur said, "that the trains go every ten minutes——"

"Nonsense!" I said. "It isn't the Metropolitan Railway!"

"It *is* the Metropolitan Railway," the Earl insisted. "This is a part of Kensington."

"Why do you talk with your eyes shut?" said Arthur. "Wake up!"

"I think it's the heat that makes me so drowsy," I said, hoping, but not feeling quite sure, that I was talking sense. "Am I awake now?"

"I think *not*," the Earl judicially pronounced. "What do *you* think, Doctor? He's only got one eye open!"

"And he's snoring like anything!" cried Bruno. "Do wake up, you dear old thing!" And he and Sylvie set to work, rolling the heavy head from side to side, as if its connection with the shoulders was a matter of no sort of importance.

And at last the Professor opened his eyes, and sat up, blinking at us with eyes of utter bewilderment. "Would you have the kindness to mention", he said, addressing me with his usual old-fashioned courtesy, "whereabouts we are just now—and *who* we are, beginning with me?"

I thought it best to begin with the children. "This is Sylvie, Sir; and *this* is Bruno."

"Ah, yes! I know *them* well enough!" the old man murmured. "It's *myself* I'm most anxious about. And perhaps you'll be good enough to mention, at the same time, how I got here?"

"A harder problem occurs to *me*," I ventured to say: "and that is, how you're to get back again."

"True, true!" the Professor replied. "That's *the* Problem, no doubt. Viewed *as* a Problem, outside of oneself, it is a *most* interesting one. Viewed as a portion of one's own biography, it is, I must admit, very distressing!" He groaned, but instantly added, with a chuckle, "As to *myself*, I think you mentioned that I am——"

"Oo're the *Professor*!" Bruno shouted in his ear. "Didn't

oo know *that*? Oo've come from *Outland*! And it's *ever* so far away from here!"

The Professor leapt to his feet with the agility of a boy. "Then there's no time to lose!" he exclaimed anxiously. "I'll just ask this guileless peasant, with his brace of buckets that contain (apparently) water, if he'll be so kind as to direct us. Guileless peasant!" he proceeded in a louder voice. "Would you tell us the way to Outland?"

The guileless peasant turned with a sheepish grin. "Hey?" was all he said.

"The—way—to—Outland!" the Professor repeated.

The guileless peasant set down his buckets and considered. "Ah, dunnot——"

"I ought to mention," the Professor hastily put in, "that whatever you say will be used in evidence against you."

The guileless peasant instantly resumed his buckets. "Then ah says nowt!" he answered briskly, and walked away at a great pace.

The children gazed sadly at the rapidly vanishing figure. "He goes very quick!" the Professor said with a sigh. "But I *know* that was the right thing to say. I've studied your English Laws. However, let's ask this next man that's coming. He is *not* guileless, and he is *not* a peasant —but I don't know that either point is of vital importance."

It was, in fact, the Honourable Eric Lindon, who had apparently fulfilled his task of escorting Lady Muriel home, and was now strolling leisurely up and down the road outside the house, enjoying a solitary cigar.

"Might I trouble you, Sir, to tell us the nearest way to Outland!" Oddity as he was, in outward appearance, the Professor was, in that essential nature which no outward disguise could conceal, a thorough gentleman.

And, as such, Eric Lindon accepted him instantly. He took the cigar from his mouth, and delicately shook off the ash, while he considered. "The name sounds strange to me," he said. "I doubt if I can help you."

"It is not *very* far from *Fairyland*," the Professor suggested.

Eric Lindon's eye-brows were slightly raised at these words, and an amused smile, which he courteously tried to repress, flitted across his handsome face. "A trifle *cracked!*" he muttered to himself. "But what a jolly old patriarch it is!" Then he turned to the children. "And ca'n't *you* help him, little folk?" he said, with a gentleness of tone that seemed to win their hearts at once. "Surely *you* know all about it?

> *'How many miles to Babylon?*
> *Three-score miles and ten.*
> *Can I get there by candlelight?*
> *Yes, and back again!'* "

To my surprise, Bruno ran forwards to him, as if he were some old friend of theirs, seized the disengaged hand and hung on to it with both of his own: and there stood this tall dignified officer in the middle of the road, gravely swinging a little boy to and fro, while Sylvie stood ready to push him, exactly as if a real swing had suddenly been provided for their pastime.

"We don't want to get to *Babylon*, oo know!" Bruno explained as he swung.

"And it isn't *candlelight*: it's *daylight!*" Sylvie added, giving the swing a push of extra vigour, which nearly took the whole machine off its balance.

By this time it was clear to me that Eric Lindon was quite unconscious of my presence. Even the Professor and the children seemed to have lost sight of me: and I stood in the midst of the group, as unconcernedly as a ghost, seeing but unseen.

"How perfectly isochronous!" the Professor exclaimed with enthusiasm. He had his watch in his hand, and was carefully counting Bruno's oscillations. "He measures time quite as accurately as a pendulum!"

"Yet even pendulums," the good-natured young soldier observed, as he carefully released his hand from Bruno's grasp, "are not a joy *for ever!* Come, that's enough for one bout, little man! Next time we meet, you shall have another. Meanwhile you'd better take this old gentleman to Queer Street, Number——"

"*We'll* find it!" cried Bruno eagerly, as they dragged the Professor away.

"We are much indebted to you!" the Professor said, looking over his shoulder.

"Don't mention it!" replied the officer, raising his hat as a parting salute.

"*What* number did you say!" the Professor called from the distance.

The officer made a trumpet of his two hands. "Forty!" he shouted in stentorian tones. "And not *piano*, by any means!" he added to himself. "It's a mad world, my masters, a mad world!" He lit another cigar, and strolled on towards his hotel.

"What a lovely evening!" I said, joining him as he passed me.

"Lovely indeed," he said. "Where did *you* come from? Dropped from the clouds?"

"I'm strolling your way," I said: and no further explanation seemed necessary.

"Have a cigar?"

"Thanks: I'm not a smoker."

"Is there a Lunatic Asylum near here?"

"Not that I know of."

"Thought there might be. Met a lunatic just now. Queer old fish as ever I saw!"

And so, in friendly chat, we took our homeward ways, and wished each other "good-night" at the door of his hotel.

Left to myself, I felt the "eerie" feeling rush over me again, and saw, standing at the door of Number Forty, the three figures I knew so well.

"Then it's the wrong house?" Bruno was saying.

"No, no! It's the right *house*," the Professor cheerfully replied: "but it's the wrong *street*. *That's* where we've made our mistake! Our best plan, now will be to——"

It was over. The street was empty. Commonplace life was around me, and the "eerie" feeling had fled.

Chapter XIX

How to Make a Phlizz

The week passed without any further communication with the "Hall", as Arthur was evidently fearful that we might "wear out our welcome"; but when, on Sunday morning, we were setting out for church, I gladly agreed to his proposal to go round and enquire after the Earl, who was said to be unwell.

Eric, who was strolling in the garden, gave us a good report of the invalid, who was still in bed, with Lady Muriel in attendance.

"Are you coming with us to church?" I enquired.

"Thanks, no," he courteously replied. "It's not—exactly—in my line, you know. It's an excellent institution—for the *poor*. When I'm with my own folk, I go, just to set them an example. But I'm not known *here:* so I think I'll excuse myself sitting out a sermon. Country-preachers are always so dull!"

Arthur was silent till we were out of hearing. Then he said to himself, almost inaudibly, *"Where two or three are gathered together in my name, there am I in the midst of them."*

"Yes," I assented: "no doubt that *is* the principle on which church-going rests."

"And when he *does* go," he continued (our thoughts ran so much together, that our conversation was often slightly elliptical), "I suppose he repeats the words '*I believe in the Communion of Saints*'?"

But by this time we had reached the little church, into which a goodly stream of worshippers, consisting mainly of fishermen and their families, was flowing.

The service would have been pronounced by any modern æsthetic religionist—or religious æsthete, which is it?—to be crude and cold: to me, coming fresh from the ever-advancing developments of a London church under a *soi-disant* "Catholic" Rector, it was unspeakably refreshing.

There was no theatrical procession of demure little choristers, trying their best not to simper under the admiring gaze of the congregation: the people's share in the service was taken by the people themselves, unaided, except that a few good voices, judiciously posted here and there among them, kept the singing from going too far astray.

There was no murdering of the noble music, contained in the Bible and the Liturgy, by its recital in a dead monotone, with no more expression than a mechanical talking-doll.

No, the prayers were *prayed*, the lessons were *read*, and—best of all—the sermon was *talked*; and I found myself repeating, as we left the church, the words of Jacob, when he *"awaked out of his sleep"*. " *'Surely the Lord is in this place! This is none other but the house of God, and this is the gate of heaven.'* "

"Yes," said Arthur, apparently in answer to my thoughts, "those 'high' services are fast becoming pure Formalism. More and more the people are beginning to regard them as 'performances', in which they only 'assist' in the French sense. And it is *specially* bad for the little boys. They'd be much less self-conscious as pantomime-fairies. With all that dressing-up, and stagy-entrances and exits, and being always *en evidence*, no wonder if they're eaten up with vanity, the blatant little coxcombs!"

When we passed the Hall on our return, we found the Earl and Lady Muriel sitting out in the garden. Eric had gone for a stroll.

We joined them, and the conversation soon turned on the sermon we had just heard, the subject of which was "selfishness".

"What a change has come over our pulpits", Arthur remarked, "since the time when Paley gave that utterly selfish definition of virtue, *'the doing good to mankind, in obedience to the will of God, and for the sake of ever-lasting happiness'*!"

Lady Muriel looked at him enquiringly, but she seemed to have learned by intuition, what years of experience had taught *me*, that the way to elicit Arthur's deepest thoughts was neither to assent nor dissent, but simply to *listen*.

"At that time," he went on, "a great tidal wave of selfishness was sweeping over human thought. Right and Wrong had somehow been transformed into Gain and Loss, and Religion had become a sort of commercial transaction. We may be thankful that our preachers are beginning to take a nobler view of life."

"But is it not taught again and again in the *Bible?*" I ventured to ask.

"Not in the Bible, as a *whole*," said Arthur. "In the Old Testament, no doubt, rewards and punishments are constantly appealed to as motives for action. That teaching is best for *children*, and the Israelites seem to have been, mentally, *utter* children. We guide our children thus, at first: but we appeal, as soon as possible, to their innate sense of Right and Wrong: and, when *that* stage is safely past, we appeal to the highest motive of all, the desire for likeness to, and union with, the Supreme Good. I think you will find that to be the teaching of the Bible, *as a whole*, beginning with *'that thy days may be long in the land'*, and ending with *'be ye perfect, even as your Father which is in heaven is perfect'*."

We were silent for awhile, and then Arthur went off on another tack. "Look at the literature of Hymns, now. How cankered it is, through and through, with selfishness! There are few human compositions more utterly degraded than some modern Hymns!"

I quoted the stanza.

> *"Whatever, Lord, we lend to Thee,*
> *Repaid a thousandfold shall be,*
> *Then gladly will we give to Thee,*
> *Giver of all!"*

"Yes," he said grimly: "that is the typical stanza. And the very last charity-sermon I heard was infected with it. After giving many good reasons for charity, the preacher wound up with 'and, for all you give, you will be repaid a thousandfold!' Oh, the utter meanness of such a motive, to be put before men who *do* know what self-sacrifice is, who *can* appreciate generosity and heroism! Talk of Original *Sin!*" he went on with increasing bitterness. "Can you have a stronger proof of the Original Goodness there must be in this nation, than the fact that Religion has been preached to us, as a commercial speculation, for a century, and that we still believe in a God?"

"It couldn't have gone on so long", Lady Muriel musingly remarked, "if the Opposition hadn't been practically silenced—put under what the French call *la clôture*. Surely in any lecture-hall, or in private society, such teaching would soon have been hooted down?"

"I trust so," said Arthur: "and, though I don't want to see 'brawling in church' legalized, I must say that our preachers enjoy an *enormous* privilege—which they ill deserve, and which they misuse terribly. We put our man into a pulpit, and we virtually tell him 'Now, you may stand there and talk to us for half-an-hour. We wo'n't interrupt you by so much as a *word!* You shall have it all your own way!' And what does he give us in return? Shallow twaddle, that, if it were addressed to you over a dinner-table, you would think 'Does the man take me for a *fool?*' "

The return of Eric from his walk checked the tide of Arthur's eloquence, and, after a few minutes' talk on more conventional topics, we took our leave. Lady Muriel walked with us to the gate. "You have given me much to think about," she said earnestly, as she gave Arthur her hand. "I'm so glad you came in!" And her words brought a real glow of pleasure into that pale worn face of his.

On the Tuesday, as Arthur did not seem equal to more walking, I took a long stroll by myself, having stipulated that he was not to give the *whole* day to his books, but was to meet me at the Hall at about tea-time. On my way back, I passed the Station just as the afternoon-train came in sight, and sauntered down the stairs to see it come in. But there was little to gratify my idle curiosity: and, when the train was empty, and the platform clear, I found it was about time to be moving on, if I meant to reach the Hall by five.

As I approached the end of the platform, from which a steep irregular wooden staircase conducted to the upper world, I noticed two passengers, who had evidently arrived by the train, but who, oddly enough, had entirely escaped my notice, though the arrivals had been so few. They were a young woman and a little girl: the former, so far as one could judge by appearances, was a nurse-maid, or possibly a nursery-governess, in attendance on the child, whose refined face, even more than her dress, distinguished her as of a higher class than her companion.

The child's face was refined, but it was also a worn and sad one, and told a tale (or so I seemed to read it) of much illness and suffering, sweetly and patiently borne. She had a little crutch to help herself along with: and she was now standing, looking wistfully up the long staircase, and apparently waiting till she could muster courage to begin the toilsome ascent.

There are some things one *says* in life—as well as things one *does*—which come automatically, by *reflex action*, as the physiologists say (meaning, no doubt, action *without* reflection, just as *lucus* is said to be derived *"a non lucendo"*). Closing one's eyelids, when something seems to be flying into the eye, is one of those actions, and saying "May I carry the little girl up the stairs?" was another. It wasn't that any thought of offering help occurred to me, and that *then* I spoke: the first intimation I had, of being likely to make that offer, was the sound of my own voice, and the discovery that the offer had been made. The servant paused, doubtfully glancing from her charge to me, and then back again to the child. "Would you like it, dear?" she asked her. But no such doubt appeared to cross the child's mind: she lifted her arms eagerly to be taken up. "Please!" was all she said, while a faint smile flickered on the weary little face. I took her up with scrupulous care, and her little arm was at once clasped trustfully round my neck.

She was a *very* light weight—so light, in fact, that the ridiculous idea crossed my mind that it was rather easier going up, with her in my arms, than it would have been without her: and, when we reached the road above, with its cart-ruts and loose stones—all formidable obstacles for a lame child—I found that I had said "I'd better carry her over this rough place", before I had formed any *mental* connection between its roughness and my gentle little burden. "Indeed it's troubling you too much, Sir!" the maid exclaimed. "She can walk very well on the flat." But the arm, that was twined about my neck, clung just an atom more closely at the suggestion, and decided me to say "She's no weight, really. I'll carry her a little further. I'm going your way."

The nurse raised no further objection: and the next speaker was a ragged little boy, with bare feet, and a broom over his shoulder, who ran across the road, and pretended to sweep the perfectly dry road in front of us. "Give us a 'ap'ny!" the little urchin pleaded, with a broad grin on his dirty face.

"*Don't* give him a 'ap'ny!" said the little lady in my arms. The *words* sounded harsh: but the *tone* was gentleness itself. "He's an *idle* little boy!" And she laughed a laugh of such silvery sweetness as I had never yet heard from any lips but Sylvie's. To my astonishment, the boy actually *joined* in the laugh, as if there were some subtle sympathy between them, as he ran away down the road and vanished through a gap in the hedge.

But he was back in a few moments, having discarded his broom and provided himself, from some mysterious source, with an exquisite bouquet of flowers. "Buy a posy, buy a posy! Only a 'ap'ny!" he chanted, with the melancholy drawl of a professional beggar.

"*Don't* buy it!" was Her Majesty's edict as she looked down, with a lofty scorn that seemed curiously mixed with tender interest, on the ragged creature at her feet.

But this time I turned rebel, and ignored the royal commands. Such lovely flowers, and of forms so entirely new to me, were not to be abandoned at the bidding of any little maid, however imperious. I bought the bouquet: and the little boy, after popping the halfpenny into his mouth, turned head-over-heels, as if to ascertain whether the human mouth is really adapted to serve as a money-box.

With wonder, that increased every moment, I turned over the flowers, and examined them one by one: there was not a single one among them that I could remember having ever seen before. At last I turned to the nursemaid. "Do these flowers grow wild about here? I never saw——" but the speech died away on my lips. The nursemaid had vanished!

"You can put me down, *now*, if you like," Sylvie quietly remarked.

I obeyed in silence, and could only ask myself "Is this a *dream*?", on finding Sylvie and Bruno walking one on either side of me, and clinging to my hands with the ready confidence of childhood.

"You're larger than when I saw you last!" I began. "Really I think we ought to be introduced again! There's so much of you that I never met before, you know."

"Very well!" Sylvie merrily replied. "This is *Bruno*. It doesn't take long. He's only got one name!"

"There's *another* name to me!" Bruno protested, with a reproachful look at the Mistress of the Ceremonies. "And it's—'*Esquire*'!"

"Oh, of course. I forgot," said Sylvie. "Bruno—*Esquire*!"

"And did you come here to meet *me*, my children?" I enquired.

"You know I *said* we'd come on Tuesday," Sylvie explained. "Are we the proper size for common children?"

"Quite the right size for *children*," I replied, (adding mentally "though not *common* children, by any means!") "But what became of the nursemaid?"

"It are *gone!*" Bruno solemnly replied.

"Then it wasn't solid, like Sylvie and you?"

"No. Oo couldn't *touch* it, oo know. If oo walked *at* it, oo'd go right froo!"

"I quite expected you'd find it out, once," said Sylvie. "Bruno ran it against a telegraph post, by accident. And it went in two halves. But you were looking the other way."

I felt that I had indeed missed an opportunity: to witness such an event as a nursemaid going "in two halves" does not occur twice in a life-time!

"When did oo guess it were Sylvie?" Bruno enquired.

"I didn't guess it, till it *was* Sylvie," I said. "But how did you manage the nursemaid?"

"*Bruno* managed it," said Sylvie. "It's called a Phlizz."

"And how do you make a Phlizz, Bruno?"

"The Professor teached me how," said Bruno. "First oo takes a lot of air——"

"Oh, *Bruno!*" Sylvie interposed. "The Professor said you weren't to tell!"

"But who did her *voice*?" I asked.

"Indeed it's troubling you too much, Sir! She can walk very well on the flat."

Bruno laughed merrily as I turned hastily from side to side, looking in all directions for the speaker. "That were *me!*" he gleefully proclaimed, in his own voice.

"She can indeed walk very well on the flat," I said. "And I think *I* was the Flat."

By this time we were near the Hall. "This is where my friends live," I said. "Will you come in and have some tea with them?"

Bruno gave a little jump of joy: and Sylvie said "Yes, please. You'd like some tea, Bruno, wouldn't you? He hasn't tasted *tea*", she explained to me, "since we left Outland."

"And *that* weren't *good* tea!" said Bruno. "It were so *welly* weak!"

Chapter XX

Light Come, Light Go

LADY MURIEL's smile of welcome could not *quite* conceal the look of surprise with which she regarded my new companions.

I presented them in due form. "This is *Sylvie*, Lady Muriel. And this is *Bruno*."

"Any surname?" she enquired, her eyes twinkling with fun.

"No," I said gravely. "No surname."

She laughed, evidently thinking I said it in fun; and stooped to kiss the children—a salute to which *Bruno* submitted with reluctance: *Sylvie* returned it with interest.

While she and Arthur (who had arrived before me) supplied the children with tea and cake, I tried to engage the Earl in conversation: but he was restless and *distrait*, and we made little progress. At last, by a sudden question, he betrayed the cause of his disquiet.

"*Would* you let me look at those flowers you have in your hand?"

"Willingly!" I said, handing him the bouquet. Botany was, I knew, a favourite study of his: and these flowers were to me so entirely new and mysterious, that I was really curious to see what a botanist would say of them.

They did *not* diminish his disquiet. On the contrary, he became every moment more excited as he turned them over. "*These* are all from Central India!" he said, laying aside part of the bouquet. "They are rare, even there: and I have never seen them in any other part of the world. *These* two are Mexican—*This* one——" (He rose hastily and carried it to the window, to examine it in a better light, the flush of excitement mounting to his very forehead) "—is, I am nearly sure—but I have a book of Indian Botany here——" He took a volume from the book-shelves, and turned the leaves with trembling fingers. "Yes! Compare it with this picture! It is the exact duplicate! This is the flower of the Upas-tree, which usually grows only in the depths of forests; and the flower fades so quickly after being plucked, that it is scarcely possible to keep its form or colour even so far as the outskirts of the forest! Yet this is in full bloom! *Where* did you get these flowers?" he added with breathless eagerness.

I glanced at Sylvie, who, gravely and silently, laid her finger on her lips, then beckoned to Bruno to follow her, and ran out into the garden; and I found myself in the position of a defendant whose two most important witnesses have been suddenly taken away. "Let me give you the flowers!" I stammered out at last, quite "at my wit's end" as to how to get out of the difficulty. "You know much more about them than I do!"

"I accept them most gratefully! But you have not yet told me——" the Earl was beginning, when we were interrupted, to my great relief, by the arrival of Eric Lindon.

To *Arthur*, however, the newcomer was, I saw clearly, anything but welcome. His face clouded over: he drew a little back from the circle, and took no further part in the conversation, which was wholly maintained, for some minutes, by Lady Muriel and her lively cousin, who were discussing some new music that had just arrived from London.

"Do just try this one!" he pleaded. "The music looks easy to sing at sight, and the song's quite appropriate to the occasion."

"Then I suppose it's

> *'Five o'clock tea!*
> *Ever to thee*
> *Faithful I'll be,*
> *Five o'clock tea!'* "

laughed Lady Muriel, as she sat down to the piano, and lightly struck a few random chords.

"Not quite: and yet it *is* a kind of 'ever to thee faithfull I'll be!' It's a pair of hapless lovers: *he* crosses the briny deep: and *she* is left lamenting."

"That is *indeed* appropriate!" she replied mockingly, as he placed the song before her. "And am *I* to do the lamenting? And who for, if you please?"

She played the air once or twice through, first in quick, and finally in slow, time; and then gave us the whole song with as much graceful ease as if she had been familiar with it all her life:

> "*He steps so lightly to the land,*
> *All in his manly pride:*
> *He kissed her cheek, he pressed her hand,*
> *Yet still she glanced aside.*
> '*Too gay he seems,' she darkly dreams,*
> '*Too gallant and too gay*
> *To think of me—poor simple me—*
> *When he is far away!*'
>
> '*I bring my Love this goodly pearl*
> *Across the seas,' he said:*
> '*A gem to deck the dearest girl*
> *That ever sailor wed!*'
> *She clasps it tight: her eyes are bright:*
> *Her throbbing heart would say*
> '*He thought of me—he thought of me—*
> *When he was far away!*'
>
> *The ship has sailed into the West:*
> *Her ocean-bird is flown:*
> *A dull dead pain is in her breast,*
> *And she is weak and lone:*
> *Yet there's a smile upon her face,*
> *A smile that seems to say*
> '*He'll think of me—he'll think of me—*
> *When he is far away!*
>
> '*Though waters wide between us glide,*
> *Our lives are warm and near:*

No distance parts two faithful hearts—
Two hearts that love so dear:
And I will trust my sailor-lad,
For ever and a day,
To think of me—to think of me—
When he is far away!'"

The look of displeasure, which had begun to come over Arthur's face when the young Captain spoke of Love so lightly, faded away as the song proceeded, and he listened with evident delight. But his face darkened again when Eric demurely remarked "Don't you think 'my *soldier*-lad' would have fitted the tune just as well?"

"Why, so it would!" Lady Muriel gaily retorted. "Soldiers, sailors, tinkers, tailors, what a lot of words would fit in! I think 'my *tinker*-lad' sounds best. Don't *you*?"

To spare my friend further pain, I rose to go, just as the Earl was beginning to repeat his particularly embarrassing question about the flowers.

"You have not yet——"

"Yes, I've *had* some tea, thank you!" I hastily interrupted him. "And now we really *must* be going. Good evening, Lady Muriel!" And we made our adieux, and escaped, while the Earl was still absorbed in examining the mysterious bouquet.

Lady Muriel accompanied us to the door. "You *couldn't* have given my father a more acceptable present!" she said, warmly. "He is so passionately fond of Botany. I'm afraid *I* know nothing of the *theory* of it, but I keep his *Hortus Siccus* in order. I must get some sheets of blotting-paper, and dry these new treasures for him before they begin to fade."

"*That* wo'n't be no good at all!" said Bruno, who was waiting for us in the garden.

"Why wo'n't it?" said I. "You know I *had* to give the flowers, to stop questions."

"Yes, it ca'n't be helped," said Sylvie: "but they *will* be sorry when they find them gone!"

"But how will they go?"

"Well, I don't know *how*. But they *will* go. The nose-gay was only a *Phlizz*, you know. Bruno made it up."

These last words were in a whisper, as she evidently did not wish Arthur to hear. But of this there seemed to be little risk: he hardly seemed to notice the children, but paced on, silent and abstracted; and when, at the entrance to the wood, they bid us a hasty farewell and ran off, he seemed to wake out of a day-dream.

The bouquet vanished, as Sylvie had predicted; and when, a day or two afterwards, Arthur and I once more visited the Hall, we found the Earl and his daughter, with the old housekeeper, out in the garden, examining the fastenings of the drawing-room window.

"We are holding an Inquest," Lady Muriel said, advancing to meet us: "and we admit you, as Accessories before the Fact, to tell us all you know about those flowers."

"The Accessories before the Fact decline to answer *any* questions," I gravely replied. "And they reserve their defence."

"Well then, turn Queen's Evidence, please! The flowers have disappeared in the night," she went on, turning to Arthur, "and we are *quite* sure no one in the house has meddled with them. Somebody must have entered by the window——"

"But the fastenings have not been tampered with," said the Earl.

"It must have been while you were dining, my Lady," said the housekeeper.

"That was it," said the Earl. "The thief must have seen you bring the flowers", turning to me, "and have noticed that you did *not* take them away. And he must have known their great value—they are simply *priceless*!" he exclaimed, in sudden excitement.

"And you never told us how you got them!" said Lady Muriel.

"Some day," I stammered, "I may be free to tell you. Just now, would you excuse me?"

The Earl looked disappointed, but kindly said "Very well, we will ask no questions".

"But we consider you a *very* bad Queen's Evidence," Lady Muriel added playfully, as we entered the arbour. "We pronounce you to be an accomplice: and we sentence you to solitary confinement, and to be fed on bread and—butter. Do you take sugar?"

"It is disquieting, certainly," she resumed, when all "creature-comforts" had been duly supplied, "to find that the house has been entered by a thief—in this out-of-the-way place. If only the flowers had been *eatables*, one might have suspected a thief of quite another shape——"

"You mean that universal explanation for all mysterious disappearances, 'the *cat* did it'?" said Arthur.

"Yes," she replied. "What a convenient thing it would be if all thieves had the same shape! It's so confusing to have some of them quadrupeds and others bipeds!"

"It has occurred to me", said Arthur, "as a curious problem in Teleology—the Science of Final Causes," he added, in answer to an enquiring look from Lady Muriel.

"And a Final Cause is——?"

"Well, suppose we say—the last of a series of connected events—each of the series being the cause of the next—for whose sake the first event takes place."

"But the last event is practically an *effect* of the first, isn't it? And yet you call it a *cause* of it!"

Arthur pondered a moment. "The words are rather confusing, I grant you," he said. "Will this do? The last event is an effect of the first: but the *necessity* for that event is a cause of the *necessity* for the first."

"That seems clear enough," said Lady Muriel. "Now let us have the problem."

"It's merely this. What object can we imagine in the arrangement by which each different size (roughly speaking) of living creatures has its special shape? For instance, the human race has one kind of shape—bipeds. Another set, ranging from the lion to the mouse, are quadrupeds. Go down a step or two further, and you come to insects with six legs—hexapods—a beautiful name, is it not? But beauty, in our sense of the word, seems to diminish as we go down: the creature becomes more—I won't say 'ugly' of any of God's creatures— more uncouth. And, when we take the microscope, and go a few steps lower still, we come upon animalculæ, terribly uncouth, and with a terrible number of legs!"

"The other alternative," said the Earl, "would be a *diminuendo* series of repetitions of the same type. Never mind the monotony of it: let's see how it would work in other ways. Begin with the race of men, and the creatures they require: let us say horses, cattle, sheep, and dogs—we don't exactly require frogs and spiders, do we, Muriel?"

Lady Muriel shuddered perceptibly: it was evidently a painful subject. "We can dispense with *them*," she said gravely.

"Well, then we'll have a second race of men, half-a-yard high——"

"—who would have *one* source of exquisite enjoyment, not possessed by ordinary men!" Arthur interrupted.

"*What* source?" said the Earl.

"Why, the grandeur of scenery! Surely the grandeur of a mountain, to *me*, depends on its *size*, relative to me? Double the height of the mountain, and of course it's twice as grand. Halve *my* height, and you produce the same effect."

"Happy, happy, happy Small!" Lady Muriel murmured rapturously. "None but the Short, none but the Short, none but the Short enjoy the Tall!"

"But let me go on," said the Earl. "We'll have a third race of men, five inches high; a fourth race, an inch high——"

"They couldn't eat common beef and mutton, I'm sure!" Lady Muriel interrupted.

"True, my child, I was forgetting. Each set must have its own cattle and sheep."

"And its own vegetation," I added. "What could a cow, an inch high, do with grass that waved far above its head?"

"That is true. We must have a pasture within a pasture, so to speak. The common grass would serve our inch-high cows as a green forest of palms, while round the root of each tall stem would stretch a tiny carpet of microscopic grass. Yes, I think our scheme will work fairly well. And it would be very interesting, coming into contact with the races below us. What sweet little things the inch-high bull-dogs would be! I doubt if even *Muriel* would run away from one of them!"

"Don't you think we ought to have a *crescendo* series, as well?" said Lady Muriel. "Only fancy being a hundred yards high! One could use an elephant as a paper-weight, and a crocodile as a pair of scissors!"

"And would you have races of different sizes communicate with one another?" I enquired. "Would they make war on one another, for instance, or enter into treaties?"

"*War* we must exclude, I think. When you could crush a whole nation with one blow of your fist, you couldn't conduct war on equal terms. But anything, involving a collision of *minds* only, would be possible in our ideal world—for of course we must allow *mental* powers to all, irrespective of size. Perhaps the fairest rule would be that, the *smaller* the race, the *greater* should be its intellectual development!"

"Do you mean to say", said Lady Muriel, "that these manikins of an inch high are to *argue* with me?"

"Surely, surely!" said the Earl. "An argument doesn't depend for its logical force on the *size* of the creature that utters it!"

She tossed her head indignantly. "I would *not* argue with any man less than six inches high!" she cried. "I'd make him *work*!"

"What at?" said Arthur, listening to all this nonsense with an amused smile.

"*Embroidery*!" she readily replied. "What *lovely* embroidery they would do!"

"Yet, if they did it wrong," I said, "you couldn't *argue* the question. I don't know *why:* but I agree that it couldn't be done."

"The reason is," said Lady Muriel, "one couldn't sacrifice one's *dignity* so far."

"Of course one couldn't!" echoed Arthur. "Any more than one could argue with a potato. It would be altogether—excuse the ancient pun—*infra dig.*!"

"I doubt it," said I. "Even a pun doesn't *quite* convince me."

"Well, if that is *not* the reason," said Lady Muriel, "what reason would you give?"

I tried hard to understand the meaning of this question: but the persistent humming of the bees confused me, and there was a drowsiness in the air that made every thought stop and go to sleep before it had got well thought out: so all I could say was "That must depend on the *weight* of the potato".

I felt the remark was not so sensible as I should have liked it to be. But Lady Muriel seemed to take it quite as a matter of course. "In that case——" she began, but suddenly started, and turned away to listen. "Don't you hear him?" she said. "He's crying. We must go to him, somehow."

And I said to myself "That's very strange! I quite thought it was *Lady Muriel* talking to me. Why, it's *Sylvie* all the while!" And I made another great effort to say something that should have some meaning in it. "Is it about the potato?"

CHAPTER XXI

Through the Ivory Door

"I DON'T know," said Sylvie. "Hush! I must think. I could go to him, by myself, well enough. But I want *you* to come too."

"Let me go with you," I pleaded. "I can walk as fast as *you* can, I'm sure."

Sylvie laughed merrily. "What nonsense!" she cried. "Why, you ca'n't walk a bit! You're lying quite flat on your back! You don't understand these things."

"I can walk as well as *you* can," I repeated. And I tried my best to walk a few steps: but the ground slipped away backwards, quite as fast as I could walk, so that I made no progress at all. Sylvie laughed again.

"There, I told you so! You've no idea how funny you look, moving your feet about in the air, as if you were walking! Wait a bit. I'll ask the Professor what we'd better do." And she knocked at his study-door.

The door opened, and the Professor looked out. "What's that crying I heard just now?" he asked. "Is it a human animal?"

"It's a boy," Sylvie said.

"I'm afraid you've been teasing him?"

"No, *indeed* I haven't!" Sylvie said, very earnestly. "I *never* tease him!"

"Well, I must ask the Other Professor about it." He went back into the study, and we heard him whispering "small human animal—says she hasn't been teasing him —the kind that's called Boy——"

"Ask her *which* Boy," said a new voice. The Professor came out again.

"*Which* Boy is it that you haven't been teasing?"

Sylvie looked at me with twinkling eyes. "You dear old thing!" she exclaimed, standing on tip-toe to kiss him, while he gravely stooped to receive the salute. "How you *do* puzzle me! Why, there are *several* boys I haven't been teasing!"

The Professor returned to his friend: and this time the voice said "Tell her to bring them here—*all* of them!"

"I ca'n't, and I wo'n't!" Sylvie exclaimed, the moment he reappeared. "It's *Bruno* that's crying: and he's my brother: and, please, we *both* want to go: he ca'n't walk, you know: he's—he's *dreaming*, you know" (this in a whisper, for fear of hurting my feelings). *"Do* let's go through the Ivory Door!"

"I'll ask him," said the Professor, disappearing again. He returned directly. "He says you may. Follow me, and walk on tip-toe."

The difficulty with me would have been, just then, *not* to walk on tip-toe. It seemed very hard to reach down far enough to just touch the floor, as Sylvie led me through the study.

The Professor went before us to unlock the Ivory Door. I had just time to glance at the Other Professor, who was sitting reading, with his back to us, before the Professor showed us out through the door, and locked it behind us. Bruno was standing with his hands over his face, crying bitterly.

"What's the matter, darling?" said Sylvie, with her arms round his neck.

"Hurted mine self *welly* much!" sobbed the poor little fellow.

"I'm *so* sorry, darling! How ever *did* you manage to hurt yourself so?"

"Course I managed it!" said Bruno, laughing through his tears. "Does oo think nobody else but *oo* ca'n't manage things?"

Matters were looking distinctly brighter, now Bruno had begun to argue. "Come, let's hear all about it!" I said.

"My foot took it into its head to slip——" Bruno began.

"A foot hasn't got a head!" Sylvie put in, but all in vain.

"I slipted down the bank. And I tripted over a stone. And the stone hurted my foot! And I trod on a Bee. And the Bee stinged my finger!" Poor Bruno sobbed again. The complete list of woes was too much for his feelings. "And it knewed I didn't *mean* to trod on it!" he added, as the climax.

"That Bee should be ashamed of itself!" I said severely,

and Sylvie hugged and kissed the wounded hero till all tears were dried.

"My finger's quite unstung now!" said Bruno. "Why doos there be stones? Mister Sir, doos oo know?"

"They're good for *something*," I said: "even if we don't know *what*. What's the good of *dandelions*, now?"

"Dindledums?" said Bruno. "Oh, they're ever so pretty! And stones aren't pretty, one bit. Would oo like some dindledums, Mister Sir?"

"Bruno!" Sylvie murmured reproachfully. "You mustn't say 'Mister' and 'Sir' both at once! Remember what I told you!"

"You telled me I were to say 'Mister' when I spoked *about* him, and I were to say 'Sir' when I spoked *to* him!"

"Well, you're not doing *both*, you know."

"Ah, but I *is* doing bofe, Miss Praticular!" Bruno exclaimed triumphantly. "I wishted to speak *about* the Gemplun—and I wishted to speak *to* the Gemplun. So a course I said 'Mister Sir'!"

"That's all right, Bruno," I said.

"*Course* it's all right!" said Bruno. "Sylvie just knows nuffin at all!"

"There never *was* an impertinenter boy!" said Sylvie, frowning till her bright eyes were nearly invisible.

"And there never was an ignoranter girl!" retorted Bruno. "Come along and pick some dindledums. *That's all she's fit for!*" he added in a very loud whisper to me.

"But why do you say 'Dindledums', Bruno? *Dandelions* is the right word."

"It's because he jumps about so," Sylvie said, laughing.

"Yes, that's it," Bruno assented. "Sylvie tells me the words, and then, when I jump about, they get shooken up in my head—till they're all froth!"

I expressed myself as perfectly satisfied with this explanation. "But aren't you going to pick me any dindledums, after all?"

"Course we will!" cried Bruno. "Come along, Sylvie!"

And the happy children raced away, bounding over the turf with the fleetness and grace of young antelopes.

"Then you didn't find your way back to Outland?" I said to the Professor.

"Oh yes, I did!" he replied, "We never got to Queer Street; but I found another way. I've been backwards and forwards several times since then. I had to be present at the Election, you know, as the author of the new Money-Act. The Emperor was so kind as to wish that *I* should have the credit of it. 'Let come what come may,' (I remember the very words of the Imperial Speech) 'if it *should* turn out that the Warden *is* alive, *you* will bear witness that the change in the coinage is the *Professor's* doing, not *mine!*' I never was so glorified in my life, before!" Tears trickled down his cheeks at the recollection, which apparently was not *wholly* a pleasant one.

"Is the Warden supposed to be *dead?*"

"Well, it's *supposed* so: but, mind you, *I* don't believe it! The evidence is *very* weak—mere hear-say. A wandering Jester, with a Dancing-Bear (they found their way into the Palace, one day) has been telling people he comes from Fairyland, and that the Warden died there. *I* wanted the Vice-Warden to question him, but, most unluckily, he and my Lady were always out walking when the Jester came round. Yes, the Warden's supposed to be dead!" And more tears trickled down the old man's cheeks.

"But what is the new Money-Act?"

The Professor brightened up again. "The Emperor started the thing," he said. "He wanted to make everybody in Outland twice as rich as he was before—just to make the new Government popular. Only there wasn't nearly enough money in the Treasury to do it. So *I* suggested that he might do it by doubling the value of every coin and bank-note in Outland. It's the simplest thing possible. I wonder nobody ever thought of it before! And you never saw such universal joy. The shops are full from morning to night. Everybody's buying everything!"

"And how was the glorifying done?"

A sudden gloom overcast the Professor's jolly face. "They did it as I went home after the Election," he mournfully replied. "It was kindly meant—but I didn't like it! They waved flags all round me till I was nearly blind: and they rang bells till I was nearly deaf: and they strewed the road so thick with flowers that I lost my way!" And the poor old man sighed deeply.

"How far is it to Outland?" I asked, to change the subject.

"About five days' march. But one *must* go back— occasionally. You see, as Court-Professor, I have to be *always* in attendance on Prince Uggug. The Empress would be *very* angry if I left him, even for an hour."

"But surely, every time you come here, you are absent ten days, at least?"

"Oh, more than that!" the Professor exclaimed. "A fortnight, sometimes. But of course I keep a memorandum of the exact time when I started, so that I can put the Court-time back to the very moment!"

"Excuse me," I said. "I don't understand."

Silently the Professor drew from his pocket a square gold watch, with six or eight hands, and held it out for my inspection. "This", he began, "is an Outlandish Watch——"

"So I should have thought."

"—which has the peculiar property that, instead of *its* going with the *time*, the *time* goes with *it*. I trust you understand me now?"

"Hardly," I said.

"Permit me to explain. So long as it is let alone, it takes its own course. Time has *no* effect upon it."

"I have known such watches," I remarked.

"It *goes*, of course, at the usual rate. Only the time has to go *with* it. Hence, if I move the hands, I change the time. To move them *forwards*, in *advance* of the true time, is impossible: but I can move them as much as a month *backwards*—that is the limit. And then you have the events all over again—with any alterations experience may suggest."

"*What* a blessing such a watch would be", I thought, "in real life! To be able to unsay some heedless word—to undo some reckless deed! Might I see the thing done?"

"With pleasure!" said the good natured Professor. "When I move *this* hand back to *here*", pointing out the place, "History goes back fifteen minutes!"

Trembling with excitement, I watched him push the hand round as he described.

"Hurted mine self *welly* much!"

Shrilly and suddenly the words rang in my ears, and, more startled than I cared to show, I turned to look for the speaker.

Yes! There was Bruno, standing with the tears running down his cheeks, just as I had seen him a quarter of an hour ago; and there was Sylvie with her arms round his neck!

I had not the heart to make the dear little fellow go through his troubles a second time, so hastily begged the Professor to push the hands round into their former position. In a moment Sylvie and Bruno were gone again, and I could just see them in the far distance, picking "dindledums".

"Wonderful, indeed!" I exclaimed.

"It has another property, yet more wonderful," said the Professor. "You see this little peg? That is called the 'Reversal Peg'. If you push it in, the events of the next hour happen in the reverse order. Do not try it now. I will lend you the Watch for a few days, and you can amuse yourself with experiments."

"Thank you very much!" I said as he gave me the Watch. "I'll take the greatest care of it—why, here are the children again!"

"We could only but find *six* dindledums," said Bruno, putting them into my hands, " 'cause Sylvie said it were time to go back. And here's a big blackberry for *ooself*! We couldn't only find but *two*!"

"Thank you: it's *very* nice," I said. "And I suppose *you* ate the other, Bruno?"

"No, I didn't," Bruno said, carelessly. "*Aren't* they pretty dindledums, Mister Sir?"

"Yes, very: but what makes you limp so, my child?"

"Mine foot's come *hurted* again!" Bruno mournfully replied. And he sat down on the ground, and began nursing it.

The Professor held his head between his hands—an attitude that I knew indicated distraction of mind. "Better rest a minute," he said. "It may be better then—or it may be worse. If only I had some of my medicines here! I'm Court-Physician, you know," he added, aside to me.

"Shall I go and get you some blackberries, darling?" Sylvie whispered, with her arms round his neck; and she kissed away a tear that was trickling down his cheek.

Bruno brightened up in a moment. "That *are* a good plan!" he exclaimed. "I thinks my foot would come *quite* unhurted, if I eated a blackberry—two or three black-berries—six or seven blackberries——"

Sylvie got up hastily. "I'd better go", she said, aside to me, "before he gets into the double figures!"

"Let me come and help you," I said. "I can reach higher up than you can."

"Yes, please," said Sylvie, putting her hand into mine: and we walked off together.

"Bruno *loves* blackberries," she said, as we paced slowly along by a tall hedge, that looked a promising place for them, "and it was so *sweet* of him to make me eat the only one!"

"Oh, it was *you* that ate it, then? Bruno didn't seem to like to tell me about it."

"No; I saw that," said Sylvie. "He's always afraid of being praised. But he *made* me eat it, really! I would much rather he—oh, what's that?" And she clung to my hand, half-frightened, as we came in sight of a hare, lying on its side with legs stretched out, just in the entrance to the wood.

"It's a *hare*, my child. Perhaps it's asleep."

"No, it isn't asleep," Sylvie said, timidly going nearer to look at it: "it's eyes are open. Is it—is it——" her voice dropped to an awe-struck whisper. "is it *dead*, do you think?"

"Yes, it's quite dead," I said, after stooping to examine it. "Poor thing! I think it's been hunted to death. I know the harriers were out yesterday. But they haven't touched it. Perhaps they caught sight of another, and left it to die of fright and exhaustion."

"Hunted to *death*?" Sylvie repeated to herself, very slowly and sadly. "I thought hunting was a thing they *played* at—like a game. Bruno and I hunt snails: but we never hurt them when we catch them!"

"Sweet angel!" I thought. "How am I to get the idea of *Sport* into your innocent mind?" And as we stood, hand-in-hand, looking down at the dead hare, I tried to put the thing into such words as she could understand. "You know what fierce wild-beasts lions and tigers are?" Sylvie nodded. "Well, in some countries men *have* to kill them, to save their own lives, you know."

"Yes," said Sylvie: "if one tried to kill *me*, Bruno would kill *it*—if he could."

"Well, and so the men—the hunters—get to enjoy it, you know: the running, and the fighting, and the shouting, and the danger."

"Yes," said Sylvie. "Bruno likes danger."

"Well, but, in *this* country, there aren't any lions and tigers, loose: so they hunt other creatures, you see." I hoped, but in vain, that this would satisfy her, and that she would ask no more questions.

"They hunt *foxes*," Sylvie said, thoughtfully. "And I think they *kill* them, too. Foxes are very fierce. I daresay men don't love them. Are hares fierce?"

"No," I said, "A hare is a sweet, gentle, timid animal— almost as gentle as a lamb."

"But, if men *love* hares, why—why——" her voice quivered, and her sweet eyes were brimming over with tears.

"I'm afraid they *don't* love them, dear child."

"All *children* love them," Sylvie said. "All *ladies* love them."

"I'm afraid even *ladies* go to hunt them sometimes."

Sylvie shuddered. "Oh, no, not *ladies*!" she earnestly pleaded. "Not Lady Muriel!"

"No, *she* never does, I'm sure—but this is too sad a sight for *you*, dear. Let's try and find some——"

But Sylvie was not satisfied yet. In a hushed, solemn tone, with bowed head and clasped hands, she put her final question. "Does GOD love hares?"

"Yes!" I said. "I'm *sure* He does! He loves every living thing. Even sinful *men*. How much more the animals, that cannot sin!"

"I don't know what 'sin' means," said Sylvie. And I didn't try to explain it.

"Come, my child," I said, trying to lead her away. "Wish good-bye to the poor hare, and come and look for blackberries."

"Good-bye, poor hare!" Sylvie obediently repeated, looking over her shoulder at it as we turned away. And then, all in a moment, her self-command gave way. Pulling her hand out of mine, she ran back to where the dead hare was lying, and flung herself down at its side in such an agony of grief as I could hardly have believed possible in so young a child.

"Oh, my darling, my darling!" she moaned over and over again. "And GOD meant your life to be so beautiful!"

Sometimes, but always keeping her face hidden on the ground, she would reach out one little hand, to stroke the poor dead thing, and then once more bury her face in her hands, and sob as if her heart would break.

I was afraid she would really make herself ill: still I thought it best to let her weep away the first sharp agony of grief: and, after a few minutes, the sobbing gradually ceased, and Sylvie rose to her feet, and looked calmly at me, though tears were still streaming down her cheeks.

I did not dare to speak again, just yet; but simply held out my hand to her, that we might quit the melancholy spot.

"Yes, I'll come now," she said. Very reverently she kneeled down, and kissed the dead hare; then rose and gave me her hand, and we moved on in silence.

A child's sorrow is violent, but short; and it was almost in her usual voice that she said, after a minute, "Oh, stop, stop! Here are some *lovely* blackberries!"

We filled our hands with fruit, and returned in all haste to where the Professor and Bruno were seated on a bank, awaiting our return.

Just before we came within hearing-distance, Sylvie checked me. "Please don't tell *Bruno* about the hare!" she said.

"Very well, my child! But why not?"

Tears again glittered in those sweet eyes, and she turned her head away, so that I could scarcely hear her reply. "He's—he's very *fond* of gentle creatures, you know. And he'd—he'd be so sorry! I don't want him to be made sorry."

"And *your* agony of sorrow is to count for nothing, then, sweet unselfish child!" I thought to myself. But no more was said till we had reached our friends; and Bruno was far too much engrossed, in the feast we had brought him, to take any notice of Sylvie's unusually grave manner.

"I'm afraid it's getting rather late, Professor?" I said.

"Yes, indeed," said the Professor. "I must take you all through the Ivory Door again. You've stayed your full time."

"Mightn't we stay a *little* longer!" pleaded Sylvie.

"Just *one* minute!" added Bruno.

But the Professor was unyielding. "It's a great privilege, coming through at all," he said. "We must go now." And we followed him obediently to the Ivory Door, which he threw open, and signed to me to go through first.

"You're coming too, aren't you?" I said to Sylvie.

"Yes," she said: "but you wo'n't see us after you've gone through."

"But suppose I wait for you outside?" I asked, as I stepped through the doorway.

"In that case," said Sylvie, "I think the potato would be *quite* justified in asking *your* weight. I can quite imagine a really *superior* kidney-potato declining to argue with any one under *fifteen stone!*"

With a great effort I recovered the thread of my thoughts. "We lapse very quickly into nonsense!" I said.

Chapter XXII

Crossing the Line

"Let us lapse back again," said Lady Muriel. "Take another cup of tea? I hope *that's* sound common sense?"

"And all that strange adventure", I thought, "has occupied the space of a single comma in Lady Muriel's speech! A single comma, for which grammarians tell us to 'count *one*'!" (I felt no doubt that the Professor had kindly put back the time for me, to the exact point at which I had gone to sleep.)

When a few minutes afterwards, we left the house, Arthur's first remark was certainly a strange one. "We've been there just *twenty minutes,*" he said, "and I've done nothing but listen to you and Lady Muriel talking: and yet, somehow, I feel exactly as if *I* had been talking with her for an *hour* at least!"

And so he *had* been, I felt no doubt: only, as the time had been put back to the beginning of the *tête-à-tête* he referred to, the whole of it had passed into oblivion, if not into nothingness! But I valued my own reputation for sanity too highly to venture on explaining to *him* what had happened.

For some cause, which I could not at the moment divine, Arthur was unusually grave and silent during our walk home. It could not be connected with Eric Lindon, I thought, as he had for some days been away in London: so that, having Lady Muriel almost "all to himself"—for *I* was only too glad to hear those two conversing, to have any wish to intrude any remarks of my own—he *ought*, theoretically, to have been specially radiant and contented with life. "Can he have heard any bad news?" I said to myself. And, almost as if he had read my thoughts, he spoke.

"He will be here by the last train," he said, in the tone of one who is continuing a conversation rather than beginning one.

"Captain Lindon, do you mean?"

"Yes—Captain Lindon," said Arthur: "I said 'he', because I fancied we were talking about him. The Earl told me he comes to-night, though *to-morrow* is the day when he will know about the Commission that he's hoping for. I wonder he doesn't stay another day to hear the result, if he's really so anxious about it as the Earl believes he is."

"He can have a telegram sent after him," I said: "but it's not very soldier-like, running away from possible bad news!"

"He's a very good fellow," said Arthur: "but I confess it would be good news for *me*, if he got his Commission, and his Marching Orders all at once! I wish him all happiness—with *one* exception. Good night!" (We had reached home by this time.) "I'm not good company to-night—better be alone."

It was much the same, next day. Arthur declared he wasn't fit for Society, and I had to set forth alone for an afternoon-stroll. I took the road to the Station, and, at the point where the road from the "Hall" joined it, I paused, seeing my friends in the distance, seemingly bound for the same goal.

"Will you join us?" the Earl said, after I had exchanged greetings with him, and Lady Muriel, and Captain Lindon. "This restless young man is expecting a telegram, and we are going to the Station to meet it."

"There is also a restless young woman in the case," Lady Muriel added.

"That goes without saying, my child," said her father. "Women are *always* restless!"

"For generous appreciation of all one's *best* qualities," his daughter impressively remarked, "there's nothing to compare with a father, is there, Eric?"

"Cousins are not 'in it'," said Eric: and then somehow the conversation lapsed into two duologues, the younger folk taking the lead, and the two old men following with less eager steps.

"And when are we to see your little friends again?" said the Earl. "They are singularly attractive children."

"I shall be delighted to bring them, when I can," I said. "But I don't know, myself, when I am likely to see them again."

"I'm not going to question you," said the Earl: "but there's no harm in mentioning that Muriel is simply tormented with curiosity! We know most of the people about here, and she has been vainly trying to guess what house they can possibly be staying at."

"Some day I may be able to enlighten her: but just at present——"

"Thanks. She must bear it as best she can. *I* tell her it's a grand opportunity for practising *patience*. But she hardly sees it from that point of view. Why, there *are* the children!"

So indeed they were: waiting (for *us*, apparently) at a stile, which they could not have climbed over more than a few moments, as Lady Muriel and her cousin had passed it without seeing them. On catching sight of us, Bruno ran to meet us, and to exhibit to us, with much pride, the handle of a clasp-knife—the blade having been broken off—which he had picked up in the road.

"And what shall you use it for, Bruno?" I said.

"Don't know," Bruno carelessly replied: "must think."

"A child's first view of life", the Earl remarked, with that sweet sad smile of his, "is that it is a period to be spent in accumulating portable property. That view gets modified as the years glide away." And he held out his hand to Sylvie, who had placed herself by me, looking a little shy of him.

But the gentle old man was not one with whom any child, human of fairy, could be shy for long; and she had very soon deserted my hand for his—Bruno alone remaining faithful to his first friend. We overtook the other couple just as they reached the Station, and both Lady Muriel and Eric greeted the children as old friends—the latter with the words "So you got to Babylon by candle-light, after all?"

"Yes, and back again!" cried Bruno.

Lady Muriel looked from one to the other in blank astonishment. "What, *you* know them, Eric?" she exclaimed. "This mystery grows deeper every day!"

"Then we must be somewhere in the Third Act," said Eric. "You don't expect the mystery to be cleared up till the Fifth Act, do you?"

"But it's such a *long* drama!" was the plaintive reply. "We *must* have got to the Fifth Act by this time!"

"*Third* Act, I assure you," said the young soldier mercilessly. "Scene, a railway-platform. Lights down. Enter Prince (in disguise, of course) and faithful Attendant. *This* is the Prince—" (taking Bruno's hand) "and here stands his humble Servant! What is your Royal Highness's next command?" And he made a most courtier-like low bow to his puzzled little friend.

"Oo're *not* a Servant!" Bruno scornfully exclaimed. "Oo're a *Gemplun*!"

"*Servant*, I assure your Royal Highness!" Eric respectfully insisted. "Allow me to mention to your Royal Highness my various situations—past, present, and future."

"What did oo begin wiz?" Bruno asked, beginning to enter into the jest. "Was oo a shoe-black?"

"Lower than that, your Royal Highness! Years ago, I offered myself as a *Slave*—as a '*Confidential* Slave', I think it's called?" he asked, turning to Lady Muriel.

But Lady Muriel heard him not: something had gone wrong with her glove, which entirely engrossed her attention.

"Did oo get the place?" said Bruno.

"Sad to say, your Royal Highness, I did *not*! So I had to take a situation as—as *Waiter*, which I have now held for some years—haven't I?" He again glanced at Lady Muriel.

"Sylvie dear, *do* help me to button this glove!" Lady Muriel whispered, hastily stooping down, and failing to hear the question.

"And what will oo be *next*?" said Bruno.

"My next place will, I hope, be that of *Groom*. And after that——"

"Don't puzzle the child so!" Lady Muriel interrupted. "What nonsense you talk!"

"—after that," Eric persisted, "I hope to obtain the situation of *Housekeeper*, which—*Fourth Act!*" he proclaimed, with a sudden change of tone. "Lights turned up. Red lights. Green lights. Distant rumble heard. Enter a passenger-train!"

And in another minute the train drew up alongside of the platform, and a stream of passengers began to flow out from the booking office and waiting-rooms.

"Did you ever make *real* life into a drama?" said the Earl. "Now just try. I've often amused myself that way. Consider this platform as our stage. Good entrances and exits on *both* sides, you see. Capital background scene: real engine moving up and down. All this bustle, and people passing to and fro, must have been most carefully rehearsed! How naturally they do it! With never a glance at the audience! And every grouping is quite fresh, you see. No repetition!"

It really was admirable, as soon as I began to enter into it from this point of view. Even a porter passing, with a barrow piled with luggage, seemed so realistic that one was tempted to applaud. He was followed by an angry mother, with hot red face, dragging along two screaming children, and calling, to some one behind, "John! Come on!" Enter, John, very meek, very silent, and loaded with parcels. And he was followed, in his turn, by a frightened little nursemaid, carrying a fat baby, also screaming. All the children screamed.

"Capital byplay!" said the old man aside. "Did you notice the nursemaid's look of terror? It was simply *perfect*!"

"You have struck quite a new vein," I said. "To most of us Life and its pleasures seem like a mine that is nearly worked out."

"Worked out!" exclaimed the Earl. "For any one with true dramatic instincts, it is only the Overture that is ended! The real treat has yet to begin. You go to a theatre, and pay your ten shillings for a stall, and what do you get for your money? Perhaps it's a dialogue between a couple of farmers—unnatural in their overdone caricature of farmers' dress—more unnatural in their constrained attitudes and gestures—most unnatural in their attempts at ease and geniality in their talk. Go instead and take a seat in a third-class railway-carriage, and you'll get the same dialogue done *to the life*! Front-seats—no orchestra to block the view—and nothing to pay!"

"Which reminds me," said Eric. "There is nothing to pay on receiving a telegram! Shall we enquire for one?" And he and Lady Muriel strolled off in the direction of the Telegraph-Office.

"I wonder if Shakespeare had that thought in his mind", I said, "when he wrote 'All the world's a stage'?"

The old man sighed. "And so it is," he said, "look at it as you will. Life is indeed a drama; a drama with but few *encores*—and no *bouquets*!" he added dreamily. "We spend one half of it in regretting the things we did in the other half!"

"And the secret of *enjoying* it", he continued, resuming his cheerful tone, "is *intensity!*"

"But not in the modern æsthetic sense, I presume? Like the young lady, in Punch, who begins a conversation with 'Are you *intense?*'"

"By no means!" replied the Earl. "What I mean is intensity of *thought*—a concentrated *attention*. We lose half the pleasure we might have in Life, by not really *attending*. Take any instance you like: it doesn't matter *how* trivial the pleasure may be—the principle is the same. Suppose *A* and *B* are reading the same second-rate circulating-library novel. *A* never troubles himself to master the relationships of the characters, on which perhaps all the interest of the story depends: he 'skips' over all the descriptions of scenery, and every passage that looks rather dull: he doesn't half attend to the passages he does read: he goes on reading—merely from want of resolution to find another occupation—for hours after he ought to have put the book aside: and reaches the 'FINIS' in a state of utter weariness and depression! *B* puts his whole soul *into* the thing—on the principle that 'whatever is worth doing is worth doing *well*': he masters the genealogies: he calls up pictures before his 'mind's eye' as he reads about the scenery: best of all, he resolutely shuts the book at the end of some chapter, while his interest is yet at its keenest, and turns to other subjects; so that, when next he allows himself an hour at it, it is like a hungry man sitting down to dinner: and, when the book is finished, he returns to the work of his daily life like 'a giant refreshed'!"

"But suppose the book were really *rubbish*—nothing to repay attention?"

"Well, suppose it," said the Earl. "My theory meets *that* case, I assure you! *A* never finds out that it *is* rubbish, but maunders on to the end, trying to believe he's enjoying himself. *B* quietly shuts the book, when he's read a dozen pages, walks off to the Library, and changes it for a better! I have yet *another* theory for adding to the enjoyment of Life—that is, if I have not exhausted your patience? I'm afraid you find me a very garrulous old man."

"No indeed!" I exclaimed earnestly. And indeed I felt as if one *could* not easily tire of the sweet sadness of that gentle voice.

"It is, that we should learn to take our pleasures *quickly*, and our pains *slowly*."

"But why? I should have put it the other way, myself."

"By taking *artificial* pain—which can be as trivial as you please—*slowly*, the result is that, when *real* pain comes, however severe, all you need do is to let it go at its *ordinary* pace, and it's over in a moment!"

"Very true," I said, "but how about the *pleasure*?"

"Why, by taking it quick, you can get so much more into life. It takes *you* three hours and a half to hear and enjoy an opera. Suppose *I* can take it in, and enjoy it, in half-an-hour. Why, I can enjoy *seven* operas, while you are listening to *one*!"

"Always supposing you have an orchestra capable of *playing* them," I said. "And that orchestra has yet to be found!"

The old man smiled. "I have heard an air played," he said, "and by no means a short one—played right through, variations and all, in three seconds!"

"When? And how?" I asked eagerly, with a half-notion that I was dreaming again.

"It was done by a little musical-box," he quietly replied. "After it had been wound up, the regulator, or something, broke, and it ran down, as I said, in about three seconds. But it *must* have played all the notes, you know!"

"Did you *enjoy* it?" I asked, with all the severity of a cross-examining barrister.

"No, I didn't!" he candidly confessed. "But then, you know, I hadn't been trained to that kind of music!"

"I should much like to *try* your plan," I said, and, as Sylvie and Bruno happened to run up to us at the moment, I left them to keep the Earl company, and strolled along the platform, making each person and event play its part in an *extempore* drama for my especial benefit. "What, is the Earl tired of you already?" I said, as the children ran past me.

"No!" Sylvie replied with great emphasis. "He wants the evening-paper. So Bruno's going to be a little news-boy!"

"Mind you charge a good price for it!" I called after them.

Returning up the platform, I came upon Sylvie alone.

"Well, child," I said, "where's your little news-boy? Couldn't he get you an evening-paper?"

"He went to get one at the book-stall at the other side," said Sylvie; "and he's coming across the line with it—oh, Bruno, you ought to cross by the bridge!" for the distant thud, thud, of the Express was already audible. Suddenly a look of horror came over her face. "Oh, he's fallen down on the rails!" she cried, and darted past me at a speed that quite defied the hasty effort I made to stop her.

But the wheezy old Station-Master happened to be close behind me: he wasn't good for much, poor old man, but he was good for this; and, before I could turn round, he had the child clasped in his arms, saved from the certain death she was rushing to. So intent was I in watching this scene, that I hardly saw a flying figure in a light grey suit, who shot across from the back of the plat-form, and was on the line in another second. So far as one could take note of time in such a moment of horror, he had about ten clear seconds, before the Express would be upon him, in which to cross the rails and to pick up Bruno. Whether he did so or not it was quite impossible to guess: the next thing one knew was that the Express had passed, and that, whether for life or death, all was over. When the cloud of dust had cleared away, and the line was once more visible, we saw with thankful hearts that the child and his deliverer were safe.

"All right!" Eric called to us cheerfully, as he recrossed the line. "He's more frightened than hurt!"

He lifted the little fellow up into Lady Muriel's arms, and mounted the platform as gaily as if nothing had happened: but he was as pale as death, and leaned heavily on the arm I hastily offered him, fearing he was about to faint. "I'll just—sit down a moment——" he said dreamily: "—where's Sylvie?"

Sylvie ran to him, and flung her arms round his neck, sobbing as if her heart would break. "Don't do that, my darling!" Eric murmured, with a strange look in his eyes. "Nothing to cry about now, you know. But you very nearly got yourself killed for nothing!"

"For Bruno!" the little maiden sobbed. "And he would have done it for me. Wouldn't you, Bruno?"

"Course I would!" Bruno said, looking round with a bewildered air.

Lady Muriel kissed him in silence as she put him down out of her arms. Then she beckoned Sylvie to come and take his hand, and signed to the children to go back to where the Earl was seated. "Tell him," she whispered with quivering lips, "tell him—all is well!" Then she turned to the hero of the day. "I thought it was *death*," she said. "Thank God, you are safe! Did you see how near it was?"

"I saw there was just time," Eric said lightly. "A soldier must learn to carry his life in his hand, you know. I'm all right now. Shall we go to the telegraph-office again? I daresay it's come by this time."

I went to join the Earl and the children, and we waited —almost in silence, for no one seemed inclined to talk, and Bruno was half-asleep on Sylvie's lap—till the others joined us. No telegram had come.

"I'll take a stroll with the children," I said, feeling that we were a little *de trop*, "and I'll look in, in the course of the evening."

"We must go back into the wood, now," Sylvie said, as soon as we were out of hearing. "We ca'n't stay this size any longer."

"Then you will be quite tiny Fairies, again, next time we meet?"

"Yes," said Sylvie: "but we'll be children again some day—if you'll let us. Bruno's very anxious to see Lady Muriel again."

"She are *welly* nice," said Bruno.

"I shall be very glad to take you to see her again," I said. "Hadn't I better give you back the Professor's Watch? It'll be too large for you to carry when you're Fairies, you know."

Bruno laughed merrily. I was glad to see he had quite recovered from the terrible scene he had gone through. "Oh, no, it wo'n't!" he said. "When *we* go small, *it'll* go small!"

"And then it'll go straight to the Professor," Sylvie added, "and you wo'n't be able to use it any more: so you'd better use it all you can, *now*. We *must* go small when the sun sets. Good-bye!"

"Good-bye!" cried Bruno. But their voices sounded very far away, and, when I looked round, both children had disappeared.

"And it wants only two hours to sunset!" I said as I strolled on. "I must make the best of my time!"

Chapter XXIII

An Outlandish Watch

As I entered the little town, I came upon two of the fishermen's wives interchanging that last word "which never was the last": and it occurred to me, as an experiment with the Magic Watch, to wait till the little scene was over, and then to "encore" it.

"Well, good night t'ye! And ye winna forget to send us word when your Martha writes?"

"Nay, ah winna forget. An' if she isn't suited, she can but coom back. Good night t'ye!"

A casual observer might have thought "and there ends

the dialogue!" That casual observer would have been mistaken.

"Ah, she'll like 'em, I war'n' ye! *They'll* not treat her bad, yer may depend. They're varry canny fowk. Good night!"

"Ay, they *are* that! Good night!"

"Good night! And ye'll send us word if she writes?"

"Aye, ah will, yer may depend! Good night t'ye!"

And at last they parted. I waited till they were some twenty yards apart, and then put the Watch a minute back. The instantaneous change was startling: the two figures seemed to flash back into their former places.

"—isn't suited, she can but coom back. Good night t'ye!" one of them was saying: and so the whole dialogue was repeated, and, when they had parted for the second time, I let them go their several ways, and strolled on through the town.

"But the real usefulness of this magic power", I thought, "would be to undo some harm, some painful event, some accident——" I had not long to wait for an opportunity of testing *this* property also of the Magic Watch, for, even as the thought passed through my mind, the accident I was imagining occurred. A light cart was standing at the door of the "Great Millinery Depôt" of Elveston, laden with card-board packing-cases, which the driver was carrying into the shop, one by one. One of the cases had fallen into the street. but it scarcely seemed worth while to step forward and pick it up, as the man would be back again in a moment. Yet, in that moment, a young man riding a bicycle came sharp round the corner of the street and, in trying to avoid running over the box, upset his machine, and was thrown headlong against the wheel of the spring-cart. The driver ran out to his assistance, and he and I together raised the unfortunate cyclist and carried him into the shop. His head was cut and bleeding; and one knee seemed to be badly injured; and it was speedily settled that he had better be conveyed at once to the only Surgery in the place. I helped them in emptying the cart, and placing in it some pillows for the wounded man to rest on; and it was only when the driver had mounted to his place, and was starting for the Surgery, that I bethought me of the strange power I possessed of undoing all this harm.

"Now is my time!" I said to myself, as I moved back the hand of the Watch, and saw, almost without surprise this time, all things restored to the places they had occupied at the critical moment when I had first noticed the fallen packing-case.

Instantly I stepped out into the street, picked up the box, and replaced it in the cart: in the next moment the bicycle had spun round the corner, passed the cart without let or hindrance, and soon vanished in the distance, in a cloud of dust.

"Delightful power of magic!" I thought. "How much of human suffering I have—not only relieved, but actually annihilated!" And, in a glow of conscious virtue, I stood watching the unloading of the cart, still holding the Magic Watch open in my hand, as I was curious to see what would happen when we again reached the exact time at which I had put back the hand.

The result was one that, if only I had considered the thing carefully, I might have foreseen: as the hand of the Watch touched the mark, the spring-cart—which had driven off, and was by this time half-way down the street, was back again at the door, and in the act of starting, while—oh woe for the golden dream of world-wide benevolence that had dazzled my dreaming fancy!—the wounded youth was once more reclining on the heap of pillows, his pale face set rigidly in the hard lines that told of pain resolutely endured.

"Oh mocking Magic Watch!" I said to myself, as I passed out of the little town, and took the seaward road that led to my lodgings. "The good I fancied I could do is vanished like a dream: the evil of this troublesome world is the only abiding reality!"

And now I must record an experience so strange, that I

think it only fair, before beginning to relate it, to release my much-enduring reader from any obligation he may feel to believe this part of my story, *I* would not have believed it, I freely confess, if I had not seen it with my own eyes: then why should I expect it of my reader, who, quite possibly, has never seen anything of the sort?

I was passing a pretty little villa, which stood rather back from the road, in its own grounds, with bright flower-beds in front—creepers wandering over the walls and hanging in festoons about the bow-windows—an easy-chair forgotten on the lawn, with a newspaper lying near it—a small pug-dog "couchant" before it, resolved to guard the treasure even at the sacrifice of life—and a front-door standing invitingly half-open. "Here is my chance", I thought, "for testing the reverse action of the Magic Watch!" I pressed the "reversal-peg" and walked in. In *another* house, the entrance of a stranger might cause surprise—perhaps anger, even going so far as to expel the said stranger with violence: but *here*, I knew, nothing of the sort could happen. The *ordinary* course of events—first, to think nothing about me; then, hearing my footsteps to look up and see me; and then to wonder what business I had there—would be reversed by the action of my Watch. They would *first* wonder who I was, *then* see me, then look down, and think no more about me. And as to being expelled with violence, *that* event would necessarily come *first* in this case. "So, if I can once get *in*," I said to myself, "all risk of *expulsion* will be over!"

The pug-dog sat up, as a precautionary measure, as I passed; but, as I took no notice of the treasure he was guarding, he let me go by without even one remonstrant bark. "He that takes my life," he seemed to be saying, wheezily, to himself, "takes trash: But he that takes the *Daily Telegraph*——!" But this awful contingency I did not face.

The party in the drawing-room—I had walked straight in, you understand, without ringing the bell, or giving any notice of my approach—consisted of four laughing rosy children, of ages from about fourteen down to ten, who were, apparently, all coming towards the door (I found they were really walking *backwards*), while their mother, seated by the fire with some needle-work on her lap, was saying, just as I entered the room, "Now, girls, you may get your things on for a walk."

To my utter astonishment—for I was not yet accustomed to the action of the Watch—"all smiles ceased" (as Browning says) on the four pretty faces, and they all got out pieces of needle-work, and sat down. No one noticed *me* in the least, as I quietly took a chair and sat down to watch them.

When the needle-work had been unfolded, and they were all ready to begin, their mother said "Come, *that's* done, at last! You may fold up your work, girls." But the children took no notice whatever of the remark; on the contrary, they set to work at once sewing—if that is the proper word to describe an operation such as *I* had never before witnessed. Each of them threaded her needle with a short end of thread attached to the work, which was instantly pulled by an invisible force through the stuff, dragging the needle after it: the nimble fingers of the little sempstress caught it at the other side, but only to lose it again the next moment. And so the work went on, steadily undoing itself, and the neatly-stitched little dresses, or whatever they were, steadily falling to pieces. Now and then one of the children would pause, as the recovered thread became inconveniently long, wind it on a bobbin, and start again with another short end.

At last all the work was picked to pieces and put away, and the lady led the way into the next room, walking backwards, and making the insane remark "Not yet, dear: we *must* get the sewing done first." After which, I was not surprised to see the children skipping backwards after her, exclaiming "Oh, mother, it *is* such a lovely day for a walk!"

In the dining-room, the table had only dirty plates and empty dishes on it. However the party—with the addition of a gentleman, as good-natured, and as rosy, as the children—seated themselves at it very contentedly.

You have seen people eating cherry-tart, and every now and then cautiously conveying a cherry-stone from their lips to their plates? Well, something like that went on all through this ghastly—or shall we say "ghostly"?—banquet. An empty fork is raised to the lips: there it receives a neatly-cut piece of mutton, and swiftly conveys it to the plate, where it instantly attaches itself to the mutton already there. Soon one of the plates, furnished with a complete slice of mutton and two potatoes, was handed up to the presiding gentleman, who quietly replaced the slice on the joint, and the potatoes in the dish.

Their conversation was, if possible, more bewildering than their mode of dining. It began by the youngest girl suddenly, and without provocation, addressing her eldest sister. "Oh, you *wicked* story-teller!" she said.

I expected a sharp reply from the sister; but, instead of this, she turned laughingly to her father, and said, in a very loud stage-whisper, "To be a bride!"

The father, in order to do *his* part in a conversation that seemed only fit for lunatics, replied "Whisper it to me, dear."

But she *didn't* whisper (these children never did anything they were told): she said, quite loud, "Of course not! Everybody knows what *Dolly* wants!"

And little Dolly shrugged her shoulders, and said, with a pretty pettishness, "Now, Father, you're not to tease! You know I don't want to be bride's-maid to *anybody*!"

"And Dolly's to be the fourth," was her father's idiotic reply.

Here Number Three put in her oar. "Oh, it *is* settled, Mother dear, really and truly! Mary told us all about it. It's to be next Tuesday four weeks—and three of her cousins are coming to be bride's-maids—and——"

"*She* doesn't forget it Minnie!" the Mother laughingly replied. "I do wish they'd get it settled! I don't like long engagements."

And Minnie wound up the conversation—if so chaotic a series of remarks deserves the name—with "Only think! We passed the Cedars this morning, just exactly as Mary Davenant was standing at the gate, wishing good-bye to Mister—I forget his name. Of course we looked the other way."

By this time I was so hopelessly confused that I gave up listening, and followed the dinner down into the kitchen.

But to you, O hypercritical reader, resolute to believe no item of this weird adventure, what need to tell how the mutton was placed on the spit, and slowly unroasted— how the potatoes were wrapped in their skins, and handed over to the gardener to be buried—how, when the mutton had at length attained to rawness, the fire, which had gradually changed from red-heat to a mere blaze, died down so suddenly that the cook had only just time to catch its last flicker on the end of a match—or how the maid, having taken the mutton off the spit, carried it (backwards, of course) out of the house, to meet the butcher, who was coming (also backwards) down the road?

The longer I thought over this strange adventure, the more hopelessly tangled the mystery became: and it was a real relief to meet Arthur in the road, and get him to go with me up to the Hall, to learn what news the telegraph had brought. I told him, as we went, what had happened at the Station, but as to my further adventures I thought it best, for the present, to say nothing.

The Earl was sitting alone when we entered. "I am glad you are come in to keep me company," he said. "Muriel is gone to bed—the excitement of that terrible scene was too much for her—and Eric has gone to the hotel to pack his things, to start for London by the early train."

"Then the telegram has come!" I said.

"Did you not hear? Oh, I had forgotten: it came in after you left the Station. Yes, it's all right: Eric has got his commission; and, now that he has arranged matters with Muriel, he has business in town that must be seen to at once."

"What arrangement do you mean?" I asked with a sinking heart, as the thought of Arthur's crushed hopes came to my mind. "Do you mean that they are *engaged*?"

"They have been engaged—in a sense—for two years," the old man gently replied: "that is, he has had my promise to consent to it, so soon as he could secure a permanent and settled line in life. I could never be happy with my child married to a man without an object to live for— without even an object to die for!"

"I hope they will be happy," a strange voice said. The speaker was evidently in the room, but I had not heard the door open, and I looked around in some astonishment. The Earl seemed to share my surprise. "Who spoke?" he exclaimed.

"It was I," said Arthur, looking at us with a worn, haggard face, and eyes from which the light of life seemed suddenly to have faded. "And let me wish *you* joy also, dear friend," he added, looking sadly at the Earl, and speaking in the same hollow tones that had startled us so much.

"Thank you," the old man said, simply and heartily.

A silence followed: then I rose, feeling sure that Arthur would wish to be alone, and bade our gentle host "Good night": Arthur took his hand, but said nothing: nor did he speak again, as we went home, till we were in the house and had lit our bed-room candles. Then he said, more to himself than to me, *"The heart knoweth its own bitterness.* I never understood those words till now."

The next few days passed wearily enough. I felt no inclination to call again, by myself, at the Hall; still less to propose that Arthur should go with me: it seemed better to wait till Time—that gentle healer of our bitterest sorrows—should have helped him to recover from the first shock of the disappointment that had blighted his life.

Business, however, soon demanded my presence in town; and I had to announce to Arthur that I must leave him for a while. "But I hope to run down again in a month," I added. "I would stay now, if I could. I don't think it's good for you to be alone."

"No, I ca'n't face solitude, *here*, for long," said Arthur. "But don't think about *me*. I have made up my mind to accept a post in India, that has been offered me. Out there, I suppose I shall find something to live for; I ca'n't see *anything* at present. '*This life of mine I guard, as God's high gift, from scathe and wrong, Not greatly care to lose!*' "

"Yes," I said: "your name-sake bore as heavy a blow, and lived through it."

"A far heavier one than *mine*," said Arthur. "The woman *he* loved proved false. There is no such cloud as *that* on my memory of—of——" He left the name unuttered, and went on hurriedly. "But *you* will return, will you not?"

"Yes, I shall come back for a short time."

"Do," said Arthur: "and you shall write and tell me of our friends. I'll send you my address when I'm settled down."

CHAPTER XXIV

The Frogs' Birthday-Treat

AND so it came to pass that, just a week after the day when my Fairy-friends first appeared as Children, I found myself taking a farewell-stroll through the wood, in the hope of meeting them once more. I had but to stretch myself on the smooth turf, and the "eerie" feeling was on me in a moment.

"Put oor ear *welly* low down," said Bruno, "and I'll tell oo a secret! It's the Frogs' Birthday-Treat—and we've lost the Baby!"

"*What* Baby?" I said, quite bewildered by this complicated piece of news.

"The *Queen's* Baby, a course!" said Bruno. "Titania's Baby. And we's *welly* sorry. Sylvie, she's—oh so sorry!"

"*How* sorry is she?" I asked, mischievously.

"Three-quarters of a yard," Bruno replied with perfect solemnity. "And *I'm* a little sorry too," he added, shutting his eyes so as not to see that he was smiling.

"And what are you doing about the Baby?"

"Well, the *soldiers* are all looking for it—up and down —everywhere."

"The *soldiers*?" I exclaimed.

"Yes, a course!" said Bruno. "When there's no fighting to be done, the soldiers doos any little odd jobs, oo know."

I was amused at the idea of its being a "little odd job" to find the Royal Baby. "But how did you come to lose it?" I asked.

"We put it in a flower," Sylvie, who had just joined us, explained with her eyes full of tears. "Only we ca'n't remember *which*!"

"She says *us* put it in a flower," Bruno interrupted, " 'cause she doesn't want *I* to get punished. But it were really *me* what put it there. *Sylvie* were picking Dindle-dums."

"You shouldn't say '*us* put it in a flower'," Sylvie very gravely remarked.

"Well, *hus*, then," said Bruno. "I never *can* remember those horrid H's!"

"Let me help you to look for it," I said. So Sylvie and I made a "voyage of discovery" among all the flowers; but there was no Baby to be seen.

"What's become of Bruno?" I said, when we had completed our tour.

"He's down in the ditch there," said Sylvie, "amusing a young Frog."

I went down on my hands and knees to look for him, for I felt very curious to know how young Frogs *ought* to be amused. After a minute's search, I found him sitting at the edge of the ditch, by the side of the little Frog, and looking rather disconsolate.

"How are you getting on, Bruno?" I said, nodding to him as he looked up.

"Ca'n't amuse it no more," Bruno answered, very dolefully, " 'cause it wo'n't say what it would like to do next! I've showed it all the duck-weeds—and a live caddisworm—but it wo'n't say nuffin! What—would oo—like?" he shouted into the ear of the Frog: but the little creature sat quite still, and took no notice of him. "It's deaf, I think!" Bruno said, turning away with a sigh. "And it's time to get the Theatre ready."

"Who are the audience to be?"

"Only but Frogs," said Bruno. "But they haven't comed yet. They wants to be drove up, like sheep."

"Would it save time", I suggested, "if *I* were to walk round with Sylvie, to drive up the Frogs, while *you* get the Theatre ready?"

"That *are* a good plan!" cried Bruno. "But where *are* Sylvie?"

"I'm here!" said Sylvie, peeping over the edge of the bank. "I was just watching two Frogs that were having a race."

"Which won it?" Bruno eagerly inquired.

Sylvie was puzzled. "He *does* ask such hard questions!" she confided to me.

"And what's to happen in the Theatre?" I asked.

"First they have their Birthday-Feast," Sylvie said: "then Bruno does some Bits of Shakespeare; then he tells them a Story."

"I should think the Frogs like the Feast best. Don't they?"

"Well, there's generally very few of them that get any. They *will* keep their mouths shut so tight! And it's just as well they *do*," she added, "because Bruno likes to cook it himself: and he cooks *very* queerly. Now they're all in. Would you just help me to put them with their heads the right way?"

We soon managed this part of the business, though the Frogs kept up a most discontented croaking all the time.

"What *are* they saying?" I asked Sylvie.

"They're saying 'Fork! Fork!' It's very silly of them! You're not going to *have* forks!" she announced with some severity. "Those that want any Feast have just got to open their mouths, and Bruno'll put some of it in!"

At this moment Bruno appeared, wearing a little white apron to show that he was a Cook, and carrying a tureen full of very queer-looking soup. I watched very carefully as he moved about among the Frogs; but I could not see that *any* of them opened their mouths to be fed—except one very young one, and I'm nearly sure it did it accidentally, in yawning. However, Bruno instantly put a large spoonful of soup into its mouth, and the poor little thing coughed violently for some time.

So Sylvie and I had to share the soup between us, and to *pretend* to enjoy it, for it certainly was *very* queerly cooked.

I only ventured to take *one* spoonful of it ("Sylvie's Summer-Soup," Bruno said it was), and must candidly confess that it was not *at all* nice; and I could not feel surprised that so many guests had kept their mouths shut up tight.

"What's the soup *made* of, Bruno?" said Sylvie, who had put a spoonful of it to her lips, and was making a wry face over it.

And Bruno's answer was anything but encouraging. "Bits of things!"

The entertainment was to conclude with "Bits of Shakespeare", as Sylvie expressed it, which were all to be done by Bruno, Sylvie being fully engaged in making the Frogs keep their heads towards the stage: after which Bruno was to appear in his real character, and tell them a Story of his own invention.

"Will the Story have a Moral to it?" I asked Sylvie, while Bruno was away behind the hedge, dressing for the first "Bit".

"I *think* so," Sylvie replied doubtfully. "There generally *is* a Moral, only he puts it in too soon."

"And will he *say* all the Bits of Shakespeare?"

"No, he'll only *act* them," said Sylvie. "He knows hardly any of the words. When I see what he's dressed like, I've to tell the Frogs what character it is. They're always in such a hurry to guess! Don't you hear them all saying 'What? What?'" And so indeed they were: it had only sounded like croaking, till Sylvie explained it, but I could now make out the "Wawt? Wawt?" quite distinctly.

"But why do they try to guess it before they see it?"

"I don't know," Sylvie said: "but they always *do*. Sometimes they begin guessing weeks and weeks before the day!"

(So now, when you hear the Frogs croaking in a particularly melancholy way, you may be sure they're trying to guess Bruno's next Shakespeare "Bit". Isn't *that* interesting?)

However, the chorus of guessing was cut short by Bruno, who suddenly rushed on from behind the scenes, and took a flying leap down among the Frogs, to re-arrange them.

For the oldest and fattest Frog—who had never been properly arranged so that he could see the stage, and so had no idea what was going on—was getting restless, and had upset several of the Frogs, and turned others round with their heads the wrong way. And it was no good at all, Bruno said, to do a "Bit" of Shakespeare when there was nobody to look at it (you see he didn't count *me* as anybody). So he set to work with a stick, stirring them up, very much as you would stir up tea in a cup, till most of them had at least *one* great stupid eye gazing at the stage.

"*Oo* must come and sit among them, Sylvie," he said in despair, "I've put these two side-by-side, with their noses the same way, ever so many times, but they *do* squarrel so!"

So Sylvie took her place as "Mistress of the Ceremonies", and Bruno vanished again behind the scenes, to dress for the first "Bit".

"Hamlet!" was suddenly proclaimed, in the clear sweet tones I knew so well. The croaking all ceased in a moment, and I turned to the stage, in some curiosity to see what Bruno's ideas were as to the behaviour of Shakespeare's greatest Character.

According to this eminent interpreter of the Drama, Hamlet wore a short black cloak (which he chiefly used for muffling up his face, as if he suffered a good deal from toothache), and turned out his toes very much as he walked. "To be or not to be!" Hamlet remarked in a cheerful tone, and then turned head-over-heels several times, his cloak dropping off in the performance.

I felt a little disappointed: Bruno's conception of the part seemed so wanting in dignity. "Wo'n't he say any more of the speech?" I whispered to Sylvie.

"I *think* not," Sylvie whispered in reply. "He generally turns head-over-heels when he doesn't know any more words."

Bruno had meanwhile settled the question by disappearing from the stage; and the Frogs instantly began inquiring the name of the next Character.

"You'll know directly!" cried Sylvie, as she adjusted two or three young Frogs that had struggled round with their backs to the stage. "Macbeth!" she added, as Bruno re-appeared.

Macbeth had something twisted round him, that went over one shoulder and under the other arm, and was meant, I believe, for a Scotch plaid. He had a thorn in his hand, which he held out at arm's length, as if he were a little afraid of it. "Is this a *dagger*?" Macbeth inquired, in a puzzled sort of tone: and instantly a chorus of "Thorn! Thorn!" arose from the Frogs (I had quite learned to understand their croaking by this time).

"It's a *dagger*!" Sylvie proclaimed in a peremptory tone. "Hold your tongues!" and the croaking ceased at once.

Shakespeare has not told us, so far as I know, that Macbeth had any such eccentric habit as turning head-over-

heels in private life: but Bruno evidently considered it
quite an essential part of the character, and left the stage
in a series of somersaults. However, he was back again in
a few moments, having tucked under his chin the end of
a tuft of wool (probably left on the thorn by a wandering
sheep), which made a magnificent beard, that reached
nearly down to his feet.

"Shylock!" Sylvie proclaimed. "No, I beg your pardon!" she hastily corrected herself, "King Lear! I hadn't
noticed the crown." (Bruno had very cleverly provided
one, which fitted him exactly, by cutting out the centre of
a dandelion to make room for his head.)

King Lear folded his arms (to the imminent peril of
his beard) and said, in a mild explanatory tone, "Ay,
every *inch* a king!" and then paused, as if to consider how
this could best be proved. And here, with all possible
deference to Bruno as a Shakespearean critic, I *must*
express my opinion that the poet did *not* mean his three
great tragic heroes to be so strangely alike in their personal habits; nor do I believe that he would have accepted
the faculty of turning head-over-heels as any proof at all
of royal descent. Yet it appeared that King Lear, after
deep meditation, could think of no other argument by
which to prove his kingship: and, as this was the last of
the "Bits" of Shakespeare ("We never do more than
three," Sylvie explained in a whisper), Bruno gave the
audience quite a long series of somersaults before he
finally retired, leaving the enraptured Frogs all crying out
"More! More!" which I suppose was their way of encoring
a performance. But Bruno wouldn't appear again, till the
proper time came for telling the Story.

When he appeared at last in his *real* character, I
noticed a remarkable change in his behaviour. He tried no
more somersaults. It was clearly his opinion that, however
suitable the habit of turning head-over-heels might be to
such petty individuals as Hamlet and King Lear, it
would never do for *Bruno* to sacrifice his dignity to such
an extent. But it was equally clear that he did not feel

entirely at his ease, standing all alone on the stage, with no costume to disguise him: and though he began, several times, "There were a Mouse——", he kept glancing up and down, and on all sides, as if in search of more comfortable quarters from which to tell the Story. Standing on one side of the stage, and partly overshadowing it, was a tall fox-glove, which seemed, as the evening breeze gently swayed it hither and thither, to offer exactly the sort of accommodation that the orator desired. Having once decided on his quarters, it needed only a second or two for him to run up the stem like a tiny squirrel, and to seat himself astride on the topmost bend, where the fairy-bells clustered most closely, and from whence he could look down on his audience from such a height that all shyness vanished, and he began his Story merrily.

"Once there were a Mouse and a Crocodile and a Man and a Goat and a Lion." I had never heard the "dramatis personæ" tumbled into a story with such profusion and in such reckless haste; and it fairly took my breath away. Even Sylvie gave a little gasp, and allowed three of the Frogs, who seemed to be getting tired of the entertainment, to hop away into the ditch, without attempting to stop them.

"And the Mouse found a Shoe, and it thought it were a Mouse-trap. So it got right in, and it stayed in ever so long."

"Why did it *stay* in?" said Sylvie. Her function seemed to be much the same as that of the Chorus in a Greek Play: she had to encourage the orator, and draw him out, by a series of intelligent questions.

" 'Cause it thought it couldn't get out again," Bruno explained. "It were a clever mouse. It knew it couldn't get out of traps!"

"But why did it go in at all?" said Sylvie.

"—and it jamp, and it jamp," Bruno proceeded, ignoring this question, "and at last it got right out again. And it looked at the mark in the Shoe. And the Man's name were in it. So it knew it wasn't its own Shoe."

"Had it thought it *was*?" said Sylvie.

"Why, didn't I tell oo it thought it were a *Mouse-trap*?" the indignant orator replied. "Please, Mister Sir, will oo make Sylvie attend?" Sylvie was silenced, and was all attention: in fact, she and I were most of the audience now, as the Frogs kept hopping away, and there were very few of them left.

"So the Mouse gave the Man his Shoe. And the Man were welly glad, 'cause he hadn't got but one Shoe, and he were hopping to get the other."

Here I ventured on a question. "Do you mean 'hopping', or 'hoping'?"

"Bofe," said Bruno. "And the Man took the Goat out of the Sack." ("We haven't heard of the *sack* before," I said. "Now you wo'n't hear of it again," said Bruno.) "And he said to the Goat, 'Oo will walk about here till I comes back.' And he went and he tumbled into a deep hole. And the Goat walked round and round. And it walked under the Tree. And it wug its tail. And it looked up in the Tree. And it sang a sad little Song. Oo never heard such a sad little Song!"

"Can you sing it, Bruno?" I asked.

"Iss, I can," Bruno readily replied. "And I sa'n't. It would make Sylvie cry——"

"It wouldn't!" Sylvie interrupted in great indignation. "And I don't believe the Goat sang it at all!"

"It did, though!" said Bruno. "It singed it right froo. I *sawed* it singing with its long beard——"

"It couldn't sing with its *beard*," I said, hoping to puzzle the little fellow: "a beard isn't a *voice*."

"Well then, *oo* couldn't walk with Sylvie!" Bruno cried triumphantly. "Sylvie isn't a *foot*!"

I thought I had better follow Sylvie's example, and be silent for a while. Bruno was too sharp for us.

"And when it had singed all the Song, it ran away—for to get along to look for the Man, oo know. And the Crocodile got along after it—for to bite it, oo know. And the Mouse got along after the Crocodile."

"Wasn't the Crocodile *running?*" Sylvie enquired. She appealed to me. "Crocodiles do run, don't they?"

I suggested "crawling" as the proper word.

"He wasn't running," said Bruno, "and he wasn't crawling. He went struggling along like a portmanteau. And he held his chin ever so high in the air——"

"What did he do *that* for?" said Sylvie.

"'Cause he hadn't got a toofache!" said Bruno. "Ca'n't oo make out *nuffin* wizout I 'splain it? Why, if he'd had a toofache, a course he'd have held his head down—like this—and he'd have put a lot of warm blankets round it!"

"If he'd *had* any blankets," Sylvie argued.

"Course he *had* blankets!" retorted her brother. "Doos oo think Crocodiles goes walks wizout blankets? And he frowned with his eyebrows. And the Goat was welly flightened at his eyebrows!"

"I'd never be afraid of *eyebrows!*" exclaimed Sylvie.

"I should think oo *would*, though, if they'd got a Crocodile fastened to them, like these had! And so the Man jamp, and he jamp, and at last he got right out of the hole."

Sylvia gave another little gasp: this rapid dodging about among the characters of the Story had taken away her breath.

"And he runned away—for to look for the Goat, oo know. And he heard the Lion grunting——"

"Lions don't grunt," said Sylvie.

"This one did," said Bruno. "And its mouth were like a large cupboard. And it had plenty of room in its mouth. And the Lion runned after the Man—for to eat him, oo know. And the Mouse runned after the Lion."

"But the Mouse was running after the *Crocodile,*" I said: "he couldn't run after *both!*"

Bruno sighed over the density of his audience, but explained very patiently. "He *did* runned after *bofe*: 'cause they went the same way! And first he caught the Crocodile, and then he didn't catch the Lion. And when he'd caught the Crocodile, what doos oo think he did—'cause he'd got pincers in his pocket?"

"I ca'n't guess," said Sylvie.

"Nobody couldn't guess it!" Bruno cried in high glee. "Why, he wrenched out that Crocodile's toof!"

"*Which* tooth?" I ventured to ask.

But Bruno was not to be puzzled. "The toof he were going to bite the Goat with, a course!"

"He couldn't be sure about that", I argued, "unless he wrenched out *all* its teeth."

Bruno laughed merrily, and half sang, as he swung himself backwards and forwards, "He did—wrenched—out—*all* its teef!"

"Why did the Crocodile wait to have them wrenched out?" said Sylvie.

"It had to wait," said Bruno.

I ventured on another question. "But what became of the Man who said 'You may wait here till I come back'?"

"He didn't say 'Oo *may*'," Bruno explained. "He said, 'Oo *will*.' Just like Sylvie says to me 'Oo will do oor lessons till twelve o'clock.' Oh, I *wiss*," he added with a little sigh, "I *wiss* Sylvie would say 'Oo *may* do oor lessons'!"

This was a dangerous subject for discussion, Sylvie seemed to think. She returned to the Story. "But what became of the Man?"

"Well, the Lion springed at him. But it came so slow, it were three weeks in the air——"

"Did the Man wait for it all that time?" I said.

"Course he didn't!" Bruno replied, gliding head-first down the stem of the fox-glove, for the Story was evidently close to its end. "He sold his house, and he packed up his things, while the Lion were coming. And he went and he lived in another town. So the Lion ate the wrong man."

This was evidently the Moral: so Sylvie made her final proclamation to the Frogs. "The Story's finished! And whatever is to be *learned* from it," she added, aside to me, "I'm sure *I* don't know!"

I did not feel *quite* clear about it myself, so made no
suggestion: but the Frogs seemed quite content, Moral or
no Moral, and merely raised a husky chorus of "Off!
Off!" as they hopped away.

Chapter XXV

Looking Eastward

"It's just a week", I said, three days later, to Arthur,
"since we heard of Lady Muriel's engagement. I think *I*
ought to call, at any rate, and offer my congratulations.
Wo'n't you come with me?"

A pained expression passed over his face. "When must
you leave us?" he asked.

"By the first train on Monday."

"Well—yes, I *will* come with you. It would seem
strange and unfriendly if I didn't. But this is only Friday.
Give me till Sunday afternoon. I shall be stronger then."

Shading his eyes with one hand, as if half-ashamed of
the tears that were coursing down his cheeks, he held
the other out to me. It trembled as I clasped it.

I tried to frame some words of sympathy; but they
seemed poor and cold, and I left them unspoken. "Good
night!" was all I said.

"Good night, dear friend!" he replied. There was a
manly vigour in his tone that convinced me he was
wrestling with, and triumphing over, the great sorrow
that had so nearly wrecked his life—and that, on the
stepping-stone of his dead self, he would surely rise to
higher things!

There was no chance, I was glad to think, as we set out
on Sunday afternoon, of meeting *Eric* at the Hall, as he
had returned to town the day after his engagement was
announced. *His* presence might have disturbed the calm
—the almost unnatural calm—with which Arthur met

the woman who had won his heart, and murmured the few graceful words of sympathy that the occasion demanded.

Lady Muriel was perfectly radiant with happiness: sadness could not live in the light of such a smile: and even Arthur brightened under it, and, when she remarked "You see I'm watering my flowers, though it *is* the Sabbath-Day," his voice had almost its old ring of cheerfulness as he replied "Even on the Sabbath-Day works of mercy are allowed. But this *isn't* the Sabbath-Day. The Sabbath-Day has ceased to exist."

"I know it's not *Saturday*," Lady Muriel replied: "but isn't Sunday often called 'the Christian Sabbath'?"

"It is so called, I think, in recognition of the *spirit* of the Jewish institution, that one day in seven should be a day of *rest*. But I hold that Christians are freed from the *literal* observance of the Fourth Commandment."

"Then where is our *authority* for Sunday observance?"

"We have, first, the fact that the seventh day was 'sanctified', when God rested from the work of Creation. That is binding on us as *Theists*. Secondly, we have the fact that 'the Lord's Day' is a *Christian* institution. That is binding on us as *Christians*."

"And your practical rules would be——?"

"First, as Theists, to keep it *holy* in some special way, and to make it, so far as is reasonably possible, a day of *rest*. Secondly, as *Christians*, to attend public worship."

"And what of *amusements*?"

"I would say of them, as of all kinds of *work*, whatever is innocent on a week-day, is innocent on Sunday, provided it does not interfere with the duties of the day."

"Then you would allow children to *play* on Sunday?"

"Certainly I should. Why make the day irksome to their restless natures?"

"I have a letter somewhere," said Lady Muriel, "from an old friend, describing the way in which Sunday was kept in her younger days. I will fetch it for you."

"I had a similar description, *vivâ voce*, years ago," Arthur said when she had left us, "from a little girl. It was really touching to hear the melancholy tone in which she said 'On Sunday I mustn't play with my doll! On Sunday I mustn't run on the sands! On Sunday I mustn't dig in the garden!' Poor child! She had indeed abundant cause for hating Sunday!"

"Here is the letter," said Lady Muriel, returning. "Let me read you a piece of it."

' *When, as a child, I first opened my eyes on a Sunday-morning, a feeling of dismal anticipation, which began at least on the Friday, culminated. I knew what was before me, and my wish, if not my word, was 'Would God it were evening!' It was no day of rest, but a day of texts, of catechisms (Watts'), of tracts about converted swearers, godly char-women, and edifying deaths of sinners saved.*

"*Up with the lark, hymns and portions of Scripture had to be learned by heart till 8 o'clock, when there were family-prayers, then breakfast, which I was never able to enjoy, partly from the fast already undergone, and partly from the outlook I dreaded.*

"*At 9 came Sunday-School; and it made me indignant to be put into the class with the village-children, as well as alarmed lest, by some mistake of mine, I should be put below them.*

"*The Church-Service was a veritable Wilderness of Zin. I wandered in it, pitching the tabernacle of my thoughts on the lining of the square family-pew, the fidgets of my small brothers, and the horror of knowing that, on the Monday, I should have to write out, from memory, jottings of the rambling disconnected extempore sermon, which might have any text but its own, and to stand or fall by the result.*

"*This was followed by a cold dinner at 1 (servants to have no work), Sunday-School again from 2 to 4, and Evening-Service at 6. The intervals were perhaps the greatest trial of all, from the efforts I had to make, to be less than usually sinful, by reading books and sermons as barren as the Dead Sea. There was but one rosy spot, in the distance, all that day: and that was 'bed-time', which never could come too early!*"

"Such teaching was well meant, no doubt," said Arthur; "but it must have driven many of its victims into deserting the Church-Services altogether."

"I'm afraid *I* was a deserter this morning," she gravely said. "I had to write to Eric. Would you—would you mind my telling you something he said about *prayer*? It had never struck me in that light before."

"In what light?" said Arthur.

"Why, that all Nature goes by fixed, regular laws— Science has proved *that*. So that asking God to *do* anything (except of course praying for *spiritual* blessings) is to expect a miracle: and we've no right to do *that*. I've not put it as well as *he* did: but that was the outcome of it, and it has confused me. Please tell me what you can say in answer to it."

"I don't propose to discuss *Captain Lindon's* difficulties," Arthur gravely replied; "specially as he is not present. But, if it is *your* difficulty," (his voice unconsciously took a tender tone) "then I will speak."

"It *is* my difficulty," she said anxiously.

"Then I will begin by asking 'Why did you except *spiritual* blessings?' Is not your mind a part of Nature?"

"Yes, but Free-Will comes in there—I can *choose* this or that; and God can influence my choice."

"Then you are not a Fatalist?"

"Oh, no!" she earnestly exclaimed.

"Thank God!" Arthur said to himself, but in so low a whisper that only *I* heard it. "You grant then that I can, by an act of free choice, move this cup", suiting the action to the word, "*this* way or *that* way?"

"Yes, I grant it."

"Well, let us see how far the result is produced by fixed laws. The *cup* moves because certain mechanical forces are impressed on it by my *hand*. My *hand* moves because certain forces—electric, magnetic, or whatever 'nerve-force' may prove to be—are impressed on it by my *brain*. This nerve-force, stored in the brain, would probably be traceable, if Science were complete, to chemical forces supplied to the brain by the blood, and ultimately derived from the food I eat and the air I breathe."

"But would not that be Fatalism? Where would Free-Will come in?"

"In *choice* of nerves," replied Arthur. "The nerve-force in the brain may flow just as naturally down one nerve as down another. We need something more than a fixed Law of Nature to settle *which* nerve shall carry it. That 'something' is Free-Will."

Her eyes sparkled. "I see what you mean!" she exclaimed. "Human Free-Will is an exception to the system of fixed Law. Eric said something like that. And then I think he pointed out that God can only influence Nature by influencing Human Wills. So that we *might* reasonably pray '*give us this day our daily bread*', because many of the causes that produce bread are under Man's control. But to pray for rain, or fine weather, would be as unreasonable as——" she checked herself, as if fearful of saying something irreverent.

In a hushed, low tone, that trembled with emotion, and with the solemnity of one in the presence of death, Arthur slowly replied "*Shall he that contendeth with the Almighty instruct him?* Shall we, 'the swarm that in the noon-tide beam were born,' feeling in ourselves the power to direct, this way or that, the forces of Nature—of *Nature*, of which we form so trivial a part—shall we, in our boundless arrogance, in our pitiful conceit, *deny* that power to the Ancient of Days? Saying, to our Creator, 'Thus far and no further. Thou madest, but thou canst not rule!'?"

Lady Muriel had covered her face in her hands, and did not look up. She only murmured "Thanks, thanks!" again and again.

We rose to go. Arthur said, with evident effort, "One word more. If you would *know* the power of Prayer—in anything and everything that Man can need—*try* it. *Ask, and it shall be given you.* I—*have* tried it. I *know* that God answers prayer!"

Our walk home was a silent one, till we had nearly

reached the lodgings: then Arthur murmured—and it was almost an echo of my own thoughts—"*What knowest thou, O wife, whether thou shalt save thy husband?*"

The subject was not touched on again. We sat on, talking, while hour after hour, of this our last night together, glided away unnoticed. He had much to tell me about India, and the new life he was going to, and the *work* he hoped to do. And his great generous soul seemed so filled with noble ambition as to have no space left for any vain regret or selfish repining.

"Come, it is nearly morning!" Arthur said at last, rising and leading the way upstairs. "The sun will be rising in a few minutes: and, though I *have* basely defrauded you of your last chance of a night's rest here, I'm sure you'll forgive me: for I really *couldn't* bring myself to say 'Good night' sooner. And God knows whether you'll ever see me again, or hear of me!"

"*Hear* of you I am certain I shall!" I warmly responded, and quoted the concluding lines of that strange poem "Waring":

> "*Oh, never star*
> *Was lost here, but it rose afar!*
> *Look East, where whole new thousands are!*
> *In Vishnu-land what Avatar?*"

"Aye, look Eastward!" Arthur eagerly replied, pausing at the stair-case window, which commanded a fine view of the sea and the eastward horizon. "The West is the fitting tomb for all the sorrow and the sighing, all the errors and the follies of the Past: for all its withered Hopes and all its buried Loves! From the East comes new strength, new ambition, new Hope, new Life, new Love! Look Eastward! Aye, look Eastward!"

His last words were still ringing in my ears as I entered my room, and undrew the window-curtains, just in time to see the sun burst in glory from his ocean-prison, and clothe the world in the light of a new day.

"So may it be for him, and me, and all of us!" I mused.

"All that is evil, and dead, and hopeless, fading with the Night that is past! All that is good, and living, and hopeful, rising with the dawn of Day!

"Fading, with the Night, the chilly mists, and the noxious vapours, and the heavy shadows, and the wailing gusts, and the owl's melancholy hootings: rising, with the Day, the darting shafts of light, and the wholesome morning breeze, and the warmth of a dawning life, and the mad music of the lark! Look Eastward!

"Fading, with the Night, the clouds of ignorance, and the deadly blight of sin, and the silent tears of sorrow: and ever rising, higher, higher, with the Day, the radiant dawn of knowledge, and the sweet breath of purity, and the throb of a world's ecstasy! Look Eastward!

"Fading, with the Night, the memory of a dead love, and the withered leaves of a blighted hope, and the sickly repinings and moody regrets that numb the best energies of the soul: and rising, broadening, rolling upward like a living flood, the manly resolve, and the dauntless will, and the heavenward gaze of faith—*the substance of things hoped for, the evidence of things not seen!*

"Look Eastward! Aye, look Eastward!"

IV
Sylvie and Bruno
Concluded

Dreams, that elude the Maker's frenzied grasp—
Hands, stark and still, on a dead Mother's breast,
Which nevermore shall render clasp for clasp,
Or deftly soothe a weeping Child to rest—
In suchlike forms me listeth to portray
My Tale, here ended. Thou delicious Fay—
The guardian of a Sprite that lives to tease thee—
Loving in earnest, chiding but in play
The merry mocking Bruno! Who, that sees thee,
Can fail to love thee, Darling, even as I?—
My sweetest Sylvie, we must say "Good-bye!"

PREFACE

LET me here express my sincere gratitude to the many
Reviewers who have noticed, whether favourably or un-
favourably, the previous Volume. Their unfavourable remarks were, most probably, well-deserved; the favourable
ones less probably so. Both kinds have no doubt served
to make the book known, and have helped the reading
Public to form their opinions of it. Let me also here assure
them that it is not from any want of respect for their
criticisms, that I have carefully forborne from reading
any of them. I am strongly of opinion that an author had
far better *not* read any reviews of his books: the unfavourable ones are almost certain to make him cross, and the
favourable ones conceited; and *neither* of these results is
desirable.

Criticisms have, however, reached me from private
sources, to some of which I propose to offer a reply.

One such critic complains that Arthur's strictures, on
sermons and on choristers, are too severe. Let me say, in
reply, that I do *not* hold myself responsible for *any* of the
opinions expressed by the characters in my book. They
are simply opinions which, it seemed to me, might probably be held by the persons into whose mouths I put
them, and which were worth consideration.

Other critics have objected to certain innovations in
spelling, such as "ca'n't", "wo'n't", "traveler". In reply,
I can only plead my firm conviction that the popular
usage is *wrong*. As to "ca'n't", it will not be disputed
that, in all *other* words ending in "n't", these letters are
an abbreviation of "not"; and it is surely absurd to suppose that, in this solitary instance, "not" is represented
by " 't"! In fact "can't" is the *proper* abbreviation for
"can it", just as "is't" is for "is it". Again, in "wo'n't",
the first apostrophe is needed, because the word "would"

461

is here *abridged* into "wo": but I hold it proper to spell "don't" with only *one* apostrophe, because the word "do" is here *complete*. As to such words as "traveler", I hold the correct principle to be, to *double* the consonant when the accent falls on that syllable; otherwise to leave it *single*. This rule is observed in most cases (e.g. we double the "r" in "preferred", but leave it single in "offered"), so that I am only extending, to other cases, an existing rule. I admit, however, that I do not spell "parallel", as the rule would have it; but here we are constrained, by the etymology, to insert the double "l".

In the Preface to Vol. I. were two puzzles, on which my readers might exercise their ingenuity. One was, to detect the 3 lines of "padding", which I had found it necessary to supply in the passage extending from the top of p. 280 to the middle of p. 282. They are the 23rd, 24th and 25th lines of p. 281. The other puzzle was, to determine which (if any) of the 8 stanzas of the Gardener's Song (see pp. 294, 301, 303, 306, 314, 318, 342, 344) were adapted to the context, and which (if any) had the context adapted to them. The last of them is the only one that was adapted to the context, the "Garden-Door that opened with a key" having been substituted for some creature (a Cormorant, I think) "that nestled in a tree". At pp. 301, 314, and 342, the context was adapted to the stanza. At p. 306, neither stanza nor context was altered: the connection between them was simply a piece of good luck.

In the Preface to Vol. I., at pp. 255, 256, I gave an account of the making-up of the story of "Sylvie and Bruno". A few more details may perhaps be acceptable to my Readers.

It was in 1873, as I *now* believe, that the idea first occurred to me that a little fairy-tale (written, in 1867, for "Aunt Judy's Magazine", under the title "Bruno's Revenge") might serve as the nucleus of a longer story. This I surmise, from having found the original draft of the last paragraph of Vol. II., dated 1873. So that this paragraph has been waiting 20 years for its chance of emerging into print—more than twice the period so cautiously recommended by Horace for "repressing" one's literary efforts!

It was in February, 1885, that I entered into negotiations, with Mr. Harry Furniss, for illustrating the book. Most of the substance of *both* Volumes was then in existence in manuscript: and my original intention was to publish the *whole* story at once. In September, 1885, I received from Mr. Furniss the first set of drawings—the four which illustrate "Peter and Paul": in November, 1886, I received the second set—the three which illustrate the Professor's song about the "little man" who had "a little gun": and in January, 1887, I received the third set —the four which illustrate the "Pig-Tale".

So we went on, illustrating first one bit of the story, and then another, without any idea of sequence. And it was not till March, 1889, that, having calculated the number of pages the story would occupy, I decided on dividing it into *two* portions, and publishing it half at a time. This necessitated the writing of a *sort* of conclusion for the first Volume: and *most* of my Readers, I fancy, regarded this as the *actual* conclusion, when that Volume appeared in December, 1889. At any rate, among all the letters I received about it, there was only *one* which expressed *any* suspicion that it was not a *final* conclusion. This letter was from a child. She wrote "we were so glad, when we came to the end of the book, to find that there was no ending-up, for that shows us that you are going to write a sequel."

It may interest some of my Readers to know the *theory* on which this story is constructed. It is an attempt to show what might *possibly* happen, supposing that Fairies really existed; and that they were sometimes visible to us, and we to them; and that they were sometimes able to assume human form: and supposing, also, that human beings might sometimes become conscious of what goes on in the Fairy-world—by actual transference of their immaterial essence, such as we meet with in "Esoteric Buddhism".

I have supposed a Human being to be capable of various psychical states, with varying degrees of consciousness, as follows:

(a) the ordinary state, with no consciousness of the presence of Fairies;

(b) the "eerie" state, in which, while conscious of actual surroundings, he is *also* conscious of the presence of Fairies;

(c) a form of trance, in which, while *un*conscious of actual surroundings, and apparently asleep, he (i.e. his immaterial essence) migrates to other scenes, in the actual world, or in Fairyland, and is conscious of the presence of Fairies.

I have also supposed a Fairy to be capable of migrating from Fairyland into the actual world, and of assuming, at pleasure, a Human form; and also to be capable of various psychical states, viz.

(a) the ordinary state, with no consciousness of the presence of Human beings;

(b) a sort of "eerie" state, in which he is conscious, if in the actual world, of the presence of actual Human beings; if in Fairyland, of the presence of the immaterial essences of Human beings.

I will here tabulate the passages, in both Volumes, where abnormal states occur.

Vol. I.	Historian's Locality and	State.	Other Characters.
pp. 264–270	In train	c	Chancellor (b) p. 264.
277–289	do.	c	
294–301	do.	c	
303–310	At lodgings	c	
314–318	On beach	c	
319–350	At lodgings	c	S. and B. (b) pp. 338–341. Professor (b) p. 344.
355–370	In wood	b	Bruno (b) pp. 358–370.

Vol. I.	Historian's Locality and	State.	Other characters.
pp. 372–376	In wood, sleep-walking	c	S. and B. (b).
383–385	Among ruins	c	do. (b).
389, 390	do. dreaming	a	
391–393	do. sleep-walking	c	S. B. and Professor in Human form.
393	In street...........	b	
398–406	At station, &c.	b	S. and B. (b)
410–421	In garden..........	c	S. B. and Professor(b)
423–431	On road, &c.	a	S. and B. in Human form.
431–437	In street, &c........	a	
439–450	In wood	b	S. and B. (b).
Vol. II.			
pp. 474–482	In garden..........	b	S. and B. (b).
496–498	On road	b	do. (b).
498–511	do.	b	do. in Human form.
511–517	do.	b	do. (b).
547–578	In drawing-room ...	a	do. in Human form.
578–595	do. ...	c	do. (b).
603–607	In smoking-room ...	c	do. (b).
623–626	In wood	b	do. (a); Lady Muriel (b).
627–644	At lodgings	c	
646–669	do.	c	
673–end.	do.	b	

In the Preface to Vol. I., at pp. 255 and 256, I gave an account of the *origination* of some of the ideas embodied in the book. A few more such details may perhaps interest my Readers:

I. p. 361. The very peculiar use, here made of a dead mouse, comes from real life. I once found two very small boys, in a garden, playing a microscopic game of "Single-Wicket". The bat was, I think, about the size of a table-spoon; and the utmost distance attained by the ball, in its most daring flights, was some 4 or 5 yards. The *exact* length was of course a matter of *supreme* importance; and it was always carefully measured out (the batsman and the bowler amicably sharing the toil) with a dead mouse!

I. p. 388. The two quasi-mathematical Axioms, quoted

by Arthur at p. 388 of Vol. I. ("Things that are greater than the same are greater than one another", and "All angles are equal") were actually enunciated, in all seriousness, by undergraduates at a University situated not 100 miles from Ely.

II. p. 477. Bruno's remark ("I can, if I like, &c.") was actually made by a little boy.

II. p. 478. So also was his remark ("I know what it *doesn't* spell"). And his remark ("I just twiddled my eyes, &c.") I heard from the lips of a little girl, who had just solved a puzzle I had set her.

II. p. 501. Bruno's soliloquy ("For its father, &c.") was actually spoken by a little girl, looking out of the window of a railway-carriage.

II. p. 540. The remark, made by a guest at the dinner-party, when asking for a dish of fruit ("I've been wishing for them, &c.") I heard made by the great Poet-Laureate, whose loss the whole reading-world has so lately had to deplore.

II. p. 553. Bruno's speech, on the subject of the age of "Mein Herr", embodies the reply of a little girl to the question "Is your grandmother an *old* lady?" "I don't know if she's an *old* lady," said this cautious young person; "she's *eighty-three*."

II. p. 573. The speech about "Obstruction" is no mere creature of my imagination! It is copied *verbatim* from the columns of the Standard, and was spoken by Sir William Harcourt, who was, at the time, a member of the "Opposition", at the "National Liberal Club", on July the 16th, 1890.

II. p. 636. The Professor's remark, about a dog's tail, that "it doesn't bite at *that* end", was actually made by a child, when warned of the danger he was incurring by pulling the dog's tail.

II. p. 657. The dialogue between Sylvie and Bruno, which occupies lines 28 to 36, is a *verbatim* report (merely substituting "cake" for "penny") of a dialogue overheard between two children.

One story in this Volume—"Bruno's Picnic"—I can vouch for as suitable for telling to children, having tested it again and again; and, whether my audience has been a dozen little girls in a village-school, or some thirty or forty in a London drawing-room, or a hundred in a High School, I have always found them earnestly attentive, and keenly appreciative of such fun as the story supplied.

May I take this opportunity of calling attention to what I flatter myself was a successful piece of name-coining, at p. 283 of Vol. I. Does not the name "Sibimet" fairly embody the character of the Sub-Warden? The gentle Reader has no doubt observed what a singularly useless article in a house a brazen trumpet is, if you simply leave it lying about, and never blow it!

Readers of the first Volume, who have amused themselves by trying to solve the two puzzles propounded at page 257 of the Preface, may perhaps like to exercise their ingenuity in discovering which (if any) of the following parallelisms were intentional, and which (if any) accidental.

"Little Birds".   Events, and Persons.
Stanza 1. Banquet.
        2. Chancellor.
        3. Empress and Spinach (II. 635).
        4. Warden's Return.
        5. Professor's Lecture (II. 640).
        6. Other Professor's Song (I. 329).
        7. Petting of Uggug.
        8. Baron Doppelgeist.
        9. Jester and Bear (I. 321). Little Foxes.
       10. Bruno's Dinner-Bell; Little Foxes.

I will publish the answer to this puzzle in the Preface to a little book of "Original Games and Puzzles", now in course of preparation.

I have reserved, for the last, one or two rather more serious topics.

I had intended, in this Preface, to discuss more fully, than I had done in the previous Volume, the "Morality of Sport", with special reference to letters I have received from lovers of Sport, in which they point out the many great advantages which men get from it, and try to prove that the suffering, which it inflicts on animals, is too trivial to be regarded.

But, when I came to think the subject out, and to arrange the whole of the arguments "pro" and "con", I found it much too large for treatment here. Some day, I hope to publish an essay on this subject. At present, I will content myself with stating the net result I have arrived at.

It is, that God has given to Man an absolute right to take the *lives* of other animals, for *any* reasonable cause, such as the supply of food: but that He has *not* given to Man the right to inflict *pain*, unless when *necessary*: that mere pleasure, or advantage, does not constitute such a necessity: and, consequently, that pain, inflicted for the purposes of *Sport*, is cruel, and therefore wrong. But I find it a far more complex question than I had supposed; and that the "case", on the side of the Sportsman, is a much stronger one than I had supposed. So, for the present, I say no more about it.

Objections have been raised to the severe language I have put into the mouth of "Arthur", at p. 397, on the subject of "Sermons", and at pp. 395, 396, on the subjects of Choral Services and "Choristers".

I have already protested against the assumption that I am ready to endorse the opinions of characters in my story. But, in these two instances, I admit that I am much in sympathy with "Arthur". In my opinion, far too many sermons are expected from our preachers; and, as a consequence, a great many are preached, which are not worth listening to; and, as a consequence of *that*, we are very apt *not* to listen. The reader of this paragraph probably heard a sermon last Sunday morning? Well, let him, if he can, name the text, and state how the preacher treated it!

Then, as to "Choristers", and all the other accessories —of music, vestments, processions, &c.—which have come, along with them, into fashion—while freely admitting that the "Ritual" movement was sorely needed, and that it has effected a vast improvement in our Church-Services, which had become dead and dry to the last degree, I hold that, like many other desirable movements, it has gone too far in the opposite direction, and has introduced many new dangers.

For the Congregation this new movement involves the danger of learning to think that the Services are done *for* them; and that their bodily *presence* is all they need contribute. And, for Clergy and Congregation alike, it involves the danger of regarding these elaborate Services as *ends in themselves*, and of forgetting that they are simply *means*, and the very hollowest of mockeries, unless they bear fruit in our *lives*.

For the Choristers it seems to involve the danger of self-conceit, as described at p. 395 (N.B. "stagy-entrances" is a misprint for "stage-entrances"), the danger of regarding those parts of the Service, where their help is not required, as not worth attending to, the danger of coming to regard the Service as a mere outward form—a series of postures to be assumed, and of words to be said or sung, while the *thoughts* are elsewhere—and the danger of "familiarity" breeding "contempt" for sacred things.

Let me illustrate these last two forms of danger, from my own experience. Not long ago, I attended a Cathedral-Service, and was placed immediately behind a row of men, members of the Choir; and I could not help noticing that they treated the *Lessons* as a part of the Service to which they needed not to give *any* attention, and as affording them a convenient opportunity for arranging music-books, &c., &c. Also I have frequently seen a row of little choristers, after marching in procession to their places, kneel down, as if about to pray, and rise from their knees after a minute spent in looking about them, it being but too evident that the attitude was a mere mockery. Surely it is very dangerous, for these children, to thus accustom them to *pretend* to pray? As an instance of irreverent treatment of holy things, I will mention a custom, which no doubt many of my readers have noticed in Churches where the Clergy and Choir enter in procession, viz. that, at the end of the private devotions, which are carried on in the vestry, and which are of course inaudible to the Congregation, the final "Amen" is *shouted*, loud enough to be heard all through the Church. This serves as a signal, to the Congregation, to prepare to rise when the procession appears: and it admits of no dispute that it is for this purpose that it is thus shouted. When we remember to Whom that "Amen" is *really* addressed, and consider that it is here *used* for the same purpose as one of the Church-bells, we must surely admit that it is a piece of gross irreverence? To *me* it is much as if I were to see a Bible used as a footstool.

As an instance of the dangers, for the Clergy themselves, introduced by this new movement, let me mention the fact that, according to *my* experience, Clergymen of this school are *specially* apt to retail comic anecdotes, in which the most sacred names and words—sometimes actual texts from the Bible—are used as themes for jesting. Many such things are repeated as having been originally said by *children*, whose utter ignorance of evil must no doubt acquit *them*, in the sight of God, of all blame; but it must be otherwise for those who *consciously* use such innocent utterances as material for their unholy mirth.

Let me add, however, *most* earnestly, that I fully believe that this profanity is, in many cases, *un*conscious: the "environment" (as I have tried to explain at pp. 532, 533) makes all the difference between man and man; and I rejoice to think that many of these profane stories— which *I* find so painful to listen to, and should feel it a sin to repeat—give to *their* ears no pain, and to *their* consciences no shock; and that *they* can utter, not less sincerely than myself, the two prayers, *"Hallowed be Thy Name,"* and *"from hardness of heart, and contempt of Thy Word and Commandment, Good Lord, deliver us!"* To which I would desire to add, for their sake and for my own, Keble's beautiful petition, *"help us, this and every day, To live more nearly as we pray!"* It is, in fact, for its *consequences*—for the grave dangers, both to speaker and to hearer, which it involves—rather than for what it is *in itself*, that I mourn over this clerical habit of profanity in social talk. To the *believing* hearer it brings the danger of loss of reverence for holy things, by the mere act of listening to, and enjoying, such jests; and also the temptation to retail them for the amusement of others. To the *unbelieving* hearer it brings a welcome confirmation of his theory that religion is a fable, in the spectacle of its accredited champions thus betraying their trust. And to the speaker himself it must surely bring the danger of *loss of faith*. For surely such jests, if uttered with no consciousness of harm, must necessarily be also uttered with no consciousness, at the moment, of the *reality* of God, as a *living being*, who hears all we say. And he, who allows himself the habit of thus uttering holy words, with no thought of their meaning, is but too likely to find that, for him, God has become a myth, and heaven a poetic fancy—that, for him, the light of life is gone, and that he is at heart an atheist, lost in *"a darkness that may be felt"*.

There is, I fear, at the present time, an increasing tendency to irreverent treatment of the name of God and of subjects connected with religion. Some of our theatres are helping this downward movement by the gross caricatures of clergymen which they put upon the stage: some of our clergy are themselves helping it, by showing that they can lay aside the spirit of reverence, along with their surplices, and can treat as jests, when *outside* their churches, names and things to which they pay an almost superstitious veneration when *inside*: the "Salvation Army" has, I fear, with the best intentions, done much to help it, by the coarse familiarity with which they treat holy things: and surely every one, who desires to *live* in the spirit of the prayer *"Hallowed be Thy Name"*, ought to do what he can, however little that may be, to check it. So I have gladly taken this unique opportunity, however unfit the topic may seem for the Preface to a book of this kind, to express some thoughts which have weighed on my mind for a long time. I did not expect, when I wrote the Preface to Vol. I, that it would be read to any appreciable extent: but I rejoice to believe, from evidence that has reached me, that it *has* been read by many, and to hope that this Preface will also be so: and I think that, among them, some will be found ready to sympathize with the views I have put forwards, and ready to help, with their prayers and their example, the revival, in Society, of the waning spirit of reverence.

Christmas, 1893.

CHAPTER I

Bruno's Lessons

DURING the next month or two my solitary town-life seemed, by contrast, unusually dull and tedious. I missed the pleasant friends I had left behind at Elveston—the genial interchange of thought—the sympathy which gave to one's ideas a new and vivid reality: but, perhaps more than all, I missed the companionship of the two Fairies— or Dream-Children, for I had not yet solved the problem as to who or what they were—whose sweet playfulness had shed a magic radiance over my life.

In office-hours—which I suppose reduce most men to the mental condition of a coffee-mill or a mangle—time sped along much as usual: it was in the pauses of life, the desolate hours when books and newspapers palled on the sated appetite, and when, thrown back upon one's own dreary musings, one strove—all in vain—to people the vacant air with the dear faces of absent friends, that the real bitterness of solitude made itself felt.

One evening, feeling my life a little more wearisome than usual, I strolled down to my Club, not so much with the hope of meeting any friend there, for London was now "out of town", as with the feeling that here, at least, I should hear "sweet words of human speech", and come into contact with human thought.

However, almost the first face I saw there *was* that of a friend. Eric Lindon was lounging, with rather a "bored" expression of face, over a newspaper; and we fell into conversation with a mutual satisfaction which neither of us tried to conceal.

After a while I ventured to introduce what was just then the main subject of my thoughts. "And so the Doc- tor" (a name we had adopted by a tacit agreement, as a convenient compromise between the formality of "Doctor Forester" and the intimacy—to which Eric Lindon hardly seemed entitled—of "Arthur") "has gone abroad by this time, I suppose? Can you give me his present address?"

"He is still at Elveston—I believe," was the reply. "But I have not been there since I last met you."

I did not know which part of this intelligence to wonder at most. "And might I ask—if it isn't taking too much of a liberty—when your wedding-bells are to—or perhaps they *have* rung, already?"

"No," said Eric, in a steady voice, which betrayed scarcely a trace of emotion: "*that* engagement is at an end. I am still 'Benedick the *un*married man'."

After this, the thick-coming fancies—all radiant with new possibilities of happiness for Arthur—were far too bewildering to admit of any further conversation, and I was only too glad to avail myself of the first decent excuse, that offered itself, for retiring into silence.

The next day I wrote to Arthur, with as much of a reprimand for his long silence as I could bring myself to put into words, begging him to tell me how the world went with him.

Needs must that three or four days—possibly more—should elapse before I could receive his reply; and never had I known days drag their slow length along with a more tedious indolence.

To while away the time, I strolled, one afternoon, into Kensington Gardens, and, wandering aimlessly along any path that presented itself, I soon became aware that I had somehow strayed into one that was wholly new to me. Still, my elfish experiences seemed to have so completely faded out of my life that nothing was further from my thoughts than the idea of again meeting my fairy-friends, when I chanced to notice a small creature, moving among the grass that fringed the path, that did not seem to be an insect, or a frog, or any other living thing that I could think of. Cautiously kneeling down, and making an *ex tempore* cage of my two hands, I imprisoned the little wanderer, and felt a sudden thrill of surprise and delight on discovering that my prisoner was no other than *Bruno* himself!

Bruno took the matter *very* coolly, and, when I had replaced him on the ground, where he would be within easy conversational distance, he began talking, just as if it were only a few minutes since last we had met.

"Doos oo know what the *Rule* is", he enquired, "when oo catches a Fairy, withouten its having tolded oo where it was?" (Bruno's notions of English Grammar had certainly *not* improved since our last meeting.)

"No," I said. "I didn't know there was any Rule about it."

"I *think* oo've got a right to *eat* me," said the little fellow, looking up into my face with a winning smile. "But I'm not pruffickly sure. Oo'd better not do it wizout asking."

It did indeed seem reasonable not to take so irrevocable a step as *that*, without due enquiry. "I'll certainly *ask* about it, first," I said. "Besides, I don't know yet whether you would be *worth* eating!"

"I guess I'm *deliciously* good to eat," Bruno remarked in a satisfied tone, as if it were something to be rather proud of.

"And what are you doing here, Bruno?"

"*That's* not my name!" said my cunning little friend. "Don't oo know my name's 'Oh Bruno!'? That's what Sylvie always calls me, when I says mine lessons."

"Well then, what are you doing here, oh Bruno?"

"Doing mine lessons, a-course!" With that roguish twinkle in his eye, that always came when he knew he was talking nonsense.

"Oh, *that's* the way you do your lessons, is it? And do you remember them well?"

"Always can 'member *mine* lessons," said Bruno. "It's *Sylvie's* lessons that's so *dreffully* hard to 'member!" He frowned, as if in agonies of thought, and tapped his fore-

head with his knuckles. "I *ca'n't* think enough to understand them!" he said despairingly. "It wants *double*
thinking, I believe!"

"But where's Sylvie gone?"

"That's just what *I* want to know!" said Bruno dis-
consolately. "What ever's the good of setting me lessons,
when she isn't here to 'splain the hard bits?"

"*I'll* find her for you!" I volunteered; and, getting up,
I wandered round the tree under whose shade I had been
reclining, looking on all sides for Sylvie. In another minute I *again* noticed some strange thing moving among the
grass, and, kneeling down, was immediately confronted
with Sylvie's innocent face, lighted up with a joyful surprise at seeing me, and was accosted, in the sweet voice I
knew so well, with what seemed to be the *end* of a sentence
whose beginning I had failed to catch.

"——and I think he ought to have *finished* them by
this time. So I'm going back to him. Will you come too?
It's only just round at the other side of this tree."

It was but a few steps for *me*; but it was a great
many for Sylvie; and I had to be very careful to walk
slowly, in order not to leave the little creature so far behind as to lose sight of her.

To find Bruno's *lessons* was easy enough: they appeared to be neatly written out on large smooth ivy-
leaves, which were scattered in some confusion over a
little patch of ground where the grass had been worn
away; but the pale student, who ought by rights to have
been bending over them, was nowhere to be seen: we
looked in all directions, for some time in vain; but
at last Sylvie's sharp eyes detected him, swinging on a
tendril of ivy, and Sylvie's stern voice commanded
his instant return to *terra firma* and to the business of
Life.

"Pleasure first and business afterwards" seemed to be
the motto of these tiny folk, so many hugs and kisses
had to be interchanged before anything else could be
done.

"Now, Bruno," Sylvie said reproachfully, "didn't I tell you you were to go on with your lessons, unless you heard to the contrary?"

"But I *did* heard to the contrary!" Bruno insisted, with a mischievous twinkle in his eye.

"*What* did you hear, you wicked boy?"

"It were a sort of noise in the air," said Bruno: "a sort of a scrambling noise. Didn't *oo* hear it, Mister Sir?"

"Well, anyhow, you needn't go to *sleep* over them, you lazy-lazy!" For Bruno had curled himself up, on the largest "lesson", and was arranging another as a pillow.

"I *wasn't* asleep!" said Bruno, in a deeply-injured tone. "When I shuts mine eyes, it's to show that I'm *awake*!"

"Well, how much have you learned, then?"

"I've learned a little tiny bit," said Bruno, modestly, being evidently afraid of overstating his achievement. "*Ca'n't* learn no more!"

"Oh Bruno! You know you *can*, if you like."

"Course I can, if I *like*," the pale student replied; "but I ca'n't if I *don't* like!"

Sylvie had a way—which I could not too highly admire —of evading Bruno's logical perplexities by suddenly striking into a new line of thought; and this masterly stratagem she now adopted.

"Well, I must say *one* thing——"

"Did oo know, Mister Sir," Bruno thoughtfully remarked, "that Sylvie ca'n't count? Whenever she says 'I must say *one* thing', I *know* quite well she'll say *two* things! And she always doos."

"Two heads are better than one, Bruno," I said, but with no very distinct idea as to what I meant by it.

"I shouldn't mind having two *heads*," Bruno said softly to himself: "one head to eat mine dinner, and one head to argue wiz Sylvie—doos oo think oo'd look prettier if oo'd got *two* heads, Mister Sir?"

The case did not, I assured him, admit of a doubt.

"The reason why Sylvie's so cross——" Bruno went on very seriously, almost sadly.

Sylvie's eyes grew large and round with surprise at this new line of enquiry—her rosy face being perfectly radiant with good humour. But she said nothing.

"Wouldn't it be better so tell me after the lessons are over?" I suggested.

"Very well," Bruno said with a resigned air: "only she wo'n't be cross then."

"There's only three lessons to do," said Sylvie. "Spelling, and Geography, and Singing."

"Not *Arithmetic*?" I said.

"No, he hasn't a head for Arithmetic——"

"Course I haven't!" said Bruno. "Mine head's for *hair*. I haven't got a *lot* of heads!"

"—and he ca'n't learn his Multiplication-table——"

"I like *History* ever so much better," Bruno remarked. "Oo has to *repeat* that Muddlecome table——"

'Well, and you have to repeat——"

"No, oo hasn't!" Bruno interrupted. "History repeats itself. The Professor said so!"

Sylvie was arranging some letters on a board—E—V—I—L. "Now, Bruno," she said, "what does *that spell*?"

Bruno looked at it, in solemn silence, for a minute. "I know what it *doesn't* spell!" he said at last.

"That's no good," said Sylvie. "What *does* it spell?"

Bruno took another look at the mysterious letters. "Why, it's 'LIVE', backwards!" he exclaimed. (I thought it was, indeed.)

"How *did* you manage to see that?" said Sylvie.

"I just twiddled my eyes," said Bruno, "and then I saw it directly. Now may I sing the King-fisher Song?"

"Geography next," said Sylvie. "Don't you know the Rules?"

"I think there oughtn't to be such a lot of Rules, Sylvie! I thinks——"

"Yes, there *ought* to be such a lot of Rules, you wicked,

wicked boy! And how dare you *think* at all about it? And shut up that mouth directly!"

So, as "that mouth" didn't seem inclined to shut up of itself, Sylvie shut it for him—with both hands—and sealed it with a kiss, just as you would fasten up a letter.

"Now that Bruno is fastened up from talking," she went on, turning to me, "I'll show you the Map he does his lessons on."

And there it was, a large Map of the World, spread out on the ground. It was so large that Bruno had to crawl about on it, to point out the places named in the "King-fisher Lesson".

"When a King-fisher sees a Lady-bird flying away, he says '*Ceylon*, if you *Candia*!' And when he catches it, he says 'Come to *Media*! And if you're *Hungary* or thirsty, I'll give you some *Nubia*!' When he takes it in his claws, he says '*Europe*!' When he puts it into his beak, he says '*India*!' When he's swallowed it, he says '*Eton*!' That's all."

"That's *quite* perfect," said Sylvie. "Now, you may sing the King-fisher Song."

"Will *oo* sing the chorus?" Bruno said to me.

I was just beginning to say "I'm afraid I don't know the *words*", when Sylvie silently turned the map over, and I found the words were all written on the back. In one respect it was a *very* peculiar song: the chorus to each verse came in the *middle*, instead of at the *end* of it. However, the tune was so easy that I soon picked it up, and managed the chorus as well, perhaps, as it is possible for *one* person to manage such a thing. It was in vain that I signed to Sylvie to help me: she only smiled sweetly and shook her head.

> "*King Fisher courted Lady Bird*—
> **Sing Beans, sing Bones, sing Butterflies!**
> '*Find me my match*,' *he said*,
> '*With such a noble head*—
> *With such a beard, as white as curd*—
> *With such expressive eyes*!'

" *'Yet pins have heads,' said Lady Bird*—
Sing Prunes, sing Prawns, sing Primrose-Hill!
'And, where you stick them in,
They stay, and thus a pin
Is very much to be preferred
To one that's never still!'

" *'Oysters have beards,' said Lady Bird*—
Sing Flies, sing Frogs, sing Fiddle-strings!
'I love them, for I know
They *never chatter so:*
They would not say one single word—
Not if you crowned them Kings!'

" *'Needles have eyes,' said Lady Bird*—
Sing Cats, sing Corks, sing Cowslip-tea!
'And they are sharp—*just what*
Your Majesty is not:
So get you gone—'*tis too absurd*
To come a-courting me!' "

"So he went away," Bruno added as a kind of post-script, when the last note of the song had died away, "Just like he always did."

"Oh, my *dear* Bruno!" Sylvie exclaimed, with her hands over her ears. "You shouldn't say 'like': you should say *'what'*".

To which Bruno replied, doggedly, "I only says 'what!' when oo doesn't speak loud, so as I can hear oo."

"Where did he go to?" I asked, hoping to prevent an argument.

"He went more far than he'd never been before," said Bruno.

"You should never say 'more far'," Sylvie corrected him: "you should say *'farther'*."

"Then *oo* shouldn't say 'more broth', when we're at dinner," Bruno retorted: "oo should say *'brother'*!"

This time Sylvie evaded an argument by turning away, and beginning to roll up the Map. "Lessons are over!" she proclaimed in her sweetest tones.

"And has there been no *crying* over them?" I enquired. "Little boys *always* cry over their lessons, don't
they?"

"I never cries after twelve o'clock," said Bruno:
" 'cause then it's getting so near to dinner-time."

"Sometimes, in the morning," Sylvie said in a low
voice; "when it's Geography-day, and when he's been
disobe———"

"*What* a fellow you are to talk, Sylvie!" Bruno hastily
interposed. "Doos oo think the world was *made* for oo to
talk in?"

"Why, where would you *have* me talk, then?" Sylvie
said, evidently quite ready for an argument.

But Bruno answered resolutely. "I'm not going to
argue about it, 'cause it's getting late, and there wo'n't
be time—but oo's as 'ong as ever oo can be!" And he
rubbed the back of his hand across his eyes, in which
tears were beginning to glitter.

Sylvie's eyes filled with tears in a moment. "I didn't
mean it, Bruno, *darling!*" she whispered; and the rest of
the argument was lost "amid the tangles of Neæra's
hair", while the two disputants hugged and kissed each
other.

But this new form of argument was brought to a sudden end by a flash of lightning, which was closely followed by a peal of thunder, and by a torrent of rain-
drops, which came hissing and spitting, almost like live
creatures, through the leaves of the tree that sheltered us.
"Why, it's raining cats and dogs!" I said.

"And all the *dogs* has come down *first*," said Bruno:
"there's nothing but *cats* coming down now!"

In another minute the pattering ceased, as suddenly as
it had begun. I stepped out from under the tree, and
found that the storm was over; but I looked in vain, on
my return, for my tiny companions. They had vanished
with the storm, and there was nothing for it but to make
the best of my way home.

On the table lay, awaiting my return, an envelope of

that peculiar yellow tint which always announces a telegram, and which must be, in the memories of so many
of us, inseparably linked with some great and sudden
sorrow—something that has cast a shadow, never in this
world to be wholly lifted off, on the brightness of Life.
No doubt it has *also* heralded—for many of us—some
sudden news of joy; but this, I think, is less common:
human life seems, on the whole, to contain more of sorrow than of joy. And yet the world goes on. Who knows
why?

This time, however, there was no shock of sorrow to be
faced: in fact, the few words it contained ("Could not
bring myself to write. Come soon. Always welcome. A
letter follows this. Arthur.") seemed so like Arthur himself speaking, that it gave me quite a thrill of pleasure,
and I at once began the preparations needed for the
journey.

CHAPTER II

Love's Curfew

"FAYFIELD Junction! Change for Elveston!"

What subtle memory could there be, linked to these
commonplace words, that caused such a flood of happy
thoughts to fill my brain? I dismounted from the carriage in a state of joyful excitement for which I could not
at first account. True, I had taken this very journey, and
at the same hour of the day, six months ago; but many
things had happened since then, and an old man's memory has but a slender hold on recent events: I sought "the
missing link" in vain. Suddenly I caught sight of a bench
—the only one provided on the cheerless platform—with
a lady seated on it, and the whole forgotten scene flashed
upon me as vividly as if it were happening over again.

"Yes," I thought. "This bare platform is, for me, rich with the memory of a dear friend! She was sitting on that very bench, and invited me to share it, with some quotation from Shakespeare—I forget what. I'll try the Earl's plan for the Dramatization of Life, and fancy that figure to be Lady Muriel; and I wo'n't undeceive myself too soon!"

So I strolled along the platform, resolutely "making-believe" (as children say) that the casual passenger, seated on that bench, was the Lady Muriel I remembered so well. She was facing away from me, which aided the elaborate cheatery I was practising on myself: but, though I was careful, in passing the spot, to look the other way, in order to prolong the pleasant illusion, it was inevitable that, when I turned to walk back again, I should see who it was. It was Lady Muriel herself!

The whole scene now returned vividly to my memory; and, to make this repetition of it stranger still, there was the same old man, whom I remembered seeing so roughly ordered off, by the Station-Master, to make room for his titled passenger. The same, but "with a difference": no longer tottering feebly along the platform, but actually seated at Lady Muriel's side, and in conversation with her! "Yes, put it in your purse," she was saying, "and remember you're to spend it all for *Minnie*. And mind you bring her something nice, that'll do her real good! And give her my love!" So intent was she on saying these words, that, although the sound of my footstep had made her lift her head and look at me, she did not at first recognize me.

I raised my hat as I approached, and then there flashed across her face a genuine look of joy, which so exactly recalled the sweet face of Sylvie, when last we met in Kensington Gardens, that I felt quite bewildered.

Rather than disturb the poor old man at her side, she rose from her seat, and joined me in my walk up and down the platform, and for a minute or two our conversation was as utterly trivial and commonplace as if we were merely two casual guests in a London drawing-room. Each of us seemed to shrink, just at first, from touching on the deeper interests which linked our lives together.

The Elveston train had drawn up at the platform, while we talked; and, in obedience to the Station-Master's obsequious hint of "This way, my Lady! Time's up!", we were making the best of our way towards the end which contained the sole first-class carriage, and were just passing the now-empty bench, when Lady Muriel noticed, lying on it, the purse in which her gift had just been so carefully bestowed, the owner of which, all unconscious of his loss, was being helped into a carriage at the other end of the train. She pounced on it instantly. "Poor old man!" she cried. "He mustn't go off, and think he's lost it!"

"Let *me* run with it! I can go quicker than you!" I said. But she was already half-way down the platform, flying ("running" is much too mundane a word for such fairy-like motion) at a pace that left all possible efforts of *mine* hopelessly in the rear.

She was back again before I had well completed my audacious boast of speed in running, and was saying, quite demurely, as we entered our carriage, "and you really think *you* could have done it quicker?"

"No, indeed!" I replied. "I plead 'Guilty' of gross exaggeration, and throw myself on the mercy of the Court!"

"The Court will overlook it—for this once!" Then her manner suddenly changed from playfulness to an anxious gravity.

"You are not looking your best!" she said with an anxious glance. "In fact, I think you look *more* of an invalid than when you left us. I very much doubt if London agrees with you?"

"It *may* be the London air," I said, "or it may be the hard work—or my rather lonely life: anyhow, I've *not* been feeling very well, lately. But Elveston will soon set me up again. Arthur's prescription—he's my doctor, you know, and I heard from him this morning—is 'plenty of ozone, and new milk, and *pleasant society*'!"

"Pleasant society?" said Lady Muriel, with a pretty make-believe of considering the question. "Well, really I don't know where we can find *that* for you! We have so few neighbours. But new milk we *can* manage. Do get it of my old friend Mrs. Hunter, up there, on the hill-side. You may rely upon the *quality*. And her little Bessie comes to school every day, and passes your lodgings. So it would be very easy to send it."

"I'll follow your advice with pleasure," I said; "and I'll go and arrange about it to-morrow. I know Arthur will want a walk."

"You'll find it quite an easy walk—under three miles, I think."

"Well, now that we've settled that point, let me retort your own remark upon yourself. I don't think *you're* looking quite your best!"

"I daresay not," she replied in a low voice; and a sudden shadow seemed to overspread her face. "I've had some troubles lately. It's a matter about which I've been long wishing to consult you, but I couldn't easily write about it. I'm *so* glad to have this opportunity!"

"Do you think", she began again, after a minute's silence, and with a visible embarrassment of manner most unusual in her, "that a promise, deliberately and solemnly given, is *always* binding—except, of course, where its fulfilment would involve some actual *sin*?"

"I ca'n't think of any other exception at this moment," I said. "That branch of casuistry is usually, I believe, treated as a question of truth and untruth——"

"Surely that *is* the principle?" she eagerly interrupted. "I always thought the Bible-teaching about it consisted of such texts '*lie not one to another*'?"

"I have thought about that point," I replied; "and it seems to me that the essence of *lying* is the intention of *deceiving*. If you give a promise, fully *intending* to fulfil it, you are certainly acting truthfully *then*; and, if you afterwards break it, that does not involve any *deception*. I cannot call it *untruthful*."

Another pause of silence ensued. Lady Muriel's face was hard to read: she looked pleased, I thought, but also puzzled; and I felt curious to know whether her question had, as I began to suspect, some bearing on the breaking off of her engagement with Captain (now Major) Lindon.

"You have relieved me from a great fear," she said; "but the thing is of course *wrong*, somehow. What texts would *you* quote, to prove it wrong?"

"Any that enforce the payment of *debts*. If *A* promises something to *B*, *B* has a claim upon *A*. And *A*'s sin, if he breaks his promise, seems to me more analogous to *stealing* than to *lying*."

"It's a new way of looking at it—to me," she said; "but it seems a *true* way, also. However, I wo'n't deal in generalities, with an old friend like you! For we *are* old friends, somehow. Do you know, I think we *began* as old friends?" she said with a playfulness of tone that ill accorded with the tears that glistened in her eyes.

"Thank you very much for saying so," I replied. "I like to think of you as an *old* friend," ("—though you don't look it!" would have been the almost necessary sequence, with any other lady; but she and I seemed to have long passed out of the time when compliments, or any such trivialities, were possible).

Here the train paused at a station, where two or three passengers entered the carriage; so no more was said till we had reached our journey's end.

On our arrival at Elveston, she readily adopted my suggestion that we should walk up together; so, as soon as our luggage had been duly taken charge of—hers by the servant who met her at the station, and mine by one of the porters—we set out together along the familiar lanes, now linked in my memory with so many delightful associations. Lady Muriel at once recommenced the conversation at the point where it had been interrupted.

"You knew of my engagement to my cousin Eric. Did you also hear——"

"Yes," I interrupted, anxious to spare her the pain of giving any details. "I heard it had all come to an end."

"I would like to tell you how it happened," she said; "as that is the very point I want your advice about. I had long realized that we were not in sympathy in religious belief. His ideas of Christianity are very shadowy; and even as to the existence of a God he lives in a sort of dreamland. But it has not affected his life! I feel sure, now, that the most absolute Atheist *may* be leading, though walking blindfold, a pure and noble life. And if you knew half the good deeds——" she broke off suddenly, and turned away her head.

"I entirely agree with you," I said. "And have we not our Saviour's own promise that such a life shall surely lead to the light?"

"Yes, I know it," she said in a broken voice, still keeping her head turned away. "And so I told him. He said he would believe, for *my* sake, if he could. And he wished for *my* sake, he could see things as I did. But that is all wrong!" she went on passionately. "God *cannot* approve such low motives as that! Still it was not *I* that broke it off. I knew he loved me; and I had *promised*; and——"

"Then it was *he* that broke it off?"

"He released me unconditionally." She faced me again now, having quite recovered her usual calmness of manner.

"Then what difficulty remains?"

"It is *this*, that I don't believe he did it of his own free will. Now, supposing he hid it *against* his will, merely to satisfy my scruples, would not his claim on me remain just as strong as ever? And would not my promise be as binding as ever? My father says 'no'; but I ca'n't help fearing he is biased by his love for me. And I've asked no one else. I have many friends—friends for the bright sunny weather; not friends for the clouds and storms of life; not *old* friends like you!"

"Let me think a little," I said: and for some minutes we walked on in silence, while, pained to the heart at seeing the bitter trial that had come upon this pure and gentle soul, I strove in vain to see my way through the tangled skein of conflicting motives.

"If she loves him truly", (I seemed at last to grasp the clue to the problem) "is not *that*, for her the voice of God? May she not hope that she is sent to him, even as Ananias was sent to Saul in his blindness, that he may receive his sight?" Once more I seemed to hear Arthur whispering *"What knowest thou, O wife, whether thou shalt save thy husband?"* and I broke the silence with the words "If you still love him truly——"

"I do *not!*" she hastily interrupted. "At least—not in *that* way. I *believe* I loved him when I promised; but I was very young: it is hard to know. But, whatever the feeling was, it is dead *now*. The motive on *his* side is Love: on *mine* it is—Duty!"

Again there was a long silence. The whole skein of thought was tangled worse than ever. This time *she* broke the silence. "Don't misunderstand me!" she said. "When I said my heart was not *his*, I did not mean it was any one else's! At present I feel bound to *him*; and, till I know I am absolutely free, in the sight of God, to love any other than him, I'll never even *think* of any one else—in *that* way, I mean. I would die sooner!" I had never imagined my gentle friend capable of such passionate utterances.

I ventured on no further remark until we had nearly arrived at the Hall-gate; but, the longer I reflected, the clearer it became to me that no call of Duty demanded the sacrifice—possibly of the happiness of a life—which she seemed ready to make. I tried to make this clear to *her* also, adding some warnings on the dangers that surely awaited a union in which mutual love was wanting. "The only argument for it, worth considering," I said in conclusion, "seems to be his supposed *reluctance* in releasing you from your promise. I have tried to give to that argument its *full* weight, and my conclusion is that it does *not* affect the rights of the case, or invalidate the release he has given you. My belief is that you are *entirely* free to act as *now* seems right."

"I am *very* grateful to you," she said earnestly. "Believe it, please! I ca'n't put it into proper words!" and the subject was dropped by mutual consent: and I only learned, long afterwards, that our discussion had really served to dispel the doubts that had harassed her so long.

We parted at the Hall-gate, and I found Arthur eagerly awaiting my arrival; and, before we parted for the night, I had heard the whole story—how he had put off his journey from day to day, feeling that he *could* not go away from the place till his fate had been irrevocably settled by the wedding taking place: how the preparations for the wedding, and the excitement in the neighbourhood, had suddenly come to an end, and he had learned (from Major Lindon, who called to wish him good-bye) that the engagement had been broken off by mutual consent: how he had instantly abandoned all his plans for going abroad, and had decided to stay on at Elveston, for a year or two at any rate, till his newly-awakened hopes should prove true or false; and how, since that memorable day, he had avoided all meetings with Lady Muriel, fearing to betray his feelings before he had had any sufficient evidence as to how she regarded him. "But it is nearly six weeks since all that happened," he said in conclusion, "and we can meet in the ordinary way, now, with no need for any painful allusions. I would have written to tell you all this: only I kept hoping from day to day that—that there would be *more* to tell!"

"And how should there be *more*, you foolish fellow," I fondly urged, "if you never even go near her? Do you expect the offer to come from *her*?"

Arthur was betrayed into a smile. "No," he said, "I hardly expect *that*. But I'm a desperate coward. There's no doubt about it!"

"And what *reasons* have you heard of for breaking off the engagement?"

"A good many," Arthur replied, and proceeded to count them on his fingers. "First, it was found that she was dying of—something; so *he* broke it off. Then it was found that *he* was dying of—some other thing; so *she* broke it off. Then the Major turned out to be a confirmed gamester; so the *Earl* broke it off. Then the Earl insulted him; so the *Major* broke it off. It got a good deal broken off, all things considered!"

"You have all this on the very best authority, of course?"

"Oh, certainly! And communicated in the strictest confidence! Whatever defects Elveston society suffers from, *want of information* isn't one of them!"

"Nor *reticence*, either, it seems. But, seriously, do you know the real reason?"

"No, I'm quite in the dark."

I did not feel that I had any right to enlighten him; so I changed the subject, to the less engrossing one of "new milk", and we agreed that I should walk over, next day, to Hunter's farm, Arthur undertaking to set me part of the way, after which he had to return to keep a business engagement.

Chapter III

Streaks of Dawn

NEXT day proved warm and sunny, and we started early, to enjoy the luxury of a good long chat before he would be obliged to leave me.

"This neighbourhood has more than its due proportion of the *very* poor," I remarked, as we passed a group of hovels, too dilapidated to deserve the name of "cottages".

"But the few rich", Arthur replied, "give more than

their due proportion of help in charity. So the balance is kept."

"I suppose the *Earl* does a good deal?"

"He *gives* liberally; but he has not the health or strength to do more. Lady Muriel does more in the way of school-teaching and cottage-visiting than she would like me to reveal."

"Then *she*, at least, is not one of the 'idle mouths' one so often meets with among the upper classes. I have sometimes thought they would have a hard time of it, if suddenly called on to give their *raison d'être*, and to show cause why they should be allowed to live any longer!"

"The whole subject", said Arthur, "of what we may call 'idle mouths' (I mean persons who absorb some of the material *wealth* of a community—in the form of food, clothes, and so on—without contributing its equivalent in the form of productive *labour*) is a complicated one, no doubt. I've tried to think it out. And it seemed to me that the simplest form of the problem, to start with, is a community without *money*, who buy and sell by *barter* only; and it makes it yet simpler to suppose the food and other things to be capable of *keeping* for many years without spoiling."

"Yours is an excellent plan," I said. "What is your solution of the problem?"

"The commonest type of 'idle mouths' ", said Arthur, "is no doubt due to money being left by parents to their own children. So I imagined a man—either exceptionally clever, or exceptionally strong and industrious—who had contributed so much valuable labour to the needs of the community that its equivalent, in clothes, etc., was (say) five times as much as he needed for himself. We cannot deny his *absolute* right to give the superfluous wealth as he chooses. So, if he leaves *four* children behind him (say two sons and two daughters), with enough of all the necessaries of life to last them a life-time, I cannot see that the *community* is in any way wronged if they choose to do nothing in life but to 'eat, drink, and be merry'.

Most certainly, the community could not fairly say, in reference to *them*, '*if a man will not work, neither let him eat.*' Their reply would be crushing. 'The labour has already been *done*, which is a fair equivalent for the food we are eating; and you have had the benefit of it. On what principle of justice can you demand *two* quotas of work for *one* quota of food?' "

"Yet surely", I said, "there is something wrong *somewhere*, if these four people are well able to do useful work, and if that work is actually *needed* by the community, and they elect to sit idle?"

"I think there *is*," said Arthur: "but it seems to me to arise from a Law of God—that every one shall do as much as he can to help others—and not from any *rights*, on the part of the community, to exact labour as an equivalent for food that has already been fairly earned."

"I suppose the *second* form of the problem is where the 'idle mouths' possess *money* instead of *material* wealth?"

"Yes," replied Arthur: "and I think the simplest case is that of *paper*-money. *Gold* is itself a form of material wealth; but a bank-note is merely a *promise* to hand over so much *material* wealth when called upon to do so. The father of these four 'idle mouths', had done (let us say) five thousand pounds' worth of useful work for the community. In return for this, the community had given him what amounted to a written promise to hand over, whenever called upon to do so, five thousand pounds' worth of food, etc. Then, if he only uses *one* thousand pounds' worth himself, and leaves the rest of the notes to his children, surely they have a full right to *present* these written promises, and to say 'hand over the food, for which the equivalent labour has been already done'. Now I think *this* case well worth stating, publicly and clearly. I should like to drive it into the heads of those Socialists who are priming our ignorant paupers with such sentiments as 'Look at them bloated haristocrats! Doing not a stroke o' work for theirselves, and living on the sweat of *our* brows!' I should like to *force* them to see that the *money*, which those 'haristocrats' are spending, represents so much labour *already* done for the community, and whose equivalent, in *material* wealth, is *due from the community.*"

"Might not the Socialists reply 'Much of this money does not represent *honest* labour *at all*. If you could trace it back, from owner to owner, though you might begin with several legitimate steps, such as gifts, or bequeathing by will, or 'value received', you would soon reach an owner who had no moral right to it but had got it by fraud or other crimes; and of course his successors in the line would have no better right to it than *he* had.''

"No doubt, no doubt," Arthur replied. "But surely that involves the logical fallacy of *proving too much*? It is *quite* as applicable to *material* wealth, as it is to *money*. If we once begin to go back beyond the fact that the *present* owner of certain property came by it honestly, and to ask whether any previous owner, in past ages, got it by fraud, would *any* property be secure?''

After a minute's thought, I felt obliged to admit the truth of this.

"My general conclusion," Arthur continued, "from the mere standpoint of human *rights*, man against man, was this—that if some wealthy 'idle mouth', who has come by his money in a lawful way, even though not one atom of the labour it represents has been his own doing, chooses to spend it on his own needs, without contributing any labour to the community from whom he buys his food and clothes, that community has no *right* to interfere with him. But it's quite another thing, when we come to consider the *divine* law. Measured by *that* standard, such a man is undoubtedly doing wrong, if he fails to use, for the good of those in need, the strength or the skill, that God has given him. That strength and skill do *not* belong to the community, to be paid to *them* as a *debt*: they do *not* belong to the man *himself*, to be used for his *own* enjoyment: they *do* belong to God, to be used according to

His will; and we are not left in doubt as to what this will is. '*Do good, and lend, hoping for nothing again.*' "

"Anyhow," I said, "an 'idle mouth' very often gives away a great deal in charity."

"In *so-called* 'charity'," he corrected me. "Excuse me if I seem to speak *un*charitably. I would not dream of *applying* the term to any *individual*. But I would say, *generally*, that a man who gratifies every fancy that occurs to him— denying himself in *nothing*—and merely gives to the poor some part, or even *all*, of his *superfluous* wealth, is only deceiving himself if he calls it *charity*."

"But, even in giving away *superfluous* wealth, he *may* be denying himself the miser's pleasure in hoarding?"

"I grant you that, gladly," said Arthur. "Given that he *has* that morbid craving, he is doing a good deed in restraining it."

"But, even in spending on *himself*", I persisted, "our typical rich man often does good, by employing people who would otherwise be out of work: and that is often better than pauperizing them by *giving* the money."

"I'm glad you've said that!" said Arthur. "I would not like to quit the subject without exposing the *two* fallacies of that statement—which have gone so long uncontradicted that Society now accepts it as an axiom!"

"What are they?" I said. "I don't even see *one*, myself."

"One is merely the fallacy of *ambiguity*—the assumption that '*doing good*' (that is, benefiting somebody) is necessarily *a good thing to do* (that is, a *right* thing). The other is the assumption that, if one of two specified acts is *better* than another, it is necessarily a *good* act in itself. I should like to call this the fallacy of *comparison*—meaning that it assumes that what is *comparatively* good is therefore *positively* good."

"Then what is *your* test of a good act?"

"That it shall be *our best*," Arthur confidently replied. "And even *then* '*we are unprofitable servants*'. But let me illustrate the two fallacies. Nothing illustrates a fallacy so well as an extreme case, which fairly comes under it.

Suppose I find two children drowning in a pond. I rush in, and save one of the children, and then walk away, leaving the other to drown. Clearly I have *'done good'*, in saving a child's life? But—— Again, supposing I meet an inoffensive stranger, and knock him down and walk on. Clearly that is *'better'* than if I had proceeded to jump upon him and break his ribs? But——"

"Those 'buts' are quite unanswerable," I said. "But I should like an instance from *real* life."

"Well, let us take one of those abominations of modern Society, a Charity-Bazaar. It's an interesting question to think out—how much of the money, that reaches the object in view, is *genuine* charity; and whether even *that* is spent in the *best* way. But the subject needs regular classification, and analysis, to understand it properly."

"I should be glad to *have* it analysed," I said: "it has often puzzled me."

"Well, if I am really not boring you. Let us suppose our Charity-Bazaar to have been organized to aid the funds of some Hospital: and that A, B, C *give* their services in making articles to sell, and in acting as salesmen, while X, Y, Z buy the articles, and the money so paid goes to the Hospital.

"There are two distinct species of such Bazaars: one, where the payment exacted is merely the *market-value* of the goods supplied, that is, exactly what you would have to pay at a shop: the other, where *fancy-prices* are asked. We must take these separately.

"First, the 'market-value' case. Here A, B, C are exactly in the same position as ordinary shopkeepers; the only difference being that they give the proceeds to the Hospital. Practically, they are *giving their skilled labour* for the benefit of the Hospital. This seems to me to be genuine charity. And I don't see how they could use it better. But X, Y, Z are exactly in the same position as any ordinary purchasers of goods. To talk of 'charity' in connection with *their* share of the business, is sheer nonsense. Yet they are very likely to do so.

"Secondly, the case of 'fancy-prices'. Here I think the simplest plan is to divide the payment into two parts, the 'market-value' and the excess over that. The 'market-value' part is on the same footing as in the first case: the *excess* is all we have to consider. Well, A, B, C do not *earn* it; so we may put *them* out of the question: it is a *gift*, from X, Y, Z, to the Hospital. And my opinion is that it is not given in the best way: far better buy what they choose to *buy*, and give what they choose to *give*, as two *separate* transactions: then there is *some* chance that their motive in giving may be real charity, instead of a mixed motive—half charity, half self-pleasing. 'The trail of the serpent is over it all.' And *therefore* it is that I hold all such spurious 'Charities' in *utter* abomination!" He ended with unusual energy, and savagely beheaded, with his stick, a tall thistle at the road-side, behind which I was startled to see Sylvie and Bruno standing. I caught at his arm, but too late to stop him. Whether the stick reached them, or not, I could not feel sure: at any rate they took not the smallest notice of it, but smiled gaily, and nodded to me: and I saw at once that they were only visible to *me*: the "eerie" influence had not reached to *Arthur*.

"Why did you try to save it?" he said. "*That's* not the wheedling Secretary of a Charity-Bazaar! I only wish it were!" he added grimly.

"Does oo know, that stick went right froo my head!" said Bruno. (They had run round to me by this time, and each had secured a hand.) "Just under my chin! I *are* glad I aren't a thistle!"

"Well, we've threshed *that* subject out, anyhow!" Arthur resumed. "I'm afraid I've been talking too much, for *your* patience and for my strength. I must be turning soon. This is about the end of my tether."

> "*Take, O boatman, thrice thy fee;*
> *Take, I give it willingly;*
> *For, invisible to thee,*
> *Spirits twain have crossed with me!*"

I quoted, involuntarily.

"For utterly inappropriate and irrelevant quotations," laughed Arthur, "you are 'ekalled by few, and excelled by none'!" And we strolled on.

As we passed the head of the lane that led down to the beach, I noticed a single figure moving slowly along it, seawards. She was a good way off, and had her back to us: but it was Lady Muriel, unmistakably. Knowing that Arthur had not seen her, as he had been looking, in the other direction, at a gathering rain-cloud, I made no remark, but tried to think of some plausible pretext for sending him back by the sea.

The opportunity instantly presented itself. "I'm getting tired," he said. "I don't think it would be prudent to go further. I had better turn here."

I turned with him, for a few steps, and as we again approached the head of the lane, I said, as carelessly as I could, "Don't go back by the road. It's too hot and dusty. Down this lane, and along the beach, is nearly as short; and you'll get a breeze off the sea."

"Yes, I think I will," Arthur began; but at that moment we came into sight of Lady Muriel, and he checked himself. "No, it's too far round. Yet it certainly *would* be cooler——" He stood, hesitating, looking first one way and then the other—a melancholy picture of utter infirmity of purpose!

How long this humiliating scene would have continued, if *I* had been the only external influence, it is impossible to say; for at this moment Sylvie, with a swift decision worthy of Napoleon himself, took the matter into her own hands. "You go and drive *her*, up this way," she said to Bruno. "I'll get *him* along!" And she took hold of the stick that Arthur was carrying, and gently pulled him down the lane.

He was totally unconscious that any will but his own was acting on the stick, and appeared to think it had taken a horizontal position simply because he was pointing with it. "Are not those *orchises* under the hedge there?" he said. "I think that decides me. I'll gather some as I go along."

Meanwhile Bruno had run on behind Lady Muriel, and, with much jumping about and shouting (shouts audible to no one but Sylvie and myself), much as if he were driving sheep, he managed to turn her round and make her walk, with eyes demurely cast upon the ground, in our direction.

The victory was ours! And, since it was evident that the lovers, thus urged together, *must* meet in another minute, I turned and walked on, hoping that Sylvie and Bruno would follow my example, as I felt sure that the fewer the spectators the better it would be for Arthur and his good angel.

"And what sort of meeting was it?" I wondered, as I paced dreamily on.

Chapter IV

The Dog-King

"THEY shooked hands," said Bruno, who was trotting at my side, in answer to the unspoken question.

"And they looked *ever* so pleased!" Sylvie added from the other side.

"Well, we must get on, now, as quick as we can," I said. "If only I knew the best way to Hunter's farm!"

"They'll be sure to know in this cottage," said Sylvie.

"Yes, I suppose they will. Bruno, would you run in and ask?"

Sylvie stopped him, laughingly, as he ran off. "Wait a minute," she said. "I must make you *visible* first, you know."

"And *audible* too, I suppose?" I said, as she took the

jewel, that hung round her neck, and waved it over his head, and touched his eyes and lips with it.

"Yes," said Sylvie: "and *once*, do you know, I made him *audible*, and forgot to make him *visible*! And he went to buy some sweeties in a shop. And the man *was* so frightened! A voice seemed to come out of the air, 'Please, I want two ounces of barley-sugar drops!' And a shilling came *bang* down upon the counter! And the man said 'I ca'n't *see* you!' And Bruno said 'It doosn't sinnify seeing *me*, so long as oo can see the *shilling*!' But the man said he never sold barley-sugar drops to people he couldn't *see*. So we had to—*Now*, Bruno, you're ready!" And away he trotted.

Sylvie spent the time, while we were waiting for him, in making *herself* visible also. "It's rather awkward, you know," she explained to me, "when we meet people, and they can see *one* of us, and ca'n't see the *other*!"

In a minute or two Bruno returned, looking rather disconsolate. "He'd got friends with him, and he were *cross*!" he said. "He asked me who I were. And I said 'I'm Bruno: who is *these* peoples?' And he said 'One's my half-brother, and t'other's my half-sister: and I don't want no more company! Go along with yer!' And I said 'I ca'n't go along *wizout* mine self!' And I said 'Oo shouldn't have *bits* of peoples lying about like that! It's welly untidy!' And he said 'Oh, don't talk to *me*!' And he pushted me outside! And he shutted the door!"

"And you never asked where Hunter's farm was?" queried Sylvie.

"Hadn't room for any questions," said Bruno. "The room were so crowded."

"Three people *couldn't* crowd a room," said Sylvie.

"They *did*, though," Bruno persisted. "*He* crowded it most. He's such a welly *thick* man—so as oo couldn't knock him down."

I failed to see the drift of Bruno's argument. "Surely *anybody* could be knocked down," I said: "thick or thin wouldn't matter."

"Oo couldn't knock *him* down," said Bruno. "He's more wide than he's high: so, when he's lying down he's more higher than when he's standing: so a-course oo couldn't knock him *down!*"

"Here's another cottage," I said: "*I'll* ask the way, *this* time."

There was no need to go in, this time, as the woman was standing in the doorway, with a baby in her arms, talking to a respectably dressed man—a farmer, as I guessed—who seemed to be on his way to the town.

"—and when there's *drink* to be had," he was saying, "he's just the worst o' the lot, is your Willie. So they tell me. He gets fairly mad wi' it!"

"I'd have given 'em the lie to their faces, a twelve-month back!" the woman said in a broken voice. "But a' canna noo! A' canna noo!" She checked herself on catching sight of us, and hastily retreated into the house, shutting the door after her.

"Perhaps you can tell me where Hunter's farm is?" I said to the man, as he turned away from the house.

"I can *that*, Sir!" he replied with a smile. "I'm John Hunter hissel, at your sarvice. It's nobbut half a mile further—the only house in sight, when you get round bend o' the road yonder. You'll find my good woman within, if so be you've business wi' *her*. Or mebbe I'll do as well?"

"Thanks," I said. "I want to order some milk. Perhaps I had better arrange it with your wife?"

"Aye," said the man. "*She* minds all *that*. Good day t'ye, Master—and to your bonnie childer, as well!" And he trudged on.

"He should have said '*child*', not '*childer*'," said Bruno. "Sylvie's not a *childer!*"

"He meant *both* of us," said Sylvie.

"No, he didn't!" Bruno persisted. " 'cause he said 'bonnie', oo know!"

"Well, at any rate he *looked* at us both," Sylvie maintained.

"Well, then he *must* have seen we're not *both* bonnie!"

Bruno retorted. "A-*course* I'm much uglier than *oo*! Didn't he mean *Sylvie*, Mister Sir?" he shouted over his shoulder, as he ran off.

But there was no use in replying, as he had already vanished round the bend of the road. When we overtook him he was climbing a gate, and was gazing earnestly into the field, where a horse, a cow, and a kid were browsing amicably together. "For its father, a *Horse*," he murmured to himself. "For its mother, a *Cow*. For their dear little child, a *little* Goat, is the most curiousest thing I ever seen in my world!"

"Bruno's World!" I pondered. "Yes, I suppose every child has a world of his own—and every man, too, for the matter of that. I wonder if *that's* the cause for all the misunderstanding there is in Life?"

"That *must* be Hunter's farm!" said Sylvie, pointing to a house on the brow of the hill, led up to by a cart-road. "There's no other farm in sight, *this* way; and you *said* we must be nearly there by this time."

I had *thought* it, while Bruno was climbing the gate, but I couldn't remember having *said* it. However, Sylvie was evidently in the right. "Get down, Bruno," I said, "and open the gate for us."

"It's a good thing we's with oo, *isn't* it, Mister Sir?" said Bruno, as we entered the field. "That big dog might have bited oo, if oo'd been alone! Oo needn't be *flightened* of it!" he whispered, clinging tight to my hand to encourage me. "It aren't fierce!"

"Fierce!" Sylvie scornfully echoed, as the dog—a magnificent Newfoundland—that had come galloping down the field to meet us, began curveting round us, in gambols full of graceful beauty, and welcoming us with short joyful barks. "Fierce! Why, it's as gentle as a lamb! It's— why, Bruno, don't you know? It's——"

"So it *are*!" cried Bruno, rushing forwards and throwing his arms round its neck. "Oh, you *dear* dog!" And it seemed as if the two children would never have done hugging and stroking it.

"And how *ever* did he get *here?*" said Bruno. "Ask him, Sylvie. I doosn't know how."

And then began an eager talk in Doggee, which of course was lost upon *me*; and I could only *guess*, when the beautiful creature, with a sly glance at me, whispered something in Sylvie's ear, that *I* was now the subject of conversation. Sylvie looked round laughingly.

"He asked me who you are," she explained. "And I said '*He's our friend*'. And he said 'What's his name?' And I said 'It's *Mister Sir*'. And he said 'Bosh!' "

"What is 'Bosh!' in Doggee," I enquired.

"It's the same as in English," said Sylvie. "Only, when a *dog* says it, it's a sort of whisper, that's half a *cough* and half a *bark*. Nero, say '*Bosh!*' "

And Nero, who had now begun gamboling round us again, said "*Bosh!*" several times; and I found that Sylvie's description of the sound was perfectly accurate.

"I wonder what's behind this long wall?" I said, as we walked on.

"It's the *Orchard*," Sylvie replied, after a consultation with Nero. "See, there's a boy getting down off the wall, at that far corner. And now he's running away across the field. I do believe he's been stealing the apples!"

Bruno set off after him, but returned to us in a few moments, as he had evidently no chance of overtaking the young rascal.

"I couldn't catch him!" he said. "I wiss I'd started a little sooner. His pockets *was* full of apples!"

The Dog-King looked up at Sylvie, and said something in Doggee.

"Why, of *course* you can!" Sylvie exclaimed. "How stupid not to think of it! *Nero*'ll hold him for us, Bruno! But I'd better make him invisible, first." And she hastily got out the Magic Jewel, and began waving it over Nero's head, and down along his back.

"That'll do!" cried Bruno, impatiently. "After him, good Doggie!"

"Oh, Bruno!" Sylvie exclaimed reproachfully. "You

shouldn't have sent him off so quick! I hadn't done the tail!"

Meanwhile Nero was coursing like a greyhound down the field: so at least I concluded from all *I* could see of him—the long feathery tail, which floated like a meteor through the air—and in a very few seconds he had come up with the little thief.

"He's got him safe, by one foot!" cried Sylvie, who was eagerly watching the chase. "Now there's no hurry, Bruno!"

So we walked, quite leisurely, down the field, to where the frightened lad stood. A more curious sight I had seldom seen, in all my "eerie" experiences. Every bit of him was in violent action, except the left foot, which was apparently glued to the ground—there being nothing visibly holding it: while, at some little distance, the long feathery tail was waving gracefully from side to side, showing that Nero, at least, regarded the whole affair as nothing but a magnificent game of play.

"What's the matter with you?" I said, as gravely as I could.

"Got the crahmp in me ahnkle!" the thief groaned in reply. "An' me fut's gone to sleep!" And he began to blubber aloud.

"Now, look here!" Bruno said in a commanding tone, getting in front of him. "Oo've got to give up those apples!"

The lad glanced at me, but didn't seem to reckon *my* interference as worth anything. Then he glanced at Sylvie: *she* clearly didn't count for very much, either. Then he took courage. "It'll take a better man than any of *yer* to get 'em!" he retorted defiantly.

Sylvie stooped and patted the invisible Nero. "A *little* tighter!" she whispered. And a sharp yell from the ragged boy showed how promptly the Dog-King had taken the hint.

"What's the matter *now*?" I said. "Is your ankle worse?"

"And it'll get worse, and worse, and worse," Bruno solemnly assured him, "till oo gives up those apples!"

Apparently the thief was convinced of this at last, and he sulkily began emptying his pockets of the apples. The children watched from a little distance, Bruno dancing with delight at every fresh yell extracted from Nero's terrified prisoner.

"That's all," the boy said at last.

"It *isn't* all!" cried Bruno. "There's three more in that pocket!"

Another hint from Sylvie to the Dog-King—another sharp yell from the thief, now convicted of lying also—and the remaining three apples were surrendered.

"Let him go, please," Sylvie said in Doggee, and the lad limped away at a great pace, stooping now and then to rub the ailing ankle in fear, seemingly, that the "crahmp" might attack it again.

Bruno ran back, with his booty, to the orchard wall, and pitched the apples over it one by one. "I's welly afraid *some* of them's gone under the wrong trees!" he panted, on overtaking us again.

"The *wrong* trees!" laughed Sylvie. "Trees *ca'n't* do wrong! There's no such things as *wrong* trees!"

"Then there's no such things as *right* trees, neither!" cried Bruno. And Sylvie gave up the point.

"Wait a minute, please!" she said to me. "I must make Nero *visible*, you know!"

"No, *please* don't!" cried Bruno, who had by this time mounted on the Royal back, and was twisting the Royal hair into a bridle. "It'll be *such* fun to have him like this!"

"Well, it *does* look funny," Sylvie admitted, and led the way to the farm-house, where the farmer's wife stood, evidently much perplexed at the weird procession now approaching her. "It's summat gone wrong wi' my spectacles, I doubt!" she murmured, as she took them off, and began diligently rubbing them with a corner of her apron.

Meanwhile Sylvie had hastily pulled Bruno down from

his steed, and had just time to make His Majesty wholly visible before the spectacles were resumed.

All was natural, now; but the good woman still looked a little uneasy about it. "My eyesight's getting bad," she said, "but I see you *now*, my darlings! You'll give me a kiss, won't you?"

Bruno got behind me, in a moment: however Sylvie put up *her* face, to be kissed, as representative of *both*, and we all went in together.

CHAPTER V

Matilda Jane

"COME to me, my little gentleman," said our hostess, lifting Bruno into her lap, "and tell me everything."

"I ca'n't," said Bruno. "There wouldn't be time. Besides, I don't know everything."

The good woman looked a little puzzled, and turned to Sylvie for help. "Does he like *riding*?" she asked.

"Yes, I *think* so," Sylvie gently replied. "He's just had a ride on *Nero*."

"Ah, Nero's a grand dog, isn't he? Were you ever outside a *horse*, my little man?"

"*Always!*" Bruno said with great decision. "Never was *inside* one. Was *oo*?"

Here I thought it well to interpose, and to mention the business on which we had come, and so relieved her, for a few minutes, from Bruno's perplexing questions.

"And those dear children will like a bit of cake, *I'll* warrant!" said the farmer's hospitable wife, when the business was concluded, as she opened her cupboard, and brought out a cake. "And don't you waste the crust, little gentleman!" she added, as she handed a good slice of it to Bruno. "You know what the poetry-book says about wilful waste?"

"No, I don't," said Bruno. "What doos he say about it?"

"Tell him, Bessie!" And the mother looked down, proudly and lovingly, on a rosy little maiden, who had just crept shyly into the room, and was leaning against her knee. "What's that your poetry-book says about wilful waste?"

"*For wilful waste makes woeful want,*" Bessie recited, in an almost inaudible whisper: "*and you may live to say 'How much I wish I had the crust that then I threw away!'* "

"Now try if *you* can say it, my dear! *For wilful——*"

"*For wifful*—sumfinoruvver——" Bruno began, readily enough; and then there came a dead pause. "Ca'n't remember no more!"

"Well, what do you *learn* from it, then? You can tell us *that*, at any rate?"

Bruno ate a little more cake, and considered: but the moral did not seem to him to be a very obvious one.

"Always to——" Sylvie prompted him in a whisper.

"Always to——" Bruno softly repeated: and then, with sudden inspiration, "always to look where it goes to!"

"Where *what* goes to, darling?"

"Why the *crust*, a course!" said Bruno. "Then, if I lived to say '*How much I wiss I had the crust——*' (and all that), I'd know where I frew it to!"

This new interpretation quite puzzled the good woman. She returned to the subject of "Bessie". "Wouldn't you like to see Bessie's doll, my dears! Bessie, take the little lady and gentleman to see Matilda Jane!"

Bessie's shyness thawed away in a moment. "Matilda Jane has just woke up," she stated, confidentially, to Sylvie. "Won't you help me on with her frock? Them strings *is* such a bother to tie!"

"I can tie *strings*," we heard, in Sylvie's gentle voice, as the two little girls left the room together. Bruno ignored the whole proceeding, and strolled to the window, quite with the air of a fashionable gentleman. Little girls, and dolls, were not at all in his line.

And forthwith the fond mother proceeded to tell me (as what mother is not ready to do?) of all Bessie's virtues (and vices too, for the matter of that) and of the many fearful maladies which, notwithstanding those ruddy cheeks and that plump little figure, had nearly, time and again, swept her from the face of the earth.

When the full stream of loving memories had nearly run itself out, I began to question her about the working men of that neighbourhood, and specially the "Willie'" whom we had heard of at his cottage. "He was a good fellow once," said my kind hostess: "but it's the drink has ruined him! Not that I'd rob them of the drink—it's good for the most of them—but there's some as is too weak to stand agin' temptations: it's a thousand pities, for *them*, as they ever built the Golden Lion at the corner there!"

"The Golden Lion?" I repeated.

"It's the new Public," my hostess explained. "And it stands right in the way, and handy for the workmen, as they come back from the brickfields, as it might be to-day, with their week's wages. A deal of money gets wasted that way. And some of 'em gets drunk."

"If only they could have it in their own houses——" I mused, hardly knowing I had said the words out loud.

"That's it!" she eagerly exclaimed. It was evidently a solution, of the problem, that she had already thought out. "If only you could manage, so's each man to have his own little barrel in his own house—there'd hardly be a drunken man in the length and breadth of the land!"

And then I told her the old story—about a certain cottager who bought himself a little barrel of beer, and installed his wife as bar-keeper: and how, every time he wanted his mug of beer, he regularly paid her over the counter for it: and how she never would let him go on "tick", and was a perfectly inflexible bar-keeper in never letting him have more than his proper allowance: and how, every time the barrel needed refilling, she had plenty to do it with, and something over for her money-box: and how, at the end of the year, he not only found

himself in first-rate health and spirits, with that unde-
finable but quite unmistakable air which always distin-
guishes the sober man from the one who takes "a drop
too much", but had quite a box full of money, all saved
out of his own pence!

"If only they'd all do like that!" said the good woman,
wiping her eyes, which were overflowing with kindly
sympathy. "Drink hadn't need to be the curse it is to
some——"

"Only a *curse*", I said, "when it is used wrongly. Any
of God's gifts may be turned into a curse, unless we use it
wisely. But we must be getting home. Would you call the
little girls? Matilda Jane has seen enough of company,
for *one* day, I'm sure!"

"I'll find 'em in a minute," said my hostess, as she rose
to leave the room. "Maybe that young gentleman saw
which way they went?"

"Where are they, Bruno?" I said.

"They ain't in the field," was Bruno's rather evasive
reply, " 'cause there's nothing but *pigs* there, and Sylvie
isn't a pig. Now don't interrupt me any more, 'cause I'm
telling a story to this fly; and it wo'n't attend!"

"They're among the apples, I'll warrant 'em!" said the
Farmer's wife. So we left Bruno to finish his story, and
went out into the orchard, where we soon came upon the
children, walking sedately side by side, Sylvie carrying
the doll, while little Bess carefully shaded its face, with a
large cabbage-leaf for a parasol.

As soon as they caught sight of us, little Bess dropped
her cabbage-leaf and came running to meet us, Sylvie
following more slowly, as her precious charge evidently
needed great care and attention.

"I'm its Mamma, and Sylvie's the Head-Nurse," Bessie
explained: "and Sylvie's taught me ever such a pretty
song, for me to sing to Matilda Jane!"

"Let's hear it once more, Sylvie," I said, delighted at
getting the chance I had long wished for, of hearing her
sing. But Sylvie turned shy and frightened in a moment.

"No, *please not!*" she said, in an earnest "aside" to me. "Bessie knows it quite perfect now. Bessie can sing it!"

"Aye, aye! Let Bessie sing it!" said the proud mother. "Bessie has a bonny voice of her own," (this again was an "aside" to me) "though I say it as shouldn't!"

Bessie was only too happy to accept the "encore". So the plump little Mamma sat down at our feet, with her hideous daughter reclining stiffly across her lap (it was one of a kind that wo'n't sit down, under *any* amount of persuasion), and, with a face simply beaming with delight, began the lullaby, in a shout that *ought* to have frightened the poor baby into fits. The Head-Nurse crouched down behind her, keeping herself respectfully in the background, with her hands on the shoulders of her little mistress, so as to be ready to act as Prompter, if required, and to supply *"each gap in faithless memory void"*.

The shout, with which she began, proved to be only a momentary effort. After a very few notes, Bessie toned down, and sang on in a small but very sweet voice. At first her great black eyes were fixed on her mother, but soon her gaze wandered upwards, among the apples, and she seemed to have quite forgotten that she had any other audience than her Baby, and her Head-Nurse, who once or twice supplied, almost inaudibly, the right note, when the singer was getting a little "flat".

> *"Matilda Jane, you never look*
> *At any toy or picture-book:*
> *I show you pretty things in vain—*
> *You must be blind, Matilda Jane!*

> *"I ask you riddles, tell you tales,*
> *But* all *our conversation fails:*
> *You* never *answer me again—*
> *I fear you're dumb, Matilda Jane!*

> *"Matilda, darling, when I call,*
> *You never seem to hear at all:*
> *I shout with all my might and main—*
> *But you're so deaf, Matilda Jane!*

"Matilda Jane, you needn't mind:
For, though you're deaf, and dumb, and blind,
There's some one *loves you, it is plain—*
And that is me, *Matilda Jane!"*

She sang three of the verses in a rather perfunctory style, but the last stanza evidently excited the little maiden. Her voice rose, ever clearer and louder: she had a rapt look on her face, as if suddenly inspired, and, as she sang the last few words, she clasped to her heart the inattentive Matilda Jane.

"Kiss it now!" prompted the Head-Nurse. And in a moment the simpering meaningless face of the Baby was covered with a shower of passionate kisses.

"What a bonny song!" cried the Farmer's wife. "Who made the words, dearie?"

'I—I think I'll look for Bruno," Sylvie said demurely, and left us hastily. The curious child seemed always afraid of being praised, or even noticed.

"Sylvie planned the words," Bessie informed us, proud of her superior information: "and Bruno planned the music—and *I* sang it!" (this last circumstance, by the way, we did not need to be told).

So we followed Sylvie, and all entered the parlour together. Bruno was still standing at the window, with his elbows on the sill. He had, apparently, finished the story that he was telling to the fly, and had found a new occupation. "Don't imperrupt!" he said as we came in. "I'm counting the Pigs in the field!"

"How many are there?" I enquired.

"About a thousand and four," said Bruno.

"You mean 'about a thousand'," Sylvie corrected him. "There's no good saying '*and four*': you *ca'n't* be sure about the four!"

"And you're as wrong as ever!" Bruno exclaimed triumphantly. "It's just the *four* I *can* be sure about; 'cause they're here, grubbling under the window! It's the *thousand* I isn't pruffickly sure about!"

"But some of them have gone into the sty," Sylvie said, leaning over him to look out of the window.

"Yes," said Bruno; "but they went so slowly and so fewly, I didn't care to count *them*."

"We must be going, children," I said. "Wish Bessie good-bye." Sylvie flung her arms round the little maiden's neck, and kissed her: but Bruno stood aloof, looking unusually shy. ("I never kiss *nobody* but Sylvie!" he explained to me afterwards.) The Farmer's wife showed us out: and we were soon on our way back to Elveston.

"And that's the new public-house that we were talking about, I suppose?" I said, as we came in sight of a long low building, with the words "THE GOLDEN LION" over the door.

"Yes, that's it," said Sylvie. "I wonder if *her* Willie's inside? Run in, Bruno, and see if he's there."

I interposed, feeling that Bruno was, in a sort of way, in *my* care. "That's not a place to send a child into." For already the revellers were getting noisy: and a wild discord of singing, shouting, and meaningless laughter came to us through the open windows.

"They wo'n't *see* him, you know," Sylvie explained. "Wait a minute, Bruno!" She clasped the jewel, that always hung round her neck, between the palms of her hands, and muttered a few words to herself. What they were I could not at all make out, but some mysterious change seemed instantly to pass over us. My feet seemed to me no longer to press the ground, and the dream-like feeling came upon me, that I was suddenly endowed with the power of floating in the air. I could still just *see* the children: but their forms were shadowy and unsubstantial, and their voices sounded as if they came from some distant place and time, they were so unreal. However, I offered no further opposition to Bruno's going into the house. He was back again in a few moments. "No, he isn't come yet," he said. "They're talking about him inside, and saying how drunk he was last week."

While he was speaking, one of the men lounged out

through the door, a pipe in one hand and a mug of beer in the other, and crossed to where we were standing, so as to get a better view along the road. Two or three others leaned out through the open window, each holding his mug of beer, with red faces and sleepy eyes. "Canst see him, lad?" one of them asked.

"I dunnot know," the man said, taking a step forwards, which brought us nearly face to face. Sylvie hastily pulled me out of his way. "Thanks, child," I said. "I had forgotten he couldn't see us. What would have happened if I had stayed in his way?"

"I don't know," Sylvie said gravely. "It wouldn't matter to *us*; but *you* may be different." She said this in her usual voice, but the man took no sort of notice, though she was standing close in front of him, and looking up into his face as she spoke.

"He's coming now!" cried Bruno, pointing down the road.

"He be a-coomin noo!" echoed the man, stretching out his arm exactly over Bruno's head, and pointing with his pipe.

"Then *chorus* agin!" was shouted out by one of the red-faced men in the window: and forthwith a dozen voices yelled, to a harsh discordant melody, the refrain:

> "*There's him, an' yo', an' me,*
> *Roarin' laddies!*
> *We loves a bit o' spree,*
> *Roarin' laddies we,*
> *Roarin' laddies*
> *Roarin' laddies!*"

The man lounged back again to the house, joining lustily in the chorus as he went: so that only the children and I were in the road when "Willie" came up.

Chapter VI

Willie's Wife

HE made for the door of the public-house, but the children intercepted him. Sylvie clung to one arm; while Bruno, on the opposite side, was pushing him with all his strength, and many inarticulate cries of "Gee-up! Gee-back! Woah then!" which he had picked up from the waggoners.

"Willie" took not the least notice of them: he was simply conscious that *something* had checked him: and, for want of any other way of accounting for it, he seemed to regard it as his own act.

"I wunnut coom in," he said: "not to-day."

"A mug o' beer wunnut hurt 'ee!" his friends shouted in chorus. "*Two* mugs wunnut hurt 'ee! Nor a dozen mugs!"

"Nay," said Willie. "I'm agoan whoam."

"What, withouten thy drink, Willie man?" shouted the others. But "Willie man" would have no more discussion, and turned doggedly away, the children keeping one on each side of him, to guard him against any change in his sudden resolution.

For a while he walked on stoutly enough, keeping his hands in his pockets, and softly whistling a tune, in time to his heavy tread: his success, in appearing entirely at his ease, was *almost* complete; but a careful observer would have noted that he had forgotten the second part of the air, and that, when it broke down, he instantly began it again, being too nervous to think of another, and too restless to endure silence.

It was not the old fear that possessed him now—the old fear that had been his dreary companion every Saturday night he could remember as he had reeled along, steadying himself against gates and garden-palings, and when the shrill reproaches of his wife had seemed to his dazed brain only the echo of a yet more piercing voice within,

513

the intolerable wail of a hopeless remorse: it was a wholly new fear that had come to him now: life had taken on itself a new set of colours, and was lighted up with a new and dazzling radiance, and he did not see, as yet, how his home-life, and his wife and child, would fit into the new order of things: the very novelty of it all was, to his simple mind, a perplexity and an overwhelming terror.

And now the tune died into sudden silence on the trembling lips, as he turned a sharp corner, and came in sight of his own cottage, where his wife stood, leaning with folded arms on the wicket-gate, and looking up the road with a pale face, that had in it no glimmer of the light of hope—only the heavy shadow of a deep stony despair.

"Fine an' early, lad! Fine an' early!" the words might have been words of welcoming, but oh, the bitterness of the tone in which she said it! "What brings thee from thy merry mates, and all the fiddling and the jigging? Pockets empty, I doubt? Or thou'st come, mebbe, for to see thy little one die? The bairnie's clemmed, and I've nor bite nor sup to gie her. But what does *thou* care?" She flung the gate open, and met him with blazing eyes of fury.

The man said no word. Slowly, and with downcast eyes, he passed into the house, while she, half terrified at his strange silence, followed him in without another word; and it was not till he had sunk into a chair, with his arms crossed on the table and with drooping head, that she found her voice again.

It seemed entirely natural for us to go in with them: at another time one would have asked leave for this, but I felt, I knew not why, that we were in some mysterious way invisible, and as free to come and to go as disembodied spirits.

The child in the cradle woke up, and raised a piteous cry, which in a moment brought the children to its side: Bruno rocked the cradle, while Sylvie tenderly replaced the little head on the pillow from which it had slipped. But the mother took no heed of the cry, nor yet of the satisfied "coo" that it set up when Sylvie had made it happy again: she only stood gazing at her husband, and vainly trying, with white quivering lips (I believe she thought he was mad), to speak in the old tones of shrill upbraiding that he knew so well.

"And thou'st spent all thy wages—I'll swear thou hast —on the devil's own drink—and thou'st been and made thysen a beast again—as thou allus dost——"

"Hasna!" the man muttered, his voice hardly rising above a whisper, as he slowly emptied his pockets on the table. "There's th' wage, Missus, every penny on't."

The woman gasped and put one hand to her heart, as if under some great shock of surprise. "Then *how's* thee gotten th' drink?"

"*Hasna* gotten it," he answered her, in a tone more sad than sullen. "I hanna touched a drop this blessed day. No!" he cried aloud, bringing his clenched fist heavily down upon the table, and looking up at her with gleaming eyes, "nor I'll never touch another drop o' the cursed drink—till I die—so help me God my Maker!" His voice, which had suddenly risen to a hoarse shout, dropped again as suddenly: and once more he bowed his head, and buried his face in his folded arms.

The woman had dropped upon her knees by the cradle, while he was speaking. She neither looked at him nor seemed to hear him. With hands clasped above her head, she rocked herself wildly to and fro. "Oh my God! Oh my God!" was all she said, over and over again.

Sylvie and Bruno gently unclasped her hands and drew them down—till she had an arm round each of them, though she took no notice of them, but knelt on with eyes gazing upwards, and lips that moved as if in silent thanksgiving. The man kept his face hidden, and uttered no sound: but one could *see* the sobs that shook him from head to foot.

After a while he raised his head—his face all wet with tears. "Polly!" he said softly; and then, louder, "Old Poll!"

Then she rose from her knees and came to him, with a dazed look, as if she were walking in her sleep. "Who was it called me old Poll?" she asked: her voice took on it a tender playfulness: her eyes sparkled; and the rosy light of Youth flushed her pale cheeks, till she looked more like a happy girl of seventeen than a worn woman of forty. "Was that my own lad, my Willie, a-waiting for me at the stile?"

His face too was transformed, in the same magic light, to the likeness of a bashful boy: and boy and girl they seemed, as he wound an arm about her, and drew her to his side, while with the other hand he thrust from him the heap of money, as though it were something hateful to the touch. "Tak it, lass," he said, "tak it all! An' fetch us summat to eat: but get a sup o' milk, first, for t' bairn.'

"My *little* bairn!" she murmured as she gathered up the coins. "My own little lassie!" Then she moved to the door, and was passing out, but a sudden thought seemed to arrest her: she hastily returned—first to kneel down and kiss the sleeping child, and then to throw herself into her husband's arms and be strained to his heart. The next moment she was on her way, taking with her a jug that hung on a peg near the door: we followed close behind.

We had not gone far before we came in sight of a swinging sign-board bearing the word "DAIRY" on it, and here she went in, welcomed by a little curly white dog, who, not being under the "eerie" influence, saw the children, and received them with the most effusive affection. When I got inside, the dairyman was in the act of taking the money. "Is't for thysen, Missus, or for t' bairn?" he asked, when he had filled the jug, pausing with it in his hand.

"For t' *bairn*!" she said, almost reproachfully. "Think'st tha I'd touch a drop *mysen*, while as *she* hadna got her fill?"

"All right, Missus," the man replied, turning away with the jug in his hand. "Let's just mak sure it's good measure." He went back among his shelves of milk-bowls, carefully keeping his back towards her while he emptied a little measure of cream into the jug, muttering to himself "mebbe it'll hearten her up a bit, the little lassie!"

The woman never noticed the kind deed, but took back the jug with a simple "Good evening, Master," and went her way: but the children had been more observant, and, as we followed her out, Bruno remarked "That were *welly* kind: and I loves that man: and if I was welly rich I'd give him a hundred pounds—and a bun. That little grummeling dog doesn't know its business!" He referred to the dairyman's little dog, who had apparently quite forgotten the affectionate welcome he had given us on our arrival, and was now following at a respectful distance, doing his best to *"speed the parting guest"* with a shower of little shrill barks, that seemed to tread on one another's heels.

"What *is* a dog's business?" laughed Sylvie. "Dogs ca'n't keep shops and give change!"

"Sisters' businesses *isn't* to laugh at their brothers," Bruno replied with perfect gravity. "And dogs' businesses is to *bark*—not like that: it should finish one bark before it begins another: and it should—Oh Sylvie, there's some dindledums!"

And in another moment the happy children were flying across the common, racing for the patch of dandelions.

While I stood watching them, a strange dreamy feeling came upon me: a railway-platform seemed to take the place of the green sward, and, instead of the light figure of Sylvie bounding along, I seemed to see the flying form of Lady Muriel; but whether Bruno had also undergone a transformation, and had become the old man whom she was running to overtake, I was unable to judge, so instantaneously did the feeling come and go.

When I re-entered the little sitting-room which I shared with Arthur, he was standing with his back to me, looking out of the open window, and evidently had not heard me enter. A cup of tea, apparently just tasted and pushed aside, stood on the table, on the opposite side of which was a letter, just begun, with the pen lying across it: an open book lay on the sofa: the London paper occupied the easy chair; and on the little table which stood by it, I noticed an unlighted cigar and an open box of cigar-lights: all things betokened that the Doctor, usually so methodical and so self-contained, had been trying every form of occupation, and could settle to none!

"This is very unlike *you*, Doctor!" I was beginning, but checked myself, as he turned at the sound of my voice, in sheer amazement at the wonderful change that had taken place in his appearance. Never had I seen a face so radiant with happiness, or eyes that sparkled with such unearthly light! "Even thus", I thought, "must the herald-angel have looked, who brought to the shepherds, watching over their flocks by night, that sweet message of '*peace on earth, good-will to men*'!"

"Yes, dear friend!" he said, as if in answer to the question that I suppose he read in my face. "It is true! It is true!"

No need to ask *what* was true. "God bless you both!" I said, as I felt the happy tears brimming to my eyes. "You were made for each other!"

"Yes," he said, simply, "I believe we were. And *what* a change it makes in one's Life! This isn't the same world! That isn't the sky I saw yesterday! Those clouds— I never saw such clouds in all my life before! They look like troops of hovering angels!"

To *me* they looked very ordinary clouds indeed: but then I had not fed "*on honeydew, And drunk the milk of Paradise*"!

"She wants to see you—at once," he continued, descending suddenly to the things of earth. "She says *that* is the *one* drop yet wanting in her cup of happiness!"

"I'll go at once," I said, as I turned to leave the room. "Wo'n't you come with me?"

"No, Sir!" said the Doctor, with a sudden effort— which proved an utter failure—to resume his professional manner. "Do I *look* like coming with you? Have you never heard that two is company, and——"

"Yes," I said, "I *have* heard it: and I'm painfully aware that *I* am *Number Three*! But, *when* shall we three meet again?"

"*When the hurly-burly's done!*" he answered with a happy laugh, such as I had not heard from him for many a year.

Chapter VII

Mein Herr

So I went on my lonely way, and, on reaching the Hall, I found Lady Muriel standing at the garden-gate waiting for me.

"No need to *give* you joy, or to *wish* you joy?" I began.

"None *whatever*!" she replied, with the joyous laugh of a child. "We *give* people what they haven't got: we *wish* for something that is yet to come. For me, it's all *here*! It's all *mine*! Dear friend," she suddenly broke off, "do you think Heaven ever begins on *Earth*, for any of us?"

"For *some*," I said. "For some, perhaps, who are simple and childlike. You know he said 'of such is the Kingdom of Heaven'."

Lady Muriel clasped her hands, and gazed up into the cloudless sky, with a look I had often seen in Sylvie's eyes. "I feel as if it had begun for *me*," she almost whispered. "I feel as if *I* were one of the happy children, whom He bid them bring near to Him, though the people would have kept them back. Yes, He has seen me in the throng. He has read the wistful longing in my eyes. He has beckoned me to Him. They have *had* to make way for me. He has taken me up in His arms. He has put His hands upon me and blessed me!" She paused, breathless in her perfect happiness.

"Yes," I said. "I think He has!"

"You must come and speak to my father," she went on, as we stood side by side at the gate, looking down the shady lane. But, even as she said the words, the "eerie" sensation came over me like a flood: I saw the dear old Professor approaching us, and also saw, what was stranger still, that he was visible to *Lady Muriel*!

What was to be done? Had the fairy-life been merged in the real life? Or was Lady Muriel "eerie" also, and thus able to enter into the fairy-world along with me? The words were on my lips ("I see an old friend of mine in the lane: if you don't know him, may I introduce him to you?") when the strangest thing of all happened: Lady Muriel spoke.

"I see an old friend of mine in the lane," she said: "if you don't know him, may I introduce him to you?"

I seemed to wake out of a dream: for the "eerie" feeling was still strong upon me, and the figure outside seemed to be changing at every moment, like one of the shapes in a kaleidoscope: now he was the *Professor*, and now he was somebody else! By the time he had reached the gate, he certainly was somebody else: and I felt that the proper course was for *Lady Muriel*, not for *me*, to introduce him. She greeted him kindly, and, opening the gate, admitted the venerable old man—a German, obviously—who looked about him with dazed eyes, as if *he*, too, had but just awaked from a dream!

No, it was certainly *not* the Professor! My old friend *could* not have grown that magnificent beard since last we met: moreover, he would have recognised *me*, for I was certain that *I* had not changed much in the time.

As it was, he simply looked at me vaguely, and took off his hat in response to Lady Muriel's words "Let me introduce Mein Herr to you"; while in the words, spoken in a strong German accent, "proud to make your acquaintance, Sir!" I could detect no trace of an idea that we had ever met before.

Lady Muriel led us to the well-known shady nook,

where preparations for afternoon-tea had already been made, and, while she went in to look for the Earl, we seated ourselves in two easy-chairs, and "Mein Herr" took up Lady Muriel's work, and examined it through his large spectacles (one of the adjuncts that made him so provokingly like the Professor). "Hemming pocket-hand-kerchiefs?" he said, musingly. "So *that* is what the English miladies occupy themselves with, is it?"

"It is the one accomplishment", I said, "in which Man has never yet rivalled Woman!"

Here Lady Muriel returned with her father; and, after he had exchanged some friendly words with "Mein Herr", and we had all been supplied with the needful "creature-comforts", the newcomer returned to the suggestive subject of Pocket-handkerchiefs.

"You have heard of Fortunatus's Purse, Miladi? Ah, so! Would you be surprised to hear that, with three of these leetle handkerchiefs, you shall make the Purse of Fortunatus, quite soon, quite easily?"

"Shall I indeed?" Lady Muriel eagerly replied, as she took a heap of them into her lap, and threaded her needle. "*Please* tell me how, Mein Herr! I'll make one before I touch another drop of tea!"

"You shall first," said Mein Herr, possessing himself of two of the handkerchiefs, spreading one upon the other, and holding them up by two corners, "you shall first join together these upper corners, the right to the right, the left to the left; and the opening between them shall be the *mouth* of the Purse."

A very few stitches sufficed to carry out *this* direction. "Now, if I sew the other three edges together", she suggested, "the bag is complete?"

"Not so, Miladi: the *lower* edges shall *first* be joined— ah, not so!" (as she was beginning to sew them together). "Turn one of them over, and join the *right* lower corner of the one to the *left* lower corner of the other, and sew the lower edges together in what you would call *the wrong way*."

"*I* see!" said Lady Muriel, as she deftly executed the order. "And a very twisted, uncomfortable, uncanny-looking bag it makes! But the *moral* is a lovely one. Unlimited wealth can only be attained by doing things *in the wrong way!* And how are we to join up these mysterious—no, I mean *this* mysterious opening?" (twisting the thing round and round with a puzzled air). "Yes, it *is* one opening. I thought it was *two*, at first."

"You have seen the puzzle of the Paper Ring?" Mein Herr said, addressing the Earl. "Where you take a slip of paper, and join its ends together, first twisting one, so as to join the *upper* corner of *one* end to the *lower* corner of the *other*?"

"I saw one made, only yesterday," the Earl replied. "Muriel, my child, were you not making one, to amuse those children you had to tea?"

"Yes, I know that Puzzle," said Lady Muriel. "The Ring has only *one* surface, and only *one* edge, It's very mysterious!"

"The *bag* is just like that, isn't it?" I suggested. "Is not the *outer* surface of one side of it continuous with the *inner* surface of the other side?"

"So it is!" she exclaimed. "Only it *isn't* a bag, just yet. How shall we fill up this opening, Mein Herr?"

"Thus!" said the old man impressively, taking the bag from her, and rising to his feet in the excitement of the explanation. "The edge of the opening consists of *four* handkerchief edges, and you can trace it continuously, round and round the opening: down the right edge of *one* handkerchief, up the left edge of the *other*, and then down the left edge of the *one*, and up the right edge of the *other*!"

"So you can!" Lady Muriel murmured thoughtfully, leaning her head on her hand, and earnestly watching the old man. "And that *proves* it to be only *one* opening!"

She looked so strangely like a child, puzzling over a difficult lesson, and Mein Herr had become, for the moment, so strangely like the old Professor, that I felt utter-

ly bewildered: the "eerie" feeling was on me in its full
force, and I felt almost *impelled* to say "Do you understand it, Sylvie?" However I checked myself by a great
effort, and let the dream (if indeed it *was* a dream) go on
to its end.

"Now, this *third* handkerchief", Mein Herr proceeded,
"has *also* four edges, which you can trace continuously
round and round: all you need do is to join its four edges
to the four edges of the opening. The Purse is then complete, and its outer surface——"

"*I* see!" Lady Muriel eagerly interrupted. "Its *outer*
surface will be continuous with its *inner* surface! But it
will take time. I'll sew it up after tea." She laid aside the
bag, and resumed her cup of tea. "But why do you call it
Fortunatus's Purse, Mein Herr?"

The dear old man beamed upon her, with a jolly smile,
looking more exactly like the Professor than ever. "Don't
you see, my child—I should say Miladi? Whatever is *inside* that Purse, is *outside* it; and whatever is *outside* it, is
inside it. So you have all the wealth of the world in that
leetle Purse!"

His pupil clapped her hands, in unrestrained delight.
"I'll certainly sew the third handkerchief in—*some* time,"
she said: "but I wo'n't take up your time by trying it now.
Tell us some more wonderful things, please!" And her
face and her voice so *exactly* recalled Sylvie, that I could
not help glancing round, half-expecting to see *Bruno*
also!

Mein Herr began thoughtfully balancing his spoon on
the edge of his teacup, while he pondered over this request. "Something wonderful—like Fortunatus's Purse?
That will give you—when it is made—wealth beyond
your wildest dreams: but it will not give you *Time!*"

A pause of silence ensued—utilized by Lady Muriel for
the very practical purpose of refilling the teacups.

"In *your* country", Mein Herr began with a startling
abruptness, "what becomes of all the wasted Time?"

Lady Muriel looked grave. "Who can tell?" she half-whispered to herself. "All one knows is that it is gone—past recall!"

"Well, in *my*—I mean in a country *I* have visited", said the old man, "they store it up: and it comes in *very* useful, years afterwards! For example, suppose you have a long tedious evening before you: nobody to talk to: nothing you care to do: and yet hours too soon to go to bed. How do *you* behave then?"

"I get *very* cross," she frankly admitted: "and I want to throw things about the room!"

"When that happens to—to the people I have visited, they never act *so*. By a short and simple process—which I cannot explain to you—they store up the useless hours: and, on some *other* occasion, when they happen to *need* extra time, they get them out again."

The Earl was listening with a slightly incredulous smile. "Why cannot you *explain* the process?" he enquired.

Mein Herr was ready with a quite unanswerable reason. "Because you have no *words*, in *your* language, to convey the ideas which are needed. I could explain it in—in—but you would not understand it!"

"No indeed!" said Lady Muriel, graciously dispensing with the *name* of the unknown language. "I never learnt it—at least, not to speak it *fluently*, you know. *Please* tell us some more wonderful things!"

"They run their railway-trains without any engines—nothing is needed but machinery to *stop* them with. Is *that* wonderful enough, Miladi?"

"But where does the *force* come from?" I ventured to ask.

Mein Herr turned quickly round, to look at the new speaker. Then he took off his spectacles, and polished them, and looked at me again, in evident bewilderment. I could see he was thinking—as indeed *I* was also—that we *must* have met before.

"They use the force of *gravity*," he said. "It is a force known also in *your* country, I believe?"

"But that would need a railway going *down-hill*," the Earl remarked. "You ca'n't have *all* your railways going down-hill?"

"They *all* do", said Mein Herr.

"Not from *both* ends?"

"From *both* ends."

"Then I give it up!" said the Earl.

"Can you explain the process?" said Lady Muriel. "Without using that language, that I ca'n't speak fluently?"

"Easily," said Mein Herr. "Each railway is in a long tunnel, perfectly straight: so of course the *middle* of it is nearer the centre of the globe than the two ends: so every train runs half-way *down*-hill, and that gives it force enough to run the *other* half *up*-hill."

"Thank you. I understand that perfectly," said Lady Muriel. "But the velocity, in the *middle* of the tunnel, must be something *fearful*!"

Mein Herr was evidently much gratified at the intelligent interest Lady Muriel took in his remarks. At every moment the old man seemed to grow more chatty and more fluent. "You would like to know our methods of *driving*?" he smilingly enquired. "To us, a run-away horse is of no import at all!"

Lady Muriel slightly shuddered. "To *us* it is a very real danger," she said.

"That is because your carriage is wholly *behind* your horse. Your horse runs. Your carriage follows. Perhaps your horse has the bit in his teeth. Who shall stop him? You fly, ever faster and faster! Finally comes the inevitable upset!"

"But suppose *your* horse manages to get the bit in his teeth?"

"No matter! We would not concern ourselves. Our horse is harnessed in the very centre of our carriage. Two wheels are in front of him, and two behind. To the roof is attached one end of a broad belt. This goes under the horse's body, and the other end is attached to a leetle—

what you call a 'windlass', I think. The horse takes the bit in his teeth. He runs away. We are flying at ten miles an hour! We turn our little windlass, five turns, six turns, seven turns, and—poof! Our horse is off the ground! *Now* let him gallop in the air as much as he pleases: our *carriage* stands still. We sit round him, and watch him till he is tired. Then we let him down. Our horse is glad, very much glad, when his feet once more touch the ground!"

"Capital!" said the Earl, who had been listening attentively. "Are there any other peculiarities in your carriages?"

"In the *wheels*, sometimes, my Lord. For your health, *you* go to sea: to be pitched, to be rolled, occasionally to be drowned. *We* do all that on land: we are pitched, as you; we are rolled, as you; but *drowned*, no! There is no water!"

"What are the wheels like, then?"

"They are *oval*, my Lord. Therefore the carriages rise and fall."

"Yes, and pitch the carriage backwards and forwards: but how do they make it *roll*?"

"They do not match, my Lord. The *end* of one wheel answers to the side of the opposite wheel. So first one side of the carriage rises, then the other. And it pitches all the while. Ah, you must be a good sailor, to drive in our boat-carriages!"

"I can easily believe it," said the Earl.

Mein Herr rose to his feet. "I must leave you now, Miladi," he said, consulting his watch. "I have another engagement."

"I only wish we had stored up some extra time!" Lady Muriel said, as she shook hands with him. "Then we could have kept you a little longer!"

"In *that* case I would gladly stay," replied Mein Herr. "As it is—I fear I must say goodbye!"

"Where did you first meet him?" I asked Lady Muriel, when Mein Herr had left us. "And where does he live? And what is his real name?"

"We first—met—him——" she musingly replied, "really, I ca'n't remember *where*! And I've no idea where he lives! And I never heard any other name! It's very curious. It never occurred to me before to consider what a mystery he is!"

"I hope we shall meet again," I said: "he interests me very much."

"He will be at our farewell-party, this day fortnight," said the Earl. "Of course you will come? Muriel is anxious to gather all our friends around us once more, before we leave the place."

And then he explained to me—as Lady Muriel had left us together—that he was so anxious to get his daughter away from a place full of so many painful memories connected with the now-cancelled engagement with Major Lindon, that they had arranged to have the wedding in a month's time, after which Arthur and his wife were to go on a foreign tour.

"Don't forget Tuesday week!" he said as we shook hands at parting. "I only wish you could bring with you those charming children, that you introduced to us in the summer. Talk of the mystery of Mein Herr! That's *nothing* to the mystery that seems to attend *them*! I shall never forget those marvellous flowers!"

"I will bring them if I possibly can," I said. But how to *fulfil* such a promise, I mused to myself on my way back to our lodgings, was a problem entirely beyond my skill!

CHAPTER VIII

In a Shady Place

THE ten days glided swiftly away: and, the day before the great party was to take place, Arthur proposed that we should stroll down to the Hall, in time for afternoon-tea.

"Hadn't you better go *alone?*" I suggested. "Surely *I* shall be very much *de trop?*"

"Well, it'll be a kind of *experiment,*" he said. "*Fiat experimentum in corpore vili!*" he added, with a graceful bow of mock politeness towards the unfortunate victim. "You see I shall have to bear the sight, to-morrow night, of my lady-love making herself agreeable to everybody *except* the right person, and I shall bear the agony all the better if we have a dress-rehearsal beforehand!"

"*My* part in the play being, apparently, that of the sample *wrong* person?"

"Well, no," Arthur said musingly, as we set forth: "there's no such part in a regular company. 'Heavy Father'? *That* wo'n't do: that's filled already. 'Singing Chambermaid'? Well, the 'First Lady' doubles *that* part. 'Comic Old Man'? You're not comic enough. After all, I'm afraid there's no part for you but the 'Well-dressed Villain': only", with a critical side-glance, "I'm a *leetle* uncertain about the dress!"

We found Lady Muriel alone, the Earl having gone out to make a call, and at once resumed old terms of intimacy, in the shady arbour where the tea-things seemed to be always waiting. The only novelty in the arrangements (one which Lady Muriel seemed to regard as *entirely* a matter of course), was that two of the chairs were placed *quite* close together, side by side. Strange to say, *I* was not invited to occupy *either* of them!

"We have been arranging, as we came along, about letter-writing," Arthur began. "He will want to know how we're enjoying our Swiss tour: and of course we must pretend we *are?*"

"Of course," she meekly assented.

"And the skeleton-in-the-cupboard——" I suggested.

"——is always a difficulty", she quickly put in, "when you're travelling about, and when there are no cupboards in the hotels. However, *ours* is a *very* portable one; and will be neatly packed, in a nice leather case——"

"But please don't think about *writing*", I said, "when

you've anything more attractive on hand. I delight in *reading* letters, but I know well how tiring it is to *write* them."

"It *is*, sometimes," Arthur assented. "For instance, when you're very shy of the person you have to write to."

"Does that show itself in the *letter*?" Lady Muriel enquired. "Of course, when I hear any one *talking*—*you*, for instance—I can see how *desperately* shy he is! But can you see that in a *letter*?"

"Well, of course, when you hear any one talk *fluently*—*you*, for instance—you can see how desperately *un*-shy she is—not to say saucy! But the shyest and most intermittent talker must *seem* fluent in letter-writing. He may have taken half-an-hour to *compose* his second sentence; but there it is, close after the first!"

"Then letters don't express all that they *might* express?"

"That's merely because our system of letter-writing is incomplete. A shy writer *ought* to be able to show that he is so. Why shouldn't he make *pauses* in writing, just as he would do in speaking? He might leave blank spaces—say half a page at a time. And a *very* shy girl—if there *is* such a thing—might write a sentence on the *first* sheet of her letter—then put in a couple of blank sheets—then a sentence on the *fourth* sheet: and so on."

"I quite foresee that *we*—I mean this clever little boy and myself—" Lady Muriel said to me, evidently with the kind wish to bring me into the conversation, "—are going to become famous—of course all our inventions are common property now—for a new Code of Rules for Letter-writing! Please invent some more, little boy!"

"Well, another thing *greatly* needed, little girl, is some way of expressing that we *don't* mean anything."

"Explain yourself, little boy! Surely *you* can find no difficulty in expressing a *total* absence of meaning?"

"I mean that you should be able, when you *don't* mean a thing to be taken seriously, to express that wish. For human nature is so constituted that whatever you write seriously is taken as a joke, and whatever you mean as a joke is taken seriously! At any rate, it is so in writing to a *lady*!"

"Ah! you're not used to writing to ladies!" Lady Muriel remarked, leaning back in her chair, and gazing thoughtfully into the sky. "You should try."

"Very good," said Arthur. "How many ladies may I begin writing to? As many as I can count on the fingers of both hands?"

"As many as you can count on the *thumbs* of *one* hand!" his lady-love replied with much severity. "What a *very* naughty little boy he is! *Isn't* he?" (with an appealing glance at me).

"He's a little fractious," I said. "Perhaps he's cutting a tooth." While to myself I said "How *exactly* like Sylvie talking to Bruno!"

"He wants his tea." (The naughty little boy volunteered the information.) "He's getting very tired, at the mere *prospect* of the great party to-morrow!"

"Then he shall have a good rest before-hand!" she soothingly replied. "The tea isn't made yet. Come, little boy, lean well back in your chair, and think about nothing —or about *me*, whichever you prefer!"

"All the same, all the same!" Arthur sleepily murmured, watching her with loving eyes, as she moved her chair away to the tea table, and began to make the tea. "Then he'll wait for his tea, like a good, patient little boy!"

"Shall I bring you the London Papers?" said Lady Muriel. "I saw them lying on the table as I came out, but my father said there was nothing in them, except that horrid murder-trial." (Society was just then enjoying its daily thrill of excitement in studying the details of a specially sensational murder in a thieve's den in the East of London.)

"I have no appetite for horrors," Arthur replied. "But I hope we have learned the lesson they should teach us— though we are very apt to read it backwards!"

"You speak in riddles," said Lady Muriel. "Please explain yourself. See now," suiting the action to the word, "I am sitting at your feet, just as if you were a second Gamaliel! Thanks, no." (This was to me, who had risen to bring her chair back to its former place.) "Pray don't disturb yourself. This tree and the grass make a very nice easy-chair. *What* is the lesson that one always reads wrong?"

Arthur was silent for a minute. "I would like to be clear what it *is* I mean," he said, slowly and thoughtfully, "before I say anything to *you*—because you *think* about it."

Anything approaching to a compliment was so unusual an utterance for Arthur, that it brought a flush of pleasure to her cheek, as she replied "It is *you*, that give me the ideas to think about."

"One's first thought", Arthur proceeded, "in reading anything specially vile or barbarous, as done by a fellow-creature, is apt to be that we see a new depth of Sin revealed *beneath* us: and we seem to gaze down into that abyss from some higher ground, far apart from it."

"I think I understand you now. You mean that one ought to think—not 'God, I thank Thee that I am not as other men are'—but 'God, be merciful to me also, who might be, but for Thy grace, a sinner as vile as he!' "

"No," said Arthur. "I meant a great deal more than that."

She looked up quickly, but checked herself, and waited in silence.

"One must begin further back, I think. Think of some other man, the same age as this poor wretch. Look back to the time when they both began life—before they had sense enough to know Right from Wrong. *Then*, at any rate, they were equal in God's sight?"

She nodded assent.

"We have, then, two distinct epochs at which we may contemplate the two men whose lives we are comparing. At the first epoch they are, so far as moral responsibility is concerned, on precisely the same footing: they are alike

incapable of doing right or wrong. At the second epoch
the one man—I am taking an extreme case, for contrast
—has won the esteem and love of all around him: his
character is stainless, and his name will be held in honour
hereafter: the other man's history is one unvaried record
of crime, and his life is at last forfeited to the outraged
laws of his country. Now what have been the causes, in
each case, of each man's condition being what it is at the
second epoch? They are of two kinds—one acting from
within, the other from without. These two kinds need to
be discussed separately—that is, if I have not already
tired you with my prosing?"

"On the contrary," said Lady Muriel, "it is a special
delight to me to have a question discussed in this way—
analysed and arranged so that one can understand it.
Some books, that profess to argue out a question, are to
me intolerably wearisome, simply because the ideas are
all arranged haphazard—a sort of 'first come, first
served'."

"You are very encouraging," Arthur replied, with a
pleased look. "The causes, acting from *within*, which
make a man's character what it is at any given moment,
are his successive acts of volition—that is, his acts of
choosing whether he will do this or that."

"We are to assume the existence of Free-Will?" I said,
in order to have that point made quite clear.

"If not," was the quiet reply, "*cadit quaestio:* and I
have no more to say."

"We *will* assume it!" the rest of the audience—the
majority, I may say, looking at it from Arthur's point of
view—imperiously proclaimed. The orator proceeded.

"The causes, acting from *without*, are his surroundings
—what Mr. Herbert Spencer calls his 'environment'. Now
the point I want to make clear is this, that a man is responsible for his act of choosing, but *not* responsible for
his environment. Hence, if these two men make, on some
given occasion, when they are exposed to equal temptation, equal efforts to resist and to choose the right, their

condition, in the sight of God, must be the same. If He is pleased in the one case, so will He be in the other; if displeased in the one case, so also in the other."

"That is so, no doubt: I see it quite clearly," Lady Muriel put in.

"And yet, owing to their different environments, the one may win a great victory over the temptation, while the other falls into some black abyss of crime."

"But surely you would not say those men were equally guilty in the sight of God?"

"Either that", said Arthur, "or else I must give up my belief in God's perfect justice. But let me put one more case, which will show my meaning even more forcibly. Let the one man be in a high social position—the other, say, a common thief. Let the one be tempted to some trivial act of unfair dealing—something which he can do with the absolute certainty that it will never be discovered—something which he can with perfect ease forbear from doing—and which he distinctly knows to be a sin. Let the other be tempted to some terrible crime—as men would consider it—but under an almost overwhelming pressure of motives—of course not *quite* overwhelming, as that would destroy all responsibility. Now, in this case, let the second man make a *greater* effort at resistance than the first. Also suppose *both* to fall under the temptation—I say that the second man is, in God's sight, *less* guilty than the other."

Lady Muriel drew a long breath. "It upsets all one's ideas of Right and Wrong—just at first! Why, in that dreadful murder-trial, you would say, I suppose, that it was possible that the least guilty man in the Court was the murderer, and that possibly the judge who tried him, by yielding to the temptation of making one unfair remark, had committed a crime outweighing the criminal's whole career!"

"Certainly I should," Arthur firmly replied. "It sounds like a paradox, I admit. But just think what a grievous sin it must be, in God's sight, to yield to some very slight

temptation, which we could have resisted with perfect
ease, and to do it deliberately, and in the full light of
God's Law. What penance can atone for a sin like *that*?"

"I ca'n't reject your theory," I said. "But how it seems
to widen the possible area of Sin in the world!"

"Is that so?" Lady Muriel anxiously enquired.

"Oh, not so, not so!" was the eager reply. "To me it
seems to clear away much of the cloud that hangs over
the world's history. When this view first made itself clear
to me, I remember walking out into the fields, repeating
to myself that line of Tennyson *'There seemed no room for
sense of wrong!'* The thought, that perhaps the real guilt
of the human race was infinitely less than I fancied it—
that the millions, whom I had thought of as sunk in hopeless depths of sin, were perhaps, in God's sight, scarcely
sinning at all—was more sweet than words can tell! Life
seemed more bright and beautiful, when once that
thought had come! *'A livelier emerald twinkles in the grass,
A purer sapphire melts into the sea!'* " His voice trembled
as he concluded, and the tears stood in his eyes.

Lady Muriel shaded her face with her hand, and was
silent for a minute. "It is a beautiful thought," she said,
looking up at last. "Thank you—Arthur, for putting it
into my head!"

The Earl returned in time to join us at tea, and to give
us the very unwelcome tidings that a fever had broken
out in the little harbour-town that lay below us—a fever
of so malignant a type that, though it had only appeared
a day or two ago, there were already more than a dozen
down in it, two or three of whom were reported to be in
imminent danger.

In answer to the eager questions of Arthur—who of
course took a deep scientific interest in the matter—he
could give very few *technical* details, though he had met
the local doctor. It appeared, however, that it was an
almost *new* disease—at least in *this* century, though it
might prove to be identical with the "Plague" recorded in
History—*very* infectious, and frightfully rapid in its

action. "It will not, however, prevent our party to-morrow," he said in conclusion. "None of the guests belong to the infected district, which is, as you know, exclusively peopled by fishermen: so you may come with out any fear."

Arthur was very silent, all the way back, and, on reaching our lodgings, immediately plunged into medical studies, connected with the alarming malady of whose arrival he had just heard.

CHAPTER IX

The Farewell-Party

On the following day, Arthur and I reached the Hall in good time, as only a few of the guests—it was to be a party of eighteen—had as yet arrived; and these were talking with the Earl, leaving us the opportunity of a few words apart with our hostess.

"Who is that *very* learned-looking man with the large spectacles?" Arthur enquired. "I haven't met him here before, have I?"

"No, he's a new friend of ours," said Lady Muriel: "a German, I believe. He *is* such a dear old thing! And quite the most learned man I ever met—with *one* exception, of course!" she added humbly, as Arthur drew himself up with an air of offended dignity.

"And the young lady in blue, just beyond him, talking to that foreign-looking man. Is *she* learned, too?"

"I don't know," said Lady Muriel. "But I'm told she's a wonderful piano-forte-player. I hope you'll hear her to-night. I asked that foreigner to take her in, because *he's* very musical, too. He's a French Count, I believe; and he sings *splendidly*!"

"Science—music—singing—you have indeed got a

complete party!" said Arthur. "I feel quite a privileged person, meeting all these stars. I *do* love music!"

"But the party isn't *quite* complete!" said Lady Muriel. "You haven't brought us those two beautiful children," she went on, turning to me. "He brought them here to tea, you know, one day last summer," again addressing Arthur: "and they *are* such darlings!"

"They are, *indeed*," I assented.

"But why haven't you brought them with you? You promised my father you *would*."

"I'm very sorry," I said; "but really it was impossible to bring them with me." Here I most certainly *meant* to conclude the sentence: and it was with a feeling of utter amazement, which I cannot adequately describe, that I heard myself *going on speaking*. "—but they are to join me here in the course of the evening" were the words, uttered in *my* voice, and seeming to come from *my* lips.

"I'm *so* glad!" Lady Muriel joyfully replied. "I *shall* enjoy introducing them to some of my friends here! When do you expect them?"

I took refuge in silence. The only *honest* reply would have been "That was not *my* remark. *I* didn't say it, and *it isn't true*!" But I had not the moral courage to make such a confession. The character of a "lunatic" is not, I believe, very difficult to *acquire*: but it is amazingly difficult to *get rid of:* and it seemed quite certain that any such speech as *that* would *quite* justify the issue of a writ *"de lunatico inquirendo"*.

Lady Muriel evidently thought I had failed to hear her question, and turned to Arthur with a remark on some other subject; and I had time to recover from my shock of surprise—or to awake out of my momentary "eerie" condition, whichever it was.

When things around me seemed once more to be real, Arthur was saying "I'm afraid there's no help for it: they *must* be finite in number."

"I should be sorry to have to believe it," said Lady Muriel. "Yet, when one comes to think of it, there *are* no new melodies, now-a-days. What people talk of as 'the last new song' always recalls to *me* some tune I've known as a child!"

"The day must come—if the world lasts long enough —" said Arthur, "when every possible tune will have been composed—every possible pun perpetrated—" (Lady Muriel wrung her hands, like a tragedy-queen) "and, worse than that, every possible *book* written! For the number of *words* is finite."

"It'll make very little difference to the *authors*," I suggested. "Instead of saying '*what* book shall I write?' an author will ask himself '*which* book shall I write?' A mere verbal distinction!"

Lady Muriel gave me an approving smile. "But *lunatics* would always write new books, surely?" she went on. "They *couldn't* write the sane books over again!"

"True," said Arthur. "But their books would come to an end, also. The number of lunatic *books* is as finite as the number of lunatics."

"And *that* number is becoming greater every year," said a pompous man, whom I recognized as the self-appointed showman on the day of the picnic.

"So they say," replied Arthur. "And, when ninety per cent. of us are lunatics," (he seemed to be in a wildly nonsensical mood) "the asylums will be put to their proper use."

"And that is——?" the pompous man gravely enquired

"*To shelter the sane!*" said Arthur. "*We* shall bar ourselves in. The lunatics will have it all their own way, *outside*. They'll do it a little queerly, no doubt. Railway-collisions will be always happening: steamers always blowing up: most of the towns will be burnt down: most of the ships sunk——"

"And most of the men *killed*!" murmured the pompous man, who was evidently hopelessly bewildered.

"Certainly," Arthur assented. "Till at last there will be *fewer* lunatics than sane men. Then *we* come out: *they* go in: and things return to their normal condition!"

The pompous man frowned darkly, and bit his lip, and folded his arms, vainly trying to think it out. "He is *jesting!*" he muttered to himself at last, in a tone of withering contempt, as he stalked away.

By this time the other guests had arrived; and dinner was announced. Arthur of course took down Lady Muriel: and *I* was pleased to find myself seated at her other side, with a severe-looking old lady (whom I had not met before, and whose name I had, as is usual in introductions, entirely failed to catch, merely gathering that it sounded like a compound-name) as my partner for the banquet.

She appeared, however, to be acquainted with Arthur, and confided to me in a low voice her opinion that he was "a very argumentative young man". Arthur, for his part, seemed well inclined to show himself worthy of the character she had given him, and, hearing her say "I never take wine with my soup!" (this was *not* a confidence to me, but was launched upon Society, as a matter of general interest), he at once challenged a combat by asking her "*when* would you say that property *commence* in a plate of soup?"

"This is *my* soup," she sternly replied: "and what is before you is *yours.*"

"No doubt," said Arthur: "but *when* did I begin to own it? Up to the moment of its being put into the plate, it was the property of our host: while being offered round the table, it was, let us say, held in trust by the waiter: did it become mine when I accepted it? Or when it was placed before me? Or when I took the first spoonful?"

"He is a *very* argumentative young man!" was all the old lady would say: but she said it audibly, this time, feeling that Society had a right to know it.

Arthur smiled mischievously. "I shouldn't mind betting you a shilling", he said, "that the Eminent Barrister next you" (It certainly *is* possible to say words so as to make them begin with capitals!) "ca'n't answer me!"

"I *never* bet," she sternly replied.

"Not even sixpenny points at *whist*?"

"*Never!*" she repeated. "*Whist* is innocent enough: but whist played for *money!*" She shuddered.

Arthur became serious again. "I'm afraid I ca'n't take that view," he said. "I consider that the introduction of small stakes for card-playing was one of the most *moral* acts Society ever did, *as* Society."

"How was it so?" said Lady Muriel.

"Because it took Cards, once for all, out of the category of games at which *cheating* is possible. Look at the way Croquet is demoralizing Society. Ladies are beginning to cheat at it, terribly: and, if they're found out, they only laugh, and call it fun. But when there's *money* at stake, that is out of the question. The swindler is *not* accepted as a wit. When a man sits down to cards, and cheats his friends out of their money, he doesn't get much *fun* out of it—unless he thinks it fun to be kicked down stairs!"

"If all gentlemen thought as badly of ladies as *you* do," my neighbour remarked with some bitterness, "there would be very few—very few——". She seemed doubtful how to end her sentence, but at last took "honeymoons" as a safe word.

"On the contrary," said Arthur, the mischievous smile returning to his face, "if only people would adopt *my* theory, the number of honeymoons—quite of a new kind —would be greatly increased!"

"May we hear about this new kind of honeymoon?" said Lady Muriel.

"Let X be the gentleman," Arthur began, in a slightly raised voice, as he now found himself with an audience of *six*, including "Mein Herr", who was seated at the other side of my polynomial partner. "Let X be the gentleman, and Y the lady to whom he thinks of proposing. He applies for an Experimental Honeymoon. It is granted. Forthwith the young couple—accompanied by the great-aunt of Y, to act as chaperone—start for a month's tour, during which they have many a moonlight-walk, and many a *tête-à-tête* conversation, and each can form a more correct estimate of the other's character, in four *weeks*, than would have been possible in as many *years*, when meeting under the ordinary restrictions of Society. And it is only after their *return* that X finally decides whether he will, or will not, put the momentous question to Y!"

"In nine cases out of ten", the pompous man proclaimed, "he would decide to break it off!"

"Then, in nine cases out of ten," Arthur rejoined, "an unsuitable match would be prevented, and *both* parties saved from misery!"

"The only really *unsuitable* matches", the old lady remarked, "are those made without sufficient *Money*. Love may come *afterwards*. Money is needed *to begin with*!"

This remark was cast loose upon Society, as a sort of general challenge; and, as such, it was at once accepted by several of those within hearing: *Money* became the keynote of the conversation for some time: and a fitful echo of it was again heard, when the dessert had been placed upon the table, the servants had left the room, and the Earl had started the wine in its welcome progress round the table.

"I'm very glad to see you keep up the old customs," I said to Lady Muriel as I filled her glass. "It's really delightful to experience, once more, the peaceful feeling that comes over one when the waiters have left the room— when one can converse without the feeling of being overheard, and without having dishes constantly thrust over one's shoulder. How much more sociable it is to be able to pour out the wine for the ladies, and to hand the dishes to those who wish for them!"

"In that case, kindly send those peaches down here," said a fat red-faced man, who was seated beyond our pompous friend. "I've been wishing for them—diagonally —for some time!"

"Yes, it *is* a ghastly innovation", Lady Muriel replied, "letting the waiters carry round the wine at dessert. For one thing, they *always* take it the wrong way round— which of course brings bad luck to *everybody* present!"

"Better go the *wrong* way than not go *at all!*" said our host. "Would you kindly help yourself?" (This was to the fat red-faced man.) "You are not a teetotaler, I think?"

"Indeed but I *am!*" he replied, as he pushed on the bottles. "Nearly twice as much money is spent in England on *Drink*, as on any other article of food. Read this card." (What faddist ever goes about without a pocketful of the appropriate literature?) "The stripes of different colours represent the amounts spent of various articles of food. Look at the highest three. Money spent on butter and on cheese, thirty-five millions: on bread, seventy millions: on *intoxicating liquors*, one hundred and thirty-six millions! If I had my way, I would close every public-house in the land! Look at that card, and read the motto. *That's where all the money goes to!*"

"Have you seen the *Anti-Teetotal Card?*" Arthur innocently enquired.

"No, Sir, I have not!" the orator savagely replied. "What is it like?"

"Almost exactly like this one. The coloured stripes are the same. Only, instead of the words 'Money spent on', it has 'Incomes derived from sale of'; and, instead of 'That's where all the money goes to', its motto is '*That's where all the money comes from!*'"

The red-faced man scowled, but evidently considered Arthur beneath his notice. So Lady Muriel took up the cudgels. "Do you hold the theory", she enquired, "that people can preach teetotalism more effectually by being teetotalers themselves?"

"Certainly I do!" replied the red-faced man. "Now, here is a case in point," unfolding a newspaper-cutting: "let me read you this letter from a teetotaler. *To the Editor. Sir, I was once a moderate drinker, and knew a man who drank to excess. I went to him. 'Give up this drink,' I said. 'It will ruin your health!' 'You drink,' he said: 'why shouldn't I?' 'Yes,' I said, 'but I know when to leave off.' He turned away from me. 'You drink in your way,' he said: 'let me drink in mine. Be off!' Then I saw that, to do any*

*good with him, I must forswear drink. From that hour I
haven't touched a drop!"*

"There! What do you say to *that?*" He looked round
triumphantly, while the cutting was handed round for
inspection.

"How very curious!" exclaimed Arthur when it had
reached him. "Did you happen to see a letter, last week,
about early rising? It was strangely like this one."

The red-faced man's curiosity was roused. "Where did
it appear?" he asked.

"Let me read it to you," said Arthur. He took some
papers from his pocket, opened one of them, and read as
follows. *To the Editor. Sir, I was once a moderate sleeper,
and knew a man who slept to excess. I pleaded with him.
'Give up this lying in bed,' I said. 'It will ruin your health!'
'You go to bed,' he said: 'why shouldn't I?' 'Yes,' I said,
'but I know when to get up in the morning.' He turned away
from me. 'You sleep in your way,' he said: 'let me sleep in
mine. Be off!' Then I saw that to do any good with him, I
must forswear sleep. From that hour I haven't been to bed!"*

Arthur folded and pocketed his paper, and passed on
the newspaper-cutting. None of us dared to laugh, the
red-faced man was evidently so angry. "Your parallel
doesn't run on all fours!" he snarled.

"*Moderate* drinkers never do so!" Arthur quietly
replied. Even the stern old lady laughed at this.

"But it needs many other things to make a *perfect*
dinner!" said Lady Muriel, evidently anxious to change
the subject. "Mein Herr! What is *your* idea of a perfect
dinner party?"

The old man looked around smilingly, and his gigantic
spectacles seemed more gigantic than ever. "A *perfect*
dinner-party?" he repeated. "First, it must be presided
over by our present hostess!"

"That of *course!*" she gaily interposed. "But what *else*,
Mein Herr?"

"I can but tell you what I have seen," said Mein Herr,
"in mine own—in the country I have traveled in."

He paused for a full minute, and gazed steadily at the ceiling—with so dreamy an expression on his face, that I feared he was going off into a reverie, which seemed to be his normal state. However, after a minute, he suddenly began again.

"That which chiefly causes the failure of a dinner-party, is the running-short—not of meat, nor yet of drink, but of *conversation*."

"In an *English* dinner-party", I remarked, "I have never known *small-talk* run short!"

"Pardon me," Mein Herr respectfully replied, "I did not say 'small-talk'. I said 'conversation'. All such topics as the weather, or politics, or local gossip, are unknown among us. They are either vapid or controversial. What we need for *conversation* is a topic of *interest* and of *novelty*. To secure these things we have tried various plans— Moving-Pictures, Wild-Creatures, Moving-Guests, and a Revolving-Humorist. But this last is only adapted to *small* parties."

"Let us have it in four separate Chapters, please!" said Lady Muriel, who was evidently deeply interested—as, indeed, most of the party were, by this time: and, all down the table, talk had ceased, and heads were leaning forwards, eager to catch fragments of Mein Herr's oration.

"Chapter One! Moving-Pictures!" was proclaimed in the silvery voice of our hostess.

"The dining-table is shaped like a circular ring," Mein Herr began, in low dreamy tones, which, however, were perfectly audible in the silence. "The guests are seated at the inner side as well as the outer, having ascended to their places by a winding-staircase, from the room below. Along the middle of the table runs a little railway; and there is an endless train of trucks, worked round by machinery; and on each truck there are two pictures, leaning back to back. The train makes two circuits during dinner; and, when it has been *once* round, the waiters turn the pictures round in each truck, making them face the other way. Thus *every* guest sees *every* picture!"

He paused, and the silence seemed deader than ever. Lady Muriel looked aghast. "Really, if this goes on," she exclaimed, "I shall have to drop a pin! Oh, it's *my* fault, is it?" (In answer to an appealing look from Mein Herr.) "I was forgetting my duty. Chapter Two! Wild-Creatures!"

"We found the Moving-Pictures a *little* monotonous," said Mein Herr. "People didn't care to talk Art through a whole dinner; so we tried Wild-Creatures. Among the flowers, which we laid (just as *you* do) about the table, were to be seen, here a mouse, there a beetle; here a spider" (Lady Muriel shuddered), "there a wasp; here a toad, there a snake"; ("Father!" said Lady Muriel, plaintively. "Did you hear *that*?"); "so we had plenty to talk about!"

"And when you got stung——" the old lady began.

"They were all chained-up, dear Madam!"

And the old lady gave a satisfied nod.

There was no silence to follow, *this* time. "Third Chapter!" Lady Muriel proclaimed at once. "Moving-Guests!"

"Even the Wild-Creatures proved monotonous," the orator proceeded. "So we left the guests to choose their own subjects; and, to avoid monotony, we changed *them*. We made the table of *two* rings; and the inner ring moved slowly round, all the time, along with the floor in the middle and the inner row of guests. Thus *every* inner guest was brought face-to-face with *every* outer guest. It was a little confusing, sometimes, to have to *begin* a story to one friend and *finish* it to another; but *every* plan has its faults, you know."

"Fourth Chapter!" Lady Muriel hastened to announce. "The Revolving-Humorist!"

"For a *small* party we found it an excellent plan to have a round table, with a hole cut in the middle large enough to hold *one* guest. Here we placed our *best* talker. He revolved slowly, facing every other guest in turn: and he told lively anecdotes the whole time!"

"I shouldn't like it!" murmured the pompous man. "It would make me giddy, revolving like that! I should decline to——" here it appeared to dawn upon him that perhaps the assumption he was making was not warranted by the circumstances: he took a hasty gulp of wine, and choked himself.

But Mein Herr had relapsed into reverie, and made no further remark. Lady Muriel gave the signal, and the ladies left the room.

Chapter X

Jabbering and Jam

WHEN the last lady had disappeared, and the Earl, taking his place at the head of the table, had issued the military order "Gentlemen! Close up the ranks, if you please!" and when, in obedience to his command, we had gathered ourselves compactly round him, the pompous man gave a deep sigh of relief, filled his glass to the brim, pushed on the wine, and began one of his favourite orations. "They are charming, no doubt! Charming, but very frivolous. They drag us down, so to speak, to a lower level. They——"

"Do not all pronouns require antecedent *nouns*?" the Earl gently enquired.

"Pardon me," said the pompous man, with lofty condescension. "I had overlooked the noun. The ladies. We regret their absence. Yet we console ourselves. *Thought is free*. With them, we are limited to *trivial* topics—Art, Literature, Politics, and so forth. One can bear to discuss *such* paltry matters with a lady. But no man, in his senses —" (he looked sternly round the table, as if defying contradiction) "—ever yet discussed *WINE* with a lady!" He sipped his glass of port, leaned back in his chair, and slowly raised it up to his eye, so as to look through it at the lamp. "The vintage, my Lord?" he enquired, glancing at his host.

The Earl named the date.

"So I had supposed. But one likes to be certain. The *tint* is, perhaps, slightly pale. But the *body* is unquestionable. And as for the *bouquet*——"

Ah, that magic Bouquet! How vividly that magic word recalled the scene! The little beggar boy turning his somersault in the road—the sweet little crippled maiden in my arms—the mysterious evanescent nursemaid—all rushed tumultuously into my mind, like the creatures of a dream: and through this mental haze there still boomed on, like the tolling of a bell, the solemn voice of the great connoisseur of *WINE!*

Even *his* utterances had taken on themselves a strange and dream-like form. "No," he resumed—and *why* is it, I pause to ask, that, in taking up the broken thread of a dialogue, one *always* begins with this cheerless monosyllable? After much anxious thought, I have come to the conclusion that the object in view is the same as that of the schoolboy, when the sum he is working has got into a hopeless muddle, and when in despair he takes the sponge, washes it all out, and begins again. Just in the same way the bewildered orator, by the simple process of denying *everything* that has been hitherto asserted, makes a clean sweep of the whole discussion, and can "start fair" with a fresh theory. "No," he resumed: "there's nothing like cherry-jam, after all. That's what *I* say!"

"Not for *all* qualities!" an eager little man shrilly interposed. "For *richness* of general tone I don't say that it *has* a rival. But for *delicacy* of modulation—for what one may call the *'harmonics'* of flavour—give *me* good old *raspberry*-jam!"

"Allow me one word!" The fat red-faced man, quite hoarse with excitement, broke into the dialogue. "It's too important a question to be settled by Amateurs! I can give you the views of a *Professional*—perhaps the most experienced jam-taster now living. Why, I've known him fix the age of strawberry-jam, to a *day*—and we all know what a difficult jam it is to give a date to—on a single tasting! Well, I put to him the *very* question you are discussing. His words were '*cherry*-jam is best, for mere *chiaroscuro* of flavour: *raspberry*-jam lends itself best to those resolved discords that linger so lovingly on the tongue: but, for rapturous *utterness* of saccharine perfection, it's *apricot-jam first and the rest nowhere*!' That was well put, *wasn't it*?"

"Consummately put!" shrieked the eager little man.

"I know your friend well," said the pompous man. "As a jam-taster, he has no rival! Yet I scarcely think——"

But here the discussion became general: and his words were lost in a confused medley of names, every guest sounding the praises of his own favourite jam. At length, through the din, our host's voice made itself heard. "Let us join the ladies!" These words seemed to recall me to waking life; and I felt sure that, for the last few minutes, I had relapsed into the "eerie" state.

"A strange dream!" I said to myself as we trooped upstairs. "Grown men discussing, as seriously as if they were matters of life and death, the hopelessly trivial details of mere *delicacies*, that appeal to no higher human function than the nerves of the tongue and palate! What a humiliating spectacle such a discussion would be in waking life!"

When, on our way to the drawing-room, I received from the housekeeper my little friends, clad in the daintiest of evening costumes, and looking, in the flush of expectant delight, more radiantly beautiful than I had ever seen them before. I felt no shock of surprise, but accepted the fact with the same unreasoning apathy with which one meets the events of a dream, and was merely conscious of a vague anxiety as to how they would acquit themselves in so novel a scene—forgetting that Court-life in Outland was as good training as they could need for Society in the more substantial world.

It would be best, I thought, to introduce them as soon

as possible to some good-natured lady-guest, and I selected the young lady whose piano-forte-playing had been so much talked of. "I am sure you like children," I said. "May I introduce two little friends of mine? This is Sylvie—and this is Bruno."

The young lady kissed Sylvie very graciously. She would have done the same for *Bruno*, but he hastily drew back out of reach. "Their faces are new to me," she said. "Where do you come from, my dear?"

I had not anticipated so inconvenient a question; and, fearing that it might embarrass Sylvie, I answered for her. "They come from some distance. They are only here just for this one evening."

"How far have you come, dear?" the young lady persisted.

Sylvie looked puzzled. "A mile or two, I *think*," she said doubtfully.

"A mile or *three*," said Bruno.

"You shouldn't say 'a mile or *three*'," Sylvie corrected him.

The young lady nodded approval. "Sylvie's quite right. It isn't usual to say 'a mile or *three*'."

"It would be usual—if we said it often enough," said Bruno.

It was the young lady's turn to look puzzled now. "He's very quick, for his age!" she murmured. "You're not more than seven, are you, dear?" she added aloud.

"I'm not so many as *that*," said Bruno. "I'm *one*. Sylvie's *one*. Sylvie and me is *two*. *Sylvie* taught me to count."

"Oh, I wasn't *counting* you, you know!" the young lady laughingly replied.

"Hasn't oo *learnt* to count?" said Bruno.

The young lady bit her lip. "Dear! What embarrassing questions he *does* ask!" she said in a half-audible "aside".

"Bruno, you shouldn't!" Sylvie said reprovingly.

"Shouldn't *what*?" said Bruno.

"You shouldn't ask—that sort of questions."

"*What* sort of questions?" Bruno mischievously persisted.

"What *she* told you not," Sylvie replied, with a shy glance at the young lady, and losing all sense of grammar in her confusion.

"Oo ca'n't pronounce it!" Bruno triumphantly cried. And he turned to the young lady, for sympathy in his victory. "I *knewed* she couldn't pronounce 'umbrella-sting'!"

The young lady thought it best to return to the arithmetical problem. "When I asked if you were *seven*, you know, I didn't mean 'how many *children*?' I meant 'how many *years*——'"

"Only got *two* ears," said Bruno. "Nobody's got *seven* ears."

"And you belong to this little girl?" the young lady continued, skilfully evading the anatomical problem.

"No I doosn't belong to *her*!" said Bruno. "Sylvie belongs to *me*!" And he clasped his arms round her as he added "She are my very mine!"

"And, do you know," said the young lady, "I've a little sister at home, exactly like *your* sister? I'm sure they'd love each other."

"They'd be very extremely useful to each other," Bruno said, thoughtfully. "And they wouldn't want no looking-glasses to brush their hair wiz."

"Why not, my child?"

"Why, each one would do for the other one's looking-glass a-course!" cried Bruno.

But here Lady Muriel, who had been standing by, listening to this bewildering dialogue, interrupted it to ask if the young lady would favour us with some music; and the children followed their new friend to the piano.

Arthur came and sat down by me. "If rumour speaks truly," he whispered, "we are to have a real treat!" And then, amid a breathless silence, the performance began.

She was one of those players whom Society talks of as "brilliant", and she dashed into the loveliest of Haydn's

Symphonies in a style that was clearly the outcome of years of patient study under the best masters. At first it seemed to be the perfection of piano-forte-playing; but in a few minutes I began to ask myself, wearily, *"What* is it that is wanting? *Why* does one get no pleasure from it?"

Then I set myself to listen intently to every note; and the mystery explained itself. There *was* an almost perfect mechanical *correctness*—and there was nothing else! False notes, of course, did not occur: she knew the piece too well for *that*; but there was just enough irregularity of *time* to betray that the player had no real "ear" for music—just enough inarticulateness in the more elaborate passages to show that she did not think her audience worth taking real pains for—just enough mechanical monotony of accent to take all *soul* out of the heavenly modulations she was profaning—in short, it was simply irritating; and, when she had rattled off the finale and had struck the final chord as if, the instrument being now done with, it didn't matter how many wires she broke, I could not even *affect* to join in the stereotyped "Oh, *thank* you!" which was chorused around me.

Lady Muriel joined us for a moment. "Isn't it *beautiful?*" she whispered to Arthur, with a mischievous smile.

"No, it isn't!" said Arthur. But the gentle sweetness of his face quite neutralized the apparent rudeness of the reply.

"Such execution, you know!" she persisted.

"That's what she *deserves*," Arthur doggedly replied: "but people are so prejudiced against capital——"

"Now you're beginning to talk nonsense!" Lady Muriel cried. "But you *do* like Music, don't you? You said so just now."

"Do I like *Music?*" the Doctor repeated softly to himself. "My dear Lady Muriel, there is Music and Music. Your question is painfully vague. You might as well ask 'Do you like *People?*'"

Lady Muriel bit her lip, frowned, and stamped with one tiny foot. As a dramatic, representation of ill-temper, it was distinctly *not* a success. However, it took in *one* of her audience, and Bruno hastened to interpose, as peacemaker in a rising quarrel, with the remark "*I* likes Peoples!"

Arthur laid a loving hand on the little curly head. "What? *All* Peoples?" he enquired.

"Not *all* Peoples," Bruno explained. "Only but Sylvie —and Lady Muriel—and him—" (pointing to the Earl) "and oo—and oo!"

"You shouldn't point at people," said Sylvie. "It's very rude."

"In Bruno's World," I said, "there are only *four* People—worth mentioning!"

"In Bruno's World!" Lady Muriel repeated thoughtfully. "A bright and flowery world. Where the grass is always green, where the breezes always blow softly, and the rain-clouds never gather; where there are no wild beasts, and no deserts——"

"There *must* be deserts," Arthur decisively remarked. "At least if it was *my* ideal world."

"But what possible use is there in a *desert*?" said Lady Muriel. "*Surely* you would have no wilderness in your ideal world?"

Arthur smiled. "But indeed I *would*!" he said. "A wilderness would be more necessary than a railway; and *far* more conducive to general happiness than church-bells!"

"But what would you use it for?"

"*To practise music in*," he replied. "All the young ladies, that have no ear for music, but insist on learning it, should be conveyed, every morning, two or three miles into the wilderness. There each would find a comfortable room provided for her, and also a cheap second-hand piano-forte, on which she might play for hours, without adding one needless pang to the sum of human misery!"

Lady Muriel glanced round in alarm, lest these barbarous sentiments should be overheard. But the fair musician was at a safe distance. "At any rate you must allow that she's a sweet girl?" she resumed.

"Oh, certainly. As sweet as *eau sucrée*, if you choose—and nearly as interesting!"

"You are incorrigible!" said Lady Muriel, and turned to me. "I hope you found Mrs. Mills an interesting companion?"

"Oh, *that's* her name, is it?" I said. "I fancied there was *more* of it."

"So there is: and it will be 'at your proper peril' (whatever that may mean) if you ever presume to address her as 'Mrs. Mills'. She is 'Mrs. Ernest—Atkinson—Mills'!"

"She is one of those would-be grandees," said Arthur, "who think that, by tacking on to their surname all their spare Christian-names, with hyphens between, they can give it an aristocratic flavour. As if it wasn't trouble enough to remember *one* surname!"

By this time the room was getting crowded, as the guests, invited for the evening-party, were beginning to arrive, and Lady Muriel had to devote herself to the task of welcoming them, which she did with the sweetest grace imaginable. Sylvie and Bruno stood by her, deeply interested in the process.

"I hope you like my friends?" she said to them. "Specially my dear old friend, Mein Herr (What's become of him, I wonder? Oh, there he is!), that old gentleman in spectacles, with a long beard!"

"He's a grand old gentleman!" Sylvie said, gazing admiringly at "Mein Herr", who had settled down in a corner, from which his mild eyes beamed on us through a gigantic pair of spectacles. "And what a lovely beard!"

"What does he call his-self?" Bruno whispered.

"He calls himself 'Mein Herr'," Sylvie whispered in reply.

Bruno shook his head impatiently. "That's what he calls his *hair*, not his *self*, oo silly!" He appealed to me. "What doos he call his *self*, Mister Sir?"

"That's the only name *I* know of," I said. "But he looks very lonely. Don't you pity his grey hairs?"

"I pities his *self*," said Bruno, still harping on the misnomer; "but I doosn't pity his *hair*, one bit. His *hair* ca'n't feel!"

"We met him this afternoon," said Sylvie. "We'd been to see Nero, and we'd had *such* fun with him, making him invisible again! And we saw that nice old gentleman as we came back."

"Well, let's go and talk to him, and cheer him up a little," I said: "and perhaps we shall find out what he calls himself."

CHAPTER XI

The Man in the Moon

THE children came willingly. With one of them on each side of me, I approached the corner occupied by "Mein Herr". "You don't object to *children*, I hope?" I began.

"*Crabbed age and youth cannot live together!*" the old man cheerfully replied, with a most genial smile. "Now take a good look at me, my children! You would guess me to be an *old* man, wouldn't you?"

At first sight, though his face had reminded me so mysteriously of "the Professor", he had seemed to be decidedly a *younger* man: but, when I came to look into the wonderful depth of those large dreamy eyes, I felt, with a strange sense of awe, that he was incalculably *older*: he seemed to gaze at us out of some by-gone age, centuries away.

"I don't know if oo're an *old* man," Bruno answered, as the children, won over by the gentle voice, crept a little closer to him. "I thinks oo're *eighty-three*."

"He is very exact!" said Mein Herr.

"Is he anything like right?" I said.

"There are reasons," Mein Herr gently replied, "reasons which I am not at liberty to explain, for not mentioning *definitely* any Persons, Places, or Dates. One remark only

I will permit myself to make—that the period of life, between the ages of a hundred-and-sixty-five and a hundred-and-seventy-five, is a specially *safe* one."

"How do you make that out?" I said.

"Thus. You would consider swimming to be a very safe amusement, if you scarcely ever heard of any one dying of it. Am I not right in thinking that you never heard of any one dying between those two ages?"

"I see what you mean," I said: "but I'm afraid you ca'n't prove *swimming* to be safe, on the same principle. It is no uncommon thing to hear of some one being *drowned*."

"In *my* country," said Mein Herr. "no one is *ever* drowned."

"Is there no water deep enough?"

"Plenty! But we ca'n't *sink*. We are all *lighter than water*. Let me explain," he added, seeing my look of surprise. "Suppose you desire a race of *pigeons* of a particular shape or colour, do you not select, from year to year, those that are nearest to the shape or colour you want, and keep those, and part with the others?"

"We do," I replied. "We call it 'Artificial Selection'."

"Exactly so," said Mein Herr. "Well, *we* have practised that for some centuries—constantly selecting the *lightest* people: so that, now, *everybody* is lighter than water."

"Then you never can be drowned at *sea*?"

"Never! It is only on the *land*—for instance, when attending a play in a theatre—that we are in such a danger."

"How can that happen at a *theatre*?"

"Our theatres are all *underground*. Large tanks of water are placed above. If a fire breaks out, the taps are turned, and in one minute the theatre is flooded, up to the very roof! Thus the fire is extinguished."

"*And* the audience, I presume?"

"That is a minor matter," Mein Herr carelessly replied. "But they have the comfort of knowing that, whether drowned or not, they are all *lighter than water*. We have not yet reached the standard of making people lighter than *air*: but we are *aiming* at it; and, in another thousand years or so——"

"What doos oo do wiz the peoples that's too heavy?" Bruno solemnly enquired.

"We have applied the same process," Mein Herr continued, not noticing Bruno's question, "to many other purposes. We have gone on selecting *walking-sticks*—always keeping those that walked *best*—till we have obtained some, that can walk by themselves! We have gone on selecting *cotton-wool*, till we have got some lighter than air! You've no idea what a useful material it is! We call it 'Imponderal'."

"What do you use it for?"

"Well, chiefly for *packing* articles, to go by Parcel-Post. It makes them weigh *less than nothing*, you know."

"And how do the Post Office people know what you have to pay?"

"That's the beauty of the new system!" Mein Herr cried exultingly. "They pay *us*: we don't pay *them*! I've often got as much as five shillings for sending a parcel."

"But doesn't your Government object?"

"Well, they *do* object a little. They say it comes so expensive, in the long run. But the thing's as clear as daylight, by their own rules. If I send a parcel, that weighs a pound *more* than nothing, I *pay* three-pence: so, of course, if it weighs a pound *less* than nothing, I ought to *receive* three-pence."

"It is *indeed* a useful article!" I said.

"Yet even 'Imponderal' has its disadvantages," he resumed. "I bought some, a few days ago, and put it into my *hat*, to carry it home, and the hat simply floated away!"

"Had oo some of that funny stuff in oor hat *to-day*?" Bruno enquired. "Sylvie and me saw oo in the road, and oor hat were ever so high up! Weren't it, Sylvie?"

"No, that was quite another thing," said Mein Herr. "There was a drop or two of rain falling: so I put my hat on the top of my stick—as an umbrella, you know. As I came along the road", he continued, turning to me, "I was overtaken by——"

"—a shower of rain?" said Bruno.

"Well, it *looked* more like the tail of a dog," Mein Herr replied. "It was the most curious thing! Something rubbed affectionately against my knee. And I looked down. And I could see *nothing*! Only, about a yard off, there was a dog's tail, wagging, all by itself!"

"Oh, *Sylvie*!" Bruno murmured reproachfully. "Oo didn't finish making him visible!"

"I'm *so* sorry!" Sylvie said, looking very penitent. "I meant to rub it along his back, but we were in such a hurry. We'll go and finish him to-morrow. Poor thing! Perhaps he'll get no supper to-night!"

"*Course* he won't!" said Bruno. "Nobody never gives bones to a dog's tail!"

Mein Herr looked from one to the other in blank astonishment. "I do not understand you," he said. "I had lost my way, and I was consulting a pocket-map, and somehow I had dropped one of my gloves, and this invisible *Something*, that had rubbed against my knee, actually brought it back to me!"

"Course he did!" said Bruno. "He's *welly* fond of fetching things."

Mein Herr looked so thoroughly bewildered that I thought it best to change the subject. "What a useful thing a pocket-map is!" I remarked.

"That's another thing we've learned from *your* Nation," said Mein Herr, "map-making. But we've carried it much further than *you*. What do you consider the *largest* map that would be really useful?"

"About six inches to the mile."

"Only *six inches*!" exclaimed Mein Herr. "We very soon got to six *yards* to the mile. Then we tried a *hundred* yards to the mile. And then came the grandest idea of all! We actually made a map of the country, on the scale of *a mile to the mile*!"

"Have you used it much?" I enquired.

"It has never been spread out, yet," said Mein Herr: "the farmers objected: they said it would cover the whole country, and shut out the sunlight! So we now use the country itself, as its own map, and I assure you it does nearly as well. Now let me ask you *another* question. What is the smallest *world* you would care to inhabit?"

"*I* know!" cried Bruno, who was listening intently. "I'd like a little teeny-tiny world, just big enough for Sylvie and me!"

"Then you would have to stand on opposite side of it," said Mein Herr. "And so you would never see your sister *at all*!"

"And I'd have no *lessons*," said Bruno.

"You don't mean to say you've been trying experiments in *that* direction!" I said.

"Well, not *experiments* exactly. We do not profess to *construct* planets. But a scientific friend of mine, who has made several balloon-voyages, assures me he has visited a planet so small that he could walk right round it in twenty minutes! There had been a great battle, just before his visit, which had ended rather oddly: the vanquished army ran away at full speed, and in a very few minutes found themselves face-to-face with the victorious army, who were marching home again, and who were so frightened at finding themselves between *two* armies, that they surrendered at once! Of course that lost them the battle, though, as a matter of fact, they had killed *all* the soldiers on the other side."

"Killed soldiers *ca'n't* run away," Bruno thoughtfully remarked.

" 'Killed' is a technical word," replied Mein Herr. "In the little planet I speak of, the bullets were made of soft black stuff, which marked everything it touched. So, after a battle, all you had to do was to count how many soldiers on each side were 'killed'—that means 'marked on the *back*', for marks in *front* didn't count."

"Then you couldn't 'kill' any, unless they ran away?" I said.

"My scientific friend found out a better plan than *that*. He pointed out that, if only the bullets were sent *the other way round the world*, they would hit the enemy in the *back*. After that, the *worst* marksmen were considered the *best* soldiers; and *the very worst of all* always got First Prize."

"And how did you decide which was *the very worst of all*?"

"Easily. The *best* possible shooting is, you know, to hit what is exactly in *front* of you: so of course the *worst* possible is to hit what is exactly *behind* you."

"They were strange people in that little planet!" I said.

"They were indeed! Perhaps their method of *government* was the strangest of all. In *this* planet, I am told, a Nation consists of a number of Subjects, and one King: but, in the little planet I speak of, it consisted of a number of *Kings*, and one *Subject*!"

"You say you are 'told' what happens in *this* planet," I said. "May I venture to guess that you yourself are a visitor from some *other* planet?"

Bruno clapped his hands in his excitement. "Is oo the Man-in-the-Moon?" he cried.

Mein Herr looked uneasy. "I am *not* in the Moon, my child," he said evasively. "To return to what I was saying. I think *that* method of government ought to answer *well*. You see, the Kings would be sure to make Laws contradicting each other: so the Subject could never be punished, because, *whatever* he did he'd be obeying *some* Law."

"And, whatever he did, he'd be *dis*obeying *some* Law!" cried Bruno. "So he'd *always* be punished!"

Lady Muriel was passing at the moment, and caught the last word. "Nobody's going to be punished *here*!" she said, taking Bruno in her arms. "This is Liberty-Hall! Would you lend me the children for a minute?"

"The children desert us, you see," I said to Mein Herr,

as she carried them off: "so we old folk must keep each other company!"

The old man sighed. "Ah, well! We're old folk *now*; and yet I was a child myself, once—at least I fancy so."

It *did* seem a rather unlikely fancy, I could not help owning to myself—looking at the shaggy white hair, and the long beard—that he could *ever* have been a child. "You are fond of young people?" I said.

"Young *men*," he replied. "Not of *children* exactly. I used to teach young men—many a year ago—in my dear old University!"

"I didn't quite catch its *name*?" I hinted.

"I did not name it," the old man replied mildly. "Nor would you know the name if I did. Strange tales I could tell you of all the changes I have witnessed there! But it would weary you, I fear."

"No, *indeed*!" I said. "Pray go on. What kind of changes?"

But the old man seemed to be more in a humour for questions than for answers. "Tell me," he said, laying his hand impressively on my arm, "tell me something. For I am a stranger in your land. and I know little of *your* modes of education: yet something tells me *we* are further on than *you* in the eternal cycle of change—and that many a theory *we* have tried and found to fail, *you* also will try, with a wilder enthusiasm: you also will find to fail, with a bitterer despair!"

It was strange to see how, as he talked, and his words flowed more and more freely, with a certain rhythmic eloquence, his features seemed to glow with an inner light, and the whole man seemed to be transformed, as if he had grown fifty years younger in a moment of time.

CHAPTER XII

Fairy-Music

THE silence that ensued was broken by the voice of the musical young lady, who had seated herself near us, and was conversing with one of the newly-arrived guests. "Well!" she said in a tone of scornful surprise. "We *are* to have something new in the way of music, it appears!"

I looked round for an explanation, and was nearly as much astonished as the speaker herself: it was *Sylvie* whom Lady Muriel was leading to the piano!

"Do try it, my darling!" she was saying. "I'm sure you can play very nicely!"

Sylvie looked round at me, with tears in her eyes. I tried to give her an encouraging smile, but it was evidently a great strain on the nerves of a child so wholly unused to be made an exhibition of, and she was frightened and unhappy. Yet here came out the perfect sweetness of her disposition: I could see that she was resolved to forget herself, and do her best to give pleasure to Lady Muriel and her friends. She seated herself at the instrument, and began instantly. Time and expression, so far as one could judge, were perfect: but her touch was one of such extraordinary lightness that it was at first scarcely possible, through the hum of conversation which still continued, to catch a note of what she was playing.

But in a minute the hum had died away into absolute silence, and we all sat, entranced and breathless, to listen to such heavenly music as none then present could ever forget.

Hardly touching the notes at first, she played a sort of introduction in a minor key—like an embodied twilight; one felt as though the lights were growing dim, and a mist were creeping through the room. Then there flashed through the gathering gloom the first few notes of a melody so lovely, so delicate, that one held one's breath,

560

fearful to lose a single note of it. Ever and again the music dropped into the pathetic minor key with which it had begun, and, each time that the melody forced its way, so to speak, through the enshrouding gloom into the light of day, it was more entrancing, more magically sweet. Under the airy touch of the child, the instrument actually seemed to *warble*, like a bird. *"Rise up, my love, my fair one,"* it seemed to sing, *"and come away! For lo, the winter is past, the rain is over and gone; the flowers appear on the earth; the time of the singing of birds is come!"* One could fancy one heard the tinkle of the last few drops, shaken from the trees by a passing gust—that one saw the first glittering rays of the sun, breaking through the clouds.

The Count hurried across the room in great excitement. "I *cannot* remember myself", he exclaimed, "of the name of this so charming an air! It is of an opera, most surely. Yet not even will the *opera* remind his name to me! What you call him, dear child?"

Sylvie looked round at him with a rapt expression of face. She had ceased playing, but her fingers still wandered fitfully over the keys. All fear and shyness had quite passed away now, and nothing remained but the pure joy of the music that had thrilled our hearts.

"The title of it!" the Count repeated impatiently. "How call you the opera?"

"I don't know what an opera *is*," Sylvie half-whispered.

"How, then, call you the *air*?"

"I don't know any name for it," Sylvie replied, as she rose from the instrument.

"But this is marvellous!" exclaimed the Count, following the child, and addressing himself to me, as if I were the proprietor of this musical prodigy, and so *must* know the origin of her music. "You have heard her play this, sooner—I would say 'before this occasion'? How call you the air?"

I shook my head; but was saved from more questions

by Lady Muriel, who came up to petition the Count for a song.

The Count spread out his hands apologetically, and ducked his head. "But, Milady, I have already respected —I would say prospected—all your songs; and there shall be none fitted to my voice! They are not for basso voices!"

"Wo'n't you look at them again?" Lady Muriel implored.

"Let's help him!" Bruno whispered to Sylvie. "Let's get him—*you* know!"

Sylvie nodded. "Shall *we* look for a song for you?" she said sweetly to the Count.

"Mais *oui*!" the little man exclaimed.

"Of course we may!" said Bruno, while, each taking a hand of the delighted Count, they led him to the music-stand.

"There is still hope!" said Lady Muriel over her shoulder, as she followed them.

I turned to "Mein Herr", hoping to resume our interrupted conversation. "You were remarking——" I began: but at this moment Sylvie came to call Bruno, who had returned to my side, looking unusually serious. "*Do* come, Bruno!" she entreated. "You know we've nearly found it!" Then, in a whisper, "The locket's in my *hand*, now. I couldn't get it out while they were looking!"

But Bruno drew back. "The man called me names," he said with dignity.

"What names?" I enquired with some curiosity.

"I asked him", said Bruno, "which sort of song he liked. And he said '*A* song of *a* man, not of *a* lady'. And I said 'Shall Sylvie and me find you the song of Mister Tottles?' And he said 'Wait, eel!' And I'm *not* an eel, oo know!"

"I'm *sure* he didn't mean it!" Sylvie said earnestly. "It's something French—you know he ca'n't talk English so well as——"

Bruno relented visibly. "Course he knows no better, if he's Flench! Flenchmen *never* can speak English so goodly as *us*!" And Sylvie led him away, a willing captive.

"Nice children!" said the old man, taking off his spectacles and rubbing them carefully. Then he put them on again, and watched with an approving smile, while the children tossed over the heap of music, and we just caught Sylvie's reproving words, "We're *not* making hay, Bruno!"

"This has been a long interruption to our conversation," I said. "Pray let us go on!"

"Willingly!" replied the gentle old man. "I was much interested in what you——" He paused a moment, and passed his hand uneasily across his brow. "One forgets," he murmured. "What was I saying? Oh! Something you were to tell me. Yes. Which of your teachers do you value the most highly, those whose words are easily understood, or those who puzzle you at every turn?"

I felt obliged to admit that we generally admired most the teachers we couldn't quite understand.

"Just so," said Mein Herr. "That's the way it begins. Well, *we* were at that stage some eighty years ago—or was it ninety? Our favourite teacher got more obscure every year; and every year we admired him more—just as *your* Art-fanciers call *mist* the fairest feature in a landscape, and admire a view with frantic delight when they can see nothing! Now I'll tell you how it ended. It was Moral Philosophy that our idol lectured on. Well, his pupils couldn't make head or tail of it, but they got it all by heart; and, when Examination-time came, they wrote it down; and the Examiners said 'Beautiful! What depth!' "

"But what good was it to the young men *afterwards*?"

"Why, don't you see?" replied Mein Herr. "*They* became teachers in their turn, and *they* said all these things over again; and *their* pupils wrote it all down; and the Examiners accepted it; and nobody had the ghost of an idea what it all meant!"

"And how did it end?"

"It ended this way. We woke up one fine day, and found there was no one in the place that knew *anything* about Moral Philosophy. So we abolished it, teachers, classes, examiners, and all. And if any one wanted to learn anything about it, he had to make it out for himself; and after another twenty years or so there were several men that really knew something about it! Now tell me another thing. How long do you teach a youth before you examine him, in your Universities?"

I told him, three or four years.

"Just so, just what *we* did!" he exclaimed. "We taught 'em a bit, and, just as they were beginning to take it in, we took it all out again! We pumped our wells dry before they were a quarter full—we stripped our orchards while the apples were still in blossom—we applied the severe logic of arithmetic to our chickens, while peacefully slumbering in their shells! Doubtless it's the early bird that picks up the worm—but if the bird gets up so outrageously early that the worm is still deep underground, what *then* is its chance of a breakfast?"

Not much, I admitted.

"Now see how that works!" he went on eagerly. "If you want to pump your wells so soon—and I suppose you tell me that is what you *must* do?"

"We must," I said. "In an over-crowded country like this, nothing but Competitive Examinations——"

Mein Herr threw up his hands wildly. "What, *again*?" he cried. "I thought it was dead, fifty years ago! Oh this Upas tree of Competitive Examinations! Beneath whose deadly shade all the original genius, all the exhaustive research, all the untiring life-long diligence by which our fore-fathers have so advanced human knowledge, must slowly but surely wither away, and give place to a system of Cookery, in which the human mind is a sausage, and all we ask is, how much indigestible stuff can be crammed into it!"

Always, after these bursts of eloquence, he seemed to forget himself for a moment, and only to hold on to the thread of thought by some single word. "Yes, *crammed*," he repeated. "We went through all that stage of the disease—had it bad, I warrant you! Of course, as the Examination was all in all, we tried to put in just what was wanted—and the *great* thing to aim at was, that the Candidate should know absolutely *nothing* beyond the needs of the Examination! I don't say it was ever *quite* achieved: but one of my own pupils (pardon an old man's egotism) came very near it. After the Examination, he mentioned to me the few facts which he knew but had *not* been able to bring in, and I can assure you they were trivial, Sir, absolutely trivial!"

I feebly expressed my surprise and delight.

The old man bowed, with a gratified smile, and proceeded. "At that time, no one had hit on the much more rational plan of watching for the individual scintillations of genius, and rewarding them as they occurred. As it was, we made our unfortunate pupil into a Leyden-jar, charged him up to the eyelids—then applied the knob of a Competitive Examination, and drew off one magnificent spark, which very often cracked the jar! What mattered *that*? Ee labeled it 'First Class Spark', and put it away on the shelf."

"But the more rational system——?" I suggested.

"Ah, yes! *that* came next. Instead of giving the whole reward of learning in one lump, we used to pay for every good answer as it occurred. How well I remember lecturing in those days, with a heap of small coins at my elbow! It was 'A *very* good answer, Mr. Jones!' (that meant a shilling, mostly). 'Bravo, Mr. Robinson!' (that meant half-a-crown). Now I'll tell you how *that* worked. Not one single fact would any of them take in, without a fee! And when a clever boy came up from school, he got paid more for learning than we got paid for teaching him! Then came the wildest craze of all."

"What, *another* craze?" I said.

"It's the last one," said the old man. "I must have tired you out with my long story. Each College wanted to get the clever boys: so we adopted a system which we had heard was very popular in England: the Colleges competed against each other, and the boys let themselves out to the highest bidder! What geese we were! Why, they were bound to come to the University *somehow*. We needn't have paid 'em! And all our money went in getting clever boys to come to one College rather than another! The competition was so keen, that at last mere money-payments were not enough. Any College, that wished to secure some specially clever young man, had to waylay him at the Station, and hunt him through the streets. The first who touched him was allowed to have him."

"That hunting-down of the scholars, as they arrived, must have been a curious business," I said. "Could you give me some idea of what it was like?"

"Willingly!" said the old man. "I will describe to you the very last Hunt that took place, before that form of Sport (for it was actually reckoned among the *Sports* of the day: we called it 'Cub-Hunting') was finally abandoned. I witnessed it myself, as I happened to be passing by at the moment, and was what we called 'in at the death'. I can see it now!" he went on in an excited tone, gazing into vacancy with those large dreamy eyes of his "It seems like yesterday; and yet it happened——" He checked himself hastily, and the remaining words died away into a whisper.

"*How* many years ago did you say?" I asked, much interested in the prospect of at last learning *some* definite fact in his history.

"*Many* years ago," he replied. "The scene at the Railway-Station had been (so they told me) one of wild excitement. Eight or nine Heads of Colleges had assembled at the gates (no one was allowed inside), and the Station-Master had drawn a line on the pavement, and insisted on their all standing behind it. The gates were flung open! The young man darted through them, and fled like lightning down the street, while the Heads of Colleges actually *yelled* with excitement on catching sight of him! The Proctor gave the word, in the old statutory form, *'Semel! Bis! Ter! Currite!'*, and the Hunt began! Oh, it was a fine sight, believe me! At the first corner he dropped his Greek Lexicon: further on, his railway-rug: then various small articles: then his umbrella: lastly, what I suppose he prized most, his hand-bag; but the game was up: the spherical Principal of—of——"

"Of *which* College?" I said.

"—of *one* of the Colleges", he resumed, "had put into operation the Theory—his own discovery—of Accelerated Velocity, and captured him just opposite to where I stood. I shall never forget that wild breathless struggle! But it was soon over. Once in those great bony hands, escape was impossible!"

"May I ask why you speak of him as the *'spherical'* Principal?" I said.

"The epithet referred to his *shape*, which was a perfect *sphere*. You are aware that a bullet, another instance of a perfect sphere, when falling in a perfectly straight line, moves with Accelerated Velocity?"

I bowed assent.

"Well, my spherical friend (as I am proud to call him) set himself to investigate the *causes* of this. He found them to be *three*. One; that it is a perfect *sphere*. Two; that it moves in a *straight line*. Three; that its direction is *not upwards*. When these three conditions are fulfilled, you get Accelerated Velocity."

"Hardly," I said: "if you will excuse my differing from you. Suppose we apply the theory to *horizontal* motion. If a bullet is fired *horizontally*, it——"

"—it does *not* move in a *straight line*," he quietly finished my sentence for me.

"I yield the point," I said. "What did your friend do next?"

"The next thing was to apply the theory, as you rightly suggest, to *horizontal* motion. But the moving body, ever tending to *fall*, needs *constant support*, if it is to move in a true horizontal line. 'What, then,' he asked himself, 'will give *constant support to a moving body*?' And his answer was '*Human legs*!' *That* was the discovery that immortalized his name!"

"His name being——?" I suggested.

"I had not mentioned it," was the gentle reply of my most unsatisfactory informant. "His next step was an obvious one. He took to a diet of suet-dumplings, until his body had become a perfect sphere. *Then* he went out for his first experimental run—which nearly cost him his life!"

"How was *that*?"

"Well, you see, he had no idea of the *tremendous* new Force in Nature that he was calling into play. He began too fast. In a very few minutes he found himself moving at a hundred miles an hour! And, if he had not had the presence of mind to charge into the middle of a hay-stack (which he scattered to the four winds) there can be no doubt that he would have left the Planet he belonged to, and gone right away into Space!"

"And how came that to be the *last* of the Cub-Hunts?" I enquired.

"Well, you see, it led to a rather scandalous dispute between two of the Colleges. *Another* Principal had laid his hand on the young one, so nearly at the same moment as the *spherical* one, that there was no knowing which had touched him first. The dispute got into print, and did us no credit, and, in short, Cub-Hunts came to an end. Now I'll tell you what cured us of that wild craze of ours, the bidding against each other, for the clever scholars, just as if they were articles to be sold by auction! Just when the craze had reached its highest point, and when one of the Colleges had actually advertised a Scholarship of one thousand pounds *per annum*, one of our tourists brought us the manuscript of an old African legend—I happen to have a copy of it in my pocket. Shall I translate it for you?"

"Pray go on," I said, though I felt I was getting *very* sleepy.

CHAPTER XIII

What Tottles Meant

MEIN HERR unrolled the manuscript, but, to my great surprise, instead of *reading* it, he began to *sing* it, in a rich mellow voice that seemed to ring through the room.

> "*One thousand pounds per annuum*
> *Is not so bad a figure, come!*"
> *Cried Tottles. "And I tell you, flat,*
> *A man may marry well on that!*
> *To say 'the Husband needs the Wife'*
> *Is* not *the way to represent it.*
> *The crowning joy of Woman's life*
> *Is* Man!" *said Tottles (and he meant it).*
>
> *The blissful Honey-moon is past:*
> *The Pair have settled down at last:*
> *Mamma-in-law their home will share,*
> *And make their happiness her care.*
> "*Your income is an ample one:*
> *Go it, my children!*" *(And they went it).*
> "*I* rayther think this kind of fun
> *Wo'n't last!*" *said Tottles (and he meant it).*
>
> *They took a little country-box—*
> *A box at Covent Garden also:*
> *They lived a life of double-knocks,*
> *Acquaintances began to call so:*
> *Their London house was much the same*
> *(It took three hundred, clear, to rent it):*
> "*Life is a very jolly game!*"
> *Cried happy Tottles (and he meant it).*
>
> "*Contented with a frugal lot*"
> *(He always used that phrase at Gunter's),*
> *He bought a handy little yacht—*
> *A dozen serviceable hunters—*

569

The fishing of a Highland Loch—
A sailing-boat to circumvent it—
"The sounding of that Gaelic 'och'
Beats me!" said Tottles (and he meant it).

Here, with one of those convulsive starts that wake
one up in the very act of dropping off to sleep, I became
conscious that the deep musical tones that thrilled me
did *not* belong to Mein Herr, but to the French Count.
The old man was still conning the manuscript.

"I *beg* your pardon for keeping you waiting!" he said.
"I was just making sure that I knew the English for all
the words. I am quite ready now." And he read me the
following Legend:

"In a city that stands in the very centre of Africa, and
is rarely visited by the casual tourist, the people had always bought eggs—a daily necessary in a climate where
egg-flip was the usual diet—from a Merchant who came
to their gates once a week. And the people always bid
wildly against each other: so there was quite a lively
auction every time the Merchant came, and the last egg
in his basket used to fetch the value of two or three
camels, or thereabouts. And eggs got dearer every week.
And still they drank their egg-flip, and wondered where
all their money went to.

"And there came a day when they put their heads together. And they understood what donkeys they had
been.

"And next day, when the Merchant came, only *one*
Man went forth. And he said 'Oh, thou of the hook-nose
and the goggle-eyes, thou of the measureless beard, how
much for that lot of eggs?'

"And the Merchant answered him 'I *could* let thee have
that lot at ten thousand piastres the dozen'.

"And the Man chuckled inwardly, and said '*Ten*
piastres the dozen I offer thee, and no more, oh descen-
dant of a distinguished grandfather!'

"And the Merchant stroked his beard, and said 'Hum!

I will await the coming of thy friends.' So he waited. And the Man waited with him. And they waited both together."

"The manuscript breaks off here," said Mein Herr, as he rolled it up again; "but it was enough to open our eyes. We saw what simpletons we had been—buying our Scholars much as those ignorant savages bought their eggs—and the ruinous system was abandoned. If only we could have abandoned, along with it, all the *other* fashions we had borrowed from you, instead of carrying them to their logical results! But it was not to be. What ruined my country, and drove me from my home, was the introduction—into the *Army*, of all places—of your theory of Political Dichotomy!"

"Shall I trouble you too much," I said, "if I ask you to explain what you mean by 'the Theory of Political Dichotomy'?"

"No trouble at all!" was Mein Herr's most courteous reply. "I quite enjoy talking, when I get so good a listener. What started the thing, with us, was the report brought to us, by one of our most eminent statesmen, who had stayed some time in England, of the way affairs were managed there. It was a political necessity (so he assured us, and we believed him, though we had never discovered it till that moment) that there should be *two* Parties, in every affair and on every subject. In *Politics*, the two Parties, which you had found it necessary to institute, were called, he told us, 'Whigs' and 'Tories'."

"That must have been some time ago?" I remarked.

"It *was* some time ago," he admitted. "And this was the way the affairs of the British Nation were managed. (You will correct me if I misrepresent it. I do but repeat what our traveler told us.) These two Parties—which were in chronic hostility to each other—took turns in conducting the Government; and the Party, that happened *not* to be in power, was called the 'Opposition', I believe?"

"That is the right name," I said. "There have always

been, so long as we have had a **Parliament** at all, *two* Parties, one 'in', and one 'out'.''

"Well, the function of the 'Ins' (if I may so call them) was to do the best they could for the national welfare— in such things as making war or peace, commercial treaties, and so forth?''

"Undoubtedly," I said.

"And the function of the 'Outs' was (so our traveler assured us, though we were very incredulous at first) to *prevent* the 'Ins' from succeeding in any of these things?''

"To *criticize* and to *amend* their proceedings," I corrected him. "It would be *unpatriotic* to *hinder* the Government in doing what was for the good of the Nation! We have always held a *Patriot* to be the greatest of heroes, and an *unpatriotic* spirit to be one of the worst of human ills!''

"Excuse me for a moment," the old gentleman courteously replied, taking out his pocket-book. "I have a few memoranda here, of a correspondence I had with our tourist, and, if you will allow me, I'll just refresh my memory—although I quite agree with you—it is, as you say, one of the worst of human ills——" And, here Mein Herr began singing again:

> *But oh, the worst of human ills*
> *(Poor Tottles found) are "little bills"!*
> *And, with no balance in the Bank,*
> *What wonder that his spirits sank?*
> *Still, as the money flowed away,*
> *He wondered how on earth she spent it.*
> *"You cost me twenty pounds a day,*
> *At least!" cried Tottles (and he meant it).*
>
> *She sighed. "Those Drawing Rooms, you know!*
> *I really never thought about it:*
> *Mamma declared we ought to go——*
> *We should be Nobodies without it.*
> *That diamond-circlet for my brow——*
> *I quite believed that she had sent it,*

Until the Bill came in just now——"
*"*Viper!*" cried Tottles (and he meant it).*

Poor Mrs. T. could bear no more,
But fainted flat upon the floor.
Mamma-in-law, with anguish wild,
Seeks, all in vain, to rouse her child.
"Quick! Take this box of smelling-salts!
Don't scold her, James, or you'll repent it,
She's a dear girl, with all her faults——"
"She is!" groaned Tottles (and he meant it).

"I was a donkey", Tottles cried,
"To choose your daughter for my bride!
'Twas you that bid us cut a dash!
'Tis you have brought us to this smash!
You don't suggest one single thing
That can in any way prevent it——"
"Then what's the use of arguing?"
*"*Shut up!*" cried Tottles (and he meant it).*

Once more I started into wakefulness, and realized that
Mein Herr was not the singer. He was still consulting his
memoranda.

"It is exactly what my friend told me," he resumed,
after conning over various papers. " *'Unpatriotic'* is the
very word I had used, in writing to him, and *'hinder'* is
the very word he used in his reply! Allow me to read you
a portion of his letter:

" 'I can assure you,' he writes, 'that, unpatriotic as you may
think it, the recognized function of the 'Opposition' is to hinder
in every manner not forbidden by the Law, the action of the
Government. This process is called 'Legitimate Obstruction':
and the greatest triumph the 'Opposition' can ever enjoy, is
when they are able to point out that, owing to their 'Obstruction',
the Government have failed in everything they have tried to do
for the good of the Nation!' "

"Your friend has not put it *quite* correctly," I said.
"The Opposition would no doubt be glad to point out

that the Government had failed *through their own fault*; but *not* that they had failed on account of *Obstruction!*"

"You think so?" he gently replied. "Allow me now to read to you this newspaper-cutting, which my friend enclosed in his letter. It is part of the report of a public speech, made by a Statesman who was at the time a member of the 'Opposition':

" '*At the close of the Session, he thought they had no reason to be discontented with the fortunes of the campaign. They had routed the enemy at every point. But the pursuit must be continued. They had only to follow up a disordered and dispirited foe.*' "

"Now to what portion of your national history would you guess that the speaker was referring?"

"Really, the number of *successful* wars we have waged during the last century", I replied, with a glow of British pride, "is *far* too great for me to guess, with any chance of success, *which* it was we were then engaged in. However, I will name '*India*' as the most probable. The Mutiny was no doubt, all but crushed, at the time that speech was made. What a fine, manly, *patriotic* speech it must have been!" I exclaimed in an outburst of enthusiasm.

"You think so?" he replied, in a tone of gentle pity. "Yet my friend tells me that the '*disordered and dispirited foe*' simply meant the Statesmen who happened to be in power at the moment; that the '*pursuit*' simply meant 'Obstruction'; and that the words '*they had routed the enemy*' simply meant that the 'Opposition' had succeeded in hindering the Government from doing any of the work which the Nation had empowered them to do!"

I thought it best to say nothing.

"It seemed queer to *us*, just at first," he resumed, after courteously waiting a minute for me to speak: "but, when once we had mastered the idea, our respect for your Nation was so great that we carried it into every department of life! It was '*the beginning of the end*' with us. My country never held up its head again!" And the poor old gentleman sighed deeply.

"Let us change the subject," I said. "Do not distress yourself, I beg!"

"No, no!" he said, with an effort to recover himself. "I had rather finish my story! The next step (after reducing our Government to impotence, and putting a stop to all useful legislation, which did not take us long to do) was to introduce what we called 'the glorious British Principle of Dichotomy' into *Agriculture*. We persuaded many of the well-to-do farmers to divide their staff of labourers into two Parties, and to set them one against the other. They were called, like our political Parties, the 'Ins' and the 'Outs': the business of the 'Ins' was to do as much of ploughing, sowing, or whatever might be needed, as they could manage in a day, and at night they were paid according to the amount they had *done*: the business of the 'Outs' was to hinder them, and *they* were paid for the amount they had *hindered*. The farmers found they had to pay only *half* as much wages as they did before, and they didn't observe that the amount of work done was only a *quarter* as much as was done before: so they took it up quite enthusiastically, *at first*."

"And *afterwards*——?" I enquired.

"Well, *afterwards* they didn't like it quite so well. In a very short time, things settled down into a regular routine. No work *at all* was done. So the 'Ins' got no wages, and the 'Outs' got full pay. And the farmers never discovered, till most of them were ruined, that the rascals had agreed to manage it so, and had shared the pay between them! While the thing lasted, there were funny sights to be seen! Why, I've often watched a ploughman, with two horses harnessed to the plough, doing his best to get it *forwards*; while the opposition-ploughman, with three donkeys harnessed at the *other* end, was doing *his* best to get it *backwards*! And the plough never moving an inch, *either* way!"

"But *we* never did anything like *that*!" I exclaimed.

"Simply because you were less *logical* than we were," replied Mein Herr. "There is *sometimes* an advantage in being a donk—Excuse me! No *personal* allusion intended. All this happened *long ago*, you know!"

"Did the Dichotomy-Principle succeed in *any* direction?" I enquired.

"In *none*," Mein Herr candidly confessed. "It had a *very* short trial in *Commerce*. The shop-keepers *wouldn't* take it up, after once trying the plan of having half the attendants busy in folding up and carrying away the goods which the other half were trying to spread out upon the counters. They said the Public didn't like it!"

"I don't wonder at it," I remarked.

"Well, we tried 'the British Principle' for some years. And the end of it all was——" His voice suddenly dropped, almost to a whisper; and large tears began to roll down his cheeks. "—the end was that we got involved in a war; and there was a great battle, in which we far out-numbered the enemy. But what could one expect, when only *half* of our soldiers were fighting, and the other half pulling them back? It ended in a crushing defeat—an utter rout. This caused a Revolution; and most of the Government were banished. I myself was accused of Treason, for having so strongly advocated 'the British Principle'. My property was all forfeited, and—and—I was driven into exile! 'Now the mischief's done,' they said, 'perhaps you'll kindly leave the country?' It nearly broke my heart, but I had to go!"

The melancholy tone became a wail: the wail became a chant: the chant became a song—though whether it was *Mein Herr* that was singing, this time, or somebody else, I could not feel certain.

> *"And, now the mischief's done, perhaps*
> *You'll kindly go and pack your traps?*
> *Since* two (*your daughter and your son*)
> *Are Company, but* three *are none.*
> *A course of saving we'll begin:*
> *When change is needed, I'll invent it:*

*Don't think to put your finger in
This pie!" cried Tottles (and he meant it).*

The music seemed to die away. Mein Herr was again speaking in his ordinary voice. "Now tell me one thing more," he said. "Am I right in thinking that in *your* Universities, though a man may reside some thirty or forty years, you examine him, once for all, at the end of the first three or four?"

"That is so, undoubtedly," I admitted.

"Practically, then, you examine a man at the *beginning* of his career!" the old man said to himself rather than to me. "And what guarantee have you that he *retains* the knowledge for which you have rewarded him—beforehand, as *we* should say?"

"None," I admitted, feeling a little puzzled at the drift of his remarks. "How do *you* secure that object?"

"By examining him at the *end* of his thirty or forty years—not at the beginning," he gently replied. "On an average, the knowledge then found is about one-fifth of what it was at first—the process of forgetting going on at a very steady uniform rate—and he, who forgets *least*, gets *most* honour, and most rewards."

"Then you give him the money when he needs it no longer? And you make him live most of his life on *nothing!*"

"Hardly that. He gives his orders to the tradesmen: they supply him, for forty, sometimes fifty years, at their own risk: then he gets his Fellowship—which pays him in *one* year as much as *your* Fellowships pay in fifty— and then he can easily pay all his bills, with interest."

"But suppose he fails to get his Fellowship? That must occasionally happen."

"That occasionally happens." It was Mein Herr's turn, now, to make admissions.

"And what becomes of the tradesmen?"

"They calculate accordingly. When a man appears to be getting alarmingly ignorant, or stupid, they will some-

times refuse to supply him any longer. You have no idea
with what enthusiasm a man will begin to rub up his
forgotten sciences or languages, when his butcher has cut
off the supply of beef and mutton!"

"And who are the Examiners?"

"The young men who have just come, brimming over
with knowledge. You would think it a curious sight," he
went on, "to see mere boys examining such old men. I
have known a man set to examine his own grandfather.
It was a little painful for both of them, no doubt. The
old gentleman was as bald as a coot——"

"How bald would that be?" I've no idea why I asked
this question. I felt I was getting foolish.

Chapter XIV

Bruno's Picnic

"As *bald* as bald," was the bewildering reply. "Now,
Bruno, I'll tell you a story."

"And I'll tell *oo* a story," said Bruno, beginning in a
great hurry for fear of Sylvie getting the start of him:
"once there were a Mouse—a little tiny Mouse—such a
tiny little Mouse! Oo never saw such a tiny Mouse——"

"Did nothing ever happen to it, Bruno?" I asked.
"Haven't you anything more to tell us, besides its being
so tiny?"

"Nothing never happened to it," Bruno solemnly replied.

"Why did nothing never happen to it?" said Sylvie,
who was sitting, with her head on Bruno's shoulder,
patiently waiting for a chance of beginning *her* story.

"It were too tiny," Bruno explained.

"*That's* no reason!" I said. "However tiny it was,
things might happen to it."

Bruno looked pityingly at me, as if he thought me very

stupid. "It were too tiny," he repeated. "If anything happened to it, it would die—it were so *very* tiny!"

"Really that's enough about its being tiny!" Sylvie put in. "Haven't you invented any more about it?"

"Haven't invented no more yet."

"Well, then, you shouldn't begin a story till you've invented more! Now be quiet, there's a good boy, and listen to *my* story."

And Bruno, having quite exhausted all his inventive faculty, by beginning in too great a hurry, quietly resigned himself to listening. "Tell about the other Bruno, please," he said coaxingly.

Sylvie put her arms round his neck, and began:—

"The wind was whispering among the trees," ("That wasn't good manners!" Bruno interrupted. "Never mind about manners," said Sylvie) "and it was evening—a nice moony evening, and the Owls were hooting——"

"Pretend they weren't Owls!" Bruno pleaded, stroking her cheek with his fat little hand. "I don't like Owls. Owls have such great big eyes. Pretend they were Chickens!"

"Are you afraid of their great big eyes, Bruno?" I said.

"Aren't *'fraid* of nothing," Bruno answered in as careless a tone as he could manage: "they're ugly with their great big eyes. I think if they cried, the tears would be as big—oh, as big as the moon!" And he laughed merrily. "Doos Owls cry ever, Mister Sir?"

"Owls cry never," I said gravely, trying to copy Bruno's way of speaking: "they've got nothing to be sorry for, you know."

"Oh, but they have!" Bruno exclaimed. "They're ever so sorry, 'cause they killed the poor little Mouses!"

"But they're not sorry when they're *hungry*, I suppose?"

"Oo don't know nothing about Owls!" Bruno scornfully remarked. "When they're hungry, they're very, *very* sorry they killed the little Mouses, 'cause if they *hadn't* killed them there'd be sumfin for supper, oo know!''

Bruno was evidently getting into a dangerously inventive state of mind, so Sylvie broke in with "Now I'm going on with the story. So the Owls—the Chickens, I mean —were looking to see if they could find a nice fat Mouse for their supper——"

"Pretend it was a nice 'abbit!" said Bruno.

"But it *wasn't* a nice habit, to kill Mouses," Sylvie argued. "I ca'n't pretend *that*!"

"I didn't say '*habit*', oo silly fellow!" Bruno replied with a merry twinkle in his eye. " '*abbits*—that runs about in the fields!"

"Rabbit? Well it can be a Rabbit, if you like. But you mustn't alter my story so much, Bruno. A Chicken *couldn't* eat a Rabbit!"

"But it might have wished to see if it could try to eat it."

"Well, it wished to see if it could try—oh, really, Bruno, that's nonsense! I shall go back to the Owls."

"Well, then, pretend they hadn't great eyes!"

"And they saw a little Boy," Sylvie went on, disdaining to make any further corrections. "And he asked them to tell him a story. And the Owls hooted and flew away——" ("Oo shouldn't say '*flewed*'; oo should say '*flied*'," Bruno whispered. But Sylvie wouldn't hear.) "And he met a Lion. And he asked the Lion to tell him a story. And the Lion said 'yes', it would. And, while the Lion was telling him the story, it nibbled some of his head off——"

"Don't say 'nibbled'!" Bruno entreated. "Only little things nibble—little thin sharp things, with edges——"

"Well, then, it '*nubbled*'," said Sylvie. "And when it had nubbled *all* his head off, he went away, and he never said 'thank you'!"

"That were very rude," said Bruno. "If he couldn't speak, he might have nodded—no, he couldn't nod. Well, he might have shaked *hands* with the Lion!"

"Oh, I'd forgotten that part!" said Sylvie. "He *did*

shake hands with it. He came back again, you know, and he thanked the Lion very much, for telling him the story."

"Then his head had growed up again?" said Bruno.

"Oh yes, it grew up in a minute. And the Lion begged pardon, and said it wouldn't nubble off little boys' heads —not never no more!"

Bruno looked much pleased at this change of events. "Now that are a *really* nice story!" he said. "*Aren't* it a nice story, Mister Sir?"

"Very," I said. "I would like to hear another story about that Boy."

"So would *I*," said Bruno, stroking Sylvie's cheek again. "*Please* tell about Bruno's Picnic; and don't talk about *nubbly* Lions!"

"I wo'n't, if it frightens you," said Sylvie.

"*Flightens* me!" Bruno exclaimed indignantly. "It isn't *that*! It's 'cause 'nubbly' 's such a grumbly word to say— when one person's got her head on another person's shoulder. When she talks like that," he exclaimed to me, "the talking goes down bofe sides of my face—all the way to my chin—and it *doos* tickle so! It's enough to make a beard grow, that it is!"

He said this with great severity, but it was evidently meant for a joke: so Sylvie laughed—a delicious musical little laugh, and laid her soft cheek on the top of her brother's curly head, as if it were a pillow, while she went on with the story. "So this Boy——"

"But it wasn't *me*, oo know!" Bruno interrupted. "And oo needn't try to look as if it was, Mister Sir!"

I represented, respectfully, that I was trying to look as if it wasn't.

"——he was a middling good Boy——"

"He were a *welly* good Boy!" Bruno corrected her. "And he never did nothing he wasn't told to do——"

"*That* doesn't make a good Boy!" Sylvie said contemptuously.

"That *do* make a good Boy!" Bruno insisted.

Sylvie gave up the point. "Well, he was a *very* good Boy, and he always kept his promises, and he had a big cupboard——"

"—for to keep all his promises in!" cried Bruno.

"If he kept *all* his promises," Sylvie said, with a mischievous look in her eyes, "he wasn't like *some* Boys I know of!"

"He had to put *salt* with them, a-course," Bruno said gravely: "oo cá'n't keep promises when there isn't any salt. And he kept his birthday on the second shelf."

"How long did he keep his birthday?" I asked. "I never can keep *mine* more than twenty-four hours."

"Why, a birthday *stays* that long by itself!" cried Bruno. "Oo doosn't know how to keep birthdays! This Boy kept *his* a whole year!"

"And then the next birthday would begin," said Sylvie. "So it would be his birthday *always*."

"So it were," said Bruno. "Doos *oo* have treats on *oor* birthday, Mister Sir?"

"Sometimes," I said.

"When oo're *good*, I suppose?"

"Why, it *is* a sort of treat, being good, isn't it?" I said.

"A sort of *treat!*" Bruno repeated. "It's a sort of *punishment, I* think!"

"Oh, Bruno!" Sylvie interrupted, almost sadly. "How *can* you?"

"Well, but it *is*," Bruno persisted. "Why, look here, Mister Sir! *This* is being good!" And he sat bolt upright, and put on an absurdly solemn face. "First oo must sit up as straight as pokers——"

"—as *a* poker," Sylvie corrected him.

"—as straight as *pokers*," Bruno firmly repeated. "Then oo must clasp oor hands—*so*. Then—'Why hasn't oo brushed oor hair? Go and brush it *toreckly!*' Then—'Oh, Bruno, oo mustn't dog's-ear the daisies!' Did oo learn *oor* spelling wiz daisies, Mister Sir?"

"I want to hear about that Boy's *Birthday*," I said.

Bruno returned to the story instantly. "Well, so this Boy said 'Now it's my Birthday!' And so—I'm tired!" he suddenly broke off, laying his head in Sylvie's lap. "Sylvie knows it best. Sylvie's grown-upper than me. Go on, Sylvie!"

Sylvie patiently took up the thread of the story again. "So he said 'Now it's my Birthday. Whatever shall I do to keep my Birthday?' All *good* little Boys—" (Sylvie turned away from Bruno, and made a great pretence of whispering to *me*) "—all *good* little Boys—Boys that learn their lessons quite perfect—they always keep their birthdays, you know. So of course *this* little Boy kept *his* Birthday."

"Oo may call him Bruno, if oo like," the little fellow carelessly remarked. "It weren't *me*, but it makes it more interesting."

"So Bruno said to himself 'The properest thing to do is to have a Picnic, all by myself, on the top of the hill. And I'll take some Milk, and some Bread, and some Apples: and first and foremost, I want some *Milk*!' So, first and foremost, Bruno took a milk-pail——"

"And he went and milkted the Cow!" Bruno put in.

"Yes," said Sylvie, meekly accepting the new verb. "And the Cow said 'Moo! What are you going to do with all that Milk?' And Bruno said 'Please'm, I want it for my Picnic.' And the Cow said 'Moo! But I hope you wo'n't *boil* any of it?' And Bruno said 'No, *indeed* I wo'n't! New Milk's so nice and so warm, it wants no boiling!' "

"It doesn't want no boiling,' Bruno offered as an amended version.

"So Bruno put the Milk in a bottle. And then Bruno said 'Now I want some Bread!' So he went to the Oven, and he took out a delicious new Loaf. And the Oven——".

"—ever so light and so puffy!" Bruno impatiently corrected her. "Oo shouldn't leave out so many words!"

Sylvie humbly apologized. "—a delicious new Loaf,

ever so light and so puffy. And the Oven said——" Here
Sylvie made a long pause. "Really I don't know *what* an
Oven begins with, when it wants to speak!"

Both children looked appealingly at me; but I could
only say, helplessly, "I haven't the least idea! *I* never
heard an Oven speak!"

For a minute or two we all sat silent; and then Bruno
said, very softly, "Oven begins wiz 'O'."

"*Good* little boy!" Sylvie exclaimed. "He does his spelling *very* nicely. *He's cleverer than he knows!*" she added,
aside, to *me*. "So the Oven said 'O! What are you going
to do with all that Bread?' And Bruno said 'Please—'
Is an Oven 'Sir' or ' 'm', would you say?" She looked to
me for a reply.

"*Both*, I think," seemed to me the safest thing to say.

Sylvie adopted the suggestion instantly. "So Bruno
said 'Please, Sirm, I want it for my Picnic.' And the Oven
said 'O! But I hope you wo'n't *toast* any of it?' And Bruno
said, 'No, *indeed* I wo'n't! New Bread's so light and so
puffy, it wants no toasting!' "

"It never doesn't want no toasting," said Bruno. "I
wiss oo wouldn't say it so short!"

"So Bruno put the Bread in the hamper. Then Bruno
said 'Now I want some Apples!' So he took the hamper,
and he went to the Apple-Tree, and he picked some
lovely ripe Apples. And the Apple-Tree said——" Here
followed another long pause.

Bruno adopted his favourite expedient of tapping his
forehead; while Sylvie gazed earnestly upwards, as if she
hoped for some suggestion from the birds, who were
singing merrily among the branches overhead. But no
result followed.

"What *does* an Apple-Tree begin with, when it wants
to speak?" Sylvie murmured despairingly, to the irre-
sponsive birds.

At last, taking a leaf out of Bruno's book, I ventured
on a remark. "Doesn't 'Apple-Tree' always begin with
'Eh!'?"

"Why, of *course* it does! How *clever* of you!" Sylvie cried delightedly.

Bruno jumped up, and patted me on the head. I tried not to feel conceited.

"So the Apple-Tree said 'Eh! What are you going to do with all those Apples?' And Bruno said 'Please, Sir, I want them for my Picnic.' And the Apple-Tree said 'Eh! But I hope you wo'n't *bake* any of them?' And Bruno said 'No, *indeed* I wo'n't! Ripe Apples are so nice and so sweet, they want no baking!' "

"They never doesn't——" Bruno was beginning, but Sylvie corrected herself before he could get the words out.

" 'They never doesn't nohow want no baking.' So Bruno put the Apples in the hamper, along with the Bread, and the bottle of Milk. And he set off to have a Picnic, on the top of the hill, all by himself——"

"He wasn't greedy, oo know, to have it all by himself," Bruno said, patting me on the cheek to call my attention; " 'cause he hadn't got no brothers and sisters."

"It was very sad to have no *sisters*, wasn't it?" I said.

"Well, I don't know," Bruno said thoughtfully; " 'cause he hadn't no lessons to do. So he didn't mind."

Sylvie went on. "So, as he was walking along the road, he heard behind him such a curious sort of noise—a sort of a Thump! Thump! Thump! 'Whatever *is* that?' said Bruno. 'Oh, I know!' said Bruno. 'Why, it's only my Watch a-ticking!' "

"*Were* it his Watch a-ticking?" Bruno asked me, with eyes that fairly sparkled with mischievous delight.

"No doubt of it!" I replied. And Bruno laughed exultingly.

"Then Bruno thought a little harder. And he said 'No! it *ca'n't* be my Watch a-ticking; because I haven't *got* a Watch!' "

Bruno peered up anxiously into my face, to see how I took it. I hung my head, and put a thumb into my mouth, to the evident delight of the little fellow.

"So Bruno went a little further along the road. And

then he heard it again, that queer noise—Thump! Thump! Thump! 'Whatever *is* that?' said Bruno. 'Oh, I know!' said Bruno. 'Why, it's only the Carpenter a-mending my Wheelbarrow!' "

"*Were* it the Carpenter a-mending his Wheelbarrow?" Bruno asked me.

I brightened up, and said "It *must* have been!" in a tone of absolute conviction.

Bruno threw his arms round Sylvie's neck. "Sylvie!" he said, in a perfectly audible whisper. "He says it *must* have been!"

"Then Bruno thought a little harder. And he said 'No! It *ca'n't* be the Carpenter a-mending my Wheelbarrow, because I haven't *got* a Wheelbarrow!' "

This time I hid my face in my hands, quite unable to meet Bruno's look of triumph.

"So Bruno went a little further along the road. And then he heard that queer noise again—Thump! Thump! Thump! So he thought he'd look round, *this* time, just to *see* what it was. And what should it be but a great Lion!"

"A great big Lion," Bruno corrected her.

"A great big Lion. And Bruno was ever so frightened, and he ran——"

"No, he wasn't *flightened* a bit!" Bruno interrupted. (He was evidently anxious for the reputation of his namesake.) "He runned away to get a good look at the Lion; 'cause he wanted to see if it were the same Lion what used to nubble little Boys' heads off; and he wanted to know how big it was!"

"Well, he ran away, to get a good look at the Lion. And the Lion trotted slowly after him. And the Lion called after him, in a very gentle voice, 'Little Boy, little Boy! You needn't be afraid of *me*! I'm a very *gentle* old Lion now. I *never* nubble little Boys' heads off, as I used to do.' And so Bruno said 'Don't you *really*, Sir? Then what do you live on?' And the Lion——"

"Oo *see* he weren't a bit flightened!" Bruno said to me,

patting my cheek again. " 'cause he remembered to call it 'Sir', oo know."

I said that no doubt that was the *real* test whether a person was frightened or not.

"And the Lion said 'Oh, I live on bread-and-butter, and cherries, and marmalade, and plum-cake——' "

"—and *apples*!" Bruno put in.

"Yes, 'and apples'. And Bruno said 'Wo'n't you come with me to my Picnic?' And the Lion said 'Oh, I should like it *very much indeed*!' And Bruno and the Lion went away together." Sylvie stopped suddenly.

"Is that *all*?" I asked, despondingly.

"Not *quite* all," Sylvie slily replied "There's a sentence or two more. Isn't there, Bruno?"

"Yes," with a carelessness that was evidently put on: "just a sentence or two more."

"And, as they were walking along, they looked over a hedge, and who should they see but a little black Lamb! And the Lamb was ever so frightened. And it ran——"

"It were *really* flightened!" Bruno put in.

"It ran away. And Bruno ran after it. And he called 'Little Lamb! You needn't be afraid of *this* Lion! It *never* kills things! It lives on cherries, and marmalade——' "

"—and *apples*!" said Bruno. 'Oo *always* forgets the apples!"

"And Bruno said 'Wo'n't you come with us to my Picnic?' And the Lamb said 'Oh, I should like it *very much indeed*, if my Ma will let me!' And Bruno said 'Let's go and ask your Ma!' And they went to the old Sheep. And Bruno said 'Please, may your little Lamb come to my Picnic?' And the Sheep said 'Yes, if it's learnt all its lessons.' And the Lamb said 'Oh yes, Ma! I've learnt *all* my lessons!' "

"Pretend it hadn't any lessons!" Bruno earnestly pleaded.

"Oh, that would never do!" said Sylvie. "I ca'n't leave out all about the lessons! And the old Sheep said 'Do you know your A B C yet? Have you learnt A?' And the

Lamb said 'Oh yes, Ma! I went to the A-field, and I helped them to make A!' 'Very good, my child! And have you learnt B?' 'Oh yes, Ma! I went to the B-hive, and the B gave me some honey!' 'Very good, my child! And have you learnt C?' 'Oh yes, Ma! I went to the C-side, and I saw the ships sailing on the C!' 'Very good, my child! You may go to Bruno's Picnic.' "

"So they set off. And Bruno walked in the middle, so that the Lamb mightn't see the Lion——"

"It were *flightened*," Bruno explained.

"Yes, and it trembled so; and it got paler and paler; and, before they'd got to the top of the hill, it was a *white* little Lamb—as white as snow!"

"But *Bruno* weren't flightened!" said the owner of that name. "So *he* staid black!"

"No, he *didn't* stay black! He staid *pink*!" laughed Sylvie. "I shouldn't kiss you like this, you know, if you were *black*!"

"Oo'd *have* to!" Bruno said with great decision. "Besides, Bruno wasn't *Bruno*, oo know—I mean, Bruno wasn't *me*—I mean—don't talk nonsense, Sylvie!"

"I wo'n't do it again!" Sylvie said very humbly. "And so, as they went along, the Lion said 'Oh, I'll tell you what I used to do when I was a young Lion. I used to hide behind trees, to watch for little Boys.' " (Bruno cuddled a little closer to her.) " 'And, if a little thin scraggy Boy came by, why, I used to let him go. But, if a little fat juicy——' "

Bruno could bear no more. "Pretend he wasn't juicy!" he pleaded, half-sobbing.

"Nonsense, Bruno!" Sylvie briskly replied. "It'll be done in a moment! '—if a little fat juicy Boy came by, why, I used to spring out and gobble him up! Oh, you've no *idea* what a delicious thing it is—a little juicy Boy!' And Bruno said 'Oh, if you please, Sir, *don't* talk about eating little boys! It makes me so *shivery*!' "

The real Bruno shivered, in sympathy with the hero.

"And the Lion said 'Oh, well, we wo'n't talk about it,

then! I'll tell you what happened on my wedding-day——' "

"I like *this* part better," said Bruno, patting my cheek to keep me awake.

" 'There was, oh, such a lovely wedding-breakfast! At *one* end of the table there was a large plum-pudding. And at the other end there was a nice roasted *Lamb*! Oh, you've no *idea* what a delicious thing it is—a nice roasted Lamb!' And the Lamb said 'Oh, if you please, Sir, *don't* talk about eating Lambs! It makes me so *shivery*!' And the Lion said 'Oh, well, we wo'n't talk about it, then!' "

CHAPTER XV

The Little Foxes

"So, when they got to the top of the hill, Bruno opened the hamper: and he took out the Bread, and the Apples, and the Milk: and they ate, and they drank. And when they'd finished the Milk, and eaten half the Bread and half the Apples, the Lamb said 'Oh, my paws is so sticky! I want to wash my paws!' And the Lion said 'Well, go down the hill, and wash them in the brook, yonder. We'll wait for you!' "

"It never comed back!" Bruno solemnly whispered to me.

But Sylvie overheard him. "You're not to whisper, Bruno! It spoils the story! And when the Lamb had been gone a long time, the Lion said to Bruno 'Do go and see after that silly little Lamb! It must have lost its way.' And Bruno went down the hill. And when he got to the brook, he saw the Lamb sitting on the bank: and who should be sitting by it but an old Fox!"

"Don't know who *should* be sitting by it," Bruno

said thoughtfully to himself. "A old Fox *were* sitting by it."

"And the old Fox were saying," Sylvie went on, for once conceding the grammatical point. " 'Yes, my dear, you'll be ever so happy with us, if you'll only come and see us! I've got three little Foxes there, and we do love little Lambs so dearly!' And the Lamb said 'But you never *eat* them, do you, Sir?' And the Fox said 'Oh, no! What, *eat* a Lamb? We never *dream* of doing such a thing!' So the Lamb said 'Then I'll come with you.' And off they went, hand in hand."

"That Fox were welly extremely wicked, *weren't* it?" said Bruno.

"No, no!" said Sylvie, rather shocked at such violent language. "It wasn't quite so bad as that!"

"Well, I mean, it wasn't nice," the little fellow corrected himself.

"And so Bruno went back to the Lion. 'Oh, come quick!' he said. 'The Fox has taken the Lamb to his house with him! I'm *sure* he means to eat it!' And the Lion said 'I'll come as quick as ever I can!' And they trotted down the hill."

"Do oo think he caught the Fox, Mister Sir?" said Bruno. I shook my head, not liking to speak: and Sylvie went on.

"And when they got to the house, Bruno looked in at the window. And there he saw the three little Foxes sitting round the table, with their clean pinafores on, and spoons in their hands——"

"Spoons in their hands!" Bruno repeated in an ecstasy of delight.

"And the Fox had got a great big knife—all ready to kill the poor little Lamb——" ("Oo needn't be flightened, Mister Sir!" Bruno put in, in a hasty whisper.)

"And just as he was going to do it, Bruno heard a great ROAR——" (The real Bruno put his hand into mine, and held tight), "and the Lion came *bang* through the door, and the next moment it had bitten off the old

Fox's head! And Bruno jumped in at the window, and went leaping round the room, and crying out 'Hooray! Hooray! The old Fox is dead! The old Fox is dead!' "

Bruno got up in some excitement. "May I do it now?" he enquired.

Sylvie was quite decided on this point. "Wait till afterwards," she said. "The speeches come next, don't you know? You always love the speeches, *don't* you?"

"Yes, I doos," said Bruno: and sat down again.

"The Lion's speech. 'Now, you silly little Lamb, go home to your mother, and never listen to old Foxes again. And be very good and obedient.' "

"The Lamb's speech. 'Oh, indeed, Sir, I will, Sir!' and the Lamb went away." ("But *oo* needn't go away!" Bruno explained. "It's quite the nicest part—what's coming now!" Sylvie smiled. She liked having an appreciative audience.)

"The Lion's speech to Bruno. 'Now, Bruno, take those little Foxes home with you, and teach them to be good obedient little Foxes! Not like that wicked old thing there, that's got no head!' " ("That hasn't got no head," Bruno repeated.)

"Bruno's speech to the Lion. 'Oh, indeed, Sir, I will, Sir!' And the Lion went away." ("It gets betterer and betterer, now," Bruno whispered to me, "right away to the end!")

"Bruno's speech to the little Foxes. 'Now, little Foxes, you're going to have your first lesson in being good. I'm going to put you into the hamper, along with the Apples and the Bread: and you're not to eat the Apples: and you're not to eat the Bread: and you're not to eat *anything*—till we get to my house: and then you'll have your supper.' "

"The little Foxes' speech to Bruno. The little Foxes said nothing.

"So Bruno put the Apples into the hamper—and the little Foxes—and the Bread—" ("They had picnicked all the Milk," Bruno explained in a whisper) "—and he set off to go to his house." ("We're getting near the end now," said Bruno.)

"And, when he had got a little way, he thought he would look into the hamper, and see how the little Foxes were getting on."

"So he opened the door——" said Bruno.

"Oh, Bruno!" Sylvie exclaimed, *"you're* not telling the story! So he opened the door, and behold, there were no Apples! So Bruno said 'Eldest little Fox, have *you* been eating the Apples?' And the eldest little Fox said 'No no no!' " (It is impossible to give the tone in which Sylvie repeated this rapid little 'No no no!' The nearest I can come to it is to say that it was much as if a young and excited duck had tried to quack the words. It was too quick for a quack, and yet too harsh to be anything else.) "Then he said 'Second little Fox, have *you* been eating the Apples?' And the second little Fox said 'No no no!' Then he said 'Youngest little Fox, have *you* been eating the Apples?' And the youngest little Fox *tried* to say 'No no no!' but its mouth was so full, it couldn't, and it only said 'Wauch! Wauch! Wauch!' And Bruno looked into its mouth. And its mouth was full of Apples! And Bruno shook his head, and he said 'Oh dear, oh dear! What bad creatures these Foxes are!' "

Bruno was listening intently: and, when Sylvie paused to take breath, he could only just gasp out the words "About the Bread?"

"Yes," said Sylvie, "the Bread comes next. So he shut the door again; and he went a little further; and then he thought he'd just peep in once more. And behold, there was no Bread!" ("What do 'behold' *mean?*" said Bruno. "Hush!" said Sylvie.) "And he said 'Eldest little Fox, have *you* been eating the Bread?' And the eldest little Fox said 'No no no!' 'Second little Fox, have *you* been eating the Bread?' And the second little Fox only said 'Wauch! Wauch! Wauch!' And Bruno looked into its mouth, and its mouth was full of Bread!" ("It might have chokeded it," said Bruno.) "So he said 'Oh dear, oh dear! What *shall* I do with these Foxes?' And he went a little further." ("Now comes the most interesting part," Bruno whispered.)

"And when Bruno opened the hamper again, what do you think he saw?" ("Only *two* Foxes!" Bruno cried in a great hurry.) "You shouldn't tell it so quick. However, he *did* see only *two* Foxes. And he said 'Eldest little Fox, have you been eating the youngest little Fox?' And the eldest little Fox said 'No no no!' 'Second little Fox, have *you* been eating the youngest little Fox?' And the second little Fox did its very best to say 'No no no!' but it could only say 'Weuchk! Weuchk! Weuchk!' And when Bruno looked into its mouth, it was half full of Bread, and half full of Fox!" (Bruno said nothing in the pause this time. He was beginning to pant a little, as he knew the crisis was coming.)

"And when he'd got nearly home, he looked once more into the hamper, and he saw——"

"Only——" Bruno began, but a generous thought struck him, and he looked at me. "*Oo* may say it, *this* time, Mister Sir!" he whispered. It was a noble offer, but I wouldn't rob him of the treat. "Go on, Bruno," I said, "you say it much the best." "Only—but—*one*—Fox!" Bruno said with great solemnity.

" 'Eldest little Fox,' " Sylvie said, dropping the narrative-form in her eagerness, " 'you've been *so* good that I can hardly believe *you've* been disobedient: but I'm *afraid* you've been eating your little sister?' And the eldest little Fox said 'Whihuauch! Whihuauch!' and then it choked. And Bruno looked into its mouth, and it *was* full!" (Sylvie paused to take breath, and Bruno lay back among the daisies, and looked at me triumphantly. "Isn't it *grand*, Mister Sir?" said he. I tried hard to assume a critical tone. "It's grand," I said: "but it frightens one so!" "Oo may sit a little closer to *me*, if oo like," said Bruno.)

"And so Bruno went home: and took the hamper into the kitchen, and opened it. And he saw——" Sylvie looked at *me*, this time, as if she thought I had been rather neglected and ought to be allowed *one* guess, at any rate.

"He ca'n't guess!" Bruno cried eagerly. "I 'fraid I *must* tell him! There weren't—*nuffin* in the hamper!" I shivered in terror, and Bruno clapped his hands with delight. "He *is* flightened, Sylvie! Tell the rest!"

"So Bruno said 'Eldest little Fox, have you been eating *yourself*, you wicked little Fox?' And the eldest little Fox said 'Whihuauch!' And then Bruno saw there was only its *mouth* in the hamper! So he took the mouth, and he opened it, and shook, and shook! And at last he shook the little Fox out of its own mouth! And then he said 'Open your mouth again, you wicked little thing!' And he shook, and shook! And he shook out the second little Fox! And he said 'Now open *your* mouth!' And he shook, and shook! And he shook out the youngest little Fox, and all the Apples, and all the Bread!

"And then Bruno stood the little Foxes up against the wall: and he made them a little speech. 'Now, little Foxes, you've begun very wickedly—and you'll have to be punished. First you'll go up to the nursery, and wash your faces, and put on clean pinafores. Then you'll hear the bell ring for supper. Then you'll come down: and *you wo'n't have any supper*: but you'll have a good *whipping*! Then you'll go to bed. Then in the morning you'll hear the bell ring for breakfast. *But you wo'n't have any breakfast!* You'll have a good *whipping*! Then you'll have your lessons. And, perhaps, if you're *very* good, when dinner-time comes, you'll have a little dinner, and no more whipping!' " ("How *very* kind he was!" I whispered to Bruno. "*Middling* kind," Bruno corrected me gravely.)

"So the little Foxes ran up to the nursery. And soon Bruno went into the hall, and rang the big bell. 'Tingle, tingle, tingle! Supper, supper, supper!' Down came the little Foxes, in such a hurry for their supper! Clean pinafores! Spoons in their hands! And, when they got into the dining-room, there was ever such a white table-cloth on the table! But there was nothing on it but a big whip. And they had *such* a whipping!" (I put my handkerchief to my eyes, and Bruno hastily climbed upon my knee and stroked my face. "Only *one* more whipping, Mister Sir!" he whispered. "Don't cry more than oo ca'n't help!")

"And the next morning early, Bruno rang the big bell again. 'Tingle, tingle, tingle! Breakfast, breakfast, break-fast!' Down came the little Foxes! Clean pinafores! Spoons in their hands! No breakfast! Only the big whip! Then came lessons," Sylvie hurried on, for I still had my handkerchief to my eyes. "And the little Foxes were ever so good! And they learned their lessons backwards, and forwards, and upside-down. And at last Bruno rang the big bell again. 'Tingle, tingle, tingle! Dinner, dinner, dinner!' And when the little Foxes came down——" ("Had they clean pinafores on?" Bruno enquired. "Of course!" said Sylvie. "And spoons?" "Why, you *know* they had!" "Couldn't be *certain*," said Bruno.) "— they came as slow as slow! And they said 'Oh! There'll be no dinner! There'll only be the big whip!' But, when they got into the room, they saw the most *lovely* dinner!" ("Buns?" cried Bruno, clapping his hands.) "Buns, and cake, and——" ("—and jam?" said Bruno.) "Yes, jam— and soup—and——" ("—and *sugar plums*!" Bruno put in once more; and Sylvie seemed satisfied.)

"And ever after that, they *were* such good little Foxes! They did their lessons as good as gold—and they never did what Bruno told them not to—and they never ate each other any more—and *they never ate themselves*!"

The story came to an end so suddenly, it almost took my breath away; however I did my best to make a pretty speech of thanks. "I'm sure it's very—very—very much so, I'm sure!" I seemed to hear myself say.

Chapter XVI

Beyond These Voices

"I DIDN'T quite catch what you said!" were the next words that reached my ear, but certainly *not* in the voice either of Sylvie or of Bruno, whom I could just see, through the crowd of guests, standing by the piano, and listening to the Count's song. Mein Herr was the speaker. "I didn't quite catch what you said!" he repeated. "But I've no doubt you take *my* view of it. Thank you *very* much for your kind attention. There is only but *one* verse left to be sung!" These last words were not in the gentle voice of Mein Herr, but in the deep bass of the French Count. And, in the silence that followed, the final stanza of "Tottles" rang through the room.

> *See now this couple settled down*
> *In quiet lodgings, out of town:*
> *Submissively the tearful wife*
> *Accepts a plain and humble life:*
> *Yet begs one boon on bended knee:*
> *"My ducky-darling, don't resent it!*
> *Mamma might come for two or three——"*
> *"NEVER!" yelled Tottles. And he meant it.*

The conclusion of the song was followed by quite a chorus of thanks and compliments from all parts of the room, which the gratified singer responded to by bowing low in all directions. "It is to me a great privilege", he said to Lady Muriel, "to have met with this so marvellous a song. The accompaniment to him is so strange, so mysterious: it is as if a new music were to be invented! I will play him once again so as that to show you what I mean." He returned to the piano, but the song had vanished.

The bewildered singer searched through the heap of music lying on an adjoining table, but it was not there, either. Lady Muriel helped in the search: others soon

596

joined: the excitement grew. "What *can* have become of it?" exclaimed Lady Muriel. Nobody knew: one thing only was certain, that no one had been near the piano since the Count had sung the last verse of the song.

"Nevare mind him!" he said, most good-naturedly. "I shall give it you with memory alone!" He sat down, and began vaguely fingering the notes; but nothing resembling the tune came out. Then he, too, grew excited. "But what oddness! How much of singularity! That I might lose, not the words alone, but the tune also—that is quite curious, I suppose?"

We all supposed it, heartily.

"It was that sweet little boy, who found it for me," the Count suggested. "Quite perhaps *he* is the thief?"

"Of course he is!" cried Lady Muriel. "Bruno! Where are you, my darling?"

But no Bruno replied: it seemed that the two children had vanished as suddenly, and as mysteriously, as the song.

"They are playing us a trick?" Lady Muriel gaily exclaimed. "This is only an *ex tempore* game of Hide-and-Seek! That little Bruno is an embodied Mischief!"

The suggestion was a welcome one to most of us, for some of the guests were beginning to look decidedly uneasy. A general search was set on foot with much enthusiasm: curtains were thrown back and shaken, cupboards opened, and ottomans turned over; but the number of possible hiding-places proved to be strictly limited; and the search came to an end almost as soon as it had begun.

"They must have run out, while we were wrapped up in the song," Lady Muriel said, addressing herself to the Count, who seemed more agitated than the others; "and no doubt they've found their way back to the housekeeper's room."

"Not by *this* door!" was the earnest protest of a knot of two or three gentlemen, who had been grouped round the door (one of them actually leaning against it) for the last half-hour, as they declared. *"This* door has not been opened since the song began!"

An uncomfortable silence followed this announcement. Lady Muriel ventured no further conjectures, but quietly examined the fastenings of the windows, which opened as doors. They all proved to be well fastened, *inside.*

Not yet at the end of her resources, Lady Muriel rang the bell. "Ask the housekeeper to step here," she said, "and to bring the children's walking-things with her."

"I've brought them, my Lady," said the obsequious housekeeper, entering after another minute of silence. "I thought the young lady would have come to my room to put on her boots. Here's your boots, my love!" she added cheerfully, looking in all directions for the children. There was no answer, and she turned to Lady Muriel with a puzzled smile. "Have the little darlings hid themselves?"

"I don't see them, just now," Lady Muriel replied, rather evasively. "You can leave their things here, Wilson. *I'll* dress them, when they're ready to go."

The two little hats, and Sylvie's walking-jacket, were handed round among the ladies, with many exclamations of delight. There certainly was a sort of witchery of beauty about them. Even the little boots did not miss their share of favourable criticism. "Such natty little things!" the musical young lady exclaimed, almost fondling them as she spoke. "And what tiny tiny feet they must have!"

Finally, the things were piled together on the centre-ottoman, and the guests, despairing of seeing the children again, began to wish good-night and leave the house.

There were only some eight or nine left—to whom the Count was explaining, for the twentieth time, how he had had his eye on the children during the last verse of the song; how he had then glanced round the room, to see what effect "de great chest-note" had had upon his audience; and how, when he looked back again, they had both disappeared—when exclamations of dismay began to be heard on all sides, the Count hastily bringing his story to an end to join in the outcry.

The walking-things had all disappeared!

After the utter failure of the search for the *children*, there was a very half-hearted search made for their *apparel*. The remaining guests seemed only too glad to get away, leaving only the Count and our four selves.

The Count sank into an easy-chair, and panted a little.

"Who then *are* these dear children, I pray you?" he said. "Why come they, why go they, in this so little ordinary a fashion? That the music should make itself vanish—that the hats, the boots, should make themselves to vanish—how is it, I pray you?"

"I've no idea where they are!" was all I could say, on finding myself appealed to, by general consent, for an explanation.

The Count seemed about to ask further questions, but checked himself.

"The hour makes himself to become late," he said. "I wish to you a very good night, my Lady. I betake myself to my bed—to dream—if that indeed I be not dreaming now!" And he hastily left the room.

"Stay awhile, stay awhile!" said the Earl, as I was about to follow the Count. "*You* are not a guest, you know! Arthur's friend is at *home* here!"

"Thanks!" I said, as with true English instincts, we drew our chairs together round the fire-place, though no fire was burning—Lady Muriel having taken the heap of music on her knee, to have one more search for the strangely-vanished song.

"Don't you sometimes feel a wild longing", she said, addressing herself to me, "to have something more to do with your hands, while you talk, than just holding a cigar, and now and then knocking off the ash? Oh, I know all that you're going to say!" (This was to Arthur, who appeared about to interrupt her.) "The Majesty of Thought supersedes the work of the fingers. A Man's severe thinking, *plus* the shaking-off a cigar-ash, comes to the same total as a Woman's trivial fancies, *plus* the most elaborate embroidery. *That's* your sentiment, isn't it, only better expressed?"

Arthur looked into the radiant, mischievous face, with a grave and very tender smile. "Yes," he said resignedly: "that is my sentiment, exactly."

"Rest of body, and activity of mind," I put in. "Some writer tells us *that* is the acme of human happiness."

"Plenty of *bodily* rest, at any rate!" Lady Muriel replied, glancing at the three recumbent figures around her. "But what you call activity of *mind*——"

"—is the privilege of young Physicians *only*," said the Earl. "We old men have no claim to be active. *What can an old man do but die?*"

"A good many other things, I should *hope*," Arthur said earnestly.

"Well, maybe. Still you have the advantage of me in many ways, dear boy! Not only that *your* day is dawning while *mine* is setting, but your *interest* in Life—somehow I ca'n't help envying you *that*. It will be many a year before you lose your hold of *that*."

"Yet surely many human interests *survive* human Life?" I said.

"Many do, no doubt. And *some* forms of Science; but only *some*, I think. Mathematics, for instance: *that* seems to possess an endless interest: one ca'n't imagine *any* form of Life, or *any* race of intelligent beings, where Mathematical truth would lose its meaning. But I fear *Medicine* stands on a different footing. Suppose you discover a remedy for some disease hitherto supposed to be incurable. Well, it is delightful for the moment, no doubt —full of interest—perhaps it brings you fame and fortune. But what then? Look on, a few years, into a life where disease has no existence. What is your discovery worth, *then*? Milton makes Jove promise too much. '*Of so much fame in heaven expect thy meed.*' Poor comfort when one's 'fame' concerns matters that will have ceased to have a meaning!"

"At any rate one wouldn't care to make any *fresh*

medical discoveries," said Arthur. "I see no help for *that* —though I shall be sorry to give up my favourite studies. Still, medicine, disease, pain, sorrow, sin—I fear they're all linked together. Banish sin, and you banish them all!"

"*Military* science is a yet stronger instance," said the Earl. "Without sin, *war* would surely be impossible. Still any mind, that has had in this life any keen interest, not in *itself* sinful, will surely find itself *some* congenial line of work hereafter. Wellington may have no more *battles* to fight—and yet—

> '*We doubt not that, for one so true,*
> *There must be other, nobler work to do,*
> *Than when he fought at Waterloo,*
> *And Victor he must ever be!*' "

He lingered over the beautiful words, as if he loved them: and his voice, like distant music, died away into silence.

After a minute or two he began again. "If I'm not wearying you, I would like to tell you an idea of the future Life which has haunted me for years, like a sort of waking nightmare—I ca'n't reason myself out of it."

"Pray do," Arthur and I replied, almost in a breath. Lady Muriel put aside the heap of music, and folded her hands together.

"The one idea", the Earl resumed, "that has seemed to me to overshadow all the rest, is that of *Eternity*—involving, as it seems to do, the necessary *exhaustion* of all subjects of human interest. Take Pure Mathematics, for instance—a Science independent of our present surroundings. I have studied it, myself, a little. Take the subject of circles and ellipses—what we call 'curves of the second degree'. In a future Life, it would only be a question of so many years (or *hundreds* of years, if you like), for a man to work out *all* their properties. Then he *might* go to curves of the third degree. Say *that* took ten times as long (you see we have *unlimited* time to deal with). I can hardly imagine his *interest* in the subject holding out even for those; and, though there is no limit to the *degree* of the curves he might study, yet surely the time, needed to exhaust *all* the novelty and interest of the subject, would be absolutely *finite*? And so of all other branches of Science. And, when I transport myself, in thought, through some thousands or millions of years, and fancy myself possessed of as much Science as one created reason can carry, I ask myself 'What then? With nothing more to learn, can one rest content on *knowledge*, for the eternity yet to be lived through?' It has been a very wearying thought to me. I have sometimes fancied one *might*, in that event, say 'It is better *not* to be', and pray for personal *annihilation*—the Nirvana of the Buddhists.''

"But that is only half the picture," I said. "Besides working for *oneself*, may there not be the helping of *others*?"

"Surely, surely!" Lady Muriel exclaimed in a tone of relief, looking at her father with sparkling eyes.

"Yes," said the Earl, "so long as there *were* any others needing help. But, given ages and ages more, surely all created reasons would at length reach the same dead level of *satiety*. And *then* what is there to look forward to?"

"I know that weary feeling," said the young Doctor. "I have gone through it all, more than once. Now let me tell you how I have put it to myself. I have imagined a little child, playing with toys on his nursery-floor, and yet able to *reason*, and to look on, thirty years ahead. Might he not say to himself 'By that time I shall have had enough of bricks and ninepins. How weary Life will be!' Yet, if we look forward through those thirty years, we find him a great statesman, full of interests and joys far more intense than his baby-life could give—joys wholly inconceivable to his baby-mind—joys such as no baby-language could in the faintest degree describe. Now, may not our life, a million years hence, have the same relation, to our life now, that the man's life has to the child's? And, just as one might try, all in vain, to express to that child, in the language of bricks and ninepins, the meaning of 'politics', so perhaps all those descriptions of Heaven, with its music, and its feasts, and its streets of gold, may be only attempts to describe, in *our* words, things for which we *really* have no words at all. Don't you think that, in *your* picture of another life, you are in fact transplanting that child into political life, without making any allowance for his growing up?"

'I think I understand you," said the Earl. "The music of Heaven *may* be something beyond our powers of thought. Yet the music of Earth is sweet! Muriel, my child, sing us something before we go to bed!"

"Do," said Arthur, as he rose and lit the candles on the cottage-piano, lately banished from the drawing-room to make room for a "semi-grand". "There is a song here, that I have never heard you sing.

> *'Hail to thee, blithe spirit!*
> *Bird thou never wert,*
> *That from Heaven, or near it,*
> *Pourest thy full heart!'* "

he read from the page he had spread open before her.

"And our little life here", the Earl went on, "is, to that grand time, like a child's summer-day! One gets tired as night draws on," he added, with a touch of sadness in his voice, "and one gets to long for bed! For those welcome words 'Come, child, 'tis bed-time!' "

Chapter XVII

To the Rescue!

"IT *isn't* bed-time!" said a sleepy little voice. "The owls hasn't gone to bed, and I s'a'n't go to seep wizout oo sings to me!"

"Oh, Bruno!" cried Sylvie. "Don't you know the owls

have only just got up? But the *frogs* have gone to bed, ages ago.'

"Well, *I* aren't a frog," said Bruno.

"What shall I sing?" said Sylvie, skilfully avoiding the argument.

"Ask Mister Sir," Bruno lazily replied, clasping his hands behind his curly head, and lying back on his fern-leaf, till it almost bent over with his weight. "This aren't a comfable leaf, Sylvie. Find me a comfabler—please!" he added, as an after-thought, in obedience to a warning finger held up by Sylvie. "I doosn't like being feet-up-wards!"

It was a pretty sight to see—the motherly way in which the fairy-child gathered up her little brother in her arms, and laid him on a stronger leaf. She gave it just a touch to set it rocking, and it went on vigorously by it-self, as if it contained some hidden machinery. It cer-tainly wasn't the wind, for the evening-breeze had quite died away again, and not a leaf was stirring over our heads.

"Why does that one leaf rock so, without the others?" I asked Sylvie. She only smiled sweetly and shook her head. "I don't know *why*," she said. "It always does, if it's got a fairy-child on it. It *has* to, you know."

"And can people see the leaf rock, who ca'n't see the Fairy on it?"

"Why, of course!" cried Sylvie. "A leaf's a leaf, and everybody can see it; but Bruno's Bruno, and they ca'n't see *him*, unless they're eerie, like you."

Then I understood how it was that one sometimes sees —going through the woods in a still evening—one fern-leaf rocking steadily on, all by itself. Haven't you ever seen that? Try if you can see the fairy-sleeper on it, next time; but don't *pick* the leaf, whatever you do; let the little one sleep on!

But all this time Bruno was getting sleepier and sleep-ier. "Sing, sing!" he murmured fretfully, Sylvie looked to me for instructions. "What shall it be?" she said.

"Could you sing him the nursery-song you once told me of?" I suggested. "The one that had been put through the mind-mangle, you know. '*The little man that had a little gun,*' I think it was."

"Why, that are one of the *Professor's* songs!" cried Bruno. "I likes the little man; and I likes the way they spinned him—like a teetle-totle-tum." And he turned a loving look on the gentle old man who was sitting at the other side of his leaf-bed, and who instantly began to sing, accompanying himself on his Outlandish guitar, while the snail, on which he sat, waved its horns in time to the music.

> *In stature the Manlet was dwarfish—*
> *No burly big Blunderbore he:*
> *And he wearily gazed on the crawfish*
> *His Wifelet had dressed for his tea.*
> *"Now reach me, sweet Atom, my gunlet,*
> *And hurl the old shoelet for luck:*
> *Let me hie to the bank of the runlet,*
> *And shoot thee a Duck!"*

> *She has reached him his minikin gunlet:*
> *She has hurled the old shoelet for luck:*
> *She is busily baking a bunlet,*
> *To welcome him home with his Duck.*
> *On he speeds, never wasting a wordlet,*
> *Though thoughtlets cling, closely as wax,*
> *To the spot where the beautiful birdlet*
> *So quietly quacks.*

> *Where the Lobsterlet lurks, and the Crablet*
> *So slowly and sleepily crawls:*
> *Where the Dolphin's at home, and the Dablet*
> *Pays long ceremonious calls:*
> *Where the Grublet is sought by the Froglet:*
> *Where the Frog is pursued by the Duck:*
> *Where the Ducklet is chased by the Doglet—*
> *So runs the world's luck!*

He has loaded with bullet and powder:
His footfall is noiseless as air:
But the Voices grow louder and louder,
And bellow, and bluster, and blare.
They bristle before him and after,
They flutter above and below,
Shrill shriekings of lubberly laughter,
Weird wailings of woe!

They echo without him, within him:
They thrill through his whiskers and beard:
Like a teetotum seeming to spin him,
With sneers never hitherto sneered.
"Avengement," they cry, "on our Foelet!
Let the Manikin weep for our wrongs!
Let us drench him, from toplet to toelet,
With Nursery-Songs!

"He shall muse upon 'Hey! Diddle! Diddle!'
On the Cow that surmounted the Moon:
He shall rave of the Cat and the Fiddle,
And the Dish that eloped with the Spoon:
And his soul shall be sad for the Spider,
When Miss Muffet was sipping her whey,
That so tenderly sat down beside her,
And scared her away!

"The music of Midsummer-madness
Shall sting him with many a bite,
Till, in rapture of rollicking sadness,
He shall groan with a gloomy delight:
He shall swathe him, like mists of the morning,
In platitudes luscious and limp,
Such as deck, with a deathless adorning,
The Song of the Shrimp!

"When the Ducklet's dark doom is decided,
We will trundle him home in a trice:
And the banquet, so plainly provided,
Shall round into rose-buds and rice:

In a blaze of pragmatic invention
  He shall wrestle with Fate, and shall reign:
But he has not a friend fit to mention,
    So hit him again!"

He has shot it, the delicate darling!
  And the Voices have ceased from their strife:
Not a whisper of sneering or snarling,
  As he carries it home to his wife:
Then, cheerily champing the bunlet
  His spouse was so skilful to bake,
He hies him once more to the runlet,
    To fetch her the Drake!

"He's sound asleep now," said Sylvie, carefully tucking in the edge of a violet-leaf, which she had been spreading over him as a sort of blanket: "good night!"

"Good night!" I echoed.

"You may well say 'good night'!" laughed Lady Muriel, rising and shutting up the piano as she spoke. "When you've been nid—nid—nodding all the time I've been singing for your benefit! What was it all about, now?" she demanded imperiously.

"Something about a duck?" I hazarded. "Well, a bird of some kind?" I corrected myself, perceiving at once that *that* guess was wrong, at any rate.

"*Something about a bird of some kind!*" Lady Muriel repeated, with as much withering scorn as her sweet face was capable of conveying. "And that's the way he speaks of Shelley's Sky-Lark, is it? When the Poet particularly says '*Hail to thee, blithe spirit! Bird thou never wert!*'"

She led the way to the smoking-room, where, ignoring all the usages of Society and all the instincts of Chivalry, the three Lords of the Creation reposed at their ease in low rocking-chairs, and permitted the one lady who was present to glide gracefully about among us, supplying our wants in the form of cooling drinks, cigarettes, and lights. Nay, it was only *one* of the three who had the chivalry to go beyond the common-place "thank you", and to quote the Poet's exquisite description of how Geraint, when waited on by Enid, was moved

> *"To stoop and kiss the tender little thumb*
> *That crossed the platter as she laid it down,"*

and to suit the action to the word—an audacious liberty for which, I feel bound to report, he was *not* duly reprimanded.

As no topic of conversation seemed to occur to any one, and as we were, all four, on those delightful terms with one another (the only terms, I think, on which any friendship, that deserves the name of *intimacy*, can be maintained) which involve no sort of necessity for *speaking* for mere speaking's sake, we sat in silence for some minutes.

At length I broke the silence by asking "Is there any fresh news from the harbour about the Fever?"

"None since this morning," the Earl said, looking very grave. "But that was alarming enough. The Fever is spreading fast: the London doctor has taken fright and left the place, and the only one now available isn't a regular doctor at all: he is apothecary, and doctor, and dentist, and I don't know what other trades, all in one. It's a bad outlook for those poor fishermen—and a worse one for all the women and children."

"How many are there of them altogether?" Arthur asked.

"There were nearly one hundred, a week ago," said the Earl: "but there have been twenty or thirty deaths since then."

"And what religious ministrations are there to be had?"

"There are three brave men down there," the Earl replied, his voice trembling with emotion, "gallant heroes as ever won the Victoria Cross! I am certain that no one of the three will ever leave the place merely to save his own life. There's the Curate: his wife is with him: they have no children. Then there's the Roman Catholic Priest. And there's the Wesleyan Minister. They go amongst their own flocks mostly; but I'm told that those who are dying like to have *any* of the three with them. How slight the barriers seem to be that part Christian from Christian, when one has to deal with the great facts of Life and the reality of Death!"

"So it must be, and so it should be——" Arthur was beginning, when the front-door bell rang, suddenly and violently.

We heard the front-door hastily opened, and voices outside: then a knock at the door of the smoking-room, and the old house-keeper appeared, looking a little scared.

"Two persons, my Lord, to speak with Dr. Forester."

Arthur stepped outside at once, and we heard his cheery "Well, my men?" but the answer was less audible, the only words I could distinctly catch being "ten since morning, and two more just——"

"But there *is* a doctor there?" we heard Arthur say: and a deep voice, that we had not heard before, replied "Dead, Sir. Died three hours ago."

Lady Muriel shuddered, and hid her face in her hands: but at this moment the front-door was quietly closed, and we heard no more.

For a few minutes we sat quite silent: then the Earl left the room, and soon returned to tell us that Arthur had gone away with the two fishermen, leaving word that he would be back in about an hour. And, true enough, at the end of that interval—during which very little was said, none of us seeming to have the heart to talk—the front-door once more creaked on its rusty hinges, and a step was heard in the passage, hardly to be recognized as Arthur's, so slow and uncertain was it, like a blind man feeling his way.

He came in, and stood before Lady Muriel, resting one hand heavily on the table, and with a strange look in his eyes, as if he were walking in his sleep.

"Muriel—my love——" he paused, and his lips quivered: but after a minute he went on more steadily.

"Muriel—my darling—they—*want* me—down in the harbour."

"*Must* you go?" she pleaded, rising and laying her hands on his shoulders, and looking up into his face with her great eyes brimming over with tears. "Must *you* go, Arthur? It may mean—death!"

He met her gaze without flinching. "It *does* mean death," he said, in a husky whisper: "but—darling—I am *called*. And even my life itself——" His voice failed him, and he said no more.

For a minute she stood quite silent, looking upwards with a helpless gaze, as if even prayer were now useless, while her features worked and quivered with the great agony she was enduring. Then a sudden inspiration seemed to come upon her and light up her face with a strange sweet smile. "*Your* life?" she repeated. "It is not *yours* to give!"

Arthur had recovered himself by this time, and could reply quite firmly, "That is true," he said. "It is not *mine* to give. It is *yours*, now, my—wife that is to be! And you —do *you* forbid me to go? Will you not spare me, my own beloved one?"

Still clinging to him, she laid her head softly on his breast. She had never done such a thing in my presence before, and I knew how deeply she must be moved. "I *will* spare you", she said, calmly and quietly, "to God."

"And to God's poor," he whispered.

"And to God's poor," she added. "When must it be, sweet love?"

"To-morrow morning," he replied. "And I have much to do before then."

And then he told us how he had spent his hour of absence. He had been to the Vicarage, and had arranged for the wedding to take place at eight the next morning (there was no legal obstacle, as he had, some time before this, obtained a Special Licence) in the little church we knew so well. "My old friend here", indicating me, "will act as 'Best Man', I know: your father will be there to give you away: and—and—you will dispense with bride's-maids, my darling?"

She nodded: no words came.

"And then I can go with a willing heart—to do God's work—knowing that we are *one*—and that we are together in *spirit*, though not in bodily presence—and are most of all together when we pray! Our *prayers* will go up together——"

"Yes, yes!" sobbed Lady Muriel. "But you must not stay longer now, my darling! Go home and take some rest. You will need all your strength to-morrow——"

"Well, I will go," said Arthur. "We will be here in good time to-morrow. Good night, my own own darling!"

I followed his example, and we two left the house together. As we walked back to our lodgings, Arthur sighed deeply once or twice, and seemed about to speak— but no words came, till we had entered the house, and had lit our candles, and were at our bedroom-doors. Then Arthur said "Good night, old fellow! God bless you!"

"God bless you!" I echoed from the very depths of my heart.

We were back again at the Hall by eight in the morning, and found Lady Muriel and the Earl, and the old Vicar, waiting for us. It was a strangely sad and silent party that walked up to the little church and back; and I could not help feeling that it was much more like a funeral than a wedding: to Lady Muriel it *was* in fact, a funeral rather than a wedding, so heavily did the presentiment weigh upon her (as she told us afterwards) that her newly-won husband was going forth to his death.

Then we had breakfast; and, all too soon, the vehicle was at the door, which was to convey Arthur, first to his lodgings, to pick up the things he was taking with him, and then as far towards the death-stricken hamlet as it was considered safe to go. One or two of the fishermen were to meet him on the road, to carry his things the rest of the way.

"And are you quite sure you are taking all that you will need?" Lady Muriel asked.

"All that I shall need as a *doctor*, certainly. And my own personal needs are few: I shall not even take any of my own wardrobe—there is a fisherman's suit, ready-made, that is waiting for me at my lodgings. I shall only take my watch, and a few books, and—stay—there *is* one book I should like to add, a pocket-Testament—to use at the bedsides of the sick and dying——"

"Take mine!" said Lady Muriel: and she ran upstairs to fetch it. "It has nothing written in it but 'Muriel'," she said as she returned with it: "shall I inscribe——"

"No, my own one," said Arthur, taking it from her. "What *could* you inscribe better than that? Could any human name mark it more clearly as my own individual property? Are *you* not mine? Are you not," (with all the old playfulness of manner) "as Bruno would say, 'my *very mine*'?"

He bade a long and loving adieu to the Earl and to me, and left the room, accompanied only by his wife, who was bearing up bravely, and was—*outwardly*, at least—less overcome than her old father. We waited in the room a minute or two, till the sounds of wheels had told us that Arthur had driven away; and even then we waited still, for the step of Lady Muriel, going upstairs to her room, to die away in the distance. Her step, usually so light and joyous, now sounded slow and weary, like one who plods on under a load of hopeless misery; and I felt almost as hopeless, and almost as wretched as she. "Are we four destined *ever* to meet again, on this side the grave?" I asked myself, as I walked to my home. And the tolling of a distant bell seemed to answer me, "No! No! No!"

Chapter XVIII

A Newspaper-Cutting

EXTRACT FROM THE "FAYFIELD CHRONICLE"

Our readers will have followed with painful interest, the accounts we have from time to time published of the terrible epidemic which has, during the last two months, carried off most of the inhabitants of the little fishing-harbour adjoining the village of Elveston. The last survivors, numbering twenty-three only, out of a population which, three short months ago, exceeded one hundred and twenty, were removed on Wednesday last, under the authority of the Local Board, and safely lodged in the County Hospital: and the place is now veritably "a city of the dead", without a single human voice to break its silence.

The rescuing party consisted of six sturdy fellows—fishermen from the neighbourhood—directed by the resident Physician of the Hospital, who came over for that purpose, heading a train of hospital-ambulances. The six men had been selected—from a much larger number who had volunteered for this peaceful "forlorn hope"—for their strength and robust health, as the expedition was considered to be, even now, when the malady has expended its chief force, not unattended with danger.

Every precaution that science could suggest, against the risk of infection, was adopted: and the sufferers were tenderly carried on litters, one by one, up the steep hill, and placed in the ambulances which, each provided with a hospital nurse, were waiting on the level road. The fifteen miles, to the Hospital, were done at a walking-pace, as some of the patients were in too prostrate a condition to bear jolting, and the journey occupied the whole afternoon.

The twenty-three patients consist of nine men, six women, and eight children. It has not been found possible to identify them all, as some of the children—left with no surviving relatives—are infants: and two men and one woman are not yet able to make rational replies, the brain-powers being entirely in abeyance. Among a more well-to-do race, there would no doubt have been names marked on the clothes; but here no such evidence is forthcoming.

Besides the poor fishermen and their families, there were but five persons to be accounted for: and it was ascertained, beyond

613

a doubt, that all five are numbered with the dead. It is a melancholy pleasure to place on record the names of these genuine martyrs—than whom none, surely, are more worthy to be entered on the glory-roll of England's heroes! They are as follows:

The Rev. James Burgess, M.A., and Emma his wife. He was the Curate at the Harbour, not thirty years old, and had been married only two years. A written record was found in their house, of the dates of their deaths.

Next to theirs we will place the honoured named of Dr. Arthur Forester, who, on the death of the local physician, nobly faced the imminent peril of death, rather than leave these poor folk uncared for in their last extremity. No record of his name, or of the date of his death, was found: but the corpse was easily identified, although dressed in the ordinary fisherman's suit (which he was known to have adopted when he went down there), by a copy of the New Testament, the gift of his wife, which was found, placed next his heart, with his hands crossed over it. It was not thought prudent to remove the body, for burial elsewhere: and accordingly it was at once committed to the ground, along with four others found in different houses, with all due reverence. His wife, whose maiden name was Lady Muriel Orme, had been married to him on the very morning on which he undertook his self-sacrificing mission.

Next we record the Rev. Walter Saunders, Wesleyan Minister. His death is believed to have taken place two or three weeks·ago, as the words "Died October 5" were found written on the wall of the room which he is known to have occupied—the house being shut up, and apparently not having been entered for some time.

Last—though not a whit behind the other four in glorious self-denial and devotion to duty—let us record the name of Father Francis, a young Jesuit Priest who had been only a few months in the place. He had not been dead many hours when the exploring party came upon the body, which was identified, beyond the possibility of doubt, by the dress, and by the crucifix which was, like the young Doctor's Testament, clasped closely to his heart.

Since reaching the hospital, two of the men and one of the children have died. Hope is entertained for all the others: though there are two or three cases where the vital powers seem to be so entirely exhausted that it is but "hoping against hope" to regard ultimate recovery as even possible.

Chapter XIX

A Fairy-Duet

THE year—what an eventful year it had been for me!—
was drawing to a close, and the brief wintry day hardly
gave light enough to recognize the old familiar objects,
bound up with so many happy memories, as the train
glided round the last bend into the station, and the hoarse
cry of "Elveston! Elveston!" resounded along the platform.

It was sad to return to the place, and to feel that I
should never again see the glad smile of welcome, that
had awaited me here so few months ago. "And yet, if I
were to find him here," I muttered, as in solitary state I
followed the porter, who was wheeling my luggage on a
barrow, "and if he *were* to '*strike a sudden hand in mine,
And ask a thousand things of home,*' I should not—no, '*I
should not feel it to be strange*'!"

Having given directions to have my luggage taken to
my old lodgings, I strolled off alone, to pay a visit, before
settling down in my own quarters, to my dear old friends
—for such I indeed felt them to be, though it was barely
half a year since first we met—the Earl and his widowed
daughter.

The shortest way, as I well remembered, was to cross
through the churchyard. I pushed open the little wicket-
gate and slowly took my way among the solemn mem-
orials of the quiet dead, thinking of the many who had,
during the past year, disappeared from the place, and had
gone to "join the majority". A very few steps brought me
in sight of the object of my search. Lady Muriel, dressed
in the deepest mourning, her face hidden by a long crape
veil, was kneeling before a little marble cross, round
which she was fastening a wreath of flowers.

The cross stood on a piece of level turf, unbroken by
any mound, and I knew that it was simply a memorial-

615

cross, for one whose dust reposed elsewhere, even before reading the simple inscription:

In loving Memory of
ARTHUR FORESTER, M.D.
whose mortal remains lie buried by the sea:
whose spirit has returned to God who gave it.

———

"GREATER LOVE HATH NO MAN THAN THIS, THAT
A MAN LAY DOWN HIS LIFE FOR HIS FRIENDS."

She threw back her veil on seeing me approach, and came forwards to meet me, with a quiet smile, and far more self-possessed than I could have expected.

"It is quite like old times, seeing *you* here again!" she said, in tones of genuine pleasure. "Have you been to see my father?"

"No," I said: "I was on my way there, and came through here as the shortest way. I hope he is well, and you also?"

"Thanks, we are both quite well. And you? Are you any better yet?"

"Not much better, I fear: but no worse, I am thankful to say."

"Let us sit here awhile, and have a quiet chat," she said. The calmness—almost indifference—of her manner quite took me by surprise. I little guessed what a fierce restraint she was putting upon herself.

"One can be so quiet here," she resumed. "I come here every—every day."

"It is very peaceful," I said.

"You got my letter?"

"Yes, but I delayed writing. It is so hard to say—on *paper*——"

"I know. It was kind of you. You were with us when we saw the last of——" She paused a moment, and went on more hurriedly. "I went down to the harbour several times, but no one knows which of those vast graves it is. However, they showed me the house he died in: that was

some comfort. I stood in the very room where—where——"
She struggled in vain to go on. The flood-gates had given
way at last, and the outburst of grief was the most terrible I had ever witnessed. Totally regardless of my presence, she flung herself down on the turf, burying her face
in the grass, and with her hands clasped round the little
marble cross. "Oh, my darling, my darling!" she sobbed.
"And God meant your life to be so beautiful!"

I was startled to hear, thus repeated by Lady Muriel,
the very words of the darling child whom I had seen
weeping so bitterly over the dead hare. Had some mysterious influence passed, from that sweet fairy-spirit, ere she
went back to Fairyland, into the human spirit that loved
her so dearly? The idea seemed too wild for belief. And
yet, are there not "*more things in heaven and earth than are
dreamt of in our philosophy*"?

"God *meant* it to be beautiful," I whispered, "and surely it *was* beautiful? God's purpose never fails!" I dared
say no more, but rose and left her. At the entrance-gate
to the Earl's house I waited, leaning on the gate and
watching the sun set, revolving many memories—some
happy, some sorrowful—until Lady Muriel joined me.

She was quite calm again now. "Do come in," she said.
"My father will be so pleased to see you!"

The old man rose from his chair, with a smile, to welcome me; but his self-command was far less than his
daughter's, and the tears coursed down his face as he
grasped both my hands in his, and pressed them warmly.

My heart was too full to speak; and we all sat silent for
a minute or two. Then Lady Muriel rang the bell for tea.
"You *do* take five o'clock tea, I know!" she said to me,
with the sweet playfulness of manner I remembered so
well, "even though you *ca'n't* work your wicked will on
the Law of Gravity, and make the teacups descend into
Infinite Space, a little faster than the tea!"

This remark gave the tone to our conversation. By a
tacit mutual consent, we avoided, during this our first
meeting after her great sorrow, the painful topics that

filled our thoughts, and talked like light-hearted children who had never known a care.

"Did you ever ask yourself the question," Lady Muriel began, *à propos* of nothing, "what is the *chief* advantage of being a Man instead of a Dog?"

"No, indeed," I said: "but I think there are advantages on the *Dog's* side of the question as well.

"No doubt," she replied, with that pretty mock-gravity that became her so well: "but, on *Man's* side, the chief advantage seems to me to consist in *having pockets*! It was borne in upon me—upon *us*, I should say; for my father and I were returning from a walk—only yesterday. We met a dog carrying home a bone. What it wanted it for, I've no idea: certainly there was no *meat* on it——"

A strange sensation came over me, that I had heard all this, or something exactly like it, before: and I almost expected her next words to be "perhaps he meant to make a cloak for the winter?" However what she really said was "and my father tried to account for it by some wretched joke about *pro bono publico*. Well, the dog laid down the bone—*not* in disgust with the pun, which would have shown it to be a dog of taste—but simply to rest its jaws, poor thing! I *did* pity it so! Won't you join my *Charitable Association for supplying dogs with pockets?* How would *you* like to have to carry your walking-stick in your mouth?"

Ignoring the difficult question as to the *raison d'être* of a walking-stick, supposing one had no *hands*, I mentioned a curious instance, I had once witnessed, of reasoning by a dog. A gentleman, with a lady, and child, and a large dog, were down at the end of a pier on which I was walking. To amuse his child, I suppose, the gentleman put down on the ground his umbrella and the lady's parasol, and then led the way to the other end of the pier, from which he sent the dog back for the deserted articles. I was watching with some curiosity. The dog came racing back to where I stood, but found an unexpected difficulty in picking up the things it had come for. With the umbrella in its mouth, its jaws were so far apart that it could get no firm grip on the parasol. After two or three failures, it paused and considered the matter.

Then it put down the umbrella and began with the parasol. Of course that didn't open its jaws nearly so wide, and it was able to get a good hold of the umbrella, and galloped off in triumph. One couldn't doubt that it had gone through a real train of logical thought.

"I entirely agree with you," said Lady Muriel: "but don't orthodox writers condemn that view, as putting Man on the level of the lower animals? Don't they draw a sharp boundary-line between Reason and Instinct?"

"That certainly *was* the orthodox view, a generation ago," said the Earl. "The truth of Religion seemed ready to stand or fall with the assertion that Man was the only reasoning animal. But that is at an end now. Man can still claim *certain* monopolies—for instance, such a use of *language* as enables us to utilize the work of many, by 'division of labour'. But the belief, that we have a monopoly of *Reason*, has long been swept away. Yet no catastrophe has followed. As some old poet says, '*God is where he was*'."

"Most religious believers would *now* agree with Bishop Butler," said I, "and not reject a line of argument, even if it led straight to the conclusion that animals have some kind of *soul*, which survives their bodily death."

"I *would* like to know *that* to be true!" Lady Muriel exclaimed. "If only for the sake of the poor horses. Sometimes I've thought that, if anything *could* make me cease to believe in a God of perfect justice, it would be the sufferings of horses—without guilt to deserve it, and without any compensation!"

"It is only part of the great Riddle," said the Earl, "why innocent beings *ever* suffer. It *is* a great strain on Faith—but not a *breaking* strain, I think."

"The sufferings of *horses*", I said, "are chiefly caused by *Man's* cruelty. So *that* is merely one of the many instances of Sin causing suffering to others than the Sinner himself. But don't you find a greater difficulty in sufferings inflicted by animals upon each other? For instance, a cat playing with a mouse. Assuming it to have no *moral* responsibility, isn't that a greater mystery than a man over-driving a horse?"

"I think it *is*," said Lady Muriel, looking a mute appeal to her father.

"What right have we to make that assumption?" said the Earl. *"Many* of our religious difficulties are merely deductions from unwarranted assumptions. The wisest answer to most of them, is, I think, *'behold, we know not anything'."*

"You mentioned 'division of labour', just now," I said. "Surely it is carried to a wonderful perfection in a hive of bees?"

"So wonderful—so entirely super-human—" said the Earl, "and so entirely inconsistent with the intelligence they show in other ways—that I feel no doubt at all that it is *pure* Instinct, and *not*, as some hold, a very high order of Reason. Look at the utter stupidity of a bee, trying to find its way out of an open window! It *doesn't* try, in any reasonable sense of the word: it simply bangs itself about! We should call a puppy *imbecile*, that behaved so. And yet we are asked to believe that its intellectual level is above Sir Isaac Newton!"

"Then you hold that *pure* Instinct contains no *Reason* at all?"

"On the contrary," said the Earl, "I hold that the work of a bee-hive involves Reason of the *highest* order. But none of it is done by the *Bee*. *God* has reasoned it all out, and has put into the mind of the Bee the *conclusions*, only, of the reasoning process."

"But how do their minds come to work *together*?" I asked.

"What right have we to assume that they *have* minds?"

"Special pleading, special pleading!" Lady Muriel cried, in a most unfilial tone of triumph. "Why, you yourself said, just now, 'the mind of the Bee'!"

"But I did *not* say *'minds'*, my child," the Earl gently replied. "It has occurred to me, as the most probable solution of the 'Bee'-mystery, that a swarm of Bees *have only one mind among them*. We often see one mind animating a most complex collection of limbs and organs, *when joined together*. How do we know that any material connection is necessary? May not mere neighbourhood be enough? If so, a swarm of bees is simply a single animal whose many limbs are not quite close together!"

"It is a bewildering thought," I said, "and needs a night's rest to grasp it properly. Reason and Instinct *both* tell me I ought to go home. So, good-night!"

"I'll 'set' you part of the way," said Lady Muriel. "I've had no walk to-day. It will do me good, and I have more to say to you. Shall we go through the wood? It will be pleasanter than over the common, even though it *is* getting a little dark."

We turned aside into the shade of interlacing boughs, which formed an architecture of almost perfect symmetry, grouped into lovely groined arches, or running out, far as the eye could follow, into endless aisles, and chancels, and naves, like some ghostly cathedral, fashioned out of the dream of a moon-struck poet.

"Always, in this wood," she began after a pause (silence seemed natural in this dim solitude), "I begin thinking of Fairies! May I ask you a question?" she added hesitatingly. "Do you believe in Fairies?"

The momentary impulse was so strong to tell her of my experiences in this very wood, that I had to make a real effort to keep back the words that rushed to my lips. "If you mean, by 'believe', 'believe in their *possible* existence', I say 'Yes'. For their *actual existence*, of course, one would need *evidence*."

"You were saying, the other day", she went on, "that you would accept *anything*, on good evidence, that was not *à priori* impossible. And I think you named *Ghosts* as an instance of a *provable* phenomenon. Would *Fairies* be another instance?"

"Yes, I think so." And again it was hard to check the wish to say more: but I was not yet sure of a sympathetic listener.

"And have you any theory as to what sort of place they would occupy in Creation? Do tell me what you think about them! Would they, for instance (supposing such beings to exist), would they have any moral responsibility? I mean" (and the light bantering tone suddenly changed to one of deep seriousness) "would they be capable of *sin*?"

"They can reason—on a lower level, perhaps, than men and women—never rising, I think, above the faculties of a child; and they have a moral sense, most surely. Such a being, without *free will*, would be an absurdity. So I am driven to the conclusion that they *are* capable of sin."

"You believe in them?" she cried delightedly, with a sudden motion as if about to clap her hands. "Now tell me, have you any reason for it?"

And still I strove to keep back the revelation I felt sure was coming. "I believe that there is *life* everywhere—not *material* only, not merely what is palpable to our senses—but immaterial and invisible as well. We believe in our own immaterial essence—call it 'soul', or 'spirit', or what you will. Why should not other similar essences exist around us, *not* linked on to a visible and *material* body? Did not God make this swarm of happy insects, to dance in this sunbeam for one hour of bliss, for no other object, that we can imagine, than to swell the sum of conscious happiness? And where shall we dare to draw the line, and say 'He has made all these and no more'?"

"Yes, yes"! she assented, watching me with sparkling eyes. "But these are only reasons for not *denying*. You have more reasons than this, have you not?"

"Well, yes," I said, feeling I might safely tell all now. "And I could not find a fitter time or place to say it. I have *seen* them—and in this very wood!"

Lady Muriel asked no more questions. Silently she paced at my side, with head bowed down and hands clasped tightly together. Only, as my tale went on, she drew a little short quick breath now and then, like a child panting with delight. And I told her what I had never yet breathed to any other listener, of my double life, and, more than that (for *mine* might have been but a noonday-dream), of the double life of those two dear children.

And when I told her of Bruno's wild gambols, she laughed merrily; and when I spoke of Sylvie's sweetness and her utter unselfishness and trustful love, she drew a deep breath, like one who hears at last some precious tidings for which the heart has ached for a long while; and the happy tears chased one another down her cheeks.

"I have often longed to meet an angel," she whispered, so low that I could hardly catch the words. "I'm *so* glad I've seen Sylvie! My heart went out to the child the first moment that I saw her—Listen!" she broke off suddenly. "That's Sylvie singing! I'm sure of it! Don't you know her voice?"

"I have heard *Bruno* sing, more than once," I said: "but I never heard Sylvie."

"I have only heard her *once*," said Lady Muriel. "It was that day when you brought us those mysterious flowers. The children had run out into the garden; and I saw Eric coming in that way, and went to the window to meet him: and Sylvie was singing, under the trees, a song I had never heard before. The words were something like 'I think it is Love, I feel it is Love'. Her voice sounded far away, like a dream, but it was beautiful beyond all words—as sweet as an infant's first smile, or the first gleam of the white cliffs when one is coming *home* after weary years—a voice that seemed to fill one's whole being with peace and heavenly thoughts—Listen!" she cried, breaking off again in her excitement. "That *is* her voice, and that's the very song!"

I could distinguish no words, but there was a dreamy sense of music in the air that seemed to grow ever louder and louder, as if coming nearer to us. We stood quite silent, and in another minute the two children appeared, coming straight towards us through an arched opening among the trees. Each had an arm round the other, and the setting sun shed a golden halo round their heads, like what one sees in pictures of saints. They were looking in our direction, but evidently did not see us, and I soon made out that Lady Muriel had for once passed into a condition familiar to *me*, that we were both of us "eerie", and that, though we could see the children so plainly, we were quite invisible to *them*.

The song ceased just as they came into sight: but, to my delight, Bruno instantly said "Let's sing it all again, Sylvie! It *did* sound so pretty!" And Sylvie replied "Very well. It's *you* to begin, you know."

So Bruno began, in the sweet childish treble I knew so well:

"Say, what is the spell, when her fledgelings are cheeping,
*   That lures the bird home to her nest?*
Or wakes the tired mother, whose infant is weeping,
*   To cuddle and croon it to rest?*
What's the magic that charms the glad babe in her arms,
*   Till it cooes with the voice of the dove?"*

And now ensued quite the strangest of all the strange experiences that marked the wonderful year whose history I am writing—the experience of *first* hearing Sylvie's voice in song. Her part was a very short one—only a few words—and she sang it timidly, and very low indeed, scarcely audibly, but the *sweetness* of her voice was simply indescribable; I have never heard any earthly music like it.

" 'Tis a secret, and so let us whisper it low—
*   And the name of the secret is Love!"*

On me the first effect of her voice was a sudden sharp pang that seemed to pierce through one's very heart. (I had felt such a pang only once before in my life, and it had been from *seeing* what, at the moment, realized one's idea of perfect beauty—it was in a London exhibition, where, in making my way through a crowd, I suddenly met, face to face, a child of quite unearthly beauty.) Then came a rush of burning tears to the eyes, as though one could weep one's soul away for pure delight. And lastly there fell on me a sense of awe that was almost terror—some such feeling as Moses must have had when he heard the words *"Put off thy shoes from off thy feet, for the place whereon thou standest is holy ground"*. The figures of the children became vague and shadowy, like glimmering meteors: while their voices rang together in exquisite harmony as they sang:

> *"For I think it is Love,*
> *For I feel it is Love,*
> *For I'm sure it is nothing but Love!"*

By this time I could see them clearly once more. Bruno again sang by himself:

> *"Say, whence is the voice that, when anger is burning,*
> *Bids the whirl of the tempest to cease?*
> *That stirs the vexed soul with an aching—a yearning*
> *For the brotherly hand-grip of peace?*
> *Whence the music that fills all our being—that thrills*
> *Around us, beneath, and above?"*

Sylvie sang more courageously, this time: the words seemed to carry her away, out of herself:

> *" 'Tis a secret: none knows how it comes, how it goes:*
> *But the name of the secret is Love!"*

And clear and strong the chorus rang out:

> *"For I think it is Love,*
> *For I feel it is Love,*
> *For I'm sure it is nothing but Love!"*

Once more we heard Bruno's delicate little voice alone:

"Say whose is the skill that paints valley and hill,
Like a picture so fair to the sight?
That flecks the green meadow with sunshine and shadow,
Till the little lambs leap with delight?"

And again uprose that silvery voice, whose angelic sweetness I could hardly bear:

" 'Tis a secret untold to hearts cruel and cold,
Though 'tis sung, by the angels above,
In notes that ring clear for the ears that can hear—
And the name of the secret is Love!"

And then Bruno joined in again with

"For I think it is Love,
For I feel it is Love,
For I'm sure it is nothing but Love!"

"That *are* pretty!" the little fellow exclaimed, as the children passed us—so closely that we drew back a little to make room for them, and it seemed we had only to reach out a hand to touch them: but this we did not attempt.

"No use to try and stop them!" I said, as they passed away into the shadows. "Why, they could not even *see* us!"

"No use at all," Lady Muriel echoed with a sigh. "One would *like* to meet them again, in living form! But I feel, somehow, *that* can never be. They have passed out of *our* lives!" She sighed again; and no more was said, till we came out into the main road, at a point near my lodgings.

"Well, I will leave you here," she said. "I want to get back before dark: and I have a cottage-friend to visit, first. Good night, dear friend! Let us see you soon—and often!" she added, with an affectionate warmth that went to my very heart. *"For those are few we hold as dear!"*

"Good night!" I answered. "Tennyson said that of a worthier friend than me."

"Tennyson didn't know what he was talking about!" she saucily rejoined, with a touch of her old childish gaiety; and we parted.

Chapter XX

Gammon and Spinach

My landlady's welcome had an extra heartiness about it: and though, with a rare delicacy of feeling, she made no direct allusion to the friend whose companionship had done so much to brighten life for me, I felt sure that it was a kindly sympathy with my solitary state that made her so specially anxious to do all she could think of to ensure my comfort, and make me feel at home.

The lonely evening seemed long and tedious: yet I lingered on, watching the dying fire, and letting Fancy mould the red embers into the forms and faces belonging to bygone scenes. Now it seemed to be Bruno's roguish smile that sparkled for a moment, and died away: now it was Sylvie's rosy cheek: and now the Professor's jolly round face, beaming with delight. "You're welcome, my little ones!" he seemed to say. And then the red coal, which for the moment embodied the dear old Professor, began to wax dim, and with its dying lustre the words seemed to die away into silence. I seized the poker, and with an artful touch or two revived the waning glow, while Fancy—no coy minstrel she—sang me once again the magic strain I loved to hear.

"You're welcome, little ones!" the cheery voice repeated. "I told them you were coming. Your rooms are all ready for you. And the Emperor and the Empress— well, I think they're rather pleased than otherwise! In fact, Her Highness said 'I hope they'll be in time for the Banquet!' Those were her very words, I assure you!"

"Will Uggug be at the Banquet?" Bruno asked. And both children looked uneasy at the dismal suggestion.

"Why, of course he will!" chuckled the Professor. "Why, it's his *birthday*, don't you know? And his health will be drunk, and all that sort of thing. What would the Banquet be without *him*?"

"Ever so much nicer," said Bruno. But he said it in a *very* low voice, and nobody but Sylvie heard him.

The Professor chuckled again. "It'll be a jolly Banquet, now *you've* come, my little man! I *am* so glad to see you again!"

"I 'fraid we've been very long in coming," Bruno politely remarked.

"Well, yes," the Professor assented. "However, you're very short, now you're come: that's *some* comfort." And he went on to enumerate the plans for the day. "The Lecture comes first," he said. "*That* the Empress *insists* on. She says people will eat so much at the Banquet, they'll be too sleepy to attend to the Lecture afterwards— and perhaps she's right. There'll just be a little *refreshment*, when the people first arrive—as a kind of surprise for the Empress, you know. Ever since she's been—well, not *quite so* clever as she once was—we've found it desirable to concoct little surprises for her. *Then* comes the Lecture——"

"What? The Lecture you were getting ready—ever so long ago?" Sylvie enquired.

"Yes—that's the one," the Professor rather reluctantly admitted. "It *has* taken a goodish time to prepare. I've got so many other things to attend to. For instance, I'm Court-Physician. I have to keep all the Royal Servants in good health—and that reminds me!" he cried, ringing the bell in a great hurry. "This is Medicine-Day! We only give Medicine once a week. If we were to begin giving it every day, the bottles would *soon* be empty!"

"But if they were ill on the *other* days?" Sylvie suggested.

"What, ill on the wrong *day*!" exclaimed the Professor.

"Oh, that would never do! A Servant would be dismissed *at once*, who was ill on the wrong day! This is the Medicine for *to-day*," he went on, taking down a large jug from a shelf. "I mixed it, myself, first thing this morning. Taste it!" he said, holding out the jug to Bruno. "Dip in your finger, and taste it!"

Bruno did so, and made such an excruciatingly wry face that Sylvie exclaimed in alarm, "Oh, Bruno, you mustn't!"

"It's welly extremely nasty!" Bruno said, as his face resumed its natural shape.

"Nasty?" said the Professor. "Why, of *course* it is! What would Medicine be, if it wasn't *nasty*?"

"Nice," said Bruno.

"I was going to say—" the Professor faltered, rather taken aback by the promptness of Bruno's reply, "—that *that* would never do! Medicine *has* to be nasty, you know. Be good enough to take this jug, down into the Servants' Hall," he said to the footman who answered the bell: "and tell them it's their Medicine for *to-day*."

"Which of them is to drink it?" the footman asked, as he carried off the jug.

"Oh, I've not settled *that* yet!" the Professor briskly replied. "I'll come and settle that, soon. Tell them not to begin, on any account, till I come! It's really *wonderful*", he said, turning to the children, "the success I've had in curing Diseases! Here are some of my memoranda." He took down from the shelf a heap of little bits of paper, pinned together in twos and threes. "Just look at *this* set, now. '*Under-Cook Number Thirteen recovered from Common Fever—Febris Communis*.' And now see what's pinned to it. '*Gave Under-Cook Number Thirteen a Double Dose of Medicine*.' *That's* something to be proud of, *isn't* it?"

"But which happened *first*?" said Sylvie, looking very much puzzled.

The Professor examined the papers carefully. "They are not *dated*, I find," he said with a slightly dejected air: "so I fear I ca'n't tell you. But they *both* happened: there's no doubt of *that*. The *Medicine's* the great thing, you know. The *Diseases* are much less important. You can keep a *Medicine*, for years and years: but nobody ever wants to keep a *Disease*! By the way, come and look at the platform. The Gardener asked me to come and see if it would do. We may as well go before it gets dark."

"We'd like to, very much!" Sylvie replied. "Come, Bruno, put on your hat. Don't keep the dear Professor waiting!"

"Ca'n't find my hat!" the little fellow sadly replied. "I were rolling it about. And it's rolled itself away!"

"Maybe it's rolled in *there*," Sylvie suggested, pointing to a dark recess, the door of which stood half open: and Bruno ran in to look. After a minute he came slowly out again, looking very grave, and carefully shut the cupboard door after him.

"It aren't in there," he said, with such unusual solemnity, that Sylvie's curiosity was aroused.

"What *is* in there, Bruno?"

"There's cobwebs—and two spiders—" Bruno thoughtfully replied, checking off the catalogue on his fingers, "—and the cover of a picture-book—and a tortoise—and a dish of nuts—and an old man."

"An old man!" cried the Professor, trotting across the room in great excitement. "Why, it must be the Other Professor, that's been lost for ever so long!"

He opened the door of the cupboard wide: and there he was, the Other Professor, sitting in a chair, with a book on his knee, and in the act of helping himself to a nut from a dish, which he had taken down off a shelf just within his reach. He looked round at us, but said nothing till he had cracked and eaten the nut. Then he asked the old question. "Is the Lecture all ready?"

"It'll begin in an hour," the Professor said, evading the question. "First, we must have something to surprise the Empress. And then comes the Banquet——"

"The Banquet!" cried the Other Professor, springing up, and filling the room with a cloud of dust. Then I'd better go and—and brush myself a little. What a state I'm in!"

"He *does* want brushing!" the Professor said, with a critical air. "Here's your hat, little man! I had put it on by mistake. I'd quite forgotten I had *one* on, already. Let's go and look at the platform."

"And there's that nice old Gardener singing still!" Bruno exclaimed in delight, as we went out into the garden. "I do believe he's been singing that very song ever since we went away!"

"Why, of course he has!" replied the Professor. "It wouldn't be the thing to leave off, you know."

"Wouldn't be *what* thing?" said Bruno: but the Professor thought it best not to hear the question. "What are you doing with that hedgehog?" he shouted at the Gardener, whom they found standing upon one foot, singing softly to himself, and rolling a hedgehog up and down with the other foot.

"Well, I wanted fur to know what hedgehogs lives on: so I be a-keeping this here hedgehog—fur to see if it eats potatoes——"

"Much better keep a potato," said the Professor; "and see if hedgehogs eat it!"

"That be the roight way, sure-ly!" the delighted Gardener exclaimed. "Be you come to see the platform?"

"Aye, aye!" the Professor cheerily replied. "And the children have come back, you see!"

The Gardener looked round at them with a grin. Then he led the way to the Pavilion; and as he went he sang:

> "*He looked again, and found it was*
> *A Double Rule of Three:*
> '*And all its Mystery*', *he said,*
> '*Is clear as day to me!*' "

"You've been *months* over that song," said the Professor. "Isn't it finished yet?"

"There be only one verse more," the Gardener sadly replied. And, with tears streaming down his cheeks, he sang the last verse:

> "*He thought he saw an Argument*
> *That proved he was the Pope:*
> *He looked again, and found it was*
> *A Bar of Mottled Soap.*
> '*A fact so dread*', *he faintly said*,
> '*Extinguishes all hope!*' "

Choking with sobs, the Gardener hastily stepped on a few yards ahead of the party, to conceal his emotion.

"Did *he* see the Bar of Mottled Soap?" Sylvie enquired, as we followed.

"Oh, certainly!" said the Professor. "That song is his own history, you know."

Tears of an ever-ready sympathy glittered in Bruno's eyes. "I's *welly* sorry he isn't the Pope!" he said. "Aren't *you* sorry, Sylvie?"

"Well—I hardly know," Sylvie replied in the vaguest manner. "Would it make him any happier?" she asked the Professor.

"It wouldn't make the *Pope* any happier," said the Professor. "Isn't the platform *lovely*?" he asked, as we entered the Pavilion.

"I've put an extra beam under it!" said the Gardener, patting it affectionately as he spoke. "And now it's that strong, as—as a mad elephant might dance upon it!"

"Thank you *very* much!" the Professor heartily rejoined. "I don't know that we shall exactly require—but it's convenient to know." And he led the children upon the platform, to explain the arrangements to them. "Here are three seats, you see, for the Emperor and the Empress and Prince Uggug. But there must be two more chairs here!" he said, looking down at the Gardener. "One for Lady Sylvie, and one for the smaller animal!"

"And may I help in the Lecture?" said Bruno. "I can do some conjuring tricks."

"Well, it's not exactly a *conjuring* lecture," the Professor said, as he arranged some curious-looking machines on the table. "However, what can you do? Did you ever go through a table, for instance?"

"Often!" said Bruno. "*Haven't* I, Sylvie?"

The Professor was evidently surprised, though he tried not to show it. "This must be looked into," he muttered to himself, taking out a note-book. "And first—what kind of table?"

"Tell him!" Bruno whispered to Sylvie, putting his arms round her neck.

"Tell him yourself," said Sylvie.

"Ca'n't," said Bruno. "It's a *bony* word."

"Nonsense!" laughed Sylvie. "You can say it well enough, if you only try. Come!"

"Muddle——" said Bruno. "That's a bit of it."

"*What* does he say?" cried the bewildered Professor.

"He means the multiplication-table," Sylvie explained.

The Professor looked annoyed, and shut up his note-book again. "Oh, that's *quite* another thing," he said.

"It are ever so many other things," said Bruno. "*Aren't* it, Sylvie?"

A loud blast of trumpets interrupted this conversation. "Why, the entertainment has *begun*!" the Professor exclaimed, as he hurried the children into the Reception-Saloon. "I had no idea it was so late!"

A small table, containing cake and wine, stood in a corner of the Saloon; and here we found the Emperor and Empress waiting for us. The rest of the Saloon had been cleared of furniture, to make room for the guests. I was much struck by the great change a few months had made in the faces of the Imperial Pair. A vacant stare was now the *Emperor's* usual expression; while over the face of the *Empress* there flitted, ever and anon, a meaningless smile.

"So you're come at last!" the Emperor sulkily remarked, as the Professor and the children took their places. It was evident that he was *very* much out of temper: and we were not long in learning the cause of this. He did not consider the preparations, made for the Imperial party, to be such as suited their rank. "A common mahogany table!" he growled, pointing to it contemptuously with his thumb. "Why wasn't it made of gold, I should like to know?"

"It would have taken a very long——" the Professor began, but the Emperor cut the sentence short.

"Then the cake! Ordinary plum! Why wasn't it made of—of——" He broke off again. "Then the wine! Merely old Madeira! Why wasn't it——? Then this chair! That's worst of all. Why wasn't it a throne? One *might* excuse the other omissions, but I *ca'n't* get over the chair!"

"What *I* ca'n't get over", said the Empress, in eager sympathy with her angry husband, "is the *table!*"

"Pooh!" said the Emperor.

"It is much to be regretted!" the Professor mildly replied, as soon as he had a chance of speaking. After a moment's thought he strengthened the remark. "*Everything*", he said, addressing Society in general, "is *very much* to be regretted!"

A murmur of "Hear, hear!" rose from the crowded Saloon.

There was a rather awkward pause: the Professor evidently didn't know how to begin. The Empress leant forwards, and whispered to him. "A few jokes, you know, Professor—just to put people at their ease!"

"True, true, Madam!" the Professor meekly replied. "This little boy——"

"*Please* don't make any jokes about me!" Bruno exclaimed, his eyes filling with tears.

"I wo'n't if you'd rather I didn't," said the kind-hearted Professor. "It was only something about a Ship's Buoy: a harmless pun—but it doesn't matter." Here he turned to the crowd and addressed them in a loud voice. "Learn your A's!" he shouted. "Your B's! Your C's! and your D's! *Then* you'll be at your ease!"

There was a roar of laughter from all the assembly,

and then a great deal of confused whispering. *"What* was it he said? Something about bees, I fancy——"

The Empress smiled in her meaningless way, and fanned herself. The poor Professor looked at her timidly: he was clearly at his wits' end again, and hoping for another hint. The Empress whispered again.

"Some spinach, you know, Professor, as a surprise."

The Professor beckoned to the Head-Cook, and said something to him in a low voice. Then the Head-Cook left the room, followed by all the other cooks.

"It's difficult to get things started," the Professor remarked to Bruno. "When once we get started, it'll go on all right, you'll see."

"If oo want to startle people", said Bruno, "oo should put live frogs on their backs."

Here the cooks all came in again, in a procession, the Head-Cook coming last and carrying something, which the others tried to hide by waving flags all round it. "Nothing but flags, Your Imperial Highness! Nothing but flags!" he kept repeating, as he set it before her. Then all the flags were dropped in a moment, as the Head-Cook raised the cover from an enormous dish.

"What is it?" the Empress said faintly, as she put her spy-glass to her eye. "Why, it's *Spinach*, I declare!"

"Her Imperial Highness is surprised," the Professor explained to the attendants: and some of them clapped their hands. The Head-Cook made a low bow, and in doing so dropped a spoon on the table, as if by accident, just within reach of the Empress, who looked the other way and pretended not to see it.

"I *am* surprised!" the Empress said to Bruno. "Aren't you?"

"Not a bit," said Bruno. "I heard——" but Sylvie put her hand over his mouth, and spoke for him. "He's rather tired, I think. He wants the Lecture to begin."

"I want the *supper* to begin," Bruno corrected her.

The Empress took up the spoon in an absent manner, and tried to balance it across the back of her hand, and in doing this she dropped it into the dish: and, when she took it out again, it was full of spinach. "How curious!" she said, and put it into her mouth. "It tastes just like *real* spinach! I thought it was an imitation—but I do believe it's real!" And she took another spoonful.

"It wo'n't be real much longer," said Bruno.

But the Empress had had enough spinach by this time, and somehow—I failed to notice the exact process—we all found ourselves in the Pavilion, and the Professor in the act of beginning the long-expected Lecture.

Chapter XXI

The Professor's Lecture

"In Science—in fact, in most things—it is usually best *to begin at the beginning*. In *some* things, of course, it's better to begin at the *other* end. For instance, if you wanted to paint a dog green, it *might* be best to begin with the *tail*, as it doesn't bite at *that* end. And so——"

"May *I* help oo?" Bruno interrupted.

"Help me to do *what*?" said the puzzled Professor, looking up for a moment, but keeping his finger on the book he was reading from, so as not to lose his place.

"To paint a dog green!" cried Bruno. "Oo can begin wiz its *mouf*, and I'll——"

"No, no!" said the Professor. "We haven't got to the *Experiments* yet. And so", returning to his note-book, "I'll give you the Axioms of Science. After that I shall exhibit some Specimens. Then I shall explain a Process or two. And I shall conclude with a few Experiments. An *Axiom*, you know, is a thing that you accept without contradiction. For instance, if I were to say 'Here we are!', that would be accepted without any contradiction, and it's a nice sort of remark to *begin* a conversation with. So it would be an *Axiom*. Or again, supposing I were to say, 'Here we are not!', *that* would be——"

"—a fib!" cried Bruno.

"Oh, *Bruno!*" said Sylvie in a warning whisper. "Of course it would be an *Axiom*, if the Professor said it!"

"—that would be accepted, if people were civil," continued the Professor; "so it would be *another* Axiom."

"It *might* be an Axledum," Bruno said: "but it wouldn't be *true!*"

"Ignorance of Axioms", the Lecturer continued, "is a great drawback in life. It wastes so much time to have to say them over and over again. For instance, take the Axiom, '*Nothing is greater than itself*'; that is, '*Nothing can contain itself.*' How often you hear people say 'He was so excited, he was quite unable to contain himself.' Why, *of course* he was unable! The *excitement* had nothing to do with it!"

"I say, look here, you know!" said the Emperor, who was getting a little restless. "How many Axioms are you going to give us? At *this* rate, we sha'n't get to the *Experiments* till to-morrow-week!"

"Oh, sooner than *that*, I assure you!" the Professor replied, looking up in alarm. "There are only," (he referred to his notes again) "only *two* more, that are really *necessary.*"

"Read 'em out, and get on to the *Specimens*," grumbled the Emperor.

"The *First* Axiom", the Professor read out in a great hurry, "consists of these words, '*Whatever is, is.*' And the Second consists of *these* words, '*Whatever isn't, isn't.*' We will now go on to the *Specimens*. The first tray contains Crystals and other Things." He drew it towards him, and again referred to his notebook. "Some of the labels —owing to insufficient adhesion——" Here he stopped again, and carefully examined the page with his eyeglass. "I ca'n't read the rest of the sentence," he said at last, "but it *means* that the labels have come loose, and the Things have got mixed——"

"Let *me* stick 'em on again!" cried Bruno eagerly, and began licking them, like postage-stamps, and dabbing them down upon the *Crystals* and the other Things. But the Professor hastily moved the tray out of his reach. "They *might* get fixed to the *wrong* Specimens, you know!" he said.

"Oo shouldn't have any *wrong* peppermints in the tray!" Bruno boldly replied. "*Should* he, Sylvie?"

But Sylvie only shook her head.

The Professor heard him not. He had taken up one of the bottles, and was carefully reading the label through his eye-glass. "Our first Specimen——" he announced, as he placed the bottle in front of the other Things, "is— that is, it is called——" here he took it up, and examined the label again, as if he thought it might have changed since he last saw it, "is called Aqua Pura—common water—the fluid that cheers—"

"Hip! Hip! Hip!" the Head-Cook began enthusiastically.

"—but *not* inebriates!" the Professor went on quickly, but only just in time to check the "Hooroar!" which was beginning.

"Our second Specimen", he went on, carefully opening a small jar, "is—" here he removed the lid, and a large beetle instantly darted out, and with an angry buzz went straight out of the Pavilion, "—is—or rather, I should say," looking sadly into the empty jar, "it *was*— a curious kind of Blue Beetle. Did anyone happen to remark—as it went past—three blue spots under each wing?"

Nobody had remarked them.

"Ah, well!" the Professor said with a sigh. "It's a pity. Unless you remark that kind of thing *at the moment*, it's very apt to get overlooked! The *next* Specimen, at any rate, will not fly away! It is—in short, or perhaps, more correctly, at *length*—an *Elephant*. You will observe——" Here he beckoned to the Gardener to come up on the platform, and with his help began putting together what looked like an enormous dog-kennel, with short tubes projecting out of it on both sides.

"But we've seen *Elephants* before," the Emperor grumbled.

"Yes, but not through a *Megaloscope!*" the Professor eagerly replied. "You know you ca'n't see a *Flea*, properly, without a *magnifying*-glass—what we call a *Microscope*. Well, just in the same way, you ca'n't see an *Elephant*, properly without a *minimifying*-glass. There's one in each of these little tubes. And *this* is a *Megaloscope!* The Gardener will now bring in the next Specimen. Please open *both* curtains, down at the end there, and make way for the Elephant!"

There was a general rush to the sides of the Pavilion, and all eyes were turned to the open end, watching for the return of the Gardener, who had gone away singing *"He thought he saw an Elephant That practised on a Fife!"* There was silence for a minute: and then his harsh voice was heard again in the distance. *"He looked again*—come up then! *He looked again, and found it was*—woa back! *and found it was A letter from his*—make way there! He's a-coming!"

And in marched or waddled—it is hard to say which is the right word—an Elephant, on its hind-legs, and playing on an enormous fife which it held with its fore-feet.

The Professor hastily threw open a large door at the end of the Megaloscope, and the huge animal, at a signal from the Gardener, dropped the fife, and obediently trotted into the machine, the door of which was at once shut by the Professor. "The Specimen is now ready for observation!" he proclaimed. "It is exactly the size of the common Mouse—*Mus Communis!*"

There was a general rush to the tubes, and the spectators watched with delight the minikin creature, as it playfully coiled its trunk round the Professor's extended finger, finally taking its stand upon the palm of his hand, while he carefully lifted it out, and carried it off to exhibit to the Imperial party.

"Isn't it a *darling*?" cried Bruno. "May I stroke it, please? I'll touch it *welly* gently!"

The Empress inspected it solemnly with her eye-glass. "It is very small," she said in a deep voice. "Smaller than elephants usually are, I believe?"

The Professor gave a start of delighted surprise. "Why, that's *true*!" he murmured to himself. Then louder, turning to the audience, "Her Imperial Highness has made a remark which is perfectly sensible!" And a wild cheer arose from that vast multitude.

"The next Specimen", the Professor proclaimed, after carefully placing the little elephant in the tray, among the Crystals and other things, "is a *Flea*, which we will enlarge for the purposes of observation." Taking a small pill-box from the tray, he advanced to the Megaloscope, and reversed all the tubes. "The Specimen is ready!" he cried, with his eye at one of the tubes, while he carefully emptied the pill-box through a little hole at the side. "It is now the size of the Common Horse—*Equus Communis!*"

There was another general rush, to look through the tubes, and the Pavilion rang with shouts of delight, through which the Professor's anxious tones could scarcely be heard. "Keep the door of the Microscope *shut*!" he cried. "If the creature were to escape, *this size*, it would——" But the mischief was done. The door had swung open, and in another moment the Monster had got out, and was trampling down the terrified, shrieking spectators.

But the Professor's presence of mind did not desert him. "Undraw those curtains!" he shouted. It was done. The Monster gathered its legs together, and in one tremendous bound vanished into the sky.

"Where *is* it?" said the Emperor, rubbing his eyes.

"In the next Province, I fancy," the Professor replied. "That jump would take it at *least* five miles! The next thing is to explain a Process or two. But I find there is hardly room enough to operate—the smaller animal is rather in my way——"

"Who does he mean?" Bruno whispered to Sylvie.

"He means *you*!" Sylvie whispered back. "Hush!"

"Be kind enough to move—angularly—to *this* corner," the Professor said, addressing himself to Bruno.

Bruno hastily moved his chair in the direction indicated. "Did I move angrily enough?" he inquired. But the Professor was once more absorbed in his Lecture, which he was reading from his note-book.

"I will now explain the process of—the name is blotted, I'm sorry to say. It will be illustrated by a number of— of——" here he examined the pages for some time, and at last said "It seems to be either 'Experiments' or 'Specimens'——"

"Let it be *Experiments*," said the Emperor. "We've seen plenty of *Specimens*."

"Certainly, certainly!" the Professor assented. "We will have some Experiments."

"May *I* do them?" Bruno eagerly asked.

"Oh dear no!" The Professor looked dismayed. "I really don't know what would happen if *you* did them!"

"Nor nobody doosn't know what'll happen if *oo* doos them!" Bruno retorted.

"Our First Experiment requires a Machine. It has two knobs—only *two*—you can count them, if you like."

The Head-Cook stepped forwards, counted them, and retired satisfied.

"Now you *might* press those two knobs together—but that's not the way to do it. Or you *might* turn the Machine upside-down—but *that's* not the way to do it!"

"What *are* the way to do it?" said Bruno, who was listening very attentively.

The Professor smiled benignantly. "Ah, yes!" he said, in a voice like the heading of a chapter. "The Way To Do It! Permit me!" and in a moment he had whisked Bruno upon the table. "I divide my subject", he began, "into three parts——"

"I think I'll get down!" Bruno whispered to Sylvie. "It aren't nice to be divided!"

"He hasn't got a knife, silly boy!" Sylvie whispered in reply. "Stand still! You'll break all the bottles!"

"The first part is to take hold of the knobs," putting them into Bruno's hands. "The second part is——" Here he turned the handle, and, with a loud "Oh!", Bruno dropped both the knobs, and began rubbing his elbows.

The Professor chuckled in delight. "It had a sensible effect. *Hadn't* it?" he enquired.

"No, it hadn't a *sensible* effect!" Bruno said indignantly. "It were very silly indeed. It jingled my elbows, and it banged my back, and it crinkled my hair, and it buzzed among my bones!"

"I'm sure it *didn't*!" said Sylvie. "You're only inventing!"

"Oo doesn't know nuffin about it!" Bruno replied. "Oo wasn't there to see. Nobody ca'n't go among my bones. There isn't room!"

"Our Second Experiment", the Professor announced, as Bruno returned to his place, still thoughtfully rubbing his elbows, "is the production of that seldom-seen-but-greatly-to-be-admired phenomenon, Black Light! You have seen White Light, Red Light, Green Light, and so on: but never, till this wonderful day, have any eyes but mine seen *Black Light*! This box", carefully lifting it upon the table, and covering it with a heap of blankets, "is quite full of it. The way I made it was this—I took a lighted candle into a dark cupboard and shut the door. Of course the cupboard was then full of *Yellow* Light. Then I took a bottle of Black ink, and poured it over the candle: and, to my delight, every atom of the Yellow Light turned *Black*! That was indeed the proudest moment of my life! Then I filled a box with it. And now —would anyone like to get under the blankets and see it?"

Dead silence followed this appeal: but at last Bruno said "*I'll* get under, if it won't jingle my elbows."

Satisfied on this point, Bruno crawled under the blankets, and, after a minute or two, crawled out again, very hot and dusty, and with his hair in the wildest confusion.

"What did you see in the box?" Sylvie eagerly enquired.

"I saw *nuffin!*" Bruno sadly replied. "It were too dark!"

"He has described the appearance of the thing exactly!" the Professor exclaimed with enthusiasm. "Black Light, and Nothing, look so extremely alike, at first sight, that I don't wonder he failed to distinguish them! We will now proceed to the Third Experiment."

The Professor came down, and led the way to where a post had been driven firmly into the ground. To one side of the post was fastened a chain, with an iron weight hooked on to the end of it, and from the other side projected a piece of whalebone, with a ring at the end of it. "This is a *most* interesting Experiment!" the Professor announced. "It will need *time*, I'm afraid: but that is a trifling disadvantage. Now observe. If I were to unhook this weight, and let go, it would fall to the ground. You do not deny *that*?"

Nobody denied it.

"And in the same way, if I were to bend this piece of whalebone round the post—thus—and put the ring over this hook—thus—it stays bent: but, if I unhook it, it straightens itself again. You do not deny *that*?"

Again, nobody denied it.

"Well, now, suppose we left things just as they are, for a long time. The force of the *whalebone* would get exhausted, you know, and it would stay bent, even when you unhooked it. Now, *why* shouldn't the same thing happen with the *weight*? The *whalebone* gets so used to being bent, that it ca'n't *straighten* itself any more. Why shouldn't the *weight* get so used to being held up, that it ca'n't *fall* any more? That's what *I* want to know!"

"That's what *we* want to know!" echoed the crowd.

"How long must we wait?" grumbled the Emperor.

The Professor looked at his watch. "Well, I *think* a thousand years will do to *begin* with," he said. "Then we will cautiously unhook the weight: and, if it *still* shows (as perhaps it will) a *slight* tendency to fall, we will hook it on to the chain again, and leave it for *another* thousand years."

Here the Empress experienced one of those flashes of Common Sense which were the surprise of all around her. "Meanwhile there'll be time for another Experiment," she said.

"There will *indeed*!" cried the delighted Professor. "Let us return to the platform, and proceed to the *Fourth* Experiment!"

"For this concluding Experiment, I will take a certain Alkali, or Acid—I forget which. Now you'll see what will happen when I mix it with Some—" here he took up a bottle, and looked at it doubtfully, "—when I mix it with—with Something——"

Here the Emperor interrupted. "What's the *name* of the stuff?" he asked.

"I don't remember the *name*," said the Professor: "and the label has come off." He emptied it quickly into the other bottle, and, with a tremendous bang, both bottles flew to pieces, upsetting all the machines, and filling the Pavilion with thick black smoke. I sprang to my feet in terror, and—and found myself standing before my solitary hearth, where the poker, dropping at last from the hand of the sleeper, had knocked over the tongs and the shovel, and had upset the kettle, filling the air with clouds of steam. With a weary sigh, I betook myself to bed.

CHAPTER XXII

The Banquet

"*Heaviness may endure for a night: but joy cometh in the morning.*" The next day found me quite another being. Even the memories of my lost friend and companion were sunny as the genial weather that smiled around me. I did not venture to trouble Lady Muriel, or her father, with another call so soon: but took a walk into the country, and only turned homewards when the low sunbeams warned me that day would soon be over.

On my way home, I passed the cottage where the old man lived, whose face always recalled to me the day when I first met Lady Muriel; and I glanced in as I passed, half-curious to see if he were still living there.

Yes: the old man was still alive. He was sitting out in the porch, looking just as he did when I first saw him at Fayfield Junction—it seemed only a few days ago!

"Good evening!" I said, pausing.

"Good evening, Maister!" he cheerfully responded. "Wo'n't ee step in?"

I stepped in, and took a seat on the bench in the porch. "I'm glad to see you looking so hearty," I began. "Last time, I remember, I chanced to pass just as Lady Muriel was coming away from the house. Does she still come to see you?"

"Ees," he answered slowly. "She has na forgotten me. I don't lose her bonny face for many days together. Well I mind the very first time she come, after we'd met at Railway Station. She told me as she come to mak' amends. Dear child! Only think o' that! To mak' amends!"

"To make amends for what?" I enquired. "What could *she* have done to need it?"

"Well, it were loike this, you see? We were both on us a-waiting fur t' train at t' Junction. And I had setten mysen down upat t' bench. And Station-Maister, *he* comes and he orders me off—fur t' mak' room for her Ladyship, you understand?"

"I remember it all," I said. "I was there myself, that day."

"*Was* you, now? Well, an' she axes my pardon fur 't. Think o' that, now! *My* pardon! An owd ne'er-do-weel like me! Ah! She's been here many a time, sin' then.

Why, she were in here only yestere'en, as it were, a-sittin', as it might be, where you're a-sitting now, an' lookin' sweeter and kinder nor an angel! An' she says 'You've not got your Minnie, now,' she says, 'to fettle for ye.' Minnie was my grand-daughter, Sir, as lived wi' me. She died, a matter of two months ago—or it may be three. She was a bonny lass—and a good lass, too. Eh, but life has been rare an' lonely without her!"

He covered his face in his hands: and I waited a minute or two, in silence, for him to recover himself.

"So she says, 'Just tak' *me* fur your Minnie!' she says. 'Didna Minnie mak' your tea fur you?' says she. 'Ay,' says I. An' she mak's the tea. 'An' didna Minnie light your pipe?' says she. 'Ay,' says I. An' she lights the pipe for me. 'An' didna Minnie set out your tea in t' porch?' An' I says 'My dear,' I says, 'I'm thinking you're Minnie hersen!' An' she cries a bit. We both on us cries a bit——"

Again I kept silence for a while.

"An' while I smokes my pipe, she sits an' talks to me— as loving an' as pleasant! I'll be bound I thowt it were Minnie come again! An' when she gets up to go, I says 'Winnot ye shak' hands wi' me?' says I. An' she says 'Na,' she says: 'a cannot *shak' hands* wi' thee!' she says."

"I'm sorry she said *that*," I put in, thinking it was the only instance I had ever known of pride of rank showing itself in Lady Muriel.

"Bless you, it werena *pride*!" said the old man, reading my thoughts. "She says '*Your* Minnie never *shook hands* wi' you!' she says. 'An' *I'm* your Minnie now,' she says. An' she just puts her dear arms about my neck—and she kisses me on t' cheek—an' may God in Heaven bless her!" And here the poor old man broke down entirely, and could say no more.

"God bless her!" I echoed. "And good night to you!" I pressed his hand, and left him. "Lady Muriel," I said softly to myself as I went homewards, "truly you know how to 'mak' amends'!"

Seated once more by my lonely fireside, I tried to recall

the strange vision of the night before, and to conjure up the face of the dear old Professor among the blazing coals. "That black one—with just a touch of red—would suit him well," I thought. "After such a catastrophe, it would be sure to be covered with black stains—and he would say:

"The result of *that* combination—you may have noticed?—was an *Explosion!* Shall I repeat the Experiment?"

"No, no! Don't trouble yourself!" was the general cry. And we all trooped off, in hot haste, to the Banqueting-Hall, where the feast had already begun.

No time was lost in helping the dishes, and very speedily every guest found his plate filled with good things.

"I have always maintained the principle," the Professor began, "that it is a good rule to take some food—occasionally. The great advantage of dinner-parties——" he broke off suddenly. "Why, actually here's the Other Professor!" he cried. "And there's no place left for him!"

The Other Professor came in reading a large book, which he held close to his eyes. One result of his not looking where he was going was that he tripped up, as he crossed the Saloon, flew up into the air, and fell heavily on his face in the middle of the table.

"*What* a pity!" cried the kind-hearted Professor, as he helped him up.

"It wouldn't be *me*, if I didn't trip," said the Other Professor.

The Professor looked much shocked. "Almost *anything* would be better than *that!*" he exclaimed. "It never does", he added, aside to Bruno, "to be anybody else, does it?"

To which Bruno gravely replied "I's got nuffin on my plate."

The Professor hastily put on his spectacles, to make sure that the *facts* were all right, to begin with: then he turned his jolly round face upon the unfortunate owner of the empty plate. "And what would you like next, my little man?"

"Well," Bruno said, a little doubtfully, "I think I'll take some plum-pudding, please—while I think of it."

"Oh, Bruno!" (This was a whisper from Sylvie.) "It isn't good manners to ask for a dish before it comes!"

And Bruno whispered back "But I might forget to ask for some, when it comes, oo know—I *do* forget things, sometimes," he added, seeing Sylvie about to whisper more.

And *this* assertion Sylvie did not venture to contradict.

Meanwhile a chair had been placed for the Other Professor, between the Empress and Sylvie. Sylvie found him a rather uninteresting neighbour: in fact, she couldn't afterwards remember that he had made more than *one* remark to her during the whole banquet, and that was "What a comfort a Dictionary is!" (She told Bruno, afterwards, that she had been too much afraid of him to say more than "Yes, Sir" in reply: and that had been the end of their conversation. On which Bruno expressed a very decided opinion that *that* wasn't worth calling a "conversation" at all. "Oo should have asked him a riddle!" he added triumphantly. "Why, *I* asked the Professor *three* riddles! One was that one you asked me in the morning, 'How many pennies is there in two shillings?' And another was——" "Oh, Bruno!" Sylvie interrupted. "*That* wasn't a riddle!" "It *were*!" Bruno fiercely replied.)

By this time a waiter had supplied Bruno with a plateful of *something*, which drove the plum-pudding out of his head.

"Another advantage of dinner-parties", the Professor cheerfully explained, for the benefit of anyone that would listen, "is that it helps you to *see* your friends. If you want to *see* a man, offer him something to eat. It's the same rule with a mouse."

"This Cat's very kind to the Mouses," Bruno said, stooping to stroke a remarkably fat specimen of the race, that had just waddled into the room, and was rubbing itself affectionately against the leg of his chair. "Please, Sylvie, pour some milk in your saucer. Pussie's ever so thirsty!"

"Why do you want *my* saucer?" said Sylvie. "You've got one yourself!"

"Yes, I know," said Bruno: "but I wanted *mine* for to give it some *more* milk in."

Sylvie looked unconvinced: however it seemed quite impossible for her *ever* to refuse what her brother asked: so she quietly filled her saucer with milk, and handed it to Bruno, who got down off his chair to administer it to the cat.

"The room's very hot, with all this crowd," the Professor said to Sylvie. "I wonder why they don't put some lumps of ice in the grate? You fill it with lumps of coal in the winter, you know, and you sit around it and enjoy the warmth. How jolly it would be to fill it now with lumps of ice, and sit round it and enjoy the coolth!"

Hot as it was, Sylvie shivered a little at the idea. "It's very cold *outside*," she said. "My feet got almost frozen to-day."

"That's the *shoemaker's* fault!" the Professor cheerfully replied. "How often I've explained to him that he *ought* to make boots with little iron frames under the soles, to hold lamps! But he never *thinks*. No one would suffer from cold, if only they would *think* of those little things. I always use hot ink, myself, in the winter. Very few people ever think of *that*! Yet how simple it is!"

"Yes, it's very simple," Sylvie said politely. "Has the cat had enough?" This was to Bruno, who had brought back the saucer only half-emptied.

But Bruno did not hear the question. "There's somebody scratching at the door and wanting to come in," he said. And he scrambled down off his chair, and went and cautiously peeped out through the door-way.

"Who was it wanted to come in?" Sylvie asked, as he returned to his place.

"It were a Mouse," said Bruno. "And it peepted in. And it saw the Cat. And it said 'I'll come in another day.' And I said 'Oo needn't be flightened. The Cat's *welly* kind to Mouses.' And it said 'But I's got some imporkant business, what I *must* attend to.' And it said 'I'll call again to-morrow.' And it said 'Give my love to the Cat.' ''

"What a fat cat it is!" said the Lord Chancellor, leaning across the Professor to address his small neighbour. "It's quite a wonder!"

"It was awfully fat when it camed in," said Bruno: "so it would be more wonderfuller if it got thin all in a minute."

"And that was the reason, I suppose," the Lord Chancellor suggested, "why you didn't give it the rest of the milk?"

"No," said Bruno. "It was a betterer reason. I tooked the saucer up 'cause it were so discontented!"

"It doesn't look so to *me*," said the Lord Chancellor. "What made you think it was discontented?"

" 'Cause it grumbled in its throat."

"Oh, Bruno!" cried Sylvie. "Why, that's the way cats show they're *pleased*!"

Bruno looked doubtful. "It's not a good way," he objected. "Oo wouldn't say *I* were pleased, if I made that noise in my throat!"

"What a singular boy!" the Lord Chancellor whispered to himself: but Bruno had caught the words.

"What do it mean to say 'a *singular* boy'?" he whispered to Sylvie.

"It means *one* boy," Sylvie whispered in return. "And *plural* means two or three."

"Then I's welly glad I *is* a singular boy!" Bruno said with great emphasis. "It would be *horrid* to be two or three boys! P'raps they wouldn't play with me!"

"Why *should* they?" said the Other Professor, suddenly waking up out of a deep reverie. "They might be asleep, you know."

"Couldn't, if *I* was awake," Bruno said cunningly.

"Oh, but they might indeed!" the Other Professor protested. "Boys don't all go to sleep at once, you know. So these boys—but who are you talking about?"

"He *never* remembers to ask that first!" the Professor whispered to the children.

"Why, the rest of *me*, a-course!" Bruno exclaimed triumphantly. "Supposing I was two or three boys!"

The Other Professor sighed, and seemed to be sinking back into his reverie; but suddenly brightened up again, and addressed the Professor. "There's nothing more to be done *now*, is there?"

"Well, there's the dinner to finish," the Professor said with a bewildered smile: "and the heat to bear. I hope you'll enjoy the dinner—such as it is; and that you wo'n't mind the heat—such as it isn't."

The sentence *sounded* well, but somehow I couldn't quite understand it; and the Other Professor seemed to be no better off. "Such as it isn't *what*?" he peevishly enquired.

"It isn't as hot as it might be," the Professor replied, catching at the first idea that came to hand.

"Ah, I see what you mean *now*!" the Other Professor graciously remarked. "It's very badly expressed, but I quite see it *now*! Thirteen minutes and a half ago," he went on, looking first at Bruno and then at his watch as he spoke, "you said 'this Cat's very kind to the Mouses.' It must be a singular animal!"

"So it *are*," said Bruno, after carefully examining the Cat, to make sure how many there were of it.

"But how do you know it's kind to the Mouses—or, more correctly speaking, the *Mice*?"

" 'Cause it *plays* with the Mouses," said Bruno; "for to amuse them, oo know."

"But that is just what I *don't* know," the Other Professor rejoined. "My belief is, it plays with them to *kill* them!"

"Oh, that's quite a *accident*!" Bruno began, so eagerly, that it was evident he had already propounded this very difficulty to the Cat. "It 'splained all that to me, while it were drinking the milk. It said 'I teaches the Mouses new games: the Mouses likes it ever so much.' It said 'Sometimes little accidents happens: sometimes the Mouses kills theirselves.' It said 'I's always *welly* sorry, when the Mouses kills theirselves.' It said——"

"If it was so *very* sorry," Sylvie said, rather disdainfully, "it wouldn't *eat* the Mouses after they'd killed themselves!"

But this difficulty, also, had evidently not been lost sight of in the exhaustive ethical discussion just concluded. "It said——" (the orator constantly omitted, as superfluous, his own share in the dialogue, and merely gave us the replies of the Cat) "It said 'Dead Mouses *never* objecks to be eaten.' It said 'There's no use wasting good Mouses.' It said 'Wifful——' sumfinoruvver. It said 'And oo may live to say "How much I wiss I had the Mouse that then I frew away!"' It said——"

"It hadn't *time* to say such a lot of things!" Sylvie interrupted indignantly.

"Oo doesn't know how Cats speaks!" Bruno rejoined contemptuously. "Cats speaks *welly* quick!"

Chapter XXIII

The Pig-Tale

By this time the appetites of the guests seemed to be nearly satisfied, and even *Bruno* had the resolution to say, when the Professor offered him a fourth slice of plum-pudding, "I thinks three helpings is enough!"

Suddenly the Professor started as if he had been electrified. "Why, I had nearly forgotten the most important part of the entertainment! The Other Professor is to recite a Tale of a Pig—I mean a Pig-Tale," he corrected himself. "It has Introductory Verses at the beginning, and at the end."

"It ca'n't have Introductory Verses at the *end*, can it?" said Sylvie.

"Wait till you hear it," said the Professor: "then you'll see. I'm not sure it hasn't some in the *middle*, as well." Here he rose to his feet, and there was an instant silence through the Banqueting-Hall: they evidently expected a speech.

"Ladies, and gentlemen," the Professor began, "the Other Professor is so kind as to recite a Poem. The title of it is 'The Pig-Tale'. He never recited it before!" (General cheering among the guests.) "He will never recite it again!" (Frantic excitement, and wild cheering all down the hall, the Professor himself mounting the table in hot haste, to lead the cheering, and waving his spectacles in one hand and a spoon in the other.)

Then the Other Professor got up, and began:

> *Little Birds are dining*
> *Warily and well,*
> *Hid in mossy cell:*
> *Hid, I say, by waiters*
> *Gorgeous in their gaiters—*
> *I've a Tale to tell.*

> *Little Birds are feeding*
> *Justices with jam,*
> *Rich in frizzled ham:*
> *Rich, I say, in oysters*
> *Haunting shady cloisters—*
> *That is what I am.*

> *Little Birds are teaching*
> *Tigresses to smile,*
> *Innocent of guile:*
> *Smile, I say, not smirkle—*
> *Mouth a semicircle,*
> *That's the proper style.*

Little Birds are sleeping
    All among the pins,
    Where the loser wins:
Where, I say, he sneezes
When and how he pleases—
    So the Tale begins.

There was a Pig that sat alone
    Beside a ruined Pump:
By day and night he made his moan—
It would have stirred a heart of stone
To see him wring his hoofs and groan,
    Because he could not jump.

A certain Camel heard him shout—
    A Camel with a hump.
"Oh, is it Grief, or is it Gout?
What is this bellowing about?"
That Pig replied, with quivering snout,
    "Because I cannot jump!"

That Camel scanned him, dreamy-eyed.
    "Methinks you are too plump.
I never knew a Pig so wide—
That wobbled so from side to side—
Who could, however much he tried,
    Do such a thing as jump!

"Yet mark those trees, two miles away,
    All clustered in a clump:
If you could trot there twice a day,
Nor ever pause for rest or play,
In the far future—Who can say?—
    You may be fit to jump."

That Camel passed, and left him there,
    Beside the ruined Pump.
Oh, horrid was that Pig's despair!
His shrieks of anguish filled the air.
He wrung his hoofs, he rent his hair,
    Because he could not jump.

There was a Frog that wandered by—
  A sleek and shining lump:
Inspected him with fishy eye,
And said "O Pig, what makes you cry?"
And bitter was that Pig's reply,
  "Because I cannot jump!"

That Frog he grinned a grin of glee,
  And hit his chest a thump.
"O Pig," he said, "be ruled by me,
And you shall see what you shall see.
This minute, for a trifling fee,
  I'll teach you how to jump!

"You may be faint from many a fall,
  And bruised by many a bump:
But, if you persevere through all,
And practise first on something small,
Concluding with a ten-foot wall,
  You'll find that you can *jump!"*

That Pig looked up with joyful start:
  "Oh Frog, you are *a trump!*
Your words have healed my inward smart—
Come, name your fee and do your part:
Bring comfort to a broken heart,
  By teaching me to jump!"

"My fee shall be a mutton-chop,
  My goal this ruined Pump.
Observe with what an airy flop
I plant myself upon the top!
Now bend your knees and take a hop,
  For that's the way to jump!"

Uprose that Pig, and rushed, full whack,
  Against the ruined Pump:
Rolled over like an empty sack,
And settled down upon his back,
While all his bones at once went "Crack!"
  It was a fatal jump.

When the Other Professor had recited this Verse, he went across to the fire-place, and put his head up the chimney. In doing this, he lost his balance, and fell head-first into the empty grate, and got so firmly fixed there that it was some time before he could be dragged out again.

Bruno had had time to say "I thought he wanted to see how many peoples was up the chimbley."

And Sylvie had said "*Chimney*—not chimbley."

And Bruno had said "Don't talk 'ubbish!"

All this, while the Other Professor was being extracted.

"You must have blacked your face!" the Empress said anxiously. "Let me send for some soap?"

"Thanks, no," said the Other Professor, keeping his face turned away. "Black's quite a respectable colour. Besides, soap would be no use without water——"

Keeping his back well turned away from the audience, he went on with the Introductory Verses:

> *Little Birds are writing*
>   *Interesting books,*
>   *To be read by cooks:*
> *Read, I say, not roasted—*
> *Letterpress, when toasted,*
>   *Loses its good looks.*
>
> *Little Birds are playing*
>   *Bagpipes on the shore,*
>   *Where the tourists snore:*
> *"Thanks!" they cry. "'Tis thrilling!*
> *Take, oh take this shilling!*
>   *Let us have no more!"*
>
> *Little Birds are bathing*
>   *Crocodiles in cream,*
>   *Like a happy dream:*
> *Like, but not so lasting—*
> *Crocodiles, when fasting,*
>   *Are not all they seem!*

That Camel passed, as Day grew dim
Around the ruined Pump.
"O broken heart! O broken limb!
It needs", that Camel said to him,
"Something more fairy-like and slim,
To execute a jump!"

That Pig lay still as any stone,
And could not stir a stump:
Nor ever, if the truth were known,
Was he again observed to moan,
Nor ever wring his hoofs and groan,
Because he could not jump.

That Frog made no remark, for he
Was dismal as a dump:
He knew the consequence must be
That he would never get his fee—
And still he sits, in miserie,
Upon that ruined Pump!

"It's a miserable story!" said Bruno. "It begins miserably, and it ends miserablier. I think I shall cry. Sylvie, please lend me your handkerchief."

"I haven't got it with me," Sylvie whispered.

"Then I wo'n't cry," said Bruno manfully.

"There are more Introductory Verses to come," said the Other Professor, "but I'm hungry." He sat down, cut a large slice of cake, put it on Bruno's plate, and gazed at his own empty plate in astonishment.

"Where did you get that cake?" Sylvie whispered to Bruno.

"He gived it me," said Bruno.

"But you shouldn't ask for things! You *know* you shouldn't!"

"I *didn't* ask," said Bruno, taking a fresh mouthful: "he *gived* it me."

Sylvie considered this for a moment: then she saw her way out of it. "Well, then, ask him to give *me* some!"

"You seem to enjoy that cake?" the Professor remarked.

"Doos that mean 'munch'?" Bruno whispered to Sylvie.

Sylvie nodded. "It means 'to munch' and 'to *like* to munch'."

Bruno smiled at the Professor. "I *doos* enjoy it," he said.

The Other Professor caught the word. "And I hope you're enjoying *yourself*, little Man?" he enquired.

Bruno's look of horror quite startled him. "No, *indeed* I aren't!" he said.

The Other Professor looked thoroughly puzzled. "Well, well!" he said. "Try some cowslip wine!" And he filled a glass and handed it to Bruno. "Drink this, my dear, and you'll be quite another man!"

"Who shall I be?" said Bruno, pausing in the act of putting it to his lips.

"Don't ask so many questions!" Sylvie interposed, anxious to save the poor old man from further bewilderment. "Suppose we get the Professor to tell us a story."

Bruno adopted the idea with enthusiasm. "*Please* do!" he cried eagerly. "Sumfin about tigers—and bumble-bees—and robin-redbreasts, oo knows!"

"Why should you always have *live* things in stories?" said the Professor. "Why don't you have events, or circumstances?"

"Oh, *please* invent a story like that!" cried Bruno.

The Professor began fluently enough. "Once a coincidence was taking a walk with a little accident, and they met an explanation—a *very* old explanation—so old that it was quite doubled up, and looked more like a conundrum——" he broke off suddenly.

"*Please* go on!" both children exclaimed.

The Professor made a candid confession. "It's a very difficult sort to invent, I find. Suppose Bruno tells one, first."

Bruno was only too happy to adopt the suggestion.

"Once there were a Pig, and a Accordion, and two jars of Orange-marmalade——"

"The *dramatis personæ*," murmured the Professor. "Well, what then?"

"So, when the Pig played on the Accordion," Bruno went on, "one of the Jars of Orange-marmalade didn't like the tune, and the other Jar of Orange-marmalade did like the tune—I *know* I shall get confused among those Jars of Orange-marmalade, Sylvie!" he whispered anxiously.

"I will now recite the other Introductory Verses," said the Other Professor.

> *Little Birds are choking*
> *Baronets with bun,*
> *Taught to fire a gun:*
> *Taught, I say, to splinter*
> *Salmon in the winter—*
> *Merely for the fun.*
>
> *Little Birds are hiding*
> *Crimes in carpet-bags,*
> *Blessed by happy stags:*
> *Blessed, I say, though beaten—*
> *Since our friends are eaten*
> *When the memory flags.*
>
> *Little Birds are tasting*
> *Gratitude and gold,*
> *Pale with sudden cold:*
> *Pale, I say, and wrinkled—*
> *When the bells have tinkled,*
> *And the Tale is told.*

"The next thing to be done", the Professor cheerfully remarked to the Lord Chancellor, as soon as the applause, caused by the recital of the Pig-Tale, had come to an end, "is to drink the Emperor's health, is it not?"

"Undoubtedly!" the Lord Chancellor replied with much solemnity, as he rose to his feet to give the necessary directions for the ceremony. "Fill your glasses!" he thundered. All did so, instantly. "Drink the Emperor's

health!'' A general gurgling resounded all through the
Hall. "Three cheers for the Emperor!" The faintest possible sound followed *this* announcement: and the Chancellor, with admirable presence of mind, instantly proclaimed "A speech from the Emperor!"

The Emperor had begun his speech almost before the
words were uttered. "However unwilling to be Emperor
—since you all wish me to be Emperor—you know how
badly the late Warden managed things—with such
enthusiasm as you have shown—he persecuted you—he
taxed you too heavily—you know who is fittest man to
be Emperor—my brother had no sense——"

How long this curious speech might have lasted it is
impossible to say, for just at this moment a hurricane
shook the palace to its foundations, bursting open the
windows, extinguishing some of the lamps, and filling the
air with clouds of dust, which took strange shapes in the
air, and seemed to form words.

But the storm subsided as suddenly as it had risen—
the casements swung into their places again: the dust
vanished: all was as it had been a minute ago—with the
exception of the Emperor and Empress, over whom had
come a wondrous change. The vacant stare, the meaningless smile, had passed away: all could see that these two
strange beings had returned to their senses.

The Emperor continued his speech as if there had been
no interruption. "And we have behaved—my wife and I
—like two arrant Knaves. We deserve no better name.
When my brother went away, you lost the best Warden
you ever had. And I've been doing my best, wretched
hypocrite that I am, to cheat you into making me an
Emperor. Me! One that has hardly got the wits to be a
shoe-black!"

The Lord Chancellor wrung his hands in despair. "He
is mad, good people!" he was beginning. But both
speeches stopped suddenly—and, in the dead silence that
followed, a knocking was heard at the outer door.

"What is it?" was the general cry. People began running in and out. The excitement increased every moment. The Lord Chancellor, forgetting all the rules of Court-ceremony, ran full speed down the hall, and in a minute returned, pale and gasping for breath.

Chapter XXIV

The Beggar's Return

"Your Imperial Highnesses!" he began. "It's the old Beggar again! Shall we set the dogs at him?"

"Bring him here!" said the Emperor.

The Chancellor could scarcely believe his ears. "*Here*, your Imperial Highness? Did I rightly understand——"

"Bring him here!" the Emperor thundered once more. The Chancellor tottered down the hall—and in another minute the crowd divided, and the poor old Beggar was seen entering the Banqueting-Hall.

He was indeed a pitiable object: the rags, that hung about him, were all splashed with mud: his white hair and his long beard were tossed about in wild disorder. Yet he walked upright, with a stately tread, as if used to command: and—strangest sight of all—Sylvie and Bruno came with him, clinging to his hands, and gazing at him with looks of silent love.

Men looked eagerly to see how the Emperor would receive the bold intruder. Would he hurl him from the steps of the daïs? But no. To their utter astonishment, the Emperor knelt as the beggar approached, and with bowed head murmured "Forgive us!"

"Forgive us!" the Empress, kneeling at her husband's side, meekly repeated.

The Outcast smiled. "Rise up!" he said. "I forgive you!" And men saw with wonder that a change had passed over the old beggar, even as he spoke. What had seemed, but now, to be vile rags and splashes of mud, were seen to be in truth kingly trappings, broidered with gold, and sparkling with gems. All knew him now, and bent low before the Elder Brother, the true Warden.

"Brother mine, and Sister mine!" the Warden began, in a clear voice that was heard all through that vast hall. "I come not to disturb you. Rule on, as Emperor, and rule wisely. For I am chosen King of Elfland. To-morrow I return there, taking nought from thence, save only—save only——" his voice trembled, and with a look of ineffable tenderness, he laid his hands in silence on the heads of the two little ones who clung around him.

But he recovered himself in a moment, and beckoned to the Emperor to resume his place at the table. The company seated themselves again—room being found for the Elfin-King between his two children—and the Lord Chancellor rose once more, to propose the next toast.

"The next toast—the hero of the day—why, he isn't here!" he broke off in wild confusion.

Good gracious! Everybody had forgotten Prince Uggug!

"He was told of the Banquet, of course?" said the Emperor.

"Undoubtedly!" replied the Chancellor. "*That* would be the duty of the Gold Stick in Waiting."

"Let the Gold Stick come forwards!" the Emperor gravely said.

The Gold Stick came forwards. "I attended on His Imperial Fatness," was the statement made by the trembling official. "I told him of the Lecture and the Banquet——."

"What followed!" said the Emperor: for the unhappy man seemed almost too frightened to go on.

"His Imperial Fatness was graciously pleased to be sulky. His Imperial Fatness was graciously pleased to box my ears. His Imperial Fatness was graciously pleased to say 'I don't care!' "

" 'Don't-care' came to a bad end," Sylvie whispered to Bruno. "I'm not sure, but I *believe* he was hanged."

The Professor overheard her. "*That* result", he blandly remarked, "was merely a case of mistaken identity."

Both children looked puzzled.

"Permit me to explain. 'Don't-care' and 'Care' were twin-brothers. 'Care', you know, killed the Cat. And they caught 'Don't-care' by mistake, and hanged him instead. And so 'Care' is alive still. But he's very unhappy without his brother. That's why they say 'Begone, dull Care!' "

"Thank you!" Sylvie said, heartily. "It's very extremely interesting. Why, it seems to explain *everything*!"

"Well, not quite *everything*," the Professor modestly rejoined. "There are two or three scientific difficulties—"

"What was your general impression as to His Imperial Fatness?" the Emperor asked the Gold Stick.

"My impression was that His Imperial Fatness was getting more——"

"More *what*?"

All listened breathlessly for the next word.

"More PRICKLY!"

"He must be sent for *at once*!" the Emperor exclaimed. And the Gold Stick went off like a shot. The Elfin-King sadly shook his head. "No use, no use!" he murmured to himself. "Loveless, loveless!"

Pale, trembling, speechless, the Gold Stick came slowly back again.

"Well?" said the Emperor. "Why does not the Prince appear?"

"One can easily guess," said the Professor. "His Imperial Fatness is, without doubt, a little preoccupied."

Bruno turned a look of solemn enquiry on his old friend. "What do that word mean?"

But the Professor took no notice of the question. He was eagerly listening to the Gold Stick's reply.

"Please your Highness! His Imperial Fatness is——" Not a word more could he utter.

The Empress rose in an agony of alarm. "Let us go to him!" she cried. And there was a general rush for the door.

Bruno slipped off his chair in a moment. "May we go too?" he eagerly asked. But the King did not hear the question, as the Professor was speaking to him. *"Preoccupied*, your Majesty!" he was saying. "That is what he is, no doubt!"

"May we go and see him?" Bruno repeated. The King nodded assent, and the children ran off. In a minute or two they returned, slowly and gravely. "Well?" said the King. "What's the matter with the Prince?"

"He's—what *you* said," Bruno replied looking at the Professor. "That hard word." And he looked to Sylvie for assistance.

"Porcupine," said Sylvie.

"No, no!" the Professor corrected her. " '*Pre-occupied,*' you mean."

"No, it's *porcupine*," persisted Sylvie. "Not that other word at all. And please will you come? The house is all in an uproar." ("And oo'd better bring an uproar-glass wiz oo!" added Bruno.)

We got up in great haste, and followed the children upstairs. No one took the least notice of *me*, but I wasn't at all surprised at this, as I had long realized that I was quite invisible to them all—even to Sylvie and Bruno.

All along the gallery, that led to the Prince's apartment, an excited crowd was surging to and fro, and the Babel of voices was deafening: against the door of the room three strong men were leaning, vainly trying to shut it—for some great animal inside was constantly bursting it half open, and we had a glimpse, before the men could push it back again, of the head of a furious wild beast, with great fiery eyes and gnashing teeth. Its voice was a sort of mixture—there was the roaring of a lion, and the bellowing of a bull, and now and then a scream like a gigantic parrot. "There is no judging by the voice!" the Professor cried in great excitement. "What is it?" he shouted to the men at the door. And a general chorus of voices answered him "Porcupine! Prince Uggug has turned into a Porcupine!"

"A new Specimen!" exclaimed the delighted Professor. "Pray let me go in. It should be labeled at once!"

But the strong men only pushed him back. "Label it, indeed! Do you want to be eaten up?" they cried.

"Never mind about Specimens, Professor!" said the Emperor, pushing his way through the crowd. "Tell us how to keep him safe!"

"A large cage!" the Professor promptly replied. "Bring a large cage," he said to the people generally, "with strong bars of steel, and a portcullis made to go up and down like a mouse-trap! Does anyone happen to have such a thing about him?"

It didn't sound a likely sort of thing for anyone to have about him; however, they brought him one directly: curiously enough, there happened to be one standing in the gallery.

"Put it facing the opening of the door, and draw up the portcullis!" This was done in a moment.

"Blankets now!" cried the Professor. "This is a most interesting Experiment!"

There happened to be a pile of blankets close by: and the Professor had hardly said the word, when they were all unfolded and held up like curtains all around. The Professor rapidly arranged them in two rows, so as to make a dark passage, leading straight from the door to the mouth of the cage.

"Now fling the door open!" This did not need to be done: the three men had only to leap out of the way, and the fearful monster flung the door open for itself, and, with a yell like the whistle of a steam-engine, rushed into the cage.

"Down with the portcullis!" No sooner said than done: and all breathed freely once more, on seeing the Porcupine safely caged.

The Professor rubbed his hands in childish delight. "The Experiment has succeeded!" he proclaimed. "All that is needed now is to feed it three times a day, on chopped carrots and——"

"Never mind about its food, just now!" the Emperor interrupted. "Let us return to the Banquet. Brother, will you lead the way?" And the old man, attended by his children, headed the procession down stairs. "See the fate of a loveless life!" he said to Bruno, as they returned to their places. To which Bruno made reply, "I always loved Sylvie, so I'll never get prickly like that!"

"He *is* prickly, certainly," said the Professor, who had caught the last words, "but we must remember that, however porcupiny, he is royal still! After this feast is over, I'm going to take a little present to Prince Uggug—just to soothe him, you know: it isn't pleasant living in a cage."

"What'll you give him for a birthday-present?" Bruno enquired.

"A small saucer of chopped carrots," replied the Professor. "In giving birthday-presents, *my* motto is—cheapness! I should think I save forty pounds a year by giving —oh, *what* a twinge of pain!"

"What is it?" said Sylvie anxiously.

"My old enemy!" groaned the Professor. "Lumbago— rheumatism—that sort of thing. I think I'll go and lie down a bit." And he hobbled out of the Saloon, watched by the pitying eyes of the two children.

"He'll be better soon!" the Elfin-King said cheerily. "Brother!" turning to the Emperor, "I have some business to arrange with you to-night. The Empress will take care of the children." And the two Brothers went away together, arm-in-arm.

The Empress found the children rather sad company. They could talk of nothing but "the dear Professor", and "what a pity he's so ill", till at last she made the welcome proposal "Let's go and see him!"

The children eagerly grasped the hands she offered them: and we went off to the Professor's study, and found him lying on the sofa, covered up with blankets, and reading a little manuscript-book. "Notes on Vol. Three!" he murmured, looking up at us. And there, on a table near him, lay the book he was seeking when first I saw him.

"And how are you now, Professor?" the Empress asked, bending over the invalid.

The Professor looked up, and smiled feebly. "As devoted to your Imperial Highness as ever!" he said in a weak voice. "All of me, that is not Lumbago, is Loyalty!"

"A sweet sentiment!" the Empress exclaimed with tears in her eyes. "You seldom hear anything so beautiful as that—even in a Valentine!"

"We must take you to stay at the seaside," Sylvie said, tenderly. "It'll do you ever so much good! And the Sea's so grand!"

"But a Mountain's grander!" said Bruno.

"What is there grand about the Sea?" said the Professor. "Why, you could put it all into a teacup!"

"*Some* of it," Sylvie corrected him.

"Well, you'd only want a certain number of teacups to hold it *all*. And *then* where's the grandeur? Then as to a Mountain—why, you could carry it all away in a wheelbarrow, in a certain number of years!"

"It wouldn't look grand—the bits of it in the wheelbarrow," Sylvie candidly admitted.

"But when oo put it together again——" Bruno began.

"When you're older," said the Professor, "you'll know that you *ca'n't* put Mountains together again so easily! One lives and one learns, you know!"

"But it needn't be the *same* one, need it?" said Bruno. "Wo'n't it do, if *I* live, and if *Sylvie* learns?"

"I *ca'n't* learn without living!" said Sylvie.

"But I *can* live without learning!" Bruno retorted. "Oo just try me!"

"What I meant, was—" the Professor began, looking much puzzled, "—was—that you don't know *everything*, you know."

"But I *do* know everything I know!" persisted the little fellow. "I know ever so many things! Everything, 'cept the things I *don't* know. And Sylvie knows all the rest."

The Professor sighed, and gave it up. "Do you know what a Boojum is?"

"*I* know!" cried Bruno. "It's the thing what wrenches people out of their boots!"

"He means 'bootjack'," Sylvie explained in a whisper.

"You ca'n't wrench people out of *boots*," the Professor mildly observed.

Bruno laughed saucily. "Oo *can*, though! Unless they're *welly* tight in."

"Once upon a time there was a Boojum——" the Professor began, but stopped suddenly. "I forget the rest of the Fable," he said. "And there was a lesson to be learned from it. I'm afraid I forget *that* too."

"*I'll* tell oo a Fable!" Bruno began in a great hurry. "Once there were a Locust, and a Magpie, and a Engine-driver. And the Lesson is, to learn to get up early——"

"It isn't a bit interesting!" Sylvie said contemptuously. "You shouldn't put the Lesson so soon."

"When did you invent that Fable?" said the Professor. "Last week?"

"No!" said Bruno. "A deal shorter ago than that, Guess again!"

"I ca'n't guess," said the Professor. "How long ago?"

"Why, it isn't invented yet!" Bruno exclaimed triumphantly. "But I *have* invented a lovely one! Shall I say it?"

"If you've *finished* inventing it," said Sylvie. "And let the Lesson be 'to try again'!"

"No," said Bruno with great decision. "The Lesson are '*not* to try again'!" "Once there were a lovely china man, what stood on the chimbley-piece. And he stood, and he stood. And one day he tumbleded off, and he didn't hurt his self one bit. Only he *would* try again. And the next time he tumbleded off, he hurted his self welly much, and breaked off ever so much varnish."

"But how did he come back on the chimney-piece after his first tumble?" said the Empress. (It was the first sensible question she had asked in all her life.)

"*I* put him there!" cried Bruno.

"Then I'm afraid you know something about his tumbling," said the Professor. "Perhaps you pushed him?"

To which Bruno replied, very seriously, "Didn't pushed him *much*—he were a *lovely* china man," he added hastily, evidently very anxious to change the subject.

"Come, my children!" said the Elfin-King, who had just entered the room. "We must have a little chat together, before you go to bed." And he was leading them away, but at the door they let go his hands, and ran back again to wish the Professor good night.

"Good night, Profesor, good night!" And Bruno solemnly shook hands with the old man, who gazed at him with a loving smile, while Sylvie bent down to press her sweet lips upon his forehead.

"Good night, little ones!" said the Professor. "You may leave me now—to ruminate. I'm as jolly as the day is long, except when it's necessary to ruminate on some very difficult subject. All of me," he murmured sleepily as we left the room, "all of me, that isn't *Bonhommie*, is Rumination!"

"*What* did he say, Bruno?" Sylvie enquired, as soon as we were safely out of hearing.

"I *think* he said 'All of me that isn't Bone-disease is Rheumatism.' Whatever *are* that knocking, Sylvie?"

Sylvie stopped, and listened anxiously. It sounded like some one kicking at a door, "I *hope* it isn't that Porcupine breaking loose!" she exclaimed.

"Let's go on!" Bruno said hastily. "There's nuffin to wait for, oo know!"

Chapter XXV

Life Out of Death

THE sound of kicking, or knocking, grew louder every moment: and at last a door opened somewhere near us. "Did you say 'come in!' Sir?" my landlady asked timidly.

"Oh yes, come in!" I replied. "What's the matter?"

"A note has just been left for you, Sir, by the baker's boy. He said he was passing the Hall, and they asked him to come round and leave it here."

The note contained five words only. "Please come at once. Muriel."

A sudden terror seemed to chill my very heart. "The Earl is ill!" I said to myself. "Dying, perhaps!" And I hastily prepared to leave the house.

"No bad news, Sir, I hope?" my landlady said, as she saw me out. "The boy said as some one had arrived unexpectedly——"

"I hope that is it!" I said. But my feelings were those of fear rather than of hope: though, on entering the house, I was somehat reassured by finding luggage lying in the entrance, bearing the initials "E. L."

"It's only Eric Lindon after all!" I thought, half relieved and half annoyed. "Surely she need not have sent for me for *that*!"

Lady Muriel met me in the passage. Her eyes were gleaming—but it was the excitement of joy, rather than of grief. "I have a surprise for you!" she whispered.

"You mean that Eric Lindon is here?" I said, vainly trying to disguise the involuntary bitterness of my tone. " '*The funeral baked meats did coldly furnish forth the marriage-tables,*' " I could not help repeating to myself. How cruelly I was misjudging her!

"No, no!" she eagerly replied. "At least—Eric *is* here. But——" her voice quivered, "but there is *another*!"

No need for further question. I eagerly followed her in. There on the bed, he lay—pale and worn—the mere

670

shadow of his old self—my old friend come back again from the dead!

"Arthur!" I exclaimed. I could not say another word.

"Yes, back again, old boy!" he murmured, smiling as I grasped his hand. *"He"*, indicating Eric, who stood near, "saved my life—*He* brought me back. Next to God, we must thank *him*, Muriel, my wife!"

Silently I shook hands with Eric, and with the Earl: and with one consent we moved into the shaded side of the room, where we could talk without disturbing the invalid, who lay, silent and happy, holding his wife's hand in his, and watching her with eyes that shone with the deep steady light of Love.

"He has been delirious till to-day," Eric explained in a low voice: "and even to-day he has been wandering more than once. But the sight of *her* has been new life to him." And then he went on to tell us, in would-be careless tones —I knew how he hated any display of feeling—how he had insisted on going back to the plague-stricken town, to bring away a man whom the doctor had abandoned as dying, but who *might*, he fancied, recover if brought to the hospital: how he had seen nothing in the wasted features to remind him of Arthur, and only recognized him when he visited the hospital a month after: how the doctor had forbidden him to announce the discovery, saying that any shock to the over-taxed brain might kill him at once: how he had stayed on at the hospital, and nursed the sick man by night and day—all this with the studied indifference of one who is relating the common-place acts of some chance acquaintance!

"And this was his *rival*!" I thought. "The man who had won from him the heart of the woman he loved!"

"The sun is setting," said Lady Muriel, rising and leading the way to the open window. "Just look at the western sky! What lovely crimson tints! We shall have a glorious day to-morrow——" We had followed her across the room, and were standing in a little group, talking in low tones in the gathering gloom, when we were startled by the voice of the sick man, murmuring words too indistinct for the ear to catch.

"He is wandering again," Lady Muriel whispered, and returned to the bedside. We drew a little nearer also: but no, this had none of the incoherence of delirium. *"What reward shall I give unto the Lord"*, the tremulous lips were saying, *"for all the benefits that He hath done unto me? I will receive the cup of salvation, and call—and call——"* but here the poor weakened memory failed, and the feeble voice died into silence.

His wife knelt down at the bedside, raised one of his arms, and drew it across her own, fondly kissing the thin white hand that lay so listlessly in her loving grasp. It seemed to me a good opportunity for stealing away without making her go through any form of parting: so, nodding to the Earl and Eric, I silently left the room. Eric followed me down the stairs, and out into the night.

"Is it Life or Death?" I asked him, as soon as we were far enough from the house for me to speak in ordinary tones.

"It is *Life!*" he replied with eager emphasis. "The doctors are quite agreed as to *that*. All he needs now, they say, is rest, and perfect quiet, and good nursing. He's quite sure to get rest and quiet, here: and, as for the nursing, why, I think it's just *possible*——" (he tried hard to make his trembling voice assume a playful tone) "he may even get fairly well nursed, in his present quarters!"

"I'm sure of it!" I said. "Thank you so much for coming out to tell me!" And, thinking he had now said all he had come to say, I held out my hand to bid him good night. He grasped it warmly, and added, turning his face away as he spoke, "By the way, there is one other thing I wanted to say, I thought you'd like to know that—that I'm not—not in the mind I was in when last we met. It isn't—that I can accept Christian belief—at least, not yet. But all this came about so strangely. And she had prayed, you know. And I had prayed. And—and" his voice broke, and I could only just catch the concluding words, *"there is a God that answers prayer! I know it for* certain now." He wrung my hand once more, and left me suddenly. Never before had I seen him so deeply moved.

So, in the gathering twilight, I paced slowly homewards, in a tumultuous whirl of happy thoughts: my heart seemed full, and running over, with joy and thankfulness: all that I had so fervently longed for, and prayed for, seemed now to have come to pass. And, though I reproached myself, bitterly, for the unworthy suspicion I had for one moment harboured against the true-hearted Lady Muriel, I took comfort in knowing it had been but a passing thought.

Not Bruno himself could have mounted the stairs with so buoyant a step, as I felt my way up in the dark, not pausing to strike a light in the entry, as I knew I had left the lamp burning in my sitting-room.

But it was no common *lamplight* into which I now stepped, with a strange, new, dreamy sensation of some subtle witchery that had come over the place. Light, richer and more golden than any lamp could give, flooded the room, streaming in from a window I had somehow never noticed before, and lighting up a group of three shadowy figures, that grew momently more distinct—a grave old man in royal robes, leaning back in an easy chair, and two children, a girl and a boy, standing at his side.

"Have you the Jewel still, my child?" the old man was saying.

"Oh, *yes!*" Sylvie exclaimed with unusual eagerness. "Do you think I'd *ever* lose it or forget it?" She undid the ribbon round her neck, as she spoke, and laid the Jewel in her father's hand.

Bruno looked at it admiringly. "What a lovely brightness!" he said. "It's just like a little red star! May I take it in my hand?"

Sylvie nodded: and Bruno carried it off to the window, and held it aloft against the sky, whose deepening blue was already spangled with stars. Soon he came running back in some excitement. "Sylvie! Look here!" he cried. "I can see right through it when I hold it up to the sky.

And it isn't red a bit: it's, oh such a lovely blue! And the words are all different! Do look at it!"

Sylvie was quite excited, too, by this time; and the two children eagerly held up the Jewel to the light, and spelled out the legend between them, "ALL WILL LOVE SYLVIE."

"Why, this is the *other* Jewel!" cried Bruno. "Don't you remember, Sylvie? The one you *didn't* choose!"

Sylvie took it from him, with a puzzled look, and held it, now up to the light, now down. "It's blue, *one* way," she said softly to herself, "and it's red the *other* way! Why, I thought there were *two* of them—Father!" she suddenly exclaimed, laying the Jewel once more in his hand, "I do believe it was the *same* Jewel all the time!"

"Then you chose it from *itself*," Bruno thoughtfully remarked. "Father, *could* Sylvie choose a thing from itself?"

"Yes, my own one," the old man replied to Sylvie, not noticing Bruno's embarrassing question, "it *was* the same Jewel—but you chose quite right." And he fastened the ribbon round her neck again.

"SYLVIE WILL LOVE ALL—ALL WILL LOVE SYLVIE." Bruno murmured, raising himself on tiptoe to kiss the "little red star". "And, when you look *at* it, it's red and fierce like the sun—and, when you look *through* it, it's gentle and blue like the sky!"

"God's own sky," Sylvie said, dreamily.

"God's own sky," the little fellow repeated, as they stood, lovingly clinging together, and looking out into the night. "But oh, Sylvie, what makes the sky such a *darling* blue?"

Sylvie's sweet lips shaped themselves to reply, but her voice sounded faint and very far away. The vision was fast slipping from my eager gaze: but it seemed to me, in that last bewildering moment, that not Sylvie but an angel was looking out through those trustful brown eyes, and that not Sylvie's but an angel's voice was whispering

"IT IS LOVE."

V
Verse

PREFACE TO
THE HUNTING OF THE SNARK

IF—and the thing is wildly possible—the charge of writing nonsense were ever brought against the author of this brief but instructive poem, it would be based, I feel convinced, on the line (in p. 684)

"Then the bowsprit got mixed with the rudder sometimes:"

In view of this painful possibility, I will not (as I might) appeal indignantly to my other writings as a proof that I am incapable of such a deed: I will not (as I might) point to the strong moral purpose of this poem itself, to the arithmetical principles so cautiously inculcated in it, or to its noble teachings in Natural History—I will take the more prosaic course of simply explaining how it happened.

The Bellman, who was almost morbidly sensitive about appearances, used to have the bowsprit unshipped once or twice a week to be revarnished; and it more than once happened, when the time came for replacing it, that no one on board could remember which end of the ship it belonged to. They knew it was not of the slightest use to appeal to the Bellman about it—he would only refer to his Naval Code, and read out in pathetic tones Admiralty Instructions which none of them had ever been able to understand—so it generally ended in its being fastened on, anyhow, across the rudder. The helmsman[1] used to stand by with tears in his eyes: *he* knew it was all wrong, but alas! Rule 42 of the Code, *"No one shall speak to the*

---

[1] This office was usually undertaken by the Boots, who found in it a refuge from the Baker's constant complaints about the insufficient blacking of his three pairs of boots.

Man at the Helm," had been completed by the Bellman himself with the words *"and the Man at the Helm shall speak to no one."* So remonstrance was impossible, and no steering could be done till the next varnishing day. During these bewildering intervals the ship usually sailed backwards.

As this poem is to some extent connected with the lay of the Jabberwock, let me take this opportunity of answering a question that has often been asked me, how to pronounce "slithy toves". The "i" in "slithy" is long, as in "writhe"; and "toves" is pronounced so as to rhyme with "groves". Again, the first "o" in "borogoves" is pronounced like the "o" in "borrow". I have heard people try to give it the sound of the "o" in "worry". Such is Human Perversity.

This also seems a fitting occasion to notice the other hard words in that poem. Humpty-Dumpty's theory, of two meanings packed into one word like a portmanteau, seems to me the right explanation for all.

For instance, take the two words "fuming" and "furious". Make up your mind that you will say both words, but leave it unsettled which you will say first. Now open your mouth and speak. If your thoughts incline ever so little towards "fuming", you will say "fuming-furious"; if they turn, by even a hair's breadth, towards "furious", you will say "furious-fuming"; but if you have that rarest of gifts, a perfectly balanced mind, you will say "frumious".

Supposing that, when Pistol uttered the well-known words—

"Under which king, Bezonian? Speak or die!"

Justice Shallow had felt certain that it was either William or Richard, but had not been able to settle which, so that he could not possibly say either name before the other, can it be doubted that, rather than die, he would have gasped out "Rilchiam!"

INSCRIBED TO A DEAR CHILD:
IN MEMORY OF GOLDEN SUMMER HOURS
AND WHISPERS OF A SUMMER SEA

Girt with a boyish garb for boyish task,
 Eager she wields her spade: yet loves as well
Rest on a friendly knee, intent to ask
 The tale he loves to tell.

Rude spirits of the seething outer strife,
 Unmeet to read her pure and simple spright,
Deem, if you list, such hours a waste of life,
 Empty of all delight!

Chat on, sweet Maid, and rescue from annoy
 Hearts that by wiser talk are unbeguiled.
Ah, happy he who owns that tenderest joy,
 The heart-love of a child!

Away, fond thoughts, and vex my soul no more!
 Work claims my wakeful nights, my busy days—
Albeit bright memories of that sunlit shore
 Yet haunt my dreaming gaze!

THE HUNTING OF THE SNARK

The Landing

"Just the place for a Snark!" the Bellman cried,
  As he landed his crew with care;
Supporting each man on the top of the tide
  By a finger entwined in his hair.

"Just the place for a Snark! I have said it twice:
  That alone should encourage the crew.
Just the place for a Snark! I have said it thrice:
  What I tell you three times is true."

The crew was complete: it included a Boots—
  A maker of Bonnets and Hoods—
A Barrister, brought to arrange their disputes—
  And a Broker, to value their goods.

A Billiard-marker, whose skill was immense,
  Might perhaps have won more than his share—
But a Banker, engaged at enormous expense,
  Had the whole of their cash in his care.

There was also a Beaver, that paced on the deck,
  Or would sit making lace in the bow:
And had often (the Bellman said) saved them from wreck
  Though none of the sailors knew how.

There was one who was famed for the number of things
  He forgot when he entered the ship:
His umbrella, his watch, all his jewels and rings,
  And the clothes he had bought for the trip.

He had forty-two boxes, all carefully packed,
    With his name painted clearly on each:
But, since he omitted to mention the fact,
    They were all left behind on the beach.

The loss of his clothes hardly mattered, because
    He had seven coats on when he came,
With three pair of boots—but the worst of it was,
    He had wholly forgotten his name.

He would answer to "Hi!" or to any loud cry,
    Such as "Fry me!" or "Fritter my wig!"
To "What-you-may-call-um!" or "What-was-his-name!"
    But especially "Thing-um-a-jig!"

While, for those who preferred a more forcible word,
    He had different names from these:
His intimate friends called him "Candle-ends",
    And his enemies "Toasted-cheese"

"His form is ungainly—his intellect small—"
    (So the Bellman would often remark)—
"But his courage is perfect! And that, after all,
    Is the thing that one needs with a Snark."

He would joke with hyænas, returning their stare
    With an impudent wag of the head:
And he once went a walk, paw-in-paw, with a bear,
    "Just to keep up its spirits," he said.

He came as a Baker: but owned, when too late—
    And it drove the poor Bellman half-mad—
He could only bake Bridecake—for which, I may state,
    No materials were to be had.

The last of the crew needs especial remark,
    Though he looked an incredible dunce:
He had just one idea—but, that one being "Snark",
    The good Bellman engaged him at once.

He came as a Butcher: but gravely declared,
　　When the ship had been sailing a week,
He could only kill Beavers. The Bellman looked scared,
　　And was almost too frightened to speak:

But at length he explained, in a tremulous tone,
　　There was only one Beaver on board;
And that was a tame one he had of his own,
　　Whose death would be deeply deplored.

The Beaver, who happened to hear the remark,
　　Protested, with tears in its eyes,
That not even the rapture of hunting the Snark
　　Could atone for that dismal surprise!

It strongly advised that the Butcher should be
　　Conveyed in a separate ship:
But the Bellman declared that would never agree
　　With the plans he had made for the trip:

Navigation was always a difficult art,
　　Though with only one ship and one bell:
And he feared he must really decline, for his part,
　　Undertaking another as well.

The Beaver's best course was, no doubt, to procure
　　A second-hand dagger-proof coat—
So the Baker advised it—and next, to insure
　　Its life in some Office of note:

This the Baker suggested, and offered for hire
　　(On moderate terms), or for sale,
Two excellent Policies, one Against Fire
　　And one Against Damage From Hail.

Yet still, ever after that sorrowful day,
　　Whenever the Butcher was by,
The Beaver kept looking the opposite way,
　　And appeared unaccountably shy.

FIT THE SECOND

The Bellman's Speech

THE Bellman himself they all praised to the skies—
    Such a carriage, such ease and such grace!
Such solemnity, too! One could see he was wise,
    The moment one looked in his face!

He had bought a large map representing the sea,
    Without the least vestige of land:
And the crew were much pleased when they found it to be
    A map they could all understand.

"What's the good of Mercator's North Poles and Equa-
        tors,
    Tropics, Zones, and Meridian Lines?"
So the Bellman would cry: and the crew would reply
    "They are merely conventional signs!

"Other maps are such shapes, with their islands and
        capes!
    But we've got our brave Captain to thank"
(So the crew would protest) "that he's bought *us* the
        best—
    A perfect and absolute blank!"

This was charming, no doubt: but they shortly found out
    That the Captain they trusted so well
Had only one notion for crossing the ocean,
    And that was to tingle his bell.

He was thoughtful and grave—but the orders he gave
    Were enough to bewilder a crew.
When he cried "Steer to starboard, but keep her head
        larboard!"
    What on earth was the helmsman to do?

Then the bowsprit got mixed with the rudder sometimes:
    A thing, as the Bellman remarked,
That frequently happens in tropical climes,
    When a vessel is, so to speak, "snarked".

But the principal failing occurred in the sailing,
    And the Bellman, perplexed and distressed,
Said he *had* hoped, at least, when the wind blew due East,
    That the ship would *not* travel due West!

But the danger was past—they had landed at last,
    With their boxes, portmanteaus, and bags:
Yet at first sight the crew were not pleased with the view
    Which consisted of chasms and crags.

The Bellman perceived that their spirits were low,
    And repeated in musical tone
Some jokes he had kept for a season of woe—
    But the crew would do nothing but groan.

He served out some grog with a liberal hand,
    And bade them sit down on the beach:
And they could not but own that their Captain looked
       grand,
    As he stood and delivered his speech.

"Friends, Romans, and countrymen, lend me your ears!"
    (They were all of them fond of quotations:
So they drank to his health, and they gave him three
       cheers,
    While he served out additional rations).

"We have sailed many months, we have sailed many
       weeks,
    (Four weeks to the month you may mark),
But never as yet ('tis your Captain who speaks)
    Have we caught the least glimpse of a Snark!

"We have sailed many weeks, we have sailed many days,
　(Seven days to the week I allow),
But a Snark, on the which we might lovingly gaze,
　We have never beheld till now!

"Come, listen, my men, while I tell you again
　The five unmistakable marks
By which you may know, wheresoever you go,
　The warranted genuine Snarks.

"Let us take them in order. The first is the taste,
　Which is meagre and hollow, but crisp:
Like a coat that is rather too tight in the waist,
　With a flavour of Will-o'-the-Wisp.

"Its habit of getting up late you'll agree
　That it carries too far, when I say
That it frequently breakfasts at five-o'clock tea,
　And dines on the following day.

"The third is its slowness in taking a jest.
　Should you happen to venture on one,
It will sigh like a thing that is deeply distressed:
　And it always looks grave at a pun.

"The fourth is its fondness for bathing-machines,
　Which it constantly carries about,
And believes that they add to the beauty of scenes—
　A sentiment open to doubt.

"The fifth is ambition. It next will be right
　To describe each particular batch:
Distinguishing those that have feathers, and bite,
　From those that have whiskers, and scratch.

"For, although common Snarks do no manner of harm,
　Yet I feel it my duty to say
Some are Boojums——" The Bellman broke off in alarm,
　For the Baker had fainted away.

Fit the Third

The Baker's Tale

THEY roused him with muffins—they roused him with
    ice—
They roused him with mustard and cress—
They roused him with jam and judicious advice—
    They set him conundrums to guess.

When at length he sat up and was able to speak,
    His sad story he offered to tell;
And the Bellman cried "Silence! Not even a shriek!"
    And excitedly tingled his bell.

There was silence supreme! Not a shriek, not a scream,
    Scarcely even a howl or a groan,
As the man they called "Ho!" told his story of woe
    In an antediluvian tone.

"My father and mother were honest, though poor——"
    "Skip all that!" cried the Bellman in haste.
"If it once becomes dark, there's no chance of a Snark—
    We have hardly a minute to waste!"

"I skip forty years," said the Baker in tears,
    "And proceed without further remark
To the day when you took me aboard of your ship
    To help you in hunting the Snark.

"A dear uncle of mine (after whom I was named)
    Remarked, when I bade him farewell——"
"Oh, skip your dear uncle!" the Bellman exclaimed,
    As he angrily tingled his bell.

"He remarked to me then," said that mildest of men,
    " 'If your Snark be a Snark, that is right:

Fetch it home by all means—you may serve it with greens
    And it's handy for striking a light.

" 'You may seek it with thimbles—and seek it with care—
    You may hunt it with forks and hope;
You may threaten its life with a railway-share;
    You may charm it with smiles and soap——' "

("That's exactly the method," the Bellman bold
    In a hasty parenthesis cried,
"That's exactly the way I have always been told
    That the capture of Snarks should be tried!")

" 'But oh, beamish nephew, beware of the day,
    If your Snark be a Boojum! For then
You will softly and suddenly vanish away,
    And never be met with again!'

"It is this, it is this that oppresses my soul,
    When I think of my uncle's last words:
And my heart is like nothing so much as a bowl
    Brimming over with quivering curds!

"It is this, it is this——" "We have had that before!"
    The Bellman indignantly said.
And the Baker replied "Let me say it once more.
    It is this, it is this that I dread!

"I engage with the Snark—every night after dark—
    In a dreamy delirious fight:
I serve it with greens in those shadowy scenes,
    And I use it for striking a light:

"But if ever I meet with a Boojum, that day,
    In a moment (of this I am sure),
I shall softly and suddenly vanish away—
    And the notion I cannot endure!"

Fit the Fourth

The Hunting

The Bellman looked uffish, and wrinkled his brow.
　　"If only you'd spoken before!
It's excessively awkward to mention it now,
　　With the Snark, so to speak, at the door!

"We should all of us grieve, as you well may believe,
　　If you never were met with again—
But surely, my man, when the voyage began,
　　You might have suggested it then?

"It's excessively awkward to mention it now—
　　As I think I've already remarked."
And the man they called "Hi!" replied, with a sigh,
　　"I informed you the day we embarked.

"You may charge me with murder—or want of sense—
　　(We are all of us weak at times):
But the slightest approach to a false pretence
　　Was never among my crimes!

"I said it in Hebrew—I said it in Dutch—
　　I said it in German and Greek:
But I wholly forgot (and it vexes me much)
　　That English is what you speak!"

" 'Tis a pitiful tale," said the Bellman, whose face
　　Had grown longer at every word:
"But, now that you've stated the whole of your case,
　　More debate would be simply absurd.

"The rest of my speech" (he exclaimed to his men)
　　"You shall hear when I've leisure to speak it.
But the Snark is at hand, let me tell you again!
　　'Tis your glorious duty to seek it!

"To seek it with thimbles, to seek it with care;
   To pursue it with forks and hope;
To threaten its life with a railway-share;
   To charm it with smiles and soap!

"For the Snark's a peculiar creature, that wo'n't
   Be caught in a commonplace way.
Do all that you know, and try all that you don't:
   Not a chance must be wasted to-day!

"For England expects—I forbear to proceed:
   'Tis a maxim tremendous, but trite:
And you'd best be unpacking the things that you need
   To rig yourselves out for the fight."

Then the Banker endorsed a blank cheque (which he
      crossed),
   And changed his loose silver for notes:
The Baker with care combed his whiskers and hair.
   And shook the dust out of his coats:

The Boots and the Broker were sharpening a spade—
   Each working the grindstone in turn:
But the Beaver went on making lace, and displayed
   No interest in the concern:

Though the Barrister tried to appeal to its pride,
   And vainly proceeded to cite
A number of cases, in which making laces
   Had been proved an infringement of right.

The maker of Bonnets ferociously planned
   A novel arrangement of bows:
While the Billiard-marker with quivering hand
   Was chalking the tip of his nose.

But the Butcher turned nervous, and dressed himself fine,
   With yellow kid gloves and a ruff—

Said he felt it exactly like going to dine,
    Which the Bellman declared was all "stuff".

"Introduce me, now there's a good fellow," he said,
    "If we happen to meet it together!"
And the Bellman, sagaciously nodding his head,
    Said "That must depend on the weather."

The Beaver went simply galumphing about,
    At seeing the Butcher so shy:
And even the Baker, though stupid and stout,
    Made an effort to wink with one eye.

"Be a man!" said the Bellman in wrath, as he heard
    The Butcher beginning to sob.
"Should we meet with a Jubjub, that desperate bird,
    We shall need all our strength for the job!"

Fit the Fifth

The Beaver's Lesson

THEY sought it with thimbles, they sought it with care;
    They pursued it with forks and hope;
They threatened its life with a railway-share;
    They charmed it with smiles and soap.

Then the Butcher contrived an ingenious plan
    For making a separate sally;
And had fixed on a spot unfrequented by man,
    A dismal and desolate valley.

But the very same plan to the Beaver occurred:
    It had chosen the very same place:
Yet neither betrayed, by a sign or a word,
    The disgust that appeared in his face.

Each thought he was thinking of nothing but "Snark"
    And the glorious work of the day;
And each tried to pretend that he did not remark
    That the other was going that way.

But the valley grew narrower and narrower still,
    And the evening got darker and colder,
Till (merely from nervousness, not from good will)
    They marched along shoulder to shoulder.

Then a scream, shrill and high, rent the shuddering sky
    And they knew that some danger was near:
The Beaver turned pale to the tip of its tail,
    And even the Butcher felt queer.

He thought of his childhood, left far behind—
    That blissful and innocent state—
The sound so exactly recalled to his mind
    A pencil that squeaks on a slate!

" 'Tis the voice of the Jubjub!" he suddenly cried.
    (This man, that they used to call "Dunce".)
"As the Bellman would tell you," he added with pride,
    "I have uttered that sentiment once.

" 'Tis the note of the Jubjub! Keep count, I entreat.
    You will find I have told it you twice.
'Tis the song of the Jubjub! The proof is complete.
    If only I've stated it thrice."

The Beaver had counted with scrupulous care,
    Attending to every word:
But it fairly lost heart, and outgrabe in despair,
    When the third repetition occurred.

It felt that, in spite of all possible pains,
    It had somehow contrived to lose count,
And the only thing now was to rack its poor brains
    By reckoning up the amount.

"Two added to one—if that could but be done",
  It said, "with one's fingers and thumbs!"
Recollecting with tears how, in earlier years,
  It had taken no pains with its sums.

"The thing can be done," said the Butcher, "I think.
  The thing must be done, I am sure.
The thing shall be done! Bring me paper and ink,
  The best there is time to procure."

The Beaver brought paper, portfolio, pens,
  And ink in unfailing supplies:
While strange creepy creatures came out of their dens,
  And watched them with wondering eyes.

So engrossed was the Butcher, he heeded them not,
  As he wrote with a pen in each hand,
And explained all the while in a popular style
  Which the Beaver could well understand.

"Taking Three as the subject to reason about—
  A convenient number to state—
We add Seven, and Ten, and then multiply out
  By One Thousand diminished by Eight.

"The result we proceed to divide, as you see,
  By Nine Hundred and Ninety and Two:
Then subtract Seventeen, and the answer must be
  Exactly and perfectly true.

"The method employed I would gladly explain,
  While I have it so clear in my head,
If I had but the time and you had but the brain—
  But much yet remains to be said.

"In one moment I've seen what has hitherto been
  Enveloped in absolute mystery,
And without extra charge I will give you at large
  A Lesson in Natural History."

In his genial way he proceeded to say
   (Forgetting all laws of propriety,
And that giving instruction, without introduction,
   Would have caused quite a thrill in Society),

"As to temper the Jubjub's a desperate bird.
   Since it lives in perpetual passion:
Its taste in costume is entirely absurd—
   It is ages ahead of the fashion:

"But it knows any friend it has met once before:
   It never will look at a bribe:
And in charity-meetings it stands at the door,
   And collects—though it does not subscribe.

"Its flavour when cooked is more exquisite far
   Than mutton, or oysters, or eggs:
(Some think it keeps best in an ivory jar,
   And some, in mahogany kegs:)

"You boil it in sawdust: you salt it in glue:
   You condense it with locusts and tape:
Still keeping one principal object in view—
   To preserve its symmetrical shape."

The Butcher would gladly have talked till next day,
   But he felt that the Lesson must end,
And he wept with delight in attempting to say
   He considered the Beaver his friend:

While the Beaver confessed, with affectionate looks
   More eloquent even than tears,
It had learned in ten minutes far more than all books
   Would have taught it in seventy years.

They returned hand-in-hand, and the Bellman, unmanned
   (For a moment) with noble emotion,
Said "This amply repays all the wearisome days
   We have spent on the billowy ocean!"

Such friends, as the Beaver and Butcher became,
    Have seldom if ever been known;
In winter or summer, 'twas always the same—
    You could never meet either alone.

And when quarrels arose—as one frequently finds
    Quarrels will, spite of every endeavour—
The song of the Jubjub recurred to their minds,
    And cemented their friendship for ever!

Fit the Sixth

The Barrister's Dream

THEY sought it with thimbles, they sought it with care;
    They pursued it with forks and hope;
They threatened its life with a railway-share;
    They charmed it with smiles and soap.

But the Barrister, weary of proving in vain
    That the Beaver's lace-making was wrong,
Fell asleep, and in dreams saw the creature quite plain
    That his fancy had dwelt on so long.

He dreamed that he stood in a shadowy Court,
    Where the Snark, with a glass in its eye,
Dressed in gown, bands, and wig, was defending a pig
    On the charge of deserting its sty.

The Witnesses proved, without error or flaw,
    That the sty was deserted when found:
And the Judge kept explaining the state of the law
    In a soft under-current of sound.

The indictment had never been clearly expressed,
    And it seemed that the Snark had begun,
And had spoken three hours, before any one guessed
    What the pig was supposed to have done.

The Jury had each formed a different view
    (Long before the indictment was read),
And they all spoke at once, so that none of them knew
    One word that the others had said.

"You must know——" said the Judge: but the Snark ex-
        claimed "Fudge!
    That statute is obsolete quite!
Let me tell you, my friends, the whole question depends
    On an ancient manorial right.

"In the matter of Treason the pig would appear
    To have aided, but scarcely abetted:
While the charge of Insolvency fails, it is clear,
    If you grant the plea 'never indebted'.

"The fact of Desertion I will not dispute:
    But its guilt, as I trust, is removed
(So far as relates to the costs of this suit)
    By the Alibi which has been proved.

"My poor client's fate now depends on your votes."
    Here the speaker sat down in his place,
And directed the Judge to refer to his notes
    And briefly to sum up the case.

But the Judge said he never had summed up before;
    So the Snark undertook it instead,
And summed it so well that it came to far more
    Than the Witnesses ever had said!

When the verdict was called for, the Jury declined,
    As the word was so puzzling to spell;
But they ventured to hope that the Snark wouldn't mind
    Undertaking that duty as well.

So the Snark found the verdict, although, as it owned,
    It was spent with the toils of the day:

When it said the word "GUILTY!" the Jury all groaned
  And some of them fainted away.

Then the Snark pronounced sentence, the Judge being
      quite
  Too nervous to utter a word:
When it rose to its feet, there was silence like night,
  And the fall of a pin might be heard.

"Transportation for life" was the sentence it gave,
  "And *then* to be fined forty pound."
The Jury all cheered, though the Judge said he feared
  That the phrase was not legally sound.

But their wild exultation was suddenly checked
  When the jailer informed them, with tears,
Such a sentence would have not the slightest effect,
  As the pig had been dead for some years.

The Judge left the Court, looking deeply disgusted
  But the Snark, though a little aghast,
As the lawyer to whom the defence was intrusted,
  Went bellowing on to the last.

Thus the Barrister dreamed, while the bellowing seemed
  To grow every moment more clear:
Till he woke to the knell of a furious bell,
  Which the Bellman rang close at his ear.

Fit the Seventh

The Banker's Fate

THEY sought it with thimbles, they sought it with care;
  They pursued it with forks and hope;
They threatened its life with a railway-share;
  They charmed it with smiles and soap.

And the Banker, inspired with a courage so new
  It was matter for general remark,
Rushed madly ahead and was lost to their view
  In his zeal to discover the Snark.

But while he was seeking with thimbles and care,
  A Bandersnatch swiftly drew nigh
And grabbed at the Banker, who shrieked in despair,
  For he knew it was useless to fly.

He offered large discount—he offered a cheque
  (Drawn "to bearer") for seven-pounds-ten:
But the Bandersnatch merely extended its neck
  And grabbed at the Banker again.

Without rest or pause—while those frumious jaws
  Went savagely snapping around—
He skipped and he hopped, and he floundered and flopped,
  Till fainting he fell to the ground.

The Bandersnatch fled as the others appeared
  Led on by that fear-stricken yell:
And the Bellman remarked "It is just as I feared!"
  And solemnly tolled on his bell.

He was black in the face, and they scarcely could trace
  The least likeness to what he had been:
While so great was his fright that his waistcoat turned
        white—
  A wonderful thing to be seen!

To the horror of all who were present that day,
  He uprose in full evening dress,
And with senseless grimaces endeavoured to say
  What his tongue could no longer express.

Down he sank in a chair—ran his hands through his
        hair—
  And chanted in mimsiest tones

Words whose utter inanity proved his insanity,
   While he rattled a couple of bones.

"Leave him here to his fate—it is getting so late!"
   The Bellman exclaimed in a fright.
"We have lost half the day. Any further delay,
   And we sha'n't catch a Snark before night!"

FIT THE EIGHTH

The Vanishing

THEY sought it with thimbles, they sought it with care;
   They pursued it with forks and hope;
They threatened its life with a railway-share;
   They charmed it with smiles and soap.

They shuddered to think that the chase might fail,
   And the Beaver, excited at last,
Went bounding along on the tip of its tail,
   For the daylight was nearly past.

"There is Thingumbob shouting!" the Bellman said.
   "He is shouting like mad, only hark!
He is waving his hands, he is wagging his head,
   He has certainly found a Snark!"

They gazed in delight, while the Butcher exclaimed
   "He was always a desperate wag!"
They beheld him—their Baker—their hero unnamed—
   On the top of a neighbouring crag,

Erect and sublime, for one moment of time,
   In the next, that wild figure they saw
(As if stung by a spasm) plunge into a chasm,
   While they waited and listened in awe.

"It's a Snark!" was the sound that first came to their ears,
    And seemed almost too good to be true.
Then followed a torrent of laughter and cheers:
    Then the ominous words "It's a Boo——"

Then, silence. Some fancied they heard in the air
    A weary and wandering sigh
That sounded like "—jum!" but the others declare
    It was only a breeze that went by.

They hunted till darkness came on, but they found
    Not a button, or feather, or mark,
By which they could tell that they stood on the ground
    Where the Baker had met with the Snark.

In the midst of the word he was trying to say,
    In the midst of his laughter and glee,
He had softly and suddenly vanished away—
    For the Snark *was* a Boojum, you see.

EARLY VERSE

MY FAIRY
(1845)

I HAVE a fairy by my side
  Which says I must not sleep,
When once in pain I loudly cried
  It said "You must not weep".

If, full of mirth, I smile and grin,
  It says "You must not laugh";
When once I wished to drink some gin
  It said "You must not quaff".

When once a meal I wished to taste
  It said "You must not bite";
When to the wars I went in haste
  It said "You must not fight".

"What may I do?" at length I cried,
  Tired of the painful task.
The fairy quietly replied,
  And said "You must not ask".

    Moral: "You mustn't."

PUNCTUALITY

MAN naturally loves delay,
  And to procrastinate;
Business put off from day to day
  Is always done too late.

Let every hour be in its place
  Firm fixed, nor loosely shift,
And well enjoy the vacant space,
  As though a birthday gift.

And when the hour arrives, be *there*,
  Where'er that "there" may be;
Uncleanly hands or ruffled hair
  Let no one ever see.

If dinner at "half-past" be placed,
  At "half-past" then be dressed.
If at a "quarter-past" make haste
  To be down with the rest.

Better to be before your time,
  Than e'er to be behind;
To ope the door while strikes the chime,
  That shows a punctual mind.

Moral

Let punctuality and care
  Seize every flitting hour,
So shalt thou cull a floweret fair,
  E'en from a fading flower.

MELODIES

I

THERE was an old farmer of Readall,
Who made holes in his face with a needle,
    Then went *far* deeper in
    Than to pierce through the skin,
And yet strange to say he was made beadle.

II

There was an eccentric old draper,
Who wore a hat made of brown paper,
    It went up to a point,
    Yet it looked out of joint,
The cause of which *he* said was "vapour".

III

There was once a young man of Oporta,
Who daily got shorter and shorter,
    The reason he said
    Was the hod on his head,
Which was filled with the *heaviest* mortar.

His sister, named Lucy O'Finner,
Grew constantly thinner and thinner;
    The reason was plain,
    She slept out in the rain,
And was never allowed any dinner.

BROTHER AND SISTER

"SISTER, sister, go to bed!
Go and rest your weary head."
Thus the prudent brother said.

"Do you want a battered hide,
Or scratches to your face applied?"
Thus his sister calm replied.

"Sister, do not raise my wrath.
I'd make you into mutton broth
As easily as kill a moth!"

The sister raised her beaming eye
And looked on him indignantly
And sternly answered, "Only try!"

Off to the cook he quickly ran.
"Dear Cook, please lend a frying-pan
To me as quickly as you can."

"And wherefore should I lend it you?"
"The reason, Cook, is plain to view.
I wish to make an Irish stew."

"What meat is in that stew to go?"
"My sister'll be the contents!"
                              "Oh!"
"You'll lend the pan to me, Cook?"
                              "No!"
Moral: Never stew your sister.

FACTS

WERE I to take an iron gun,
And fire it off towards the sun;
I grant 'twould reach its mark at last,
But not till many years had passed.

But should that bullet change its force,
And to the planets take its course,
'Twould *never* reach the *nearest* star,
Because it is so *very* far.

RULES AND REGULATIONS

A SHORT direction
To avoid dejection,
By variations
In occupations,
And prolongation
Of relaxation,
And combinations
Of recreations,
And disputation
On the state of the nation
In adaptation
To your station,
By invitations
To friends and relations,
By evitation
Of amputation,
By permutation
In conversation,
And deep reflection
You'll avoid dejection.

Learn well your grammar,
And never stammer,
Write well and neatly,
And sing most sweetly,
Be enterprising,
Love early rising,
Go walk of six miles,
Have ready quick smiles,
With lightsome laughter,
Soft flowing after.
Drink tea, not coffee;
Never eat toffy.
Eat bread with butter.
Once more, don't stutter.

Don't waste your money,
Abstain from honey.
Shut doors behind you,
(Don't slam them, mind you.)
Drink beer, not porter.
Don't enter the water
Till to swim you are able.
Sit close to the table.
Take care of a candle.
Shut a door by the handle,
Don't push with your shoulder
Until you are older.
Lose not a button.
Refuse cold mutton.
Starve your canaries.
Believe in fairies.
If you are able,
Don't have a stable
With any mangers.
Be rude to strangers.

Moral: Behave.

HORRORS
(1850)

METHOUGHT I walked a dismal place
   Dim horrors all around;
The air was thick with many a face,
   And black as night the ground.

I saw a monster come with speed,
   Its face of grimmliest green,
On human beings used to feed,
   Most dreadful to be seen.

I could not speak, I could not fly,
  I fell down in that place,
I saw the monster's horrid eye
  Come leering in my face!

Amidst my scarcely-stifled groans,
  Amidst my moanings deep,
I heard a voice, "Wake! Mr. Jones,
  You're screaming in your sleep!"

MISUNDERSTANDINGS

If such a thing had been my thought,
I should have told you so before,
But as I didn't, then you ought
To ask for such a thing no more,
For to teach one who has been taught
Is always thought an awful bore.

Now to commence my argument,
I shall premise an observation,
On which the greatest kings have leant
When striving to subdue a nation,
And e'en the wretch who pays no rent
By it can solve a hard equation.

Its truth is such, the force of reason
Can not avail to shake its power,
Yet e'en the sun in summer season
Doth not dispel so mild a shower
As this, and he who sees it, sees on
Beyond it to a sunny bower—
No more, when ignorance is treason,
Let wisdom's brows be cold and sour.

AS IT FELL UPON A DAY

As I was sitting on the hearth
(*And O, but a hog is fat!*)
A man came hurrying up the path,
(*And what care I for that?*)

When he came the house unto,
His breath both quick and short he drew.

When he came before the door,
His face grew paler than before.

When he turned the handle round,
The man fell fainting to the ground.

When he crossed the lofty hall,
Once and again I heard him fall.

When he came up to the turret stair,
He shrieked and tore his raven hair.

When he came my chamber in,
(*And O, but a hog is fat!*)
I ran him through with a golden pin,
(*And what care I for that?*)

YE FATTALE CHEYSE

YTTE wes a mirke an dreiry cave,
  Weet scroggis[1] owr ytte creepe.
Gurgles withyn ye flowan wave
  Throw channel braid an deep

[1] bushes.

Never withyn that dreir recesse
 Wes sene ye lyghte of daye,
Quhat bode azont[1] yts mirkinesse[2]
 Nane kend an nane mote saye.

Ye monarche rade owr brake an brae
 An drave ye yellynge packe,
Hiz meany[3] au' richte cadgily[4]
 Are wendynge[5] yn hiz tracke.

Wi' eager iye, wi' yalpe an crye
 Ye hondes yode[6] down ye rocks,
Ahead of au' their companye
 Renneth ye panky[7] foxe.

Ye foxe hes soughte that cave of awe
 Forewearied[8] wi' hiz rin.
Quha nou ys he sae bauld an braw[9]
 To dare to enter yn?

Wi' eager bounde hes ilka honde
 Gane till that caverne dreir,
Fou[10] many a yowl[11] ys[12] hearde arounde,
 Fou[10] many a screech of feir.

Like ane wi' thirstie appetite
 Quha swalloweth orange pulp,
Wes hearde a huggle an a bite,
 A swallow an a gulp.

Ye kynge hes lap frae aff hiz steid,
 Outbrayde[13] hiz trenchant brande;

[1] beyond.
[2] darkness.
[3] company.
[4] merrily.
[5] going journeying.
[6] went.
[7] cunning.
[8] much wearied.
[9] brave.
[10] full.
[11] howl.
[12] is.
[13] drawn.

"Quha on my packe of hondes doth feed,
 Maun deye benead thilke hande."

Sae sed, sae dune: ye stonderes[1] hearde
 Fou many a mickle[2] stroke,
Sowns[3] lyke ye flappynge of a birde,
 A struggle an a choke.

Owte of ye cave scarce fette[4] they ytte,
 Wi pow[5] an push an hau'[6]—
Whereof Y've drawne a littel bytte,
 Bot durst not draw ytte au.[7]

LAYS OF SORROW

No. 1

THE day was wet, the rain fell souse
 Like jars of strawberry jam,[8] a
Sound was heard in the old henhouse,
 A beating of a hammer.
Of stalwart form, and visage warm,
 Two youths were seen within it,
Splitting up an old tree into perches for their poultry
 At a hundred strokes[9] a minute.

The work is done, the hen has taken
Possession of her nest and eggs,
Without a thought of eggs and bacon,[10]
(Or I am very much mistaken:)

[1] bystanders.
[2] heavy.
[3] sounds.
[4] fetched.
[5] pull.
[6] haul.
[7] all.
[8] *I.e.* the jam without the jars, Observe the beauty of this rhyme.
[9] At the rate of a stroke and two-thirds in a second.
[10] Unless the hen was a poacher, which is unlikely.

She turns over each shell,
To be sure that all's well,
Looks into the straw
  To see there's no flaw,
  Goes once round the house,[1]
  Half afraid of a mouse,
  Then sinks calmly to rest
  On the top of her nest,
First doubling up each of her legs.
Time rolled away, and so did every shell,
  "Small by degrees and beautifully less,"
As the sage mother with a powerful spell[2]
  Forced each in turn its contents to express,[3]
But ah! "imperfect is expression,"
  Some poet said, I don't care who,
If you want to know you must go elsewhere,
  One fact I can tell, if you're willing to hear,
  He never attended a Parliament Session,
  For I'm certain that if he had ever been there,
  Full quickly would he have changed his ideas,
  With the hissings, the hootings, the groans and the
    cheers.
  And as to his name it is pretty clear
  That it wasn't me and it wasn't you!

And so it fell upon a day,
  (That is, it never rose again)
A chick was found upon the hay,
Its little life had ebbed away.
No longer frolicsome and gay,
No longer could it run or play.
"And must we, chicken, must we part?"
Its master[4] cried with bursting heart,
  And voice of agony and pain.

---

[1] The henhouse.   [2] Beak and claw.
[3] Press out.
[4] Probably one of the two stalwart youths.

So one, whose ticket's marked "Return",[1]
When to the lonely roadside station
He flies in fear and perturbation,
Thinks of his home—the hissing urn—
Then runs with flying hat and hair,
And, entering, finds to his despair
    He's missed the very latest train.[2]

Too long it were to tell of each conjecture
    Of chicken suicide, and poultry victim,
The deadly frown, the stern and dreary lecture,
    The timid guess, "perhaps some needle pricked him!"
The din of voice, the words both loud and many,
    The sob, the tear, the sigh that none could smother,
Till all agreed "a shilling to a penny
    It killed itself, and we acquit the mother!"
    Scarce was the verdict spoken,
    When that still calm was broken,
A childish form hath burst into the throng;
    With tears and looks of sadness,
    That bring no news of gladness,
But tell too surely something hath gone wrong!
"The sight that I have come upon
    The stoutest heart[3] would sicken,
That nasty hen has been and gone
    And killed another chicken!"

[1] The system of return tickets is an excellent one. People are conveyed, on particular days, there and back again for one fare.

[2] An additional vexation would be that his "Return" ticket would be no use the next day.

[3] Perhaps even the "bursting" heart of its master.

LAYS OF SORROW

No. 2

F AI R stands the ancient[1] Rectory,
    The Rectory of Croft,
The sun shines bright upon it,
    The breezes whisper soft.

From all the house and garden,
    Its inhabitants come forth,
And muster in the road without,
And pace in twos and threes about,
    The children of the North.

Some are waiting in the garden,
    Some are waiting at the door,
And some are following behind,
    And some have gone before.
But wherefore all this mustering?
    Wherefore this vast array?
A gallant feat of horsemanship
    Will be performed to-day.

To eastward and to westward,
    The crowd divides amain,
Two youths are leading on the steed,
    Both tugging at the rein;
And sorely do they labour,
    For the steed[2] is very strong,

[1] This Rectory has been supposed to have been built in the time of Edward VI, but recent discoveries clearly assign its origin to a much earlier period. A stone has been found in an island formed by the river Tees on which is inscribed the letter "A", which is justly conjectured to stand for the name of the great King Alfred, in whose reign this house was probably built.

[2] The poet entreats pardon for having represented a donkey under this dignified name.

And backward moves its stubborn feet,
And backward ever doth retreat,
 And drags its guides along.

And now the knight hath mounted,
 Before the admiring band,
Hath got the stirrups on his feet,
 The bridle in his hand.
Yet, oh! beware, sir horseman!
 And tempt thy fate no more,
For such a steed as thou hast got
 Was never rid before!

The rabbits bow before thee,
 And cower in the straw;
The chickens[1] are submissive,
 And own thy will for law;
Bullfinches and canary
 Thy bidding do obey;
And e'en the tortoise in its shell
 Doth never say thee nay.

But thy steed will hear no master,
 Thy steed will bear no stick,
And woe to those that beat her,
 And woe to those that kick![2]
For though her rider smite her,
 As hard as he can hit,
And strive to turn her from the yard,
She stands in silence, pulling hard
 Against the pulling bit.

And now the road to Dalton
 Hath felt their coming tread,

---

[1] A full account of the history and misfortunes of these interesting creatures may be found in the first "Lay of Sorrow".

[2] It is a singular fact that a donkey makes a point of returning any kicks offered to it.

The crowd are speeding on before,
    And all have gone ahead.
Yet often look they backward,
    And cheer him on, and bawl,
For slower still, and still more slow,
That horseman and that charger go,
    And scarce advance at all.

And now two roads to choose from
    Are in that rider's sight:
In front the road to Dalton,
    And New Croft upon the right.
"I ca'n't get by!" he bellows,
    "I really am not able!
Though I pull my shoulder out of joint,
I cannot get him past this point,
    For it leads unto his stable!"

Then out spake Ulfrid Longbow,[1]
    A valiant youth was he,
"Lo! I will stand on thy right hand
    And guard the pass for thee!"
And out spake fair Flureeza,[2]
    His sister eke was she,
"I will abide on thy other side,
    And turn thy steed for thee!"

And now commenced a struggle
    Between that steed and rider,
For all the strength that he hath left
    Doth not suffice to guide her.
Though Ulfrid and his sister
    Have kindly stopped the way,
And all the crowd have cried aloud,
    "We can't wait here all day!"

[1] This valiant knight, besides having a heart of steel and nerves of iron, has been lately in the habit of carrying a brick in his eye.
[2] She was sister to both.

Round turned he as not deigning
　　Their words to understand,
But he slipped the stirrups from his feet
　　The bridle from his hand,
And grasped the mane full lightly,
　　And vaulted from his seat,
And gained the road in triumph,[1]
　　And stood upon his feet.

All firmly till that moment
　　Had Ulfrid Longbow stood,
And faced the foe right valiantly,
　　As every warrior should.
But when safe on terra firma
　　His brother he did spy,
"What *did* you do that for?" he cried,
Then unconcerned he stepped aside
　　And let it canter by.

They gave him bread and butter,[2]
　　That was of public right,
As much as four strong rabbits
　　Could munch from morn to night,
For he'd done a deed of daring,
　　And faced that savage steed,
And therefore cups of coffee sweet,
And everything that was a treat,
　　Were but his right and meed.

And often in the evenings,
　　When the fire is blazing bright,
When books bestrew the table
　　And moths obscure the light,

[1] The reader will probably be at a loss to discover the nature of this triumph, as no object was gained, and the donkey was obviously the victor; on this point, however, we are sorry to say we can offer no good explanation.

[2] Much more acceptable to a true knight than "corn-land" which the Roman people were so foolish as to give to their daring champion, Horatius.

When crying children go to bed,
　　A struggling, kicking load;
We'll talk of Ulfrid Longbow's deed,
How, in his brother's utmost need,
Back to his aid he flew with speed,
And how he faced the fiery steed,
　　And kept the New Croft Road.

THE TWO BROTHERS
(1853)

THERE were two brothers at Twyford school,
　　And when they had left the place,
It was, "Will ye learn Greek and Latin?
　　Or will ye run me a race?
Or will ye go up to yonder bridge,
　　And there we will angle for dace?"

"I'm too stupid for Greek and for Latin,
　　I'm too lazy by half for a race,
So I'll even go up to yonder bridge,
　　And there we will angle for dace."

He has fitted together two joints of his rod,
　　And to them he has added another,
And then a great hook he took from his book,
　　And ran it right into his brother.

Oh much is the noise that is made among boys
　　When playfully pelting a pig,
But a far greater pother was made by his brother
　　When flung from the top of the brigg.

The fish hurried up by the dozens,
　　All ready and eager to bite,
For the lad that he flung was so tender and young,
　　It quite gave them an appetite.

Said he, "Thus shall he wallop about
   And the fish take him quite at their ease,
For me to annoy it was ever his joy,
   Now I'll teach him the meaning of 'Tees'!"

The wind to his ear brought a voice,
   "My brother, you didn't had ought ter!
And what have I done that you think it such fun
   To indulge in the pleasure of slaughter?

"A good nibble or bite is my chiefest delight,
   When I'm merely expected to *see*,
But a bite from a fish is not quite what I wish,
   When I get it performed upon *me*;
And just now here's a swarm of dace at my arm,
   And a perch has got hold of my knee.

"For water my thirst was not great at the first,
   And of fish I have quite sufficien——"
"Oh fear not!" he cried, "for whatever betide,
   We are both in the selfsame condition!

"I am sure that our state's very nearly alike
   (Not considering the question of slaughter),
For I have my perch on the top of the bridge,
   And you have your perch in the water.

"I stick to my perch and your perch sticks to you,
   We are really extremely alike;
I've a turn-pike up here, and I very much fear
   You may soon have a turn with a pike."

"Oh, grant but one wish! If I'm took by a fish
   (For your bait is your brother, good man!)
Pull him up if you like, but I hope you will strike
   As gently as ever you can."

"If the fish be a trout, I'm afraid there's no doubt
  I must strike him like lightning that's greased;
If the fish be a pike, I'll engage not to strike,
  Till I've waited ten minutes at least."

"But in those ten minutes to desolate Fate
  Your brother a victim may fall!"
"I'll reduce it to five, so *perhaps* you'll survive,
  But the chance is exceedingly small."

"Oh hard is your heart for to act such a part;
  Is it iron, or granite, or steel?"
"Why, I really can't say—it is many a day
  Since my heart was accustomed to feel.

" 'Twas my heart-cherished wish for to slay many fish
  Each day did my malice grow worse,
For my heart didn't soften with doing it so often
  But rather, I should say, the reverse."

"Oh would I were back at Twyford school,
  Learning lessons in fear of the birch!"
"Nay, brother!" he cried, "for whatever betide,
  You are better off here with your perch!

"I am sure you'll allow you are happier now,
  With nothing to do but to play;
And this single line here, it is perfectly clear,
  Is much better than thirty a day!

"And as to the rod hanging over your head,
  And apparently ready to fall,
That, you know, was the case, when you lived in that
    place,
  So it need not be reckoned at all.

"Do you see that old trout with a turn-up-nose snout?
  (Just to speak on a pleasanter theme),
Observe, my dear brother, our love for each other—
  He's the one I like best in the stream.

"To-morrow I mean to invite him to dine
   (We shall all of us think it a treat);
If the day should be fine, I'll just *drop him a line*,
   And we'll settle what time we're to meet.

"He hasn't been into society yet,
   And his manners are not of the best,
So I think it quite fair that it should be *my* care,
   To see that he's properly dressed."

Many words brought the wind of "cruel" and "kind",
   And that "man suffers more than the brute":
Each several word with patience he heard,
   And answered with wisdom to boot.

"What? prettier swimming in the stream,
   Than lying all snugly and flat?
Do but look at that dish filled with glittering fish,
   Has Nature a picture like that?

"What? a higher delight to be drawn from the sight
   Of fish full of life and of glee?
What a noodle you are! 'tis delightfuller far
   To kill them than let them go free!

"I know there are people who prate by the hour
   Of the beauty of earth, sky, and ocean;
Of the birds as they fly, of the fish darting by,
   Rejoicing in Life and in Motion.

"As to any delight to be got from the sight,
   It is all very well for a flat,
But *I* think it all gammon, for hooking a salmon
   Is better than twenty of that!

"They say that a man of a right-thinking mind
   Will *love* the dumb creatures he sees—
What's the use of his mind, if he's never inclined
   To pull a fish out of the Tees?

"Take my friends and my home—as an outcast I'll roam:
　　Take the money I have in the Bank;
It is just what I wish, but deprive me of *fish*,
　　And my life would indeed be a blank!"

Forth from the house his sister came,
　　Her brothers for to see,
But when she saw that sight of awe,
　　The tear stood in her e'e.

"Oh what bait's that upon your hook,
　　My brother, tell to me?"
"It is but the fantailed pigeon,
　　He would not sing for me."

"Whoe'er would expect a pigeon to sing,
　　A simpleton he must be!
But a pigeon-cote is a different thing
　　To the coat that there I see!"

"Oh what bait's that upon your hook,
　　Dear brother, tell to me?"
"It is my younger brother," he cried,
　　"Oh woe and dole is me!

"I's mighty wicked, that I is!
　　Or how could such things be?
Farewell, farewell, sweet sister,
　　I'm going o'er the sea."

"And when will you come back again,
　　My brother, tell to me?"
"When chub is good for human food,
　　And that will never be!"

She turned herself right round about,
　　And her heart brake into three,
Said, "One of the two will be wet through and through,
　　And t'other'll be late for his tea!"

THE LADY OF THE LADLE
(1854)

THE Youth at Eve had drunk his fill,
Where stands the "Royal" on the Hill,
And long his mid-day stroll had made,
On the so-called "Marine Parade"—
(Meant, I presume, for Seamen brave,
Whose "march is on the Mountain wave";
'Twere just the bathing-place for him
Who stays on land till he can swim)—
And he had strayed into the Town,
And paced each alley up and down,
Where still, so narrow grew the way,
The very houses seemed to say,
Nodding to friends across the Street,
"One struggle more and we shall meet."
And he had scaled that wondrous stair
That soars from earth to upper air,
Where rich and poor alike must climb,
And walk the treadmill for a time.
That morning he had dressed with care,
And put Pomatum on his hair;
He was, the loungers all agreed,
A very heavy swell indeed:
Men thought him, as he swaggered by,
Some scion of nobility,
And never dreamed, so cold his look,
That he had loved—and loved a Cook.
Upon the beach he stood and sighed
Unheedful of the treacherous tide;
Thus sang he to the listening main,
And soothed his sorrow with the strain!

CORONACH

"She is gone by the Hilda,
  She is lost unto Whitby,
And her name is Matilda,
  Which my heart it was smit by;
Tho' I take the Goliah,
  I learn to my sorrow
That 'it wo'n't', said the crier,
  'Be off till to-morrow.'

"She called me her 'Neddy',
  (Tho' there mayn't be much in it,)
And I should have been ready,
  If she'd waited a minute;
I was following behind her
  When, if you recollect, I
Merely ran back to find a
  Gold pin for my neck-tie.

"Rich dresser of suet!
  Prime hand at a sausage!
I have lost thee, I rue it,
  And my fare for the passage!
Perhaps *she* thinks it funny,
  Aboard of the Hilda,
But I've lost purse and money,
  And thee, oh, my 'Tilda!"

His pin of gold the youth undid
And in his waistcoat-pocket hid,
Then gently folded hand in hand,
And dropped asleep upon the sand.

SHE'S ALL MY FANCY PAINTED HIM

[This affecting fragment was found in MS. among the papers of the well-known author of "Was it You or I?" a tragedy, and the two popular novels, "Sister and Son", and "The Niece's Legacy, or the Grateful Grandfather".]

SHE'S all my fancy painted him
(I make no idle boast);
If he or you had lost a limb,
Which would have suffered most?

He said that you had been to her,
And seen me here before;
But, in another character,
She was the same of yore.

There was not one that spoke to us,
Of all that thronged the street:
So he sadly got into a 'bus,
And pattered with his feet.

They sent him word I had not gone
(We know it to be true);
If she should push the matter on,
What would become of you?

They gave her one, they gave me two,
They gave us three or more;
They all returned from him to you,
Though they were mine before.

If I or she should chance to be
Involved in this affair,
He trusts to you to set them free,
Exactly as we were.

It seemed to me that you had been
   (Before she had this fit)
An obstacle, that came between
   Him, and ourselves, and it.

Don't let him know she liked them best,
   For this must ever be
A secret, kept from all the rest,
   Between yourself and me.

PHOTOGRAPHY EXTRAORDINARY

The Milk-and-Water School

ALAS! she would not hear my prayer!
Yet it were rash to tear my hair;
Disfigured, I should be less fair.

She was unwise, I may say blind;
Once she was lovingly inclined;
Some circumstance has changed her mind.

The Strong-Minded or Matter-of-Fact School

Well! so my offer was no go!
She might do worse, I told her so;
She was a fool to answer "No".

However, things are as they stood;
Nor would I have her if I could,
For there are plenty more as good.

The Spasmodic or German School

Firebrands and daggers! hope hath fled!
To atoms dash the doubly dead!
My brain is fire—my heart is lead!

Her soul is flint, and what am I?
Scorch'd by her fierce, relentless eye,
Nothingness is my destiny!

LAYS OF MYSTERY,
IMAGINATION, AND HUMOUR

Number 1

THE PALACE OF HUMBUG

I DREAMT I dwelt in marble halls,
And each damp thing that creeps and crawls
Went wobble-wobble on the walls.

Faint odours of departed cheese,
Blown on the dank, unwholesome breeze,
Awoke the never-ending sneeze.

Strange pictures decked the arras drear,
Strange characters of woe and fear,
The humbugs of the social sphere.

One showed a vain and noisy prig,
That shouted empty words and big
At him that nodded in a wig.

And one, a dotard grim and gray,
Who wasteth childhood's happy day
In work more profitless than play.

Whose icy breast no pity warms,
Whose little victims sit in swarms,
And slowly sob on lower forms.

And one, a green thyme-honoured Bank,
Where flowers are growing wild and rank,
Like weeds that fringe a poisoned tank.

All birds of evil omen there
Flood with rich Notes the tainted air,
The witless wanderer to snare.

The fatal Notes neglected fall,
No creature heeds the treacherous call,
For all those goodly Strawn Baits Pall.

The wandering phantom broke and fled,
Straightway I saw within my head
A vision of a ghostly bed,

Where lay two worn decrepit men,
The fictions of a lawyer's pen,
Who never more might breathe again.

The serving-man of Richard Roe
Wept, inarticulate with woe:
She wept, that waited on John Doe.

"Oh rouse", I urged, "the waning sense
With tales of tangled evidence,
Of suit, demurrer, and defence."

"Vain", she replied, "such mockeries:
For morbid fancies, such as these,
No suits can suit, no plea can please."

And bending o'er that man of straw,
She cried in grief and sudden awe,
Not inappropriately, "Law!"

The well-remembered voice he knew,
He smiled, he faintly muttered "Sue!"
(Her very name was legal too.)

The night was fled, the dawn was nigh:
A hurricane went raving by,
And swept the Vision from mine eye.

Vanished that dim and ghostly bed,
(The hangings, tape; the tape was red:)
'Tis o'er, and Doe and Roe are dead!

Oh, yet my spirit inly crawls,
What time it shudderingly recalls
That horrid dream of marble halls!

Oxford, 1855.

THE MOCK TURTLE'S SONG

BENEATH the waters of the sea
Are lobsters thick as thick can be—
They love to dance with you and me,
  My own, my gentle Salmon!

CHORUS

Salmon, come up! Salmon, go down!
Salmon, come twist your tail around!
Of all the fishes of the sea
  There's none so good as Salmon!

UPON THE LONELY MOOR
(1856)

[It is always interesting to ascertain the sources from which our great poets obtained their ideas: this motive has dictated the publication of the following: painful as its appearance must be to the admirers of Wordsworth and his poem of "Resolution and Independence".]

I MET an aged, aged man
  Upon the lonely moor:
I knew I was a gentleman,
  And he was but a boor.

So I stopped and roughly questioned him,
   "Come, tell me how you live!"
But his words impressed my ear no more
   Than if it were a sieve.

He said, "I look for soap-bubbles,
   That lie among the wheat,
And bake them into mutton-pies,
   And sell them in the street.
I sell them unto men", he said,
   "Who sail on stormy seas;
And that's the way I get my bread—
   A trifle, if you please."

But I was thinking of a way
   To multiply by ten,
And always, in the answer, get
   The question back again.
I did not hear a word he said,
   But kicked that old man calm,
And said, "Come, tell me how you live!"
   And pinched him in the arm.

His accents mild took up the tale:
   He said, "I go my ways,
And when I find a mountain-rill,
   I set it in a blaze.
And thence they make a stuff they call
   Rowland's Macassar Oil;
But fourpence-halfpenny is all
   They give me for my toil."

But I was thinking of a plan
   To paint one's gaiters green,
So much the colour of the grass
   That they could ne'er be seen.

I gave his ear a sudden box,
   And questioned him again,
And tweaked his grey and reverend locks,
   And put him into pain.

He said, "I hunt for haddocks' eyes
   Among the heather bright,
And work them into waistcoat-buttons
   In the silent night.
And these I do not sell for gold,
   Or coin of silver-mine,
But for a copper-halfpenny,
   And that will purchase nine.

"I sometimes dig for buttered rolls,
   Or set limed twigs for crabs;
I sometimes search the flowery knolls
   For wheels of hansom cabs.
And that's the way" (he gave a wink)
   "I get my living here,
And very gladly will I drink
   Your Honour's health in beer."

I heard him then, for I had just
   Completed my design
To keep the Menai bridge from rust
   By boiling it in wine.
I duly thanked him, ere I went,
   For all his stories queer,
But chiefly for his kind intent
   To drink my health in beer.

And now if e'er by chance I put
   My fingers into glue,
Or madly squeeze a right-hand foot
   Into a left-hand shoe;

Or if a statement I aver
Of which I am not sure,
I think of that strange wanderer
Upon the lonely moor.

MISS JONES

(This frolicsome verse was written for a medley of twenty-two tunes that ranged from "The Captain and His Whiskers" to "Rule Britannia".)

'T<small>IS</small> a melancholy song, and it will not keep you long,
Tho I specs it will work upon your feelings very strong,
For the agonizing moans of Miss Arabella Jones
Were warranted to melt the hearts of any paving stones.
Simon Smith was tall and slim, and she doted upon him,
But he always called her *Miss* Jones—he never got so far,
As to use her Christian name—it was too familiar.
When she called him "Simon dear" he pretended not to
    hear,
And she told her sister Susan he behaved extremely queer,
Who said, "Very right! very right! Shews his true affec-
    tion.
If you'd prove your Simon's love follow my direction.
I'd certainly advise you just to write a simple letter,
And to tell him that the cold he kindly asked about is
    better.
And say that by the tanyard you will wait in loving hope,
At nine o'clock this evening if he's willing to elope
With his faithful Arabella."
So she wrote it, & signed it, & sealed it, & sent it, &
    dressed herself out in her holiday things.
With bracelets & brooches, & earrings, & necklace, a
    watch, & an eyeglass, & diamond rings,
For man is a creature weak and impressible, thinks such a
    deal of appearance, my dear.

So she waited for her Simon beside the tanyard gate, re-
    gardless of the pieman, who hinted it was late.
Waiting for Simon, she coughed in the chilly night, until
    the tanner found her,
And kindly brought a light old coat to wrap around her.
She felt her cold was getting worse,
Yet still she fondly whispered, "Oh, take your time, my
    Simon, although I've waited long.
I do not fear my Simon dear will fail to come at last,
Although I know that long ago the time I named is past.
My Simon! My Simon! Oh, charming man! Oh, charming
    man!
Dear Simon Smith, sweet Simon Smith."
Oh, there goes the church-clock, the town-clock, the sta-
    tion-clock and there go the other clocks, they are all
    striking twelve!
Oh, Simon, it is getting late, it's very dull to sit and wait.
And really I'm in such a state, I hope you'll come at any
    rate, quite early in the morning, quite early in the
    morning.
Then with prancing bays & yellow chaise, we'll away to
    Gretna Green.
For when I am with my Simon Smith—oh, that common
    name! Oh that vulgar name!
I shall never rest happy till he's changed that name, but
    when he has married me, maybe he'll love me to that
    degree, that he'll grant me my prayer
And will call himself "Clare"—
So she talked all alone, as she sat upon a stone,
Still hoping he would come and find her, and she started
    most unkimmon, when instead of darling "Simmon"
    'twas a strange man that stood behind her,
Who civilly observed "Good evening, M'am,
I really am surprised to see that you're out here alone, for
    you must own from thieves you're not secure.
A watch, I see. Pray lend it me (I hope the gold is pure).
And all those rings, & other things—Don't scream, you
    know, for long ago

The policeman off from his beat has gone.

In the kitchen——" "Oh, you desperate villain! Oh, you treacherous thief!"

And these were the words of her anger and grief.

"When first to Simon Smith I gave my hand I never could have thought he would have acted half so mean as this.

And where's the new police? Oh, Simon, Simon! how could you treat your love so ill?"

They sit & chatter, they chatter with the cook, the guardians, so they're called, of public peace.

Through the tanyard was heard the dismal sound, "How on earth is it policemen never, never, never, can be found?"

PUZZLES FROM WONDERLAND

I

DREAMING of apples on a wall,
And dreaming often, dear,
I dreamed that, if I counted all,
—How many would appear?

II

A stick I found that weighed two pound:
I sawed it up one day
In pieces eight of equal weight!
How much did each piece weigh?
(Everybody says "a quarter of a pound", which is wrong.)

III

John gave his brother James a box:
About it there were many locks.

James woke and said it gave him pain;
So gave it back to John again.

The box was not with lid supplied,
Yet caused two lids to open wide:

And all these locks had never a key—
What kind of a box, then, could it be?

IV

What is most like a bee in May?
"Well, let me think: perhaps——" you say.
Bravo! You're guessing well to-day!

V

Three sisters at breakfast were feeding the cat,
The first gave it sole—Puss was grateful for that:
The next gave it salmon—which Puss thought a treat:
The third gave it herring—which Puss wouldn't eat.
(Explain the conduct of the cat.)

VI

Said the Moon to the Sun,
"Is the daylight begun?"
Said the Sun to the Moon,
"Not a minute too soon."

"You're a Full Moon," said he.
She replied with a frown,
"Well! I never *did* see
So uncivil a clown!"
(Query. Why was the moon so angry?)

VII

WHEN the King found that his money was nearly all
gone, and that he really *must* live more economically, he
decided on sending away most of his Wise Men. There
were some hundreds of them—very fine old men, and
magnificently dressed in green velvet gowns with gold
buttons: if they *had* a fault, it was that they always contradicted one another when he asked for their advice—
and they certainly ate and drank enormously. So, on the
whole, he was rather glad to get rid of them. But there
was an old law, which he did not dare to disobey, which
said that there must always be

"Seven blind of both eyes:
Two blind of one eye:
Four that see with both eyes:
Nine that see with one eye."
(Query. How many did he keep?)

SOLUTIONS TO PUZZLES FROM WONDERLAND

I

Ten.

II

In Shylock's bargain for the flesh was found
   No mention of the blood that flowed around:
So when the stick was sawed in eight,
   The sawdust lost diminished from the weight.

III

As curly-headed Jemmy was sleeping in bed,
His brother John gave him a blow on the head;
James opened his eyelids, and spying his brother,
Doubled his fist, and gave him another.
This kind of box then is not so rare;
The lids are the eyelids, the locks are the hair,
And so every schoolboy can tell to his cost,
The key to the tangles is constantly lost.

IV

   'Twixt "Perhaps" and "May be"
      Little difference we see:
   Let the question go round,
      The answer is found.

V

That salmon and sole Puss should think very grand
   Is no such remarkable thing.
For more of these dainties Puss took up her stand;
But when the third sister stretched out her fair hand
   Pray why should Puss swallow her ring?

VI

"In these degenerate days", we oft hear said,
　"Manners are lost and chivalry is dead!"
No wonder, since in high exalted spheres
　The same degeneracy, in fact, appears.
The Moon, in social matters interfering,
　Scolded the Sun, when early in appearing;
And the rude Sun, her gentle sex ignoring,
　Called her a fool, thus her pretensions flooring.

VII

Five seeing, and seven blind
　Give us twelve, in all, we find;
But all of these, 'tis very plain,
　Come into account again.
For take notice, it may be true,
　That those blind of one eye are blind for two;
And consider contrariwise,
　That to see with your eye you may have your eyes;
So setting one against the other—
　For a mathematician no great bother—
And working the sum, you will understand
　That sixteen wise men still trouble the land.

PROLOGUES TO PLAYS

PROLOGUE TO "LA GUIDA DI BRAGIA"

(From an opera written for Carroll's Marionette Theatre.)

SHALL soldiers tread the murderous path of war,
Without a notion what they do it for?
Shall pallid mercers drive a roaring trade,
And sell the stuffs their hands have never made?
And shall not we, in this our mimic scene,
Be all that better actors e'er have been?
Awake again a Kemble's tragic tone,
And make a Liston's humour all our own?
Or vie with Mrs. Siddons in the art
To rouse the feelings and to charm the heart?
While Shakespeare's self, with all his ancient fires,
Lights up the forms that tremble on our wires?
Why ca'n't we have, in theatres ideal,
The good, without the evil of the real?
Why may not Marionettes be just as good
As larger actors made of flesh and blood?
Presumptuous thought! to you and your applause
In humbler confidence we trust our cause.

PROLOGUE

(Misses Beatrice and Ethel Hatch, daughters of Dr. Edwin
Hatch, Vice-principal of St. Mary Hall, were friends of the
author. He wrote two plays for performance at their house.)

*Curtain rises and discovers the Speaker, who comes for-
ward, thinking aloud,*

"Ladies and Gentlemen" seems stiff and cold.
There's something personal in "Young and Old";
I'll try "Dear Friends" (*addresses audience*)
                Oh! let me call you so.

Dear friends, look kindly on our little show.
Contrast us not with giants in the Art,
Nor say "You should see Sothern in that part";
Nor yet, unkindest cut of all, in fact,
Condemn the actors, while you praise the Act.
Having by coming proved you find a charm in it,
Don't go away, and hint there may be harm in it.

．　　　．　　　．　　　．　　　．　　　．

Miss Crabb. My dear Miss Verjuice, can it really be?
You're just in time, love, for a cup of tea;
And so, you went to see those people play.
Miss Verjuice. Well! yes, Miss Crabb, and I may truly
say
You showed your wisdom when you stayed *away*.
Miss C. Doubtless! Theatricals in *our* quiet town!
I've always said, "The law should put them down,"
They mean no harm, tho' I begin to doubt it—
But now sit down and tell me all about it.
Miss V. Well then, Miss Crabb, I won't deceive you,
dear;
I heard some things I——didn't like to hear:
Miss C. But don't omit them now.
Miss V.   Well! No! I'll try
To tell you *all* the painful history.
(*They whisper alternately behind a small fan.*)
Miss V. And then, my dear, Miss Asterisk and he
Pretended they were lovers!!
Miss C.   Gracious me!!
(*More whispering behind fan.*)

．　　　．　　　．　　　．　　　．　　　．

Speaker.

What! *Acting* love!! And has that ne'er been seen
Save with a row of footlights placed between?
My gentle censors, let me roundly ask,
Do none but actors ever wear a mask?
Or have we reached at last that golden age

That finds deception only on the Stage?
Come, let's confess all round before we budge,
When all are guilty, none should play the Judge.
We're actors all, a motley company,
Some on the Stage, and others—on the sly—
And guiltiest he who paints so well his phiz
His brother actors scarce know what he is.
A truce to moralizing; we invite
The goodly company we see to-night
To have the little banquet we have got,
Well dressed, we hope, and served up *hot & hot*.
"Loan of a Lover" is the leading dish,
Concluding with a dainty course of fish;
"Whitebait at Greenwich" in the best condition
(By Mr. Gladstone's very kind permission),
Before the courses will be handed round
An *Entrée* made of Children, nicely browned.

Bell rings.

But hark! The bell to summon me away;
They're anxious to begin their little Play.
One word before I go—We'll do our best,
And crave your kind indulgence for the rest;
Own that at least we've striven to succeed,
And take the good intention for the deed.

 Nov. 1871

PROLOGUE

*Enter Beatrice, leading Wilfred. She leaves him at centre
(front), and after going round on tip-toe, to make sure they
are not overheard, returns and takes his arm.*

B. "Wiffie! I'm *sure* that something *is* the matter,
  All day there's been—oh, *such* a fuss and clatter!
  Mamma's been trying on a funny dress—
  I never *saw* the house in such a mess!
      (*puts her arm round his neck*)
  Is there a secret, Wiffie?"

W. (*shaking her off*) "Yes, of course!"

B. "And you won't tell it? (*whimpers*) Then you're very
       cross!
       (*turns away from him and clasps her hands, looking
       up ecstatically*)
    I'm sure of *this*! It's something *quite* uncommon!"

W. (*stretching up his arms, with a mock-heroïc air*)
    "Oh, Curiosity! Thy name is Woman!
       (*puts his arm round her coaxingly*)
    Well, Birdie, then I'll tell! (*mysteriously*) What
       should you say
    If they were going to act—a little play?"

B. (*jumping and clapping her hands*)
    "I'd say 'HOW NICE!'"

W. (*pointing to audience*)
                    "But will it please the rest?"

B. "Oh *yes*! Because, you know, they'll do their best!
       (*turns to audience*)
    You'll praise them, won't you, when you've seen the
       play?
    Just say 'HOW NICE!' before you go away!"
       (*They run away hand in hand.*)

   Feb. 14, 1873.

PHANTASMAGORIA

Canto I

The Trystyng

O NE winter night, at half-past nine,
   Cold, tired, and cross, and muddy,
I had come home, too late to dine,
And supper, with cigars and wine,
   Was waiting in the study.

There was a strangeness in the room,
   And Something white and wavy
Was standing near me in the gloom—
I took it for the carpet-broom
   Left by that careless slavey.

But presently the Thing began
   To shiver and to sneeze:
On which I said "Come, come, my man!
That's a most inconsiderate plan,
   Less noise there, if you please!"

"I've caught a cold", the Thing replies,
   "Out there upon the landing."
I turned to look in some surprise,
And there, before my very eyes,
   A little Ghost was standing!

He trembled when he caught my eye,
   And got behind a chair.
"How came you here," I said, "and why?
I never saw a thing so shy.
   Come out! Don't shiver there!"

He said "I'd gladly tell you how,
    And also tell you why;
But" (here he gave a little bow)
"You're in so bad a temper now,
    You'd think it all a lie.

"And as to being in a fright,
    Allow me to remark
That Ghosts have just as good a right,
In every way, to fear the light,
    As Men to fear the dark."

"No plea", said I, "can well excuse
    Such cowardice in you:
For Ghosts can visit when they choose,
Whereas we Humans ca'n't refuse
    To grant the interview."

He said "A flutter of alarm
    Is not unnatural, is it?
I really feared you meant some harm:
But, now I see that you are calm,
    Let me explain my visit.

"Houses are classed, I beg to state,
    According to the number
Of Ghosts that they accommodate:
(The Tenant merely counts as *weight*,
    With Coals and other lumber).

"This is a 'one-ghost' house, and you,
    When you arrived last summer,
May have remarked a Spectre who
Was doing all that Ghosts can do
    To welcome the new-comer.

"In Villas this is always done—
    However cheaply rented:

For, though of course there's less of fun
When there is only room for one,
    Ghosts have to be contented.

"That Spectre left you on the Third—
    Since then you've not been haunted:
For, as he never sent us word,
'Twas quite by accident we heard
    That any one was wanted.

"A Spectre has first choice, by right,
    In filling up a vacancy;
Then Phantom, Goblin, Elf, and Sprite—
If all these fail them, they invite
    The nicest Ghoul that they can see.

"The Spectres said the place was low,
    And that you kept bad wine:
So, as a Phantom had to go,
And I was first, of course, you know,
    I couldn't well decline."

"No doubt", said I, "they settled who
    Was fittest to be sent:
Yet still to choose a brat like you,
To haunt a man of forty-two,
    Was no great compliment!"

"I'm not so young, Sir," he replied,
    "As you might think. The fact is,
In caverns by the water-side,
And other places that I've tried,
    I've had a lot of practice:

"But I have never taken yet
    A strict domestic part,
And in my flurry I forget
The Five Good Rules of Etiquette
    We have to know by heart."

My sympathies were warming fast
    Towards the little fellow:
He was so utterly aghast
At having found a Man at last,
    And looked so scared and yellow.

"At least", I said, "I'm glad to find
    A Ghost is not a *dumb* thing!
But pray sit down: you'll feel inclined
(If, like myself, you have not dined)
    To take a snack of something:

"Though, certainly, you don't appear
    A thing to offer *food* to!
And then I shall be glad to hear—
If you will say them loud and clear—
    The Rules that you allude to."

"Thanks! You shall hear them by and by.
    This *is* a piece of luck!"
"What may I offer you?" said I.
"Well, since you *are* so kind, I'll try
    A little bit of duck.

"*One* slice! And may I ask you for
    Another drop of gravy?"
I sat and looked at him in awe,
For certainly I never saw
    A thing so white and wavy.

And still he seemed to grow more white,
    More vapoury, and wavier—
Seen in the dim and flickering light,
As he proceeded to recite
    His "Maxims of Behaviour".

Canto II

Hys Fyve Rules

"M y First—but don't suppose", he said,
 "I'm setting you a riddle—
Is—if your Victim be in bed,
Don't touch the curtains at his head,
 But take them in the middle,

"And wave them slowly in and out,
 While drawing them asunder;
And in a minute's time, no doubt,
He'll raise his head and look about
 With eyes of wrath and wonder.

"And here you must on no pretence
 Make the first observation.
Wait for the Victim to commence:
No Ghost of any common sense
 Begins a conversation.

"If he should say '*How came you here?*'
 (The way that *you* began, Sir),
In such a case your course is clear—
'*On the bat's back, my little dear!*'
 Is the appropriate answer.

"If after this he says no more,
 You'd best perhaps curtail your
Exertions—go and shake the door,
And then, if he begins to snore,
 You'll know the thing's a failure.

"By day, if he should be alone—
 At home or on a walk—

You merely give a hollow groan,
To indicate the kind of tone
　　In which you mean to talk.

"But if you find him with his friends,
　　The thing is rather harder.
In such a case success depends
On picking up some candle-ends,
　　Or butter, in the larder.

"With this you make a kind of slide
　　(It answers best with suet),
On which you must contrive to glide,
And swing yourself from side to side—
　　One soon learns how to do it.

"The Second tells us what is right
　　In ceremonious calls:—
'*First burn a blue or crimson light*'
(A thing I quite forgot to-night),
　　'*Then scratch the door or walls.*'"

I said "You'll visit *here* no more,
　　If you attempt the Guy.
I'll have no bonfires on *my* floor—
And, as for scratching at the door,
　　I'd like to see you try!"

"The Third was written to protect
　　The interests of the Victim,
And tells us, as I recollect,
To treat him with a grave respect,
　　And not to contradict him."

"That's plain", said I, "as Tare and Tret,
　　To any comprehension:
I only wish *some* Ghosts I've met
Would not so *constantly* forget
　　The maxim that you mention!"

"Perhaps", he said, "*you* first transgressed
    The laws of hospitality:
All Ghosts instinctively detest
The Man that fails to treat his guest
    With proper cordiality.

"If you address a Ghost as 'Thing!'
    Or strike him with a hatchet,
He is permitted by the King
To drop all *formal* parleying—
    And then you're *sure* to catch it!

"The Fourth prohibits trespassing
    Where other Ghosts are quartered:
And those convicted of the thing
(Unless when pardoned by the King)
    Must instantly be slaughtered.

"That simply means 'be cut up small':
    Ghosts soon unite anew:
The process scarcely hurts at all—
Not more than when *you're* what you call
    'Cut up' by a Review.

"The Fifth is one you may prefer
    That I should quote entire:—
The King must be addressed as 'Sir'.
This, from a simple courtier,
    Is all the Laws require:

"*But, should you wish to do the thing*
    With out-and-out politeness,
Accost him as 'My Goblin King!'
And always use, in answering,
    The phrase 'Your Royal Whiteness . . . . . . !'

"I'm getting rather hoarse, I fear,
    After so much reciting:
So, if you don't object, my dear,
We'll try a glass of bitter beer—
    I think it looks inviting."

Canto III

Scarmoges

"And did you really walk", said I,
    "On such a wretched night?
I always fancied Ghosts could fly—
If not exactly in the sky,
    Yet at a fairish height."

"It's very well", said he, "for Kings
    To soar above the earth:
But Phantoms often find that wings—
Like many other pleasant things—
    Cost more than they are worth.

"Spectres of course are rich, and so
    Can buy them from the Elves:
But *we* prefer to keep below—
They're stupid company, you know,
    For any but themselves:

"For, though they claim to be exempt
    From pride, they treat a Phantom
As something quite beneath contempt—
Just as no Turkey ever dreamt
    Of noticing a Bantam."

"They seem too proud", said I, "to go
    To houses such as mine.

Pray, how did they contrive to know
So quickly that 'the place was low',
  And that I 'kept bad wine'?"

"Inspector Kobold came to you——"
  The little Ghost began.
Here I broke in—"Inspector who?
Inspecting Ghosts is something new!
  Explain yourself, my man!"

"His name is Kobald," said my guest:
  "One of the Spectre order:
You'll very often see him dressed
In a yellow gown, a crimson vest,
  And a night-cap with a border.

"He tried the Brocken business first,
  But caught a sort of chill;
So came to England to be nursed,
And here it took the form of *thirst*,
  Which he complains of still.

"Port-wine, he says, when rich and sound,
  Warms his old bones like nectar:
And as the inns, where it is found,
Are his especial hunting-ground,
  We call him the *Inn-Spectre*."

I bore it—bore it like a man—
  This agonizing witticism!
And nothing could be sweeter than
My temper, till the Ghost began
  Some most provoking criticism.

"Cooks need not be indulged in waste;
  Yet still you'd better teach them
Dishes should have *some sort* of taste.
Pray, why are all the cruets placed
  Where nobody can reach them?

"That man of yours will never earn
     His living as a waiter!
Is that queer *thing* supposed to burn?
(It's far too dismal a concern
     To call a Moderator.)

"The duck was tender, but the peas
     Were very much too old:
And just remember, if you please,
The *next* time you have toasted cheese,
     Don't let them send it cold.

"You'll find the bread improved, I think,
     By getting better flour:
And have you anything to drink
That looks a *little* less like ink,
     And isn't *quite* so sour?"

Then, peering round with curious eyes,
     He muttered "Goodness gracious!"
And so went on to criticize—
"Your room's an inconvenient size:
     It's neither snug nor spacious.

"That narrow window, I expect,
     Serves but to let the dusk in——"
"But please", said I, "to recollect
'Twas fashioned by an architect
     Who pinned his faith on Ruskin!"

"I don't care who he was, Sir, or
     On whom he pinned his faith!
Constructed by whatever law,
So poor a job I never saw,
     As I'm a living Wraith!

"What a re-markable cigar!
     How much are they a dozen?"

I growled "No matter what they are!
You're getting as familiar
  As if you were my cousin!

"Now that's a thing *I will not stand*,
  And so I tell you flat."
"Aha," said he, "we're getting grand!"
(Taking a bottle in his hand)
  "I'll soon arrange for *that*!"

And here he took a careful aim,
  And gaily cried "Here goes!"
I tried to dodge it as it came,
But somehow caught it, all the same,
  Exactly on my nose.

And I remember nothing more
  That I can clearly fix,
Till I was sitting on the floor,
Repeating "Two and five are four,
  But *five and two* are six."

What really passed I never learned,
  Nor guessed: I only know
That, when at last my sense returned,
The lamp, neglected, dimly burned—
  The fire was getting low—

Through driving mists I seemed to see
  A Thing that smirked and smiled:
And found that he was giving me
A lesson in Biography,
  As if I were a child.

Canto IV

Hys Nouryture

"Oh, when I was a little Ghost,
        A merry time had we!
Each seated on his favourite post,
We chumped and chawed the buttered toast
        They gave us for our tea."

"That story is in print!" I cried
        "Don't say it's not, because
It's known as well as Bradshaw's Guide!"
(The Ghost uneasily replied
        He hardly thought it was.)

"It's not in Nursery Rhymes? And yet
        I almost think it is—
'Three little Ghosteses' were set
'On posteses', you know, and ate
        Their 'buttered toasteses'.

"I have the book; so if you doubt it——"
        I turned to search the shelf.
"Don't stir!" he cried. "We'll do without it
I now remember all about it;
        I wrote the thing myself.

"It came out in a 'Monthly', or
        At least my agent said it did:
Some literary swell, who saw
It, thought it seemed adapted for
        The Magazine he edited.

"My father was a Brownie, Sir;
        My mother was a Fairy.

The notion had occurred to her,
The children would be happier,
 If they were taught to vary.

"The notion soon became a craze;
 And, when it once began, she
Brought us all out in different ways—
One was a Pixy, two were Fays,
 Another was a Banshee;

"The Fetch and Kelpie went to school
 And gave a lot of trouble;
Next came a Poltergeist and Ghoul,
And then two Trolls (which broke the rule),
 A Goblin, and a Double—

"(If that's a snuff-box on the shelf,"
 He added with a yawn,
"I'll take a pinch)—next came an Elf,
And then a Phantom (that's myself),
 And last, a Leprechaun.

"One day, some Spectres chanced to call,
 Dressed in the usual white:
I stood and watched them in the hall,
And couldn't make them out at all,
 They seemed so strange a sight.

"I wondered what on earth they were,
 That looked all head and sack;
But Mother told me not to stare,
And then she twitched me by the hair,
 And punched me in the back.

"Since then I've often wished that I
 Had been a Spectre born.
But what's the use?" (He heaved a sigh.)
"*They* are the ghost-nobility,
 And look on *us* with scorn.

"My phantom-life was soon begun:
　　When I was barely six,
I went out with an older one—
And just at first I thought it fun,
　　And learned a lot of tricks.

"I've haunted dungeons, castles, towers—
　　Wherever I was sent:
I've often sat and howled for hours,
Drenched to the skin with driving showers,
　　Upon a battlement.

"It's quite old-fashioned now to groan
　　When you begin to speak:
This is the newest thing in tone——"
And here (it chilled me to the bone)
　　He gave an *awful* squeak.

"Perhaps", he added, "to *your* ear
　　That sounds an easy thing?
Try it yourself, my little dear!
It took *me* something like a year,
　　With constant practising.

"And when you've learned to squeak, my man,
　　And caught the double sob,
You're pretty much where you began:
Just try and gibber if you can!
　　That's something *like* a job!

"*I've* tried it, and can only say
　　I'm sure you couldn't do it, e-
ven if you practised night and day,
Unless you have a turn that way,
　　And natural ingenuity.

"Shakespeare I think it is who treats
　　Of Ghosts, in days of old,

Who 'gibbered in the Roman streets',
Dressed, if you recollect, in sheets—
    They must have found it cold.

"I've often spent ten pounds on stuff,
    In dressing as a Double;
But, though it answers as a puff,
It never has effect enough
    To make it worth the trouble.

"Long bills soon quenched the little thirst
    I had for being funny.
The setting-up is always worst:
Such heaps of things you want at first,
    One must be made of money!

"For instance, take a Haunted Tower,
    With skull, cross-bones, and sheet;
Blue lights to burn (say) two an hour,
Condensing lens of extra power,
    And set of chains complete:

"What with the things you have to hire—
    The fitting on the robe—
And testing all the coloured fire—
The outfit of itself would tire
    The patience of a Job!

"And then they're so fastidious,
    The Haunted-House Committee:
I've often known them make a fuss
Because a Ghost was French, or Russ,
    Or even from the City!

"Some dialects are objected to—
    For one, the *Irish* brogue is:
And then, for all you have to do,
One pound a week they offer you,
    And find yourself in Bogies!"

Canto V

Byckerment

"DON'T they consult the 'Victims', though?"
    I said. "They should, by rights,
Give them a chance—because, you know,
The tastes of people differ so,
    Especially in Sprites."

The Phantom shook his head and smiled.
    "Consult them? Not a bit!
'Twould be a job to drive one wild,
To satisfy one single child—
    There'd be no end to it!"

"Of course you ca'n't leave *children* free",
    Said I, " to pick and choose:
But, in the case of men like me,
I think 'Mine Host' might fairly be
    Allowed to state his views."

He said "It really wouldn't pay—
    Folk are so full of fancies.
We visit for a single day,
And whether then we go, or stay,
    Depends on circumstances.

"And, though we don't consult 'Mine Host'
    Before the thing's arranged,
Still, if he often quits his post,
Or is not a well-mannered Ghost,
    Then you can have him changed.

"But if the host's a man like you—
    I mean a man of sense;

And if the house is not too new——"
"Why, what has *that*", said I, "to do
  With Ghost's convenience?"

"A new house does not suit, you know—
    It's such a job to trim it:
But, after twenty years or so,
The wainscotings begin to go,
    So twenty is the limit."

"To trim" was not a phrase I could
    Remember having heard:
"Perhaps", I said, "you'll be so good
As tell me what is understood
    Exactly by that word?"

"It means the loosening all the doors,"
    The Ghost replied, and laughed:
"It means the drilling holes by scores
In all the skirting-boards and floors,
    To make a thorough draught.

"You'll sometimes find that one or two
    Are all you really need
To let the wind come whistling through—
But *here* there'll be a lot to do!"
    I faintly gasped "Indeed!

"If I'd been rather later, I'll
    Be bound," I added, trying
(Most unsuccessfully) to smile,
"You'd have been busy all this while,
    Trimming and beautifying?"

"Why, no," said he; "perhaps I should
    Have stayed another minute—
But still no Ghost, that's any good,
Without an introduction would
    Have ventured to begin it.

"The proper thing, as you were late,
    Was certainly to go:
But, with the roads in such a state,
I got the Knight-Mayor's leave to wait
    For half an hour or so."

"Who's the Knight-Mayor?" I cried. Instead
    Of answering my question,
"Well, if you don't know *that*," he said,
"Either you never go to bed,
    Or you've a grand digestion!

"He goes about and sits on folk
    That eat too much at night:
His duties are to pinch, and poke,
And squeeze them till they nearly choke."
    (I said "It serves them right!")

"And folk who sup on things like these—"
    He muttered, "eggs and bacon—
Lobster—and duck—and toasted cheese—
If they don't get an awful squeeze,
    I'm very much mistaken!

"He is immensely fat, and so
    Well suits the occupation:
In point of fact, if you must know,
We used to call him years ago,
    The Mayor and Corporation!

"The day he was elected Mayor
    I *know* that every Sprite meant
To vote for *me*, but did not dare—
He was so frantic with despair
    And furious with excitement.

"When it was over, for a whim,
    He ran to tell the King;

And being the reverse of slim,
A two-mile trot was not for him
    A very easy thing.

"So, to reward him for his run
    (As it was baking hot,
And he was over twenty stone),
The King proceeded, half in fun,
    To knight him on the spot."

" 'Twas a great liberty to take!"
    (I fired up like a rocket.)
"He did it just for punning's sake:
'The man', says Johnson, 'that would make
    A pun, would pick a pocket!' "

"A man", said he, "is not a King."
    I argued for a while,
And did my best to prove the thing—
The Phantom merely listening
    With a contemptuous smile.

At last, when, breath and patience spent,
    I had recourse to smoking—
"Your *aim*", he said, "is excellent:
But—when you call it *argument*—
    Of course you're only joking?"

Stung by his cold and snaky eye,
    I roused myself at length
To say, "At least I do defy
The veriest sceptic to deny
    That union is strength!"

"That's true enough," said he, "yet stay—"
    I listened in all meekness—
"*Union* is strength, I'm bound to say;
In fact, the thing's as clear as day;
    But *onions* are a weakness.'

Canto VI

Discomfyture

As one who strives a hill to climb,
　　Who never climbed before:
Who finds it, in a little time,
Grow every moment less sublime,
　　And votes the thing a bore:

Yet, having once begun to try,
　　Dares not desert his quest,
But, climbing, ever keeps his eye
On one small hut against the sky
　　Wherein he hopes to rest:

Who climbs till nerve and force are spent,
　　With many a puff and pant:
Who still, as rises the ascent,
In language grows more violent,
　　Although in breath more scant:

Who, climbing, gains at length the place
　　That crowns the upward track:
And, entering with unsteady pace,
Receives a buffet in the face
　　That lands him on his back:

And feels himself, like one in sleep,
　　Glide swiftly down again,
A helpless weight, from steep to steep,
Till, with a headlong giddy sweep,
　　He drops upon the plain—

So I, that had resolved to bring
　　Conviction to a ghost,

And found it quite a different thing
From any human arguing,
 Yet dared not quit my post.

But, keeping still the end in view
 To which I hoped to come,
I strove to prove the matter true
By putting everything I knew
 Into an axiom:

Commencing every single phrase
 With "therefore" or "because",
I blindly reeled, a hundred ways,
About the syllogistic maze,
 Unconscious where I was.

Quoth he "That's regular clap-trap:
 Don't bluster any more.
Now *do* be cool and take a nap!
Such a ridiculous old chap
 Was never seen before!

"You're like a man I used to meet,
 Who got one day so furious
In arguing, the simple heat
Scorched both his slippers off his feet!"
 I said *"That's very curious!"*

"Well, it *is* curious, I agree,
 And sounds perhaps like fibs:
But still it's true as true can be—
As sure as your name's Tibbs," said he.
 I said "My name's *not* Tibbs."

"*Not* Tibbs!" he cried—his tone became
 A shade or two less hearty—
"Why, no," said I. "My proper name
Is Tibbets—" "Tibbets?" "Aye, the same."
 "Why, then YOU'RE NOT THE PARTY!"

With that he struck the board a blow
    That shivered half the glasses.
"Why couldn't you have told me so
Three quarters of an hour ago,
    You prince of all the asses?

"To walk four miles through mud and rain,
    To spend the night in smoking,
And then to find that it's in vain—
And I've to do it all again—
    It's really *too* provoking!

"Don't talk!" he cried, as I began
    To mutter some excuse.
"Who can have patience with a man
That's got no more discretion than
    An idiotic goose?

"To keep me waiting here, instead
    Of telling me at once
That this was not the house!" he said.
"There, that'll do—be off to bed!
    Don't gape like that, you dunce!"

"It's very fine to throw the blame
    On *me* in such a fashion!
Why didn't you enquire my name
The very minute that you came?"
    I answered in a passion.

"Of course it worries you a bit
    To come so far on foot—
But how was *I* to blame for it?"
"Well, well!" said he. "I must admit
    That isn't badly put.

"And certainly you've given me
    The best of wine and victual—

Excuse my violence,'' said he,
"But accidents like this, you see,
    They put one out a little.

" 'Twas *my* fault after all, I find—
    Shake hands, old Turnip-top!''
The name was hardly to my mind,
But, as no doubt he meant it kind,
    I let the matter drop.

"Good-night, old Turnip-top, good-night!
    When I am gone, perhaps
They'll send you some inferior Sprite,
Who'll keep you in a constant fright
    And spoil your soundest naps.

"Tell him you'll stand no sort of trick;
    Then, if he leers and chuckles,
You just be handy with a stick
(Mind that it's pretty hard and thick)
    And rap him on the knuckles!

"Then carelessly remark 'Old coon!
    Perhaps you're not aware
That if you don't behave, you'll soon
Be chuckling to another tune—
    And so you'd best take care!'

"That's the right way to cure a Sprite
    Of such-like goings-on—
But gracious me! It's getting light!
Good-night, old Turnip-top, good-night!"
    A nod, and he was gone.

Canto VII

Sad Souvenaunce

"What's this?" I pondered. "Have I slept?
    Or can I have been drinking?"
But soon a gentler feeling crept
Upon me, and I sat and wept
    An hour or so, like winking.

"No need for Bones to hurry so!"
    I sobbed. "In fact, I doubt
If it was worth his while to go—
And who is Tibbs, I'd like to know,
    To make such work about?

"If Tibbs is anything like me,
    It's *possible*", I said,
"He won't be over-pleased to be
Dropped in upon at half-past three,
    After he's snug in bed.

"And if Bones plagues him anyhow—
    Squeaking and all the rest of it,
As he was doing here just now—
I prophesy there'll be a row,
    And Tibbs will have the best of it!"

Then, as my tears could never bring
    The friendly Phantom back,
It seemed to me the proper thing
To mix another glass, and sing
    The following Coronach.

And art thou gone, beloved Ghost?
    Best of Familiars!

Nay, then, farewell, my duckling roast,
Farewell, farewell, my tea and toast,
  My meerschaum and cigars!

The hues of life are dull and gray,
  The sweets of life insipid,
When thou, my charmer, art away—
Old Brick, or rather, let me say,
  Old Parallelepiped!"

Instead of singing Verse the Third,
  I ceased—abruptly, rather:
But, after such a splendid word
I felt that it would be absurd
  To try it any farther.

So with a yawn I went my way
  To seek the welcome downy,
And slept, and dreamed till break of day
Of Poltergeist and Fetch and Fay
  And Leprechaun and Brownie!

For years I've not been visited
  By any kind of Sprite;
Yet still they echo in my head,
Those parting words, so kindly said,
  "Old Turnip-top, good-night!"

ECHOES

LADY Clara Vere de Vere
  Was eight years old, she said:
Every ringlet, lightly shaken, ran itself in golden thread.

She took her little porringer:
Of me she shall not win renown:
For the baseness of its nature shall have strength to drag
    her down.

"Sisters and brothers, little Maid?
There stands the Inspector at thy door:
Like a dog, he hunts for boys who know not two and two
    are four."

"Kind hearts are more than coronets,"
She said, and wondering looked at me:
"It is the dead unhappy night, and I must hurry home to
    tea."

A SEA DIRGE

THERE are certain things—as, a spider, a ghost,
    The income-tax, gout, an umbrella for three—
That I hate, but the thing that I hate the most
    Is a thing they call the Sea.

Pour some salt water over the floor—
    Ugly I'm sure you'll allow it to be:
Suppose it extended a mile or more,
    That's very like the Sea.

Beat a dog till it howls outright—
    Cruel, but all very well for a spree:
Suppose that he did so day and night,
    That would be like the Sea.

I had a vision of nursery-maids;
    Tens of thousands passed by me—
All leading children with wooden spades,
    And this was by the Sea.

Who invented those spades of wood?
   Who was it cut them out of the tree?
None, I think, but an idiot could—
   Or one that loved the Sea.

It is pleasant and dreamy, no doubt, to float
   With "thoughts as boundless, and souls as free":
But, suppose you are very unwell in the boat,
   How do you like the Sea?

There is an insect that people avoid
   (Whence is derived the verb "to flee").
Where have you been by it most annoyed?
   In lodgings by the Sea.

If you like your coffee with sand for dregs,
   A decided hint of salt in your tea,
And a fishy taste in the very eggs—
   By all means choose the Sea.

And if, with these dainties to drink and eat,
   You prefer not a vestige of grass or tree,
And a chronic state of wet in your feet,
   Then—I recommend the Sea.

For *I* have friends who dwell by the coast—
   Pleasant friends they are to me!
It is when I am with them I wonder most
   That anyone likes the Sea.

They take me a walk: though tired and stiff,
   To climb the heights I madly agree;
And, after a tumble or so from the cliff,
   They kindly suggest the Sea.

I try the rocks, and I think it cool
   That they laugh with such an excess of glee,
As I heavily slip into every pool
   That skirts the cold cold Sea.

YE CARPETTE KNYGHTE

I HAVE a horse—a ryghte goode horse—
  Ne doe I envye those
Who scoure ye playne yn headye course
  Tyll soddayne on theyre nose
They lyghte wyth unexpected force
  Yt ys—a horse of clothes.

I have a saddel—"Say'st thou soe?
  Wyth styrruppes, Knyghte, to boote?"
I sayde not that—I answere "Noe"—
  Yt lacketh such, I woote:
Yt ys a mutton-saddel, loe!
  Parte of ye fleecye brute.

I have a bytte—a ryghte good bytte—
  As shall bee seene yn tyme.
Ye jawe of horse yt wyll not fytte;
  Yts use ys more sublyme.
Fayre Syr, how deemest thou of yt?
  Yt ys—thys bytte of rhyme.

HIAWATHA'S PHOTOGRAPHING

[In an age of imitation, I can claim no special merit for this slight attempt at doing what is known to be so easy. Any fairly practised writer, with the slightest ear for rhythm, could compose, for hours together, in the easy running metre of "The Song of Hiawatha". Having, then, distinctly stated that I challenge no attention in the following little poem to its merely verbal jingle, I must beg the candid reader to confine his criticism to its treatment of the subject.]

FROM his shoulder Hiawatha
Took the camera of rosewood,
Made of sliding, folding rosewood;

Neatly put it all together.
In its case it lay compactly,
Folded into nearly nothing;
But he opened out the hinges,
Pushed and pulled the joints and hinges,
Till it looked all squares and oblongs,
Like a complicated figure
In the Second Book of Euclid.

This he perched upon a tripod—
Crouched beneath its dusky cover—
Stretched his hand, enforcing silence—
Said, "Be motionless, I beg you!"
Mystic, awful was the process.

All the family in order
Sat before him for their pictures:
Each in turn as he was taken,
Volunteered his own suggestions,
His ingenious suggestions.

First the Governor, the Father:
He suggested velvet curtains
Looped about a massy pillar;
And the corner of a table,
Of a rosewood dining-table.
He would hold a scroll of something,
Hold it firmly in his left-hand;
He would keep his right-hand buried
(Like Napoleon) in his waistcoat;
He would contemplate the distance
With a look of pensive meaning,
As of ducks that die in tempests.

Grand, heroic was the notion:
Yet the picture failed entirely:
Failed, because he moved a little,
Moved, because he couldn't help it.

Next, his better half took courage;
She would have her picture taken.
She came dressed beyond description,
Dressed in jewels and in satin

Far too gorgeous for an empress.
Gracefully she sat down sideways,
With a simper scarcely human,
Holding in her hand a bouquet
Rather larger than a cabbage.
All the while that she was sitting,
Still the lady chattered, chattered,
Like a monkey in the forest.
"Am I sitting still?" she asked him.
"Is my face enough in profile?
Shall I hold the bouquet higher?
Will it come into the picture?"
And the picture failed completely.

Next the Son, the Stunning-Cantab:
He suggested curves of beauty,
Curves pervading all his figure,
Which the eye might follow onward,
Till they centred in the breast-pin,
Centred in the golden breast-pin.
He had learnt it all from Ruskin
(Author of "The Stones of Venice",
"Seven Lamps of Architecture",
"Modern Painters", and some others);
And perhaps he had not fully
Understood his author's meaning;
But, whatever was the reason,
All was fruitless, as the picture
Ended in an utter failure.

Next to him the eldest daughter:
She suggested very little,
Only asked if he would take her
With her look of "passive beauty".

Her idea of passive beauty
Was a squinting of the left-eye,
Was a drooping of the right-eye,
Was a smile that went up sideways
To the corner of the nostrils.

Hiawatha, when she asked him,

Took no notice of the question,
Looked as if he hadn't heard it;
But, when pointedly appealed to,
Smiled in his peculiar manner,
Coughed and said it "didn't matter",
Bit his lip and changed the subject.

Nor in this was he mistaken,
As the picture failed completely.

So in turn the other sisters.

Last, the youngest son was taken:
Very rough and thick his hair was,
Very round and red his face was,
Very dusty was his jacket,
Very fidgety his manner.
And his overbearing sisters
Called him names he disapproved of:
Called him Johnny, "Daddy's Darling",
Called him Jacky, "Scrubby School-boy".
And, so awful was the picture,
In comparison the others
Seemed, to one's bewildered fancy,
To have partially succeeded.

Finally my Hiawatha
Tumbled all the tribe together,
("Grouped" is not the right expression),
And, as happy chance would have it
Did at last obtain a picture
Where the faces all succeeded:
Each came out a perfect likeness.

Then they joined and all abused it,
Unrestrainedly abused it,
As the worst and ugliest picture
They could possibly have dreamed of.
"Giving one such strange expressions—
Sullen, stupid, pert expressions.
Really anyone would take us
(Anyone that did not know us)
For the most unpleasant people!"

(Hiawatha seemed to think so,
Seemed to think it not unlikely.)
All together rang their voices,
Angry, loud, discordant voices,
As of dogs that howl in concert,
As of cats that wail in chorus.
　　But my Hiawatha's patience,
His politeness and his patience,
Unaccountably had vanished,
And he left that happy party.
Neither did he leave them slowly,
With the calm deliberation,
The intense deliberation
Of a photographic artist:
But he left them in a hurry,
Left them in a mighty hurry,
Stating that he would not stand it,
Stating in emphatic language
What he'd be before he'd stand it.
Hurriedly he packed his boxes:
Hurriedly the porter trundled
On a barrow all his boxes:
Hurriedly he took his ticket:
Hurriedly the train received him:
Thus departed Hiawatha.

MELANCHOLETTA

WITH saddest music all day long
　　She soothed her secret sorrow:
At night she sighed "I fear 'twas wrong
　　Such cheerful words to borrow.
Dearest, a sweeter, sadder song
　　I'll sing to thee to-morrow."

I thanked her, but I could not say
    That I was glad to hear it:
I left the house at break of day,
    And did not venture near it
Till time, I hoped, had worn away
    Her grief, for nought could cheer it!

My dismal sister! Couldst thou know
    The wretched home thou keepest!
Thy brother, drowned in daily woe,
    Is thankful when thou sleepest;
For if I laugh, however low,
    When thou'rt awake, thou weepest!

I took my sister t'other day
    (Excuse the slang expression)
To Sadler's Wells to see the play
    In hopes the new impression
Might in her thoughts, from grave to gay
    Effect some slight digression.

I asked three gay young dogs from town
    To join us in our folly,
Whose mirth, I thought, might serve to drown
    My sister's melancholy:
The lively Jones, the sportive Brown,
    And Robinson the jolly.

The maid announced the meal in tones
    That I myself had taught her,
Meant to allay my sister's moans
    Like oil on troubled water:
I rushed to Jones, the lively Jones,
    And begged him to escort her.

Vainly he strove, with ready wit,
    To joke about the weather—
To ventilate the last *"on dit"*—

To quote the price of leather—
She groaned "Here I and Sorrow sit:
    Let us lament together!"

I urged "You're wasting time, you know:
    Delay will spoil the venison."
"My heart is wasted with my woe!
    There is no rest—in Venice, on
The Bridge of Sighs!" she quoted low
    From Byron and from Tennyson.

I need not tell of soup and fish
    In solemn silence swallowed,
The sobs that ushered in each dish,
    And its departure followed,
Nor yet my suicidal wish
    To *be* the cheese I hollowed.

Some desperate attempts were made
    To start a conversation;
"Madam," the sportive Brown essayed,
    "Which kind of recreation,
Hunting or fishing, have you made
    Your special occupation?"

Her lips curved downwards instantly,
    As if of india-rubber.
"Hounds *in full cry* I like," said she:
    (Oh, how I longed to snub her!)
"Of fish, a whale's the one for me,
    It is so full of blubber!"

The night's performance was "King John".
    "It's dull", she wept, "and so-so!"
Awhile I let her tears flow on,
    She said they soothed her woe so!
At length the curtain rose upon
    "Bombastes Furioso".

In vain we roared; in vain we tried
  To rouse her into laughter:
Her pensive glances wandered wide
  From orchestra to rafter—
"*Tier upon tier!*" she said, and sighed;
  And silence followed after.

A VALENTINE

[Sent to a friend who had complained that I was glad
enough to see him when he came, but didn't seem to miss
him if he stayed away.]

AND cannot pleasures, while they last,
Be actual unless, when past,
They leave us shuddering and aghast,
    With anguish smarting?
And cannot friends be firm and fast,
    And yet bear parting?

And must I then, at Friendship's call,
Calmly resign the little all
(Trifling, I grant, it is and small)
    I have of gladness,
And lend my being to the thrall
    Of gloom and sadness?

And think you that I should be dumb,
And full *dolorum omnium*,
Excepting when *you* choose to come
    And share my dinner?
At other times be sour and glum
    And daily thinner?

Must he then only live to weep,
Who'd prove his friendship true and deep,

By day a lonely shadow creep,
    At night-time languish,
Oft raising in his broken sleep
    The moan of anguish?

The lover, if for certain days
His fair one be denied his gaze,
Sinks not in grief and wild amaze,
    But, wiser wooer,
He spends the time in writing lays,
    And posts them to her.

And if the verse flow free and fast,
Till even the poet is aghast,
A touching Valentine at last
    The post shall carry,
When thirteen days are gone and past
    Of February.

Farewell, dear friend, and when we meet,
In desert waste or crowded street,
Perhaps before this week shall fleet,
    Perhaps to-morrow,
I trust to find *your* heart the seat
    Of wasting sorrow.

THE THREE VOICES

The First Voice

HE trilled a carol fresh and free,
He laughed aloud for very glee:
There came a breeze from off the sea:

It passed athwart the glooming flat—
It fanned his forehead as he sat—
It lightly bore away his hat,

All to the feet of one who stood
Like maid enchanted in a wood,
Frowning as darkly as she could.

With huge umbrella, lank and brown,
Unerringly she pinned it down,
Right through the centre of the crown.

Then, with an aspect cold and grim,
Regardless of its battered rim,
She took it up and gave it him.

A while like one in dreams he stood,
Then faltered forth his gratitude
In words just short of being rude:

For it had lost its shape and shine,
And it had cost him four-and-nine
And he was going out to dine.

"To dine!" she sneered in acid tone
"To bend thy being to a bone
Clothed in a radiance not its own!"

The tear-drop trickled to his chin:
There was a meaning in her grin
That made him feel on fire within.

"Term it not 'radiance'," said he:
" 'Tis solid nutriment to me.
Dinner is Dinner: Tea is Tea."

And she, "Yea so? Yet wherefore cease?
Let thy scant knowledge find increase.
Say 'Men are Men, and Geese are Geese'."

He moaned: he knew not what to say.
The thought "That I could get away!"
Strove with the thought "But I must stay".

"To dine!" she shrieked in dragon-wrath.
"To swallow wines all foam and froth!
To simper at a table-cloth!

"Say, can thy noble spirit stoop
To join the gormandizing troop
Who find a solace in the soup?

"Canst thou desire or pie or puff?
Thy well-bred manners were enough,
Without such gross material stuff."

"Yet well-bred men", he faintly said,
"Are not unwilling to be fed:
Nor are they well without the bread."

Her visage scorched him ere she spoke:
"There are", she said, "a kind of folk
Who have no horror of a joke.

"Such wretches live: they take their share
Of common earth and common air:
We come across them here and there:

"We grant them—there is no escape—
A sort of semi-human shape
Suggestive of the man-like Ape."

"In all such theories", said he,
"One fixed exception there must be.
That is, the Present Company."

Baffled, she gave a wolfish bark:
He, aiming blindly in the dark,
With random shaft had pierced the mark.

She felt that her defeat was plain,
Yet madly strove with might and main
To get the upper hand again.

Fixing her eyes upon the beach,
As though unconscious of his speech,
She said "Each gives to more than each".

He could not answer yea or nay:
He faltered "Gifts may pass away".
Yet knew not what he meant to say.

"If that be so," she straight replied,
"Each heart with each doth coincide.
What boots it? For the world is wide."

"The world is but a Thought," said he:
"The vast unfathomable sea
Is but a Notion—unto me."

And darkly fell her answer dread
Upon his unresisting head,
Like half a hundredweight of lead.

"The Good and Great must ever shun
That reckless and abandoned one
Who stoops to perpetrate a pun.

"The man that smokes—that reads *The Times*—
That goes to Christmas Pantomimes—
Is capable of *any* crimes!"

He felt it was his turn to speak,
And, with a shamed and crimson cheek,
Moaned "This is harder than Bezique!"

But when she asked him "Wherefore so?"
He felt his very whiskers glow,
And frankly owned "I do not know".

While, like broad waves of golden grain,
Or sunlit hues on cloistered pane,
His colour came and went again.

Pitying his obvious distress,
Yet with a tinge of bitterness,
She said "The More exceeds the Less"

"A truth of such undoubted weight",
He urged, "and so extreme in date,
It were superfluous to state."

Roused into sudden passion, she
In tone of cold malignity:
"To others, yea: but not to thee."

But when she saw him quail and quake,
And when he urged "For pity's sake!"
Once more in gentle tones she spake.

"Thought in the mind doth still abide
That is by Intellect supplied,
And within that Idea doth hide:

"And he, that yearns the truth to know
Still further inwardly may go,
And find Idea from Notion flow:

"And thus the chain, that sages sought,
Is to a glorious circle wrought,
For Notion hath its source in Thought."

So passed they on with even pace:
Yet gradually one might trace
A shadow growing on his face.

The Second Voice

THEY walked beside the wave-worn beach;
Her tongue was very apt to teach,
And now and then he did beseech

She would abate her dulcet tone,
Because the talk was all her own,
And he was dull as any drone.

She urged "No cheese is made of chalk":
And ceaseless flowed her dreary talk,
Tuned to the footfall of a walk.

Her voice was very full and rich,
And, when at length she asked him "Which?"
It mounted to its highest pitch.

He a bewildered answer gave,
Drowned in the sullen moaning wave,
Lost in the echoes of the cave.

He answered her he knew not what:
Like shaft from bow at random shot,
He spoke, but she regarded not.

She waited not for his reply,
But with a downward leaden eye
Went on as if he were not by—

Sound argument and grave defence,
Strange questions raised on "Why?" and "Whence?"
And wildly tangled evidence.

When he, with racked and whirling brain,
Feebly implored her to explain,
She simply said it all again.

Wrenched with an agony intense,
He spake, neglecting Sound and Sense,
And careless of all consequence:

"Mind—I believe—is Essence—Ent—
Abstract—that is—an Accident—
Which we—that is to say—I meant——"

When, with quick breath and cheeks all flushed,
At length his speech was somewhat hushed,
She looked at him, and he was crushed.

It needed not her calm reply:
She fixed him with a stony eye,
And he could neither fight nor fly.

While she dissected, word by word,
His speech, half-guessed at and half-heard,
As might a cat a little bird.

Then, having wholly overthrown
His views, and stripped them to the bone,
Proceeded to unfold her own.

"Shall Man be Man? And shall he miss
Of other thoughts no thought but this,
Harmonious dews of sober bliss?

"What boots it? Shall his fevered eye
Through towering nothingness descry
The grisly phantom hurry by?

"And hear dumb shrieks that fill the air:
See mouths that gape, and eyes that stare
And redden in the dusky glare?

"The meadows breathing amber light,
The darkness toppling from the height,
The feathery train of granite Night?

"Shall he, grown gray among his peers,
Through the thick curtain of his tears
Catch glimpses of his earlier years,

"And hear the sounds he knew of yore,
Old shufflings on the sanded floor,
Old knuckles tapping at the door?

"Yet still before him as he flies
One pallid form shall ever rise,
And, bodying forth in glassy eyes

"The vision of a vanished good,
Low peering through the tangled wood,
Shall freeze the current of his blood."

Still from each fact, with skill uncouth
And savage rapture, like a tooth
She wrenched some slow reluctant truth.

Till, like a silent water-mill,
When summer suns have dried the rill,
She reached a full stop, and was still.

Dead calm succeeded to the fuss,
As when the loaded omnibus
Has reached the railway terminus:

When, for the tumult of the street,
Is heard the engine's stifled beat,
The velvet tread of porters' feet.

With glance that ever sought the ground,
She moved her lips without a sound,
And every now and then she frowned.

He gazed upon the sleeping sea,
And joyed in its tranquillity,
And in that silence dead, but she

To muse a little space did seem,
Then, like the echo of a dream,
Harked back upon her threadbare theme.

Still an attentive ear he lent
But could not fathom what she meant:
She was not deep, nor eloquent.

He marked the ripple on the sand:
The even swaying of her hand
Was all that he could understand.

He saw in dreams a drawing-room,
Where thirteen wretches sat in gloom,
Waiting—he thought he knew for whom:

He saw them drooping here and there,
Each feebly huddled on a chair,
In attitudes of blank despair:

Oysters were not more mute than they,
For all their brains were pumped away,
And they had nothing more to say—

Save one, who groaned "Three hours are gone!"
Who shrieked "We'll wait no longer, John!
Tell them to set the dinner on!"

The vision passed: the ghosts were fled:
He saw once more that woman dread:
He heard once more the words she said.

He left her, and he turned aside:
He sat and watched the coming tide
Across the shores so newly dried.

He wondered at the waters clear,
The breeze that whispered in his ear,
The billows heaving far and near,

And why he had so long preferred
To hang upon her every word:
"In truth", he said, "it was absurd."

The Third Voice

N o t long this transport held its place:
Within a little moment's space
Quick tears were raining down his face.

His heart stood still, aghast with fear;
A wordless voice, nor far nor near,
He seemed to hear and not to hear.

"Tears kindle not the doubtful spark.
If so, why not? Of this remark
The bearings are profoundly dark."

"Her speech", he said, "hath caused this pain.
Easier I count it to explain
The jargon of the howling main,

"Or, stretched beside some babbling brook,
To con, with inexpressive look,
An unintelligible book."

Low spake the voice within his head,
In words imagined more than said,
Soundless as ghost's intended tread:

"If thou art duller than before,
Why quittedst thou the voice of lore?
Why not endure, expecting more?"

"Rather than that", he groaned aghast,
"I'd writhe in depths of cavern vast,
Some loathly vampire's rich repast."

" 'Twere hard," it answered, "themes immense
To coop within the narrow fence
That rings *thy* scant intelligence."

"Not so," he urged, "nor once alone:
But there was something in her tone
That chilled me to the very bone.

"Her style was anything but clear,
And most unpleasantly severe;
Her epithets were very queer.

"And yet, so grand were her replies,
I could not choose but deem her wise;
I did not dare to criticise;

"Nor did I leave her, till she went
So deep in tangled argument
That all my powers of thought were spent."

A little whisper inly slid,
"Yet truth is truth: you know you did."
A little wink beneath the lid.

And, sickened with excess of dread,
Prone to the dust he bent his head,
And lay like one three-quarters dead.

The whisper left him—like a breeze
Lost in the depths of leafy trees—
Left him by no means at his ease.

Once more he weltered in despair,
With hands, through denser-matted hair,
More tightly clenched than then they were.

When, bathed in Dawn of living red,
Majestic frowned the mountain head,
"Tell me my fault," was all he said.

When, at high Noon, the blazing sky
Scorched in his head each haggard eye,
Then keenest rose his weary cry.

And when at Eve the unpitying sun
Smiled grimly on the solemn fun,
"Alack," he sighed, "what *have* I done?"

But saddest, darkest was the sight,
When the cold grasp of leaden Night
Dashed him to earth, and held him tight.

Tortured, unaided, and alone,
Thunders were silence to his groan,
Bagpipes sweet music to its tone:

"What? Ever thus, in dismal round,
Shall Pain and Mystery profound
Pursue me like a sleepless hound,

"With crimson-dashed and eager jaws,
Me, still in ignorance of the cause,
Unknowing what I broke of laws?"

The whisper to his ear did seem
Like echoed flow of silent stream,
Or shadow of forgotten dream,

The whisper trembling in the wind:
"Her fate with thine was intertwined,"
So spake it in his inner mind:

"Each orbed on each a baleful star:
Each proved the other's blight and bar:
Each unto each were best, most far:

"Yea, each to each was worse than foe:
Thou, a scared dullard, gibbering low,
AND SHE, AN AVALANCHE OF WOE!"

THEME WITH VARIATIONS

[WHY is it that Poetry has never yet been subjected to that
process of Dilution which has proved so advantageous to her
sister-art Music? The Diluter gives us first a few notes of
some well-known Air, then a dozen bars of his own, then a
few more notes of the Air, and so on alternately: thus saving
the listener, if not from all risk of recognizing the melody at
all, at least from the too-exciting transports which it might
produce in a more concentrated form. The process is termed
"setting" by Composers, and any one, that has ever experienced the emotion of being unexpectedly set down in a heap
of mortar, will recognize the truthfulness of this happy
phrase.

For truly, just as the genuine Epicure lingers lovingly
over a morsel of supreme Venison—whose every fibre seems
to murmur "Excelsior!"—yet swallows, ere returning to the
toothsome dainty, great mouthfuls of oatmeal-porridge and
winkles: and just as the perfect Connoisseur in Claret per-
mits himself but one delicate sip, and then tosses off a pint or
more of boarding-school beer: so also——]

I NEVER loved a dear Gazelle—
  Nor anything that cost me much:
High prices profit those who sell,
  But why should I be fond of such?

To glad me with his soft black eye
  My son comes trotting home from school;
He's had a fight but can't tell why—
  He always was a little fool!

But, when he came to know me well,
  He kicked me out, her testy Sire:

And when I stained my hair, that Belle
Might note the change, and thus admire

And love me, it was sure to dye
A muddy green, or staring blue:
Whilst one might trace, with half an eye,
The still triumphant carrot through.

A GAME OF FIVES

FIVE little girls of Five, Four, Three, Two, One:
Rolling on the hearthrug, full of tricks and fun.

Five rosy girls, in years from Ten to Six:
Sitting down to lessons—no more time for tricks.

Five growing girls, from Fifteen to Eleven:
Music, Drawing, Languages, and food enough for seven!

Five winsome girls, from Twenty to Sixteen:
Each young man that calls, I say "Now tell me which you
    mean!"

Five dashing girls, the youngest Twenty-one:
But, if nobody proposes, what is there to be done?

Five showy girls—but Thirty is an age
When girls may be *engaging*, but they somehow don't
    engage.

Five dressy girls, of Thirty-one or more:
So gracious to the shy young men they snubbed so much
    before!

*   *   *   *   *   *

Five *passé* girls—Their age? Well, never mind!
We jog along together, like the rest of human kind:

But the quondam "careless bachelor" begins to think he
  knows
The answer to that ancient problem "how the money
  goes"!

POETA FIT, NON NASCITUR

"How shall I be a poet?
    How shall I write in rhyme:
You told me once 'the very wish
    Partook of the sublime'.
Then tell me how! Don't put me off
    With your 'another time'!"

The old man smiled to see him,
    To hear his sudden sally;
He liked the lad to speak his mind
    Enthusiastically;
And thought "There's no hum-drum in him,
    Nor any shilly-shally."

"And would you be a poet
    Before you've been to school?
Ah, well! I hardly thought you
    So absolute a fool.
First learn to be spasmodic—
    A very simple rule.

"For first you write a sentence,
    And then you chop it small;
Then mix the bits, and sort them out
    Just as they chance to fall:
The order of the phrases makes
    No difference at all.

"Then, if you'd be impressive,
　　Remember what I say,
That abstract qualities begin
　　With capitals alway:
The True, the Good, the Beautiful—
　　Those are the things that pay!

"Next, when you are describing
　　A shape, or sound, or tint;
Don't state the matter plainly,
　　But put it in a hint;
And learn to look at all things
　　With a sort of mental squint."

"For instance, if I wished, Sir,
　　Of mutton-pies to tell,
Should I say 'dreams of fleecy flocks
　　Pent in a wheaten cell'?"
"Why, yes," the old man said: "that phrase
　　Would answer very well.

"Then fourthly, there are epithets
　　That suit with any word—
As well as Harvey's Reading Sauce
　　With fish, or flesh, or bird—
Of these, 'wild', 'lonely', 'weary', 'strange',
　　Are much to be preferred."

"And will it do, O will it do
　　To take them in a lump—
As 'the wild man went his weary way
　　To a strange and lonely pump'?"
"Nay, nay! You must not hastily
　　To such conclusions jump.

"Such epithets, like pepper,
    Give zest to what you write;
And, if you strew them sparely,
    They whet the appetite:
But if you lay them on too thick,
    You spoil the matter quite!

"Last, as to the arrangement:
    Your reader, you should show him,
Must take what information he
    Can get, and look for no im-
mature disclosure of the drift
    And purpose of your poem.

"Therefore, to test his patience—
    How much he can endure—
Mention no places, names, or dates,
    And evermore be sure
Throughout the poem to be found
    Consistently obscure.

"First fix upon the limit
    To which it shall extend:
Then fill it up with 'Padding'
    (Beg some of any friend):
Your great SENSATION-STANZA
    You place towards the end."

"And what is a Sensation,
    Grandfather, tell me, pray?
I think I never heard the word
    So used before to-day:
Be kind enough to mention one
    'Exempli gratiâ'."

And the old man, looking sadly
 Across the garden-lawn,
Where here and there a dew-drop
 Yet glittered in the dawn,
Said "Go to the Adelphi,
 And see the 'Colleen Bawn'.

"The word is due to Boucicault—
 The theory is his,
Where life becomes a Spasm,
 And History a Whiz:
If that is not Sensation,
 I don't know what it is.

"Now try your hand, ere Fancy
 Have lost its present glow——"
"And then", his grandson added,
 "We'll publish it, you know:
Green cloth—gold-lettered at the back—
 In duodecimo!"

Then proudly smiled that old man
 To see the eager lad
Rush madly for his pen and ink
 And for his blotting-pad—
But, when he thought of *publishing*,
 His face grew stern and sad.

SIZE AND TEARS

When on the sandy shore I sit,
 Beside the salt sea-wave,
And falling into a weeping fit
 Because I dare not shave—
A little whisper at my ear
Enquires the reason of my fear.

I answer "If that ruffian Jones
   Should recognise me here,
He'd bellow out my name in tones
   Offensive to the ear:
He chaffs me so on being stout
(A thing that always puts me out)."

Ah me! I see him on the cliff!
   Farewell, farewell to hope,
If he should look this way, and if
   He's got his telescope!
To whatsoever place I flee,
My odious rival follows me!

For every night, and everywhere,
   I meet him out at dinner;
And when I've found some charming fair,
   And vowed to die or win her,
The wretch (he's thin and I am stout)
Is sure to come and cut me out!

The girls (just like them!) all agree
   To praise J. Jones, Esquire:
I ask them what on earth they see
   About him to admire?
They cry "He is so sleek and slim,
It's quite a treat to look at him!"

They vanish in tobacco smoke,
   Those visionary maids—
I feel a sharp and sudden poke
   Between the shoulder-blades—
"Why, Brown, my boy! You're growing stout!"
(I told you he would find me out!)

"My growth is not *your* business, Sir!"
    "No more it is, my boy!
But if it's *yours*, as I infer,
    Why, Brown, I give you joy!
A man, whose business prospers so,
Is just the sort of man to know!

"It's hardly safe, though, talking here—
    I'd best get out of reach:
For such a weight as yours, I fear,
    Must shortly sink the beach!"—
Insult me thus because I'm stout!
I vow I'll go and call him out!

ATALANTA IN CAMDEN-TOWN

A Y , 'twas here, on this spot,
    In that summer of yore,
Atalanta did not
    Vote my presence a bore,
Nor reply to my tenderest talk "She had heard all that
nonsense before".

She'd the brooch I had bought
    And the necklace and sash on,
And her heart, as I thought,
    Was alive to my passion;
And she'd done up her hair in the style that the Empress
had brought into fashion.

I had been to the play
    With my pearl of a Peri—
But, for all I could say,
    She declared she was weary,
That "the place was so crowded and hot, and she couldn't
abide that Dundreary".

Then I thought "Lucky boy!
   'Tis for *you* that she whimpers!"
And I noted with joy
   Those sensational simpers:
And I said "This is scrumptious!"—a phrase I had learned
  from the Devonshire shrimpers.

And I vowed " 'Twill be said
   I'm a fortunate fellow,
When the breakfast is spread,
   When the topers are mellow,
When the foam of the bride-cake is white, and the fierce
  orange blossoms are yellow!"

O that languishing yawn!
   O those eloquent eyes!
I was drunk with the dawn
   Of a splendid surmise—
I was stung by a look, I was slain by a tear, by a tempest
  of sighs.

Then I whispered "I see
   The sweet secret thou keepest.
And the yearning for *ME*
   That thou wistfully weepest!
And the question is 'License or Banns?' though undoubt-
  edly Banns are the cheapest."

"Be my Hero," said I,
   "And let *me* be Leander!"
But I lost her reply—
   Something ending with "gander"—
For the omnibus rattled so loud that no mortal could
  quite understand her.

THE LANG COORTIN'

THE ladye she stood at her lattice high,
   Wi' her doggie at her feet;
Thorough the lattice she can spy
   The passers in the street,

"There's one that standeth at the door,
   And tirleth at the pin:
Now speak and say, my popinjay,
   If I sall let him in."

Then up and spake the popinjay
   That flew abune her head:
"Gae let him in that tirls the pin:
   He cometh thee to wed."

O when he cam' the parlour in,
   A woeful man was he!
"And dinna ye ken your lover agen,
   Sae well that loveth thee?"

"And how wad I ken ye loved me, Sir,
   That have been sae lang away?
And how wad I ken ye loved me, Sir?
   Ye never telled me sae."

Said—"Ladye dear," and the salt, salt tear
   Cam' rinnin' doon his cheek,
"I have sent the tokens of my love
   This many and many a week.

"O didna ye get the rings, Ladye,
   The rings o' the gowd sae fine?
I wot that I have sent to thee
   Four score, four score and nine."

"They cam' to me," said that fair ladye.
   "Wow, they were flimsie things!"
Said—"that chain o' gowd, my doggie to howd,
   It is made o' thae self-same rings."

"And didna ye get the locks, the locks,
   The locks o' my ain black hair,
Whilk I sent by post, whilk I sent by box,
   Whilk I sent by the carrier?"

"They cam' to me," said that fair ladye;
   "And I prithee send nae mair!"
Said—"that cushion sae red, for my doggie's head,
   It is stuffed wi' thae locks o' hair."

"And didna ye get the letter, Ladye,
   Tied wi' a silken string,
Whilk I sent to thee frae the far countrie,
   A message of love to bring?"

"It cam' to me frae the far countrie
   Wi' its silken string and a';
But it wasna prepaid," said that high-born maid,
   "Sae I gar'd them tak' it awa'."

"O ever alack that ye sent it back,
   It was written sae clerkly and well!
Now the message it brought, and the boon that it sought.
   I must even say it mysel'."

Then up and spake the popinjay,
   Sae wisely counselled he.
"Now say it in the proper way:
   Gae doon upon thy knee!"

The lover he turned baith red and pale,
   Went doon upon his knee:

"O Ladye, hear the waesome tale
   That must be told to thee!

"For five lang years, and five lang years,
   I coorted thee by looks;
By nods and winks, by smiles and tears,
   As I had read in books.

"For ten lang years, O weary hours!
   I coorted thee by signs;
By sending game, by sending flowers,
   By sending Valentines.

"For five lang years, and five lang years,
   I have dwelt in the far countrie,
Till that thy mind should be inclined
   Mair tenderly to me.

"Now thirty years are gane and past,
   I am come frae a foreign land:
I am come to tell thee my love at last—
   O Ladye, gie me thy hand!"

The ladye she turned not pale nor red,
   But she smiled a pitiful smile:
"Sic' a coortin' as yours, my man," she said,
   "Takes a lang and a weary while!"

And out and laughed the popinjay,
   A laugh of bitter scorn:
"A coortin' done in sic' a way,
   It ought not to be borne!"

Wi' that the doggie barked aloud,
   And up and doon he ran,
And tugged and strained his chain o' gowd,
   All for to bite the man.

"O hush thee, gentle popinjay!
   O hush thee, doggie dear!
There is a word I fain wad say,
   It needeth he should hear!"

Aye louder screamed that ladye fair
   To drown her doggie's bark:
Ever the lover shouted mair
   To make that ladye hark:

Shrill and more shrill the popinjay
   Upraised his angry squall:
I trow the doggie's voice that day
   Was louder than them all!

The serving-men and serving-maids
   Sat by the kitchen fire:
They heard sic' a din the parlour within
   As made them much admire.

Out spake the boy in buttons
   (I ween he wasna thin),
"Now wha will tae the parlour gae,
   And stay this deadlie din?"

And they have taen a kerchief,
   Casted their kevils in,
For wha will tae the parlour gae,
   And stay that deadlie din.

When on that boy the kevil fell
   To stay the fearsome noise,
"Gae in," they cried, "whate'er betide,
   Thou prince of button-boys!"

Syne, he has taen a supple cane
   To swinge that dog sae fat:
The doggie yowled, the doggie howled
   The louder aye for that.

Syne, he has taen a mutton-bane—
    The doggie ceased his noise,
And followed doon the kitchen stair
    That prince of button-boys!

Then sadly spake that ladye fair,
    Wi' a frown upon her brow:
"O dearer to me is my sma' doggie
    Than a dozen sic' as thou!

"Nae use, nae use for sighs and tears:
    Nae use at all to fret:
Sin' ye've bided sae well for thirty years,
    Ye may bide a wee langer yet!"

Sadly, sadly he crossed the floor
    And tirlëd at the pin:
Sadly went he through the door
    Where sadly he cam' in.

"O gin I had a popinjay
    To fly abune my head,
To tell me what I ought to say,
    I had by this been wed.

"O gin I find anither ladye,"
    He said wi' sighs and tears,
"I wot my coortin' sall not be
    Anither thirty years

"For gin I find a ladye gay,
    Exactly to my taste,
I'll pop the question, aye or nay
    In twenty years at maist."

FOUR RIDDLES

[These consist of two Double Acrostics and two Charades.
No. I. was written at the request of some young friends,
who had gone to a ball at an Oxford Commemoration—and
also as a specimen of what might be done by making the
Double Acrostic *a connected poem* instead of what it has
hitherto been, a string of disjointed stanzas, on every conceivable subject, and about as interesting to read straight
through as a page of a Cyclopedia. The first two stanzas
describe the two main words, and each subsequent stanza
one of the cross "lights".
No. II. was written after seeing Miss Ellen Terry perform
in the play of "Hamlet". In this case the first stanza describes the two main words.
No. III. was written after seeing Miss Marion Terry perform in Mr. Gilbert's play of "Pygmalion and Galatea". The
three stanzas respectively describe "My First", "My Second", and "My Whole".]

I

THERE was an ancient City, stricken down
    With a strange frenzy, and for many a day
They paced from morn to eve the crowded town,
      And danced the night away.

I asked the cause: the aged man grew sad:
    They pointed to a building gray and tall,
And hoarsely answered "Step inside, my lad,
      And then you'll see it all."

———

Yet what are all such gaieties to me
    Whose thoughts are full of indices and surds?

$$x^2 + 7x + 53 = \frac{11}{3}.$$

But something whispered "It will soon be done:
   Bands cannot always play, nor ladies smile:
Endure with patience the distasteful fun
     For just a little while!"

A change came o'er my Vision—it was night:
   We clove a pathway through a frantic throng:
The steeds, wild-plunging, filled us with affright:
     The chariots whirled along.

Within a marble hall a river ran—
   A living tide, half muslin and half cloth:
And here one mourned a broken wreath or fan,
     Yet swallowed down her wrath:

And here one offered to a thirsty fair
   (His words half-drowned amid those thunders tuneful)
Some frozen viand (there were many there),
     A tooth-ache in each spoonful.

There comes a happy pause, for human strength
   Will not endure to dance without cessation;
And every one must reach the point at length
     Of absolute prostration.

At such a moment ladies learn to give,
   To partners who would urge them overmuch,
A flat and yet decided negative—
     Photographers love such.

There comes a welcome summons—hope revives,
   And fading eyes grow bright, and pulses quicken:
Incessant pop the corks, and busy knives
     Dispense the tongue and chicken.

Flushed with new life, the crowd flows back again:
   And all is tangled talk and mazy motion—
Much like a waving field of golden grain,
     Or a tempestuous ocean.

And thus they give the time, that Nature meant
  For peaceful sleep and meditative snores,
To ceaseless din and mindless merriment
    And waste of shoes and floors.

And One (we name him not) that flies the flowers,
  That dreads the dances, and that shuns the salads,
They doom to pass in solitude the hours,
    Writing acrostic-ballads.

How late it grows! The hour is surely past
  That should have warned us with its double knock?
The twilight wanes, and morning comes at last—
    "Oh, Uncle, what's o'clock?"

The Uncle gravely nods, and wisely winks.
  It *may* mean much, but how is one to know?
He opes his mouth—yet out of it, methinks,
    No words of wisdom flow.

      Answer: Commemoration, Monstrosities.

II

    EMPRESS of Art, for thee I twine
      This wreath with all too slender skill.
    Forgive my Muse each halting line,
      And for the deed accept the will!

    ———

O day of tears! Whence comes this spectre grim,
  Parting, like Death's cold river, souls that love?
Is not he bound to thee, as thou to him,
  By vows, unwhispered here, yet heard above?

And still it lives, that keen and heavenward flame,
  Lives in his eye, and trembles in his tone:
And these wild words of fury but proclaim
  A heart that beats for thee, for thee alone!

But all is lost: that mighty mind o'erthrown,
　Like sweet bells jangled, piteous sight to see!
"Doubt that the stars are fire," so runs his moan,
　"Doubt Truth herself, but not my love for thee!"

A sadder vision yet: thine aged sire
　Shaming his hoary locks with treacherous wile!
And dost thou now doubt Truth to be a liar?
　And wilt thou die, that hast forgot to smile?

Nay, get thee hence! Leave all thy winsome ways
　And the faint fragrance of thy scattered flowers:
In holy silence wait the appointed days,
　And weep away the leaden-footed hours.

Answer: Ellen Terry.

III

THE air is bright with hues of light
　And rich with laughter and with singing:
Young hearts beat high in ecstasy,
　And banners wave, and bells are ringing:
But silence falls with fading day,
And there's an end to mirth and play.
　　　Ah, well-a-day!

Rest your old bones, ye wrinkled crones!
　The kettle sings, the firelight dances.
Deep be it quaffed, the magic draught
　That fills the soul with golden fancies!
For Youth and Pleasance will not stay,
And ye are withered, worn, and gray.
　　　Ah, well-a-day!

O fair cold face! O form of grace,
　For human passion madly yearning!

O weary air of dumb despair,
    From marble won, to marble turning!
"Leave us not thus!" we fondly pray.
"We cannot let thee pass away!"
        Ah, well-a-day!

Answer: Galatea (Gala-tea).

IV

M y First is singular at best:
    More plural is my Second:
My Third is far the pluralest—
So plural-plural, I protest
    It scarcely can be reckoned!

My First is followed by a bird:
    My Second by believers
In magic art: my simple Third
Follows, not often, hopes absurd
    And plausible deceivers.

My First to get at wisdom tries—
    A failure melancholy!
My Second men revered as wise:
My Third from heights of wisdom flies
    To depths of frantic folly.

My First is ageing day by day:
    My Second's age is ended:
My Third enjoys an age, they say,
That never seems to fade away,
    Through centuries extended.

My Whole? I need a poet's pen
    To paint her myriad phases:
The monarch, and the slave, of men—
A mountain-summit, and a den
    Of dark and deadly mazes—

A flashing light—a fleeting shade—
Beginning, end, and middle
Of all that human art hath made
Or wit devised! Go, seek *her* aid,
If you would read my riddle!

Answer: Imagination (I-Magi-nation).

FAME'S PENNY-TRUMPET

[Affectionately dedicated to all "original researchers" who
pant for "endowment".]

BLOW, blow your trumpets till they crack,
Ye little men of little souls!
And bid them huddle at your back—
Gold-sucking leeches, shoals on shoals!

Fill all the air with hungry wails—
"Reward us, ere we think or write!
Without your Gold mere Knowledge fails
To sate the swinish appetite!"

And, where great Plato paced serene,
Or Newton paused with wistful eye,
Rush to the chace with hoofs unclean
And Babel-clamour of the sty.

Be yours the pay: be theirs the praise:
We will not rob them of their due,
Nor vex the ghosts of other days
By naming them along with you.

They sought and found undying fame:
They toiled not for reward nor thanks:
Their cheeks are hot with honest shame
For you, the modern mountebanks!

Who preach of Justice—plead with tears
    That Love and Mercy should abound—
While marking with complacent ears
    The moaning of some tortured hound:

Who prate of Wisdom—nay, forbear,
    Lest Wisdom turn on you in wrath,
Trampling, with heel that will not spare,
    The vermin that beset her path!

Go, throng each other's drawing-rooms,
    Ye idols of a petty clique:
Strut your brief hour in borrowed plumes
    And make your penny-trumpets squeak:

Deck your dull talk with pilfered shreds
    Of learning from a nobler time,
And oil each other's little heads
    With mutual Flattery's golden slime:

And when the topmost height ye gain,
    And stand in Glory's ether clear,
And grasp the prize of all your pain—
    So many hundred pounds a year—

Then let Fame's banner be unfurled!
    Sing Pæans for a victory won!
Ye tapers, that would light the world,
    And cast a shadow on the Sun—

Who still shall pour His rays sublime,
    One crystal flood, from East to West,
When *ye* have burned your little time
    And feebly flickered into rest!

COLLEGE RHYMES AND NOTES BY AN OXFORD CHIEL

ODE TO DAMON

(From Chloë, who Understands His Meaning.)

"Oh, do not forget the day when we met
    At the fruiterer's shop in the city:
When you *said* I was plain and *excessively* vain,
    But I knew that you *meant* I was pretty.

"Recollect, too, the hour when I purchased the flour
    (For the dumplings, you know) and the suet;
Whilst the apples I told my dear Damon to hold,
    (Just to see if you knew how to do it).

"Then recall to your mind how you left *me* behind,
    And went off in a 'bus with the pippins;
When you *said* you'd forgot, but I knew you had *not*;
    (It was merely to save the odd threepence!).

"Don't forget your delight in the dumplings that night,
    Though you *said* they were tasteless and doughy:
But you winked as you spoke, and I saw that the joke
    (*If it was one*) was meant for your Chloë!

"Then remember the day when Joe offered to pay
    For us all at the Great Exhibition;
You proposed a short cut, and we found the thing shut,
    (We were two hours too late for admission).

"Your 'short cut', dear, we found took us *seven miles
    round*
  (And Joe said exactly what *we* did):
Well, *I* helped you out then—it was just like you men—
  Not an atom of sense when it's needed!

"*You* said 'What's to be done?' and *I* thought you in fun,
  (Never *dreaming* you were such a ninny).
'*Home* directly!' said I, and you paid for the fly,
  (And I *think* that you gave him a guinea).

"Well, *that* notion, you said, had not entered your head:
  You proposed 'The best thing, as we're come, is
(Since it opens again in the morning at ten)
  To wait'—*Oh, you prince of all dummies!*

"And when Joe asked you 'Why, if a man were to die,
  Just as you ran a sword through his middle,
You'd be hung for the crime?' and you said 'Give me
    time!'
  And brought to your Chloë the riddle—

"Why, remember, you dunce, how I solved it at once—
  (The question which Joe had referred to you),
Why, I told you the cause, was 'the force of the laws',
  And you said '*It had never occurred to you.*'

"This instance will show that your brain is too slow,
  And (though your exterior is showy),
Yet so arrant a goose can be no sort of use
  To society—come to your Chloë!

"You'll find *no one* like me, who can manage to see
  Your meaning, you talk so obscurely:
Why, if once I were gone, how *would* you get on?
  Come, you know what I mean, Damon, surely."

1861.

THOSE HORRID HURDY-GURDIES!

A MONODY, BY A VICTIM

"My mother bids me bind my hair,"
　　And not go about such a figure;
It's a bother, of course, but what do I care?
　　I shall do as I please when I'm bigger.

"My lodging is on the cold, cold ground,"
　　As the first-floor and attic were taken.
I tried the garret but once, and found
　　That my wish for a change was mistaken.

"Ever of thee!" yes, "Ever of thee!"
　　They chatter more and more,
Till I groan aloud, "Oh! let me be!
　　I have heard it all before!"

"Please remember the organ, sir,"
　　What? hasn't he left me yet?
I promise, good man; for its tedious burr
　　I never can forget.

1861.

MY FANCY

I painted her a gushing thing,
　　With years perhaps a score;
I little thought to find they were
　　At least a dozen more;
My fancy gave her eyes of blue,
　　A curly auburn head:
I came to find the blue a green,
　　The auburn turned to red.

She boxed my ears this morning,
　They tingled very much;
I own that I could wish her
　A somewhat lighter touch;
And if you were to ask me how
　Her charms might be improved,
I would not have them *added to*,
　But just a few *removed*!

She has the bear's ethereal grace,
　The bland hyena's laugh,
The footstep of the elephant,
　The neck of the giraffe;
I love her still, believe me,
　Though my heart its passion hides;
"She's all my fancy painted her,"
　But oh! *how much besides*!

Mar. 15, 1862.

THE MAJESTY OF JUSTICE

AN OXFORD IDYLL

THEY passed beneath the College gate;
　And down the High went slowly on;
Then spake the Undergraduate
　To that benign and portly Don:
"They say that Justice is a Queen—
　A Queen of awful Majesty—
Yet in the papers I have seen
　Some things that puzzle me.

"A Court obscure, so rumour states,
　There is, called 'Vice-Cancellarii',
Which keeps on Undergraduates,
　Who do not pay their bills, a wary eye.

A case I'm told was lately brought
   Into that tiniest of places,
And justice in that case was sought—
   As in most other cases.

"Well! Justice as I hold, dear friend,
   Is Justice, neither more than less:
I never dreamed it could depend
   On ceremonial or dress.
I thought that her imperial sway
   In Oxford surely would appear,
But all the papers seem to say
   She's not majestic *here*."

The portly Don he made reply,
   With the most roguish of his glances,
"Perhaps she drops her Majesty
   Under peculiar circumstances."
"But that's the point!" the young man cried,
   "The puzzle that I wish to pen you in—
How are the public to decide
   Which article is genuine?

"Is't only when the Court is large
   That we for 'Majesty' need hunt?
Would what is Justice in a barge
   Be something different in a punt?
"Nay, nay!" the Don replied, amused,
   "You're talking nonsense, sir! You know it!
Such arguments were never used
   By any friend of Jowett."

"Then is it in the men who trudge
   (Beef-eaters I believe they call them)
Before each wigged and ermined judge,
   For fear some mischief should befall them?

If I should recognise in one
   (Through all disguise) my own domestic,
I fear 'twould shed a gleam of fun
   Even on the 'Majestic'!"

The portly Don replied, "Ahem!
   They can't exactly be its *essence*:
I scarcely think the want of them
   The 'Majesty of Justice' lessens.
Besides, they always march awry;
   Their gorgeous garments never fit:
Processions don't make Majesty—
   I'm quite convinced of it."

"Then is it in the *wig* it lies,
   Whose countless rows of rigid curls
Are gazed at with admiring eyes
   By country lads and servant-girls?"
Out laughed that bland and courteous Don:
   "Dear sir, I do not mean to flatter—
But surely you have hit upon
   The essence of the matter.

"They will not own the Majesty
   Of Justice, making Monarchs bow,
Unless as evidence they see
   The horsehair wig upon her brow.
Yes, yes! That makes the silliest men
   Seem wise; the meanest men look big:
The Majesty of Justice, then,
   Is seated in the WIG."

March 1863.

THE ELECTIONS TO THE HEBDOMADAL COUNCIL

[In the year 1866, a Letter with the above title was published in Oxford, addressed by Mr. Goldwin Smith to the Senior Censor of Christ Church, with the two-fold object of revealing to the University a vast political misfortune which it had unwittingly encountered, and of suggesting a remedy which should at once alleviate the bitterness of the calamity and secure the sufferers from its recurrence. The misfortune thus revealed was no less than the fact that, at a recent election of Members to the Hebdomadal Council, *two* Conservatives had been chosen, thus giving a Conservative majority in the Council; and the remedy suggested was a sufficiently sweeping one, embracing, as it did, the following details:

1. "The exclusion" (from Congregation) "of the non-academical elements which form a main part of the strength of this party domination." These "elements" are afterwards enumerated as "the parish clergy and the professional men of the city, and chaplains who are without any academical occupation".

2. The abolition of the Hebdomadal Council.

3. The abolition of the legislative functions of Convocation.

These are all the main features of this remarkable scheme of Reform, unless it be necessary to add—

4. "To preside over a Congregation with full legislative powers, the Vice-Chancellor ought no doubt to be a man of real capacity."

But it would be invidious to suppose that there was any intention of suggesting this as a novelty.

The following rhythmical version of the Letter develops its principles to an extent which possibly the writer had never contemplated.]

815

"Now is the winter of our discontent." [1]

"HEARD ye the arrow hurtle in the sky?
Heard ye the dragon-monster's dreadful cry?"—
Excuse this sudden burst of the Heroic;
The present state of things would vex a Stoic!
And just as Sairey Gamp, for pains within,
Administered a modicum of gin,
So does my mind, when vexed and ill at ease,
Console itself with soothing similes,
The "dragon-monster" (pestilential schism!)
I need not tell you is Conservatism.
The "hurtling arrow" (till we find a better)
Is represented by the present Letter.
    'Twas, I remember, but the other day,
Dear Senior Censor, that you chanced to say
You thought these party-combinations would
Be found, "though needful, no unmingled good."
Unmingled good? They are unmingled ill! [2]
I never took to them, and never will—[3]
What am I saying? Heed it not, my friend:
On the next page I mean to recommend
The very dodges that I now condemn
In the Conservatives! Don't hint to them ⎫
A word of this! (In confidence. Ahem!) ⎬
    Need I rehearse the history of Jowett? ⎭
I need not, Senior Censor, for you know it. [4]
That was the Board Hebdomadal, and oh!
Who would be free, themselves must strike the blow!

[1] Dr. Wynter, President of St. John's, one of the recently elected Conservative members of Council.
[2] "In a letter on a point connected with the late elections to the Hebdomadal Council you incidentally remarked to me that our combinations for these elections, 'though necessary were not an unmixed good'. They are an unmixed evil".
[3] "I never go to a *caucus* without reluctance: I never write a canvassing letter without a feeling of repugnance to my task."
[4] "I need not rehearse the history of the Regius Professor of Greek."

Let each that wears a beard, and each that shaves,
Join in the cry "We never will be slaves!"
"But can the University afford
To be a slave to any kind of board?
A *slave?*" you shuddering ask. "Think you it can, Sir?"
"*Not at the present moment,*" is my answer.[1]
I've thought the matter o'er and o'er again
And given to it all my powers of brain;
I've thought it out, and this is what I make it,
(And I don't care a Tory how you take it:)
It may be right to go ahead, I guess:
It may be right to stop, I do confess;
Also, it may be right to retrogress.[2]

So says the oracle, and, for myself, I
Must say it beats to fits the one at Delphi!
   To save beloved Oxford from the yoke,
(For this majority's beyond a joke),
We must combine,[3] aye! hold a *caucus*-meeting,[4]
Unless we want to get another beating.
That they should "bottle" us is nothing new—
But shall they bottle us and *caucus* too?
See the "fell unity of purpose" now
With such Obstructives plunge into the row![5]
"Factious Minorities," we used to sigh—
"Factious Majorities" is now the cry.
"Votes—ninety-two"—no combination here:

---

[1] "The University cannot afford at the present moment to be delivered over as a slave to any non-academical interest whatever."

[2] "It may be right to go on, it may be right to stand still, or it may be right to go back."

[3] "To save the University from going completely under the yoke ... we shall still be obliged to combine."

[4] "Caucus-holding and wire-pulling would still be almost inevitably carried on to some extent."

[5] "But what are we to do? Here is a great political and theological party ... labouring under perfect discipline and with fell unity of purpose, to hold the University in subjection, and fill her government with its nominees."

"Votes—ninety-three"—conspiracy, 'tis clear! [1]
You urge " 'Tis but a unit." I reply
That in that unit lurks their "unity".
Our voters often bolt, and often baulk us,
But then, they never, never go *to caucus*!
Our voters ca'n't forget the maxim famous
  "Semel electum semper eligamus":
They never can be worked into a ferment
By visionary promise of preferment,
Nor taught, by hints of "Paradise" [2] beguiled,
To whisper "C for Chairman" like a child! [3]
And thus the friends that we have tempted down
Oft take the two-o'clock Express for town. [4]

    This is our danger: this the secret foe
That aims at Oxford such a deadly blow.
What champion can we find to save the State,
To crush the plot? We darkly whisper "Wait!" [5]

    My scheme is this: remove the votes of all
The residents that are not Liberal— [6]
Leave the young Tutors uncontrolled and free,
And Oxford then shall see—what it shall see.
What next? Why then, I say, let Convocation

---

  [1] At a recent election to Council, the Liberals mustered ninety-two votes and the Conservatives ninety-three; whereupon the latter were charged with having obtained their victory by a conspiracy.

  [2] Not to mention that, as we cannot promise Paradise to our supporters, they are very apt to take the train for London just before the election.

  [3] It is not known to what the word "Paradise" was intended to allude, and therefore the hint, here thrown out, that the writer meant to recall the case of the late Chairman of Mr. Gladstone's committee, who had been recently collated to the See of Chester, is wholly wanton and gratuitous.

  [4] A case of this kind had actually occurred on the occasion of the division just alluded to.

  [5] Mr. Wayte, now President of Trinity, then put forward as the Liberal candidate for election to Council.

  [6] "You and others suggest, as the only effective remedy, that the Constituency should be reformed, by the exclusion of the non-academical elements which form a main part of the strength of this party domination."

Be shorn of all her powers of legislation.[1]
But why stop there? Let us go boldly on—
Sweep everything beginning with a "Con"
Into oblivion! Convocation first,
Conservatism next, and, last and worst,
   "Concilium Hebdomadale" must,
Consumed and conquered, be consigned to dust![2]

   And here I must relate a little fable
I heard last Saturday at our high table:—
The cats, it seems, were masters of the house,
And held their own against the rat and mouse:
Of course the others couldn't stand it long,
So held a caucus (not, in their case, wrong);
And, when they were assembled to a man,
Uprose an aged rat, and thus began:—
   "Brothers in bondage! Shall we bear to be
For ever left in a minority?
With what 'fell unity of purpose' cats
Oppose the trusting innocence of rats!
So unsuspicious are we of disguise,
Their machinations take us by surprise—[3]
Insulting and tyrannical absurdities![4]
Is it too bad by half—upon my word it is!
For, now that these Con——, cats, I should say (frizzle
    'em!),
Are masters, they exterminate like Islam![5]
How shall we deal with them? I'll tell you how:—

[1] "I confess that, having included all the really academical elements in Congregation, I would go boldly on, and put an end to the Legislative functions of Convocation."
[2] "This conviction, that while we have Elections to Council we shall not entirely get rid of party organization and its evils, leads me to venture a step further, and to raise the question whether it is really necessary that we should have an Elective Council for legislative purposes at all."
[3] "Sometimes, indeed, not being informed that the wires are at work, we are completely taken by surprise."
[4] "We are without protection against this most insulting and tyrannical absurdity."
[5] "It is as exterminating as Islam."

Let none but kittens be allowed to miaow!
The Liberal kittens seize us but in play,
And, while they frolic, we can run away;
But older cats are not so generous,
Their claws are too Conservative for us!
Then let *them* keep the stable and the oats,
While kittens, rats, and mice have all the votes,
  "Yes; banish cats! The kittens would not use
Their powers for blind obstruction,[1] nor refuse
To let us sip the cream and gnaw the cheese—
How glorious then would be our destinies![2]
Kittens and rats would occupy the throne,
And rule the larder for itself alone!"[3]

So rhymed my friend, and asked me what I thought
    of it.
I told him that so much as I had caught of it
Appeared to me (as I need hardly mention)
Entirely undeserving of attention.

But now, to guide the Congregation, when
It numbers none but really "able" men,
A "*Vice-Cancellarius*" will be needed
Of every kind of human weakness weeded!
Is such the president that we have got?
He ought no doubt to be; why should he not?[4]
I do not hint that Liberals should dare
To oust the present holder of the chair—
But surely he would not object to be

[1] "Their powers would scarcely be exercised for the purposes of fanaticism, or in a spirit of blind obstruction."
[2] "These narrow local bounds, within which our thoughts and schemes have hitherto been pent, will begin to disappear, and a far wider sphere of action will open on the view."
[3] "Those councils must be freely opened to all who can serve her well and who will serve her for herself."
[4] "To preside over a Congregation with full legislative powers, the Vice-Chancellor ought no doubt to be a man of real capacity; but why should he not? His mind ought also, for this as well as for his other high functions, to be clear of petty details, and devoted to the great matters of University business; but why should not this condition also be fulfilled?"

Gently examined by a Board of three?
Their duty being just to ascertain
That he's "all there" (I mean, of course, in brain),
And that his mind, from "petty details" clear,
Is fitted for the duties of his sphere.

All this is merely moonshine, till we get
The seal of Parliament upon it set.
A word then, Senior Censor, in your ear:
The Government is in a state of fear—
Like some old gentleman, abroad at night,
Seized with a sudden shiver of affright,
Who offers money, on his bended knees,
To the first skulking vagabond he sees—
Now is the lucky moment for our task;
They daren't refuse us anything we ask![1]

And then our Fellowships shall open be
To Intellect, no meaner quality!
No moral excellence, no social fitness
Shall ever be admissible as witness.
"Avaunt, dull Virtue!" is Oxonia's cry:
"Come to my arms, ingenious Villainy!"

For Classic Fellowships, an honour high,
Simonides and Co. will then apply—
Our Mathematics will to Oxford bring
The 'cutest members of the betting-ring—
Law Fellowships will start upon their journeys
A myriad of unscrupulous attorneys—
While prisoners, doomed till now to toil unknown,
Shall mount the Physical Professor's throne!
And thus would Oxford educate, indeed,
Men far beyond a merely local need—

---

[1] "If you apply now to Parliament for this or any other University reform, you will find the House of Commons in a propitious mood. . . . Even the Conservative Government, as it looks for the support of moderate Liberals on the one great subject, is very unwilling to present itself in such an aspect that these men may not be able decently to give it their support."

With no career before them, I may say,[1]
Unless they're wise enough to go away,
And seek far West, or in the distant East,
Another flock of pigeons to be fleeced.

I might go on, and trace the destiny
Of Oxford in an age which, though it be
Thus breaking with tradition, owns a new
Allegiance to the intellectual few—
(I mean, of course, the—pshaw! no matter who!)
But, were I to pursue the boundless theme,
I fear that I should seem to you to dream.[2]

This to fulfil, or even—humbler far—
To shun Conservatism's noxious star
And all the evils that it brings behind,
These pestilential coils must be untwined—
The party-coils, that clog the march of Mind—
Choked in whose meshes Oxford, slowly wise,
Has lain for three disastrous centuries.[3]
Away with them! (It is for this I yearn!)
Each twist untwist, each Turner overturn!
Disfranchise each Conservative, and cancel
The votes of Michell, Liddon, Wall, and Mansel!
Then, then shall Oxford be herself again,
Neglect the heart, and cultivate the brain—
Then this shall be the burden of our song,
"All change is good—whatever is, is wrong—"
Then Intellect's proud flag shall be unfurled,
And Brain, and Brain alone, shall rule the world!

[1] "With open Fellowships, Oxford will soon produce a supply of men fit for the work of high education far beyond her own local demands, and in fact with no career before them unless a career can be opened elsewhere."

[2] "I should seem to you to dream if I were to say what I think the destiny of the University may be in an age which, though it is breaking with tradition, is, from the same causes, owning a new allegiance to intellectual authority."

[3] "But to fulfil this, or even a far humbler destiny—to escape the opposite lot—the pestilential coils of party, in which the University has lain for three disastrous centuries choked, must be untwined."

THE DESERTED PARKS

"Solitudinem faciunt: Parcum appellant."

MUSEUM! loveliest building of the plain
Where Cherwell winds towards the distant main;
How often have I loitered o'er thy green,
Where humble happiness endeared the scene!
How often have I paused on every charm,
The rustic couple walking arm in arm—
The groups of trees, with seats beneath the shade
For prattling babes and whisp'ring lovers made—
The never-failing brawl, the busy mill
Where tiny urchins vied in fistic skill—
(Two phrases only have that dusky race
Caught from the learned influence of the place;
Phrases in their simplicity sublime,
"Scramble a copper!" "Please, Sir, what's the time?")
These round thy walks their cheerful influence shed;
There were thy charms—but all these charms are fled.
    Amidst thy bowers the tyrant's hand is seen,
And rude pavilions sadden all thy green;
One selfish pastime grasps the whole domain,
And half a faction swallows up the plain;
Adown thy glades, all sacrificed to cricket,
The hollow-sounding bat now guards the wicket;
Sunk are thy mounds in shapeless level all,
Lest aught impede the swiftly rolling ball;
And trembling, shrinking from the fatal blow,
Far, far away thy hapless children go.
    Ill fares the place, to luxury a prey,
Where wealth accumulates, and minds decay;
Athletic sports may flourish or may fade,
Fashion may make them, even as it has made;
But the broad parks, the city's joy and pride,
When once destroyed can never be supplied!

Ye friends to truth, ye statesmen, who survey
The rich man's joys increase, the poor's decay,
'Tis yours to judge, how wide the limits stand
Between a splendid and a happy land.
Proud swells go by with laugh of hollow joy,
And shouting Folly hails them with "Ahoy!"
Funds even beyond the miser's wish abound,
And rich men flock from all the world around.
Yet count our gains. This wealth is but a name,
That leaves our useful products still the same.
Not so the loss. The man of wealth and pride
Takes up a space that many poor supplied;
Space for the game, and all its instruments,
Space for pavilions and for scorers' tents;
The ball, that raps his shins in padding cased,
Has worn the verdure to an arid waste;
His Park, where these exclusive sports are seen,
Indignant spurns the rustic from the green;
While through the plain, consigned to silence all,
In barren splendour flits the russet ball.
    In peaceful converse with his brother Don,
Here oft the calm Professor wandered on;
Strange words he used—men drank with wondering ears
The languages called "dead", the tongues of other years.
(Enough of Heber! Let me once again
Attune my verse to Goldsmith's liquid strain.)
A man he was to undergraduates dear,
And passing rich with forty pounds a year.
And so, I ween, he would have been till now,
Had not his friends ('twere long to tell you how)
Prevailed on him, Jack-Horner-like, to try
Some method to evaluate his pie,
And win from those dark depths, with skilful thumb,
Five times a hundredweight of luscious plum—
Yet for no thirst of wealth, no love of praise,
In learned labour he consumed his days!
    O Luxury! thou cursed by Heaven's decree,
How ill exchanged are things like these for thee!

How do thy potions, with insidious joy,
Diffuse their pleasures only to destroy;
Iced cobbler, Badminton, and shandy-gaff,
Rouse the loud jest and idiotic laugh;
Inspired by them, to tipsy greatness grown,
Men boast a florid vigour not their own;
At every draught more wild and wild they grow;
While pitying friends observe "I told you so!"
Till, summoned to their post, at the first ball,
A feeble under-hand, their wickets fall.

    Even now the devastation is begun,
And half the business of destruction done;
Even now, methinks while pondering here in pity,
I see the rural Virtues leave the city.
Contented Toil, and calm scholastic Care,
And frugal Moderation, all are there;
Resolute Industry that scorns the lure
Of careless mirth—that dwells apart secure—
To science gives her days, her midnight oil,
Cheered by the sympathy of others' toil—
Courtly Refinement, and that Taste in dress
That brooks no meanness, yet avoids excess—
All these I see, with slow reluctant pace
Desert the long-beloved and honoured place!

    While yet 'tis time, Oxonia, rise and fling
The spoiler from thee: grant no parleying!
Teach him that eloquence, against the wrong,
Though very poor, may still be very strong;
That party-interests we must forgo,
When hostile to "pro bono publico";
That faction's empire hastens to its end,
When once mankind to common sense attend;
While independent votes may win the day
Even against the potent spell of "Play!"

May 1867.

EXAMINATION STATUTE

["The Statute proposed to allow candidates for a degree to forsake Classics after Moderations, except so far as was needed for a Fourth Class in the Final School of Literæ Humaniores, if they wished to graduate in science. This Dodgson considered degrading both to Classics and to Mathematics." —*Dodgson Handbook*.]

A list of those who might, could, would, or should have voted thereon in Congregation, February 2, 4681, arranged alphabetically.

A is for [Acland], who'd physic the Masses,
B is for [Brodie], who swears by the gases.
C is for [Conington], constant to Horace.
D is for [Donkin], who integrates for us.
E is for [Evans], with rifle well steadied.
F is for [Freeman], Examiner dreaded!
G's [Goldwin Smith], by the "Saturday" quoted.
H is for [Heurtley], to "Margaret" devoted.
I am the Author, a rhymer erratic—
J is for [Jowett], who lectures in Attic:
K is for [Kitchen], than attic much warmer.
L is for [Liddell], relentless reformer!
M is for [Mansel], our Logic-provider,
And [Norris] is N, once a famous rough-rider.
[Ogilvie]'s O, Orthodoxy's Mendoza!
And [Parker] is P, the amendment-proposer.
Q is the Quad, where the Dons are collecting.
R is for [Rolleston], who lives for dissecting:
S is for [Stanley], sworn foe to formality.
T's [Travers Twiss], full of civil legality.
U's University, factiously splitting—
V's the Vice-Chancellor, ceaselessly sitting.
W's [Wall], by Museum made frantic,
X the Xpenditure, grown quite gigantic.
Y are the Young men, whom nobody thought about—
Z is the Zeal that this victory brought about.

ACROSTICS, INSCRIPTIONS, AND OTHER VERSES

ACROSTIC

Little maidens, when you look
On this little story-book,
Reading with attentive eye
Its enticing history,
Never think that hours of play
Are your only HOLIDAY,
And that in a HOUSE of joy
Lessons serve but to annoy:
If in any HOUSE you find
Children of a gentle mind,
Each the others pleasing ever—
Each the others vexing never—
Daily work and pastime daily
In their order taking gaily—
Then be very sure that they
Have a life of HOLIDAY.

Christmas 1861.

TO THREE PUZZLED LITTLE GIRLS,
FROM THE AUTHOR

(To the three Misses Drury.)

THREE little maidens weary of the rail,
Three pairs of little ears listening to a tale,
Three little hands held out in readiness,
For three little puzzles very hard to guess.
Three pairs of little eyes, open wonder-wide,
At three little scissors lying side by side.
Three little mouths that thanked an unknown Friend,
For one little book, he undertook to send.
Though whether they'll remember a friend, or book, or
  day—
In three little weeks is very hard to say.

August 1869.

DOUBLE ACROSTIC

(To Miss E. M. Argles.)

I SING a place wherein agree
All things on land that fairest be,
All that is sweetest of the sea.

Nor can I break the silken knot
That binds my memory to the spot
And friends too dear to be forgot.

 . . . . .

On rocky brow we loved to stand
And watch in silence, hand in hand,

The shadows veiling sea and land.	B	luf	F

Then dropped the breeze; no vessel passed:
So silent stood each taper mast,
You would have deemed it chained and
  fast.   A ncho R

Above the blue and fleecy sky:
Below, the waves that quivering lie,
Like crispèd curls of greenery.   B roccol I

"A sail!" resounds from every lip.
Mizen, no, square-sail—ah, you trip!
Edith, it cannot be a ship!   B arqu E

So home again from sea and beach,
One nameless feeling thrilling each.
A sense of beauty, passing speech.   A ppreciatio N

Let lens and tripod be unslung!
"Dolly!" 's the word on every tongue;
Dolly must sit, for she is young!   C hil D

Photography shall change her face,
Distort it with uncouth grimace—
Make her bloodthirsty, fierce, and base.   O diou S

I end my song while scarce begun;
For I should want, ere all was done,
Four weeks to tell the tale of one: M ont H

And I should need as large a hand,
To paint a scene so wild and grand,
As he who traversed Egypt's land.   B elzon I

What say you, Edith? Will it suit ye?
Reject it, if it fails in beauty:
You know your literary duty!   E ditorshi P

On the rail between Torquay and Guildford, Sep. 28, 1869.

THREE LITTLE MAIDS

(To the three Misses Drury.)

THREE little maids, one winter day,
  While others went to feed,
To sing, to laugh, to dance, to play,
  More wisely went to—Reed.

Others, when lesson-time's begun,
  Go, half inclined to cry,
Some in a walk, some in a run;
  But *these* went in a—Fly.

I give to other little maids
  A smile, a kiss, a look,
Presents whose memory quickly fades;
  I give to these—a Book.

Happy Arcadia may blind,
  While *all abroad*, their eyes;
At home, this book (I trust) they'll find
  A *very catching* prize.

PUZZLE

(To Mary, Ina, and Harriet or "Hartie" Watson.)

WHEN . a . y and I . a told . a . . ie they'd seen a
  Small . . ea . u . e with . i . . . , dressed in crimson and
    blue,
. a . . ie cried " 'Twas a . ai . y! Why, I . a and . a . y,
  I *should* have been happy if I had been you!"

Said . a . y "You wouldn't." Said I . a "You shouldn't—
  Since *you* ca'n't be *us*, and *we* couldn't be *you*.
You are *one*, my dear . a . . ie, but *we* are a . a . . y,
  And a . i . . . e . i . tells us that *one* isn't *two*."

THREE CHILDREN

(To Miss Mary Watson.)

THREE children (their names were so fearful
    You'll excuse me for leaving them out)
Sat silent, with faces all tearful—
        What *was* it about?

They were sewing, but needles are prickly,
    And fingers were cold as could be—
So they didn't get on very quickly,
        And they wept, silly Three!

"O Mother!" said they, "Guildford's not a
    Nice place for the winter, that's flat.
If you know any country that's hotter,
        Please take us to that!"

"Cease crying," said she, "little daughter!
    And when summer comes back with the flowers,
You shall roam by the edge of the water,
        In sunshiny hours."

"And in summer", said sorrowful Mary,
    "We shall hear the shrill scream of the train
That will bring that dear writer of fairy-
        tales hither again."

(Now the person she meant to allude to
    Was—well! it is best to forget.
It was some one she *always* was rude to,
        Whenever they met.)

"It's my duty", their Mother continued,
    "To fill with things useful and right
Your small minds: if I put nothing in, you'd
        Be ignorant quite.

"But enough now of lessons and thinking:
　　Your meal is quite ready, I see—.
So attend to your eating and drinking,
　　You thirsty young Three!"

Apr. 10, 1871.

TWO THIEVES

(To the Misses Drury.)

Two thieves went out to steal one day
　　Thinking that no one knew it:
Three little maids, I grieve to say,
　　Encouraged them to do it.

'Tis said that little children should
　　Encourage men in stealing!
But these, I've always understood,
　　Have got no proper feeling.

An aged friend, who chanced to pass
　　Exactly at the minute,
Said "Children! Take this Looking-glass,
　　And see your badness in it."

Jan. 11, 1872.

TWO ACROSTICS

(To Miss Ruth Dymes.)

Round the wondrous globe I wander wild,
Up and down-hill—Age succeeds to youth—
Toiling all in vain to find a child
Half so loving, half so dear as Ruth.

(*To Miss Margaret Dymes.*)

MAIDENS, if a maid you meet
Always free from pout and pet,
Ready smile and temper sweet,
Greet my little Margaret.
And if loved by all she be
Rightly, not a pampered pet,
Easily you then may see
'Tis my little Margaret.

DOUBLE ACROSTIC

Two little girls near London dwell,
More naughty than I like to tell.

1

Upon the lawn the hoops are seen:
The balls are rolling on the green.   T   ur   F

2

The Thames is running deep and wide:
And boats are rowing on the tide.   R   ive   R

3

In winter-time, all in a row,
The happy skaters come and go.   I   c   E

4

"Papa!" they cry, "Do let us stay!"
He does not speak, but says they may.   N   o   D

5

"There is a land," he says, "my dear,
Which is too hot to skate, I fear."   A   fric   A

ACROSTIC

"ARE you deaf, Father William!" the young man said,
"Did you hear what I told you just now?
"Excuse me for shouting! Don't waggle your head
"Like a blundering, sleepy old cow!
"A little maid dwelling in Wallington Town,
"Is my friend, so I beg to remark:
"Do you think she'd be pleased if a book were sent down
"Entitled 'The Hunt of the Snark?'"

"Pack it up in brown paper!" the old man cried,
"And seal it with olive-and-dove.
"I command you to do it!" he added with pride,
"Nor forget, my good fellow, to send her beside
"Easter Greetings, and give her my love."

1876.

ACROSTIC

(To the Misses Drury.)

"MAIDENS! if you love the tale,
     If you love the Snark,
Need I urge you, spread the sail,
Now, while freshly blows the gale,
     In your ocean-barque!

"English Maidens love renown,
     Enterprise, and fuss!"
Laughingly those Maidens frown;
Laughingly, with eyes cast down;
     And they answer thus:

"English Maidens fear to roam.
  Much we dread the dark;
Much we dread what ills might come,
If we left our English home,
  Even for a Snark!"

Apr. 6, 1876.

ACROSTIC

LOVE-lighted eyes, that will not start
At frown of rage or malice!
Uplifted brow, undaunted heart
Ready to dine on raspberry-tart
Along with fairy Alice!

In scenes as wonderful as if
She'd flitted in a magic skiff
Across the sea to Calais:
Be sure this night, in Fancy's feast,
Even till Morning gilds the east,
Laura will dream of Alice!

Perchance, as long years onward haste,
Laura will weary of the taste
Of Life's embittered chalice:
May she, in such a woeful hour,
Endued with Memory's mystic power,
Recall the dreams of Alice!

June 17, 1876.

TO M. A. B.

(To Miss Marion Terry, "Mary Ann Bessie Terry.")

THE royal MAB, dethroned, discrowned
  By fairy rebels wild,
Has found a home on English ground,
  And lives an English child.
I know it, Maiden, when I see
A fairy-tale upon your knee—
And note the page that idly lingers
Beneath those still and listless fingers—
And mark those dreamy looks that stray
To some bright vision far away,
Still seeking, in the pictured story,
The memory of a vanished glory.

ACROSTIC

(To Miss Marion Terry.)

MAIDEN, though thy heart may quail
And thy quivering lip grow pale,
Read the Bellman's tragic tale!

Is it life of which it tells?
Of a pulse that sinks and swells
Never lacking chime of bells?

Bells of sorrow, bells of cheer,
Easter, Christmas, glad New Year,
Still they sound, afar, anear.

So may Life's sweet bells for thee,
In the summers yet to be,
Evermore make melody!

Aug. 15, 1876.

MADRIGAL

(To Miss May Forshall.)

He shouts amain, he shouts again,
   (Her brother, fierce, as bluff King Hal),
"I tell you flat, I shall do that!"
   She softly whispers " *'May'* for *'shall'!*"

He wistful sighed one eventide
   (Her friend, that made this Madrigal),
"And shall I kiss you, pretty Miss!"
   Smiling she answered " *'May'* for *'shall'!*"

With eager eyes my reader cries,
   "Your friend must be indeed a val-
-uable child, so sweet, so mild!
   What do you call her?" "May For shall."

Dec. 24, 1877.

LOVE AMONG THE ROSES

ACROSTIC

"Seek ye Love, ye fairy-sprites?
   Ask where reddest roses grow.
Rosy fancies he invites,
And in roses he delights,
   Have ye found him?" "No!"

"Seek again, and find the boy
   In Childhood's heart, so pure and clear."
Now the fairies leap for joy,
   Crying, "Love is here!"

"Love has found his proper nest;
    And we guard him while he dozes
In a dream of peace and rest
    Rosier than roses."

Jan. 3, 1878.

TWO POEMS TO RACHEL DANIEL

I

"OH pudgy podgy pup!
Why *did* they wake you up?
Those crude nocturnal yells
Are *not* like silver bells:
Nor ever would recall
Sweet Music's 'dying fall'.
They rather bring to mind
The bitter winter wind
Through keyholes shrieking shrilly
When nights are dark and chilly:
Or like some dire duett,
Or quarrelsome quartette,
Of cats who chant their joys
With execrable noise,
And murder Time and Tune
To vex the patient Moon!"

Nov. 1880.

II

FOR "THE GARLAND OF RACHEL" (1881)

WHAT hand may wreathe thy natal crown,
    O tiny tender Spirit-blossom,
That out of Heaven hast fluttered down
    Into this Earth's cold bosom?

And how shall mortal bard aspire—
    All sin-begrimed and sorrow-laden—
To welcome, with the Seraph-choir,
    A pure and perfect Maiden?

Are not God's minstrels ever near,
    Flooding with joy the woodland mazes?
Which shall we summon, Baby dear,
    To carol forth thy praises?

With sweet sad song the Nightingale
    May soothe the broken hearts that languish
Where graves are green—the orphans' wail,
    The widow's lonely anguish:

The Turtle-dove with amorous coo
    May chide the blushing maid that lingers
To twine her bridal wreath anew
    With weak and trembling fingers:

But human loves and human woes
    Would dim the radiance of thy glory—
Only the Lark such music knows
    As fits thy stainless story.

The world may listen as it will—
    She recks not, to the skies up-springing:
Beyond our ken she singeth still
    For very joy of singing.

THE LYCEUM

"IT is the lawyer's daughter,
    And she is grown so dear, so dear,
She costs me, in one evening,
    The income of a year!

'You ca'n't have children's love', she cried,
    'Unless you choose to fee 'em!'
'And what's your fee, child?' I replied.
    She simply said——

"We saw 'The Cup'." I *hoped* she'd say,
    "I'm grateful to you, very."
She murmured, as she turned away,
    "That lovely [Ellen Terry.]
"Compared with her, the rest", she cried,
    "Are just like two or three um-
"berellas standing side by side!
    "Oh, gem of——

"We saw Two Brothers. I confess
    To *me* they seemed one man.
"Now which is which, child? Can you guess?"
    She cried, "A-course I can!"
Bad puns like this I *always* dread,
    And am resolved to flee 'em.
And so I left her there, and fled;
    She *lives* at——

1881.

ACROSTIC

AROUND my lonely hearth to-night,
    Ghostlike the shadows wander:
Now here, now there, a childish sprite,
Earthborn and yet as angel bright,
    Seems near me as I ponder.

Gaily she shouts: the laughing air
    Echoes her note of gladness—
Or bends herself with earnest care
Round fairy-fortress to prepare
Grim battlement or turret-stair—
    In childhood's merry madness!

New raptures still hath youth in store.
  Age may but fondly cherish
Half-faded memories of yore—
Up, craven heart! repine no more!
Love stretches hands from shore to shore:
  Love is, and shall not perish!

DREAMLAND

(Verses written to the dream-music written down by C. E.
Hutchinson, of Brasenose College.)

WHEN midnight mists are creeping,
  And all the land is sleeping,
Around me tread the mighty dead,
  And slowly pass away.

Lo, warriors, saints, and sages,
  From out the vanished ages,
With solemn pace and reverend face
  Appear and pass away.

The blaze of noonday splendour,
  The twilight soft and tender,
May charm the eye: yet they shall die,
  Shall die and pass away.

But here, in Dreamland's centre,
  No spoiler's hand may enter,
These visions fair, this radiance rare,
  Shall never pass away.

I see the shadows falling,
  The forms of old recalling;
Around me tread the mighty dead,
  And slowly pass away.

1882.

TO MY CHILD-FRIEND

DEDICATION TO "THE GAME OF LOGIC"

I CHARM in vain: for never again,
All keenly as my glance I bend,
    Will Memory, goddess coy,
    Embody for my joy
Departed days, nor let me gaze
    On thee, my Fairy Friend!

Yet could thy face, in mystic grace,
A moment smile on me, 'twould send
    Far-darting rays of light
    From Heaven athwart the night,
By which to read in very deed
    Thy spirit, sweetest Friend!

So may the stream of Life's long dream
Flow gently onward to its end,
    With many a floweret gay,
    A-down its willowy way:
May no sigh vex, no care perplex,
    My loving little Friend!

1886.

A RIDDLE

(To Miss Gaynor Simpson.)

MY first lends his aid when I plunge into trade:
    My second in jollifications:
My whole, laid on thinnish, imparts a neat finish
    To pictorial representations.

Answer: Copal.

A LIMERICK

(To Miss Vera Beringer.)

THERE was a young lady of station,
"I love man" was her sole exclamation;
    But when men cried, "You flatter,"
    She replied, "Oh! no matter,
Isle of Man is the true explanation."

RHYME? AND REASON?

(To Miss Emmie Drury.)

"I'M EMInent in RHYME!" she said.
    "I make WRY Mouths of RYE-Meal gruel!"
The Poet smiled, and shook his head:
    "Is REASON, then, the missing jewel?"

A NURSERY DARLING

DEDICATION TO THE NURSERY "ALICE", 1889

    A MOTHER's breast:
Safe refuge from her childish fears,
From childish troubles, childish tears,
Mists that enshroud her dawning years!
See how in sleep she seems to sing
A voiceless psalm—an offering
Raised, to the glory of her King,
    In Love: for Love is Rest.

A Darling's kiss:
Dearest of all the signs that fleet
From lips that lovingly repeat
Again, again, their message sweet!
Full to the brim with girlish glee,
A child, a very child is she,
Whose dream of Heaven is still to be
        At Home: for Home is Bliss.

MAGGIE'S VISIT TO OXFORD

(June 9th to 13th, 1889)

(*Written for Maggie Bowman.*)

WHEN Maggie once to Oxford came,
    On tour as "Bootles' Baby",
She said, "I'll see this place of fame,
    However dull the day be."

So with her friend she visited
    The sights that it was rich in:
And first of all she popped her head
    Inside the Christ Church kitchen.

The Cooks around that little child
    Stood waiting in a ring:
And every time that Maggie smiled
    Those Cooks began to sing—
Shouting the Battle-cry of Freedom!

        "Roast, boil and bake,
            For Maggie's sake:
        Bring cutlets fine
            For *her* to dine,
        Meringues so sweet
            For her to eat—
        For Maggie may be
            Bootles' Baby!"

Then hand in hand in pleasant talk
　　They wandered and admired
The Hall, Cathedral and Broad Walk,
　　Till Maggie's feet were tired:

To Worcester Garden next they strolled,
　　Admired its quiet lake:
Then to St. John, a college old,
　　Their devious way they take.

In idle mood they sauntered round
　　Its lawn so green and flat,
And in that garden Maggie found
　　A lovely Pussy-Cat!

A quarter of an hour they spent
　　In wandering to and fro:
And everywhere that Maggie went,
　　The Cat was sure to go—
Shouting the Battle-cry of Freedom!

　　　　"Maiow! Maiow!
　　　　Come, make your bow,
　　　　Take off your hats,
　　　　Ye Pussy-Cats!
　　　　And purr and purr,
　　　　To welcome *her*,
　　　　For Maggie may be
　　　　Bootles' Baby!"

So back to Christ Church, not too late
　　For them to go and see
A Christ Church undergraduate,
　　Who gave them cakes and tea.

Next day she entered with her guide
　　The garden called "Botanic",
And there a fierce Wild Boar she spied,
　　Enough to cause a panic:

But Maggie didn't mind, not she,
    She would have faced, alone,
That fierce wild boar, because, you see,
    The thing was made of stone.

On Magdalen walls they saw a face
    That filled her with delight,
A giant face, that made grimace
    And grinned with all its might.

A little friend, industrious,
    Pulled upwards all the while
The corner of its mouth, and thus
    He helped that face to smile!

"How nice", thought Maggie, "it would be
    If *I* could have a friend
To do that very thing for *me*
And make my mouth turn up with glee,
    By pulling at one end."

In Magdalen Park the deer are wild
    With joy, that Maggie brings
Some bread a friend had given the child,
    To feed the pretty things.

They flock round Maggie without fear:
    They breakfast and they lunch,
They dine, they sup, those happy deer—
    Still, as they munch and munch,
Shouting the Battle-cry of Freedom!

        "Yes, Deer are we,
        And dear is she!
        We love this child
        So sweet and mild:

We all rejoice
At Maggie's voice:
We all are fed
With Maggie's bread . . .
For Maggie may be
Bootles' Baby!"

They met a Bishop on their way . . .
    A Bishop large as life,
With loving smile that seemed to say
    "Will Maggie be my wife?"

Maggie thought *not*, because, you see,
    She was so *very* young,
And he was old as old could be . . .
    So Maggie held her tongue.

"My Lord, she's Bootles' Baby, we
    Are going up and down",
Her friend explained, "that she may see
    The sights of Oxford Town."

"Now say what kind of place it is,"
    The Bishop gaily cried.
"The best place in the Provinces!"
    That little maid replied.

Away, next morning, Maggie went
    From Oxford town: but yet
The happy hours she there had spent
    She could not soon forget.

The train is gone, it rumbles on:
    The engine-whistle screams;
But Maggie deep in rosy sleep . . .
    And softly in her dreams,
Whispers the Battle-cry of Freedom.

"Oxford, good-bye!"
She seems to sigh.
"You dear old City,
With gardens pretty,
And lanes and flowers,
And college-towers,
And Tom's great Bell . . .
Farewell—farewell:
For Maggie may be
Bootles' Baby!"

MAGGIE B——

(*To Maggie Bowman.*)

WRITTEN by Maggie B— —
Bought by me:
A present to Maggie B——
Sent by me:
But *who* can Maggie be?
Answered by me:
"She is she."

Aug. 13, 1891.

THREE SUNSETS
AND OTHER POEMS
THREE SUNSETS

HE saw her once, and in the glance,
 A moment's glance of meeting eyes,
His heart stood still in sudden trance:
 He trembled with a sweet surprise—
All in the waning light she stood,
The star of perfect womanhood.

That summer-eve his heart was light:
 With lighter step he trod the ground:
And life was fairer in his sight,
 And music was in every sound:
He blessed the world where there could be
So beautiful a thing as she.

There once again, as evening fell
 And stars were peering overhead,
Two lovers met to bid farewell:
 The western sun gleamed faint and red,
Lost in a drift of purple cloud
That wrapped him like a funeral-shroud.

Long time the memory of that night—
 The hand that clasped, the lips that kissed,
The form that faded from his sight
 Slow sinking through the tearful mist—
In dreamy music seemed to roll
Through the dark chambers of his soul.

So after many years he came
 A wanderer from a distant shore:
The street, the house, were still the same,
 But those he sought were there no more:

His burning words, his hopes and fears,
Unheeded fell on alien ears.

Only the children from their play
   Would pause the mournful tale to hear,
Shrinking in half-alarm away,
   Or, step by step, would venture near
To touch with timid curious hands
That strange wild man from other lands.

He sat beside the busy street,
   There, where he last had seen her face;
And thronging memories, bitter-sweet,
   Seemed yet to haunt the ancient place:
Her footfall ever floated near:
Her voice was ever in his ear.

He sometimes, as the daylight waned
   And evening mists began to roll,
In half-soliloquy complained
   Of that black shadow on his soul,
And blindly fanned, with cruel care,
The ashes of a vain despair.

The summer fled: the lonely man
   Still lingered out the lessening days:
Still, as the night drew on, would scan
   Each passing face with closer gaze—
Till, sick at heart, he turned away,
And sighed "She will not come to-day."

So by degrees his spirit bent
   To mock its own despairing cry,
In stern self-torture to invent
   New luxuries of agony,
And people all the vacant space
With visions of her perfect face.

Then for a moment she was nigh,
   He heard no step, but she was there;
As if an angel suddenly
   Were bodied from the viewless air,
And all her fine ethereal frame
Should fade as swiftly as it came.

So, half in fancy's sunny trance,
   And half in misery's aching void,
With set and stony countenance
   His bitter being he enjoyed,
And thrust for ever from his mind
The happiness he could not find.

As when the wretch, in lonely room,
   To selfish death is madly hurled,
The glamour of that fatal fume
   Shuts out the wholesome living world—
So all his manhood's strength and pride
One sickly dream had swept aside.

Yea, brother, and we passed him there,
   But yesterday, in merry mood,
And marvelled at the lordly air
   That shamed his beggar's attitude,
Nor heeded that ourselves might be
Wretches as desperate as he;

Who let the thought of bliss denied
   Make havoc of our life and powers,
And pine, in solitary pride,
   For peace that never shall be ours,
Because we will not work and wait
In trustful patience for our fate.

And so it chanced once more that she
   Came by the old familiar spot:
The face he would have died to see
   Bent o'er him, and he knew it not;

Too rapt in selfish grief to hear,
Even when happiness was near.

And pity filled her gentle breast
  For him that would not stir nor speak,
The dying crimson of the west,
  That faintly tinged his haggard cheek,
Fell on her as she stood, and shed
A glory round the patient head.

Ah, let him wake! The moments fly:
  This awful tryst may be the last.
And see, the tear, that dimmed her eye,
  Had fallen on him ere she passed—
She passed: the crimson paled to gray:
And hope departed with the day.

The heavy hours of night went by,
  And silence quickened into sound,
And light slid up the eastern sky,
  And life began its daily round—
But light and life for him were fled:
His name was numbered with the dead.

Nov. 1861.

THE PATH OF ROSES

(*Florence Nightingale was at the height of her fame when this was written, after the Crimean War.*)

In the dark silence of an ancient room,
Whose one tall window fronted to the West,
Where, through laced tendrils of a hanging vine,
The sunset-glow was fading into night,
Sat a pale Lady, resting weary hands
Upon a great clasped volume, and her face

Within her hands. Not as in rest she bowed,
But large hot tears were coursing down her cheek,
And her low-panted sobs broke awefully
Upon the sleeping echoes of the night.
　Soon she unclasp'd the volume once again,
And read the words in tone of agony,
As in self-torture, weeping as she read:

　　"He crowns the glory of his race:
　　　He prayeth but in some fit place
　　　To meet his foeman face to face:

　　"And, battling for the True, the Right,
　　　From ruddy dawn to purple night,
　　　To perish in the midmost fight:

　　"Where hearts are fierce and hands are strong,
　　　Where peals the bugle loud and long,
　　　Where blood is dropping in the throng:

　　"Still, with a dim and glazing eye,
　　　To watch the tide of victory,
　　　To hear in death the battle-cry:

　　"Then, gathered grandly to his grave,
　　　To rest among the true and brave,
　　　In holy ground, where yew-trees wave:

　　"Where, from church-windows sculptured fair,
　　　Float out upon the evening air
　　　The note of praise, the voice of prayer:

　　"Where no vain marble mockery
　　　Insults with loud and boastful lie
　　　The simple soldier's memory:

　　"Where sometimes little children go,
　　　And read, in whisper'd accent slow,
　　　The name of him who sleeps below."

Her voice died out: like one in dreams she sat.
"Alas!" she sighed. "For what can Woman do?
Her life is aimless, and her death unknown:
Hemmed in by social forms she pines in vain.
Man has his work, but what can Woman do?"
　　And answer came there from the creeping gloom,
The creeping gloom that settled into night:
"Peace! For thy lot is other than a man's:
His is a path of thorns: he beats them down:
He faces death: he wrestles with despair.
Thine is of roses, to adorn and cheer
His lonely life, and hide the thorns in flowers."
　　She spake again: in bitter tone she spake:
"Aye, as a toy, the puppet of an hour,
Or a fair posy, newly plucked at morn,
But flung aside and withered ere the night."
　　And answer came there from the creeping gloom,
The creeping gloom that blackened into night:
"So shalt thou be the lamp to light his path,
What time the shades of sorrow close around."
　　And, so it seemed to her, an awful light
Pierced slowly through the darkness, orbed, and grew,
Until all passed away—the ancient room—
The sunlight dying through the trellised vine—
The one tall window—all had passed away,
And she was standing on the mighty hills.
　　Beneath, around, and far as eye could see,
Squadron on squadron, stretched opposing hosts,
Ranked as for battle, mute and motionless.
Anon a distant thunder shook the ground,
The tramp of horses, and a troop shot by—
Plunged headlong in that living sea of men—
Plunged to their death: back from that fatal field
A scattered handful, fighting hard for life,
Broke through the serried lines; but, as she gazed,
They shrank and melted, and their forms grew thin—
Grew pale as ghosts when the first morning ray
Dawns from the East—the trumpet's brazen blare

Died into silence—and the vision passed—
Passed to a room where sick and dying lay
In long, sad line—there brooded Fear and Pain—
Darkness was there, the shade of Azrael's wing.
But there was one that ever, to and fro,
Moved with light footfall: purely calm her face,
And those deep steadfast eyes that starred the gloom:
Still, as she went, she ministered to each
Comfort and counsel; cooled the fevered brow
With softest touch, and in the listening ear
Of the pale sufferer whispered words of peace.
That dying warrior, gazing as she passed,
Clasped his thin hands and blessed her. Bless her too,
Thou, who didst bless the merciful of old!
  So prayed the Lady, watching tearfully
Her gentle moving onward, till the night
Had veiled her wholly, and the vision passed.
  Then once again the solemn whisper came:
"So in the darkest path of man's despair,
Where War and Terror shake the troubled earth,
Lies woman's mission; with unblenching brow
To pass through scenes of horror and affright
Where men grow sick and tremble: unto her
All things are sanctified, for all are good.
Nothing so mean, but shall deserve her care:
Nothing so great, but she may bear her part.
No life is vain: each hath his place assigned:
Do thou thy task, and leave the rest to God."
And there was silence, but the Lady made
No answer, save one deeply-breathed "Amen".
  And she arose, and in that darkening room
Stood lonely as a spirit of the night—
Stood calm and fearless in the gathered night—
And raised her eyes to heaven. There were tears
Upon her face, but in her heart was peace,
Peace that the world nor gives nor takes away!

April 10, 1856.

THE VALLEY OF THE SHADOW OF DEATH

HARK, *said the dying man, and sighed,*
 To that complaining tone—
Like sprite condemned, each eventide,
 To walk the world alone.
At sunset, when the air is still,
I hear it creep from yonder hill:
It breathes upon me, dead and chill,
 A moment, and is gone.

My son, it minds me of a day
 Left half a life behind,
That I have prayed to put away
 For ever from my mind.
But bitter memory will not die:
It haunts my soul when none is nigh:
I hear its whisper in the sigh
 Of that complaining wind.

And now in death my soul is fain
 To tell the tale of fear
That hidden in my breast hath lain
 Through many a weary year:
Yet time would fail to utter all—
The evil spells that held me thrall,
And thrust my life from fall to fall,
 Thou needest not to hear.

The spells that bound me with a chain,
 Sin's stern behests to do,
Till Pleasure's self, invoked in vain,
 A heavy burden grew—
Till from my spirit's fevered eye,
A hunted thing, I seemed to fly
Through the dark woods that underlie
 Yon mountain-range of blue.

Deep in those woods I found a vale
   No sunlight visiteth,
Nor star, nor wandering moonbeam pale;
   Where never comes the breath
Of summer-breeze—there in mine ear,
Even as I lingered half in fear,
I heard a whisper, cold and clear,
   "That is the gate of Death.

"O bitter is it to abide
   In weariness alway:
At dawn to sigh for eventide,
   At eventide for day.
Thy noon hath fled: thy sun hath shone:
The brightness of thy day is gone:
What need to lag and linger on
   Till life be cold and gray?

"O well," it said, "beneath yon pool,
   In some still cavern deep,
The fevered brain might slumber cool,
   The eyes forget to weep:
Within that goblet's mystic rim
Are draughts of healing, stored for him
Whose heart is sick, whose sight is dim,
   Who prayeth but to sleep!"

The evening-breeze went moaning by,
   Like mourner for the dead,
And stirred, with shrill complaining sigh,
   The tree-tops overhead:
My guardian-angel seemed to stand
And mutely wave a warning hand—
With sudden terror all unmanned,
   I turned myself and fled!

A cottage-gate stood open wide:
   Soft fell the dying ray

On two fair children, side by side,
    That rested from their play—
Together bent the earnest head,
As ever and anon they read
From one dear Book: the words they said
    Come back to me to-day.

Like twin cascades on mountain-stair
    Together wandered down
The ripples of the golden hair,
    The ripples of the brown:
While, through the tangled silken haze,
Blue eyes looked forth in eager gaze,
More starlike than the gems that blaze
    About a monarch's crown.

My son, there comes to each an hour
    When sinks the spirit's pride—
When weary hands forget their power
    The strokes of death to guide:
In such a moment, warriors say,
A word the panic-rout may stay,
A sudden charge redeem the day
    And turn the living tide.

I could not see, for blinding tears,
    The glories of the west:
A heavenly music filled mine ears,
    A heavenly peace my breast.
"Come unto Me, come unto Me—
All ye that labour, unto Me—
Ye heavy-laden, come to Me—
    And I will give you rest."

The night drew onwards: thin and blue
    The evening mists arise
To bathe the thirsty land in dew,
    As erst in Paradise—

While, over silent field and town,
The deep blue vault of heaven looked down;
Not, as of old, in angry frown,
  But bright with angels' eyes.

Blest day! Then first I heard the voice
  That since hath oft beguiled
These eyes from tears, and bid rejoice
  This heart with anguish wild—
Thy mother, boy, thou hast not known;
So soon she left me here to moan—
Left me to weep and watch, alone,
  Our one beloved child.

Though, parted from my aching sight,
  Like homeward-speeding dove,
She passed into the perfect light
  That floods the world above;
Yet our twin spirits, well I know—
Though one abide in pain below—
Love, as in summers long ago,
  And evermore shall love.

So with a glad and patient heart
  I move toward mine end:
The streams, that flow awhile apart,
  Shall both in ocean blend.
I dare not weep: I can but bless
The Love that pitied my distress,
And lent me, in Life's wilderness,
  So sweet and true a friend.

But if there be—O if there be
  A truth in what they say,
That angel-forms we cannot see
  Go with us on our way;

Then surely she is with me here,
I dimly feel her spirit near—
The morning-mists grow thin and clear,
    And Death brings in the Day.

April 1868.

SOLITUDE

I LOVE the stillness of the wood:
    I love the music of the rill:
I love to couch in pensive mood
    Upon some silent hill.

Scarce heard, beneath yon arching trees,
    The silver-crested ripples pass;
And, like a mimic brook, the breeze
    Whispers among the grass.

Here from the world I win release,
    Nor scorn of men, nor footstep rude,
Break in to mar the holy peace
    Of this great solitude.

Here may the silent tears I weep
    Lull the vexed spirit into rest,
As infants sob themselves to sleep
    Upon a mother's breast.

But when the bitter hour is gone,
    And the keen throbbing pangs are still,
Oh, sweetest then to couch alone
    Upon some silent hill!

To live in joys that once have been,
    To put the cold world out of sight,
And deck life's drear and barren scene
    With hues of rainbow-light.

For what to man the gift of breath,
   If sorrow be his lot below;
If all the day that ends in death
   Be dark with clouds of woe?

Shall the poor transport of an hour
   Repay long years of sore distress—
The fragrance of a lonely flower
   Make glad the wilderness?

Ye golden hours of Life's young spring,
   Of innocence, of love and truth!
Bright, beyond all imagining,
   Thou fairy-dream of youth!

I'd give all wealth that years have piled,
   The slow result of Life's decay,
To be once more a little child
   For one bright summer-day.

March 16, 1853.

BEATRICE

IN her eyes is the living light
   Of a wanderer to earth
From a far celestial height:
   Summers five are all the span—
   Summers five since Time began
To veil in mists of human night
   A shining angel-birth.

Does an angel look from her eyes?
   Will she suddenly spring away,
And soar to her home in the skies?
   Beatrice! Blessing and blessed to be!
   Beatrice! Still, as I gaze on thee,
Visions of two sweet maids arise,
   Whose life was of yesterday:

Of a Beatrice pale and stern,
  With the lips of a dumb despair,
With the innocent eyes that yearn—
  Yearn for the young sweet hours of life,
  Far from sorrow and far from strife,
For the happy summers, that never return,
  When the world seemed good and fair:

Of a Beatrice glorious, bright—
  Of a sainted, ethereal maid,
Whose blue eyes are deep fountains of light,
  Cheering the poet that broodeth apart,
  Filling with gladness his desolate heart,
Like the moon when she shines thro' a cloudless
    night
  On a world of silence and shade.

And the visions waver and faint,
  And the visions vanish away
That my fancy delighted to paint—
  She is here at my side, a living child,
  With the glowing cheek and the tresses wild,
Nor death-pale martyr, nor radiant saint,
  Yet stainless and bright as they.

For I think, if a grim wild beast
  Were to come from his charnel-cave,
From his jungle-home in the East—
  Stealthily creeping with bated breath,
  Stealthily creeping with eyes of death—
He would all forget his dream of the feast,
  And crouch at her feet a slave.

She would twine her hand in his mane:
  She would prattle in silvery tone,
Like the tinkle of summer-rain—
  Questioning him with her laughing eyes,
  Questioning him with a glad surprise.

Till she caught from those fierce eyes again
   The love that lit her own.

And be sure, if a savage heart,
   In a mask of human guise,
Were to come on her here apart—
   Bound for a dark and a deadly deed,
   Hurrying past with pitiless speed—
He would suddenly falter and guiltily start
   At the glance of her pure blue eyes.

Nay, be sure, if an angel fair,
   A bright seraph undefiled,
Were to stoop from the trackless air,
   Fain would she linger in glad amaze—
   Lovingly linger to ponder and gaze,
With a sister's love and a sister's care,
   On the happy, innocent child.

Dec. 4, 1862.

STOLEN WATERS

THE light was faint, and soft the air
   That breathed around the place;
And she was lithe, and tall, and fair,
   And with a wayward grace
   Her queenly head she bare.

With glowing cheek, with gleaming eye,
   She met me on the way:
My spirit owned the witchery
   Within her smile that lay:
I followed her, I know not why.

The trees were thick with many a fruit,
   The grass with many a flower:
My soul was dead, my tongue was mute,
   In that accursèd hour.

And, in my dream, with silvery voice,
 She said, or seemed to say,
"Youth is the season to rejoice"—
 I could not choose but stay:
 I could not say her nay.

She plucked a branch above her head,
 With rarest fruitage laden:
"Drink of the juice, Sir Knight," she said:
 " 'Tis good for knight and maiden."

Oh, blind mine eye that would not trace—
 Oh, deaf mine ear that would not heed—
The mocking smile upon her face,
 The mocking voice of greed!

I drank the juice; and straightway felt
 A fire within my brain:
My soul within me seemed to melt
 In sweet delirious pain.

"Sweet is the stolen draught," she said:
 "Hath sweetness stint or measure?
Pleasant the secret hoard of bread:
 What bars us from our pleasure?"

"Yea, take we pleasure while we may,"
 I heard myself replying.
In the red sunset, far away,
 My happier life was dying:
My heart was sad, my voice was gay.

And unawares, I knew not how,
 I kissed her dainty finger-tips,
I kissed her on the lily brow,
 I kissed her on the false, false lips—
That burning kiss, I feel it now!

"True love gives true love of the best:
    Then take", I cried, "my heart to thee!"
The very heart from out my breast
    I plucked, I gave it willingly:
    Her very heart she gave to me—
Then died the glory from the west.

In the gray light I saw her face,
    And it was withered, old, and gray;
The flowers were fading in their place,
    Were fading with the fading day.

Forth from her, like a hunted deer,
    Through all that ghastly night I fled,
And still behind me seemed to hear
    Her fierce unflagging tread;
And scarce drew breath for fear.

Yet marked I well how strangely seemed
    The heart within my breast to sleep:
Silent it lay, or so I dreamed,
    With never a throb or leap.

For hers was now my heart, she said,
    The heart that once had been mine own:
And in my breast I bore instead
    A cold, cold heart of stone.
So grew the morning overhead.

The sun shot downward through the trees
    His old familiar flame:
All ancient sounds upon the breeze
    From copse and meadow came—
    But I was not the same.

They call me mad: I smile, I weep,
    _Uncaring how or why:

Yea, when one's heart is laid asleep,
    What better than to die?
So that the grave be dark and deep.

To die! To die? And yet, methinks,
    I drink of life, to-day,
Deep as the thirsty traveler drinks
    Of fountain by the way:
My voice is sad, my heart is gay.

When yestereve was on the wane,
    I heard a clear voice singing
So sweetly that, like summer-rain,
    My happy tears came springing:
My human heart returned again.

    "A rosy child,
Sitting and singing, in a garden fair,
    The joy of hearing, seeing,
    The simple joy of being—
Or twining rosebuds in the golden hair
    That ripples free and wild.

        "A sweet pale child—
Wearily looking to the purple West—
    Waiting the great For-ever
    That suddenly shall sever
The cruel chains that hold her from her rest—
    By earth-joys unbeguiled.

        "An angel-child—
Gazing with living eyes on a dead face:
    The mortal form forsaken,
    That none may now awaken,
That lieth painless, moveless in her place,
    As though in death she smiled!

"Be as a child—
So shalt thou sing for very joy of breath—
So shalt thou wait thy dying,
In holy transport lying—
So pass rejoicing through the gate of death,
In garment undefiled."

Then call me what they will, I know
    That now my soul is glad:
If this be madness, better so,
    Far better to be mad,
Weeping or smiling as I go.

For if I weep, it is that now
    I see how deep a loss is mine,
And feel how brightly round my brow
    The coronal might shine,
Had I but kept mine early vow:

And if I smile, it is that now
    I see the promise of the years—
The garland waiting for my brow,
    That must be won with tears,
With pain—with death—I care not how.

May 9, 1862.

THE WILLOW-TREE

THE morn was bright, the steeds were light,
    The wedding guests were gay:
Young Ellen stood within the wood
    And watched them pass away.
She scarcely saw the gallant train:
    The tear-drop dimmed her e'e:
Unheard the maiden did complain
    Beneath the Willow-Tree.

"Oh, Robin, thou didst love me well,
   Till, on a bitter day,
She came, the Lady Isabel,
   And stole thy heart away.
My tears are vain: I live again
   In days that used to be,
When I could meet thy welcome feet
   Beneath the Willow-Tree.

"Oh, Willow gray, I may not stay
   Till Spring renew thy leaf;
But I will hide myself away,
   And nurse a lonely grief.
It shall not dim Life's joy for him:
   My tears he shall not see:
While he is by, I'll come not nigh
   My weeping Willow-Tree.

"But when I die, oh, let me lie
   Beneath thy loving shade,
That he may loiter careless by,
   Where I am lowly laid.
And let the white white marble tell,
   If he should stoop to see,
'Here lies a maid that loved thee well,
   Beneath the Willow-Tree.'"

1859.

ONLY A WOMAN'S HAIR

["After the death of Dean Swift, there was found among his papers a small packet containing a single lock of hair and inscribed with the above words."]

"ONLY a woman's hair!" Fling it aside!
   A bubble on Life's mighty stream:
Heed it not, man, but watch the broadening tide
   Bright with the western beam.

Nay! In those words there rings from other years
    The echo of a long low cry,
Where a proud spirit wrestles with its tears
    In loneliest agony.

And, as I touch that lock, strange visions throng
    Upon my soul with dreamy grace—
Of woman's hair, the theme of poet's song
    In every time and place.

A child's bright tresses, by the breezes kissed
    To sweet disorder as she flies,
Veiling, beneath a cloud of golden mist,
    Flushed cheek and laughing eyes—

Or fringing, like a shadow, raven-black,
    The glory of a queen-like face—
Or from a gipsy's sunny brow tossed back
    In wild and wanton grace—

Or crown-like on the hoary head of Age,
    Whose tale of life is well-nigh told—
Or, last, in dreams I make my pilgrimage
    To Bethany of old.

I see the feast—the purple and the gold;
    The gathering crowd of Pharisees,
Whose scornful eyes are centred to behold
    Yon woman on her knees.

The stifled sob rings strangely on mine ears,
    Wrung from the depth of sin's despair:
And still she bathes the sacred feet with tears,
    And wipes them with her hair.

He scorned not then the simple loving deed
    Of her, the lowest and the last;
Then scorn not thou, but use with earnest heed
    This relic of the past.

The eyes that loved it once no longer wake:
   So lay it by with reverent care—
Touching it tenderly for sorrow's sake—
   It is a woman's hair.

Feb. 17, 1862.

THE SAILOR'S WIFE

SEE! There are tears upon her face—
   Tears newly shed, and scarcely dried:
Close, in an agonized embrace,
   She clasps the infant at her side.

Peace dwells in those soft-lidded eyes,
   Those parted lips that faintly smile—
Peace, the foretaste of Paradise,
   In heart too young for care or guile.

No peace that mother's features wear;
   But quivering lip, and knotted brow,
And broken mutterings, all declare
   The fearful dream that haunts her now,

The storm-wind, rushing through the sky,
   Wails from the depths of cloudy space;
Shrill, piercing as the seaman's cry
   When death and he are face to face.

Familiar tones are in the gale:
   They ring upon her startled ear:
And quick and low she pants the tale
   That tells of agony and fear:

"Still that phantom-ship is nigh—
   With a vexed and life-like motion,
All beneath an angry sky,
   Rocking on an angry ocean.

"Round the straining mast and shrouds
   Throng the spirits of the storm:
Darkly seen through driving clouds,
   Bends each gaunt and ghastly form.

"See! The good ship yields at last!
   Dumbly yields, and fights no more;
Driving, in the frantic blast,
   Headlong on the fatal shore.

"Hark! I hear her battered side,
   With a low and sullen shock,
Dashed, amid the foaming tide,
   Full upon a sunken rock.

"His face shines out against the sky,
   Like a ghost, so cold and white;
With a dead despairing eye
   Gazing through the gathered night.

"Is he watching, through the dark,
   Where a mocking ghostly hand
Points a faint and feeble spark
   Glimmering from the distant land?

"Sees he, in this hour of dread,
   Hearth and home and wife and child?
Loved ones who, in summers fled,
   Clung to him and wept and smiled?

"Reeling sinks the fated bark
   To her tomb beneath the wave:
Must he perish in the dark—
   Not a hand stretched out to save?

"See the spirits, how they crowd!
   Watching death with eyes that burn!
Waves rush in——" she shrieks aloud,
   Ere her waking sense return.

The storm is gone: the skies are clear:
　　Hush'd is that bitter cry of pain:
The only sound, that meets her ear,
　　The heaving of the sullen main.

Though heaviness endure the night,
　　Yet joy shall come with break of day:
She shudders with a strange delight—
　　The fearful dream is pass'd away.

She wakes: the gray dawn streaks the dark:
　　With early song the copses ring:
Far off she hears the watch-dog bark
　　A joyful bark of welcoming!

Feb. 23, 1857.

AFTER THREE DAYS

["Written after seeing Holman Hunt's picture, *The Finding of Christ in the Temple.*"]

I STOOD within the gate
Of a great temple, 'mid the living stream
Of worshippers that thronged its regal state
　　Fair-pictured in my dream.

　　Jewels and gold were there;
And floors of marble lent a crystal sheen
To body forth, as in a lower air,
　　The wonders of the scene.

　　Such wild and lavish grace
Had whispers in it of a coming doom;
As richest flowers lie strown about the face
　　Of her that waits the tomb.

The wisest of the land
Had gathered there, three solemn trysting-days,
For high debate: men stood on either hand
    To listen and to gaze.

    The aged brows were bent,
Bent to a frown, half thought, and half annoy,
That all their stores of subtlest argument
    Were baffled by a boy.

    In each averted face
I marked but scorn and loathing, till mine eyes
Fell upon one that stirred not in his place,
    Tranced in a dumb surprise.

    Surely within his mind
Strange thoughts are born, until he doubts the lore
Of those old men, blind leaders of the blind,
    Whose kingdom is no more.

    Surely he sees afar
A day of death the stormy future brings;
The crimson setting of the herald-star
    That led the Eastern kings.

    Thus, as a sunless deep
Mirrors the shining heights that crown the bay,
So did my soul create anew in sleep
    The picture seen by day.

    Gazers came and went—
A restless hum of voices marked the spot—
In varying shades of critic discontent
    Prating they knew not what.

    "Where is the comely limb,
The form attuned in every perfect part,
The beauty that we should desire in him?"
    Ah! Fools and slow of heart!

Look into those deep eyes,
Deep as the grave, and strong with love divine;
Those tender, pure, and fathomless mysteries,
    That seem to pierce through thine.

Look into those deep eyes,
Stirred to unrest by breath of coming strife,
Until a longing in thy soul arise
    That this indeed were life:

That thou couldst find Him there,
Bend at His sacred feet thy willing knee,
And from thy heart pour out the passionate prayer,
    "Lord, let me follow Thee!"

But see the crowd divide:
Mother and sire have found their lost one now:
The gentle voice, that fain would seem to chide,
    Whispers, "Son, why hast thou"—

In tone of sad amaze—
"Thus dealt with us, that art our dearest thing?
Behold, thy sire and I, three weary days,
    Have sought thee sorrowing."

And I had stayed to hear
The loving words, "How is it that ye sought?"—
But that the sudden lark, with matins clear,
    Severed the links of thought.

Then over all there fell
Shadow and silence; and my dream was fled,
As fade the phantoms of a wizard's cell
    When the dark charm is said.

Yet, in the gathering light,
I lay with half-shut eyes that would not wake,
Lovingly clinging to the skirts of night
    For that sweet vision's sake.

Feb. 16, 1861.

FACES IN THE FIRE

THE night creeps onward, sad and slow:
In these red embers' dying glow
The forms of Fancy come and go.

An island-farm—broad seas of corn
Stirred by the wandering breath of morn—
The happy spot where I was born.

The picture fadeth in its place:
Amid the glow I seem to trace
The shifting semblance of a face.

'Tis now a little childish form—
Red lips for kisses pouted warm—
And elf-locks tangled in the storm.

'Tis now a grave and gentle maid,
At her own beauty half afraid,
Shrinking, and willing to be stayed.

Oh, Time was young, and Life was warm,
When first I saw that fairy-form,
Her dark hair tossing in the storm.

And fast and free these pulses played,
When last I met that gentle maid—
When last her hand in mine was laid.

Those locks of jet are turned to gray,
And she is strange and far away
That might have been mine own to-day—

That might have been mine own, my dear,
Through many and many a happy year—
That might have sat beside me here.

Ay, changeless through the changing scene,
The ghostly whisper rings between,
The dark refrain of "might have been".

The race is o'er I might have run:
The deeds are past I might have done;
And sere the wreath I might have won.

Sunk is the last faint flickering blaze:
The vision of departed days
Is vanished even as I gaze.

The pictures, with their ruddy light,
Are changed to dust and ashes white,
And I am left alone with night.

Jan. 1860.

A LESSON IN LATIN

OUR Latin books, in motley row,
    Invite us to our task—
Gay Horace, stately Cicero:
Yet there's one verb, when once we know,
    No higher skill we ask:
This ranks all other lore above—
We've learned "'*Amare*' means '*to love*'!"

So, hour by hour, from flower to flower,
    We sip the sweets of Life:
Till, all too soon, the clouds arise,
And flaming cheeks and flashing eyes
    Proclaim the dawn of strife:
With half a smile and half a sigh,
"*Amare! Bitter One!*" we cry.

Last night we owned, with looks forlorn,
  "Too well the scholar knows
There is no rose without a thorn"—
But peace is made! We sing, this morn,
  "No thorn without a rose!"
Our Latin lesson is complete:
We've learned that Love is Bitter-Sweet!

May 1888.

PUCK LOST AND FOUND

ACROSTIC

["Inscribed in two books . . . presented to a little girl and boy, as a sort of memento of a visit paid by them to the author one day, on which occasion he taught them the pastime of folding paper 'pistols'."]

P U C K has fled the haunts of men:
  Ridicule has made him wary:
In the woods, and down the glen,
  No one meets a Fairy!

"Cream!" the greedy Goblin cries—
  Empties the deserted dairy—
Steals the spoons, and off he flies.
  Still we seek our Fairy!

Ah! What form is entering?
  Lovelit eyes and laughter airy!
Is not this a better thing,
Child, whose visit thus I sing,
  Even than a Fairy?

Nov. 22, 1891.

PUCK has ventured back agen:
    Ridicule no more affrights him:
In the very haunts of men
    Newer sport delights him.

Capering lightly to and fro,
    Ever frolicking and funning—
"Crack!" the mimic pistols go!
    Hark! The noise is stunning!

All too soon will Childhood gay
    Realize Life's sober sadness.
Let's be merry while we may,
Innocent and happy Fay!
    Elves were made for gladness!

Nov. 25, 1891.

VI
Stories

TO MY PUPIL

Beloved Pupil! Tamed by thee,
    Addish-, Subtrac-, Multiplica-tion,
Division, Fractions, Rule of Three,
    Attest thy deft manipulation!

Then onward! Let the voice of Fame
    From Age to Age repeat thy story,
Till thou hast won thyself a name
    Exceeding even Euclid's glory.

PREFACE

THIS Tale originally appeared as a serial in *The Monthly Packet* beginning in April 1880. The writer's intention was to embody in each Knot (like the medicine so dexterously, but ineffectually, concealed in the jam of our early childhood) one or more mathematical questions—in Arithmetic, Algebra, or Geometry, as the case might be—for the amusement, and possible edification, of the fair readers of that magazine.

L. C.

December 1885.

A TANGLED TALE

Knot I

Excelsior

Goblin, lead them up and down

THE ruddy glow of sunset was already fading into the sombre shadows of night, when two travelers might have been observed swiftly—at a pace of six miles in the hour—descending the rugged side of a mountain; the younger bounding from crag to crag with the agility of a fawn, while his companion, whose aged limbs seemed ill at ease in the heavy chain armour habitually worn by tourists in that district, toiled on painfully at his side.

As is always the case under such circumstances, the younger knight was the first to break the silence.

"A goodly pace, I trow!" he exclaimed. "We sped not thus in the ascent!"

"Goodly, indeed!" the other echoed with a groan. "We clomb it but at three miles in the hour."

"And on the dead level our pace is——?" the younger suggested; for he was weak in statistics, and left all such details to his aged companion.

"Four miles in the hour," the other wearily replied. "Not an ounce more," he added, with that love of metaphor so common in old age, "and not a farthing less!"

" 'Twas three hours past high noon when we left our hostelry," the young man said, musingly. "We shall scarce be back by supper-time. Perchance mine host will roundly deny us all food!"

"He will chide our tardy return," was the grave reply, "and such a rebuke will be meet."

"A brave conceit!" cried the other, with a merry laugh. "And should we bid him bring us yet another course, I trow his answer will be tart!"

883

"We shall but get our deserts," sighed the elder knight, who had never seen a joke in his life, and was somewhat displeased at his companion's untimely levity. " 'Twill be nine of the clock", he added in an undertone, "by the time we regain our hostelry. Full many a mile shall we have plodded this day!"

"How many? How many?" cried the eager youth, ever athirst for knowledge.

The old man was silent.

"Tell me", he answered, after a moment's thought, "what time it was when we stood together on yonder peak. Not exact to the minute!" he added hastily, reading a protest in the young man's face. "An thy guess be within one poor half-hour of the mark, 'tis all I ask of thy mother's son! Then will I tell thee, true to the last inch, how far we shall have trudged betwixt three and nine of the clock."

A groan was the young man's only reply; while his convulsed features and the deep wrinkles that chased each other across his manly brow, revealed the abyss of arithmetical agony into which one chance question had plunged him.

Knot II

Eligible Apartments

Straight down the crooked lane,
And all round the square.

"Let's ask Balbus about it," said Hugh.

"All right," said Lambert.

"*He* can guess it," said Hugh.

"Rather," said Lambert.

No more words were needed: the two brothers understood each other perfectly.

Balbus was waiting for them at the hotel: the journey

down had tired him, he said: so his two pupils had been
the round of the place, in search of lodgings, without the
old tutor who had been their inseparable companion from
their childhood. They had named him after the hero of
their Latin exercise-book, which overflowed with anecdotes of that versatile genius—anecdotes whose vagueness
in detail was more than compensated by their sensational
brilliance. "Balbus has overcome all his enemies" had
been marked by their tutor, in the margin of the book,
"Successful Bravery." In this way he had tried to extract
a moral from every anecdote about Balbus—sometimes
one of warning, as in, "Balbus had borrowed a healthy
dragon," against which he had written, "Rashness in
Speculation"—sometimes of encouragement, as in the
words, "Influence of Sympathy in United Action," which
stood opposite to the anecdote, "Balbus was assisting his
mother-in-law to convince the dragon"—and sometimes
it dwindled down to a single word, such as "Prudence",
which was all he could extract from the touching record
that "Balbus, having scorched the tail of the dragon, went
away". His pupils liked the short morals best, as it left
them more room for marginal illustrations, and in this
instance they required all the space they could get to
exhibit the rapidity of the hero's departure.

Their report of the state of things was discouraging.
That most fashionable of watering-places, Little Mendip,
was "chock-full" (as the boys expressed it) from end to
end. But in one Square they had seen no less than four
cards, in different houses, all announcing in flaming capitals, "ELIGIBLE APARTMENTS." "So there's plenty of
choice, after all, you see," said spokesman Hugh in conclusion.

"That doesn't follow from the data," said Balbus, as
he rose from the easy-chair, where he had been dozing
over *The Little Mendip Gazette*. "They may be all single
rooms. However, we may as well see them. I shall be glad
to stretch my legs a bit."

An unprejudiced bystander might have objected that

the operation was needless, and that this long lank creature would have been all the better with even shorter legs: but no such thought occurred to his loving pupils. One on each side, they did their best to keep up with his gigantic strides, while Hugh repeated the sentence in their father's letter, just received from abroad, over which he and Lambert had been puzzling. "He says a friend of his, the Governor of—*what* was that name again, Lambert?" ("Kgovjni," said Lambert.) "Well, yes. The Governor of—what-you-may-call-it—wants to give a *very* small dinner-party, and he means to ask his father's brother-in-law, his brother's father-in-law, his father-in-law's brother, and his brother-in-law's father: and we're to guess how many guests there will be."

There was an anxious pause. "*How* large did he say the pudding was to be?" Balbus said at last. "Take its cubical contents, divide by the cubical contents of what each man can eat, and the quotient——"

"He didn't say anything about pudding," said Hugh, "—and here's the Square," as they turned a corner and came into sight of the "eligible apartments".

"It *is* a Square!" was Balbus's first cry of delight, as he gazed around him. "Beautiful! Beau-ti-ful! Equilateral! *And* rectangular!"

The boys looked round with less enthusiasm. "Number Nine is the first with a card," said prosaic Lambert; but Balbus would not so soon awake from his dream of beauty.

"See, boys!" he cried. "Twenty doors on a side! What symmetry! Each side divided into twenty-one equal parts! It's delicious!"

"Shall I knock, or ring?" said Hugh, looking in some perplexity at a square brass plate which bore the simple inscription, "RING ALSO."

"Both," said Balbus. "That's an Ellipsis, my boy. Did you never see an Ellipsis before?"

"I couldn't hardly read it," said Hugh evasively. "It's no good having an Ellipsis, if they don't keep it clean."

"Which there is *one* room, gentlemen," said the smiling

landlady. "And a sweet room too! As snug a little back-room——"

"We will see it," said Balbus gloomily, as they followed her in. "I knew how it would be! One room in each house! No view, I suppose?"

"Which indeed there *is*, gentlemen!" the landlady indignantly protested, as she drew up the blind, and indicated the back-garden.

"Cabbages, I perceive," said Balbus. "Well, they're green, at any rate."

"Which the greens at the shops", their hostess explained, "are by no means dependable upon. Here you has them on the premises, *and* of the best."

"Does the window open?" was always Balbus's first question in testing a lodging: and, "Does the chimney smoke?" his second. Satisfied on all points, he secured the refusal of the room, and they moved on to Number Twenty-five.

This landlady was grave and stern. "I've nobbut one room left," she told them: "and it gives on the back-gyardin."

"But there are cabbages?" Balbus suggested.

The landlady visibly relented. "There is, sir," she said: "and good ones, though I say it as shouldn't. We ca'n't rely on the shops for greens. So we grows them ourselves."

"A singular advantage," said Balbus; and, after the usual questions, they went on to Fifty-two.

"And I'd gladly accommodate you all, if I could," was the greeting that met them. "We are but mortal" ("Irrelevant!" muttered Balbus), "and I've let all my rooms but one."

"Which one is a back-room, I perceive," said Balbus: "and looking out on—on cabbages, I presume?"

"Yes, indeed, sir!" said their hostess. "Whatever *other* folks may do, *we* grows our own. For the shops——"

"An excellent arrangement!" Balbus interrupted. "Then one can really depend on their being good. Does the window open?"

The usual questions were answered satisfactorily: but this time Hugh added one of his own invention—"Does the cat scratch?"

The landlady looked round suspiciously, as if to make sure the cat was not listening. "I will not deceive you, gentlemen," she said. "It *do* scratch, but not without you pulls its whiskers! It'll never do it", she repeated slowly, with a visible effort to recall the exact words of some written agreement between herself and the cat, "without you pulls its whiskers!"

"Much may be excused in a cat so treated," said Balbus, as they left the house and crossed to Number Seventy-three, leaving the landlady curtseying on the doorstep, and still murmuring to herself her parting words, as if they were a form of blessing, "—not without you pulls its whiskers!"

At Number Seventy-three they found only a small shy girl to show the house, who said "yes'm" in answer to all questions.

"The usual room," said Balbus, as they marched in "the usual back-garden, the usual cabbages. I suppose you can't get them good at the shops?"

"Yes'm," said the girl.

"Well, you may tell your mistress we will take the room, and that her plan of growing her own cabbages is simply *admirable*!"

"Yes'm," said the girl, as she showed them out.

"One day-room and three bedrooms," said Balbus, as they returned to the hotel. "We will take as our day-room the one that gives us the least walking to do to get to it."

"Must we walk from door to door, and count the steps?" said Lambert.

"No, no! Figure it out, my boys, figure it out!" Balbus gayly exclaimed, as he put pens, ink, and paper before his hapless pupils, and left the room.

"I say! It'll be a job!" said Hugh.

"Rather!" said Lambert.

Knot III

Mad Mathesis

I waited for the train

"WELL, they call me so because I *am* a little mad, I suppose," she said, good-humouredly, in answer to Clara's cautiously worded question as to how she came by so strange a nickname. "You see, I never do what sane people are expected to do nowadays. I never wear long trains (talking of trains, that's the Charing Cross Metropolitan Station—I've something to tell you about *that*), and I never play lawn-tennis. I ca'n't cook an omelette. I ca'n't even set a broken limb! *There's* an ignoramus for you!"

Clara was her niece, and full twenty years her junior; in fact, she was still attending a High School—an institution of which Mad Mathesis spoke with undisguised aversion. "Let a woman be meek and lowly!" she would say. "None of your High Schools for me!" But it was vacation-time just now, and Clara was her guest, and Mad Mathesis was showing her the sights of that Eighth Wonder of the world—London.

"The Charing Cross Metropolitan Station!" she resumed, waving her hand towards the entrance as if she were introducing her niece to a friend. "The Bayswater and Birmingham Extension is just completed, and the trains now run round and round continuously—skirting the border of Wales, just touching at York, and so round by the east coast back to London. The way the trains run is *most* peculiar. The westerly ones go round in two hours; the easterly ones take three; but they always manage to start two trains from here, opposite ways, punctually every quarter of an hour."

"They part to meet again," said Clara, her eyes filling with tears at the romantic thought.

"No need to cry about it!" her aunt grimly remarked. "They don't meet on the same line of rails, you know. Talking of meeting, an idea strikes me!" she added, changing the subject with her usual abruptness. "Let's go opposite ways round, and see which can meet most trains. No need for a chaperon—ladies' saloon, you know. You shall go whichever way you like, and we'll have a bet about it!"

"I never make bets," Clara said very gravely. "Our excellent preceptress has often warned us——"

"You'd be none the worst if you did!" Mad Mathesis interrupted. "In fact, you'd be the better, I'm certain!"

"Neither does our excellent preceptress approve of puns," said Clara. "But we'll have a match, if you like. Let me choose my train," she added after a brief mental calculation, "and I'll engage to meet exactly half as many again as you do."

"Not if you count fair," Mad Mathesis bluntly interrupted. "Remember, we only count the trains we meet *on the way*. You mustn't count the one that starts as you start, nor the one that arrives as you arrive."

"That will only make the difference of *one* train," said Clara, as they turned and entered the station. "But I never travelled alone before. There'll be no one to help me to alight. However, I don't mind. Let's have a match."

A ragged little boy overheard her remark, and came running after her. "Buy a box of cigar-lights, Miss!" he pleaded, pulling her shawl to attract her attention. Clara stopped to explain.

"I never smoke cigars," she said in a meekly apologetic tone. "Our excellent preceptress——" But Mad Mathesis impatiently hurried her on, and the little boy was left gazing after her with round eyes of amazement.

The two ladies bought their tickets and moved slowly down the central platform. Mad Mathesis prattling on as usual—Clara silent, anxiously reconsidering the calculation on which she rested her hopes of winning the match.

"Mind where you go, dear!" cried her aunt, checking

her just in time. "One step more, and you'd have been in that pail of cold water!"

"I know, I know," Clara said dreamily. "The pale, the cold, and the moony——"

"Take your places on the spring-boards!" shouted a porter.

"What are *they* for!" Clara asked in a terrified whisper.

"Merely to help us into the trains." The elder lady spoke with the nonchalance of one quite used to the process. "Very few people can get into a carriage without help in less than three seconds, and the trains only stop for one second." At this moment the whistle was heard, and two trains rushed into the station. A moment's pause, and they were gone again; but in that brief interval several hundred passengers had been shot into them, each flying straight to his place with the accuracy of a Minie bullet—while an equal number were showered out upon the side-platforms.

Three hours had passed away, and the two friends met again on the Charing Cross platform, and eagerly compared notes. Then Clara turned away with a sigh. To young impulsive hearts, like hers, disappointment is always a bitter pill. Mad Mathesis followed her, full of kindly sympathy.

"Try again, my love!" she said cheerily. "Let us vary the experiment. We will start as we did before, but not begin counting till our trains meet. When we see each other, we will say 'One!' and so count on till we come here again."

Clara brightened up. "I shall win *that*", she exclaimed eagerly, "if I may choose my train!"

Another shriek of engine whistles, another upheaving of spring-boards, another living avalanche plunging into two trains as they flashed by and the travelers were off again.

Each gazed eagerly from her carriage window, holding up her handkerchief as a signal to her friend. A rush and a roar. Two trains shot past each other in a tunnel, and

two travelers leaned back in their corners with a sigh—
or rather with *two* sighs—of relief "One!" Clara murmured to herself. "Won! It's a word of good omen. *This*
time, at any rate, the victory will be mine!"

But *was* it?

KNOT IV

The Dead Reckoning

I did dream of money-bags to-night

NOONDAY on the open sea within a few degrees of the
Equator is apt to be oppressively warm; and our two
travelers were now airily clad in suits of dazzling white
linen, having laid aside the chain-armour which they had
found not only endurable in the cold mountain air they
had lately been breathing, but a necessary precaution
against the daggers of the banditti who infested the
heights. Their holiday-trip was over, and they were now
on their way home, in the monthly packet which plied
between the two great ports of the island they had been
exploring.

Along with their armour, the tourists had laid aside
the antiquated speech it had pleased them to affect while
in knightly disguise, and had returned to the ordinary
style of two country gentlemen of the twentieth century.

Stretched on a pile of cushions, under the shade of a
huge umbrella, they were lazily watching some native
fishermen, who had come on board at the last landing-
place, each carrying over his shoulder a small but heavy
sack. A large weighing-machine, that had been used for
cargo at the last port, stood on the deck; and round this
the fishermen had gathered, and, with much unintelligible
jabber, seemed to be weighing their sacks.

"More like sparrows in a tree than human talk, isn't
it?" the elder tourist remarked to his son, who smiled

feebly, but would not exert himself so far as to speak. The old man tried another listener.

"What have they got in those sacks, Captain?" he enquired, as that great being passed them in his never-ending parade to and fro on the deck.

The Captain paused in his march, and towered over the travelers—tall, grave, and serenely self-satisfied.

"Fishermen", he explained, "are often passengers in My ship. These five are from Mhruxi—the place we last touched at—and that's the way they carry their money. The money of this island is heavy, gentlemen, but it costs little, as you may guess. We buy it from them by weight—about five shillings a pound. I fancy a ten-pound note would buy all those sacks."

By this time the old man had closed his eyes—in order, no doubt, to concentrate his thoughts on these interesting facts; but the Captain failed to realize his motive, and with a grunt resumed his monotonous march.

Meanwhile the fishermen were getting so noisy over the weighing-machine that one of the sailors took the pre-caution of carrying off all the weights, leaving them to amuse themselves with such substitutes in the form of winch-handles, belaying-pins, etc., as they could find. This brought their excitement to a speedy end: they carefully hid their sacks in the folds of the jib that lay on the deck near the tourists, and strolled away.

When next the Captain's heavy footfall passed, the younger man roused himself to speak.

"*What* did you call the place those fellows came from, Captain?" he asked.

"Mhruxi, sir."

"And the one we are bound for?"

The Captain took a long breath, plunged into the word, and came out of it nobly. "They call it Kgovjni, sir."

"K—I give it up!" the young man faintly said.

He stretched out his hand for a glass of iced water which the compassionate steward had brought him a minute ago, and had set down, unluckily, just outside the shadow of the umbrella. It was scalding hot, and he decided not to drink it. The effort of making this resolution, coming close on the fatiguing conversation he had just gone through, was too much for him; he sank back among the cushions in silence.

His father courteously tried to make amends for his nonchalance.

"Whereabout are we now, Captain?" said he. "Have you any idea?"

The Captain cast a pitying look on the ignorant landsman. "I could tell you that, sir," he said, in a tone of lofty condescension, "to an inch!"

"You don't say so!" the old man remarked, in a tone of languid surprise.

"And mean to," persisted the Captain. "Why, what do you suppose would become of My ship, if I were to lose My longitude and My latitude? Could *you* make anything of My Dead Reckoning?"

"Nobody could, I'm sure!" the other heartily rejoined. But he had overdone it.

"It's *perfectly* intelligible", the Captain said, in an offended tone, "to anyone that understands such things." With these words he moved away, and began giving orders to the men, who were preparing to hoist the jib.

Our tourists watched the operation with such interest that neither of them remembered the five money-bags, which in another moment, as the wind filled out the jib, were whirled overboard and fell heavily into the sea.

But the poor fishermen had not so easily forgotten their property. In a moment they had rushed to the spot, and stood uttering cries of fury, and pointing, now to the sea, and now to the sailors who had caused the disaster.

The old man explained it to the Captain.

"Let us make it up among us," he added in conclusion. "Ten pounds will do it, I think you said?"

But the Captain put aside the suggestion with a wave of the hand.

"No, sir!" he said, in his grandest manner. "You will

excuse Me, I am sure; but these are My passengers. The accident has happened on board My ship, and under My orders. It is for Me to make compensation." He turned to the angry fishermen. "Come here, my men!" he said, in the Mhruxian dialect. "Tell me the weight of each sack. I saw you weighing them just now."

Then ensued a perfect Babel of noise, as the five natives explained, all screaming together, how the sailors had carried off the weights, and they had done what they could with whatever came handy.

Two iron belaying-pins, three blocks, six holy stones, four winch-handles, and a large hammer, were now carefully weighed, the Captain superintending and noting the results. But the matter did not seem to be settled, even then: an angry discussion followed, in which the sailors and the five natives all joined: and at last the Captain approached our tourists with a disconcerted look, which he tried to conceal under a laugh.

"It's an absurd difficulty," he said. "Perhaps one of you gentlemen can suggest something. It seems they weighed the sacks two at a time!"

"If they didn't have five separate weighings, of course you ca'n't value them separately," the youth hastily decided.

"Let's hear all about it," was the old man's more cautious remark.

"They *did* have five separate weighings," the Captain said, "but—well, it beats *me* entirely!" he added, in a sudden burst of candour. "Here's the result: First and second sacks weighed twelve pounds; second and third, thirteen and a half; third and fourth, eleven and a half; fourth and fifth, eight; and then they say they had only the large hammer left, and it took *three* sacks to weigh it down—that's the first, third, and fifth—and *they* weighed sixteen pounds. There, gentlemen! Did you ever hear anything like *that*?"

The old man muttered under his breath, "If only my sister were here!" and looked helplessly at his son. His son looked at the five natives. The five natives looked at the Captain. The Captain looked at nobody: his eyes were cast down, and he seemed to be saying softly to himself, "Contemplate one another, gentlemen, if such be your good pleasure. *I* contemplate *Myself*!"

KNOT V

Oughts and Crosses

Look here, upon this picture, and on this

"AND what made you choose the first train, Goosey?" said Mad Mathesis, as they got into the cab. "Couldn't you count better than *that*?"

"I took an extreme case," was the tearful reply. "Our excellent preceptress always says, 'When in doubt, my dears, take an extreme case.' And I *was* in doubt."

"Does it always succeed?" her aunt inquired.

Clara sighed. "Not *always*," she reluctantly admitted. "And I ca'n't make out why. One day she was telling the little girls—they make such a noise at tea, you know—'The more noise you make, the less jam you will have, and vice versa.' And I thought they wouldn't know what 'vice versa' meant: so I explained it to them. I said, 'If you make an infinite noise, you'll get no jam: and if you make no noise, you'll get an infinite lot of jam.' But our excellent preceptress said that wasn't a good instance. *Why* wasn't it?" she added plaintively.

Her aunt evaded the question. "One sees certain objections to it," she said. "But how did you work it with the Metropolitan trains? None of them go infinitely fast, I believe."

"I called them hares and tortoises," Clara said—a little timidly, for she dreaded being laughed at. "And I thought there couldn't be so many hares as tortoises on the Line:

so I took an extreme case—one hare and an infinite number of tortoises."

"An extreme case, indeed," her aunt remarked with admirable gravity: "and a most dangerous state of things!"

"And I thought, if I went with a tortoise, there would be only *one* hare to meet: but if I went with the hare— you know there were *crowds* of tortoises!"

"It wasn't a bad idea," said the elder lady, as they left the cab, at the entrance of Burlington House. "You shall have another chance to-day. We'll have a match in marking pictures."

Clara brightened up. "I should like to try again, very much," she said. "I'll take more care this time. How are we to play?"

To this question Mad Mathesis made no reply: she was busy drawing lines down the margins of the catalogue. "See," she said after a minute, "I've drawn three columns against the names of the pictures in the long room, and I want you to fill them with oughts and crosses—crosses for good marks and oughts for bad. The first column is for choice of subject, the second for arrangement, the third for colouring. And these are the conditions of the match: You must give three crosses to two or three pictures. You must give two crosses to four or five——"

"Do you mean *only* two crosses?" said Clara. "Or may I count the three-cross pictures among the two-cross pictures?"

"Of course you may," said her aunt. "Anyone that has *three* eyes, may be said to have *two* eyes, I suppose?"

Clara followed her aunt's dreamy gaze across the crowded gallery, half-dreading to find that there was a three-eyed person in sight.

"And you must give one cross to nine or ten."

"And which wins the match?" Clara asked, as she carefully entered these conditions on a blank leaf in her catalogue.

"Whichever marks fewest pictures."

"But suppose we marked the same number?"

"Then whichever uses most marks."

Clara considered. "I don't think it's much of a match," she said. "I shall mark nine pictures, and give three crosses to three of them, two crosses to two more, and one cross each to all the rest."

"Will you, indeed?" said her aunt. "Wait till you've heard all the conditions, my impetuous child. You must give three oughts to one or two pictures, two oughts to three or four, and one ought to eight or nine. I don't want you to be *too* hard on the R.A.'s."

Clara quite gasped as she wrote down all these fresh conditions. "It's a great deal worse than Circulating Decimals!" she said. "But I'm determined to win, all the same!"

Her aunt smiled grimly. "We can begin *here*," she said, as they paused before a gigantic picture, which the catalogue informed them was the "Portrait of Lieutenant Brown, mounted on his favourite elephant".

"He looks awfully conceited!" said Clara. "I don't think he was the elephant's favourite Lieutenant. What a hideous picture it is! And it takes up room enough for twenty!"

"Mind what you say, my dear!" her aunt interposed. "It's by an R.A.!"

But Clara was quite reckless. "I don't care who it's by!" she cried. "And I shall give it three bad marks!"

Aunt and niece soon drifted away from each other in the crowd, and for the next half-hour Clara was hard at work, putting in marks and rubbing them out again, and hunting up and down for a suitable picture. This she found the hardest part of all. "I *ca'n't* find the one I want!" she exclaimed at last, almost crying with vexation.

"What is it you want to find, my dear?" The voice was strange to Clara, but so sweet and gentle that she felt attracted to the owner of it, even before she had seen her; and when she turned, and met the smiling looks of two little old ladies, whose round dimpled faces, exactly alike, seemed never to have known a care, it was as much as she

could do—as she confessed to Aunt Mattie afterwards—
to keep herself from hugging them both. "I was looking
for a picture", she said, "that has a good subject—and
that's well arranged—but badly coloured."

The little old ladies glanced at each other in some alarm.
"Calm yourself, my dear," said the one who had spoken
first, "and try to remember which it was. What *was* the
subject?"

"Was it an elephant, for instance?" the other sister
suggested. They were still in sight of Lieutenant Brown.

"I don't know, indeed!" Clara impetuously replied.
"You know it doesn't matter a bit what the subject *is*, so
long as it's a good one!"

Once more the sisters exchanged looks of alarm, and
one of them whispered something to the other, of which
Clara caught only the one word "mad".

"They mean Aunt Mattie, of course," she said to herself—fancying, in her innocence, that London was like
her native town, where everybody knew everybody else.
"If you mean my aunt," she added aloud, "she's *there*—
just three pictures beyond Lieutenant Brown."

"Ah, well! Then you'd better go to her, my dear!" her
new friend said soothingly. "*She'll* find you the picture
you want. Good-bye, dear!"

"Good-bye, dear!" echoed the other sister. "Mind you
don't lose sight of your aunt!" And the pair trotted off
into another room, leaving Clara rather perplexed at their
manner.

"They're real darlings!" she soliloquized. "I wonder
why they pity me so!" And she wandered on, murmuring
to herself, "It must have two good marks, and——"

Knot VI

Her Radiancy

One piecee thing that my have got,
Maskee[1] that thing my no can do.
You talkee you no sabey what?
Bamboo.

THEY landed, and were at once conducted to the Palace. About half-way they were met by the Governor, who welcomed them in English—a great relief to our travelers, whose guide could speak nothing but Kgovjnian.

"I don't half like the way they grin at us as we go by!" the old man whispered to his son. "And why do they say 'Bamboo' so often?"

"It alludes to a local custom," replied the Governor, who had overheard the question. "Such persons as happen in any way to displease Her Radiancy are usually beaten with rods."

The old man shuddered. "A most objectionable local custom!" he remarked with strong emphasis. "I wish we had never landed! Did you notice that black fellow, Norman, opening his great mouth at us? I verily believe he would like to eat us!"

Norman appealed to the Governor, who was walking at his other side. "Do they often eat distinguished strangers here?" he said, in as indifferent a tone as he could assume.

"Not often—not ever!" was the welcome reply. "They are not good for it. Pigs we eat, for they are fat. This old man is thin."

"And thankful to be so!" muttered the elder traveler. "Beaten we shall be without a doubt. It's a comfort to know it won't be Beaten without the B! My dear boy, just look at the peacocks!"

---

[1] "Maskee", in Pigeon-English, means "Without".

They were now walking between two unbroken lines of those gorgeous birds, each held in check, by means of a golden collar and chain, by a black slave, who stood well behind, so as not to interrupt the view of the glittering tail, with its network of rustling feathers and its hundred eyes.

The Governor smiled proudly. "In your honour," he said, "Her Radiancy has ordered up ten thousand additional peacocks. She will, no doubt, decorate you, before you go, with the usual Star and Feathers."

"It'll be Star without the S!" faltered one of his hearers.

"Come, come! Don't lose heart!" said the other. "All this is full of charm for me."

"You are young, Norman," sighed his father; "young and light-hearted. For me, it is Charm without the C."

"The old one is sad," the Governor remarked with some anxiety. "He has, without doubt, effected some fearful crime?"

"But I haven't!" the poor old gentleman hastily exclaimed. "Tell him I haven't, Norman!"

"He has not, as yet," Norman gently explained. And the Governor repeated, in a satisfied tone, "Not as yet."

"Yours is a wondrous country!" the Governor resumed, after a pause. "Now here is a letter from a friend of mine, a merchant, in London. He and his brother went there a year ago, with a thousand pounds apiece; and on New Year's Day they had sixty thousand pounds between them!"

"How did they do it?" Norman eagerly exclaimed. Even the elder traveler looked excited.

The Governor handed him the open letter. "Anybody can do it, when once they know how," so ran this oracular document. "We borrowed nought: we stole nought. We began the year with only a thousand pounds apiece: and last New Year's Day we had sixty thousand pounds between us—sixty thousand golden sovereigns!"

Norman looked grave and thoughtful as he handed

back the letter. His father hazarded one guess. "Was it by gambling?"

"A Kgovjnian never gambles," said the Governor gravely, as he ushered them through the palace gates. They followed him in silence down a long passage, and soon found themselves in a lofty hall, lined entirely with peacocks' feathers. In the centre was a pile of crimson cushions, which almost concealed the figure of Her Radiancy—a plump little damsel, in a robe of green satin dotted with silver stars, whose pale round face lit up for a moment with a half-smile as the travelers bowed before her, and then relapsed into the exact expression of a wax doll, while she languidly murmured a word or two in the Kgovjnian dialect.

The Governor interpreted: "Her Radiancy welcomes you. She notes the Impenetrable Placidity of the old one, and the Imperceptible Acuteness of the youth."

Here the little potentate clapped her hands, and a troop of slaves instantly appeared, carrying trays of coffee and sweetmeats, which they offered to the guests, who had, at a signal from the Governor, seated themselves on the carpet.

"Sugar-plums!" muttered the old man. "One might as well be at a confectioner's! Ask for a penny bun, Norman!"

"Not so loud!" his son whispered. "Say something complimentary!" For the Governor was evidently expecting a speech.

"We thank Her Exalted Potency," the old man timidly began. "We bask in the light of her smile, which——"

"The words of old men are weak!" the Governor interrupted angrily. "Let the youth speak!"

"Tell her," cried Norman, in a wild burst of eloquence, "that, like two grasshoppers in a volcano, we are shrivelled up in the presence of Her Spangled Vehemence!"

"It is well," said the Governor, and translated this into Kgovjnian. "I am now to tell you", he proceeded, "what Her Radiancy requires of you before you go. The yearly competition for the post of Imperial Scarf-maker is just ended; you are the judges. You will take account of the rate of work, the lightness of the scarves, and their warmth. Usually the competitors differ in one point only. Thus, last year, Fifi and Gogo made the same number of scarves in the trial-week, and they were equally light; but Fifi's were twice as warm as Gogo's and she was pronounced twice as good. But this year, woe is me, who can judge it? Three competitors are here, and they differ in all points! While you settle their claims, you shall be lodged, Her Radiancy bids me say, free of expense—in the best dungeon, and abundantly fed on the best bread and water."

The old man groaned. "All is lost!" he wildly exclaimed. But Norman heeded him not: he had taken out his notebook, and was calmly jotting down the particulars.

"Three they be," the Governor proceeded. "Lolo, Mimi, and Zuzu. Lolo makes 5 scarves while Mimi makes 2; but Zuzu makes 4 while Lolo makes 3! Again, so fairy-like is Zuzu's handiwork, 5 of her scarves weigh no more than one of Lolo's; yet Mimi's is lighter still—5 of hers will but balance 3 of Zuzu's! And for warmth one of Mimi's is equal to 4 of Zuzu's; yet one of Lolo's is as warm as 3 of Mimi's!"

Here the little lady once more clapped her hands.

"It is our signal of dismissal!" the Governor hastily said. "Pay Her Radiancy your farewell compliments—and walk out backwards."

The walking part was all the elder tourist could manage. Norman simply said, "Tell Her Radiancy we are transfixed by the spectacle of Her Serene Brilliance, and bid an agonized farewell to her Condensed Milkiness!"

"Her Radiancy is pleased," the Governor reported, after duly translating this. "She casts on you a glance from Her Imperial Eyes, and is confident that you will catch it!"

"That I warrant we shall!" the elder traveler moaned to himself distractedly.

Once more they bowed low, and then followed the Governor down a winding staircase to the Imperial Dungeon, which they found to be lined with coloured marble, lighted from the roof, and splendidly though not luxuriously furnished with a bench of polished malachite. "I trust you will not delay the calculation," the Governor said, ushering them in with much ceremony. "I have known great inconvenience—great and serious inconvenience—result to those unhappy ones who have delayed to execute the commands of Her Radiancy! And on this occasion she is resolute: she says the thing must and shall be done: and she has ordered up ten thousand additional bamboos!" With these words he left them, and they heard him lock and bar the door on the outside.

"I told you how it would end!" moaned the elder traveler, wringing his hands, and quite forgetting in his anguish that he had himself proposed the expedition, and had never predicted anything of the sort. "Oh, that we were well out of this miserable business!"

"Courage!" cried the younger cheerily. "*Hæc olim meminisse juvabit*! The end of all this will be glory!"

"Glory without the L!" was all the poor old man could say, as he rocked himself to and fro on the malachite bench. "Glory without the L!"

Knot VII

Petty Cash

Base is the slave that pays

"Aunt Mattie!"

"My child?"

"*Would* you mind writing it down at once? I shall be quite *certain* to forget it if you don't!"

"My dear, we really must wait till the cab stops. How

can I possibly write anything in the midst of all this
jolting?"

"But *really* I shall be forgetting it!"

Clara's voice took the plaintive tone that her aunt
never knew how to resist, and with a sigh the old lady
drew forth her ivory tablets and prepared to record the
amount that Clara had just spent at the confectioner's
shop. Her expenditure was always made out of her aunt's
purse, but the poor girl knew, by bitter experience, that
sooner or later "Mad Mathesis" would expect an exact
account of every penny that had gone, and she waited,
with ill-concealed impatience, while the old lady turned
the tablets over and over, till she had found the one
headed "PETTY CASH".

"Here's the place," she said at last, "and here we have
yesterday's luncheon duly entered. *One glass lemonade*
(Why ca'n't you drink water, like me?), *three sandwiches*
(They never put in half mustard enough. I told the young
woman so, to her face; and she tossed her head—like
her impudence!), *and seven biscuits. Total one-and-two-
pence.* Well, now for to-day's?"

"One glass of lemonade——" Clara was beginning to
say, when suddenly the cab drew up, and a courteous
railway-porter was handing out the bewildered girl before
she had had time to finish her sentence.

Her aunt pocketed the tablets instantly. "Business
first," she said: "petty cash—which is a form of pleasure,
whatever *you* may think—afterwards." And she proceeded to pay the driver, and to give voluminous orders
about the luggage, quite deaf to the entreaties of her
unhappy niece that she would enter the rest of the
luncheon account. "My dear, you really must cultivate
a more capacious mind!" was all the consolation she
vouchsafed to the poor girl. "Are not the tablets of your
memory wide enough to contain the record of one single
luncheon?"

"Not wide enough! Not half wide enough!" was the
passionate reply.

The words came in aptly enough, but the voice was not that of Clara, and both ladies turned in some surprise to see who it was that had so suddenly struck into their conversation. A fat little old lady was standing at the door of a cab, helping the driver to extricate what seemed an exact duplicate of herself: it would have been no easy task to decide which was the fatter or which looked the more good-humoured of the two sisters.

"I tell you the cab-door isn't half wide enough!" she repeated, as her sister finally emerged, somewhat after the fashion of a pellet from a pop-gun, and she turned to appeal to Clara. "Is it, dear?" she said, trying hard to bring a frown into a face that dimpled all over with smiles.

"Some folks is too wide for 'em," growled the cab-driver.

"Don't provoke me, man!" cried the little old lady, in what she meant for a tempest of fury. "Say another word and I'll put you into the County Court, and sue you for a Habeas Corpus!" the cabman touched his hat, and marched off, grinning.

"Nothing like a little Law to cow the ruffians, my dear!" she remarked confidentially to Clara. "You saw how he quailed when I mentioned the Habeas Corpus? Not that I've any idea what it means, but it sounds very grand, doesn't it?"

"It's very provoking," Clara replied, a little vaguely.

"Very!" the little old lady eagerly replied. "And we're very much provoked indeed. Aren't we, sister?"

"I never was so provoked in all my life!" the fatter sister assented radiantly.

By this time Clara had recognized her picture-gallery acquaintances, and, drawing her aunt aside, she hastily whispered her reminiscences. "I met them first in the Royal Academy—and they were very kind to me—and they were lunching at the next table to us, just now, you know—and they tried to help me to find the picture I wanted—and I'm sure they're dear old things!"

"Friends of yours, are they?" said Mad Mathesis. "Well

I like their looks. You can be civil to them, while I get the tickets. But do try and arrange your ideas a little more chronologically!"

And so it came to pass that the four ladies found themselves seated side by side on the same bench waiting for the train, and chatting as if they had known one another for years.

"Now this I call quite a remarkable coincidence!" exclaimed the smaller and more talkative of the two sisters —the one whose legal knowledge had annihilated the cab-driver. "Not only that we should be waiting for the same train, and at the same station—*that* would be curious enough—but actually on the same day, and the same hour of the day! That's what strikes *me* so forcibly!" She glanced at the fatter and more silent sister, whose chief function in life seemed to be to support the family opinion, and who meekly responded:

"And me too, sister!"

"Those are not *independent* coincidences——" Mad Mathesis was just beginning, when Clara ventured to interpose.

"There's no jolting here," she pleaded meekly. "*Would* you mind writing it down now?"

Out came the ivory tablets once more. "What was it, then?" said her aunt.

"One glass of lemonade, one sandwich, one biscuit— Oh, dear me!" cried poor Clara, the historical tone suddenly changing to a wail of agony.

"Toothache?" said her aunt calmly, as she wrote down the items. The two sisters instantly opened their reticules and produced two different remedies for neuralgia, each marked "unequalled".

"It isn't that!" said poor Clara. "Thank you very much. It's only that I *ca'n't* remember how much I paid!"

"Well, try and make it out, then," said her aunt. "You've got yesterday's luncheon to help you, you know. And here's the luncheon we had the day before—the first day we went to that shop—*one glass lemonade, four sand-*

wiches, ten biscuits. Total, one-and-fivepence." She handed the tablets to Clara, who gazed at them with eyes so dim with tears that she did not at first notice that she was holding them upside down.

The two sisters had been listening to all this with the deepest interest, and at this juncture the smaller one softly laid her hand on Clara's arm.

"Do you know, my dear," she said coaxingly, "my sister and I are in the very same predicament! Quite identically the very same predicament! Aren't we, sister?"

"Quite identically and absolutely the very——" began the fatter sister, but she was constructing her sentence on too large a scale, and the little one would not wait for her to finish it.

"Yes, my dear," she resumed; "we were lunching at the very same shop as you were—and we had two glasses of lemonade and three sandwiches and five biscuits—and neither of us has the least idea what we paid. Have we, sister?"

"Quite identically and absolutely——" murmured the other, who evidently considered that she was now a whole sentence in arrears, and that she ought to discharge one obligation before contracting any fresh liabilities; but the little lady broke in again, and she retired from the conversation a bankrupt.

"Would you make it out for us, my dear?" pleaded the little old lady.

"You can do Arithmetic, I trust?" her aunt said, a little anxiously, as Clara turned from one tablet to another, vainly trying to collect her thoughts. Her mind was a blank, and all human expression was rapidly fading out of her face.

A gloomy silence ensued.

Knot VIII

De Omnibus Rebus

This little pig went to market:
This little pig staid at home.

"By Her Radiancy's express command," said the Governor, as he conducted the travelers, for the last time, from the Imperial presence, "I shall now have the ecstasy of escorting you as far as the outer gate of the Military Quarter, where the agony of parting—if indeed Nature can survive the shock—must be endured! From that gate grurmstipths start every quarter of an hour, both ways——"

"Would you mind repeating that word?" said Norman. "Grurm——?"

"Grurmstipths," the Governor repeated. "You call them omnibuses in England. They run both ways, and you can travel by one of them all the way down to the harbour."

The old man breathed a sigh of relief; four hours of courtly ceremony had wearied him, and he had been in constant terror lest something should call into use the ten thousand additional bamboos.

In another minute they were crossing a large quadrangle, paved with marble, and tastefully decorated with a pigsty in each corner. Soldiers, carrying pigs, were marching in all directions: and in the middle stood a gigantic officer giving orders in a voice of thunder, which made itself heard above all the uproar of the pigs.

"It is the Commander-in-Chief!" the Governor hurriedly whispered to his companions, who at once followed his example in prostrating themselves before the great man. The Commander gravely bowed in return. He was covered with gold lace from head to foot: his face wore an expression of deep misery: and he had a little black pig under each arm. Still the gallant fellow did his best, in the midst of the orders he was every moment issuing to his men, to bid a courteous farewell to the departing guests.

"Farewell, O old one!—carry these three to the South corner—and farewell to thee, thou young one—put this fat one on the top of the others in the Western sty—may your shadows never be less—woe is me, it is wrongly done! Empty out all the sties, and begin again!" And the soldier leant upon his sword, and wiped away a tear.

"He is in distress," the Governor explained as they left the court. "Her Radiancy has commanded him to place twenty-four pigs in those four sties, so that, as she goes round the court, she may always find the number in each sty nearer to ten than the number in the last."

"Does she call ten nearer to ten than nine is?" said Norman.

"Surely," said the Governor. "Her Radiancy would admit that ten is nearer to ten than nine is—and also nearer than eleven is."

"Then I think it can be done," said Norman.

The Governor shook his head. "The Commander has been transferring them in vain for four months," he said. "What hope remains? And Her Radiancy has ordered up ten thousand additional——"

"The pigs don't seem to enjoy being transferred," the old man hastily interrupted. He did not like the subject of bamboos.

"They are only *provisionally* transferred, you know," said the Governor. "In most cases they are immediately carried back again: so they need not mind it. And all is done with the greatest care, under the personal super-intendence of the Commander-in-Chief."

"Of course she would only go *once* round?" said Norman.

"Alas, no!" sighed their conductor. "Round and round. Round and round. These are Her Radiancy's own words. But oh, agony! Here is the outer gate, and we must part!"

He sobbed as he shook hands with them, and the next moment was briskly walking away.

"He *might* have waited to see us off!" said the old man piteously.

"And he needn't have begun whistling the very *moment* he left us!" said the young one severely. "But look sharp—here are two what's-his-names in the act of starting!"

Unluckily, the sea-bound omnibus was full. "Never mind!" said Norman cheerily. "We'll walk on till the next one overtakes us."

They trudged on in silence, both thinking over the military problem, till they met an omnibus coming from the sea. The elder traveler took out his watch. "Just twelve minutes and a half since we started," he remarked in an absent manner. Suddenly the vacant face brightened; the old man had an idea. "My boy!" he shouted, bringing his hand down upon Norman's shoulder so suddenly as for a moment to transfer his centre of gravity beyond the base of support.

Thus taken off his guard, the young man wildly staggered forwards, and seemed about to plunge into space: but in another moment he had gracefully recovered himself. "Problem in Precession and Nutation," he remarked —in tones where filial respect only just managed to conceal a shade of annoyance. "What is it?" he hastily added, fearing his father might have been taken ill. "Will you have some brandy?"

"When will the next omnibus overtake us? When? When?" the old man cried, growing more excited every moment.

Norman looked gloomy. "Give me time," he said. "I must think it over." And once more the travelers passed on in silence—a silence only broken by the distant squeals of the unfortunate little pigs, who were still being provisionally transferred from sty to sty, under the personal superintendence of the Commander-in-Chief.

Knot IX

A Serpent with Corners

Water, water, everywhere,
Nor any drop to drink.

"It'll just take one more pebble."

"Whatever *are* you doing with those buckets?"

The speakers were Hugh and Lambert. Place, the beach of Little Mendip. Time 1:30 P.M. Hugh was floating a bucket in another a size larger, and trying how many pebbles it would carry without sinking. Lambert was lying on his back, doing nothing.

For the next minute or two Hugh was silent, evidently deep in thought. Suddenly he started. "I say, look here, Lambert!" he cried.

"If it's alive, and slimy, and with legs, I don't care to," said Lambert.

"Didn't Balbus say this morning that, if a body is immersed in liquid it displaces as much liquid as is equal to its own bulk?" said Hugh.

"He said things of that sort," Lambert vaguely replied.

"Well, just look here a minute. Here's the little bucket almost quite immersed: so the water displaced ought to be just about the same bulk. And now just look at it!" He took out the little bucket as he spoke, and handed the big one to Lambert. "Why, there's hardly a teacupful! Do you mean to say *that* water is the same bulk as the little bucket?"

"Course it is," said Lambert.

"Well, look here again!" cried Hugh, triumphantly, as he poured the water from the big bucket into the little one. "Why, it doesn't half fill it!"

"That's *its* business," said Lambert. "If Balbus says it's the same bulk, why, it *is* the same bulk, you know."

"Well, I don't believe it," said Hugh.

"You needn't," said Lambert. "Besides, it's dinner-time. Come along."

They found Balbus waiting dinner for them, and to him Hugh at once propounded his difficulty.

"Let's get you helped first," said Balbus, briskly cutting away at the joint. "You know the old proverb, 'Mutton first, mechanics afterwards'?"

The boys did *not* know the proverb, but they accepted it in perfect good faith, as they did every piece of information, however startling, that came from so infallible an authority as their tutor. They ate on steadily in silence, and, when dinner was over, Hugh set out the usual array of pens, ink, and paper, while Balbus repeated to them the problem he had prepared for their afternoon's task.

"A friend of mine has a flower-garden—a very pretty one, though no great size——"

"How big is it?" said Hugh.

"That's what *you* have to find out!" Balbus gaily replied. "All *I* tell you is that it is oblong in shape—just half a yard longer than its width—and that a gravel-walk, one yard wide, begins at one corner and runs all round it."

"Joining into itself?" said Hugh.

"*Not* joining into itself, young man. Just before doing *that*, it turns a corner, and runs round the garden again, alongside of the first portion, and then inside that again, winding in and in, and each lap touching the last one, till it has used up the whole of the area."

"Like a serpent with corners?" said Lambert.

"Exactly so. And if you walk the whole length of it, to the last inch, keeping in the centre of the path, it's exactly two miles and half a furlong. Now, while you find out the length and breadth of the garden, I'll see if I can think out that sea-water puzzle."

"You said it was a flower-garden?" Hugh inquired, as Balbus was leaving the room.

"I did," said Balbus.

"Where do the flowers grow?" said Hugh. But Balbus

thought it best not to hear the question. He left the boys to their problem, and, in the silence of his own room, set himself to unravel Hugh's mechanical paradox.

"To fix our thoughts," he murmured to himself, as, with hands deep-buried in his pockets, he paced up and down the room, "we will take a cylindrical glass jar, with a scale of inches marked up the side, and fill it with water up to the 10-inch mark: and we will assume that every inch depth of jar contains a pint of water. We will now take a solid cylinder, such that every inch of it is equal in bulk to *half* a pint of water, and plunge 4 inches of it into the water, so that the end of the cylinder comes down to the 6-inch mark. Well, that displaces 2 pints of water. What becomes of them? Why, if there were no more cylinder, they would lie comfortably on the top, and fill the jar up to the 12-inch mark. But unfortunately there *is* more cylinder, occupying half the space between the 10-inch and the 12-inch marks, so that only *one* pint of water can be accommodated there. What becomes of the other pint? Why, if there were no more cylinder, it would lie on the top, and fill the jar up to the 13-inch mark. But unfortunately—Shade of Newton!" he exclaimed, in sudden accents of terror. "When *does* the water stop rising?"

A bright idea struck him. "I'll write a little essay on it," he said.

BALBUS'S ESSAY

"When a solid is immersed in a liquid, it is well known that it displaces a portion of the liquid equal to itself in bulk, and that the level of the liquid rises just so much as it would rise if a quantity of liquid had been added to it, equal in bulk to the solid. Lardner says precisely the same process occurs when a solid is *partially* immersed: the quantity of liquid displaced, in this case, equalling the portion of the solid which is immersed, and the rise of the level being in proportion.

"Suppose a solid held above the surface of a liquid and partially immersed: a portion of the liquid is displaced, and the level of the liquid rises. But, by this rise of level, a little bit more of the solid is of course immersed, and so there is a new displacement of a second portion of the liquid, and a consequent rise of level. Again, this second rise of level causes a yet further immersion, and by consequence another displacement of liquid and another rise. It is self-evident that this process must continue till the entire solid is immersed, and that the liquid will then begin to immerse whatever holds the solid, which, being connected with it, must for the time be considered a part of it. If you hold a stick, six feet long, with its ends in a tumbler of water, and wait long enough, you must eventually be immersed. The question as to the source from which the water is supplied—which belongs to a high branch of mathematics, and is therefore beyond our present scope—does not apply to the sea. Let us therefore take the familiar instance of a man standing at the edge of the sea, at ebb-tide, with a solid in his hand, which he partially immerses: he remains steadfast and unmoved, and we all know that he must be drowned. The multitudes who daily perish in this manner to attest a philosophical truth, and whose bodies the unreasoning wave casts sullenly upon our thankless shores, have a truer claim to be called the martyrs of science than a Galileo or a Kepler. To use Kossuth's eloquent phrase, they are the unnamed demigods of the nineteenth century." [1]

"There's a fallacy *somewhere*," he murmured drowsily, as he stretched his long legs upon the sofa. "I must think it over again." He closed his eyes, in order to concentrate his attention more perfectly, and for the next hour or so his slow and regular breathing bore witness to the careful deliberation with which he was investigating this new and perplexing view of the subject.

[1] *Note by the writer.*—For the above essay I am indebted to a dear friend, now deceased.

Knot X

Chelsea Buns

Yea, buns, and buns, and buns!

Old Song.

"How very, very sad!" exclaimed Clara; and the eyes of the gentle girl filled with tears as she spoke.

"Sad—but very curious when you come to look at it arithmetically," was her aunt's less romantic reply. "Some of them have lost an arm in their country's service, some a leg, some an ear, some an eye——"

"And some, perhaps, *all!*" Clara murmured dreamily, as they passed the long rows of weather-beaten heroes basking in the sun. "Did you notice that very old one, with a red face, who was drawing a map in the dust with his wooden leg, and all the others watching? I *think* it was a plan of a battle——"

"The Battle of Trafalgar, no doubt," her aunt interrupted briskly.

"Hardly that, I think," Clara ventured to say. "You see, in that case, he couldn't well be alive——"

"Couldn't well be alive!" the old lady contemptuously repeated. "He's as lively as you and me put together! Why, if drawing a map in the dust—with one's wooden leg—doesn't prove one to be alive, perhaps you'll kindly mention what *does* prove it!"

Clara did not see her way out of it. Logic had never been her forte.

"To return to the arithmetic," Mad Mathesis resumed —the eccentric old lady never let slip an opportunity of driving her niece into a calculation—"what percentage do you suppose must have lost all four—a leg, an arm, an eye, and an ear?"

"How *can* I tell?" gasped the terrified girl. She knew well what was coming.

"You ca'n't, of course, without data," her aunt replied: "but I'm just going to give you——"

"Give her a Chelsea bun, miss! That's what most young ladies like best!" The voice was rich and musical, and the speaker dexterously whipped back the snowy cloth that covered his basket, and disclosed a tempting array of the familiar square buns, joined together in rows, richly egged and browned, and glistening in the sun.

"No, sir! I shall give her nothing so indigestible! Be off!" The old lady waved her parasol threateningly: but nothing seemed to disturb the good humour of the jolly old man, who marched on, chanting his melodious refrain:

Chel - sea buns! Chel-sea buns hot! Chel - sea buns!

Pi - ping hot! Chel - sea buns hot! Chel - sea buns!

"Far too indigestible, my love!" said the old lady. "Percentages will agree with you ever so much better!"

Clara sighed, and there was a hungry look in her eyes as she watched the basket lessening in the distance; but she meekly listened to the relentless old lady, who at once proceeded to count off the data on her fingers.

"Say that 70 per cent have lost an eye—75 per cent an ear—80 per cent an arm—85 per cent a leg—that'll do it beautifully. Now, my dear, what percentage, *at least*, must have lost all four?"

No more conversation occurred—unless a smothered exclamation of, "Piping hot!" which escaped from Clara's lips as the basket vanished round a corner could be counted as such—until they reached the old Chelsea mansion, where Clara's father was then staying, with his three sons and their old tutor.

Balbus, Lambert, and Hugh had entered the house

only a few minutes before them. They had been out walking, and Hugh had been propounding a difficulty which had reduced Lambert to the depths of gloom, and had even puzzled Balbus.

"It changes from Wednesday to Thursday at midnight, doesn't it?" Hugh had begun.

"Sometimes," said Balbus cautiously.

"Always," said Lambert decisively.

"*Sometimes*," Balbus gently insisted. "Six midnights out of seven, it changes to some other name."

"I meant, of course," Hugh corrected, "when it *does* change from Wednesday to Thursday, it does it at midnight—and *only* at midnight."

"Surely," said Balbus. Lambert was silent.

"Well, now, suppose it's midnight here in Chelsea. Then it's Wednesday *west* of Chelsea (say in Ireland or America), where midnight hasn't arrived yet: and it's Thursday *east* of Chelsea (say in Germany or Russia), where midnight has just passed by?"

"Surely," Balbus said again. Even Lambert nodded his time.

"But it isn't midnight anywhere else; so it ca'n't be changing from one day to another anywhere else. And yet, if Ireland and America and so on call it Wednesday, and Germany and Russia and so on call it Thursday, there *must* be some place—not Chelsea—that has different days on the two sides of it. And the worst of it is, the people *there* get their days in the wrong order: they've got Wednesday *east* of them, and Thursday *west*—just as if their day had changed from Thursday to Wednesday!"

"I've heard that puzzle before!" cried Lambert. "And I'll tell you the explanation. When a ship goes round the world from east to west, we know that it loses a day in its reckoning: so that when it gets home and calls its day Wednesday, it finds people here calling it Thursday, because we've had one more midnight than the ship has had. And when you go the other way round you gain a day."

"I know all that," said Hugh, in reply to this not very

lucid explanation: "but it doesn't help me, because the ship hasn't proper days. One way round, you get more than twenty-four hours to the day, and the other way you get less: so of course the names get wrong: but people that live on in one place always get twenty-four hours to the day."

"I suppose there *is* such a place," Balbus said, meditatively, "though I never heard of it. And the people must find it queer, as Hugh says, to have the old day *east* of them, and the new one *west*: because, when midnight comes round to them, with the new day in front of it and the old one behind it, one doesn't see exactly what happens. I must think it over."

So they had entered the house in the state I have described—Balbus puzzled, and Lambert buried in gloomy thought.

"Yes, m'm, Master *is* at home, m'm," said the stately old butler. (N.B.—It is only a butler of experience who can manage a series of three M's together, without any interjacent vowels.) "And the *ole* party is a-waiting for you in the libery."

"I don't like his calling your father an *old* party," Mad Mathesis whispered to her niece, as they crossed the hall. And Clara had only just time to whisper in reply, "He meant the *whole* party," before they were ushered into the library, and the sight of the five solemn faces there assembled chilled her into silence.

Her father sat at the head of the table, and mutely signed to the ladies to take the two vacant chairs, one on each side of him. His three sons and Balbus completed the party. Writing materials had been arranged round the table, after the fashion of a ghostly banquet: the butler had evidently bestowed much thought on the grim device. Sheets of quarto paper, each flanked by a pen on one side and a pencil on the other, represented the plates —penwipers did duty for rolls of bread—while ink-bottles stood in the places usually occupied by wine-glasses. The *pièce de résistance* was a large green baize bag, which gave forth, as the old man restlessly lifted it from side to side, a charming jingle, as of innumerable golden guineas.

"Sister, daughter, sons—and Balbus——" the old man began, so nervously that Balbus put in a gentle "Hear, hear!" while Hugh drummed on the table with his fists. This disconcerted the unpractised orator. "Sister——" he began again, then paused a moment, moved the bag to the other side, and went on with a rush, "I mean—this being—a critical occasion—more or less—being the year when one of my sons comes of age——" he paused again in some confusion, having evidently got into the middle of his speech sooner than he intended: but it was too late to go back. "Hear, hear!" cried Balbus. "Quite so," said the old gentleman, recovering his self-possession a little: "when first I began this annual custom—my friend Balbus will correct me if I am wrong——" (Hugh whispered, "With a strap!" but nobody heard him except Lambert, who only frowned and shook his head at him) "—this annual custom of giving each of my sons as many guineas as would represent his age—it was a critical time—so Balbus informed me—as the ages of two of you were together equal to that of the third—so on that occasion I made a speech——" He paused so long that Balbus thought it well to come to the rescue with the words, "It was a most——" but the old man checked him with a warning look: "yes, made a speech," he repeated. "A few years after that, Balbus pointed out—I say pointed out——" ("Hear, hear!" cried Balbus. "Quite so," said the grateful old man.) "—that it was *another* critical occasion. The ages of two of you were together *double* that of the third. So I made another speech—another speech. And now again it's a critical occasion—so Balbus says—and I am making——" (here Mad Mathesis pointedly referred to her watch) "all the haste I can!" the old man cried, with wonderful presence of mind. "Indeed, sister, I'm coming to the point now! The number of years that have passed since that first occasion is just two-thirds of the numbers of guineas I then gave you.

Now, my boys, calculate your ages from the data, and you shall have the money!"

"But we *know* our ages!" cried Hugh.

"Silence, sir!" thundered the old man, rising to his full height (he was exactly five-foot five) in his indignation. "I say you must use the data only! You mustn't even assume *which* it is that comes of age!" He clutched the bag as he spoke, and with tottering steps (it was about as much as he could do to carry it) he left the room.

"And *you* shall have a similar *cadeau*", the old lady whispered to her niece, "when you've calculated that per-centage!" And she followed her brother.

Nothing could exceed the solemnity with which the old couple had risen from the table, and yet was it—was it a *grin* with which the father turned away from his unhappy sons? Could it be—could it be a *wink* with which the aunt abandoned her despairing niece? And were those—were those sounds of suppressed *chuckling* which floated into the room, just before Balbus (who had followed them out) closed the door? Surely not: and yet the butler told the cook—but no, that was merely idle gossip, and I will not repeat it.

The shades of evening granted their unuttered petition, and "closed not o'er" them (for the butler brought in the lamp): the same obliging shades left them a "lonely bark" (the wail of a dog, in the back-yard, baying the moon) for "a while": but neither "morn, alas", nor any other epoch, seemed likely to "restore" them—to that peace of mind which had once been theirs ere ever these problems had swooped upon them, and crushed them with a load of unfathomable mystery!

"It's hardly fair," muttered Hugh, "to give us such a jumble as this to work out!"

"Fair?" Clara echoed bitterly. "Well!"

And to all my readers I can but repeat the last words of gentle Clara:

FARE-WELL!

Appendix

"A knot," said Alice. "Oh, do let me help to undo it!"

Problem.—Two travelers spend from 3 o'clock till 9 in walking along a level road, up a hill, and home again: their pace on the level being 4 miles an hour, up hill 3, and down hill 6. Find the distance walked: also (within half an hour) time of teaching top of hill.

Answer.—24 miles: half-past 6.

Solution.—A level mile takes $\frac{1}{4}$ of an hour, up hill $\frac{1}{3}$, down hill $\frac{1}{6}$. Hence to go and return over the same mile, whether on the level or on the hillside, takes $\frac{1}{2}$ an hour. Hence in 6 hours they went 12 miles out and 12 back. If the 12 miles out had been nearly all level, they would have taken a little over 3 hours; if nearly all up hill, a little under 4. Hence $3\frac{1}{2}$ hours must be within $\frac{1}{2}$ an hour of the time taken in reaching the peak; thus, as they started at 3, they got there within $\frac{1}{2}$ an hour of $\frac{1}{2}$ past 6.

Twenty-seven answers have come in. Of these, 9 are right, 16 partially right, and 2 wrong. The 16 give the *distance* correctly, but they have failed to grasp the fact that the top of the hill might have been reached at *any* moment between 6 o'clock and 7.

The two wrong answers are from GERTY VERNON and A NIHILIST. The former makes the distance "23 miles", while her revolutionary companion puts it at "27". GERTY VERNON says, "they had to go 4 miles along the plain, and got to the foot of the hill at 4 o'clock." They *might* have done so, I grant; but you have no ground for saying they *did* so. "It was $7\frac{1}{2}$ miles to the top of the hill, and they reached that at $\frac{1}{4}$ before 7 o'clock." Here you go wrong in your arithmetic, and I must, however reluctantly, bid you farewell. $7\frac{1}{2}$ miles, at 3 miles an hour, would *not* require $2\frac{3}{4}$ hours. A NIHILIST says, "Let x denote the whole number of miles; y the number of hours to hill-top;

∴ $3y$ = number of miles to hill-top, and $x - 3y$ = number of miles on the other side." You bewilder me. The other side of *what*? "Of the hill," you say. But then, how did they get home again? However, to accommodate your views we will build a new hostelry at the foot of the hill on the opposite side, and also assume (what I grant you is *possible*, though it is not *necessarily* true) that there was no level road at all. Even then you go wrong. You say:

$$"y = 6\,\frac{x - 3y}{6} \quad . \quad . \quad . \quad . \quad \text{(i)};$$

$$\frac{x}{4\frac{1}{2}} = 6 \quad . \quad . \quad . \quad . \quad . \quad \text{(ii).}"$$

I grant you (i), but I deny (ii): it rests on the assumption that to go *part* of the time at 3 miles an hour, and the rest at 6 miles an hour, comes to the same result as going the *whole* time at $4\frac{1}{2}$ miles an hour. But this would only be true if the *"part"* were in exact half, *i.e.* if they went up hill for 3 hours, and down hill for the other 3: which they certainly did *not* do.

The sixteen who are partially right, are AGNES BAILEY, F. K., FIFEE, G. E. B., H. P., KIT, M. E. T., MYSIE, A MOTHER'S SON, NAIRAM, A REDRUTHIAN, A SOCIALIST, SPEAR MAIDEN, T. B. C., VIS INERTIÆ, and YAK. Of these, F. K., FIFEE, T. B. C., and VIS INERTIÆ do not attempt the second part at all. F. K. and H. P. give no working. The rest make particular assumptions, such as that there was no level road—that there were 6 miles of level road— and so on, all leading to *particular* times being fixed for reaching the hill-top. The most curious assumption is that of AGNES BAILEY, who says, "Let x = number of hours occupied in ascent; then $\frac{x}{2}$ = hours occupied in descent; and $\frac{4x}{3}$ = hours occupied on the level." I suppose you were thinking of the relative *rates*, up hill and on the level; which we might express by saying that, if they went x miles up hill in a certain time, they would go $\dfrac{4x}{3}$ miles on the level *in the same time*. You have, in fact, assumed that they took *the same time* on the level that they took in ascending the hill. FIFEE assumed that, when the aged knight said they had gone "four miles in the hour" on the level, he meant that four miles was the *distance* gone, not merely the rate. This would have been—if FIFEE will excuse the slang expression—a "sell", ill-suited to the dignity of the hero.

And now, "descend, ye classic Nine!" who have solved the whole problem, and let me sing your praises. Your names are BLITHE, E. W., L. B., A MARLBOROUGH BOY, O. V. L., PUTNEY WALKER, ROSE, SEA-BREEZE, SIMPLE SUSAN, and MONEY-SPINNER. (These last two I count as one, as they send a joint answer.) ROSE and SIMPLE SUSAN and Co. do not actually state that the hill-top was reached sometime between 6 and 7, but, as they have clearly grasped the fact that a mile, ascended and descended, took the same time as two level miles, I mark them as "right". A MARLBOROUGH BOY and PUTNEY WALKER deserve honourable mention for their algebraic solutions, being the only two who have perceived that the question leads to *an indeterminate equation*. E. W. brings a charge of untruthfulness against the aged knight—a serious charge, for he was the very pink of chivalry! She says, "According to the data given, the time at the summit affords no clue to the total distance. It does not enable us to state precisely to an inch how much level and how much hill there was on the road." "Fair damsel," the aged knight replies, "—if, as I surmise, thy initials denote Early Womanhood—bethink thee that the word 'enable' is thine, not mine. I did but ask the time of reaching the hill-top as my *condition* for further parley. If *now* thou wilt not grant that I am a truth-loving man, then will I affirm that those same initials denote Envenomed Wickedness!"

CLASS LIST

I

A MARLBOROUGH BOY. PUTNEY WALKER.

II

BLITHE.	ROSE.
E. W.	SEA-BREEZE.
L. B.	SIMPLE SUSAN.
O. V. L.	MONEY-SPINNER.

BLITHE has made so ingenious an addition to the problem, and SIMPLE SUSAN and Co. have solved it in such tuneful verse, that I record both their answers in full. I have altered a word or two in BLITHE's—which I trust she will excuse; it did not seem quite clear as it stood.

"Yet say," said the youth, as a gleam of inspiration lighted up the relaxing muscles of his quiescent features. "Stay. Methinks it matters little *when* we reached that summit, the crown of our toil. For in the space of time wherein we clambered up one mile and bounded down the same on our return, we could have trudged the *twain* on the level. We have plodded, then, four-and-twenty miles in these six mortal hours; for never a moment did we stop for catching of fleeting breath or for gazing on the scene around!"

"Very good," said the old man. "Twelve miles out and twelve miles in. And we reached the top sometime between six and seven of the clock. Now mark me! For every five minutes that had fled since six of the clock when we stood on yonder peak, so many miles had we toiled upwards on the dreary mountain-side!"

The youth moaned and rushed into the hostel.

BLITHE.

The elder and the younger knight
　They sallied forth at three;
How far they went on level ground
　It matters not to me;

What time they reached the foot of hill,
　When they began to mount,
Are problems which I hold to be
　Of very small account.

The moment that each waved his hat
　Upon the topmost peak—
To trivial query such as this
　No answer will I seek.
Yet can I tell the distance well
　They must have travelled o'er:
On hill and plain, 'twixt three and nine,
　The miles were twenty-four.

Four miles an hour their steady pace
　Along the level track,
Three when they climbed—but six when they
　Came swiftly striding back
Adown the hill; and little skill
　It needs, methinks, to show,
Up hill and down together told,
　Four miles an hour they go.

For whether long or short the time
　Upon the hill they spent,
Two thirds were passed in going up,
　One third in the descent.
Two thirds at three, one third at six,
　If rightly reckoned o'er,
Will make one whole at four—the tale
　Is tangled now no more.

SIMPLE SUSAN.
MONEY-SPINNER.

ANSWERS TO KNOT II

§ I. THE DINNER PARTY

Problem.—The Governor of Kgovjni wants to give a very small dinner party, and invites his father's brother-in-law, his brother's father-in-law, his father-in-law's brother, and his brother-in-law's father. Find the number of guests.

Answer.—One.

In this genealogy, males are denoted by capitals, and females by small letters.

The Governor is E and his guest is C.

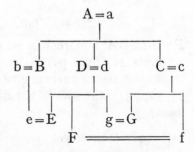

Ten answers have been received. Of these, one is wrong, GALANTHUS NIVALIS MAJOR, who insists on inviting *two* guests, one being the Governor's *wife's brother's father*. If she had taken his *sister's husband's father* instead, she would have found it possible to reduce the guests to *one*.

Of the nine who send right answers, SEA-BREEZE is the very faintest breath that ever bore the name! She simply states that the Governor's uncle might fulfil all the conditions "by intermarriages"! "Wind of the western sea", you have had a very narrow escape! Be thankful to appear in the Class List at all! BOG-OAK and BRADSHAW OF THE FUTURE use genealogies which require 16 people instead of 14, by inviting the Governor's *father's sister's husband* instead of his *father's wife's brother*. I cannot think this so good a solution as one that requires only 14. CAIUS and VALENTINE deserve special mention as the only two who have supplied genealogies.

CLASS LIST

I

| BEE. | M. M. | OLD CAT. |
| CAIUS. | MATTHEW MATTICKS. | VALENTINE. |

II

| BOG-OAK. | BRADSHAW OF THE FUTURE. |

III

SEA-BREEZE.

§ 2. THE LODGINGS

Problem.—A Square has 20 doors on each side, which contains 21 equal parts. They are numbered all round, beginning at one corner. From which of the four, Nos. 9, 25, 52, 73, is the sum of the distances, to the other three, least?

Answer.—From No. 9.

$$\begin{array}{|ccc|}
\hline
\multicolumn{3}{c}{A} \\
9 & .\ 12 & 5 \\
8 & & \\
& & \cdot B \\
D\cdot & & \\
13 & & 16 \\
9. & & 12 \\
\hline
\multicolumn{3}{c}{C} \\
\end{array}$$

Let A be No. 9, B No. 25, C No. 52, and D No. 73.

Then $AB = \sqrt{(12^2 + 5^2)} = \sqrt{169} = 13;$

$\quad AC = 21;$

$\quad AD = \sqrt{(9^2 + 8^2)} = \sqrt{145} = 12 +$
$\qquad$ (N.B. *i.e.*, "between 12 and 13")

$\quad BC = \sqrt{(16^2 + 12^2)} = \sqrt{400} = 20;$

$\quad BD = \sqrt{(3^2 + 21^2)} = \sqrt{450} = 21 +;$

$\quad CD = \sqrt{(9^2 + 13^2)} = \sqrt{250} = 15 +;$

Hence the sum of distances from A is between 46 and 47; from B, between 54 and 55; from C, between 56 and 57; from D, between 48 and 51. (Why not "between 48 and 49"? Make this out for yourselves.) Hence the sum is least for A.

Twenth-five solutions have been received. Of these, 15 must be marked "zero", 5 are partly right, and 5 right.

Of the 15, I may dismiss ALPHABETICAL PHANTOM, BOG-OAK, DINAH MITE, FIFEE, GALANTHUS NIVALIS MAJOR (I fear the cold spring has blighted our SNOWDROP), GUY, H.M.S. PINAFORE, JANET, and VALENTINE with the simple remark that they insist on the unfortunate lodgers *keeping to the pavement*. (I used the words "crossed to Number Seventy-three" for the special purpose of showing that *short cuts* were possible.) SEA-BREEZE does the same, and adds that "the result would be the same" even if they crossed the Square, but gives no proof of this. M. M. draws a diagram, and says that No. 9 is the house, "as the diagram shows". I cannot see *how* it does so. OLD CAT assumes that the house *must* be No. 9 or No. 73. She does not explain how she estimates the distances. BEE's arithmetic is faulty: she makes $\sqrt{169} + \sqrt{442} + \sqrt{130} = 741$. (I suppose you mean $\sqrt{742}$, which would be a little nearer the truth. But roots cannot be added in this manner. Do you think $\sqrt{9} + \sqrt{16}$ is 25, or even $\sqrt{25}$?) But AYR's state is more perilous still: she draws illogical conclusions with a frightful calmness. After pointing out (rightly) that AC is less than BD, she says, "therefore the nearest house to the other three must be A or C." And again, after pointing out (rightly) that B and D are both within the half-square containing A, she says, "therefore" AB + AD must be less than BC + CD. (There is no logical force in either "therefore". For the first, try Nos. 1, 21, 60, 70: this will make your premiss true, and your conclusion false. Similarly, for the second, try Nos. 1, 30, 51, 71.)

Of the five partly-right solutions, RAGS AND TATTERS and MAD HATTER (who send one answer between them) make No. 25 6 units from the corner instead of 5. CHEAM, E. R. D. L., and MEGGY POTTS leave openings at the corners of the Square, which are not in the data: moreover CHEAM gives values for the distances without any hint that they are only *approximations*. CROPHI AND MOPHI make the bold and unfounded assumption that there were really 21 houses on each side, instead of 20 as stated by

Balbus. "We may assume", they add, "that the doors of Nos. 21, 42, 63, 84, are invisible from the centre of the Square"! What is there, I wonder, that CROPHI AND MOPHI would *not* assume?

Of the five who are wholly right, I think BRADSHAW OF THE FUTURE, CAIUS, CLIFTON C., and MARTREB deserve special praise for their full *analytical* solutions. MATTHEW MATTICKS picks out No. 9, and proves it to be the right house in two ways, very neatly and ingeniously, but *why* he picks it out does not appear. It is an excellent *synthetical* proof, but lacks the analysis which the other four supply.

CLASS LIST

I

BRADSHAW OF THE FUTURE.
CAIUS.
CLIFTON C.
MARTREB.

II

MATTHEW MATTICKS.

III

CHEAM.	MEGGY POTTS.
CROPHI AND MOPHI.	⎰RAGS AND TATTERS.
E. R. D. L.	⎱MAD HATTER.

A remonstrance has reached me from SCRUTATOR on the subject of Knot I, which he declares was "no problem at all". "Two questions", he says, "are put. To solve one there is no data: the other answers itself." As to the first point, SCRUTATOR is mistaken; there *are* (not "is") data sufficient to answer the question. As to the other, it is interesting to know that the question "answers itself", and I am sure it does the question great credit: still I fear

I cannot enter it on the list of winners, as this competition is only open to human beings.

Problem.—(1) Two travelers, starting at the same time, went opposite ways round a circular railway. Trains start each way every 15 minutes, the easterly ones going round in 3 hours, the westerly in 2. How many trains did each meet on the way, not counting trains met at the terminus itself? (2) They went round, as before, each traveler counting as "one" the train containing the other traveler. How many did each meet?

Answers.—(1) 19. (2) The easterly traveler met 12; the other 8.

The trains one way took 180 minutes, the other way 120. Let us take the l.c.m., 360, and divide the railway into 360 units. Then one set of trains went at the rate of 2 units a minute and at intervals of 30 units; the other at the rate of 3 units a minute and at intervals of 45 units. An easterly train starting has 45 units between it and the first train it will meet: it does $\frac{2}{5}$ of this while the other does $\frac{3}{5}$, and thus meets it at the end of 18 units, and so all the way round. A westerly train starting has 30 units between it and the first train it will meet: it does $\frac{3}{5}$ of this while the other does $\frac{2}{5}$, and thus meets it at the end of 18 units, and so all the way round. Hence if the railway be divided, by 19 posts, into 20 parts, each containing 18 units, trains meet at every post, and, in (1) each traveler passes 19 posts in going round, and so meets 19 trains. But, in (2), the easterly traveler only begins to count after traversing $\frac{2}{5}$ of the journey, *i.e.* on reaching the 8th post, and so counts 12 posts: similarly, the other counts 8. They meet at the end of $\frac{2}{5}$ of 3 hours, or $\frac{3}{5}$ of 2 hours, *i.e.* 72 minutes.

Forty-five answers have been received. Of these, 12 are beyond the reach of discussion, as they give no working.

I can but enumerate their names, ARDMORE, E. A., F. A. D., L. D., MATTHEW MATTICKS, M. E. T., POO-POO, and THE RED QUEEN are all wrong. BETA and ROWENA have got (1) right and (2) wrong. CHEEKY BOB and NAIRAM give the right answers, but it may perhaps make the one less cheeky, and induce the other to take a less inverted view of things, to be informed that, if this had been a competition for a prize, they would have got no marks. (N.B.—I have not ventured to put E. A.'s name in full, as she only gave it provisionally, in case her answer should prove right.)

Of the 33 answers for which the working is given, 10 are wrong; 11 half-wrong and half-right; 3 right, except that they cherish the delusion that it was *Clara* who traveled in the easterly train—a point which the data do not enable us to settle; and 9 wholly right.

The 10 wrong answers are from BO-PEEP, FINANCIER, I. W. T., KATE B., M. A. H., Q. Y. Z., SEA-GULL, THISTLE-DOWN, TOM-QUAD, and an unsigned one. BO-PEEP rightly says that the easterly traveler met all trains which started during the 3 hours of her trip, as well as all which started during the previous 2 hours, *i.e.* all which started at the commencements of 20 periods of 15 minutes each; and she is right in striking out the one she met at the moment of starting; but wrong in striking out the *last* train, for she did not meet this at the terminus, but 15 minutes before she got there. She makes the same mistake in (2). FINANCIER thinks that any train, met for the second time, is not to be counted. I. W. T. finds, by a process which is not stated, that the travelers met at the end of 71 minutes and 26½ seconds. KATE B. thinks the trains which are met on starting and on arriving are *never* to be counted, even when met elsewhere. Q. Y. Z. tries a rather complex algebraic solution, and succeeds in finding the time of meeting correctly: all else is wrong. SEA-GULL seems to think that, in (1), the easterly train *stood still* for 3 hours; and says that, in (2) the travelers meet at the end of 71 minutes 40 seconds. THISTLEDOWN nobly confesses to having tried no calculation, but merely having drawn a picture of the railway and counted the trains; in (1) she counts wrong; in (2) she makes them meet in 75 minutes. TOM-QUAD omits (1); in (2) he makes Clara count the train she met on her arrival. The unsigned one is also unintelligible; it states that the travelers go "$\frac{1}{24}$ more than the total distance to be traversed"! The "Clara" theory, already referred to, is adopted by 5 of these, *viz.*, BO-PEEP, FINANCIER, KATE B., TOM-QUAD, and the nameless writer.

The 11 half-right answers are from BOG-OAK, BRIDGET, CASTOR, CHESHIRE CAT, G. E. B., GUY, MARY, M. A. H., OLD MAID, R. W., and VENDREDI. All these adopt the "Clara" theory. CASTOR omits (1). VENDREDI gets (1) right, but in (2) makes the same mistake as BO-PEEP. I notice in your solution a marvellous proportion-sum: "300 miles : 2 hours :: one mile : 24 seconds." May I venture to advise your acquiring, as soon as possible, an utter disbelief in the possibility of a ratio existing between *miles* and *hours*? Do not be disheartened by your two friends' sarcastic remarks on your "roundabout ways". Their short method, of adding 12 and 8, has the slight disadvantage of bringing the answer wrong: even a "roundabout" method is better than *that*! M. A. H., in (2), makes the travelers count "one" *after* they met, not *when* they met. CHESHIRE CAT and OLD MAID get "20" as answer for (1), by forgetting to strike out the train met on arrival. The others all get "18" in various ways. BOG-OAK, GUY, and R. W. divide the trains which the westerly traveler has to meet into 2 sets, *viz.*, those already on the line, which they (rightly) make "11", and those which started during her 2 hours' journey (exclusive of train met on arrival), which they (wrongly) make "7"; and they make a similar mistake with the easterly train. BRIDGET (rightly) says that the westerly traveler met a train every 6 minutes for 2 hours, but (wrongly) makes the number "20"; it should be "21". G. E. B. adopts BO-PEEP's method, but (wrongly) strikes out (for the easterly traveler) the train which started at the *commencement* of the previous 2 hours. MARY thinks a train met on arrival must not be counted, even when met on a *previous* occasion.

The 3 who are wholly right but for the unfortunate "Clara" theory, are F. LEE, G. S. C., and X. A. B.

And now "descend, ye classic ten!" who have solved the whole problem. Your names are AIX-LES-BAINS, ALGERNON BRAY (thanks for a friendly remark, which comes with a heart-warmth that not even the Atlantic could chill), ARVON, BRADSHAW OF THE FUTURE, FIFEE, H. L. R., J. L. O., OMEGA, S. S. G., and WAITING FOR THE TRAIN. Several of these have put Clara, provisionally, into the easterly train: but they seem to have understood that the data do not decide that point.

CLASS LIST

I

AIX-LES-BAINS.	H. L. R.
ALGERNON BRAY.	OMEGA.
BRADSHAW OF THE FUTURE.	S. S. G.
FIFEE.	WAITING FOR THE TRAIN.

II

ARVON.   J. L. O.

III

F. LEE.   G. S. C.   X. A. B.

ANSWERS TO KNOT IV

Problem.—There are 5 sacks, of which Nos. 1, 2, weigh 12 lbs.; Nos. 2, 3, $13\frac{1}{2}$ lbs.; Nos. 3, 4, $11\frac{1}{2}$ lbs.; Nos. 4, 5, 8 lbs.; Nos. 1, 3, 5, 16 lbs. Required the weight of each sack.

Answer.—$5\frac{1}{2}$, $6\frac{1}{2}$, 7, $4\frac{1}{2}$, $3\frac{1}{2}$.

The sum of all the weighings, 61 lbs., includes sack No. 3 *thrice* and each other *twice*. Deducting twice the sum of the 1st and 4th weighings, we get 21 lbs. for *thrice* No. 3, *i.e.* 7 lbs. for No. 3. Hence, the 2nd and 3rd weighings give 6½ lbs., 4½ lbs. for Nos. 2, 4; and hence again, the 1st and 4th weighings give 5½ lbs., 3½ lbs., for Nos. 1, 5.

Ninety-seven answers have been received. Of these, 15 are beyond the reach of discussion, as they give no working. I can but enumerate their names, and I take this opportunity of saying that this is the last time I shall put on record the names of competitors who give no sort of clue to the process by which their answers were obtained. In guessing a conundrum, or in catching a flea, we do not expect the breathless victor to give us afterwards, in cold blood, a history of the mental or muscular efforts by which he achieved success; but a mathematical calculation is another thing. The names of this "mute inglorious" band are COMMON SENSE, D. E. R., DOUGLAS, E. L., ELLEN, I. M. T., J. M. C., JOSEPH, KNOT I, LUCY, MEEK, M. F. C., PYRAMUS, SHAH, VERITAS.

Of the eighty-two answers with which the working, or some approach to it, is supplied, one is wrong: seventeen have given solutions which are (from one cause or another) practically valueless: the remaining sixty-four I shall try to arrange in a Class List, according to the varying degrees of shortness and neatness to which they seem to have attained.

The solitary wrong answer is from NELL. To be thus "alone in a crowd" is a distinction—a painful one, no doubt, but still a distinction. I am sorry for you, my dear young lady, and I seem to hear your tearful exclamation, when you read these lines, "Ah! This is the knell of all my hopes!" Why, oh why, did you assume that the 4th and 5th bags weighed 4 lbs. each? And why did you not test your answers? However, please try again: and please don't change your *nom-de-plume*: let us have NELL in the First Class next time!

The seventeen whose solutions are practically valueless are ARDMORE, A READY RECKONER, ARTHUR, BOG-LARK, BOG-OAK, BRIDGET, FIRST ATTEMPT, J. L. C., M. E. T.,

Rose, Rowena, Sea-Breeze, Sylvia, Thistledown, Three-Fifths Asleep, Vendredi, and Winifred. Bog-Lark tries it by a sort of "rule of false", assuming experimentally that Nos. 1, 2, weigh 6 lbs. each, and having thus produced $17\frac{1}{2}$, instead of 16, as the weight of 1, 3, and 5, she removes "the superfluous pound and a half", but does not explain how she knows from which to take it. Three-Fifths Asleep says that (when in that peculiar state) "it seemed perfectly clear" to her that, "3 out of the 5 sacks being weighed twice over, $\frac{3}{5}$ of $45 = 27$, must be the total weight of the 5 sacks." As to which I can only say, with the Captain, "it beats me entirely!" Winifred, on the plea that "one must have a starting-point", assumes (what I fear is a mere guess) that No. 1 weighed $5\frac{1}{2}$ lbs. The rest all do it, wholly or partly, by guess-work.

The problem is of course (as any algebraist sees at once) a case of "simultaneous simple equations". It is, however, easily soluble by arithmetic only; and, when this is the case, I hold that it is bad workmanship to use the more complex method. I have not, this time, given more credit to arithmetical solutions; but in future problems I shall (other things being equal) give the highest marks to those who use the simplest machinery. I have put into Class I those whose answers seemed specially short and neat, and into Class III those that seemed specially long or clumsy. Of this last set, A. C. M., Furze-Bush, James, Partridge, R. W., and Waiting for the Train, have sent long wandering solutions, the substitutions have no definite method, but seeming to have been made to see what would come of it. Chilpome and Dublin Boy omit some of the working. Arvon Marlborough Boy only finds the weight of *one* sack.

CLASS LIST

I

| B. E. D. | Number Five. |
| C. H. | Pedro. |

Constance Johnson.
Greystead.
Guy.
Hoopoe.
J. F. A.
M. A. H.

R. E. X.
Seven Old Men.
Vis Inertiæ.
Willy B.
Yahoo.

II

American Subscriber.
An Appreciative School-ma'am.
Ayr.
Bradshaw of the Future.
Cheam.
C. M. G.
Dinah Mite.
Duckwing.
E. C. M.
E. N. Lowry.
Era.
Euroclydon.
F. H. W.
Fifee.
G. E. B.
Harlequin.
Hawthorn.
Hough Green.
J. A. B.
Jack Tar.

J. B. B.
Kgovjni.
Land Lubber.
L. D.
Magpie.
Mary.
Mhruxi.
Minnie.
Money-Spinner.
Nairam.
Old Cat.
Polichinelle.
Simple Susan.
S. S. G.
Thisbe.
Verena.
Wamba.
Wolfe.
Wykehamicus.
Y. M. A. H.

III

A. C. M.
Arvon Marleborough Boy.
Chilpome.
Dublin Boy.
Furze-Bush.

James.
Partridge.
R. W.
Waiting for the Train.

ANSWERS TO KNOT V

Problem.—To mark pictures, giving 3 ×'s to 2 or 3, 2 to 4 or 5, and 1 to 9 or 10; also giving 3 o's to 1 or 2, 2 to 3 or 4, and 1 to 8 or 9; so as to mark the smallest possible number of pictures, and to give them the largest possible number of marks.

Answer.—10 pictures; 29 marks; arranged thus:

```
×   ×   ×   ×   ×   ×   ×   ×   ×   o
×   ×   ×   ×   ×           o   o   o   o
×   ×   o   o   o   o   o   o   o   o
```

Solution.—By giving all the ×'s possible, putting into brackets the optional ones, we get 10 pictures marked thus:

```
×   ×   ×   ×   ×   ×   ×   ×   ×   (×)
×   ×   ×   ×   (×)
×   ×   (×)
```

By then assigning o's in the same way, beginning at the other end, we get 9 pictures marked thus:

```
                                (o)  o
                        (o)  o   o   o
        (o)  o   o   o   o   o   o   o
```

All we have now to do is to run these two wedges as close together as they will go, so as to get the minimum number of pictures—erasing optional marks where by so doing we can run them closer, but otherwise letting them stand. There are 10 necessary marks in the 1st row, and in the 3rd; but only 7 in the 2nd. Hence we erase all optional marks in the 1st and 3rd rows, but let them stand in the 2nd.

Twenty-two answers have been received. Of these, 11 give no working; so, in accordance with what I announced in my last review of answers, I leave them unnamed, merely mentioning that 5 are right and 6 wrong.

Of the eleven answers with which some working is

supplied, 3 are wrong. C. H. begins with the rash assertion that under the given conditions "the sum is impossible. For", he or she adds (these initialed correspondents
are dismally vague beings to deal with: perhaps "it"
would be a better pronoun), "10 is the least possible number of pictures" (granted): "therefore we must either
give 2 × 's to 6, or 2 o's to 5". Why "must," O alphabetical
phantom? It is nowhere ordained that every picture
"must" have 3 marks! FIFEE sends a folio page of solution, which deserved a better fate: she offers three answers,
in each of which 10 pictures are marked, with 30 marks;
in one she gives 2 × 's to 6 pictures; in another to 7; in
the third she gives 2 o's to 5; thus in every case ignoring
the conditions. (I pause to remark that the condition "2
× 's to 4 or 5 pictures" can only mean "*either* to 4 *or else*
to 5": if, as one competitor holds, it might mean *any*
number not less than 4, the words "*or* 5" would be superfluous.) I. E. A. (I am happy to say that none of these
bloodless phantoms appear this time in the class-list. Is
it IDEA with the "D" left out?) gives 2 × 's to 6 pictures.
She then takes me to task for using the word "ought"
instead of "nought". No doubt, to one who thus rebels
against the rules laid down for her guidance, the word
must be distasteful. But does not I. E. A. remember the
parallel case of "adder"? That creature was originally "a
nadder": then the two words took to bandying the poor
"n" backwards and forwards like a shuttlecock, the final
state of the game being "an adder". May not "a nought"
have similarly become "an ought"? Anyhow, "oughts
and crosses" is a very old game. I don't think I ever heard
it called "noughts and crosses".

In the following Class List, I hope the solitary occupant
of III will sheathe her claws when she hears how narrow
an escape she has had of not being named at all. Her
account of the process by which she got the answer is so
meagre that, like the nursery tale of "Jack-a-Minory" (I
trust I. E. A. will be merciful to the spelling), it is scarcely
to be distinguished from "zero".

CLASS LIST

I

GUY. OLD CAT. SEA-BREEZE.

II

AYR. F. LEE.
BRADSHAW OF THE FUTURE. H. VERNON.

III

CAT.

ANSWERS TO KNOT VI

Problem 1.—*A* and *B* began the year with only £1000 apiece. They borrowed nought; they stole nought. On the next New Year's Day they had £60,000 between them. How did they do it?

Solution.—They went that day to the Bank of England· *A* stood in front of it, while *B* went round and stood behind it.

Two answers have been received, both worthy of much honour. ADDLEPATE makes them borrow "zero" and steal "zero", and uses both cyphers by putting them at the righthand end of the £1000, thus producing £100,000, which is well over the mark. But (or to express it in Latin) AT SPES INFRACTA has solved it even more ingeniously: with the first cypher she turns the "1" of the £1000 into a "9", and adds the result to the original sum, thus getting £10,000: and in this, by means of the other "zero", she turns the "1" into a "6" thus hitting the exact £60,000.

CLASS LIST

I

AT SPES INFRACTA.

II

ADDLEPATE.

Problem 2.—*L* makes 5 scarves, while *M* makes 2: *Z* makes 4, while *L* makes 3. Five scarves of *Z*'s weigh one of *L*'s; 5 of *M*'s weigh 3 of *Z*'s. One of *M*'s is as warm as 4 of *Z*'s and one of *L*'s as warm as 3 of *M*'s. Which is best, giving equal weight in the result of rapidity of work, lightness, and warmth?

Answer.—The order is *M, L, Z*.

Solution.—As to rapidity (other things being constant), *L*'s merit is to *M*'s in the ratio of 5 to 2: *Z*'s to *L*'s in the ratio of 4 to 3. In order to get one set of 3 numbers fulfilling these conditions, it is perhaps simplest to take the one that occurs *twice* as unity, and reduce the others to fractions: this gives, for *L*, *M*, and *Z*, the marks $1, \frac{2}{3}, \frac{4}{3}$. In estimating for *lightness*, we observe that the greater the weight, the less the merit, so that *Z*'s merit is to *L*'s as 5 to 1. Thus the marks for *lightness* are $\frac{1}{5}, \frac{5}{3}, 1$. And similarly, the marks for warmth are $3, 1, \frac{1}{4}$. To get the total result, we must *multiply L*'s 3 marks together, and do the same for *M* and for *Z*. The final numbers are $1 \times \frac{1}{5} \times 3, \frac{2}{3} \times \frac{5}{3} \times 1, \frac{4}{3} \times 1 \times \frac{1}{4}$; *i.e.* $\frac{3}{5}, \frac{2}{3}, \frac{1}{3}$; *i.e.* multiplying throughout by 15 (which will not alter the proportion), 9, 10, 5; showing the order of merit to be *M, L, Z*.

Twenty-nine answers have been received, of which five are right, and twenty-four wrong. These hapless ones have all (with three exceptions) fallen into the error of *adding* the proportional numbers together, for each candidate, instead of *multiplying*. *Why* the latter is right, rather than the former, is fully proved in textbooks, so I will not occupy space by stating it here: but it can be *illustrated* very easily by the case of length, breadth, and depth. Suppose *A* and *B* are rival diggers of rectangular tanks: the amount of work done is evidently measured by the number of *cubical feet* dug out. Let *A* dig a tank 10 feet long, 10 wide, 2 deep: let *B* dig one 6 feet long, 5 wide, 10 deep. The cubical contents are 200, 300; *i.e. B* is best digger in the ratio of 3 to 2. Now try marking for length, width, and depth, separately; giving a maximum mark of 10 to the best in each contest, and then *adding* the results!

Of the twenty-four malefactors, one gives no working, and so has no real claim to be named; but I break the rule for once, in deference to its success in Problem 1: he, she, or it, is ADDLEPATE. The other twenty-three may be divided into five groups.

First and worst are, I take it, those who put the rightful winner *last*; arranging them as "Lolo, Zuzu, Mimi". The names of these desperate wrong-doers are AYR, BRADSHAW OF THE FUTURE, FURZE-BUSH, and POLLUX (who send a joint answer), GREYSTEAD, GUY, OLD HEN, and SIMPLE SUSAN. The latter was *once* best of all; the Old Hen has taken advantage of her simplicity, and beguiled her with the chaff which was the bane of her own chicken-hood.

Secondly, I point the finger of scorn at those who have put the worst candidate at the top; arranging them as "Zuzu, Mimi, Lolo". They are GRÆCIA, M. M., OLD CAT, and R. E. X. " 'Tis Greece, but——"

The third set have avoided both these enormities, and have even succeeded in putting the worst last, their answer being "Lolo, Mimi, Zuzu". Their names are AYR (who also appears among the "quite too too"), CLIFTON C., F. B., FIFEE, GRIG, JANET, and MRS. SAIREY GAMP. F. B. has not fallen into the common error; she *multiplies* together the proportionate number she gets, but in getting them she goes wrong, by reckoning warmth as a *de-merit*. Possibly she is "Freshly Burnt", or comes "From Bombay". JANET and MRS. SAIREY GAMP have also avoided this error: the method they have adopted is shrouded in mystery—I scarcely feel competent to criticise it. MRS. GAMP says, "If Zuzu makes 4 while Lolo makes 3, Zuzu makes 6 while Lolo makes 5 [bad reasoning], while Mimi makes 2." From this she concludes, "Therefore Zuzu excels in speed by 1" (*i.e.* when compared with Lolo? but what about Mimi?). She then compares the 3 kinds of excellence, measured on this mystic scale. JANET takes the statement that "Lolo makes 5 while Mimi makes 2", to prove that "Lolo makes 3 while Mimi makes 1 and Zuzu 4" (worse reasoning than MRS. GAMP'S), and thence concludes that "Zuzu excels in speed by $\frac{1}{8}$"! JANET should have been ADELINE, "mystery of mysteries!"

The fourth set actually put Mimi at the top, arranging them as "Mimi, Zuzu, Lolo". They are MARQUIS AND CO., MARTREB, S. B. B. (first initial scarcely legible: *may* be meant for "J"), and STANZA.

The fifth set consists of AN ANCIENT FISH and CAMEL. These ill-assorted comrades, by dint of foot and fin, have scrambled into the right answer, but, as their method is wrong, of course it counts for nothing. Also AN ANCIENT FISH has very ancient and fishlike ideas as to *how* numbers represent merit: she says, "Lolo gains $2\frac{1}{2}$ on Mimi." Two and a half *what*? Fish, fish, art thou in thy duty?

Of the five winners I put BALBUS and THE ELDER TRAVELLER slightly below the other three—BALBUS for defective reasoning, the other for scanty working. BALBUS gives two reasons for saying that *addition* of marks is *not* the right method, and then adds, "It follows that the decision must be made by *multiplying* the marks together". This is hardly more logical than to say, "This is not Spring: *therefore* it must be Autumn".

CLASS LIST

I

DINAH MITE.   E. B. D. L.   JORAM.

II

BALBUS. THE ELDER TRAVELLER.

With regard to Knot V, I beg to express to VIS INERTIÆ and to any others, who, like her, understood the condition to be that *every* marked picture must have *three* marks, my sincere regret that the unfortunate phrase "*fill* the columns with oughts and crosses" should have caused them to waste so much time and trouble. I can only repeat that a *literal* interpretation of "fill" would seem to *me* to require that *every* picture in the gallery should be marked. VIS INERTIÆ would have been in the First Class if she had sent in the solution she now offers.

ANSWERS TO KNOT VII

Problem.—Given that one glass of lemonade, 3 sandwiches, and 7 biscuits, cost 1s. 2d.; and that one glass of lemonade, 4 sandwiches, and 10 biscuits, cost 1s. 5d.: find the cost of (1) a glass of lemonade, a sandwich, and a biscuit; and (2) 2 glasses of lemonade, 3 sandwiches, and 5 biscuits.

Answer.—(1) 8d.; (2) 1s. 7d.

Solution.—This is best treated algebraically. Let $x =$ the cost (in pence) of a glass of lemonade, y of a sandwich, and z of a biscuit. Then we have $x + 3y + 7z = 14$, and $x + 4y + 10z = 17$. And we require the values of $x + y + z$, and of $2x + 3y + 5z$. Now, from *two* equations only, we cannot find, *separately*, the values of *three* unknowns: certain *combinations* of them may, however, be found. Also we know that we can, by the help of the given equations, eliminate 2 of the 3 unknowns from the quantity whose value is required, which will then contain one only. If, then, the required value is ascertainable at all, it can only be by the 3rd unknown vanishing of itself: otherwise the problem is impossible.

Let us then eliminate lemonade and sandwiches, and reduce everything to biscuits—a state of things even more depressing than "if all the world were apple-pie"—by subtracting the 1st equation from the 2nd, which eliminates lemonade, and gives $y + 3z = 3$, or $y = 3 - 3z$; and then substituting this value of y in the 1st, which gives $x - 2z = 5$, i.e. $x = 5 + 2z$. Now if we substitute these values of x, y, in the quantities whose values are required, the first becomes $(5 + 2z) + (3 - 3z) + z$, i.e. 8: and the second becomes $2(5 + 2z) + 3(3 - 3z) + 5z$, i.e. 19. Hence the answers are (1) $8d.$, (2) $1s.$ $7d.$

The above is a *universal* method: that is, it is absolutely certain either to produce the answer, or to prove that no answer is possible. The question may also be solved by combining the quantities whose values are given, so as to form those whose values are required. This is merely a matter of ingenuity and good luck: and as it *may* fail, even when the thing is possible, and is of no use in proving it *im*possible, I cannot rank this method as equal in value with the other. Even when it succeeds, it may prove a very tedious process. Suppose the 26 competitors who have sent in what I may call *accidental* solutions, had had a question to deal with where every number contained 8 or 10 digits! I suspect it would have been a case of "silvered is the raven hair" (see *Patience*) before any solution would have been hit on by the most ingenious of them.

Forty-five answers have come in, of which 44 give, I am happy to say, some sort of *working*, and therefore deserve to be mentioned by name, and to have their virtues, or vices, as the case may be, discussed. Thirteen have made assumptions to which they have no right, and so cannot figure in the Class List, even though, in 10 of the 12 cases, the answer is right. Of the remaining 28, no less than 26 have sent in *accidental* solutions, and therefore fall short of the highest honours.

I will now discuss individual cases, taking the worst first, as my custom is.

Froggy gives no working—at least this is all he gives: after stating the given equations, he says, "Therefore the difference, 1 sandwich + 3 biscuits, = 3d.": then follow the amounts of the unknown bills, with no further hint as to how he got them. FROGGY has had a *very* narrow escape of not being named at all!

Of those who are wrong, VIS INERTIÆ has sent in a piece of incorrect working. Peruse the horrid details, and shudder! She takes x (call it "y") as the cost of a sandwich, and concludes (rightly enough) that a biscuit will cost $\frac{3-y}{3}$. She then subtracts the second equation from the first, and deduces $3y + 7 \times \frac{3-y}{3} - 4y + 10 \times \frac{3-y}{3} = 3$. By making two mistakes in this line, she brings out $y = \frac{3}{2}$. Try it again, O VIS INERTIÆ! Away with INERTIÆ: infuse a little more VIS: and you will bring out the correct (though uninteresting) result, $0 = 0$! This will show you that it is hopeless to try to coax any one of these 3 unknowns to reveal its *separate* value. The other competitor who is wrong throughout, is either J. M. C. or T. M. C.: but, whether he be a Juvenile Mis-Calculator or a True Mathematician Confused, he makes the answers 7d. and 1s. 5d. He assumes with Too Much Confidence, that biscuits were ½d. each, and that Clara paid for 8, though she only ate 7!

We will now consider the 13 whose working is wrong, though the answer is right: and, not to measure their demerits too exactly, I will take them in alphabetical order. ANITA finds (rightly) that "1 sandwich and 3 biscuits cost 3d." and proceeds, "therefore 1 sandwich = 1½d., 3 biscuits = 1½d., 1 lemonade = 6d." DINAH MITE begins like ANITA: and thence proves (rightly) that a biscuit costs less than 1d.: whence she concludes (wrongly) that it *must* cost ½d. F. C. W. is so beautifully resigned to the certainty of a verdict of "guilty", that I have hardly the heart to utter the word, without adding a "recommended to mercy owing to extenuating circumstances". But really, you know, where *are* the extenuating circumstances? She begins by assuming that lemonade is $4d$. a glass, and sandwiches $3d$. each (making with the 2 given equations, *four* conditions to be fulfilled by *three* miserable unknowns!) And, having (naturally) developed this into a contradiction, she then tries $5d$. and $2d$. with a similar result. (N.B.—*This* process might have been carried on through the whole of the Tertiary Period, without gratifying one single Megatherium.) She then, by a "happy thought", tries halfpenny biscuits, and so obtains a consistent result. This may be a good solution, viewing the problem as a conundrum: but it is *not* scientific. JANET identifies sandwiches with biscuits! "One sandwich + 3 biscuits" she makes equal to "4". Four *what*? MAYFAIR makes the astounding assertion that the equation, $s + 3b = 3$, "is evidently only satisfied by $s = \frac{3}{2}$, $b = \frac{1}{2}$"! OLD CAT believes that the assumption that a sandwich costs $1\frac{1}{2}d$. is "the only way to avoid unmanageable fractions". But *why* avoid them? Is there not a certain glow of triumph in taming such a fraction? "Ladies and gentlemen, the fraction now before you is one that for years defied all efforts of a refining nature: it was, in a word, hopelessly vulgar. Treating it as a circulating decimal (the treadmill of fractions) only made matters worse. As a last resource, I reduced it to its lowest terms, and extracted its square root!" Joking apart, let me thank OLD CAT for some very kind words of sympathy, in reference to a correspondent (whose name I am happy to say I have now forgotten) who had found fault with me as a discourteous critic. O. V. L. is beyond my comprehension. He takes the given equations as (1) and (2): thence, by the process [(2) − (1)], deduces (rightly) equation (3), *viz.*, $s + 3b = 3$: and thence again, by the process [× 3] (a hopeless mystery), deduces $3s + 4b = 4$. I have nothing to say about it: I give it up. SEA-BREEZE says, "It is immaterial to the answer" (why?) "in what proportion $3d$. is divided between the sandwich and the 3 biscuits": so she assumes $s = 1\frac{1}{2}d$., $b = \frac{1}{2}d$. STANZA is one of a very irregular metre.

At first she (like JANET) identifies sandwiches with biscuits. She then tries two assumptions ($s = 1$, $b = \frac{2}{3}$ and $s = \frac{1}{2}$, $b = \frac{5}{6}$,), and (naturally) ends in contradictions. Then she returns to the first assumption, and finds the 3 unknowns separately: *quod est absurdum*. STILETTO identifies sandwiches and biscuits, as "articles". Is the word ever used by confectioners? I fancied, "What is the next article, ma'am?" was limited to linendrapers. TWO SISTERS first assume that biscuits are 4 a penny, and then that they are 2 a penny, adding that "the answer will of course be the same in both cases". It is a dreamy remark, making one feel something like Macbeth grasping at the spectral dagger. "Is this a statement that I see before me?" If you were to say, "We both walked the same way this morning," and *I* were to say, "*One* of you walked the same way, but the other didn't," which of the three would be the most hopelessly confused? TURTLE PYATE (what *is* a Turtle Pyate, please?) and OLD CROW, who send a joint answer, and Y. Y., adopt the same method. Y. Y. gets the equation $s + 3b = 3$: and then says, "This sum must be apportioned in one of the three following ways." It *may* be, I grant you: but Y. Y. do you say "must"? I fear it is *possible* for Y. Y. to be *two* Y's. The other two conspirators are less positive: they say it "can" be so divided: but they add "either of the three prices being right"! This is bad grammar and bad arithmetic at once, O mysterious birds!

Of those who win honours, THE SHETLAND SNARK must have the Third Class all to himself. He has only answered half the question, viz. the amount of Clara's luncheon: the two little old ladies he pitilessly leaves in the midst of their "difficulty". I beg to assure him (with thanks for his friendly remarks) that entrance-fees and subscriptions are things unknown in that most economical of clubs, "The Knot-Untiers."

The authors of the 26 "accidental" solutions differ only in the number of steps they have taken between the data and the answers. In order to do them full justice I have arranged the Second Class in sections, according to the number of steps. The two Kings are fearfully deliberate! I suppose walking quick, or taking short cuts, is inconsistent with kingly dignity: but really, in reading THESEUS' solution, one almost fancied he was "marking time", and making no advance at all! The other King will, I hope, pardon me for having altered "Coal" into "Cole". King Coilus, or Coil, seems to have reigned soon after Arthur's time. Henry of Huntingdon identifies him with the King Coël who first built walls round Colchester, which was named after him. In the Chronicle of Robert of Gloucester we read:

> Aftur Kyng Aruirag, of wam we habbeth y told,
> Marius ys sone was kyng, quoynte mon & bold,
> And ys sone was aftur hym, *Coil* was ys name,
> Bothe it were quoynte men, & of noble fame.

BALBUS lays it down as a general principle that "in order to ascertain the cost of any one luncheon, it must come to the same amount upon two different assumptions". (*Query*. Should not "it" be "we"? Otherwise the *luncheon* is represented as wishing to ascertain its own cost!) He then makes two assumptions—one, that sandwiches cost nothing; the other, that biscuits cost nothing (either arrangement would lead to the shop being inconveniently crowded!)—and brings out the unknown luncheons as 8*d*. and 19*d*. on each assumption. He then concludes that this agreement of results "shows that the answers are correct". Now I propose to disprove his general law by simply giving *one* instance of its failing. One instance is quite enough. In logical language, in order to disprove a "universal affirmative", it is enough to prove its contradictory, which is a "particular negative". (I must pause for a digression on Logic, and especially on Ladies' Logic. The universal affirmative, "Everybody says he's a duck," is crushed instantly by proving the particular negative, "Peter says he's a goose," which is equivalent to "Peter does *not* say he's a duck".

And the universal negative, "Nobody calls on her," is well met by the particular affirmative, "*I* called yesterday." In short, either of two contradictories disproves the other: and the moral is that, since a particular proposition is much more easily proved than a universal one, it is the wisest course, in arguing with a lady, to limit one's *own* assertions to "particulars", and leave *her* to prove the "universal" contradictory, if she can. You will thus generally secure a *logical* victory: a *practical* victory is not to be hoped for, since she can always fall back upon the crushing remark, "*That* has nothing to do with it!"—a move for which Man has not yet discovered any satisfactory answer. Now let us return to BALBUS.) Here is my "particular negative", on which to test his rule: Suppose the two recorded luncheons to have been "2 buns, one queen-cake, 2 sausage-rolls, and a bottle of Zoëdone: total, one-and-ninepence", and "one bun, 2 queen-cakes, a sausage-roll, and a bottle of Zoëdone: total, one-and-fourpence". And suppose Clara's unknown luncheon to have been "3 buns, one queen-cake, one sausage-roll, and 2 bottles of Zoëdone": while the two little sisters had been indulging in "8 buns, 4 queen-cakes, 2 sausage-rolls, and 6 bottles of Zoëdone". (Poor souls, how thirsty they must have been!) If BALBUS will kindly try this by his principle of "two assumptions", first assuming that a bun is $1d$. and a queen-cake $2d$., and then that a bun is $3d$. and a queen-cake $3d$., he will bring out the other two luncheons, on each assumption, as "one-and-ninepence" and "four-and-tenpence" respectively, which harmony of results, he will say, "shows that the answers are correct." And yet, as a matter of fact, the buns were $2d$. each, the queen-cakes $3d$., the sausage-rolls $6d$., and the Zoëdone $2d$. a bottle: so that Clara's third luncheon had cost one-and-sevenpence, and her thirsty friends had spent four-and-fourpence!

Another remark of BALBUS I will quote and discuss: for I think that it also may yield a moral for some of my readers. He says, "It is the same thing in substance whether in solving this problem we use words and call it arithmetic, or use letters and signs and call it algebra." Now this does not appear to me a correct description of the two methods: the arithmetical method is that of "synthesis" only; it goes from one known fact to another, till it reaches its goal: whereas the algebraical method is that of "analysis"; it begins with the goal, symbolically represented, and so goes backwards, dragging its veiled victim with it, till it has reached the full daylight of known facts, in which it can tear off the veil and say, "I know you!"

Take an illustration: Your house has been broken into and robbed, and you appeal to the policeman who was on duty that night. "Well, mum, I did see a chap getting out over your garden wall: but I was a good bit off, so I didn't chase him, like. I just cut down the short way to the 'Chequers', and who should I meet but Bill Sykes, coming full split round the corner. So I just ups and says, 'My lad, you're wanted.' That's all I says. And he says, 'I'll go along quiet, Bobby,' he says, 'without the darbies,' he says." There's your *Arithmetical* policeman. Now try the other method: "I seed somebody a-running, but he was well gone or ever *I* got nigh the place. So I just took a look round in the garden. And I noticed the footmarks, where the chap had come right across your flower-beds. They was good big footmarks sure-ly. And I noticed as the left foot went down at the heel, ever so much deeper than the other. And I says to myself, 'The chap's been a big hulking chap: and he goes lame on his left foot'. And I rubs my hand on the wall where he got over, and there was soot on it, and no mistake. So I says to myself, 'Now where can I light on a big man, in the chimbley-sweep line, what's lame of one foot?' And I flashes up permiscuous: and I says, 'It's Bill Sykes!' says I." There is your *Algebraical* policeman—a higher intellectual type, to my thinking, than the other.

LITTLE JACK's solution calls for a word of praise, as he has written out what really is an algebraical proof *in words*, without representing any of his facts as equations.

If it is all his own, he will make a good algebraist in the time to come. I beg to thank SIMPLE SUSAN for some kind words of sympathy, to the same effect as those received from OLD CAT.

HECLA and MARTREB are the only two who have used a method *certain* either to produce the answer, or else to prove it impossible: so they must share between them the highest honours.

CLASS LIST

I

HECLA.   MARTREB.

II

§ 1 (*2 steps*)   § 2 (*3 steps*)—continued
ADELAIDE   THE RED QUEEN.
CLIFTON C. . . .   WALL-FLOWER.
E. K. C.
GUY.   § 3 (*4 steps*)
L'INCONNU.   HAWTHORN.
LITTLE JACK.   JORAM.
NIL DESPERANDUM.   S. S. G.
SIMPLE SUSAN.
YELLOW-HAMMER.   § 4 (*5 steps*)
WOOLLY ONE.   A STEPNEY COACH.

§ 2 (*3 steps*)   § 5 (*6 steps*)
A. A.   BAY LAUREL.
A CHRISTMAS CAROL.   BRADSHAW OF THE FUTURE.
AFTERNOON TEA.
AN APPRECIATIVE SCHOOL-   § 6 (*9 steps*)
    MA'AM.   OLD KING COLE.
BABY.
BALBUS.   § 7 (*14 steps*)
BOG-OAK.   THESEUS.

ANSWERS TO CORRESPONDENTS

I HAVE received several letters on the subjects of Knots II and VI, which lead me to think some further explanation desirable.

In Knot II, I had intended the numbering of the houses to begin at one corner of the Square, and this was assumed by most, if not all, of the competitors. TROJANUS, however, says, "Assuming, in default of any information, that the street enters the square in the middle of each side, it may be supposed that the numbering begins at a street." But surely the other is the more natural assumption?

In Knot VI, the first Problem was, of course a mere *jeu de mots*, whose presence I thought excusable in a series of Problems whose aim is to entertain rather than to instruct: but it has not escaped the contemptuous criticisms of two of my correspondents, who seem to think that Apollo is in duty bound to keep his bow always on the stretch. Neither of them has guessed it: and this is true human nature. Only the other day—the 31st of September, to be quite exact—I met my old friend Brown, and gave him a riddle I had just heard. With one great effort of his colossal mind, Brown guessed it. "Right!" said I. "Ah," said he, "it's very neat—very neat. And it isn't an answer that would occur to everybody. Very neat indeed." A few yards farther on, I fell in with Smith, and to him I propounded the same riddle. He frowned over it for a minute, and then gave it up. Meekly I faltered out the answer. "A poor thing, sir!" Smith growled, as he turned away. "A very poor thing! I wonder you care to repeat such rubbish!" Yet Smith's mind is, if possible, even more colossal than Brown's.

The second Problem of Knot VI is an example in ordinary Double Rule of Three, whose essential feature is that the result depends on the variation of several elements, which are so related to it that, if all but one be constant, it varies as that one: hence, if none be constant, it varies as their product. Thus, for example, the cubical contents of a rectangular tank vary as its length, if breadth and depth be constant, and so on; hence, if none be constant, it varies as the product of the length, breadth, and depth.

When the result is not thus connected with the varying elements, the problem ceases to be double Rule of Three and often becomes one of great complexity.

To illustrate this, let us take two candidates for a prize, A and B, who are to compete in French, German, and Italian:

(a) Let it be laid down that the result is to depend on their *relative* knowledge of each subject, so that, whether their marks, for French, be "1, 2" or "100, 200", the result will be the same: and let it also be laid down that, if they get equal marks on 2 papers, the final marks are to have the same ratio as those of the 3rd paper. This is a case of ordinary Double Rule of Three. We multiply A's 3 marks together, and do the same for B. Note that, if A gets a single "zero", his final mark is "zero", even if he gets full marks for 2 papers while B gets only one mark for each paper. This of course would be very unfair on A, though a correct solution under the given conditions.

(b) The result is to depend, as before, on *relative* knowledge; but French is to have twice as much weight as German or Italian. This is an unusual form of question. I should be inclined to say, "The resulting ratio is to be nearer to the French ratio than if we multiplied as in (a), and so much nearer that it would be necessary to use the other multipliers *twice* to produce the same result as in (a)": *e.g.*, if the French ratio were 9/10, and the others 4/9, 1/9, so that the ultimate ratio, by method (a), would be 3/45, I should multiply instead by 2/3, 1/3, giving the result, 1/5, which is nearer to 9/10 than if we had used method (a).

(c) The result is to depend on *actual* amount of knowledge of the 3 subjects collectively. Here we have to ask two questions: (1) What is to be the "unit" (*i.e.* "standard to measure by") in each subject? (2) Are these units to be of equal, or unequal, value? The usual "unit" is the knowledge shown by answering the whole paper correctly; calling this "100", all lower amounts are represented by numbers between "zero", and "100". Then, if these units are to be of equal value, we simply add A's 3 marks together, and do the same for B.

(*d*) The conditions are the same as (*c*), but French is to have double weight. Here we simply double the French marks, and add as before.

(*e*) French is to have such weight that, if other marks be equal, the ultimate ratio is to be that of the French paper, so that a "zero" in this would swamp the candidate: but the other two subjects are only to affect the result collectively, by the amount of knowledge shown, the two being reckoned of equal value. Here I should add A's German and Italian marks together, and multiply by his French mark.

But I need not go on: the problem may evidently be set with many varying conditions, each requiring its own method of solution. The Problem in Knot VI was meant to belong to variety (*a*), and to make this clear, I inserted the following passage:

"Usually the competitors differ in one point only. Thus, last year, Fifi and Gogo made the same number of scarves in the trial week, and they were equally light; but Fifi's were twice as warm as Gogo's, and she was pronounced twice as good."

What I have said will suffice, I hope, as an answer to BALBUS, who holds that (*a*) and (*c*) are the only possible varieties of the problem, and that to say, "We cannot use addition, therefore we must be intended to use multiplication," is "no more illogical than, from knowledge that one was not born in the night, to infer that he was born in the daytime"; and also to FIFEE, who says, "I think a little more consideration will show you that our 'error of *adding* the proportional numbers together for each candidate instead of *multiplying*' is no error at all." Why, even if addition *had* been the right method to use, not one of the writers (I speak from memory) showed any consciousness of the necessity of fixing a "unit" for each subject. "No error at all"! They were positively steeped in error!

One correspondent (I do not name him, as the communication is not quite friendly in tone) writes thus: "I wish to add, very respectfully, that I think it would be in better taste if you were to abstain from the very trenchant expressions which you are accustomed to indulge in when criticising the answer. That such a tone must not be" ("be not"?) "agreeable to the persons concerned who have made mistakes may possibly have no great weight with you, but I hope you will feel that it would be as well not to employ it, *unless you are quite certain of being correct yourself.*" The only instances the writer gives of the "trenchant expressions" are "hapless" and "malefactors". I beg to assure him (and any others who may need the assurance: I trust there are none) that all such words have been used in jest, and with no idea that they could possibly annoy any one, and that I sincerely regret any annoyance I may have thus inadvertently given. May I hope that in future they will recognize the distinction between severe language used in sober earnest, and the "words of unmeant bitterness", which Coleridge has alluded to in that lovely passage beginning, "A little child, a limber elf"? If the writer will refer to that passage, or to the Preface to *Fire, Famine, and Slaughter*, he will find the distinction, for which I plead, far better drawn out than I could hope to do in any words of mine.

The writer's insinuation that I care not how much annoyance I give to my readers I think it best to pass over in silence; but to his concluding remark I must entirely demur. I hold that to use language likely to annoy any of my correspondents would not be in the least justified by the plea that I was "quite certain of being correct". I trust that the knot-untiers and I are not on such terms as those!

I beg to thank G. B. for the offer of a puzzle—which, however, is too like the old one, "Make four 9's into 100."

ANSWERS TO KNOT VIII

§ 1. THE PIGS

Problem.—Place twenty-four pigs in four sties so that, as you go round and round, you may always find the number in each sty nearer to ten than the number in the last.

Answer.—Place 8 pigs in the first sty, 10 in the second, nothing in the third, and 6 in the fourth: 10 is nearer ten than 8; nothing is nearer ten than 10; 6 is nearer ten than nothing; and 8 is nearer ten than 6.

This problem is noticed by only two correspondents. BALBUS says, "It certainly cannot be solved mathematically, nor do I see how to solve it by any verbal quibble." NOLENS VOLENS makes Her Radiancy change the direction of going round; and even then is obliged to add, "the pig must be carried in front of her"!

§ 2. THE GRURMSTIPTHS

Problem.—Omnibuses start from a certain point, both ways, every 15 minutes. A traveler, starting on foot along with one of them, meets one in $12\frac{1}{2}$ minutes: when will he be overtaken by one?

Answer.—In $6\frac{1}{4}$ minutes.

Solution.—Let "a" be the distance an omnibus goes in 15 minutes, and "x" the distance from the starting-point to where the traveler is overtaken. Since the omnibus met is due at the starting-point in $2\frac{1}{2}$ minutes, it goes in that time as far as the traveler walks in $12\frac{1}{2}$, *i.e.*, it goes 5 times as fast. Now the overtaking omnibus is "a" behind the traveler when he starts, and therefore goes "$a + x$" while he goes "x". Hence $a + x = 5x$; *i.e.* $4x = a$, and $x = \frac{a}{4}$. This distance would be traversed by an omnibus in $\frac{15}{4}$ minutes, and therefore by the traveler in $5 \times \frac{15}{4}$.

Hence he is overtaken in $18\frac{3}{4}$ minutes after starting, *i.e.* in $6\frac{1}{4}$ minutes after meeting the omnibus.

Four answers have been received, of which two are wrong. DINAH MITE rightly states that the overtaking omnibus reached the point where they met the other omnibus 5 minutes after they left, but wrongly concludes that, going 5 times as fast, it would overtake them in another minute. The travelers are 5 minutes' walk ahead of the omnibus, and must walk $\frac{1}{4}$ of this distance farther before the omnibus overtakes them, which will be $\frac{1}{5}$ of the distance traversed by the omnibus in the same time: this will require $1\frac{1}{4}$ minutes more. NOLENS VOLENS tries it by a process like "Achilles and the Tortoise". He rightly states that, when the overtaking omnibus leaves the gate, the travelers are $\frac{1}{5}$ of "*a*" ahead, and that it will take the omnibus 3 minutes to traverse this distance; "during which time" the travelers, he tells us, go $\frac{1}{15}$ of "*a*" (this should be $\frac{1}{25}$). The travelers being now $\frac{1}{15}$ of "*a*" ahead, he concludes that the work remaining to be done is for the travelers to go $\frac{1}{60}$ of "*a*", while the omnibus goes $\frac{1}{12}$. The *principle* is correct, and might have been applied earlier.

CLASS LIST

I

BALBUS.   DELTA.

ANSWERS TO KNOT IX

§ 1. THE BUCKETS

Problem.—Lardner states that a solid, immersed in a fluid, displaces an amount equal to itself in bulk. How can this be true of a small bucket floating in a larger one?

Solution.—Lardner means, by "displaces", "occupies a space which might be filled with water without any change in the surroundings." If the portion of the floating bucket, which is above the water, could be annihilated, and the rest of it transformed into water, the surrounding water would not change its position: which agrees with Lardner's statement.

Five answers have been received, none of which explains the difficulty arising from the well-known fact that a floating body is the same weight as the displaced fluid. HECLA says that "Only that portion of the smaller bucket which descends below the original level of the water can be properly said to be immersed, and only an equal bulk of water is displaced." Hence, according to HECLA, a solid whose weight was equal to that of an equal bulk of water, would not float till the whole of it was below "the original level" of the water: but, as a matter of fact, it would float as soon as it was all under water. MAGPIE says the fallacy is "the assumption that one body can displace another from a place where it isn't", and that Lardner's assertion is incorrect, except when the containing vessel "was originally full to the brim". But the question of floating depends on the present state of things, not on past history. OLD KING COLE takes the same view as HECLA. TYMPANUM and VINDEX assume that "displaced" means "raised above its original level", and merely explain how it comes to pass that the water, so raised, is less in bulk than the immersed portion of bucket, and thus land themselves —or rather set themselves floating—in the same boat as HECLA.

I regret that there is no Class List to publish for this Problem.

§ 2. BALBUS'S ESSAY

Problem.—Balbus states that if a certain solid be immersed in a certain vessel of water, the water will rise through a series of distances, two inches, one inch, half an inch, etc., which series has no end. He concludes that the water will rise without limit. Is this true?

Solution.—No. This series can never reach 4 inches, since, however many terms we take, we are always short of 4 inches by an amount equal to the last term taken.

Three answers have been received—but only two seem to me worthy of honours.

TYMPANUM says that the statement about the stick "is merely a blind, to which the old answer may well be applied, *solvitur ambulando,* or rather *mergendo*". I trust TYMPANUM will not test this in his own person, by taking the place of the man in Balbus's Essay! He would infallibly be drowned.

OLD KING COLE rightly points out that the series, 2, 1, etc., is a decreasing geometrical progression: while VINDEX rightly identifies the fallacy as that of "Achilles and the Tortoise".

CLASS LIST

I

OLD KING COLE.   VINDEX.

§ 3. THE GARDEN

Problem.—An oblong garden, half a yard longer than wide, consists entirely of a gravel walk, spirally arranged, a yard wide and 3630 yards long. Find the dimensions of the garden.

Answer.—60, 60½.

Solution.—The number of yards and fractions of a yard traversed in walking along a straight piece of walk, is evidently the same as the number of square yards and fractions of a square yard contained in that piece of walk: and the distance traversed in passing through a square yard at a corner, is evidently a yard. Hence the area of the garden is 3630 square yards: *i.e.* if x be the width, $x(x + \frac{1}{2}) = 3630$. Solving this quadratic, we find $x = 60$. Hence the dimensions are 60, 60½.

Twelve answers have been received—seven right and five wrong.

C. G. L., NABOB, OLD CROW, and TYMPANUM assume that the number of yards in the length of the path is equal to the number of square yards in the garden. This is true, but should have been proved. But each is guilty of darker deeds. C. G. L.'s "working" consists of dividing 3630 by 60. Whence came this divisor, O Segiel? Divination? Or was it a dream? I fear this solution is worth noting. OLD CROW's is shorter, and so (if possible) worth rather less. He says the answer "is at once seen to be $60 \times 60\frac{1}{2}$"! NABOB's calculation is short, but "as rich as a NABOB" in error. He says that the square root of 3630, multiplied by 2, equals the length plus the breadth. That is $60 \cdot 25 \times 2 = 120\frac{1}{2}$. His first assertion is only true of a *square* garden. His second is irrelevant, since $60 \cdot 25$ is *not* the square root of 3630! Nay, Bob, this will *not* do! TYMPANUM says that, by extracting the square root of 3630, we get 60 yards with a remainder of 30/60, or half a yard, which we add so as to make the oblong $60 \times 60\frac{1}{2}$. This is very terrible: but worse remains behind. TYMPANUM proceeds thus: "But why should there be the half-yard at all? Because without it there would be no space at all for flowers. By means of it, we find reserved in the very centre a small plot of ground, two yards long by half a yard wide, the only space not occupied by walk." But Balbus expressly said that the walk "used up the whole of the area", O TYMPANUM! My tympa is exhausted: my brain is num! I can say no more.

HECLA indulges, again and again, in that most fatal of all habits in computation—the making *two* mistakes which cancel each other. She takes x as the width of the garden, in yards, and $x + \frac{1}{2}$ as its length, and makes her first "coil" the sum of $x - \frac{1}{2}$, $x - \frac{1}{2}$, $x - 1$, $x - 1$, *i.e.* $4x - 3$: but the fourth term should be $x - 1\frac{1}{2}$, so that her first coil is $\frac{1}{2}$ a yard too long. Her second coil is the sum of $x - 2\frac{1}{2}$, $x - 2\frac{1}{2}$, $x - 3$, $x - 3$: here the first term should be $x - 2$ and the last $x - 3\frac{1}{2}$: these two mistakes cancel and this coil is therefore right. And the same thing is true of every other coil but the last, which needs an extra half-yard to reach the *end* of the path: and this exactly balances the mistake in the first coil. Thus the sum-total of the coils comes right though the working is all wrong.

Of the seven who are right, DINAH MITE, JANET, MAG-PIE, and TAFFY make the same assumption as C. G. L. and Co. They then solve by a quadratic. MAGPIE also tries it by arithmetical progression, but fails to notice that the first and last "coils" have special values.

ALUMNUS ETONÆ attempts to prove what C. G. L. assumes by a particular instance, taking a garden 6 by $5\frac{1}{2}$. He ought to have proved it generally: what is true of one number is not always true of others. OLD KING COLE solves it by an arithmetical progression. It is right, but too lengthy to be worth as much as a quadratic.

VINDEX proves it very neatly, by pointing out that a yard of walk measured along the middle represents a square yard of garden, "whether we consider the straight stretches of walk or the square yards at the angles, in which the middle line goes half a yard in one direction and then turns a right angle and goes half a yard in another direction."

CLASS LIST

I

VINDEX.

II

ALUMNUS ETONÆ.   OLD KING COLE.

III

DINAH MITE.   MAGPIE.
JANET.   TAFFY.

ANSWERS TO KNOT X

§ 1. The Chelsea Pensioners

Problem.—If 70 per cent have lost an eye, 75 per cent an ear, 80 per cent an arm, 85 per cent a leg: what percentage, *at least*, must have lost all four?

Answer.—Ten.

Solution.—(I adopt that of Polar Star, as being better than my own.) Adding the wounds together, we get $70 + 75 + 80 + 85 = 310$, among 100 men; which gives 3 to each, and 4 to 10 men. Therefore the least percentage is 10.

Nineteen answers have been received. One is "5", but, as no working is given with it, it must, in accordance with the rule, remain "a deed without a name". Janet makes it "$35\frac{7}{10}$". I am sorry she has misunderstood the question, and has supposed that those who had lost an ear were 75 per cent *of those who had lost an eye*; and so on. Of course, on this supposition, the percentages must all be multiplied together. This she has done correctly, but I can give her no honours, as I do not think the question will fairly bear her interpretation. Three Score and Ten makes it "$19\frac{3}{8}$". Her solution has given me—I will not say "many anxious days and sleepless nights", for I wish to be strictly truthful, but—some trouble in making any sense at all of it. She makes the number of "pensioners wounded once" to be 310 ("per cent," I suppose!): dividing by 4, she gets $77\frac{1}{2}$ as "average percentage": again dividing by 4, she gets $19\frac{3}{8}$ as "percentage wounded four times". Does she suppose wounds of different kinds to "absorb" each other, so to speak? Then, no doubt, the data are equivalent to 77 pensioners with one wound each and a half-pensioner with a half-wound. And does she then suppose these concentrated wounds to be *transferable*, so that $\frac{3}{4}$ of these unfortunates can obtain perfect health by handing over their wounds to the remaining $\frac{1}{4}$? Granting these suppositions, her answer is right; or rather *if* the question had been, "A road is covered with one inch of gravel, along $77\frac{1}{2}$ per cent of it. How much of it could be covered 4 inches deep with the same material?" her answer *would* have been right. But alas, that *wasn't* the question! DELTA makes some most amazing assumptions: "let every one who has not lost an eye have lost an ear," "let every one who has not lost both eyes and ears have lost an arm." Her ideas of a battlefield are grim indeed. Fancy a warrior who would continue fighting after losing both eyes, both ears, and both arms! This is a case which she (or "it"?) evidently considers *possible*.

Next come eight writers who have made the unwarrantable assumption that, because 70 per cent have lost an eye, *therefore* 30 per cent have *not* lost one, so that they have *both* eyes. This is illogical. If you give me a bag containing 100 sovereigns, and if in an hour I come to you (my face *not* beaming with gratitude nearly so much as when I received the bag) to say, "I am sorry to tell you that 70 of these sovereigns are bad," do I thereby guarantee the other 30 to be good? Perhaps I have not tested them yet. The sides of this illogical octagon are as follows, in alphabetical order: ALGERNON BRAY, DINAH MITE, G. S. C., JANE E., J. D. W., MAGPIE (who makes the delightful remark, "Therefore 90 per cent have two of something," recalling to one's memory that fortunate monarch with whom Xerxes was so much pleased that "he gave him ten of everything"!), S. S. G., and TOKIO.

BRADSHAW OF THE FUTURE and T. R. do the question in a piecemeal fashion—on the principle that the 70 per cent and the 75 per cent, though commenced at opposite ends of the 100, must overlap by *at least* 45 per cent; and so on. This is quite correct working, but not, I think, quite the best way of doing it.

The other five competitors will, I hope, feel themselves sufficiently glorified by being placed in the first class, without my composing a Triumphal Ode for each!

CLASS LIST

I

OLD CAT.   POLAR STAR.
OLD HEN.   SIMPLE SUSAN.
                  WHITE SUGAR.

II

BRADSHAW OF THE FUTURE.   T. R.

III

ALGERNON BRAY.   J. D. W.
DINAH MITE.   MAGPIE.
G. S. C.   S. S. G.
JANE E.   TOKIO.

§ 2. CHANGE OF DAY

I must postpone, *sine die*, the geographical problem—partly because I have not yet received the statistics I am hoping for, and partly because I am myself so entirely puzzled by it; and when an examiner is himself dimly hovering between a second class and a third, how is he to decide the position of others?

§ 3. THE SON'S AGES

Problem.—At first, two of the ages are together equal to the third. A few years afterwards, two of them are together double of the third. When the number of years since the first occasion is two-thirds of the sum of the ages on that occasion, one age is 21. What are the other two?

Answer.—15 and 18.

Solution.—Let the ages at first be x, y, $(x+y)$. Now, if $a+b=2c$, then $(a-n)+(b-n)=2(c-n)$, whatever be the value of n. Hence the second relationship, if *ever* true, was *always* true. Hence it was true at first. But it cannot be true that x and y are together double of $(x+y)$. Hence it must be true of $(x+y)$, together with x or y; and it does not matter which we take. We assume, then, $(x+y)+x=2y$; *i.e.* $y=2x$. Hence the three ages were, at first, x, $2x$, $3x$; and the number of years since that time is two-thirds of $6x$, *i.e.* is $4x$. Hence the present ages are $5x$, $6x$, $7x$. The ages are clearly *integers*, since this is only "the year when one of my sons comes of age". Hence $7x=21$, $x=3$, and the other ages are 15, 18.

Eighteen answers have been received. One of the writers merely asserts that the first occasion was 12 years ago, that the ages were then 9, 6, and 3; and that on the second occasion they were 14, 11, and 8! As a Roman father, I *ought* to withhold the name of the rash writer; but respect for age makes me break the rule: it is THREE SCORE AND TEN. JANE E. also asserts that the ages at first were 9, 6, 3: then she calculates the present ages, leaving the *second* occasion unnoticed. OLD HEN is nearly as bad; she "tried various numbers till I found one that fitted *all* the conditions"; but merely scratching up the earth, and pecking about, is *not* the way to solve a problem, O venerable bird! And close after OLD HEN prowls, with hungry eyes, OLD CAT, who calmly assumes, to begin with, that the son who comes of age is the *eldest*. Eat your bird, Puss, for you will get nothing from me!

There are yet two zeroes to dispose of. MINERVA assumes that, on *every* occasion, a son comes of age; and that it is only such a son who is "tipped with gold". Is it wise thus to interpret, "Now, my boys, calculate your ages, and you shall have the money"? BRADSHAW OF THE FUTURE says "let" the ages at first be 9, 6, 3, then assumes that the second occasion was 6 years afterwards, and on these baseless assumptions brings out the right answers. Guide *future* travelers, an thou wilt; thou art no Bradshaw for *this* Age!

Of those who win honours, the merely "honourable"

are two. DINAH MITE ascertains (rightly) the relationship between the three ages at first, but then *assumes* one of them to be "6", thus making the rest of her solution tentative. M. F. C. does the algebra all right up to the conclusion that the present ages are $5z$, $6z$, and $7z$; it then assumes, without giving any reason, that $7z = 21$.

Of the more honourable, DELTA attempts a novelty— to discover *which* son comes of age by elimination: it assumes, successively, that it is the middle one, and that it is the youngest; and in each case it *apparently* brings out an absurdity. Still, as the proof contains the following bit of algebra: "$63 = 7x + 4y$; $\therefore$ $21 = x + 4/7$ of y," I trust it will admit that its proof is not *quite* conclusive. The rest of its work is good. MAGPIE betrays the deplorable tendency of her tribe—to appropriate any stray conclusion she comes across, without having any *strict* logical right to it. Assuming A, B, C, as the ages at first, and E as the number of the years that have elapsed since then, she finds (rightly) the 3 equations, $2A = B$, $C = B + A$, $D = 2B$. She then says, "Supposing that $A = 1$, then $B = 2$, $C = 3$, and $D = 4$. Therefore for A, B, C, D, four numbers are wanted which shall be to each other as 1:2:3:4." It is in the "therefore" that I detect the unconscientiousness of this bird. The conclusion *is* true, but this is only because the equations are "homogeneous" (*i.e.* having one "unknown" in each term), a fact which I strongly suspect had not been grasped—I beg pardon, clawed—by her. Were I to lay this little pitfall: "$A + 1 = B$, $B + 1 = C$; supposing $A = 1$, then $B = 2$, and $C = 3$. *Therefore* for A, B, C, three numbers are wanted which shall be to one another as 1:2:3," would you not flutter down into it, O MAGPIE! as amiably as a Dove? SIMPLE SUSAN is anything but simple to *me*. After ascertaining that the 3 ages at first are as 3:2:1, she says, "Then, as two-thirds of their sum, added to one of them, $= 21$, the sum cannot exceed 30, and consequently the highest cannot exceed 15." I suppose her (mental) argument is something like this: "Two-thirds of sum, $+$ one age, $= 21$; $\therefore$ sum, $+3$ halves of one age,

$= 31\frac{1}{2}$. But 3 halves of one age cannot be less than $1\frac{1}{2}$ [here I perceive that SIMPLE SUSAN would on no account present a guinea to a newborn baby!]; hence the sum cannot exceed 30." This is ingenious, but her proof, after that, is (as she candidly admits) "clumsy and round-about". She finds that there are 5 possible sets of ages, and eliminates four of them. Suppose that, instead of 5, there had been 5 million possible sets! Would SIMPLE SUSAN have courageously ordered in the necessary gallon of ink and ream of paper?

The solution sent in by C. R. is, like that of SIMPLE SUSAN, partly tentative, and so does not rise higher than being Clumsily Right.

Among those who have earned the highest honours, ALGERNON BRAY solves the problem quite correctly, but adds that there is nothing to exclude the supposition that all the ages were *fractional*. This would make the number of answers infinite. Let me meekly protest that I *never* intended my readers to devote the rest of their lives to writing out answers! E. M. RIX *points* out that, if fractional ages be admissible, any one of the three sons might be the one "come of age"; but she rightly rejects this supposition on the ground that it would make the problem indeterminate. WHITE SUGAR is the only one who has detected an oversight of mine: I had forgotten the possibility (which of course ought to be allowed for) that the son who came of age that *year*, need not have done so by that *day*, so that he *might* be only 20. This gives a second solution, *viz.*, 20, 24, 28. Well said, pure Crystal! Verily, thy "fair discourse hath been as sugar"!

CLASS LIST

I

ALGERNON BRAY.	S. S. G.
AN OLD FOGEY.	TOKIO.
E. M. RIX.	T. R.
G. S. C.	WHITE SUGAR.

II

C. R.	MAGPIE.
DELTA.	SIMPLE SUSAN.

III

DINAH MITE.	M. F. C.

I have received more than one remonstrance on my
assertion, in the Chelsea Pensioners' problem, that it was
illogical to assume, from the datum, "70 per cent have
lost an eye," that 30 per cent have *not*. ALGERNON BRAY
states, as a paralel case, "Suppose Tommy's father gives
him 4 apples, and he eats one of them, how many has he
left?" and says, "I think we are justified in answering, 3."
I think so too. There is no "must" here, and data are
evidently meant to fix the answer *exactly*: but, if the
question were set me, "How many *must* he have left?"
I should understand the data to be that his father gave
him 4 *at least*, but *may* have given him more.

I take this opportunity of thanking those who have
sent, along with their answers to the Tenth Knot, regrets
that there are no more Knots to come, or petitions that
I should recall my resolution to bring them to an end. I
am most grateful for their kind words; but I think it
wisest to end what, at best, was but a lame attempt. "The
stretched metre of an antique song" is beyond my compass; and my puppets were neither distinctly *in* my life
(like those I now address), nor yet (like Alice and the
Mock Turtle) distinctly *out* of it. Yet let me at least fancy,
as I lay down the pen, that I carry with me into my silent
life, dear reader, a farewell smile from your unseen face,
and a kindly farewell pressure from your unfelt hand!
And so, good night! Parting is such sweet sorrow, that I
shall say "good night!" till it be morrow.

NOVELTY AND ROMANCEMENT

I HAD grave doubts at first whether to call this passage of my life "A Wail", or "A Pæan", so much does it contain that is great and glorious, so much that is sombre and stern. Seeking for something which should be a sort of medium between the two, I decided, at last, on the above heading—wrongly, of course; I am always wrong: but let me be calm. It is a characteristic of the true orator never to yield to a burst of passion at the outset; the mildest of commonplaces are all he dare indulge in at first, and thence he mounts gradually;—*"vires acquirit eundo."* Suffice it, then, to say, in the first place, that *I am Leopold Edgar Stubbs*. I state this fact distinctly in commencing, to prevent all chance of the reader's confounding me either with the eminent shoemaker of that name, of Pottle-street, Camberwell, or with my less reputable, but more widely known, namesake, Stubbs, the light comedian, of the Provinces; both which connections I repel with horror and disdain: no offence, however, being intended to either of the individuals named—men whom I have never seen, whom I hope I never shall.

So much for commonplaces.

Tell me now, oh! man, wise in interpretation of dreams and omens, how it chanced that, on a Friday afternoon, turning suddenly out of Great Wattles-street, I should come into sudden and disagreeable collision with an humble individual of unprepossessing exterior, but with an eye that glowed with all the fire of genius? I had dreamed at night that the great idea of my life was to be fulfilled. What was the great idea of my life? I will tell you. With shame or sorrow I will tell you.

My thirst and passion from boyhood (predominating over the love of taws and running neck and neck with my appetite for toffee) has been for poetry—for poetry in its widest and wildest sense—for poetry untrammeled by the

970

laws of sense, rhyme, or rhythm, soaring through the universe, and echoing the music of the spheres! From my youth, nay, from my very cradle, I have yearned for poetry, for beauty, for novelty, for romancement. When I say "yearned", I employ a word mildly expressive of what may be considered as an outline of my feelings in my calmer moments: it is about as capable of picturing the headlong impetuosity of my life-long enthusiasm as those unanatomical paintings which adorn the outside of the Adelphi, representing Flexmore in one of the many conceivable attitudes into which the human frame has never yet been reduced, are of conveying to the speculative pit-goer a true idea of the feats performed by that extraordinary compound of humanity and Indian-rubber.

I have wandered from the point: that is a peculiarity, if I may be permitted to say so, incidental to life; and, as I remarked on an occasion which time will not suffer me more fully to specify, "What, after all, *is* life?" nor did I find any one of the individuals present (we were a party of nine, including the waiter, and it was while the soup was being removed that the above-recorded observation was made) capable of furnishing me with a rational answer to the question.

The verses which I wrote at an early period of life were eminently distinguished by a perfect freedom from conventionalism, and were thus unsuited to the present exactions of literature: in a future age they will be read and admired, "when Milton," as my venerable uncle has frequently exclaimed, "when Milton and such like are forgot!" Had it not been for this sympathetic relative, I firmly believe that the poetry of my nature would never have come out; I can still recall the feelings which thrilled me when he offered me sixpence for a rhyme to "despotism". I never succeeded, it is true, in finding the rhyme, but it was on the very next Wednesday that I penned my well known "Sonnet on a Dead Kitten", and in the course of a fortnight had commenced three epics, the titles of which I have unfortunately now forgotten.

Seven volumes of poetry have I given to an ungrateful world during my life; they have all shared the fate of true genius—obscurity and contempt. Not that any fault could be found with their contents; whatever their deficiencies may have been, *no reviewer has yet dared to criticize them.* This is a great fact.

The only composition of mine which has yet made any noise in the world, was a sonnet I addressed to one of the Corporation of Muggleton-cum-Swillside, on the occasion of his being selected Mayor of that town. It was largely circulated through private hands, and much talked of at the time; and though the subject of it, with characteristic vulgarity of mind, failed to appreciate the delicate compliments it involved, and indeed spoke of it rather disrespectfully than otherwise, I am inclined to think that it possesses all the elements of greatness. The concluding couplet was added at the suggestion of a friend, who assured me it was necessary to complete the sense, and in this point I deferred to his maturer judgment:

> "When Desolation snatched her tearful prey
> From the lorn empire of despairing day;
> When all the light, by gemless fancy thrown,
> Served but to animate the putrid stone;
> When monarchs, lessening on the wildered sight,
> Crumblingly vanished into utter night;
> When murder stalked with thirstier strides abroad,
> And redly flashed the never-sated sword;
> In such an hour thy greatness had been seen—
> That is, if such an hour had ever been—
> In such an hour thy praises shall be sung,
> If not by mine, by many a worthier tongue;
> And thou be gazed upon by wondering men,
> When such an hour arrives, but not till then!"

Alfred Tennyson is Poet Laureate, and it is not for me to dispute his claim to that eminent position; still I cannot help thinking, that if the Government had only come forward candidly at the time, and thrown the thing open to general competition, proposing some subject to test the powers of the candidate (say "Frampton's Pill of Health, an Acrostic"), a very different result might have been arrived at.

But let us return to our muttons (as our noble allies do most unromantically express themselves), and to the mechanic of Great Wattles-street. He was coming out of a small shop—rudely built it was, dilapidated exceedingly, and in its general appearance seedy—what did I see in all this to inspire a belief that a great epoch in my existence arrived? Reader, I saw the signboard!

Yes. Upon that rusty signboard, creaking awkwardly on its one hinge against the mouldering wall, was an inscription which thrilled me from head to foot with unwonted excitement. "Simon Lubkin. Dealer in Romancement." Those were the very words.

It was Friday, the fourth of June, half-past four p.m.

Three times I read that inscription through, and then took out my pocketbook, and copied it on the spot; the mechanic regarding me during the whole proceeding with a stare of serious and (as I thought at the time) respectful astonishment.

I stopped that mechanic, and entered into conversation with him; years of agony since then have gradually branded that scene upon my writhing heart, and I can repeat all that passed, word for word.

Did the mechanic (this was my first question) possess a kindred soul, or did he not?

Mechanic didn't know as he did.

Was he aware (this with thrilling emphasis) of the meaning of that glorious inscription upon his signboard?

Bless you, mechanic knew all about that 'ere.

Would mechanic (overlooking the suddenness of the invitation) object to adjourn to the neighbouring public-house, and there discuss the point more at leisure?

Mechanic would *not* object to a drain. On the contrary.

(Adjournment accordingly: brandy-and-water for two: conversation resumed.)

Did the article sell well, especially with the *"mobile vulgus"*?

Mechanic cast a look of good-natured pity on the questioner; the article sold well, he said, and the vulgars bought it most.

Why not add "Novelty" to the inscription? (This was a critical moment: I trembled as I asked the question.)

Not so bad an idea, mechanic thought: time was, it might have answered; but time flies, you see.

Was mechanic alone in his glory, or was there any one else who dealt as largely in the article?

Mechanic would pound it, there was none.

What was the article employed for? (I brought this question out with a gasp, excitement almost choking my utterance.)

It would piece almost anything together, mechanic believed, and make it solider nor stone.

This was a sentence difficult of interpretation. I thought it over a little, and then said, doubtfully, "you mean, I presume, that it serves to connect the broken threads of human destiny? to invest with a—with a sort of vital reality the chimerical products of a fertile imagination?"

Mechanic's answer was short, and anything but encouraging: "mought be—, I's no scollard, bless you."

At this point conversation certainly began to flag; I was seriously debating in my own mind whether this could really be the fulfilment of my life-cherished dream; so ill did the scene harmonize with my ideas of romance, and so painfully did I feel my companion's lack of sympathy in the enthusiasm of my nature—an enthusiasm which has found vent, ere now, in actions which the thoughtless crowd have too often attributed to mere eccentricity.

I have risen with the lark—"day's sweet harbinger"—(once, certainly, if not oftener), with the aid of a patent alarm, and have gone forth at that unseemly hour, much to the astonishment of the housemaid cleaning the door steps, to "brush with hasty steps the dewy lawn", and have witnessed the golden dawn with eyes yet half-closed in sleep. (I have always stated to my friends, in any allusion to the subject, that my raptures at that moment were such that I have never since ventured to expose myself to the influence of excitement so dangerous. In confidence, however, I admit that the reality did not come up to the idea I had formed of it over night, and by no means repaid the struggle of getting out of bed so early.)

I have wandered in the solemn woods at night, and bent me o'er the moss-grown fountain, to lave in its crystal stream my tangled locks and fevered brow. (What though I was laid up with a severe cold in consequence, and that my hair was out of curl for a week? Do paltry considerations such as these, I ask, affect the poetry of the incident?)

I have thrown open my small, but neatly furnished, cottage tenement, in the neighbourhood of St. John's Wood, and invited an aged beggar in to "sit by my fire, and talk the night away". (It was immediately after reading Goldsmith's "Deserted Village". True it is that he told me nothing interesting, and that he took the hall-clock with him when he departed in the morning; still my uncle has always said that he wishes he had been there, and that it displayed in me a freshness and greenness of fancy (or "disposition", I forget which) such as he had never expected to see.)

I feel that it is incumbent on me to enter more fully into this latter topic—the personal history of my uncle: the world will one day learn to revere the talents of that wonderful man, though a want of funds prevents, at present, the publication of the great system of philosophy of which he is the inventor. Meanwhile, out of the mass of priceless manuscripts which he has bequeathed to an ungrateful nation, I will venture to select one striking specimen. And when the day arrives that my poetry is appreciated by the world at large (distant though it now appear!) then, I feel assured, shall his genius also receive its meed of fame!

Among the papers of that respected relative, I find what appears to have been a leaf torn from some philosophical work of the day: the following passage is scored. "Is this your rose? It is mine. It is yours. Are these your houses? They are mine. Give to me (of) the bread. She gave him a box on the ear." Against this occurs a marginal note in my uncle's handwriting: "some call this unconnected writing: I have my own opinion." This last was a favourite expression of his, veiling a profundity of ethical acumen on which it would be vain to speculate; indeed, so uniformly simple was the language of this great man, that no one besides myself ever suspected his possessing more than the ordinary share of human intellect.

May I, however, venture to express what I believe would have been my uncle's interpretation of this remarkable passage? It appears that the writer intended to distinguish the provinces of Poetry, Real Property, and Personal Property. The inquirer touches first on flowers, and with what a gush of generous feeling does the answer break upon him! "It is mine. It is yours." That is the beautiful, the true, the good; these are not hampered by petty consideration of "meum" and "tuum"; these are the common property of men. (It was with some such idea as this that I drew up the once celebrated bill, entitled "An Act for exempting Pheasants from the operation of the Game Laws, on the ground of Beauty"—a bill which would, doubtless, have passed both Houses in triumph, but that the member who had undertaken the care of it was unfortunately incarcerated in a Lunatic Asylum before it had reached the second reading.) Encouraged by the success of his first question, our inquirer passes on to "houses" ("Real Property", you will observe); he is here met by the stern, chilling answer, "They are mine"—none of the liberal sentiment which dictated the former reply, but in its place a dignified assertion of the rights of property.

Had this been a genuine Socratic dialogue, and not

merely a modern imitation, the inquirer would have probably here interrupted with "To me indeed," or, "I, for my part," or, "But how otherwise?" or some other of those singular expressions, with which Plato makes his characters display at once their blind acquiescence in their instructor's opinions, and their utter inability to express themselves grammatically. But the writer takes another line of thought; the bold inquirer, undeterred by the coldness of the last reply, proceeds from questions to demands, "give me (of) the bread"; and here the conversation abruptly ceases, but the moral of the whole is pointed in the narrative: "she gave him a box on the ear." This is not the philosophy of one individual or nation, the sentiment is, if I may so say, European; and I am borne out in this theory by the fact that the book has evidently been printed in three parallel columns, English, French, and German.

Such a man was my uncle; and with such a man did I resolve to confront the suspected mechanic. I appointed the following morning for an interview, when I would personally inspect "the article" (I could not bring myself to utter the beloved word itself). I passed a restless and feverish night, crushed by a sense of the approaching crisis.

The hour came at last—the hour of misery and despair; it always does so, it cannot be put off forever; even on a visit to a dentist, as my childhood can attest with bitter experience, we are not forever getting there; the fatal door too surely dawns upon us, and our heart, which for the last half-hour has been gradually sinking lower and lower, until we almost doubt its existence, vanishes suddenly downwards into depths hitherto undreamed of. And so, I repeat it, the hour came at last.

Standing before that base mechanic's door, with a throbbing and expectant heart, my eye chanced to fall once more upon that signboard, once more I perused its strange inscription. Oh! fatal change! Oh! horror! What do I see? Have I been deluded by a heated imagination?

A hideous gap yawns between the N and the C, making it not one word but two!

And the dream was over.

At the corner of the street I turned to take a sad fond look at the spectre of a phantom hope, I once had held so dear. "Adieu!" I whispered; this was all the last farewell I took, and I leant upon my walking stick and wiped away a tear. On the following day I entered into commercial relations with the firm of Dumpy and Spagg, wholesale dealers in the wine and spirit department.

The signboard yet creaks upon the mouldering wall, but its sound shall make music in these ears nevermore—ah! nevermore.

A PHOTOGRAPHER'S DAY OUT

I AM shaken, and sore, and stiff, and bruised. As I have told you many times already, I haven't the least idea how it happened and there is no use in plaguing me with any more questions about it. Of course, if you wish it, I can read you an extract from my diary, giving a full account of the events of yesterday, but if you expect to find any clue to the mystery in *that*, I fear you are doomed to be disappointed.

August 23, *Tuesday.* They say that we Photographers are a blind race at best; that we learn to look at even the prettiest faces as so much light and shade; that we seldom admire, and never love. This is a delusion I long to break through—if I could only find a young lady to photograph, realizing *my* ideal of beauty—above all, if her name should be—(why is it, I wonder, that I dote on the name Amelia more than any other word in the English language?)—I feel sure that I could shake off this cold, philosophic lethargy.

The time has come at last. Only this evening I fell in with young Harry Glover in the Haymarket—"Tubbs!" he shouted, slapping me familiarly on the back, "my Uncle wants you down to-morrow at his Villa, camera and all!"

"But I don't know your uncle," I replied, with my characteristic caution. (N.B. If I have a virtue, it is quiet, gentlemanly caution.)

"Never mind, old boy, he knows all about *you*. You be off by the early train, and take your whole kit of bottles, for you'll find lots of faces to uglify, and——"

"Ca'n't go," I said rather gruffly, for the extent of the job alarmed me, and I wished to cut him short, having a decided objection to talking slang in the public streets.

"Well, they'll be precious cut up about it, that's all,"

979

said Harry, with rather a blank face, "and my cousin Amelia——"

"Don't say another word!" I cried enthusiastically, "I'll go!" And as my omnibus came by at the moment, I jumped in and rattled off before he had recovered his astonishment at my change of manner. So it is settled, and to-morrow I am to see an Amelia, and—Oh Destiny, what hast thou in store for me?

August 24, *Wednesday.* A glorious morning. Packed in a great hurry, luckily breaking only two bottles and three glasses in doing so. Arrived at Rosemary Villa as the party were sitting down to breakfast. Father, mother, two sons from school, a host of children from the nursery and the inevitable BABY.

But how shall I describe the daughter? Words are powerless; nothing but a Tablotype could do it. Her nose was in beautiful perspective—her mouth wanting perhaps the least possible foreshortening—but the exquisite half-tints on the cheek would have blinded one to any defects, and as to the high light on her chin, it was (photographically speaking) perfection. Oh! what a picture she would have made if fate had not—but I am anticipating.

There was a Captain Flanaghan present——

I am aware that the preceding paragraph is slightly abrupt, but when I reached that point, I remembered that the idiot actually believed himself engaged to Amelia (*my* Amelia!). I choked, and could get no further. His figure, I am willing to admit, was good: some might have admired his face; but what is face or figure without brains?

My own figure is perhaps a *little* inclined to the robust; in stature I am none of your military giraffes—but why should I describe myself? My photograph (done by myself) will be sufficient evidence to the world.

The breakfast, no doubt, was good, but I knew not what I ate or drank; I lived for Amelia only, and as I gazed on that peerless brow, those chiseled features, I clenched my fist in an involuntary transport (upsetting my coffee-cup in doing so), and mentally exclaimed, "I will photograph that woman, or perish in the attempt!"

After breakfast the work of the day commenced, which I will here briefly record.

PICTURE 1.—Paterfamilias. This I wanted to try again, but they all declared it would do very well, and had "just his usual expression"; though unless his usual expression was that of a man with a bone in his throat, endeavouring to alleviate the agony of choking by watching the end of his nose with both eyes, I must admit that this was too favourable a statement of the case.

PICTURE 2.—Materfamilias. She told us with a simper, as she sat down, that she "had been very fond of theatricals in her youth", and that she "wished to be taken in a favourite Shakespearean character". What the character was, after long and anxious thought on the subject, I have given up as a hopeless mystery, not knowing any one of his heroines in whom an attitude of such spasmodic energy could have been combined with a face of such blank indifference, or who could have been thought appropriately costumed in a blue silk gown, with a Highland scarf over one shoulder, a ruffle of Queen Elizabeth's time round the throat, and a hunting-whip.

*

PICTURE 3.—17th sitting. Placed the baby in profile. After waiting till the usual kicking had subsided, uncovered the lens. The little wretch instantly threw its head back, luckily only an inch, as it was stopped by the nurse's nose, establishing the infant's claim to "first blood" (to use a sporting phrase). This, of course, gave *two* eyes to the result, something that might be called a nose, and an unnaturally wide mouth. Called it a full-face accordingly and went on to

PICTURE 4.—The three younger girls, as they would have appeared, if by any possibility a black dose could have been administered to each of them at the same

moment, and the three tied together by the hair before
the expression produced by the medicine had subsided
from any of their faces. Of course, I kept this view of the
subject to myself, and merely said that "it reminded me
of a picture of the three Graces", but the sentence ended
in an involuntary groan, which I had the greatest difficulty in converting into a cough.

PICTURE 5.—This was to have been the great artistic
triumph of the day; a family group, designed by the two
parents, and combining the domestic with the allegorical.
It was intended to represent the baby being crowned with
flowers, by the united efforts of the children, regulated
by the advice of the father, under the personal superintendence of the mother; and to combine with this the
secondary meaning of "Victory transferring her laurel
crown to Innocence, with Resolution, Independence,
Faith, Hope and Charity, assisting in the graceful task,
while Wisdom looks benignly on, and smiles approval!"
Such, I say, was the *intention*; the result, to any unprejudiced observer, was capable of but one interpretation—
that the baby was in a fit—that the mother (doubtless
under some erroneous notions of the principles of Human
Anatomy), was endeavouring to recover it by bringing
the crown of its head in contact with its chest—that the
two boys, seeing no prospect for the infant but immediate
destruction, were tearing out some locks of its hair as
mementos of the fatal event—that two of the girls were
waiting for a chance at the baby's hair, and employing
the time in strangling the third—and that the father, in
despair at the extraordinary conduct of his family, had
stabbed himself, and was feeling for his pencil-case, to
make a memorandum of having done so.

All this time I had no opportunity of asking my Amelia
for a sitting, but during luncheon I succeeded in finding
one, and, after introducing the subject of photographs in
general, I turned to her and said, "before the day is out,
Miss Amelia, I hope to do myself the honour of coming to
you for a negative."

With a sweet smile she replied "certainly, Mr. Tubbs. There is a cottage near here, that I wish you would try after luncheon, and when you've done that, I shall be at your service."

"Faix! an' I hope she'll give you a decoisive one!" broke in that awkward Captain Flanaghan, "wo'n't you, Mely Darlint?" "I trust so, Captain Flanaghan," I interposed with great dignity; but all politeness is wasted on that animal; he broke into a great "haw! haw!" and Amelia and I could hardly refrain from laughing at his folly. She, however, with ready tact turned it off, saying to the bear, "come, come, Captain, we mustn't be *too* hard on him!" (Hard on *me*! on *me*! bless thee, Amelia!)

The sudden happiness of that moment nearly overcame me; tears rose to my eyes as I thought, "the wish of a Life is accomplished! I shall photograph an Amelia!" Indeed, I almost think I should have gone down on my knees to thank her, had not the table-cloth interfered with my so doing, and had I not known what a difficult position it is to recover from.

However, I seized an opportunity toward the close of the meal to give utterance to my overwrought feelings: turning toward Amelia, who was sitting next to me, I had just murmured the words, "there beats in this bosom a heart," when a general silence warned me to leave the sentence unfinished. With the most admirable presence of mind she said, "some tart, did you say, Mr. Tubbs? Captain Flanaghan, may I trouble you to cut Mr. Tubbs some of that tart?"

"It's nigh done," said the captain, poking his great head almost into it, "will I send him the dish, Mely?"

"No, sir!" I interrupted, with a look that ought to have crushed him, but he only grinned and said, "don't be modest now, Tubbs, me bhoy, sure there's plenty more in the larder."

Amelia was looking anxiously at me, so I swallowed my rage— and the tart.

Luncheon over, after receiving directions by which to

find the cottage, I attached to my camera the hood used for developing pictures in the open air, placed it over my shoulder, and set out for the hill which had been pointed out to me.

My Amelia was sitting in the window working, as I passed with the machine; the Irish idiot was with her. In reply to my look of undying affection, she said anxiously, "I'm sure that's too heavy for you, Mr. Tubbs. Wo'n't you have a boy to carry it?"

"Or a donkey?" giggled the captain.

I pulled up short, and faced round, feeling that now, if ever, the dignity of Man, and the liberty of the subject, must be asserted. To *her* I merely said, "thanks, thanks!" kissing my hand as I spoke; then, fixing my eyes on the idiot at her side, I hissed through my clenched teeth, *"we shall meet again, Captain!"*

"Sure, I hope so, Tubbs," said the unconscious blockhead, "sharp six is the dinner hour, mind!" A cold shiver passed over me; I had made my great effort, and had *failed*; I shouldered my camera again, and strode moodily on.

Two steps, and I was myself again; *her* eyes, I knew, were upon me, and once more I trod the gravel with an elastic tread. What mattered to me, in that moment, the whole tribe of captains? should *they* disturb my equanimity?

The hill was nearly a mile from the house, and I reached it tired and breathless. Thoughts of Amelia, however, bore me up. I selected the best point of view for the cottage, so as to include a farmer and cow in the picture, cast one fond look toward the distant villa, and, muttering, "Amelia, 'tis for thee!" removed the lid of the lens; in 1 minute and 40 seconds I replaced it: "it is over!" I cried in uncontrollable excitement, "Amelia, thou art mine!"

Eagerly, tremblingly, I covered my head with the hood, and commenced the development. Trees rather misty—well! the wind had blown them about a little; *that* wouldn't show much—the farmer? well, *he* had walked on a yard or two, and I should be sorry to state how many arms and legs he appeared with—never mind! call him a spider, a centipede, anything—the cow? I must, however reluctantly, confess that the cow had three heads, and though such an animal may be curious, it is *not* picturesque. However, there could be no mistake about the cottage; its chimneys were all that could be desired, and, "all things considered," I thought, "Amelia will——"

At this point my soliloquy was interrupted by a tap on the shoulder, more peremptory than suggestive. I withdrew myself from the hood, need I say with what quiet dignity? and turned upon the stranger. He was a thick-built man, vulgar in dress, repulsive in expression, and carried a straw in his mouth: his companion outdid him in these peculiarities. "Young man," began the first, "ye're trespassing here, and ya mun take yourself off, and no bones about it." I need hardly say that I took no notice of this remark, but took up the bottle of hypo-sulphite of soda, and proceeded to fix the picture; he tried to stop me; I resisted: the negative fell, and was broken. I remember nothing further, except that I have an indistinct notion that I hit somebody.

If you can find anything in what I have just read to you to account for my present condition, you are welcome to do so; but, as I before remarked, all I can tell you is that I am shaken, and sore, and stiff, and bruised, and that how I came so I haven't the faintest idea.

WILHELM VON SCHMITZ

CHAPTER I

" 'Twas Ever Thus"
(*Old Play*)

THE sultry glare of noon was already giving place to the cool of a cloudless evening, and the lulled ocean was washing against the Pier with a low murmur, suggestive to poetical minds of the kindred ideas of motion and lotion, when two travelers might have been seen, by such as chose to look that way, approaching the secluded town of Whitby by one of those headlong paths, dignified by the name of road, which serve as entrances into the place, and which were originally constructed, it is supposed, on the somewhat fantastic model of pipes running into a water-butt. The elder of the two was a sallow and care-worn man; his features were adorned with what had been often at a distance mistaken for a moustache, and were shaded by a beaver hat, of doubtful age, and of appearance which, if not respectable, was at least venerable. The younger, in whom the sagacious reader already recognizes the hero of my tale, possessed a form which, once seen, could scarcely be forgotten: a slight tendency to obesity proved but a trifling drawback to the manly grace of its contour, and though the strict laws of beauty might perhaps have required a somewhat longer pair of legs to make up the proportion of his figure, and that his eyes should match rather more exactly than they chanced to do, yet to those critics who are untrammeled with any laws of taste, and there are many such, to those who could close their eyes to the faults in his shape, and single out its beauties, though few were ever found capable of the task, to those above all who knew and esteemed his personal character, and believed that the powers of his mind transcended those of the age he lived in, though alas! none such has as yet turned up—to those he was a very Apollo.

What though it had not been wholly false to assert that too much grease had been applied to his hair, and too little soap to his hands? that his nose turned too much up, and his shirt collars too much down? that his whiskers had borrowed all the colour from his cheeks, excepting a little that had run down into his waistcoat? Such trivial criticisms were unworthy the notice of any who laid claim to the envied title of the connoisseur.

He had been christened William, and his father's name was Smith, but though he had introduced himself to many of the higher circles in London under the imposing name of "Mr. Smith, of Yorkshire", he had unfortunately not attracted so large a share of public notice as he was confident he merited: some had asked him how far back he traced his ancestry; others had been mean enough to hint that his position in society was not entirely unique; while the sarcastic enquiries of others touching the dormant peerage in his family, to which, it was suggested, he was about to lay claim, had awakened in the breast of the noble-spirited youth an ardent longing for that high birth and connection which an adverse Fortune had denied him.

Hence he had conceived the notion of that fiction, which perhaps in his case must be considered merely as a poetical licence, whereby he passed himself off upon the world under the sounding appellation which heads this tale. This step had already occasioned a large increase in his popularity, a circumstance which his friends spoke of under the unpoetical simile of a bad sovereign fresh gilt, but which he himself more pleasantly described as, ". . . a violet pale, At length discovered in its mossy dale, And borne to sit with kings": a destiny for which, as it is generally believed, violets are not naturally fitted.

The travelers, each buried in his own thoughts, paced in silence down the steep, save when an unusually sharp stone, or an unexpected dip in the road, produced one of those involuntary exclamations of pain, which so triumphantly demonstrate the connection between Mind and Matter. At length the young traveler, rousing himself with an effort from his painful reverie, broke upon the meditations of his companion with the unexpected question, "Think you she will be much altered in feature? I trust me not." "Think who?" testily rejoined the other: then hastily correcting himself, with an exquisite sense of grammar, he substituted the expressive phrase, "Who's the she you're after?" "Forget you then," asked the young man, who was so intensely poetical in soul that he never spoke in ordinary prose, "forget you the subject we conversed on but now? Trust me, she hath dwelt in my thoughts ever since." "But now!" his friend repeated, in sarcastic tone, "it is an hour good since you spoke last." The young man nodded assent; "An hour? true, true. We were passing Lyth, as I bethink me, and lowly in thine ear was I murmuring that touching sonnet to the sea I writ of late, beginning, 'Thou roaring, snoring, heaving, grieving main which——'" "For pity's sake!" interrupted the other, and there was real earnestness in that pleading tone, "don't let us have it all again! I have heard it with patience once already."

"Thou hast, thou hast," the baffled poet replied: "well then, she shall again be the topic of my thoughts," and he frowned and bit his lip, muttering to himself such words as cooky, hooky, and crooky, as if he were trying to find a rhyme to something. And now the pair were passing near a bridge, and shops were on their left and water on their right; and from beneath uprose a confused hubbub of sailors' voices, and, wafted on the landward breeze, came an aroma, dimly suggestive of salt herring, and all things from the heaving waters in the harbour to the light smoke that floated gracefully above the housetops, suggested nought but poetry to the mind of the gifted youth.

CHAPTER II

"And I, for One"
(*Old Play*)

"BUT about she," resumed the man of prose, "what's her name? You never told me that yet." A faint flush crossed the interesting features of the youth; could it be that her name was unpoetical, and did not consort with his ideas of the harmony of nature? He spoke reluctantly and indistinctly; "Her name", he faintly gasped, "is Sukie."

A long, low whistle was the only reply; thrusting his hands deep in his pockets, the elder speaker turned away, while the unhappy youth, whose delicate nerves were cruelly shaken by his friend's ridicule, grasped the railing near to him to steady his tottering feet. Distant sounds of melody from the cliff at this moment reached their ears, and while his unfeeling comrade wandered in the direction of the music, the distressed poet hastily sought the Bridge, to give his pent-up feelings vent, unnoticed by the passers-by.

The Sun was setting as he reached the spot, and the still surface of the waters below, as he crossed on to the Bridge, calmed his perturbed spirit, and sadly leaning his elbows on the rail, he pondered. What visions filled that noble soul, as, with features that would have beamed with intelligence, had they only possessed an expression at all, and a frown that only needed dignity to be appalling, he fixed upon the sluggish tide those fine though blood-shot eyes?

Visions of his early days; scenes from the happy time of pinafores, treacle, and innocence; through the long vista of the past came floating spectres of long-forgotten spelling-books, slates scrawled thick with dreary sums, that seldom came out at all, and never came out right; tingling and somewhat painful sensations returned to his knuckles and the roots of his hair; he was a boy once more.

"Now, young man there!" so broke a voice upon the air, "tak whether o' the two roads thou likes, but thou ca'n't stop in't middle!" The words fell idly on his ears, or served but to suggest new trains of reverie; "Roads, aye, roads," he whispered low, and then louder, as the glorious idea burst upon him, "Aye, and am I not the Colossus of Rhodes?" he raised his manly form erect at the thought, and planted his feet with a firmer stride.

. . . Was it but a delusion of his heated brain? or stern reality? slowly, slowly yawned the bridge beneath him, and now his footing is already grown unsteady, and now the dignity of his attitude is gone: he recks not, come what may; is he not a Colossus?

. . . The stride of a Colossus is possibly equal to any emergency; the elasticity of fustian is limited; it was at this critical juncture that "the force of nature could no further go", and therefore deserted him, while the force of gravity began to operate in its stead.

In other words, he fell.

And the "Hilda" went slowly on its way, and knew not that it passed a poet under the Bridge, and guessed not whose were those two feet, that disappeared through the eddying waters, kicking with spasmodic energy; and men pulled into a boat a dripping, panting form, that resembled a drowned rat rather than a Poet; and spoke to it without awe, and even said, "young feller," and something about "greenhorn", and laughed; what knew they of Poetry?

Turn we to other scenes: a long, low room, with high-backed settees, and a sanded floor: a knot of men drinking and gossiping: a general prevalence of tobacco; a powerful conviction that spirits existed somewhere: and she, the fair Sukie herself, gliding airily through the scene, and bearing in those lily hands—what? Some garland doubtless, wreathed of the most fragrant flowers that grow? Some cherished volume, morocco-bound and golden-clasped, the works immortal of the bard of eld, whereon she loveth oft to ponder? Possibly, "The Poems of William Smith," that idol of her affections, in two volumes quarto, published some years agone, whereof one copy only has as yet been sold, and that he bought himself—to give to Sukie. Which of these is it that the beauteous maiden carries with such tender care? Alas none: it is but those two "goes of arf-an-arf, warm without", which have just been ordered by the guests in the tap-room.

In a small parlour hard by, unknown, untended, though his Sukie was so near, wet, moody, and dishevelled, sat the youth: the fire had been kindled at his desire, and before it he was now drying himself, but as "the cheery blaze, Blithe harbinger of wintry days", to use his own powerful description, consisted at present of a feeble, spluttering faggot, whose only effect was to half-choke him with its smoke, he may be pardoned for not feeling, more keenly than he does, that ". . . fire of Soul, When gazing on the kindling coal, A Britain feels that, spite of fone, He wots his native hearth his own!" we again employ his own thrilling words on the subject.

The waiter, unconscious that a Poet sat before him, was talking confidingly; he dwelt on various themes, and still the youth sat heedless, but when at last he spoke of Sukie, those dull eyes flashed with fire, and cast upon the speaker a wild glance of scornful defiance, that was unfortunately wasted, as its object was stirring the fire at the moment and failed to notice it. "Say, oh say those words again!" he gasped. "I surely heard thee not aright!" The waiter looked astonished, but obligingly repeated his remark, "I were merely a saying, sir, that she's an uncommon clever girl, and as how I were 'oping some day to hacquire her Hart, if so be that——" He said no more, for the Poet with a groan of anguish, had rushed distractedly from the room.

CHAPTER III

"Nay, 'Tis Too Much!"
(*Old Play*)

NIGHT, solemn night.

On the present occasion the solemnity of night's approach was rendered far more striking than it is to dwellers in ordinary towns, by that time-honoured custom observed by the people of Whitby, of leaving their streets wholly unlighted: in thus making a stand against the deplorably swift advance of the tide of progress and civilization, they displayed no small share of moral courage and independent judgment. Was it for a people of sense to adopt every new-fangled invention of the age, merely because their neighbours did? It might have been urged, in disparagement of their conduct, that they only injured themselves by it, and the remark would have been undeniably true; but it would only have served to exalt, in the eyes of an admiring nation, their well-earned character of heroic self-denial and uncompromising fixity of purpose.

Headlong and desperate, the lovelorn Poet plunged through the night; now tumbling up against a doorstep, and now half down in a gutter, but ever onward, onward, reckless where he went.

In the darkest spot of one of those dark streets (the nearest lighted shop window being about fifty yards off), chance threw into his way the very man he fled from, the man whom he hated as a successful rival, and who had driven him to this pitch of frenzy. The waiter, not knowing what was the matter, had followed him to see that he came to no harm, and to bring him back, little dreaming of the shock that awaited him.

The instant the Poet perceived who it was, all his pent-up fury broke forth: to rush upon him, to grasp him by the throat with both hands, to dash him to the ground, and there to reduce him to the extreme verge of suffocation—all this was the work of a moment.

"Traitor! villain! malcontent! regicide!" he hissed through his closed teeth, taking any abusive epithet that came into his head, without stopping to consider its suitability. "Is it thou? Now shalt thou feel my wrath!" And doubtless the waiter did experience that singular sensation, whatever it may have been, for he struggled violently with his assailant, and bellowed "murder" the instant he recovered his breath.

"Say not so," the Poet sternly answered, as he released him; "it is thou that murderest me." The waiter gathered himself up, and began in great surprise, "Why, I never——" " 'Tis a lie!" the Poet screamed; "she loves thee not! Me, me alone." "Who ever said she did?" the other asked, beginning to perceive how matters stood. "Thou! thou saidst it," was the wild reply, "what, villain? acquire her heart? thou never shalt."

The waiter calmly explained himself: "My 'ope were, Sir, to hacquire her Hart of waiting at table, which she do perdigious well, sure-ly: seeing that I were thinking of happlying for to be 'eadwaiter at the 'otel." The Poet's wrath instantly abated, indeed, he looked rather crestfallen than otherwise; "Excuse my violence," he gently said, "and let us take a friendly glass together." "I agree," was the waiter's generous answer, "but man halive, you've ruinated my coat!"

"Courage," cried our hero gaily, "thou shalt have a new one anon: aye, and of the best cashmere." "H'm," said the other, hesitatingly, "wouldn't hany other stuff——" "I will not buy thee one of any other stuff," returned the Poet, gently but decidedly, and the waiter gave up the point.

Arrived once more at the friendly tavern, the Poet briskly ordered a jorum of Punch, and, on its being furnished, called on his friend for a toast. "I'll give you," said the waiter, who was of a sentimental turn, however little he looked like it, "I'll give you—Woman! She doubles our sorrows and 'alves our joy." The Poet drained his glass, not caring to correct his companion's mistake, and at intervals during the evening the same inspiring sentiment was repeated. And so the night wore away, and another jorum of Punch was ordered, and another.

*   *   *   *   *

"And now hallow me," said the waiter, attempting for about the tenth time to rise on his feet and make a speech, and failing even more signally than he had yet done, "to give a toast for this 'appy hoccasion. Woman! she doubles ——" but at this moment, probably in illustration of his favourite theory, he "doubled" himself up, and so effectually, that he instantly vanished under the table.

Occupying that limited sphere of observation, it is conjectured that he fell to moralizing on human ills in general, and their remedies, for a solemn voice was presently heard to issue from his retreat, proclaiming feelingly though rather indistinctly, that "when the 'art of man is hopressed with care——" here came a pause, as if he wished to leave the question open to discussion, but as no one present seemed competent to suggest the proper course to be taken in that melancholy contingency, he attempted to supply the deficiency himself with the remarkable statement "she's hall my fancy painted 'er".

Meanwhile the Poet was sitting, smiling quietly to himself, as he sipped his punch: the only notice he took of his companion's abrupt disappearance was to help himself to a fresh glass, and say, "your health!" in a cordial tone, nodding to where the waiter ought to have been. He then cried, "hear, hear!" encouragingly, and made an attempt to thump the table with his fist, but missed it. He seemed interested in the question regarding the heart oppressed with care, and winked sagaciously with one eye two or three times, as if there were a good deal he could say on that subject, if he chose; but the second quotation roused him to speech, and he at once broke into the waiter's subterranean soliloquy with an ecstatic fragment from the poem he had been just composing:

"What though the world be cross and crooky?
Of Life's fair flowers the fairest bouquet
I plucked, when I chose *thee*, my Sukie!

"Say, could'st thou grasp at nothing greater
Than to be wedded to a waiter?
And did'st thou deem thy Schmitz a traitor?

"Nay! the fond waiter was rejected,
And thou, alone, with flower-bedecked head,
Sitting, did'st sing of one expected.

"And while the waiter, crazed and silly,
Dreamed he had won that precious lily,
At length he came, thy wished-for Willie.

"And then thy music took a new key,
For whether Schmitz be boor or duke, he
Is all in all to faithful Sukie!"

He paused for a reply, but a heavy snoring from beneath the table was the only one he got.

Chapter IV

"Is This the Hend?"
(*"Nicholas Nickleby"*)

BATHED in the radiance of the newly-risen Sun, the billows are surging and bristling below the Cliff, along which the Poet is thoughtfully wending his way. It may possibly surprise the reader that he should not ere this have obtained an interview with his beloved Sukie: he may ask the reason: he will ask in vain: to record with rigid accuracy the progress of events is the sole duty of the historian: were he to go beyond that, and attempt to dive into the hidden causes of things, the why and the wherefore, he would be trespassing on the province of the metaphysician.

Presently the Poet reached a small rising ground at the

end of the gravel walk, where he found a seat commanding a view of the sea, and here he sunk down wearily.

For a while he gazed dreamily upon the expanse of ocean, then, struck by a sudden thought, he opened a small pocket book, and proceeded to correct and complete his last poem. Slowly to himself he muttered the words "death—saith—breath", impatiently tapping the ground with his foot. "Ah, that'll do," he said at last, with an air of relief, "breath":

> "His barque had perished in the storm,
>   Whirled by its fiery breath
> On sunken rocks, his stalwart form
>   Was doomed to watery death."

"That last line's good," he continued exaltingly, "and on Coleridge's principle of alliteration, too—W. D., W. D. —was doomed to watery death."

"Take care," growled a deep voice in his ear, "what you say will be used in evidence against you—now it's no use trying that, we've got you tight," this last remark being caused by the struggles of the Poet, naturally indignant at being unexpectedly collared by two men from behind.

"He's confessed to it, constable? you heard him?" said the first speaker (who rejoiced in the euphonious title of Muggle, and whom it is almost superfluous to introduce to the reader as the elder traveler of Chapter One)! "it's as much as his life is worth."

"I say, stow that——" warmly responded the other; "seems to me the gen'leman was a spouting potry."

"What—what's the matter?" here gasped our unfortunate hero, who had recovered his breath; "you— Muggle—what do you mean by it?"

"Mean by it!" blustered his quondam friend, "what do *you* mean by it, if it comes to that? You're an assassin, that's what you are! Where's the waiter you had with you last night? answer me that!"

"The—the waiter?" slowly repeated the Poet, still

stunned by the suddenness of his capture, "why, he's dr——"

"I knew it!" cried his friend, who was at him in a moment, and choked up the unfinished word in his throat, "drowned, Constable! I told you so—and who did it?" he continued, loosing his grip a moment to obtain an answer.

The Poet's answer, so far as it could be gathered (for it came out in a very fragmentary state, and as it were by crumbs, in intervals of choking), was the following: "It was my—my—you'll kill me—fault—I say, fault—I—I—gave him—you—you're suffoca—I say—I gave him——" "a push I suppose," concluded the other, who here "shut off" the slender supply of breath he had hitherto allowed his victim "and he fell in: no doubt. I heard some one had fallen off the Bridge last night," turning to the Constable; "no doubt this unfortunate waiter. Now mark my words! from this moment I renounce this man as my friend: don't pity him, constable! don't think of letting him go to spare *my* feelings!"

Some convulsive sounds were heard at this moment from the Poet, which, on attentive consideration, were found to be "the punch—was—was too much—for him—quite—it—quite——" "Miserable man!" sternly interposed Muggle; "can you jest about it? You gave him a punch, did you? and what then?"

"It quite—quite—upset him," continued the unhappy Schmitz, in a sort of rambling soliloquy, which was here cut short by the impatience of the Constable, and the party set forth on their return to the town.

But an unexpected character burst upon the scene and broke into a speech far more remarkable for energetic delivery than for grammatical accuracy: "I've only just 'erd of it—I were hasleep under table—'avin' taken more punch than I could stand—he's as hinnocent as I am—dead indeed! I'm more alive than you, a precious sight!"

This speech produced various effects on its hearers: the Constable calmly released his man, the bewildered

Muggle muttered "Impossible! conspiracy—perjury—have it tried at assizes": while the happy Poet rushed into the arms of his deliverer crying in a broken voice: "No, never from this hour to part. We'll live and love so true!" a sentiment which the waiter did not echo with the cordiality that might have been expected.

Later in the day, Wilhelm and Sukie were sitting conversing with the waiter and a few friends, when the penitent Muggle suddenly entered the room, placed a folded paper on the knees of Schmitz, pronounced in a hollow tone the affecting words "be happy!" vanished, and was seen no more.

After perusing the paper, Wilhelm rose to his feet; in the excitement of the moment he was roused into unconscious and extempore verse:

> "My Sukie! He hath bought, yea, Muggle's self,
> Convinced at last of deeds unjust and foul,
> The licence of a vacant public-house.
> We are licensed here to sell to all,
> Spirits, porter, snuff, and ale!"

So we leave him: his after happiness who dare to doubt? has he not Sukie? and having her, he is content.

THE LEGEND OF SCOTLAND

BEING a true and terrible report touching the rooms of Auckland Castell, called Scotland, and of the things there endured by Matthew Dixon, Chaffer, and of a certain Ladye, called Gaunless of some, there apparent, and how that none durst in these days sleep therein (belike through fear), all which things fell out in ye days of Bishop Bec, of chearfull memorie, and were writ down by mee in the Yeere One Thousand Three Hundred and Twenty Five, in the Month February, on a certayn Tuesday and other days.

EDGAR CUTHWELLIS.

Now the said Matthew Dixon, having fetched wares unto that place, my Loords commended the same, and bade that hee should be entertained for that night, (which in sooth hee was, supping with a grete Appetite,) and sleep in a certayn roome of that apartment now called Scotland—From whence at Midnight hee rushed forth with so grete a Screem, as awaked all men, and hastily running into those Passages, and meeting him so screeming, hee presentlie faynted away.

Whereon they hadde hym into my Loorde's parlour, and with much ado set hym on a Chaire, wherefrom hee three several times split even to the grounde, to the grete admiration of all men.

But being stayed with divers Strong Liquors, (and, chifest, wyth Gin,) he after a whyle gave foorth in a lamentable tone these following particulars, all which were presentlie sworn to by nine painful and stout farmers, who lived hard by, which witness I will heare orderlie set downe.

Witness of Matthew Dixon, Chaffer, being in my right minde, and more than Fortie Yeeres of Age, though sore affrighted by reason of Sightes and Sounds in This Castell endured by mee, as touching the Vision of Scotland, and the Ghosts, all two of them, therein contayned, and of A certayn straunge Ladye, and of the lamentable thyngs by her uttered, with other sad tunes and songs, by her and by other Ghosts devised, and of the coldness and shakyng of my Bones (through sore grete feer), and of other things very pleasant to knowe, cheefly of a Picture hereafter suddenlie to bee taken, and of what shall befall thereon, (as trulie foreshowne by Ghosts,) and of Darkness, with other things more terrible than Woordes and of that which Men call Chimera.

Matthew Dixon, Chaffer, deposeth: "that hee, having supped well over Night on a Green Goose, a Pasty, and other Condiments of the Bishop's grete bountie provided, (looking, as he spake, at my Loorde, and essaying toe pull offe hys hatte untoe hym, but missed soe doing, for that hee hadde yt not on hys hedde,) soe went untoe hys bedde, where of a long tyme hee was exercysed with sharp and horrible Dreems. That hee saw yn hys Dreem a young Ladye, habited, not (as yt seemed) yn a Gaun, but yn a certayn sorte of Wrapper, perchance a Wrap-Rascal." (Hereon a Mayde of the House affirmed that noe Ladye woold weare such a thing, and hee answered, "I stand corrected," and indeed rose from hys chaire, yet fayled to stand.)

Witness continued: "that ye sayde Ladye waved toe and froe a Grete Torche, whereat a thin Voyce shreeked 'Gaunless! Gaunless!' and Shee standyng yn the midst of the floor, a grete Chaunge befell her, her Countenance waxing ever more and more Aged, and her Hayr grayer, shee all that tyme saying yn a most sad Voyce, 'Gaunless, now, as Ladyes bee: yet yn yeeres toe come they shall not lacke for Gauns.' At whych her Wrapper seemed slowlie toe melte, chaunging into a gaun of sylk, which puckered up and down, yea, and flounced itself out not a lyttle": (at thys mye Loorde, waxing impatient, smote hym roundlie onne the hedde, bydding hym finish hys tale anon.)

Witness continued: "that the sayd Gaun thenne

chaunged ytself into divers fashyons whych shall hereafter bee, loopyng ytself uppe yn thys place and yn that,
soe gyving toe View ane pettycote of a most fiery hue,
even Crimson toe looke upon, at whych dismal and blode-
thirstie sight he both groned and wepte. That at the laste
the skyrt swelled unto a Vastness beyond Man's power
toe tell ayded (as hee judged), bye Hoops, Cartwheels,
Balloons, and the lyke, bearing yt uppe within. That yt
fylled alle that Chamber, crushing hym flat untoe hys
bedde, tylle such as she appeared toe depart, fryzzling
hys Hayre with her Torche as she went.

"That hee, awakyng from such Dreems, herd thereon
a Rush, and saw a Light." (Hereon a Mayde interrupted
hym, crying out that there was yndeed a Rush-Light
burning yn that same room, and woulde have sayde
more, but that my Loorde checkt her, and sharplie bade
her stow that, meening thereby, that she shoulde holde
her peece.)

Witness continued: "that being muche affrited thereat,
whereby hys Bones were (as hee sayde), all of a dramble,
hee essayed to leep from hys bedde, and soe quit. Yet tar-
ried hee some whyle, not, as might bee thought from
being stout of Harte, but rather of Bodye; whych tyme
she caunted snatches of old lays, as Maister Wil Shakespeare hath yt."

Hereon my Loorde questioned what lays, bydding hym
syng the same, and saying hee knew but of two lays:
" 'Twas yn Trafalgar's bay wee saw the Frenchmen lay",
and "There wee lay all that day yn the Bay of Biscay-O",
whych hee forthwyth hummed aloud, yet out of tune, at
whych somme smyled.

Witness continued: "that hee perchaunce coulde chaunt
the sayde lays wyth Music, but unaccompanied hee durst
not." On thys they hadde hym to the Schoolroom, where
was a Musical Instrument, called a Paean-o-Forty (meaning that yt hadde forty Notes, and was a Paean or
Triumph of Art), whereon two young ladyes, Nieces of
my Loorde, that abode there (lerning, as they deemed,

Lessons; but, I wot, idlynge not a lyttle), did wyth much thumpyng playe certyn Music wyth hys synging, as best they mighte, seeing that the Tunes were such as noe Man had herde before.

> Lorenzo dwelt at Heighington,
> (Hys cote was made of Dimity,)
> Least-ways yf not exactly there,
> Yet yn yts close proximity.
> Hee called on mee—hee stayed to tee—
> Yet not a word he ut-tered,
> Untyl I sayd, "D'ye lyke your bread
> Dry?" and hee answered "But-tered".

(Chorus whereyn all present joyned with fervour.)

> Noodle dumb
> Has a noodle-head,
> I hate such noodles, *I* do.

Witness continued: "that shee then appeared unto hym habited yn the same loose Wrapper, whereyn hee first saw her yn hys Dreem, and yn a stayd and piercing tone gave forth her History as followeth."

THE LADYE'S HISTORY

"On a dewie autumn evening, mighte have been seen, pacing yn the grounds harde by Aucklande Castell, a yong Ladye of a stiff and perky manner, yet not ill to look on, nay, one mighte saye, faire to a degree, save that haply that hadde been untrue.

"That yong Ladye, O miserable Man, was I" (whereon I demanded on what score shee held mee miserable, and shee replied, yt mattered not). "I plumed myself yn those tymes on my exceeding not soe much beauty as loftiness of Figure, and gretely desired that some Painter might paint my picture; but they ever were too high, not yn skyll I trow, but yn charges." (At thys I most humbly enquired at what charge the then Painters wrought, but shee loftily affirmed that money-matters were vulgar and that she knew not, no, nor cared.)

"Now yt chaunced that a certyn Artist, hight Lorenzo, came toe that Quarter, having wyth hym a merveillous machine called by men a Chimera (that ys, a fabulous and wholly incredible thing;) where wyth hee took manie pictures, each yn a single stroke of Tyme, whiles that a Man might name 'John, the son of Robin' (I asked her, what might a stroke of Tyme bee, but shee, frowning, answered not).

"He yt was that undertook my Picture: yn which I mainly required one thyng, that yt shoulde bee at full-length, for yn none other way mighte my Loftiness bee trulie set forth. Nevertheless, though hee took manie Pic-tures, yet all fayled yn thys: for some, beginning at the Hedde reeched not toe the Feet; others, takyng yn the Feet, yet left out the Hedde; whereof the former were a grief unto myself, and the latter a Laughing-Stocke unto others.

"At these thyngs I justly fumed, having at the first been frendly unto hym (though yn sooth hee was dull), and oft smote hym gretely on the Eares, rending from hys Hedde certyn Locks, whereat crying out hee was wont toe saye that I made hys lyfe a burden untoe hym, whych thyng I not so much doubted as highlie rejoyced yn.

"At the last hee counselled thys, that a Picture shoulde bee made, showing so much skyrt as mighte reasonably bee gotte yn, and a Notice set below toe thys effect: 'Item, two yards and a Half Ditto, and then the Feet.' Byt thys no Whit contented mee, and thereon I shut hym ynto the Cellar, where hee remaned three Weeks, growing dayly thinner and thinner, till at the last hee floted up and downe like a Feather.

"Now yt fell at thys tyme, as I questioned hym on a certyn Day, yf hee woulde nowe take mee at full-length, and hee replying untoe mee, yn a little moning Voyce, lyke a Gnat, one chaunced to open the Door: whereat the Draft bore hym uppe ynto a Cracke of the Cieling, and

I remaned awaytyng hym, holding uppe my Torche, until such time as I also faded ynto a Ghost, yet stickyng untoe the Wall."

Then did my Loorde and the Companie haste down ynto the Cellar, for to see thys straunge sight, to whych place when they came, my Loorde bravely drew hys sword, loudly crying "Death!" (though to whom or what he explained not); then some went yn, but the more part hung back, urging on those yn front, not soe largely bye example, as Words of cheer; yet at last all entered, my Loorde last.

Then they removed from the wall the Casks and other stuff, and founde the sayd Ghost, dredful toe relate, yet extant on the Wall, at which horrid sight such screems were raysed as yn these days are seldom or never herde; some faynted, others bye large drafts of Beer saved themselves from that Extremity, yet were they scarcely alive for Feer.

Then dyd the Ladye speak unto them yn suchwise:

> "Here I bee, and here I byde,
> Till such tyme as yt betyde
> That a Ladye of thys place,
> Lyke to mee yn name and face,
> (Though my name bee never known,
> My initials shall bee shown,)
> Shall be fotograffed aright—
> Hedde and Feet bee both yn sight—
> Then my face shall disappear,
> Nor agayn affrite you heer."

Then sayd Matthew Dixon unto her, "Wherefore holdest thou uppe that Torche?" to whych shee answered, "Candles Gyve Light": but none understood her.

After thys a thyn Voyce sayd from overhedde:

> "Yn the Auckland Castell cellar,
> Long, long ago,
> I was shut—a brisk young feller—
> Woe, woe, ah woe!

To take her at full-lengthe
I never hadde the strengthe
Tempore (and soe I tell her)
Practerito!"

(Yn thys Chorus they durst none joyn, seeing that
Latyn was untoe them a Tongue unknown.)

"She was hard—oh, she was cruel—
Long, long ago,
Starved mee here—not even gruel—
No, believe mee, no!—
Frae Scotland could I flee,
I'd gie my last bawbee,—
Arrah, bhoys, fair play's a jhewel,
Lave me, darlints, goe!"

Then my Loorde, putting bye hys Sworde (whych was
layd up thereafter, yn memory of soe grete Bravery),
bade hys Butler fetch hym presentlie a Vessel of Beer,
whych when yt was brought at hys nod (nor, as hee
merrily sayd, hys "nod, and Bec, and wreathed smyle"),
hee drank hugelie thereof: "for why?" quoth hee, "surely
a Bec ys no longer a Bec, when yt ys Dry."

VII
A Miscellany

THE OFFER OF
THE CLARENDON TRUSTEES

> *"Accommodated: That is, when a
> man is, as they say, accommodated:
> or when a man is—being—whereby
> —he may be thought to be accom-
> modated; which is an excellent
> thing."*

*(Written in 1868 as a letter suggesting, half-humorously,
half-seriously, new means for mathematical research.)*

DEAR SENIOR CENSOR:

In a desultory conversation on a point connected with
the dinner at our high table, you incidentally remarked
to me that lobster-sauce, "though a necessary adjunct to
turbot, was not entirely wholesome."

It is entirely unwholesome. I never ask for it without
reluctance: I never take a second spoonful without a feeling of apprehension on the subject of possible nightmare.
This naturally brings me to the subject of Mathematics,
and of the accommodation provided by the University
for carrying on the calculations necessary in that important branch of Science.

As Members of Convocation are called upon (whether
personally, or, as is less exasperating, by letter) to consider the offer of the Clarendon Trustees, as well as every
other subject of human, or inhuman, interest, capable of
consideration, it has occurred to me to suggest for your
consideration how desirable roofed buildings are for carrying on mathematical calculations: in fact, the variable
character of the weather in Oxford renders it highly inexpedient to attempt much occupation, of a sedentary
nature, in the open air.

Again, it is often impossible for students to carry on accurate mathematical calculations in close contiguity to one another, owing to their mutual interference, and a tendency to general conversation: consequently these processes require different rooms in which irrepressible conversationalists, who are found to occur in every branch of Society, might be carefully and permanently fixed.

It may be sufficient for the present to enumerate the following requisites: others might be added as funds permitted.

A. A very large room for calculating Greatest Common Measure. To this a small one might be attached for Least Common Multiple: this, however, might be dispensed with.

B. A piece of open ground for keeping Roots and practising their extraction: it would be advisable to keep Square Roots by themselves, as their corners are apt to damage others.

C. A room for reducing Fractions to their Lowest Terms. This should be provided with a cellar for keeping the Lowest Terms when found, which might also be available to the general body of undergraduates, for the purpose of "keeping Terms".

D. A large room, which might be darkened, and fitted up with a magic lantern, for the purpose of exhibiting Circulating Decimals in the act of circulation. This might also contain cupboards, fitted with glass-doors, for keeping the various Scales of Notation.

E. A narrow strip of ground, railed off and carefully leveled, for investigating the properties of Asymptotes, and testing practically whether Parallel Lines meet or not: for this purpose it should reach, to use the expressive language of Euclid, "ever so far".

This last process, of "continually producing the Lines", may require centuries or more: but such a period, though long in the life of an individual, is as nothing in the life of the University.

As Photography is now very much employed in recording human expressions, and might possibly be adapted to Algebraical Expressions, a small photographic room would be desirable, both for general use and for representing the various phenomena of Gravity, Disturbance of Equilibrium, Resolution, etc., which affect the features during severe mathematical operations.

May I trust that you will give your immediate attention to this most important subject?

Believe me,
Sincerely yours,
MATHEMATICUS

February 6, 1868.

THE NEW METHOD OF EVALUATION

AS APPLIED TO *Π*

"LITTLE JACK HORNER
SAT IN A CORNER
EATING HIS CHRISTMAS PIE."

THE problem of evaluating π which has engaged the attention of mathematicians from the earliest ages, had, down to our own time, been considered as purely arithmetical. It was reserved for this generation to make the discovery that it is in reality a dynamical problem: and the true value of π which appeared an *ignis fatuus* to our forefathers, has been at last obtained under pressure.

The following are the main data of the problem:

Let U = the University, G = Greek, and P = Professor. Then GP = Greek Professor; let this be reduced to its lowest terms, and call the result J.

Also let W = the work done, T = the Times, p = the

given payment, $\pi =$ the payment according to T, and S $=$ the sum required; so that $\pi = S$.

The problem is, to obtain a value for π which shall be commensurable with W.

In the early treatises on this subject, the mean value assigned to π will be found to be 40.000000. Later writers suspected that the decimal point had been accidentally shifted, and that the proper value was 400.00000: but, as the details of the process for obtaining it had been lost, no further progress was made in the subject till our own time, though several most ingenious methods were tried for solving the problem.

Of these methods we proceed to give some brief account. Those chiefly worthy of note appear to be Rationalization, the Method of Indifferences, Penrhyn's Method, and the Method of Elimination.

We shall conclude with an account of the great discovery of our own day, the Method of Evaluation under Pressure.

I. Rationalization

THE peculiarity of this process consists in its affecting all quantities alike with a negative sign.

To apply it, let H $=$ High Church, and L $=$ Low Church, then the geometric mean $= \sqrt{HL}$: call this "B" (Broad Church).

$$\therefore \ HL = B^2.$$

Also let x and y represent unknown quantities.

The process now requires the breaking up of U into its partial factions, and the introduction of certain combinations. Of the two principal factions thus formed, that corresponding with P presented no further difficulty, but it appeared hopeless to rationalize the other.

A *reductio ad absurdum* was therefore attempted, and it was asked "why should π *not* be evaluated?" The great difficulty now was, to discover y.

Several ingenious substitutions and transformations were then resorted to, with a view to simplifying the equation, and it was at one time asserted, though never actually proved, that the y's were all on one side. However, as repeated trials produced the same irrational result, the process was finally abandoned.

II. The Method of Indifferences

THIS was a modification of *"the method of finite Differences"*, and may be thus briefly described:

Let $E = $ Essays, and $R = $ Reviews: then the locus of $(E + R)$, referred to multilinear coördinates, will be found to be a superficies (*i.e.*, a locus possessing length and breadth, but no depth). Let $v = $ novelty, and assume $(E + R)$ as a function of v.

Taking this superficies as the plane of reference, we get—

$$E = R = B$$
$$\therefore EB = B^2 = HL \text{ (By the last article)}$$
$$\text{Multiplying by P, } EBP = HPL.$$

It was now necessary to investigate the locus of EBP: this was found to be a species of Catenary, called the Patristic Catenary, which is usually defined as "passing through origen, and containing many multiple points". The locus of HPL will be found almost entirely to coincide with this.

Great results were expected from the assumption of $(E + R)$ as a function of v: but the opponents of this theorem having actually succeeded in demonstrating that the v-element did not even enter into the function, it appeared hopeless to obtain any real value of π by this method.

III. Penrhyn's Method

THIS was an exhaustive process for extracting the value of π in a series of terms, by repeated divisions. The series so obtained appeared to be convergent, but the residual quantity was always negative, which of course made the process of extraction impossible.

This theorem was originally derived from a radical series in Arithmetical Progression: let us denote the series itself by A.P., and its sum by (A.P.)S. It was found that the function (A.P.)S. entered into the above process, in various forms.

The experiment was therefore tried of transforming (A.P.)S. into a new scale of notation: it had hitherto been, through a long series of terms, entirely in the senary, in which scale it had furnished many beautiful expressions: it was now transferred into the denary.

Under this modification, the process of division was repeated, but with the old negative result: the attempt was therefore abandoned, though not without a hope that future mathematicians, by introducing a number of hitherto undetermined constants, raised to the second degree, might succeed in obtaining a positive result.

IV. Elimination of J

It had long been perceived that the chief obstacle to the evaluation of π was the presence of J, and in an earlier age of mathematics J would probably have been referred to rectangular axes, and divided into two unequal parts—a process of arbitrary elimination which is now considered not strictly legitimate.

It was proposed, therefore, to eliminate J by an appeal to the principle known as *"the permanence of equivalent formularies"*: this, however, failed on application, as J became indeterminate. Some advocates of the process would have preferred that J should be eliminated *in toto*. The classical scholar need hardly be reminded that *toto* is the ablative of *tumtum*, and that this beautiful and expressive phrase embodied the wish that J should be eliminated by the compulsory religious examination.

It was next proposed to eliminate J by means of a *canonisant*. The chief objection to this process was, that it would raise J to an inconveniently high power, and would after all only give an irrational value for π.

Other processes, which we need not here describe, have been suggested for the evaluation of π. One was, that it should be treated as a *given* quantity: this theory was supported by many eminent men, at Cambridge and elsewhere; but, on application, J was found to exhibit a negative sign, which of course made the evaluation impossible.

We now proceed to describe the modern method, which has been crowned with brilliant and unexpected success, and which may be defined as

V. Evaluation Under Pressure

MATHEMATICIANS had already investigated the locus of HPL, and had introduced this function into the calculation, but without effecting the desired evaluation, even when HPL was transferred to the opposite side of the equation, with a change of sign. The process we are about to describe consists chiefly in the substitution of G for P, and the application of pressure.

Let the function ϕ (HGL) be developed into a series, and let the sum of this be assumed as a perfectly rigid body, moving in a fixed line; let "μ" be the coefficient of moral obligation, and "e" the expediency. Also let "F" be a Force acting equally in all directions, and varying inversely as T: let A = Able, and E = Enlightened.

We have now to develop ϕ (HGL) by Maclaurin's Theorem.

The function itself vanishes when the variable vanishes:

i.e.
$$\phi\,(o) = O$$
$$\phi'\,(o) = C \text{ (a prime constant)}$$
$$\phi''\,(o) = 2.J.$$
$$\phi'''\,(o) = 2.3.H$$
$$\phi''''\,(o) = 2.3.4.S$$
$$\phi'''''\,(o) = 2.3.4.5.P$$
$$\phi''''''\,(o) = 2.3.4.5.6.J$$

after which the quantities recur in the same order.

The above proof is taken from the learned treatise *"Augusti de fallibilitate historicorum"*, and occupies an entire Chapter: the evaluation of π is given in the next Chapter. The author takes occasion to point out several remarkable properties, possessed by the above series, the existence of which had hardly been suspected before.

This series is a function both of μ and of e: but, when it is considered as a body, it will be found that $\mu = 0$ and that e only remains.

We now have the equation

$$\phi \, (HGL) = O + C + J + H + S + P + J.$$

The summation of this gave a minimum value for π: this, however, was considered only as a first approximation, and the process was repeated under pressure EAF, which gave to π a partial maximum value: by continually increasing EAF, the result was at last obtained.

$$\pi = S = 500.00000.$$

The result differs considerably from the anticipated value, namely 400.00000: still there can be no doubt that the process has been correctly performed, and that the learned world may be congratulated on the final settlement of this most difficult problem.

THE DYNAMICS OF A PARTI-CLE

" 'Tis strange the mind, that very fiery particle,
Should let itself be snuff'd out by an article."

(First printed in 1865 as an Oxford pamphlet, this article concerns itself with the then existing political situation.)

INTRODUCTION

I T was a lovely Autumn evening, and the glorious effects of chromatic aberration were beginning to show them-

selves in the atmosphere as the earth revolved away from
the great western luminary, when two lines might have
been observed wending their weary way across a plane
superficies. The elder of the two had by long practice acquired the art, so painful to young and impulsive loci, of
lying evenly between his extreme points; but the younger,
in her girlish impetuosity, was ever longing to diverge and
become an hyperbola or some such romantic and boundless curve. They had lived and loved: fate and the inter-
vening superficies had hitherto kept them asunder, but
this was no longer to be: a line had intersected them,
making the two interior angles together less than two
right angles. It was a moment never to be forgotten, and,
as they journeyed on, a whisper thrilled along the superficies in isochronous waves of sound, "Yes! We shall at
length meet if continually produced!" (Jacobi's Course of
Mathematics, Chap. I.)

We have commenced with the above quotation as a
striking illustration of the advantage of introducing the
human element into the hitherto barren region of Mathematics. Who shall say what germs of romance, hitherto
unobserved, may not underlie the subject? Who can tell
whether the parallelogram, which in our ignorance we
have defined and drawn, and the whole of whose properties we profess to know, may not be all the while panting
for exterior angles, sympathetic with the interior, or
sullenly repining at the fact that it cannot be inscribed
in a circle? What mathematician has ever pondered
over an hyperbola, mangling the unfortunate curve
with lines of intersection here and there, in his efforts
to prove some property that perhaps after all is a
mere calumny, who has not fancied at last that the ill-
used locus was spreading out its asymptotes as a silent
rebuke, or winking one focus at him in contemptuous
pity?

In some such spirit as this we have compiled the following pages. Crude and hasty as they are, they yet exhibit some of the phenomena of light, or "enlightenment",

considered as a force, more fully than has hitherto been attempted by other writers.

June, 1865.

Chapter I

GENERAL CONSIDERATIONS

Definitions

I

PLAIN SUPERFICIALITY is the character of a speech, in which any two points being taken, the speaker is found to lie wholly with regard to those two points.

II

PLAIN ANGER is the inclination of two voters to one another, who meet together, but whose views are not in the same direction.

III

When a Proctor, meeting another Proctor, makes the votes on one side equal to those on the other, the feeling entertained by each side is called RIGHT ANGER.

IV

When two parties, coming together, feel a Right Anger, each is *said* to be COMPLEMENTARY to the other (though, strictly speaking, this is very seldom the case).

V

OBTUSE ANGER is that which is greater than Right Anger.

Postulates

I

Let it be granted, that a speaker may digress from any one point to any other point.

II

That a finite argument (i.e. one finished and disposed of), may be produced to any extent in subsequent debates.

III

That a controversy may be raised about any question, and at any distance from that question.

Axioms

I

Men who go halves in the same (quart) are (generally) equal to another.

II

Men who take a double in the same (term) are equal to anything.

On Voting

The different methods of voting are as follows:

I

ALTERNANDO, as in the case of Mr. —— who voted for and against Mr. Gladstone, alternate elections.

II

INVERTENDO, as was done by Mr. —— who came all the way from Edinburgh to vote, handed in a blank voting-paper, and so went home rejoicing.

III

COMPONENDO, as was done by Mr. —— whose name appeared on both committees at once, whereby he got great praise from all men, by the space of one day.

IV

DIVIDENDO, as in Mr. ——'s case, who being sorely perplexed in his choice of candidates, voted for neither.

V

CONVERTENDO, as was wonderfully exemplified by Messrs. —— and —— who held a long and fierce argument on the election, in which, at the end of two hours, each had vanquished and converted the other.

VI

EX ÆQUALI IN PROPORTIONE PERTURBATA SEU INORDINATA, as in the election, when the result was for a long time equalized, and as it were held in the balance, by reason of those who had first voted on the one side seeking to pair off with those who had last arrived on the other side, and those who were last to vote on the one side being kept out by those who had first arrived on the other side, whereby, the entry to the Convocation House being blocked up, men could pass neither in nor out.

On Representation

Magnitudes are algebraically represented by letters, men by men of letters, and so on. The following are the principal systems of representation.

1. CARTESIAN: i.e. by means of "cartes". This system represents *lines* well, sometimes too well; but fails in representing *points*, particularly good points.

2. POLAR: i.e. by means of the 2 poles, "North and South." This is a very uncertain system of representation, and one that cannot safely be depended upon.

3. TRILINEAR: i.e. by means of a line which takes 3 different courses. Such a line is usually expressed by three letters, as W.E.G.

That the principle of Representation was known to the ancients is abundantly exemplified by Thucydides, who tells us that the favourite cry of encouragement during a trireme race was that touching allusion to Polar Coördinates which is still heard during the races of our own time, "$\rho 5$, $\rho 6$, cos ϕ, they're gaining!"

CHAPTER II

DYNAMICS OF A PARTICLE

Particles are logically divided according to GENIUS and SPEECHES.

GENIUS is the higher classification, and this, combined with DIFFERENTIA (i.e. difference of opinion), produces SPEECHES. These again naturally divide themselves into three heads.

Particles belonging to the great order of GENIUS are called "able" or "enlightened".

Definitions

I

A SURD is a radical whose meaning cannot be exactly ascertained. This class comprises a very large number of particles.

II

INDEX indicates the degree, or power, to which a particle is raised. It consists of two letters, placed to the right of the symbol representing the particle. Thus, "A.A." signifies the oth degree; "B.A." the 1st degree; and so on, till we reach "M.A." the 2nd degree (the intermediate letters indicating fractions of a degree); the last two usually employed being "R.A." (the reader need hardly be reminded of that beautiful line in *The Princess* "Go dress yourself, Dinah, like a gorgeous R.A.") and "S.A." This last indicates the 360th degree, and denotes that the particle in question (which is 1/7th part of the function $E + R$ "Essays and Reviews",) has effected a complete revolution, and that the result $= 0$.

III

MOMENT is the product of the mass into the velocity. To discuss this subject fully, would lead us too far into the subject Vis Viva, and we must content ourselves with mentioning the fact that *no moment is ever really lost, by fully enlightened Particles*. It is scarcely necessary to quote the well-known passage: "Every moment, that can be snatched from academical duties, is devoted to furthering the cause of the popular Chancellor of the Exchequer."—(Clarendon, History of the Great Rebellion.)

IV

A COUPLE consists of a moving particle, raised to the degree M.A., and combined with what is technically called a "better half". The following are the principal characteristics of a Couple: (1) It may be easily transferred from point to point. (2) Whatever *force of translation* was possessed by the uncombined particle (and this is often considerable), is wholly lost when the Couple is formed. (3) The two forces constituting the Couple habitually *act in opposite directions*.

On Differentiation

The effect of Differentiation on a Particle is very remarkable, the first Differential being frequently of a greater value than the original Particle, and the second of less enlightenment.

For example, let L = "Leader", S = "Saturday", and then L.S. = "Leader in the Saturday" (a particle of no assignable value). Differentiating once, we get L.S.D., a function of great value. Similarly it will be found that, by taking a second Differential of an enlightened Particle (i.e. raising it to the Degree D.D.), the enlightenment becomes rapidly less. The effect is much increased by the addition of a C: in this case the enlightenment often vanishes altogether, and the Particle becomes conservative.

It should be observed that, whenever the symbol L is used to denote "Leader", it must be affected with the sign ±: this serves to indicate that its action is sometimes positive and sometimes negative—some particles of this class having the property of drawing others after them (as "a Leader of an army"), and others of repelling them (as "a leader of the Times").

Propositions

PROP. I. PR.

To find the value of a given Examiner.

Example. A takes in 10 books in the Final Examination, and gets a 3d Class: B takes in the Examiners, and gets a 2nd. Find the value of the Examiners in terms of books. Find also their value in terms in which no Examination is held.

PROP. II. PR.

To estimate Profit and Loss.

Example. Given a Derby Prophet, who has sent 3 different winners to 3 different betting-men, and given that none of the three horses are placed. Find the total Loss incurred by the three men (*a*) in money, (*b*) in temper. Find also the Prophet. Is this latter generally possible?

To estimate the direction of a line.

Example. Prove that the definition of a line, according to Walton, coincides with that of Salmon, only that they begin at opposite ends. If such a line be divided by Frost's method, find its value according to Price.

The end (i.e. "the product of the extremes"), justifies (i.e. "is equal to"—see Latin "æquus"), the means.

No example is appended to this Proposition, for obvious reasons.

To continue a given series.

Example. A and B who are respectively addicted to Fours and Fives, occupy the same set of rooms, which is always at Sixes and Sevens. Find the probable amount of reading done by A and B while the Eights are on.

We proceed to illustrate this hasty sketch of the Dynamics of a Parti-cle, by demonstrating the great Proposition on which the whole theory of Representation depends, namely: "To remove a given Tangent from a given Circle, and to bring another given Line into contact with it."

To work the following problem algebraically, it is best to let the circle be represented as referred to its two tangents, i.e. first to WEG, WH, and afterwards to WH, GH. When this is effected, it will be found most convenient to project WEG to infinity. The process is not given here in full, since it requires the introduction of many complicated determinants.

To remove a given Tangent from a given Circle, and to bring another given Line into contact with it.

Let UNIV be a Large Circle, whose centre is O (V being, of course, placed at the top), and let WGH be a triangle, two of whose sides, WEG and WH, are in contact with the circle, while GH (called "the base" by liberal mathematicians), is not in contact with it. (See Fig.1.) It is required to destroy the contact of WEG, and to bring GH into contact instead.

Let I be the point of maximum illumination of the circle, and therefore E the point of maximum enlightenment of the triangle. (E of course varying perversely as the square of the distance from O.)

Let WH be fixed absolutely, and remain always in contact with the circle, and let the direction of OI be also fixed.

Now, so long as WEG preserves a perfectly straight course, GH cannot possibly come into contact with the circle, but if the force of illumination, acting along OI, cause it to bend (as in Fig. 2), a partial revolution on the part of WEG and GH is effected, WEG ceases to touch the circle, and GH is immediately brought into contact with it. Q.E.F.

The theory involved in the foregoing Proposition is at present much controverted, and its supporters are called upon to show what is the fixed *point*, or *locus standi*, on which they propose to effect the necessary revolution. To make this clear, we must go to the original Greek, and remind our readers that the true point or *locus standi*, is in this case 'ἀρδις (or 'ἀρδις according to modern usage), and therefore must not be assigned to WEG. In reply to this it is urged that, in a matter like the present, a single word cannot be considered a satisfactory explanation, such as ἀρδέως.

It should also be observed that the revolution here discussed is entirely the effect of enlightenment, since particles, when illuminated to such an extent as actually to become φώς, are always found to diverge more or less widely from each other; though undoubtedly the *radical* force of the word is "union" or "friendly feeling". The reader will find in "Liddell and Scott" a remarkable illustration of this, from which it appears to be an essential condition that the feeling should be entertained φοράδην and that the particle entertaining it should belong to the genus ἀκύτυς and should therefore be, nominally at least, unenlightened.

THE NEW BELFRY
OF CHRIST CHURCH, OXFORD

A MONOGRAPH BY D. C. L.

"A thing of beauty is a joy forever."

I. ON THE ETYMOLOGICAL SIGNIFICANCE OF THE NEW BELFRY, CH. CH.

THE word "Belfry" is derived from the French *bel*, "beautiful, becoming, meet," and from the German *frei*, "free, unfettered, secure, safe." Thus the word is strictly equivalent to "meatsafe", to which the new Belfry bears a resemblance so perfect as almost to amount to coincidence.

II. ON THE STYLE OF THE NEW BELFRY, CH. CH.

THE style is that which is usually known as "Early Debased": very early, and remarkably debased.

III. ON THE ORIGIN OF THE NEW BELFRY, CH. CH.

OUTSIDERS have enquired, with a persistence verging on personality, and with a recklessness scarcely distinguishable from insanity, to *whom* we are to attribute the first grand conception of the work. Was it the Treasurer, say

they, who thus strove to force it on an unwilling House?
Was it a Professor who designed this box, which, whether
with a lid on or not, equally offends the eye? Or was it a
Censor whose weird spells evoked the horrible thing, the
bane of this and of succeeding generations? Until some
reply is given to these and similar questions, they must
and will remain—forever—unanswered!

On this point Rumour has been unusually busy. Some
say that the Governing Body evolved the idea in solemn
conclave—the original motion being to adopt the Tower
of St. Mark's at Venice as a model: and that by a series of
amendments it was reduced at last to a simple cube.
Others say that the Reader in Chemistry suggested it as a
form of crystal. There are others who affirm that the
Mathematical Lecturer found it in the Eleventh Book of
Euclid. In fact, there is no end to the various myths afloat
on the subject. Most fortunately, we are in possession of
the real story.

The true origin of the design is as follows: we have it
on the very best authority.

The head of the House, and the architect, feeling a
natural wish that their names should be embodied, in
some conspicuous way, among the alterations then in
progress, conceived the beautiful and unique idea of representing, by means of a new Belfry, a gigantic copy of a
Greek Lexicon.[1] But, before the idea had been reduced to
a working form, business took them both to London for a
few days, and during their absence, somehow (*this* part of
the business has never been satisfactorily explained) the
whole thing was put into the hands of a wandering architect, who gave the name of Jeeby. As the poor man is now
incarcerated at Hanwell, we will not be too hard upon his
memory, but will only say that he professed to have ori-
ginated the idea in a moment of inspiration, when idly
contemplating one of those highly coloured, and mysteri-

---

[1] The editor confesses to a difficulty here. No sufficient reason
has been adduced why a model of a Greek Lexicon should in any
way "embody" the names of the above illustrious individuals.

ously decorated chests which, filled with dried leaves from gooseberry bushes and quickset hedges, profess to supply the market with tea of genuine Chinese growth. Was there not something prophetic in the choice? What traveler is there, to whose lips, when first he enters the great educational establishment and gazes on its newest decoration, the words do not rise unbidden—"Thou tea-chest"?

It is plain then that Scott, the great architect to whom the work of restoration has been entrusted, is not responsible for this. He is *said* to have pronounced it a *casus belli*, which (with all deference to the Classical Tutors of the House, who insist that he meant merely "a case for a bell") we believe to have been intended as a term of reproach.

The following lines are attributed to Scott:

> "If thou wouldst view the Belfry aright,
> Go visit it at the mirk midnight—
> For the least hint of open day
> Scares the beholder quite away.
> When wall and window are black as pitch,
> And there's no deciding which is which;
> When the dark Hall's uncertain roof
> In horror seems to stand aloof;
> When corner and corner, alternately,
> Is wrought to an odious symmetry;
> When distant Thames is heard to sigh
> And shudder as he hurries by;
> Then go, if it be worth the while,
> Then view the Belfry's monstrous pile,
> And, home returning, soothly swear
> ' 'Tis more than Job himself could bear!' "

IV. ON THE CHIEF ARCHITECTURAL MERIT OF THE NEW BELFRY, CH. CH.

Its chief merit is its Simplicity—a Simplicity so pure, so profound, in a word, so *simple*, that no other word will fitly describe it. The meagre outline, and baldness of detail, of the present Chapter, are adopted in humble imitation of this great feature.

V. ON THE OTHER ARCHITECTURAL MERITS OF THE NEW BELFRY, CH. CH.

THE Belfry has no other architectural merits.

VI. ON THE MEANS OF OBTAINING THE BEST VIEWS OF THE NEW BELFRY, CH. CH.

THE visitor may place himself, in the first instance, at the opposite corner of the Great Quadrangle, and so combine, in one grand spectacle, the beauties of the North and West sides of the edifice. He will find that the converging lines forcibly suggest a vanishing point, and if that vanishing point should in its turn suggest the thought, "would that *it* were on the point of vanishing!" he may perchance, like the Soldier in the Ballad, "lean upon his sword" (if he has one: they are not commonly worn by modern tourists), "and wipe away a tear."

He may then make the circuit of the Quadrangle, drinking in new visions of beauty at every step—

> "Ever charming, ever new,
> When will the Belfry tire the view?"

as Dyer sings in his well-known poem, "Grongar Hill"— and, as he walks along from the Deanery towards the Hall staircase, and breathes more and more freely as the Belfry lessens on the view, the delicious sensation of relief, which he will experience when it has finally disappeared, will amply repay him for all he will have endured.

The *best* view of the Belfry is that selected by our Artist for the admirable frontispiece which he has furnished for the first Volume of the present work.[1] This view

[1] On further consideration, it was deemed inexpedient to extend this work beyond the compass of one Volume.

may be seen, in all its beauty, from the far end of Merton Meadow. From that point the imposing position (or, more briefly, the imposition) of the whole structure is thrilling-ly apparent. There the thoughtful passer-by, with four right angles on one side of him, and four anglers, who have no right to be there, on the other, may ponder on the mutability of human things, or recall the names of Euclid and Isaac Walton, or smoke, or ride a bicycle, or do anything that the local authorities will permit.

VII. ON THE IMPETUS GIVEN TO ART IN ENGLAND BY THE NEW BELFRY, CH. CH.

THE idea has spread far and wide, and is rapidly per-vading all branches of manufacture. Already an enter-prising maker of bonnet-boxes is advertising "the Belfry pattern": two builders of bathing machines at Ramsgate have followed his example: one of the great London houses is supplying "bar-soap" cut in the same striking and symmetrical form: and we are credibly informed that Borwick's Baking Powder and Thorley's Food for Cattle are now sold in no other shape.

VIII. ON THE FEELINGS WITH WHICH OLD CH. CH. MEN REGARD THE NEW BELFRY.

BITTERLY bitterly do all old Ch. Ch. men lament this latest lowest development of native taste. "We see the Governing Body," say they: "Where is the Governing *Mind?*" And Echo (exercising a judicious "natural selec-tion" for which even Darwin would give her credit) answers—"where?"

At the approaching "Gaudy", when a number of old Ch. Ch. men will be gathered together, it is proposed, at the conclusion of the banquet, to present to each guest a portable model of the new Belfry, tastefully executed in cheese.

IX. ON THE FEELINGS WITH WHICH RESIDENT CH. CH.
MEN REGARD THE NEW BELFRY.

WHO that has seen a Ch. Ch. man conducting his troop
of "lionesses" (so called from the savage and pitiless greed
with which they devour the various sights of Oxford)
through its ancient precincts, that has noticed the convulsive start and ghastly stare that always affect new-
comers when first they come into view of the new Belfry,
that has heard the eager questions with which they assail
their guide as to the how, the why, the what for, and the
how long, of this astounding phenomenon, can have
failed to mark the manly glow which immediately suf-
fuses the cheek of the hapless cicerone?

"Is it the glow of conscious pride—
Of pure ambition gratified—
That seeks to read in other eye
Something of its own ecstasy?
Or wrath, that worldlings should make fun
Of anything 'the House' has done?
Or puzzlement, that seeks in vain
The rigid mystery to explain?
Or is it shame that, knowing not
How to defend or cloak the blot—
The foulest blot on fairest face
That ever marred a noble place—
Burns with the pangs it will not own,
Pangs felt by loyal sons alone?"

X. ON THE LOGICAL TREATMENT OF THE NEW
BELFRY, CH. CH.

THE subject has been reduced to three Syllogisms.
The first is in "*Barbara*". It is attributed to the enemies
of the Belfry.

Wooden buildings in the midst of stone-work are barbarous;

Plain rectangular forms in the midst of arches and decora-
 tions are barbarous;
Ergo, The whole thing is ridiculous and revolting.

The second is in *"Celarent"*, and has been most carefully composed by the friends of the Belfry.

The Governing Body would conceal this appalling structure, if they could;
The Governing Body would conceal the feelings of
 chagrin with which they now regard it, if they could;
Ergo, ... (MS. *unfinished*.)

The third Syllogism is in *"Festino"*, and is the joint
composition of the friends and enemies of the Belfry.

To restore the character of Ch. Ch., a tower must be
 built;
To build a tower, ten thousand pounds must be raised;
Ergo, No time must be lost.

These three syllogisms have been submitted to the
criticism of the Professor of Logic, who writes that "he
fancies he can detect some slight want of logical sequence
in the Conclusion of the third". He adds that, according
to *his* experience of life, when people thus commit a fatal
blunder in child-like confidence that money will be forthcoming to enable them to set it right, in ten cases out of
nine the money is *not* forthcoming. This is a large percentage.

XI. ON THE DRAMATIC TREATMENT OF
THE NEW BELFRY, CH. CH.

CURTAIN rises, discovering the Dean, Canons, and Students, seated round a table, on which the mad Architect,
fantastically dressed, and wearing a Fool's cap and bells,
is placing a square block of deal.

DEAN (*as Hamlet*). Methinks I see a Bell-tower!

CANONS (*looking wildly in all directions*). Where, my good Sir?

DEAN. In my mind's eye. (*Knocking heard.*) Who's there?

FOOL. A spirit, a spirit; he says his name's poor Tom.

Enter THE GREAT BELL, *disguised as a mushroom.*

GREAT BELL. Who gives anything to poor Tom? whom the foul fiend hath led through bricks and through mortar, through rope and windlass, through plank and scaffold; that hath torn down his balustrades, and torn up his terraces; that hath made him go as a common pedlar, with a wooden box upon his back. Do poor Tom some charity. Tom's a-cold.

> Rafters, and planks, and such small deer,
> Shall be Tom's food for many a year.

CENSOR. I feared it would come to this.

DEAN (*as King Lear*). The little dons and all, Tutor, Reader, Lecturer—see, they bark at me!

CENSOR. His wits begin to unsettle.

DEAN (*as Hamlet*). Do you see yonder box, that's almost in shape of a tea-caddy?

CENSOR. By its mass, it is like a tea-caddy, indeed.

DEAN. Methinks it is like a clothes-horse.

CENSOR. It is backed like a clothes-horse.

DEAN. Or like a tub.

CENSOR. Very like a tub.

DEAN. They fool me to the top of my bent.

Enter from opposite sides THE BELFRY *as* BOX, *and* THE BODLEY LIBRARIAN *as* COX.

LIBRARIAN. Who are you, Sir?

BELFRY. If it comes to that, Sir, who are you?

They exchange cards.

LIBRARIAN. I should feel obliged to you if you would accommodate me with a more protuberant Bell-tower, Mr. B. The one you have now seems to me to consist of corners only, with nothing whatever in the middle.

BELFRY. Anything to accommodate you, Mr. Cox.

(*Places jauntily on his head a small model of the skeleton of an umbrella, upside down.*)

LIBRARIAN. Ah, tell me—in mercy tell me—have you such a thing as a redeeming feature, or the least mark of artistic design, about you?

BELFRY. No!

LIBRARIAN. Then you are my long-lost door scraper!

They rush into each other's arms.

Enter TREASURER *as* ARIEL. *Solemn music.*

SONG AND CHORUS

Five fathom square the Belfry frowns;
  All its sides of timber made;
Painted all in grays and browns;
  Nothing of it that will fade.
Christ Church may admire the change—
Oxford thinks it sad and strange.
Beauty's dead! Let's ring her knell.
Hark! now I hear them—ding-dong, bell.

XII. ON THE FUTURE OF THE NEW BELFRY, CH. CH.

THE Belfry has a great Future before it—at least, if it has not, it has very little to do with Time at all, its Past being (fortunately for our ancestors) a nonentity, and its Present a blank. The advantage of having been born in the reign of Queen Anne, and of having died in that or the subsequent reign, has never been so painfully apparent as it is now.

Credible witnesses assert that, when the bells are rung, the Belfry must come down. In that case considerable damage (the process technically described as "pulverisation") must ensue to the beautiful pillar and roof which adorn the Hall staircase. But the architect is prepared even for this emergency. "On the first symptom of deflection" (he writes from Hanwell), "let the pillar be carefully removed and placed, with its superstruent superstructure" (we cannot forbear calling attention to this beautiful phrase), "in the centre of 'Mercury'. *There* it will constitute a novel and most unique feature of the venerable House."

"Yea, and the Belfry shall serve to generations yet unborn as an aerial Ticket-office," so he cries with his eye in a fine frenzy rolling, "where the Oxford and London Balloon shall call ere it launch forth on its celestial voyage—and where expectant passengers shall while away the time with the latest edition of 'Bell's Life'!"

XIII. ON THE MORAL OF THE NEW BELFRY, CH. CH.

THE moral position of Christ Church is undoubtedly improved by it. "We have been attacked, and perhaps not without reason, on the Bread-and-Butter question," she remarks to an inattentive World (which heeds her not, but prates on of Indirect Claims and of anything but indirect Claimants), "we have been charged—and, it must be confessed, in a free and manly tone—with shortcomings in the payment of the Greek Professor, but who shall say that we are not all 'on the square' *now*?"

This, however, is not *the* Moral of the matter. Every thing has a moral, if you choose to look for it. In Wordsworth, a good half of every poem is devoted to the Moral: in Byron, a smaller proportion: in Tupper, the whole. Perhaps the most graceful tribute we can pay to the genius of the last-named writer, is to entrust to him, as an old member of Christ Church, the conclusion of this Monograph.

"Look on the Quadrangle of Christ Church, squarely, for is
   it not a Square?
And a Square recalleth a Cube; and a Cube recalleth the
   Belfry;
And the Belfry recalleth a Die, shaken by the hand of the
   gambler;
Yet, once thrown, it may not be recalled, being, so to speak,
   irrevocable.
There it shall endure for ages, treading hard on the heels
   of the Sublime——

For it is but a step, saith the wise man, from the Sublime
unto the Ridiculous:
And the Simple dwelleth midway between, and shareth the
qualities of either."

THE VISION OF THE THREE T'S

A THRENODY

Contents

CHAPTER I

*A Conference (held on the Twentieth of March, 1873)
betwixt an Angler, a Hunter, and a Professor; concerning angling and the beautifying of Thomas his Quadrangle. The Ballad of "The Wandering Burgess".*

CHAPTER II

*A Conference, with one distraught: who discourseth
strangely of many things.*

CHAPTER III

*A Conference of the Hunter with a Tutor, whilom the
Angler his eyes be closed in sleep. The Angler awaking
relateth his Vision. The Hunter chaunteth "A Baccanalian Ode."*

CHAPTER I

*A Conference betwixt an Angler, a Hunter, and a Professor; concerning angling, and the beautifying of
Thomas his Quadrangle. The Ballad of "The Wandering Burgess".*

PISCATOR. My honest Scholar, we are now arrived at the place whereof I spake, and trust me, we shall have good sport. How say you? Is not this a noble Quadrangle we see around us? And be not these lawns trimly kept, and this lake marvellous clear?

VENATOR. So marvellous clear, good Master, and withal so brief in compass, that methinks, if any fish of a reasonable bigness were therein, we must perforce espy it. I fear me there is none.

PISC. The less fish, dear Scholar, the greater the skill in catching of it. Come, let's sit down, and, while we unpack the fishing-gear, I'll deliver a few remarks, both as to the fish to be met with hereabouts, and the properest method of fishing.

But you are to note first (for, as you are pleased to be my Scholar, it is but fitting you should imitate my habits of close observation) that the margin of this lake is so deftly fashioned that each portion thereof is at one and the same distance from that tumulus which rises in the centre.

VEN. O' my word, 'tis so! You have indeed a quick eye, dear Master, and a wondrous readiness of observing.

PISC. Both may be yours in time, my Scholar, if with humility and patience you follow me as your model.

VEN. I thank you for that hope, great Master! But ere you begin your discourse, let me enquire of you one thing touching this noble Quadrangle.—Is all we see of a like antiquity? To be brief, think you that those two tall archways, that excavation in the parapet, and that quaint wooden box, belong to the ancient design of the building, or have men of our day thus sadly disfigured the place?

PISC. I doubt not they are new, dear Scholar. For indeed I was here but a few years since, and saw naught of these things. But what book is that I see lying by the water's edge?

VEN. A book of ancient ballads, and truly I am glad to

see it, as we may herewith beguile the tediousness of the day, if our sport be poor, or if we grow aweary.

PISC. This is well thought of. But now to business. And first I'll tell you somewhat of the fish proper to these waters. The Commoner kinds we may let pass: for though some of them be easily Plucked forth from the water, yet are they so slow, and withal have so little in them, that they are good for nothing, unless they be crammed up to the very eyes with such stuffing as comes readiest to hand. Of these the Stickleback, a mighty slow fish, is chiefest, and along with him you may reckon the Fluke, and divers others: all these belong to the "Mullet" genus, and be good to play, though scarcely worth examination.

I will now say somewhat of the Nobler kinds, and chiefly of the Gold-fish, which is a species highly thought of, and much sought after in these parts, not only by men, but by divers birds, as for example the King-fishers: and note that wheresoever you shall see those birds assemble, and but few insects about, there shall you ever find the Gold-fish most lively and richest in flavour: but wheresoever you perceive swarms of a certain gray fly, called the Dun-fly, there the Gold-fish are ever poorer in quality, and the King-fishers seldom seen.

A good Perch may sometimes be found hereabouts: but for a good fat Plaice (which is indeed but a magnified Perch) you may search these waters in vain. They that love such dainties must needs betake them to some distant Sea.

But for the manner of fishing, I would have you note first that your line be not thicker than an ordinary bell-rope: for look you, to flog the water, as though you laid on with a flail, is most preposterous, and will surely scare the fish. And note further, that your rod must by no means exceed ten, or at the most twenty, pounds in weight, for——

VEN. Pardon me, my Master, that I thus break in on so excellent a discourse, but there now approaches us a Collegian, as I guess him to be, from whom we may haply learn the cause of these novelties we see around us. Is not that a bone which, ever as he goes, he so cautiously waves before him?

Enter PROFESSOR

PISC. By his reverend aspect and white hair, I guess him to be some learned Professor. I give you good day, reverend Sir! If it be not ill manners to ask it, what bone is that you bear about with you? It is, methinks, a humerous whimsy to chuse so strange a companion.

PROF. Your observation, Sir, is both anthropolitically and ambidexterously opportune: for this is indeed a *Humerus* I carry with me. You are, I doubt not, strangers in these parts, for else you would surely know that a Professor doth ever carry that which most aptly sets forth his Profession. Thus, the Professor of Uniform Rotation carries with him a wheelbarrow—the Professor of Graduated Scansion a ladder—and so of the rest.

VEN. It is an inconvenient and, methinks, an ill-advised custom.

PROF. Trust me, Sir, you are absolutely and amorphologically mistaken: yet time would fail me to show you wherein lies your error, for indeed I must now leave you, being bound for this great performance of music, which even at this distance salutes your ears.

PISC. Yet, I pray you, do us one courtesy before you go: and that shall be to resolve a question, whereby my friend and I are sorely exercised.

PROF. Say on, Sir, and I will e'en answer you to the best of my poor ability.

PISC. Briefly, then, we would ask the cause for piercing the very heart of this fair building with that uncomely tunnel, which is at once so ill-shaped, so ill-sized, and so ill-lighted.

PROF. Sir, do you know German?

PISC. It is my grief, Sir, that I know no other tongue than mine own.

PROF. Then, Sir, my answer is this, Warum nicht?

Pisc. Alas, Sir, I understand you not.

Prof. The more the pity. For nowadays, all that is good comes from the German. Ask our men of science: they will tell you that any German book must needs surpass an English one. Aye, and even an English book, worth naught in this its native dress, shall become, when rendered into German, a valuable contribution to Science!

Ven. Sir, you much amaze me.

Prof. Nay, Sir, I'll amaze you yet more. No learned man doth now talk, or even so much as cough, save only in German. The time has been, I doubt not, when an honest English "Hem!" was held enough, both to clear the voice and rouse the attention of the company, but nowadays no man of Science, that setteth any store by his good name, will cough otherwise than thus, Ach! Euch! Auch!

Ven. 'Tis wondrous. But, not to stay you further, wherefore do we see that ghastly gash above us, hacked, as though by some wanton school-boy in the parapet adjoining the Hall?

Prof. Sir, do *you* know German?

Ven. Believe me, No.

Prof. Then, Sir, I need but ask you this, Wie befinden Sie Sich?

Ven. I doubt not, Sir, but you are in the right on't.

Pisc. But, Sir, I will by your favour ask you one other thing, as to that unseemly box that blots the fair heavens above. Wherefore, in this grand old City, and in so conspicuous a place, do men set so hideous a thing?

Prof. Be you mad, Sir? Why this is the very climacteric and coronal of all our architectural aspirations! In all Oxford there is naught like it!

Pisc. It joys me much to hear you say so.

Prof. And, trust me, to an earnest mind, the categorical evolution of the Abstract, ideologically considered, must infallibly develop itself in the parallelepipedisation of the Concrete! And so farewell.

Exit Professor

PISC. He is a learned man, and methinks there is much that is sound in his reasoning.

VEN. It is *all* sound, as it seems to me. But how say you? Shall I read you one of these ballads? Here is one called "The Wandering Burgess", which (being forsooth a dumpish ditty) may well suit the ears of us whose eyes are oppressed with so dire a spectacle.

PISC. Read on, good Scholar, and I will bait our hooks the while.

VENATOR readeth

THE WANDERING BURGESS

Our Willie had been sae lang awa'
    Frae bonnie Oxford toon,
The townsfolk they were greeting a'
    As they went up and doon.

He hadna been gane a year, a year,
    A year but barely ten,
When word came unto Oxford toon,
    Our Willie wad come agen.

Willie he stude at Thomas his Gate,
    And made a lustie din;
And who so blithe as the gate-porter
    To rise and let him in?

"Now enter Willie, now enter Willie,
    And look around the place,
And see the pain that we have ta'en
    Thomas his Quad to grace."

The first look that our Willie cast,
    He leuch loud laughters three,
The neist look that our Willie cast
    The tear blindit his e'e.

Sae square and stark the Tea-chest frowned
    Athwart the upper air,

But when the Trench our Willie saw,
   He thocht the Tea-chest fair.

Sae murderous-deep the Trench did gape
   The parapet aboon,
But when the Tunnel Willie saw
   He loved the Trench eftsoon.

'Twas mirk beneath the tane archway,
   'Twas mirk beneath the tither;
Ye wadna ken a man therein,
   Though it were your ain dear brither.

He turned him round and round about,
   And looked upon the Three;
And dismal grew his countenance,
   And drumlie grew his e'e.

"What cheer, what cheer, my gallant knight?"
   The gate-porter 'gan say.
"Saw ever ye sae fair a sight
   As ye have seen this day?"

"Now haud your tongue of your prating, man:
   Of your prating now let me be.
For, as I'm a true knight, a fouler sight
   I'll never live to see.

"Before I'd be the ruffian dark
   Who planned this ghastly show,
I'd serve as secretary's clerk
   To Ayrton or to Lowe.

"Before I'd own the loathly thing
   That Christ Church Quad reveals,
I'd serve as shoeblack's underling
   To Odger and to Beales!"

CHAPTER II

A Conference with one distraught: who discourseth strangely of many things.

PISCATOR, VENATOR

PISCATOR. 'Tis a marvellous pleasant ballad. But look you, another Collegian draws near. I wot not of what station he is, for indeed his apparel is new to me.

VENATOR. It is compounded, as I take it, of the diverse dresses of a jockey, a judge, and a North American Indian.

Enter LUNATIC

PISC. Sir, may I make bold to ask your name?

LUN. With all my heart, Sir. It is Jeeby, at your service.

PISC. And wherefore (if I may further trouble you, being as you see a stranger) do you wear so gaudy, but withal so ill-assorted, a garb?

LUN. Why, Sir, I'll tell you. Do you read the *Morning Post?*

PISC. Alas, Sir, I do not.

LUN. 'Tis pity of your life you do not. For, look you, not to read the *Post*, and not to know the newest and most commended fashions, are but one and the same thing. And yet this raiment, that I wear, is *not* the newest fashion. No, nor has it ever been, nor will it ever be, the fashion.

VEN. I can well believe it.

LUN. And therefore 'tis, Sir, that I wear it. 'Tis but a badge of greatness. My deeds you see around you. *Si monumentum quæris, circumspice!* You know Latin?

VEN. Not I, Sir! It shames me to say it.

LUN. You are then (let me roundly tell you) *monstrum horrendum, informe, ingens, cui lumen ademptum!*

VEN. Sir, you may tell it me roundly—or, if you list,

squarely—or again, triangularly. But if, as you affirm, I see your deeds around me, I would fain know which they be.

Lun. Aloft, Sir, stands the first and chiefest! That soaring minaret! That gorgeous cupola! That dreamlike effulgence of——

Ven. That wooden box?

Lun. The same, Sir! 'Tis mine!

Ven. (*after a pause*). Sir, it is worthy of you.

Lun. Lower now your eyes by a hairsbreadth, and straight you light upon my *second* deed. Oh Sir, what toil of brain, what cudgelling of forehead, what rending of locks, went to the fashioning of it!

Ven. Mean you that newly-made gap?

Lun. I do, Sir. 'Tis mine!

Ven. (*after a long pause*). What else, Sir? I would fain know the worst.

Lun. (*wildly*). It comes, it comes! My *third* great deed! Lend, lend your ears—your nose—any feature you can least conveniently spare! See you those twin doorways? Tall and narrow they loom upon you—severely simple their outline—massive the masonry between—black as midnight the darkness within! Sir, of what do they mind you?

Ven. Of vaults, Sir, and of charnel-houses.

Lun. This is a goodly fancy, and yet they are not vaults. No, Sir, you see before you a Railway Tunnel!

Ven. 'Tis very strange!

Lun. But no less true than strange. Mark me. 'Tis love, 'tis love, that makes the world go round. Society goes round of itself. In circles. Military society in military circles. Circles must needs have centres. Military circles military centres.

Ven. Sir, I fail to see——

Lun. Lo you, said our Rulers, Oxford shall be a military centre! Then the chiefest of them (glad in countenance, yet stony, I wot, in heart) so ordered it by his underling (I remember me not his name, yet is he one that can play a card well, and so serveth meetly the behests of that mighty one, who played of late in Ireland a game of cribbage such as no man, who saw it, may lightly forget); and then, Sir, this great College, ever loyal and generous, gave this Quadrangle as a Railway Terminus, whereby the Troops might come and go. By that Tunnel, Sir, the line will enter.

PISC. But, Sir, I see no rails.

LUN. Patience, good Sir! For railing we look to the Public! The College doth but furnish sleepers.

PISC. And the design of that Tunnel is——

LUN. Is mine, Sir! Oh, the fancy! Oh, the wit! Oh, the rich vein of humour! When came the idea? I'the mirk midnight. Whence came the idea? From a cheese-scoop! How came the idea? In a wild dream. Hearken, and I will tell. Form square, and prepare to receive a canonry! All the evening long I had seen lobsters marching around the table in unbroken order. Something sputtered in the candle—something hopped among the tea-things— something pulsated, with an ineffable yearning, beneath the enraptured hearthrug! My heart told me something was coming—and something came! A voice cried "Cheese-scoop!" and the Great Thought of my life flashed upon me! Placing an ancient Stilton cheese, to represent this venerable Quadrangle, on the chimney-piece, I retired to the further end of the room, armed only with a cheese-scoop, and with a dauntless courage awaited the word of command. Charge, Cheesetaster, charge! On, Stilton, on! With a yell and a bound I crossed the room, and plunged my scoop into the very heart of the foe! Once more! Another yell—another bound— another cavity scooped out! The deed was done!

VEN. And yet, Sir, if a cheese-scoop were your guide, these cavities must needs be circular.

LUN. They were so at the first—but, like the fickle Moon, my guardian satellite, I change as I go on. Oh, the rapture, Sir, of that wild moment! And did I reveal the Mighty Secret! Never, never! Day by day, week by week, behind a wooden screen, I wrought out that vision of beauty. The world came and went, and knew not of it. Oh, the ecstasy, when yesterday the Screen was swept away, and the Vision was a Reality! I stood by Tom-Gate, in that triumphal hour, and watched the passers-by. They stopped! They stared!! They started!!! A thrill of envy paled their cheeks! Hoarse inarticulate words of delirious rapture rose to their lips! What withheld me—what, I ask you candidly, withheld me from leaping upon them, holding them in a frantic clutch, and yelling in their ears " 'Tis mine, 'tis mine!"

PISC. Perchance, the thought that——

LUN. You are right, Sir. The thought that there is a lunatic asylum in the neighbourhood, and that two medical certificates—but I will be calm. The deed is done. Let us change the subject. Even now a great musical performance is going on within. Wilt hear it? The Chapter give it—ha, ha! They give it!

PISC. Sir, I will very gladly be their guest.

LUN. Then, guest, you have not guessed all! You shall be bled, Sir, ere you go! 'Tis love, 'tis love, that makes the hat go round! Stand and deliver! Vivat Regina! No money returned!

PISC. How mean you, Sir?

LUN. I said, Sir, "No money returned!"

PISC. And *I* said, Sir, "How mean——"

LUN. Sir, I am with you. You have heard of Bishops' Charges? Sir, what are Bishops to Chapters? Oh, it goes to my heart to see these quaint devices! First, sixpence for use of a doorscraper. Then, fivepence for right of choosing by which archway to approach the door. Then, a poor threepence for turning of the handle. Then, a shilling a head for admission, and half-a-crown for every two-headed man. Now this, Sir, is manifestly unjust: for you are to note that the double of a shilling——

PISC. I do surmise, Sir, that the case is rare.

LUN. And then, Sir, five shillings each for care of your umbrella! Hence comes it that each visitor of ready wit hides his umbrella, ere he enter, either by swallowing it (which is perilous to the health of the inner man), or by running it down within his coat, even from the nape of the neck, which indeed is the cause of that which you may have observed in me, namely, a certain stiffness in mine outward demeanour. Farewell, gentlemen, I go to hear the music.

Exit LUNATIC

CHAPTER III

A Conference of the Hunter *with a* Tutor, *whilom the* Angler *his eyes be closed in sleep. The* Angler *awaking relateth his Vision. The* Hunter *chaunteth "A Bacchanalian Ode".*

PISCATOR, VENATOR, TUTOR

VENATOR. He hath left us, but methinks we are not to lack company, for look you, another is even now at hand, gravely apparelled, and bearing upon his head Hoffmann's Lexicon in four volumes folio.

PISCATOR. Trust me, this doth symbolize his craft. Good morrow, Sir. If I rightly interpret these that you bear with you, you are a teacher in this learned place?

TUTOR. I am, Sir, a Tutor, and profess the teaching of divers unknown tongues.

PISC. Sir, we are happy to have your company, and if it trouble you not too much, we would gladly ask (as indeed we did ask another of your learned body, but understood not his reply) the cause of these new things we see around us, which indeed are as strange as they are new, and as unsightly as they are strange.

TUTOR. Sir, I will tell you with all my heart. You must know then (for herein lies the pith of the matter) that the motto of the Governing Body is this:

"Diruit, ædificat, mutat quadrata rotundis"; which I thus briefly expound.

Diruit. *"It teareth down."* Witness that fair opening which, like a glade in an ancient forest, we have made in the parapet at the sinistral extremity of the Hall. Even as a tree is the more admirable when the hewer's axe hath all but severed its trunk—or as a row of pearly teeth, enshrined in ruby lips, are yet the more lovely for the loss of one—so, believe me, this our fair Quadrangle is but enhanced by that which foolish men in mockery call "the Trench".

Ædificat. "It buildeth up." Witness that beauteous Belfry which, in its ethereal grace, seems ready to soar away even as we gaze upon it! Even as a railway-porter moves with an unwonted majesty when bearing a portmanteau on his head—or as I myself (to speak modestly) gain a new beauty from these massive tomes—or as ocean charms us most when the rectangular bathing-machine breaks the monotony of its curving marge—so are we blessed by the presence of that which an envious world hath dubbed "the Tea-chest".

Mutat quadrata rotundis. "It exchangeth square things for round." Witness that series of square-headed doors and windows, so beautifully broken in upon by that double archway! For indeed, though simple (*"simplex munditiis"*, as the poet saith) it is matchless in its beauty. Had those twin archways been greater, they would but have matched those at the corners of the Quadrangle— had they been less, they would have copied, with an abject servility, the doorways around them. In such things, it is only a vulgar mind that thinks of a *match*. The subject is lowe. *We* seek the Unique, the Eccentric! *We* glory in this two-fold excavation, which scoffers speak of as "the Tunnel".

VEN. Come, Sir, let me ask you a pleasant question. Why doth the Governing Body chuse for motto so trite a saying? It is, if I remember me aright, an example of a rule in the Latin grammar.

TUTOR. Sir, if we are not grammatical, we are nothing!

VEN. But for the Belfry, Sir. Sure none can look on it without an inward shudder?

TUTOR. I will not gainsay it. But you are to note that it is not permanent. This shall serve its time, and a fairer edifice shall succeed it.

VEN. In good sooth I hope it. Yet for the time being it doth not, in that it is not permanent, the less disgrace the place. Drunkenness, Sir, is not permanent, and yet is held in no good esteem.

TUTOR. 'Tis an apt simile.

VEN. And for these matchless arches (as you do most truly call them) would it not savour of more wholesome Art, had they matched the doorways, or the gateways?

TUTOR. Sir, do you study the Mathematics?

VEN. I trust, Sir, I can do the Rule of Three as well as another: and for Long Division——

TUTOR. You must know, then, that there be three Means treated of in Mathematics. For there is the Arithmetic Mean, the Geometric, and the Harmonic. And note further, that a Man is that which falleth between two magnitudes. Thus it is, that the entrance you here behold falleth between the magnitudes of the doorways and the gateways, and is in truth the Non-harmonic Mean, the Mean Absolute. But that the Mean, or Middle, is ever the safer course, we have a notable ensample in Egyptian history, in which land (as travelers tell us) the Ibis standeth ever in the midst of the river Nile, so best to avoid the onslaught of the ravenous alligators, which infest the banks on either side: from which habit of that wise bird is derived the ancient maxim *"In medio tutissimus Ibis"*.

VEN. But wherefore be they *two*? Surely *one* arch were at once more comely and more convenient?

TUTOR. Sir, so long as public approval be won, what matter for the arch? But that they are two, take this as sufficient explication—that they are too tall for doorways, too narrow for gateways; too light without, too dark within; too plain to be ornamental, and withal too fantastic to be useful. And if this be not enough, you are to note further that, were it all one arch, it must needs cut short one of those shafts which grace the Quadrangle on all sides—and that were a monstrous and unheard-of thing, in good sooth, look you.

VEN. In good sooth, Sir, if I look, I cannot miss seeing that there be three such shafts already cut short by doorways: so that it hath fair ensample to follow.

TUTOR. Then will I take other ground, Sir, and affirm (for I trust I have not learned Logic in vain) that to cut short the shaft were a common and vulgar thing to do. But indeed a single arch, where folk might smoothly enter in, were wholly adverse to Nature, who formeth never a mouth without setting a tongue as an obstacle in the midst thereof.

VEN. Sir, do you tell me that the block of masonry, between the gateways, was left there of set purpose, to hinder those that would enter in?

TUTOR. Trust me, it was even so; for firstly, we may thereby more easily control the entering crowds (*"divide et impera"* say the Ancients), and secondly, in this matter a wise man will ever follow Nature. Thus, in the centre of a hall-door we usually place an umbrella-stand—in the midst of a wicket-gate, a milestone—what place so suited for a watch-box as the centre of a narrow bridge?—Yea, and in the most crowded thoroughfare, where the living tide flows thickest, there, in the midst of all, the true *ideal* architect doth ever plant an obelisk! You may have observed this?

VEN. (*much bewildered*). I *may* have done so, worthy Sir: and yet, methinks——

TUTOR. I must now bid you farewell; for the music, which I would fain hear, is even now beginning.

VEN. Trust me, Sir, your discourse hath interested me hugely.

TUTOR. Yet it hath, I fear me, somewhat wearied your friend, who is, as I perceive, in a deep slumber.

VEN. I had partly guessed it, by his loud and continuous snoring.

TUTOR. You had best let him sleep on. He hath, I take it, a dull fancy, that cannot grasp the Great and the Sublime. And so farewell: I am bound for the music.

Exit TUTOR

VEN. I give you good day, good Sir. Awake, my Master! For the day weareth on, and we have catched no fish.

PISC. Think not of fish, dear Scholar, but hearken! Trust me, I have seen such things in my dreams, as words may hardly compass! Come, Sir, sit down, and I'll unfold to you, in such poor language as may best suit both my capacity and the briefness of our time,

THE VISION OF THE THREE T'S

Methought that, in some bygone Age, I stood beside the waters of Mercury, and saw, reflected on its placid face, the grand old buildings of the Great Quadrangle: near me stood one of portly form and courtly mien, with scarlet gown, and broad-brimmed hat whose strings, wide-fluttering in the breezeless air, at once defied the laws of gravity and marked the reverend Cardinal! 'Twas Wolsey's self! I would have spoken, but he raised his hand and pointed to the cloudless sky, from whence deep-muttering thunders now began to roll. I listened in wild terror.

Darkness gathered overhead, and through the gloom sobbingly down-floated a gigantic Box! With a fearful crash it settled upon the ancient College, which groaned beneath it, while a mocking voice cried "Ha! Ha!" I looked for Wolsey: he was gone. Down in those glassy depths lay the stalwart form, with scarlet mantle grandly wrapped around it: the broad-brimmed hat floated, boat-like, on the lake, while the strings with their complex tassels, still defying the laws of gravity, quivered in the air, and seemed to point a hundred fingers at the horrid Belfry! Around, on every side, spirits howled in the howling blast, blatant, stridulous!

A darker vision yet! A black gash appeared in the shud-

dering parapet! Spirits flitted hither and thither with averted face, and warning fingers pressed to quivering lips!

Then a wild shriek rang through the air, as, with volcanic roar, two murky chasms burst upon the view, and the ancient College reeled giddily around me!

Spirits in patent-leather boots stole by on tiptoe, with hushed breath and eyes of ghastly terror! Spirits with cheap umbrellas, and unnecessary goloshes, hovered over me, sublimely pendant! Spirits with carpet-bags, dressed in complete suits of dittos, sped by me, shrieking "Away! Away! To the arrowy Rhine! To the rushing Guadalquiver! To Bath! To Jericho! To anywhere!"

Stand here with me and gaze. From this thrice-favoured spot, in one rapturous glance gather in, and brand for ever on the tablets of memory, the Vision of the Three T's! To your left frowns the abysmal blackness of the tenebrous Tunnel. To your right yawns the terrible Trench. While far above, away from the sordid aims of Earth and the petty criticisms of Art, soars, tetragonal and tremendous, the tintinabulatory Tea-chest! Scholar, the Vision is complete!

VEN. I am glad on't: for in good sooth I am a-hungered. How say you, my Master? Shall we not leave fishing, and fall to eating presently? And look you, here is a song, which I have chanced on in this book of ballads, and which methinks suits well the present time and this most ancient place.

PISC. Nay then, let's sit down. We shall, I warrant you, make a good, honest, wholesome, hungry nuncheon with a piece of powdered beef and a radish or two that I have in my fish-bag. And you shall sing us this same song as we eat.

VEN. Well then, I will sing: and I trust it may content you as well as your excellent discourse hath oft profited me.

VENATOR *chaunteth*

A BACCHANALIAN ODE

Here's to the Freshman of bashful eighteen!
   Here's to the Senior of twenty!
Here's to the youth whose moustache ca'n't be seen!
   And here's to the man who has plenty!
     Let the men Pass!
     Out of the mass
I'll warrant we'll find you some fit for a Class!

Here's to the Censors, who symbolize Sense,
   Just as Mitres incorporate Might, Sir!
To the Bursar, who never expands the expense!
   And the Readers, who always do right, Sir!
     Tutor and Don,
     Let them jog on!
I warrant they'll rival the centuries gone!

Here's to the Chapter, melodious crew!
   Whose harmony surely *intends* well:
For, though it commences with "harm", it is true,
   Yet its motto is "All's well that ends well!"
     'Tis love, I'll be bound,
     That makes it go round!
For "In for a penny is in for a pound!"

Here's to the Governing Body, whose Art
   (For they're Masters of Arts to a man, Sir!)
Seeks to beautify Christ Church in every part,
   Though the method seems hardly to answer!
     With three T's it is graced—
     Which letters are placed
To stand for the names of Tact, Talent, and Taste!

Pisc. I thank you, good Scholar, for this piece of merriment, and this Song, which was well humoured by the maker, and well rendered by you.

Ven. Oh me! Look you, Master! A fish, a fish!

Pisc. Then let us hook it.

They hook it.

THE BLANK CHEQUE

A FABLE

"Vell, perhaps," said Sam, "you bought houses, vich is delicate English for goin' mad; or took to buildin', vich is a medical term for bein' incurable."

"FIVE o'clock tea" is a phrase that our "rude fore-fathers", even of the last generation, would scarcely have understood, so completely is it a thing of to-day: and yet, so rapid is the March of Mind, it has already risen into a national institution, and rivals, in its universal application to all ranks and ages, and as a specific for "all the ills that flesh is heir to", the glorious Magna Charta.

Thus, it came to pass, that, one chilly day in March, which only made the shelter indoors seem by contrast the more delicious, I found myself in the cozy little parlour of my old friend, kind hospitable Mrs. Nivers. Her broad good-humoured face wreathed itself into a sunny smile as I entered, and we were soon embarked on that wayward smooth-flowing current of chat about nothing in particular, which is perhaps the most enjoyable of all forms of conversation. John (I beg his pardon, "Mr. Nivers" I should say: but he was so constantly talked *of*, and *at*, by his better half, as "John", that his friends were apt to forget he had a surname at all) sat in a distant corner with his feet tucked well under his chair, in an attitude rather too upright for comfort, and rather too suggestive of general collapse for anything like dignity, and sipped his tea in silence. From some distant region came a sound like the roar of the sea, rising and falling, suggesting the presence of many boys; and indeed I knew that the house was full to overflowing of noisy urchins, overflowing with high spirits and mischief, but on the whole a very creditable set of little folk.

"And where are you going for your sea-side trip this summer, Mrs. Nivers?"

My old friend pursed up her lips with a mysterious smile, and nodded. "Ca'n't understand you," I said.

"You understand me, Mr. De Ciel, just as well as I understand myself, and *that's* not saying much. *I* don't know where we're going: *John* doesn't know where we're going—but we're certainly going *somewhere*; and we sha'n't even know the name of the place, till we find ourselves there! *Now* are you satisfied?"

I was more hopelessly bewildered than ever. "One of us is dreaming, no doubt," I faltered; "or—or perhaps I'm going mad, or——" The good lady laughed merrily at my discomfiture.

"Well, well! It's a shame to puzzle you so," she said. "I'll tell you all about it. You see, last year we *couldn't* settle it, do what we would. *John* said, 'Herne Bay'; and *I* said 'Brighton'; and the *boys* said 'somewhere where there's a circus'; not that we gave much weight to *that*, you know: well, and Angela (she's a growing girl, and we've got to find a new school for her, this year), *she* said 'Portsmouth, because of the soldiers'; and Susan (she's my maid, you know), *she* said 'Ramsgate'. Well, with all those contrary opinions, somehow it ended in our going *nowhere*: and John and I put our heads together last week, and we settled that it should *never* happen again. And now, how do you think we've managed it?"

"Quite impossible to guess," I said dreamily, as I handed back my empty cup.

"In the first place," said the good lady, "we need change sadly. Housekeeping worries me more every year, particularly with boarders—and John will have a couple of gentleman-boarders always on hand: he says it looks respectable, and that they talk so well they make the house quite lively. As if *I* couldn't talk enough for him!"

"It isn't that!" muttered John. "It's——"

"They're well enough sometimes," the lady went on (she never seemed to hear her husband's remarks), "but

I'm sure, when Mr. Prior Burgess was here, it was enough to turn one's hair grey! He was an open-handed gentleman enough—as liberal as could be—but *far* too particular about his meals. Why, if you'll believe me, he wouldn't sit down to dinner without there were three courses! We couldn't go on in *that* style, you know. I had to tell the next boarder he must be more hardy in his notions, or I could warrant him we shouldn't suit each other.''

"Quite right," I said. "Might I trouble you for another half cup?"

"Sea-side air we *must* have, you see," Mrs. Nivers went on, mechanically taking up the tea-pot, but too much engrossed in the subject to do more, "and as we ca'n't agree *where* to go, and yet we must go *somewhere*—did you say half a cup?"

"Thanks," said I. "You were going to tell me what it was you settled."

"We settled", said the good lady, pouring out the tea without a moment's pause in her flow of talk, "that the only course was—(cream I think you take, but no sugar? Just so)—was to put the whole matter—but stop, John shall read it all out to you. We've drawn up the agreement in writing—quite ship-shape, isn't it, John? Here's the document: John shall read it to you—and mind your stops, there's a dear!"

John put on his spectacles, and in a tone of gloomy satisfaction (it was evidently his own composition) read the following:

"Be it hereby enacted and decreed,

"That Susan be appointed for the business of choosing a watering-place for this season, and finding a New School for Angela.

"That Susan be empowered not only to procure plans, but to select a plan, to submit the estimate for the execution of such plan to the Housekeeper; and, if the Housekeeper sanction the proposed expenditure, to proceed with the execution of such plan, and to fill up the Blank Cheque for the whole expense incurred."

Before I could say another word the door burst open, and a whole army of boys tumbled into the room, headed by little Harry, the pet of the family, who hugged in his arms the much-enduring parlour cat, which, as he eagerly explained in his broken English, he had been trying to teach to stand on one leg. "Harry-Parry Ridy-Pidy Coachy-Poachy!" said the fond mother, as she lifted the little fellow to her knee and treated him to a jog-trot. "Harry's very fond of Pussy, he is, but he mustn't tease it, he mustn't! Now go and play on the stairs, there's dear children! Mr. De Ciel and I want to have a quiet talk." And the boys tumbled out of the room again, as eagerly as they had tumbled in, shouting "Let's have a Chase in the Hall!"

"A good set of Heads, are they not, Mr. De Ciel?" my friend continued, with a wave of her fat hand towards the retreating army. "Phrenologists admire them much. Look at little Sam, there. He's one of the latest arrivals, you know, but he grows—mercy on us, how that boy does grow! You've no idea what a Weight he is! Then there's Freddy, that tall boy in the corner: he's rather too big for the others, that's a fact—and he's something of a Bully at times, but the boy has a tender heart, too: give him a bit of poetry, now, and he's as maudlin as a girl! Then there's Benjy, again: a nice boy, but I daren't tell you what he costs us in pocket-money! Oh, the work we had with that boy, till we raised his allowance! Hadn't we, John?" (John grunted in acquiescence.) "It was Arthur took up his cause so much, and worried poor John and me nearly into our graves! Arthur was a very nice boy, Mr. De Ciel, and as great a favourite with the other boys as Harry is now, before he went to Westminster. He used to tell them stories, and draw them the prettiest pictures you ever saw! Houses that were all windows and chimneys—what they call 'High Art', I believe. We tried a conservatory once on the High-Art principle, and (would you believe it?) the man stuck the roof up on a lot of rods like so many knitting-needles! Of course it soon came down about our ears, and we had to do it all over again. As I said to John at the time, 'If this is High Art, give me a little more of the Art next time, and a little less of the High!' He's doing very well at Westminster, I hear, but his tutor writes that he's very asthmatic, poor fellow——"

"Æsthetic, my dear, æsthetic!" remonstrated John.

"Ah, well, my love," said the good lady, "all those long medical words are one and the same to *me*. And they come to the same thing in the Christmas bills, too: they both mean 'Draught as before'! Well, well! They're a set of dear good boys on the whole: they've only one real Vice among them—but I shall tire you, talking about the boys so much. What do you think of that agreement of ours?"

I had been turning the paper over and over in my hands, quite at a loss to know what to say to so strange a scheme. "Surely I've misunderstood you?" I said. "You don't mean to say that you've left the whole thing to your maid to settle for you?"

"But that's exactly what I *do* mean, Mr. De Ciel," the lady replied, a little testily. "She's a very sensible young person, I can assure you. So now, wherever Susan chooses to take us, *there* we go!" ("There we go! There we go!" echoed her husband in a dismal sort of chant, rocking himself backwards and forwards in his chair.) "You've no idea what a comfort it is to feel that the whole thing's in Susan's hands!"

"Go where Susan takes thee," I remarked, with a vague idea that I was quoting an old song. "Well, no doubt Susan has very correct taste, and all that—but still, if I might advise, I wouldn't leave *all* to her. She may need a little check——"

"That's the very word, dear Mr. De Ciel!" cried my old friend, clapping her hands. "And that's the very thing we've done, isn't it, John?" ("The very thing we've done," echoed John.) "I made him do it only this morning. He has signed her a Blank Cheque, so that she can go to any cost she likes. It's such a comfort to get things settled and off one's hands, you know! John's been grumbling about

it ever since, but now that I can tell him it's *your* advice
_____"

"But, my dear Madam," I faltered, "I don't mean cheque with a 'Q'!"

"—*your* advice," repeated Mrs. N., not heeding my interruption, "why, of course he'll see the reasonableness of it, like a sensible creature as he is!" Here she looked approvingly at her husband, who tried to smile a "slow wise smile", like Tennyson's "wealthy miller", but I fear the result was more remarkable for slowness than for wisdom.

I saw that it would be waste of words to argue the matter further, so took my leave, and did not see my old friends again before their departure for the sea-side. I quote the following from a letter which I received yesterday from Mrs. Nivers:

"MARGATE, *April 1.*

"*Dear Friend,*
"*You know the old story of the dinner-party, where there was nothing hot but the ices, and nothing cold but the soup? Of this place I may fairly say that there is nothing high but the prices, the staircases, and the eggs; nothing low but the sea and the company; nothing strong but the butter; and nothing weak but the tea!*"

From the general tenor of her letter I gather that they are not enjoying it.

MORAL

Is it really seriously proposed—in the University of Oxford, and towards the close of the Nineteenth Century (never yet reckoned by historians as part of the Dark Ages)—to sign a Blank Cheque for the expenses of building New Schools, before any estimate has been made of those expenses—before any plan has been laid before the University, from which such an estimate could be made—before any architect has been found to design such a plan—before any Committee has been elected to find such an architect?

TWELVE MONTHS
IN A CURATORSHIP

BY ONE WHO HAS TRIED IT

(As Curator of the Common Room at Christ Church, Oxford, C. L. Dodgson was obliged to prepare a report. He could not miss the opportunity to give these selections a Carrollean flavour.)

PREFACE

THIS book is not a plagiarism—as its name might at first suggest—of "Five Years in Penal Servitude". Nor, again, is it meant to traverse precisely the same ground as "Six Months on the Treadmill". There is a *general* resemblance, no doubt, to both the above works: still, it may be claimed for the present memoir, that it deals with *some* phases of humanity not hitherto analyzed, and narrates *some* woes that are peculiarly its own.

An apology is needed for its great length: but I have not had time to condense it into smaller compass.

The record, which I here propose to lay before the members of Ch. Ch. Common Room ... will be found largely autobiographical (a euphemism for "egotistic"), slightly apologetic, cautiously retrospective, and boldly prophetic: it will be at once financial, carbonaceous, æsthetic, chalybeate, literary, and alcoholic: it will be pervaded with mystery, and spiced with hints of thrilling plots and deeds of darkness. . . .

Would Common Room "be surprised to hear" that I have been breaking the rules ... with all the *abandon* of a bull, when critically inspecting a collection of old Dresden China? I meant, of course, the *letter* of the rules ... an instance will be found in the Rules of the Wine Committee, which have fared but badly at my hands: "Compound and comminuted fracture" is the scientific term, I believe, for the process I have put them through: but this matter is too awful to be dealt with here: it must have a section to itself. . . .

OF WINE

Whether this subject is *quite* the noblest to which Time and Thought can be devoted by Man is a question I leave on one side for the moment . . . one curious phenomenon I wish to call attention to. The consumption of Madeira (B) has been, during the past year, zero. [The total wine consumption was about 3,000 bottles for the previous year.] After careful calculation, I estimate that, if this rate of consumption be steadily maintained, our present stock will last us an infinite number of years. And although there may be something monotonous and dreary in the prospect of such vast cycles spent in drinking second-class Madeira, we may yet cheer ourselves with the thought of how economically it can be done. . . .

OF LIQUEURS

. . . The asterisks [in the accompanying list] indicate the degree of goodness according to the views of a certain Member of the Wine-Committee, who, in the noblest spirit of self-sacrifice, came day after day to taste the samples, on which views I (being one whose opinion on such points is worth absolutely nothing) entirely coincide.

OF THE WINE COMMITTEE

The Wine-Committee was a very simple organism at first—a sort of Amœba, with so brief a code of rules that it was all but structureless. But as time went on it developed and its rules grew ever more complex and stringent till they became, in the humble opinion of the present Curator, rather too tight a fit to be altogether comfortable. . . .

Perhaps the most interesting feature in the career of the Committee has been its gentle fading away in dimensions —"fine by degrees, and beautifully less".

Tune: "Ten Little Niggers"

"Four frantic Members of a chosen Commit*tee*!
    One of them resigned, then there were Three.

"Three thoughtful Members: they may pull us through!
    One was invalided—then there were Two.

"Two tranquil Members: much may yet be done!
    But they never came together, so I had to work with One."

And I find, by the records of the business transacted during the year, that much of it was done with only this very limited number of Members present besides the Curator.

OF CHALYBEATE WATERS

It is not the happy lot of every Curator to be criticized, not only by resident members of the C.R., but also by distant correspondents. I have received, during this past year, a long series of letters from one writer, of a highly critical—not to say hostile—tendency. These have been fired off at me with a monotonous regularity, having all the persistency—without the pathos—of minute-guns. ... What most amuses me in this series of projectiles is the novel view it gives me of my position as Curator. I had been weak enough to picture myself to myself as a well-worked and slightly worried individual, trying, to the best of his poor judgment, to do his duty by the friends who had entrusted their Common Room to his care—acknowledging responsibility to those friends as a body, but most certainly *not* to single members of that body, still less to outside-critics—and behold, I find I am a dark conspirator, going about in cloak and domino, with daggers and detonators, and withal liable to be put in the dark and lectured by any *soi-disant* judge that chooses to don the wig and gown! All this is, as Tennyson says "sweet and strange to me".

A VISION OF THE FUTURE

It was in 1983, and the new Curator was in an awful dilemma. . . . Only a month ago, passing the Common Room one afternoon, he had noticed the cellar door open, and strolling in had found two shabbily-dressed men filling a coal-sack with bottles of old Port. They had declined to explain their motives, and left hastily. But the Curator had been true to his duty. "It is a question of *keeping wine*", he said to himself, "and can only be decided by a majority of the Wine-Committee at a duly-summoned meeting." . . .

And now, within the last few days, the Common Room, ever anxious to oblige their Curator in all things, had devised a new Code of Rules, which fitted him to a T, like a pair of new handcuffs—a Code of Rules which, as they fondly hoped, he would welcome as something really striking and stringent. . . . [Rule 6] "Nothing shall be done, or left undone, by the Curator without the concurrence of the Wine-Committee. And, if the Curator shall complain of cold, it shall be the duty of the Committee to make things warm for him."

After this Code had passed into law, the members of the Common Room went about with elastic steps, and hearts bursting with joy and thankfulness. "The wild beast is caged at last!" they were always saying to each other, shaking hands whenever they met. The Curator appeared to be less entirely at his ease. His walk was suggestive of Tight Boots, his countenance of Toothache, while his general deportment was that of a man whose system has been demoralized by too much Tea. . . .

All this was very cheerful, but a new difficulty had arisen, and the Curator was distracted. An old member of the Common Room had just come to Oxford, who always took pale Brandy and Soda at dinner, and there was nothing but brown in the Cellar. "What *am* I to do?" groaned the Curator. "It will take 8 days to get a Committee-meeting to settle from what merchant to get samples—4 days to get the samples—8 days more to get a meeting to select the brandy and fix the price to put on it—and 4 days to get it. That is over 3 weeks, and the poor old man only stays a fortnight!'' Beads of perspiration trickled down his manly forehead. After some hours of anxious thought, he nerved himself for a truly desperate step: *he ordered a bottle of pale brandy on his own responsibility!* And forthwith came a letter from Tunbridge Wells. ''What! you're at it again, are you? . . . What's the use of my anathematizing you twice a week by post, and doing my best to make your life a burden?'' . . .

I don't quite know what became of that guilty Curator. I believe he fled to other climes; and they elected a new one: and Common Room was once more supposed to be governed on constitutional principles: and no hitch occurred—till the next time.

THREE YEARS IN A CURATORSHIP

BY ONE WHOM IT HAS TRIED

(Four paragraphs of a report submitted by the author when he was Curator of the Common Room at Oxford.)

PREFACE

LONG and painful experience has taught me one great principle in managing business for other people, *viz.*, if you want to inspire confidence, *give plenty of statistics.* It does not matter that they should be accurate, or even intelligible, so long as there is enough of them. A curator who contents himself with simply *doing* the business of a Common Room, and who puts out no statistics, is sure to be distrusted. ''He keeps us in the dark!'' men will say. ''He publishes no figures. What does it mean? Is he assisting himself?" But, only circulate some abstruse tables of figures, particularly if printed in lines and columns, so that ordinary readers can make nothing of them, and all is changed at once. "Oh, go on, go on!" they cry, satiated with facts. "Manage things as you like! We trust you entirely!"

Hence this pamphlet.

I

OF AIRS, GLARES, AND CHAIRS

The Committee . . . appointed a year ago "to consider the whole question of lighting and ventilating", have grappled with, and (it is hoped) pretty nearly solved, the two problems proposed to them—though but scantily supported by the sympathies of Common Room, who, though ready enough to ventilate our proposals as to "light" have altogether made light of our "ventilation".

The latter subject was discussed . . . and the plan adopted, of an oblique opening . . . pierced through the E. wall of the Common Room, with a valve inside, which might be opened or shut at will. . . . The valve has not only served the purpose for which it was designed—it has also furnished some most interesting illustrations of the tricks the human imagination can play, and the influence it has over physical sensations. The members of the C.R., who sit on the E. side of the room were at first terrified at the prospect of so much cold air beating down on their unsheltered heads. "It is *hair* we need—not *air*!" Thus they moaned in their anguish. But the strangest part of it was that it was usually when the valve was *shut* that they felt most keenly "the pelting of this pitiless storm": when it was open, they made no complaint. The conclusion seems to be, that the additional ventilation has not *really* produced any inconvenience, while it has conferred an undoubted benefit, by increasing the longevity of members of the C.R.—as is plain from the simple consideration that they are, all of them, six months older than they were when the change was made.

The question of "light" has been very fully and fiercely debated by the Committee, and the suggestions were so many, and so contradictory, that the great mind of the Curator nearly gave way . . . for the table, it was agreed to request Mr. Thompson to select one of Hinck's "Duplex" lamps—it being understood that that kind combined high art and high illumination. Mr. Thompson kindly did so, and the result has been "a thing of beauty", which is also (probably) "a joy forever", but it has not yet been tested quite long enough to prove this. . . .

2

DE RE NUMMARIÂ

On this topic I am nothing if not tabular. . . .

No financial statement can possibly be complete without a word or two about wine. For surely any Curator, worthy of the name, would be found, if tested by one Lee's Reader, to possess a density varying directly, and a gravity varying inversely, as the potency of the Port— if tested anatomically by a second, to have the word "WINE" neatly emblazoned on his heart—and, if finally submitted to quantitative analysis by a third, to consist principally of $C_4H_6O_2$.

There is not, however, anything specially thrilling to say about this deeply-interesting subject. Water-drinkers will be pleased to hear that we have spent during the past year, with all the recklessness of several Grand Old Men, no less than £768 18s. 9d. on wine, and that the result of this skilful financial operation has been a deficit on the year's account, of £44 19s. 9d.—while the wine-drinkers will be equally delighted to learn that the stock of pints of Y'quem has this year reached the proud position occupied, two years ago, by *Madeira* (B), and that we have enough in hand to last, at the present rate of consumption, for an infinite number of years. . . .

3

DE MERI MERITIS

... I have yet a word to say regarding one of our choicest wines, the "Mouton" Claret. On this subject we, the Wine Committee, have displayed a nervous trepidation, not to say a hysterical *hyperæsthesia*—absolutely morbid. About a year ago a panic seized us. One or two bottles had turned out bad ("corked" or whatever it might have been): and suddenly the cry went up "All is lost!": wild words, such as "It is past its prime!" "It is worth only three shillings a bottle!" hurled in the air: the very constitution of the Cellar was affected for a time: symptoms of diminished circulation and of slight consumption showed themselves. The Curator trembled, but would not quit the gory field in such frantic haste, or give the order ... to empty the remaining bottles into Mercury—thereby certainly demoralizing, and probably destroying, its scaly inmates. ... The devouring anxiety (members of the C.R. may have noticed its crushing effect on me, producing a lambent—not to say sheepish—style of conversation?) on the subject of "Mouton" is now wholly and at once removed. Those, who have not felt the anxiety, cannot fully realize the relief. The wretch, who groans with a bad tooth, is grateful to the dentist who extracts it for him: but were the same dentist to rush, pincers in hand, into the street, stop the first passer-by, and wrench from his jaw some perfectly *sound* tooth, similar expressions of gratitude could not reasonably be looked for.

4

DE LICLÆ STATISTICÆ

... Enough, enough! I have said my say, gentle reader! Turn the page, and revel, to your heart's content, in [A Table of the Present Stock of Wine.]

RESIDENT WOMEN-STUDENTS

In the bewildering multiplicity of petty side-issues, with which the question, of granting University Degrees to Women, has been overlaid, there is some danger that Members of Congregation may lose sight of the really important issues involved.

The following four propositions should, I think, be kept steadily in view by all who wish to form an independent opinion as to the matter in dispute.

(1)

One of the chief functions, if not *the* chief function, of our University, is to prepare young Men—partly by teaching, partly by discipline, partly by the personal influence of those who have charge of them, and partly by the influence they exercise on one another—for the business of Life.

> (This needs to be *specially* borne in mind in connection with the assumption, so constantly made in this controversy, that the *sole* meaning of the B.A. Degree is that it guarantees the possession of a large amount of *knowledge*.)

Consequently,

(2)

The first question to be asked, as to any Scheme proposed to our University, is, "How will it affect those for whose well-being we are responsible?" When we have assured ourselves that it will not exercise any harmful influence on our own Students, then, and not till then, may we fairly proceed to consider how it will affect those for whose well-being we are *not* responsible.

1068

(3)

Any Scheme for the recognition of Women-Students—
whether by a series of Certificates or a single Diploma—
whereby those who have resided here will have an advantage, in the keen competition for educational posts, over
those who have not, will most certainly end in making
residence *compulsory* on all. Whether they wish it or not,
whether they can afford it or not, Women-Students will
find that they *must* reside, unless they are content to be
hopelessly distanced in the race whose prize is "daily
bread".

Consequently,

(4)

Any such Scheme is certain to produce an enormous in-
flux of resident Women-Students. Considering that we
have over 3000 young Men-Students, and that the number of young Women, who are devoting themselves to
study, is increasing "by leaps and bounds", it may be
confidently predicted that any such Scheme will bring to
Oxford at least 3000 more young Women-Students. Such
an immigration will of course produce a rapid increase in
the size of Oxford, and will necessitate a large increase in
our teaching-staff and in the number of our lecture-rooms.

The main question before us is, "Will the mutual influence, of two such sets of Students, residing in such close
proximity, be for good or for evil?"

Some Members of the Congregation will reply, "For
good," some, "For evil." By all means let each form his
own independent judgment, and give effect to it by his
vote: but let him do it *deliberately*, and in the full light of
facts.

The late Dr. Liddon was strongly of opinion that such
an influence would be for *evil*, at any rate for the young
Women. I have myself heard him—no doubt many others

have done the same—express, most warmly and earnestly, his fears as to the effect the new movement, for flooding Oxford with young Women-Students, would have on the young Women themselves. And I have no doubt that, were he yet among us, his silvery tones would have been heard in Congregation last Tuesday, deprecating the introduction, into our ancient University, of that social monster, the "He-Woman".

Surely the real "way-out", from our present perplexity, is to be found in some such course as that advocated by Mr. Strachan-Davidson, that Oxford, Cambridge, and Dublin, should join in a petition to the Crown to grant a charter for a Women's University.

Such a University would very soon attract to itself the greater portion of young Women-Students. It takes no great time to build Colleges; and we might confidently expect to see "New Oxford", in the course of 20 or even of 10 years, rivaling Oxford, not only in numbers, but in attainments. At first, perhaps, they might need to borrow some teachers from the older Universities; but they would soon be able to supply all, that would be needed, from among themselves; and Women-Lecturers and Women-Professors would arise, fully as good as any that the older Universities have ever produced.

This proposal has been met by the plea that it is *not* what the Women themselves "desire". Surely no weaker plea was ever urged in any controversy. Even *men* very often fail to "desire" what is, after all, the best thing for them to *have*. And those ancients, on whom the onerous task was laid, of weighing and, if reasonably possible, satisfying the claims of the horse-leech and her two daughters, had other things to consider than the mere shrillness of their outcries.

CHARLES L. DODGSON

CH.CH.
Mar. 7th, 1896

SOME POPULAR FALLACIES
ABOUT VIVISECTION

AT a time when this painful subject is engrossing so large a share of public attention, no apology, I trust, is needed for the following attempt to formulate and classify some of the many fallacies, as they seem to me, which I have met with in the writings of those who advocate the practice. No greater service can be rendered to the cause of truth, in this fiercely contested field, than to reduce these shadowy, impalpable phantoms into definite forms, which can be seen, which can be grappled with, and which, when once fairly *laid*, we shall not need to exercise a second time.

I begin with two contradictory propositions, which seem to constitute the two extremes, containing between them the golden mean of truth—

1. *That the infliction of pain on animals is a right of man, needing no justification.*

2. *That it is in no case justifiable.*

The first of these is assumed in practice by many who would hardly venture to outrage the common feelings of humanity by stating it in terms. All who recognize the difference of right and wrong must admit, if the question be closely pressed, that the infliction of pain is in *some* cases wrong. Those who deny it are not likely to be amenable to argument. For what common ground have we? They must be restrained, like brute beasts, by physical force.

The second has been assumed by an Association lately formed for the total suppression of Vivisection, in whose manifesto it is placed in the same category with Slavery, as being an absolute evil, with which no terms can be made. I think I may assume that the proposition most generally accepted is an intermediate one, namely, that the infliction of pain is in some cases justifiable, but not in all.

3. *That our right to inflict pain on animals is co-extensive with our right to kill, or even to exterminate a race (which prevents the existence of possible animals) all being alike infringements of their rights.*

This is one of the commonest and most misleading of all the fallacies. Mr. Freeman, in an article on Field Sports and Vivisection, which appeared in the *Fortnightly Review* for May, 1874, appears to countenance this when he classes death with pain together, as if they were admitted to be homogeneous. For example—

"By cruelty then I understand, as I have understood throughout, not all infliction of death or suffering on man or beast, but their wrongful or needless infliction. . . . My positions then were two. First . . . that certain cases of the infliction of death or suffering on brute creatures may be blameworthy. The second was, that all infliction of death or suffering for the purpose of mere sport is one of those blameworthy cases."

But in justice to Mr. Freeman I ought also to quote the following sentence, in which he takes the opposite view: "I must in all cases draw a wide distinction between mere killing and torture."

In discussing the "rights of animals", I think I may pass by, as needing no remark, the so-called right of a race of animals to be perpetuated, and the still more shadowy right of a non-existent animal to come into existence. The only question worth consideration is whether the killing of an animal is a real infringement of right. Once grant this, and a *reductio ad absurdum* is imminent, unless we are illogical enough to assign rights to animals in proportion to their size. Never may we destroy, for our convenience, some of a litter of puppies—or open a score of oysters when nineteen would have sufficed—or light a candle in a summer evening for mere pleasure, lest some hapless moth should rush to an untimely end! Nay, we must not even take a walk, with the certainty of crushing many an insect in our path, unless for really important business! Surely all this is childish. In the absolute hopelessness of drawing a line anywhere, I conclude (and I believe that many, on considering the point, will agree with me) that man has an *absolute* right to inflict death on animals, without assigning any reason, provided that it be a painless death, but that any infliction of pain needs its special justification.

4. *That man is infinitely more important than the lower animals, so that the infliction of animal suffering, however great, is justifiable if it prevent human suffering, however small.*

This fallacy can be assumed only when unexpressed. To put it into words is almost to refute it. Few, even in an age where selfishness has almost become a religion, dare openly avow a selfishness so hideous as this! While there are thousands, I believe, who would be ready to assure the vivisectors that, so far as their personal interests are concerned, they are ready to forego any prospect they may have of a diminution of pain, if it can only be secured by the infliction of so much pain on innocent creatures.

But I have a more serious charge than that of selfishness to bring against the scientific men who make this assumption. They use it dishonestly, recognizing it when it tells in their favour, and ignoring it when it tells against them. For does it not pre-suppose the axiom that human and animal suffering differ *in kind*? A strange assertion this, from the lips of people who tell us that man is twin-brother to the monkey! Let them be at least consistent, and when they have proved that the lessening of the *human* suffering is an end so great and glorious as to justify any means that will secure it, let them give the anthropomorphoid ape the benefit of the argument. Further than that I will not ask them to go, but will resign them in confidence to the guidance of an exorable logic.

Had they only the candour and the courage to do it, I believe they would choose the other horn of the dilemma, and would reply, "Yes, man *is* in the same category as the brute; and just as we care not (you see it, so we cannot deny it) how much pain we inflict on the one, so we care not, unless when deterred by legal penalties, how much we inflict on the other. The lust for scientific knowledge is our real guiding principle. The lessening of human suffering is a mere dummy set up to amuse sentimental dreamers.

I now come to another class of fallacies—those involved in the comparison, so often made, between vivisection and field-sports. If the theory, that the two are essentially similar, involved no worse consequence than that sports should be condemned by all who condemn vivisection, I should be by no means anxious to refute it. Unfortunately the other consequence is just as logical, and just as likely, that vivisection should be approved of by all who approve of sport.

The comparison rests on the assumption that the main evil laid to the charge of vivisection is the pain inflicted on the animal. This assumption I propose to deal with, further on, as a fallacy: at present I will admit it for the sake of argument, hoping to show, that, even on this hypothesis, the vivisectors have a very poor case. In making this comparison their first claim is—

5. *That it is fair to compare aggregates of pain.*

"The aggregate amount of wrong"—I quote from an article in the *Pall Mall Gazette* for February 13th— "which is perpetrated against animals by sportsmen in a single year probably exceeds that which some of them endure from vivisectors in half a century." The best refutation of this fallacy would seem to be to trace it to its logical conclusion—that a very large number of trivial wrongs are equal to one great one. For instance, that a man, who by selling adulterated bread inflicts a minute injury on the health of some thousands of persons, commits a crime equal to one murder. Once grasp this *reductio ad absurdum*, and you will be ready to allow that the only fair comparison is between individual and individual.

Supposing the vivisectors are forced to abandon this position, they may then fall back on the next parallel—

6. *That the pain inflicted on an individual animal in vivisection is not greater than in sport.*

I am no sportsman, and so have no right to dogmatize, but I am tolerably sure that all sportsmen will agree with me that this is untrue of shooting, in which, whenever the animal is killed at once, it is probably as painless a form of death as could be devised; while the sufferings of one that escapes wounded ought to be laid to the charge of unskilful sport, not of sport in the abstract. Probably much of the same might be said of fishing: for other forms of sport, and especially for hunting, I have no defence to offer, believing that they involve very great cruelty.

Even if the last two fallacies were granted to advocates of vivisection, their use in the argument must depend on the following proposition being true:

7. *That the evil charged against vivisection consists chiefly in the pain inflicted on the animal.*

I maintain, on the contrary, that it consists chiefly in the effect produced on the operator. To use the words of Mr. Freeman, in the article already quoted, "the question is not as to the aggregate amount of suffering inflicted, but as to the moral character of the acts by which the suffering is inflicted." We see this most clearly, when we shift our view from the act itself to its remoter consequences. The hapless animal suffers, dies, "and there an end": but the man whose sympathies have been deadened, and whose selfishness has been fostered, by the contemplation of pain deliberately inflicted, may be the parent of others equally brutalized, and so bequeath a curse to future ages. And even if we limit our view to the present time, who can doubt that the degradation of a soul is a greater evil than the suffering of bodily frame? Even if driven to admit this, the advocates of the practice may still assert—

8. *That vivisection has no demoralizing effect on the character of the operator.*

"Look at our surgeons!" they may exclaim. "Are they a demoralized or a brutalized class? Yet you must admit,

that in the operations they have to perform, they are per-
petually contemplating pain—aye, and pain deliberately
inflicted by their own hands." The analogy is not a fair
one; since the *immediate* motive—of saving the life, or
diminishing the sufferings, of the person operated on—is
a counteracting influence in surgery, to which vivisection,
with its shadowy hope of some day relieving the sufferings of some human being yet unborn, has nothing parallel to offer. This, however, is a question to be decided
by evidence, not by argument. History furnishes us with
too many examples of the degradation of character produced by the deliberate pitiless contemplation of suffering. The effect of the national bull-fights on the Spanish
character is a case in point. But we need not go to Spain
for evidence: the following extract from the *Echo*, quoted
in the *Spectator* for March 20th, will be enough to
enable the reader to judge for himself what sort of
effect this practice is likely to have on the minds of the
students—

"But if yet more be necessary to satisfy the public
minds on this latter point" (the effect on the operators),
"the testimony of an English physiologist, known to the
writer, may be useful in conclusion. He was present some
time past at a lecture, in the course of which demonstra-
tions were made on living dogs. When the unfortunate
creatures cried and moaned under the operation, many of
the students *actually mimicked their cries in derision!* The
gentleman who related this occurrence adds that the
spectacle of the writhing animals and the fiendish behaviour of the audience so sickened him, that he could
not wait for the conclusion of the lecture, but took his
departure in disgust."

It is a humiliating but an undeniable truth, that man
has something of the wild beast in him, that a thirst for
blood can be aroused in him by witnessing a scene of car-
nage, and that the infliction of torture, when the first instincts of horror have been deadened by the familiarity
may become, first, a matter of indifference, then a subject

of morbid interest, then a positive pleasure, and then a ghastly and ferocious delight.

Here again, however, the analogy of sport is of some service to the vivisector, and he may plead that the influence we dread is already at work among our sportsmen. This I will now consider.

9. *That vivisection does not demoralize the character more than sport.*

The opponent's case would not, I think, suffer much even if this were admitted; but I am inclined to demur to to it as a universal truth. We must remember that much of the excitement and interest of sport depends on causes entirely unconnected with the infliction of pain, which is rather ignored than deliberately contemplated; whereas in vivisection the painful effects constitute in many cases a part, in some cases the whole, of the interest felt by the spectator. And all they tell us of the highly developed intellect of the anatomical student, with which they contrast so contemptuously the low animal instincts of the fox-hunter, is but another argument against themselves; for surely the nobler the being we degrade, the greater is the injury we inflict on society. *Corruptio optimi pessima.*

"But all this ignores the *motive* of the action," cry the vivisectors. "What is it in sport? Mere pleasure. In this matter we hold an impregnable position." Let us see.

10. *That, while the motive in sport is essentially selfish, in vivisection it is essentially unselfish.*

It is my conviction that the non-scientific world is far too ready to attribute to the advocates of science all the virtues they are so ready to claim; and when they put forward their favourite *ad captandum* argument that their labours are undergone for one pure motive—the good of humanity—society is far too ready to exclaim, with Mrs. Varden, "Here is a meek, righteous, thorough-going Christian, who, having dropped a pinch of salt on the tails of all the cardinal virtues, and caught them every one, makes light of their possession, and pants for more morality!" In other words, society is far too ready to ac-

cept the picture of the pale, worn devotee of science giving his days and nights to irksome and thankless toil,
spurred on by no other motive than a boundless philan-
thropy. As one who has himself devoted much time and
labour to scientific investigations, I desire to offer the
strongest possible protest against this falsely coloured
picture. I believe that any branch of science, when taken
up by one who has a natural turn for it, will soon become
as fascinating as sport to the most ardent sportsman, or
as any form of pleasure to the most refined sensualist.
The claim that hard work, or the endurance of privation,
proves the existence of an unselfish motive, is simply
monstrous. Grant to me that the miser is proved unselfish
when he stints himself of food and sleep to add one more
piece of gold to his secret hoard, that the place-hunter is
proved unselfish when he toils through long years to reach
the goal of his ambition, and I will grant to you that the
laborious pursuit of science is proof positive of an unselfish
motive. Of course I do not assert, of even a single scientific student, that his real motive is merely that craving
for more knowledge, whether useful or useless, which is as
natural an appetite as the craving for novelty or any other
form of excitement. I only say that the lower motive
would account for the observed conduct quite as well as
the higher.

Yet, after all, the whole argument, deduced from a
comparison of vivisection with sport, rests on the following proposition, which I claim to class as a fallacy—

11. *That toleration of one form of an evil necessitates the
toleration of all others.*

Grant this, and you simply paralyze all conceivable
efforts at reformation. How can we talk of putting down
cruelty to animals when drunkenness is rampant in the
land? You would propose, then, to legislate in the interests of sobriety? Shame on you! Look at the unseaworthy
ships in which our gallant sailors are risking their lives!
What! Organize a crusade against dishonest shipowners,
while our streets swarm with a population growing up in

heathen ignorance! We can but reply, *non omnia possumus omnes*. And surely the man who sees his way to diminish in any degree a single one of the myriad evils around him, may well lay to heart the saying of a wise man of old, "Whatsoever thy hand findeth to do, do it with thy might."

The last parallel to which the advocates of vivisection may be expected to retreat, supposing all these positions to be found untenable, is the assertion—

12. *That legislation would only increase the evil.*

The plea, if I understand it aright, amounts to this— that legislation would probably encourage many to go beyond the limit with which at present they are content, as soon as they found that a legal limit had been fixed beyond their own. Granting this to be the tendency of human nature, what is the remedy usually adopted in other cases? A stricter limit, or the abandonment of all limits? Suppose a case—that in a certain town it were proposed to close all taverns at midnight, and that the opponents of the measure urged, "At present some close at eleven—a most desirable hour: if you pass this law, all will keep open till midnight." What would the answer be? "Then let us do nothing," or, "Then let us fix eleven, instead of twelve, as our limit?" Surely this does not need many words: the principle of doing evil that good may come is not likely to find many defenders, even in this modern disguise of forbearing to do good lest evil should come. We may safely take our stand on the principle of doing the duty which we see before us: secondary consequences are at once out of our control and beyond our calculation.

Let us now collect into one paragraph the contradictions of some of these fallacies (which I have here rather attempted to formulate and classify than to refute, or even fully discuss), and so exhibit in one view the case of the opponents of vivisection. It is briefly this—

That while we do not deny the absolute right of man to end the lives of the lower animals by a painless death, we require good and sufficient cause for the infliction of pain.

That the prevention of suffering to a human being does not justify the infliction of a greater amount of suffering on an animal.

That the chief evil of the practice of vivisection consists in its effect on the moral character of the operator; and that this effect is distinctly demoralizing and brutalizing.

That hard work and endurance of privations are no proof of an unselfish motive.

That the toleration of one form of an evil is no excuse for tolerating another.

Lastly, that the risk of legislation increasing the evil is not enough to make all legislation undesirable.

We have now, I think, seen good reasons to suspect that the principle of selfishness lies at the root of this accursed practice. That the same principle is probably the cause of the indifference with which its growth among us is regarded, is not perhaps so obvious. Yet I believe this indifference to be based on a tacit assumption, which I propose to notice as the last of this long catalogue of fallacies—

13. *That the practice of vivisection will never be extended so as to include human subjects.*

That is, in other words, that while science arrogates to herself the right of torturing at her pleasure the whole sentient creation up to man himself, some inscrutable boundary line is there drawn, over which she will never venture to pass. "Let the galled jade wince, *our* withers are unwrung."

Not improbably, when that stately Levite of old was pacing with dainty step the road that led from Jerusalem to Jericho, "bemused with thinking of tithe-concerns," and doing his best to look unconscious of the prostrate form on the other side of the way, if it could have whispered in his ear, "*Your* turn comes next to fall among the thieves!" some sudden thrill of pity might have been aroused in him: he might even, at the risk of soiling those rich robes, have joined the Samaritan in his humane task of tending the wounded man. And surely the easy-going Levites of our own time would take an altogether new interest in this matter, could they only realize the possible advent of a day when anatomy shall claim as legitimate subjects for experiment, first, our condemned criminals—next, perhaps, the inmates of our refuges for incurables—then the hopeless lunatic, the pauper hospital-patient, and generally "him that hath no helper"—a day when successive generations of students, trained from their earliest years to the repression of all human sympathies, shall have developed a new and more hideous Frankenstein—a soulless being to whom science shall be all in all.

Homo sum! Quidvis humanum non a me alienum puto.[1]

And when that day shall come, O my brother-man, you who claim for yourself and for me so proud an ancestry—tracing our pedigree through the anthropomorphoid ape up to the primeval zoöphyte—what potent charm have *you* in store to win exemption from the common doom? Will you represent to that grim spectre, as he gloats over you, scalpel in hand, the inalienable rights of man? He will tell you that this is merely a question of relative expediency—that, with so feeble a physique as yours, you have only to be thankful that natural selection has spared you so long. Will you reproach him with the needless torture he proposes to inflict upon you? He will smilingly assure you that the *hyperæsthesia*, which he hopes to induce, is in itself a most interesting phenome-

---

[1] Quotation from letter, dated July 18, 1924, from F. Madan, of Oxford to M. L. Parrish, of Pine Valley, New Jersey.
Dear Mr. Parrish,
   I congratulate you on acquiring the "Popular Fallacies about Vivisection". Mr. Williams himself has the only other copy.
   I suppose it has Mr. Dodgson's misquotation of Terence in it: "Homo sum! Quidvis humanum non a me alienum puto." That is bad all round. It doesn't even scan. Really mathematicians should let Latin alone. It should be of course :
   "Homo sum: humani nihil a me alienum puto."

non, deserving much patient study. Will you then, gathering up all your strength for one last desperate appeal, plead with him as with a fellow-man, and with an agonized cry for "Mercy!" seek to rouse some dormant spark of pity in that icy breast? Ask it rather of the nether mill-stone.

LAWN TENNIS TOURNAMENTS

The True Method of Assigning Prizes with a Proof of the Fallacy of the Present Method

I. INTRODUCTORY

AT a Lawn Tennis Tournament, where I chanced, some while ago, to be a spectator, the present method of assigning prizes was brought to my notice by the lamentations of one of the Players, who had been beaten (and had thus lost all chance of a prize) early in the contest, and who had had the mortification of seeing the 2nd prize carried off by a Player whom he knew to be quite inferior to himself. The results of the investigations, which I was led to make, I propose to lay before the reader under the following four headings—

   (*a*) A proof that the present method of assigning prizes is, except in the case of the first prize, entirely unmeaning.

   (*b*) A proof that the present method of scoring in matches is constantly liable to lead to unjust results.

   (*c*) A system of rules for conducting Tournaments, which, while requiring even less time than the present system, shall secure equitable results.

   (*d*) An equitable system for scoring in matches.

2. *A proof that the present method of assigning prizes is, except in the case of the first prize, entirely unmeaning.*

Let us take, as an example of the present method, a Tournament of 32 competitors with 4 prizes.

On the 1st day, these contend in 16 pairs: on the 2nd day, the 16 Winners contend in 8 pairs, the Losers being excluded from further competition: on the 3rd day, the 8 Winners contend in 4 pairs: on the 4th day, the 4 Winners (who are now known to be the 4 Prize-Men) contend in 2 pairs: and on the 5th day, the 2 Winners contend together to decide which is to take the 1st prize and which the 2nd —the two Losers having no further contest, as the 3rd and 4th prizes are of equal value.

Now, if we divide the list of competitors, arranged in the order in which they are paired, into 4 sections, we may see that all that this method really does is to ascertain who is best in each section, then who is best in each half of the list, and then who is best of all. The best of all (and this is the only equitable result arrived at) wins the 1st prize: the best in the other half of the list wins the 2nd: and the best men in the two sections not yet represented by a champion win the other two prizes. If the Players had chanced to be paired in the order of merit, the 17th best Player would necessarily carry off the 2nd prize, and the 9th and 25th best the 3rd and 4th! This of course is an extreme case: but anything within these limits is possible: e.g. any competitor, from the 3rd best to the 17th best, may, by the mere accidental arrangement of pairs, and by no means as a result of his own skill, carry off the 2nd prize. As a mathematical fact, the chance that the 2nd best Player will get the prize he deserves is only $\frac{16}{31}$sts; while the chance that the best 4 shall get their proper prizes is so small, that the odds are 12 to 1 against its happening!

If any one thinks that, after all, we are merely introducing another element of chance into the game, and that no one can fairly object to *that*, let him try the experiment in a rifle competition. Let him interpose when the man, who has made the 2nd best score, is going to receive his prize, and propose that he shall draw a counter from a bag containing 16 white and 15 black, and only have his prize in case he draw a white one: and let him observe the expression of that rifleman's face.

3. *A proof that the present method of scoring in matches is constantly liable to lead to unjust results.*

To prove this, let us suppose a "set" to mean "the best of 11 games", and a "match" "the best of 5 sets": i.e. "he, who first wins 6 games, wins a set; he, who first wins 3 sets, wins a match."

Suppose A and B to play the following 50 games ("A2" means A wins 2 games, and so on)—

B2A5B4 | A6 | B3A5B2A* | B*A2B4A3B | B2A5B3A.

Here A wins 28 games to 22, and also wins the match.

But, by simply transposing A*, B*, we get

B2A5B4 | A6 | B3A5B3 | A3B4A3 | B3A5B3,

the last game of the original series not being played.

Here A still wins 27 games to 22: yet he loses the match!

4. *A system of rules for conducting Tournaments, which while requiring even less time than the present system, shall secure equitable results.*

The method for conducting Tournaments, which I have to propose, involves two departures from the present method. First, I propose to make a "match" last only half a day (the necessary reduction in the number of games I will discuss in section 5): secondly, I propose to give only 3 prizes. The rules for a Tournament of 32 Players would be as follows—

(*a*) The Tournament begins in the middle of the 1st day, so that there is only one contest that day—the 32 Players being arranged in 16 pairs.

(*b*) A list is kept, and against each name is entered, at the end of each contest, the name of any one who has been superior to him—whether by actually beating him, or by beating some one who has done so (thus, if A beats B, and B beats C, A and B are both "superiors" of C). So soon as any name has 3 "superiors" entered against it, it is struck out of the list.

(c) For the 2nd day (morning) the 16 unbeaten men are paired together, and similarly the 16 with 1 superior (the Losers in these last-named pairs will now have 3 superiors each, and will therefore be struck off the list). In all other contests they are paired in the same way; first pairing the unbeaten, then those with 1 superior, and so on, and avoiding, as far as possible, pairing two Players who have a common superior.

(d) By the middle of the 3rd day the unbeaten are reduced to two, one of whom is certainly "First-prize-man". These two do not contend in the afternoon contest that day, but have a whole-day match on the 4th day—the other Players meanwhile continuing the usual half-day matches.

(e) By the end of the 4th day, the "First-prize-man" is known (by the very same process of elimination used in the existing method): and the remaining Players are paired by the same rules as before, for the 2 contests on the 5th day. If, in section (a), the Tournament was begun in the morning, the two men named in section (d) being still allowed a whole-day match, nothing would be gained in time, as the Tournament would take $4\frac{1}{2}$ days, while much would be lost in interest, as the first prize would be settled in 3 days.

To illustrate these rules, I will give the complete history of a Tournament of 32 competitors, with 3 prizes. If the reader will draw out the following Tables, in blank, and fill them up for himself, referring, if necessary, to the accompanying directions, he will easily understand the workings of the system.

Let the Players be arranged alphabetically, and let the relative skill, with which they play in this Tournament, be—

A	B	C	D	E	F	G	H	J
19	22	14	32	16	25	15	28	3

K	L	M	N	P	Q	R	S	T
10	8	1	29	4	12	2	17	23

U	V	W	X	Y	Z	a	b	c
26	11	20	31	13	18	6	24	9

d	e	f	g	h
21	30	5	7	27

These numbers ("1" meaning "best") will enable the reader to name the victor in any contest: but of course they are not supposed to be known to the Tournament-Committee, who have nothing to guide them but the results of actual contests. In the following Tables, "I(e)" means "first day, evening", and so on: also a Player, who is *virtually* proved superior to another, is entered thus "(A)". The victor in each contest is marked *: and ⊙ means "struck out".

Directions for filling in the Tables—

Tab. I. Day I (e). The names are written out alphabetically, and paired as they stand. The victors are marked with asterisks.

Tab. II. Day I (e). As B has been beaten by A, A is entered as his "superior"; C as D's superior; and so on.

Tab. I. Day II (m). We first pair together all the unbeaten, A,C,E,G, &c. Then those who have one superior, B,D,F,H, &c.

Tab. II (m). We first enter the *actual* superiors, C,G, &c. Then, since A has a superior C, and B has a superior A, we see that B has a *virtual* superior C; and so on. We then see that D has 3 superiors, and must be struck out; and so with H, &c.

Tab. I. Day II (e). We first pair together all the unbeaten, C,G, &c. Then all with one superior, A,E, &c.; but when we come to J,L, we find we have a common superior; so we pair J with P, and L with Q. This series ends with an odd one, g, who must therefore be paired with the first of those who have two superiors each, F,T, &c.

Tab. I. Day III (m). Here, in pairing those with one superior, we again end with an odd one, g, who must therefore be paired with the first of those with two superiors, viz. T. We end with an "odd man", c.

Tab. II. Day III (m). The unbeaten are now reduced to one pair, M,f, who therefore will do nothing this afternoon, but will have a whole-day contest to-morrow.

Tab. I. Day III (e). Those who have one superior are C,J,L,R, all with a common superior M; and then V,a,g, all with a common superior f. We therefore pair C with V, and so on, leaving an odd one R, who must be paired with the only one who has two superiors, viz. c.

Tab. II. Day III (e). Enter as usual.

Tab. I. Day IV (m). We pair the 2 unbeaten, M,f, for their whole-day contest. Then those with one superior.

Tab. II. Day IV (m). M and f are still contending. V and g are struck out.

Tab. I. Day IV (e). J and R must be paired together, though they have a common superior.

Tab. I. Day IV (e). M is First-prize-man.

Tab. I. Day V (m). R and f must be paired together, though they have a common superior. J is "odd man".

Tab. II. Day V (m). R is now the only man with one superior, and is therefore Second-prize-man.

Tab. I. Day V (e). J and f contend for the Third prize.

If this Tournament were fought by the present method, the 4 Prize men would be C,M,V,f: f would get the 2nd prize, and C and V the 3rd and 4th: i.e. the 5th best man would get the 2nd prize, and the 14th and 11th best the other two.

5. *An equitable system for scoring in matches.*

In order to make "matches" more equitable, I propose to abolish "sets", and make a "match" consist of "games". Thus, instead of "best of 11 games = set; best of 5 sets = match" (i.e. he who first wins 6 games wins a set; he who first wins 3 sets wins a match), where a player *may* win with as few as 18 games, and *must* win with 28, I would substitute "he who first wins 28 games, or who

TABLE I. (Pairs.)

I. (e)	II. (m)	(e)	III. (m)	(e)	IV. (m)	(e)	V. (m)	(e)
A / B }*	A / C }	C / G }*	C / M }*	C / V }*	M / f }	M / f }*	R / f }*	J / f }*
C / D }*	E / G }*	M / R }*	V / f }*	J / a }*	J / V }*	J / R }*	J	
E / F }*	J / M }*	V / Y }	A / J }*	L / g }*	R / g }*			
G / H }*	P / R }*	a / f }*	G / L }*	R / c }*				
J / K }*	S / V }*	A / E }*	R / S }*					
L / M }*	W / Y }*	J / P }*	Y / a }*					
N / P }*	a / c }*	L / Q }*	g / T }*					
Q / R }*	f / g }*	S / W }*	c					
S / T }*	B / D }*	Z / c }*						
U / V }*	F / H }*	g / B }*						
W / X }*	K / L }*	F / T }*						
Y / Z }*	N / Q }*	d / h }*						
a / b }*	T / U }*							
c / d }*	X / Z }*							
e / f }*	b / d }*							
g / h }*	e / h }*							

TABLE II. (Superiors.)

	I.(e)	II. (m)	(e)	III. (m)	(e)	IV. (m)	(e)	V. (m)	(e)
A	...	C	...	J(M)○					
B	A	(C)	g○						
C	...	...	...	M	V(f)○				
D	C	B(A)○							
E	...	G	A(C)○						
F	E	(G)	T○						
G	...	...	C	L(M)○					
H	G	F(E)○							
J	...	M	...	...	...	...	R	...	Pr. III.
K	J	L(M)○							
L	M	...	...	...	g(f)○				
M	...	...	...	...	...	...	Pr. I.		
N	P	Q(R)○							
P	...	R	J(M)○						
Q	R	...	L(M)○						
R	...	...	M	...	...	...	...	Pr. II.	
S	...	V	...	R(f)○					
T	S	(V)	...	g○					
U	V	T(S)○							
V	...	...	...	f	...	J(M)○			
W	...	Y	S(V)○						
X	W	Z(Y)○							
Y	...	...	V	a(f)○					
Z	Y	...	c(V)○						
a	...	...	f	...	J(M)○				
b	a	d(c)○							
c	...	a	(f)	...	R○				
d	c	(a)	(f)○						
e	f	h(g)○							
f	...	...	...	...	...	...	M	R	J○
g	...	f	...	...	...	R(M)○			
h	g	(f)	d○						

gets 18 games ahead, wins the match". I therefore propose as follows: "For a whole-day, he who first wins 28
games, or who gets 18 ahead, wins the match: for a half-
day, he who first wins 14 games, or who gets 9 ahead,
wins the match."

6. *Concluding remarks.*

Let it not be supposed that, in thus proposing to make
these Tournaments a game of pure skill (like chess) instead of a game of mixed skill and chance (like whist), I
am altogether eliminating the element of luck, and making it possible to predict the prize-winners, so that no one
else would care to enter. The "chances of the board"
would still exist in full force: it would not at all follow,
because a Player was reputed best, that he was certain of
the 1st prize: a thousand accidents might occur to prevent his playing best: the 4th best, 5th best, or even a
worst Player, need not despair of winning even the 1st
prize.

Nor, again, let it be supposed that the present system,
which allows an inferior player a chance of the 2nd prize,
even though he fails to play above his reputation, is more
attractive than one which, in such a case, gives him no
hope. Let us compare the two systems, as to the attrac-
tions they hold out to (say) the 5th best Player in a Tournament of 32, with 3 prizes. The present system says, "If
you play up to your reputation, your chance of a prize is
about ¼th; and even if, by great luck and painstaking,
you play 2nd or 3rd best, it never rises above a half." My
system says, "It is admitted that, if you only play up to
your reputation, you will get nothing: but, if you play 2nd
or 3rd best, you are certain of the proper prize." Thus,
the one system offers a chance of ¼th, where the other
offers nothing; and a chance of a half, where the other
offers certainty, I am inclined to think the second the
more attractive of the two.

If, however, it be thought that, under the proposed
system, the very inferior Players would feel so hopeless of
a prize that they would not enter a Tournament, this can

easily be remedied by a process of handicapping, as is usual in races, &c. This would give every one a reasonable hope of a prize, and therefore a sufficient motive for entering.

The proposed form of Tournament, though lasting a shorter time than the present one, has a great many more contests going on at once, and consequently furnishes the spectacle-loving public with a great deal more to look at.

EIGHT OR NINE WISE WORDS
ABOUT LETTER WRITING

I. ON STAMP-CASES

SOME American writer has said "the snakes in this district may be divided into one species—the venomous". The same principle applies here. Postage-Stamp-Cases may be divided into one species, the "Wonderland". Imitations of it will soon appear, no doubt: but they cannot include the two Pictorial Surprises, which are copyright.

You don't see why I call them "Surprises"? Well, take the Case in your left-hand, and regard it attentively. You see Alice nursing the Duchess's Baby? (An entirely new combination, by the way: It doesn't occur in the book.) Now, with your right thumb and forefinger, lay hold of the little book, and suddenly pull it out. *The Baby has turned into a Pig!* If *that* doesn't surprise you, why, I suppose you wouldn't be surprised if your own Mother-in-law suddenly turned into a Gyroscope!

This Case is *not* intended to carry about in your pocket. Far from it. People seldom want any other Stamps, on an emergency, than Penny-Stamps for Letters, Sixpenny-Stamps for Telegrams, and a bit of Stamp-edging for cut fingers (it makes capital sticking-plaster, and will stand three or four washings, cautiously conducted): and all these are easily carried in a purse or pocket-book. No, *this* is meant to haunt your envelope-case, or wherever you keep your writing-materials. What made me invent it was the constantly wanting Stamps of other values, for foreign Letters, Parcel Post, etc., and finding it very bothersome to get at the kind I wanted in a hurry. Since I have possessed a "Wonderland Stamp-Case", life has been bright and peaceful, and I have used no other. I believe the Queen's laundress uses no other.

Each of the pockets will hold 6 stamps, comfortably. I would recommend you to arrange the 6, before putting them in, something like a *bouquet*, making them lean to the right and to the left alternately: thus there will always be a free *corner* to get hold of, so as to take them out, quickly and easily, one by one: otherwise you will find them apt to come out two or three at a time.

According to *my* experience, the 5*d.*, 9*d.*, and 1*s.* Stamps are hardly ever wanted, though I have constantly to replenish all the other pockets. If your experience agrees with mine, you may find it convenient to keep only a couple (say) of each of these 3 kinds, in the 1*s.* pocket, and to fill the other 2 pockets with extra 1*d.* stamps.

2. HOW TO BEGIN A LETTER

If the Letter is to be in answer to another, begin by getting out that other letter and reading it through, in order to refresh your memory, as to what it is you have to answer, and as to your correspondent's *present address* (otherwise you will be sending your letter to his regular address in *London*, though he has been careful in writing to give you his *Torquay* address in full).

Next, Address and Stamp the Envelope. "What! Before writing the *Letter*?" Most certainly. And I'll tell you what will happen if you don't. You will go on writing till the last moment, and, just in the middle of the last sentence, you will become aware that "time's up!" Then comes the hurried wind-up—the wildly-scrawled signature—the hastily-fastened envelope, which comes open in the post—the address, a mere hieroglyphic—the horrible discovery that you've forgotten to replenish your Stamp-Case—the frantic appeal, to every one in the house, to lend you a Stamp—the headlong rush to the Post Office, arriving, hot and gasping, just after the box has closed—and finally, a week afterwards, the return of the Letter, from the Dead-Letter Office, marked "address illegible"!

Next, put your own address, *in full*, at the top of the note-sheet. It is an aggravating thing—I speak from bitter experience—when a friend, staying at some new address, heads his letter "Dover", simply, assuming that you can get the rest of the address from his previous letter, which perhaps you have destroyed.

Next, put the date *in full*. It is another aggravating thing, when you wish, years afterwards, to arrange a series of letters, to find them dated "Feb. 17", "Aug. 2", without any *year* to guide you as to which comes first. And never, never, dear Madam (N.B. this remark is addressed to ladies *only*: no *man* would ever do such a thing), put "Wednesday", simply, as the date!

"That way madness lies."

3. HOW TO GO ON WITH A LETTER

Here is a golden Rule to begin with. *Write legibly.* The average temper of the human race would be perceptibly sweetened, if everybody obeyed this Rule! A great deal of the bad writing in the world comes simply from writing *too quickly*. Of course you reply, "I do it to save *time*." A very good object, no doubt: but what right have you to do it at your friend's expense? Isn't *his* time as valuable as yours? Years ago, I used to receive letters from a friend—and very interesting letters too—written in one of the most atrocious hands ever invented. It generally took me about a *week* to read one of his letters. I used to carry it about in my pocket, and take it out at leisure times, to puzzle over the riddles which composed it—holding it in different positions, and at different distances, till at last the meaning of some hopeless scrawl would flash upon me, when I at once wrote down the English under it; and, when several had been thus guessed, the context would help with the others, till at last the whole series of hieroglyphics was deciphered. If *all* one's friends wrote like that, Life would be entirely spent in reading their letters!

This Rule applies, specially, to names of people or places—and *most* specially to *foreign names*. I got a letter once, containing some Russian names, written in the same hasty scramble in which people often write "yours sincerely". The *context*, of course, didn't help in the least: and one spelling was just as likely as another, so far as *I* knew: It was necessary to write and tell my friend that I couldn't read any of them!

My second Rule is, don't fill *more* than a page and a half with apologies for not having written sooner!

The best subject, to *begin* with, is your friend's last letter. Write with the letter open before you. Answer his questions, and make any remarks his letter suggests. *Then* go on to what you want to say yourself. This arrangement is more courteous, and pleasanter for the reader, than to fill the letter with your own invaluable remarks, and then hastily answer your friend's questions in a postscript. Your friend is much more likely to enjoy your wit, *after* his own anxiety for information has been satisfied.

In referring to anything your friend has said in his letter, it is best to *quote the exact words*, and not to give a summary of them in *your* words. *A*'s impression, of what *B* has said, expressed in *A*'s words, will never convey to *B* the meaning of his own words.

This is specially necessary when some point has arisen as to which the two correspondents do not quite agree. There ought to be no opening for such writing as "You are quite mistaken in thinking I said so-and-so. It was not in the least my meaning, &c., &c.", which tends to make a correspondence last for a life-time.

A few more Rules may fitly be given here, for correspondence that has unfortunately become *controversial*.

One is, *don't repeat yourself*. When once you have said your say, fully and clearly, on a certain point, and have failed to convince your friend, *drop that subject:* to repeat your arguments, all over again, will simply lead to his doing the same; and so you will go on, like a Circulating Decimal. *Did you ever know a Circulating Decimal come to an end?*

Another Rule is, when you have written a letter that you feel may possibly irritate your friend, however necessary you may have felt it to so express yourself, *put it aside till the next day*. Then read it over again, and fancy it addressed to yourself. This will often lead to your writing it all over again, taking out a lot of the vinegar and pepper, and putting in honey instead, and thus making a *much* more palatable dish of it! If, when you have done your best to write inoffensively, you still feel that it will probably lead to further controversy, *keep a copy of it*. There is very little use, months afterwards, in pleading "I am almost sure I never expressed myself as you say: to the best of my recollection I said so-and-so". *Far* better to be able to write "I did *not* express myself so: these are the words I used".

My fifth Rule is, if your friend makes a severe remark, either leave it unnoticed, or make your reply distinctly *less* severe: and if he makes a friendly remark, tending towards "making up" the little difference that has arisen between you, let your reply be distinctly *more* friendly. If, in picking a quarrel, each party declined to go more than *three-eighths* of the way, and if, in making friends, each was ready to go *five-eighths* of the way—why, there would be more reconciliations than quarrels! Which is like the Irishman's remonstrance to his gad-about daughter—"Shure, you're *always* goin' out! You go out *three* times, for *wanst* that you come in!"

My sixth Rule (and my last remark about controversial correspondence) is, *don't try to have the last word!* How many a controversy would be nipped in the bud, if each was anxious to let the *other* have the last word! Never mind how telling a rejoinder you leave unuttered: never mind your friend's supposing that you are silent from lack of anything to say: let the thing drop, as soon as it is possible without discourtesy: remember "speech is silvern, but silence is golden"! (N.B.—If you are a gentleman, and your friend a lady, this Rule is superfluous: *you wo'n't get the last word!*)

My seventh Rule is, if it should ever occur to you to write, jestingly, in *dispraise* of your friend, be sure you exaggerate enough to make the jesting *obvious*: a word spoken in *jest*, but taken as earnest, may lead to very serious consequences. I have known it to lead to the breaking-off of a friendship. Suppose, for instance, you wish to remind your friend of a sovereign you have lent him, which he has forgotten to repay—you might quite *mean* the words "I mention it, as you seem to have a conveniently bad memory for debts", in jest; yet there would be nothing to wonder at if he took offence at that way of putting it. But, suppose you wrote "Long observation of your career, as a pickpocket and a burglar, has convinced me that my one lingering hope, for recovering that sovereign I lent you, is to say 'Pay up, or I'll summons yer!' " he would indeed be a matter-of-fact friend if he took *that* as seriously meant!

My eighth Rule. When you say, in your letter, "I enclose cheque for £5," or "I enclose John's letter for you to see", leave off writing for a moment—go and get the document referred to—and *put it into the envelope*. Otherwise, you are pretty certain to find it lying about, *after the Post has gone!*

My ninth Rule. When you get to the end of a note-sheet, and find you have more to say, take another piece of paper—a whole sheet, or a scrap, as the case may demand: but whatever you do, *don't cross!* Remember the old proverb *"Cross-writing makes cross reading"*. *"The old* proverb?" you say, inquiringly. *"How* old?" Well, not so *very* ancient, I must confess. In fact, I'm afraid I invented it while writing this paragraph! Still, you know, "old" is a *comparative* term. I think you would be *quite* justified in addressing a chicken, just out of the shell, as "Old boy!" *when compared* with another chicken, that was only half-out!

4. HOW TO END A LETTER

If doubtful whether to end with "yours faithfully", or "yours truly", or "your most truly", &c. (there are at least a dozen varieties, before you reach "yours affectionately"), refer to your correspondent's last letter, and make your winding-up *at least as friendly as his*: in fact, even if a shade *more* friendly, it will do no harm!

A Postscript is a very useful invention: but it is *not* meant (as so many ladies suppose) to contain the real *gist* of the letter: it serves rather to throw into the shade any little matter we do *not* wish to make a fuss about. For example, your friend had promised to execute a commission for you in town, but forgot it, thereby putting you to great inconvenience: and he now writes to apologize for his negligence. It would be cruel, and needlessly crushing, to make it the main subject of your reply. How much more gracefully it comes in thus! "P.S. Don't distress yourself any more about having omitted that little matter in town. I wo'n't deny that it *did* put my plans out a little, at the time: but it's all right now. I often forget things, myself: and 'those, who live in glasshouses, mustn't throw stones', you know!"

When you take your letters to the Post, *carry them in your hand*. If you put them in your pocket you will take a long country-walk (I speak from experience), passing the Post-Office *twice*, going and returning, and, when you get home, will find them *still* in your pocket.

5. ON REGISTERING CORRESPONDENCE

Let me recommend you to keep a record of Letters Received and Sent. I have kept one for many years, and have found it of the greatest possible service, in many ways: it secures my *answering* Letters, however long they have to wait; it enables me to refer, for my own guidance, to the details of previous correspondence, though the actual Letters may have been destroyed long ago; and, most valuable feature of all, if any difficulty arises, years afterwards, in connection with a half-forgotten correspondence, it enables me to say, with confidence, "I did *not* tell you that he was 'an *invaluable* servant in *every* way', and that you *couldn't* 'trust him too much'. I have a *precis* of my letter. What I said was 'he is a *valuable* servant in *many* ways, but *don't* trust him too much'. So, if he's cheated you, you really must not hold *me* responsible for it!"

I will now give you a few simple Rules for making, and keeping a Letter-Register.

Get a blank book, containing (say) 200 leaves, about 4 inches wide and 7 high. It should be *well* fastened into its cover, as it will have to be opened and shut hundreds of times. Have a line ruled, in red ink, down each margin of every page, an inch off the edge (the margin should be wide enough to contain a number of 5 digits, easily: *I* manage with a $\frac{3}{4}$ inch margin: but, unless you write very small you will find an inch more comfortable).

Write a *precis* of each Letter, received or sent, in chronological order. Let the entry of a "received" Letter reach from the left-hand edge to the right-hand marginal line; and the entry of a "sent" Letter from the left-hand marginal line to the right-hand edge. Thus the two kinds will be quite distinct, and you can easily hunt through the "received" Letters by themselves, without being bothered with the "sent" Letters; and *vice versa*.

Use the *right-hand* pages only: and, when you come to the end of the book, turn it upside-down, and begin at the other end, still using right-hand pages. You will find this much more comfortable than using left-hand pages.

You will find it convenient to write, at the top of every sheet of a "received" Letter, its Register-Number in full.

I will now give a few (ideal) specimen pages of my Letter-Register, and make a few remarks on them: after which I think you will find it easy enough to manage one for yourself.

29217	/90.	
(217) sendg, J., a	Ap. 1. (Tu) *Jones, Mrs.* am as present from self and Mr. white elephant.	27518 / 225
(218) grand	do. *Wilkins & Co.* bill, for piano, £175 10s. 6d. [pd	28743 / 221, 2
(219) "Grand to borr	do. *Scareham, H.* [writes from Hotel, Monte Carlo"] asking ow £50 for a few weeks (!)	
	(220) do. *Scareham, H.* would know *object*, for wh loan is and *security* offered.	like to asked,
218 / 246	(221) Ap. 3. *Wilkins & Co.* vious letter, now before me, undertook to supply one for decling to pay more.	in pre- / you / £120:
23514 / 218 / 228	(222) do. *Cheetham & Sharp.* written 221 — enclosing previous letter — is law on my side?	have / us let- / [
(223) G. N. dressed 'very	Ap. 4. *Manager, Goods Statn,* R. White Elephant arrived, ad- to you — send for it at once — savage.'	226
29225	/90.	
217 / 230	(225) Ap. 4 (F) *Jones, Mrs.* th but no room for it at present, am ing it to Zoological Gardens.	anks, send-

223	(226) do. *Manager, Goods Sta*	tn, G.
	N. R. please deliver, to bearer	of this
	note, case containing White Ele-	phant
	addressed to me.	
223	(227) do. *Director Zool. Garde*	ns. (en-
	closing above note to R. W. Ma	nager)
	call for valuable animal, prese	nted to
229	Gardens.	
(228)	Ap. 8. *Cheetham & Sharp*, you	222
misquot	e enclosed letter, limit named	
is £18	o.	237
(229)	Ap. 9. *Director, Zoo. Gardens.*	227
case de	livered to us contained 1 doz.	
Port—	consumed at Directors' Ban-	230
quet—	many thanks.	
225	(230) do. **T** *Jones, Mrs.* why	call a
⊙	doz. of Port a 'White Elephant'?	
(231)	do. **T** *Jones, Mrs.* 'it was a	⊙
joke.'		
29233	/90.	
	(233) Ap. 10 (Th) *Page & Co.*	orderg
	Macaulay's Essays and "Jane	Eyre"
242	(cheap edtn).	
(234)	do. *Aunt Jemina* — invitg for	
2 or 3	days after the 15th. [	236
(235)	do. *Lon. and West. Bk.* have	
recevd	£250, pd to yr Acct fm Parkins	
& Co.	Calcutta. [en	
234	(236) do. *Aunt Jemina* — can	not
	possibly come this month, will	write
239	when able.	[

228 240	(237) Ap. 11. *Cheetham and* turn letter enclosed to you.	Co. re- [×
245	(238) do. *Morton, Philip.* Co uld you lend me Browning's "Dramati s Per- sonæ" for a day or 2?	
(239) ing hou "136,	Ap. 14. *Aunt Jemina,* leav- se at end of month: address Royal Avenue, Bath." [	236
(240) returng	Ap. 15. *Cheetham and Co.,* letter as reqd, bill 6/6/8. [	237 244
29242	/90.	
(242) for boo	Ap. 15. (Tu) *Page & Co.* bill ks, as ordered, 15/6 [	233
(243)	do. ¶ *do.* books	247
240 248	(244) do. *Cheetham and Co.* c derstand the 6/8 — what is £6	an un- for?
(245) matis	Ap. 17. ¶ *Morton, P.* "Dra- Personæ," as asked for. [retd	238 249
221 250	(246) do. *Wilkins and Co.* w bill, 175/10/6, and ch. for do.	ith [en
243	(247) do. *Page and Co.* bill, postal J 107258 for 15/- and	15/6, 6 stps.
(248) was a	Ap. 18. *Cheetham and Co,* it "clerical error" (!)	244
245	(249) Ap. 19. *Morton, P.* retu Browning with many thanks.	rng
(250) bill.	do. *Wilkins and Co.* receptd	246

I begin each page by putting, at the top left-hand corner, the next entry-number I am going to use, *in full* (the last 3 digits of each entry-number are enough afterwards); and I put the date of the year, at the top, in the centre.

I begin each entry with the last 3 digits of the entry-number, enclosed in an oval (this is difficult to reproduce in print, so I have put round-parentheses here). Then, for the *first* entry in each page, I put the day of the month and the day of the week: afterwards, "do." is enough for the month-day, till it changes: I do not repeat the week-day.

Next, if the entry is *not* a letter, I put a symbol for "parcel" (see Nos. 243, 245) or "telegram" (see Nos. 230, 231) as the case may be.

Next, the name of the person, underlined (indicated here by italics).

If an entry needs special further attention, I put [at the end: and, when it has been attended to, I fill in the appropriate symbol, *e.g.*, in No. 218, it showed that the bill had to be *paid*; in No. 222, that an answer was really *needed* (the " × " means "attended to"); in No. 234, that I owed the old lady a visit; in No. 235, that the item had to be entered in my account book; in No. 236, that I must not forget to write; in No. 239, that the address had to be entered in my address-book; in No. 245, that the book had to be returned.

I give each entry the space of 2 lines, whether it fills them or not, in order to have room for references. And, at the foot of each page I leave 2 or 3 lines *blank* (often useful afterwards for entering omitted Letters) and miss one or 2 numbers before I begin the next page.

At any odd moments of leisure, I "make up" the entry-book, in various ways, as follows:

(1) I draw a *second* line, at the right-hand end of the "received" entries, and at the left-hand end of the "sent" entries. This I usually do pretty well "up to date". In my Register the first line is *red*, the second *blue*: here I dis-

tinguish them by making the first thin, and the second *thick*.

(2) Beginning with the last entry, and going backwards, I read over the names till I recognize one as having occurred already: I then link the two entries together, by giving the one, that comes first in chronological order, a "foot-reference" (see Nos. 217, 225). I do not keep this "up to date", but leave it till there are 4 or 5 pages to be done. I work back till I come among entries that are all supplied with "foot-references", when I once more glance through the last few pages, to see if there are any entries not yet supplied with head-references: *their* predecessors may need a special search. If an entry is connected, in subject, with another under a different name, I link them by cross-references, distinguished from the head- and foot-references by being written *further from the marginal line* (see No. 229). When 2 consecutive entries have the same name, and are both of the same kind (*i.e.* both "received" or both "sent") I bracket them (see Nos. 242, 243); if of different kinds, I link them with the symbol used for Nos. 219, 220.

(3) Beginning at the earliest entry not yet done with, and going forwards, I cross out every entry that has got a head- and foot-reference, and is done with, by continuing the extra line *through* it (see Nos. 221, 223, 225). Thus, wherever a *break* occurs in this extra line, it shows there is some matter still needing attention. I do not keep this anything like "up to date", but leave it till there are 30 or 40 pages to look through at a time. When the first page in the volume is thus completely crossed out, I put a mark at the foot of the page to indicate this; and so with pages 2, 3, &c. Hence, whenever I do this part of the "making-up", I need not begin at the beginning of the volume, but only at the *earliest page that has not got this mark*.

All this looks very complicated, when stated at full length: but you will find it perfectly simple, when you have had a little practice, and will come to regard the "making-up" as a pleasant occupation for a rainy day, or at any time that you feel disinclined for more severe mental work. In the Game of Whist, Hoyle gives us one golden Rule, "When in doubt, win the trick"—I find that Rule admirable for real life: when in doubt what to do, I "make-up" my Letter-Register!

WHAT THE TORTOISE
SAID TO ACHILLES

ACHILLES had overtaken the Tortoise, and had seated himself comfortably on its back.

"So you've got to the end of our race-course?" said the Tortoise. "Even though it *does* consist of an infinite series of distances? I thought some wiseacre or other had proved that the thing couldn't be done?"

"It *can* be done," said Achilles. "It *has* been done! *Solvitur ambulando.* You see the distances were constantly *diminishing*: and so——"

"But if they had been constantly *increasing*?" the Tortoise interrupted. "How then?"

"Then I shouldn't be *here*," Achilles modestly replied; "and *you* would have got several times round the world, by this time!"

"You flatter me—*flatten*, I mean," said the Tortoise; "for you *are* a heavy weight, and *no* mistake! Well now, would you like to hear of a race-course, that most people fancy they can get to the end of in two or three steps, while it *really* consists of an infinite number of distances, each one longer than the previous one?"

"Very much indeed!" said the Grecian warrior, as he drew from his helmet (few Grecian warriors possessed *pockets* in those days) an enormous note-book and a pencil. "Proceed! And speak *slowly*, please! *Short-hand* isn't invented yet!"

"That beautiful First Proposition of Euclid!" the Tortoise murmured dreamily. "You admire Euclid?"

"Passionately! So far, at least, as one *can* admire a treatise that wo'n't be published for some centuries to come!"

"Well, now, let's take a little bit of the argument in that First Proposition—just *two* steps, and the conclusion drawn from them. Kindly enter them in your note-book. And, in order to refer to them conveniently, let's call them *A*, *B*, and *Z*:

(*A*) Things that are equal to the same are equal to each other.

(*B*) The two sides of this Triangle are things that are equal to the same.

(*Z*) The two sides of this Triangle are equal to each other.

"Readers of Euclid will grant, I suppose, that *Z* follows logically from *A* and *B*, so that any one who accepts *A* and *B* as true, *must* accept *Z* as true?"

"Undoubtedly! The youngest child in a High School— as soon as High Schools are invented, which will not be till some two thousand years later—will grant *that*."

"And if some reader had *not* yet accepted *A* and *B* as true, he might still accept the *Sequence* as a *valid* one, I suppose?"

"No doubt such a reader might exist. He might say 'I accept as true the Hypothetical Proposition that, if *A* and *B* be true, *Z* must be true; but I *don't* accept *A* and *B* as true'. Such a reader would do wisely in abandoning Euclid, and taking to football."

"And might there not *also* be some reader who would say 'I accept *A* and *B* as true, but I *don't* accept the Hypothetical'?"

"Certainly there might. *He*, also, had better take to football."

"And *neither* of these readers", the Tortoise continued, "is *as yet* under any logical necessity to accept *Z* as true?"

"Quite so," Achilles assented.

"Well, now, I want you to consider *me* as a reader of the *second* kind, and to force me, logically, to accept *Z* as true."

"A tortoise playing football would be——" Achilles was beginning.

"—an anomaly, of course," the Tortoise hastily interrupted. "Don't wander from the point. Let's have *Z* first, and football afterwards!"

"I'm to force you to accept *Z*, am I?" Achilles said musingly. "And your present position is that you accept *A* and *B*, but you *don't* accept the Hypothetical——"

"Let's call it *C*," said the Tortoise.

"—but you don't accept:

(*C*) If *A* and *B* are true, *Z* must be true."

"That is my present position," said the Tortoise.

"Then I must ask you to accept *C*."

"I'll do so", said the Tortoise, "as soon as you've entered it in that note-book of yours. What else have you got in it?"

"Only a few memoranda," said Achilles, nervously fluttering the leaves: "a few memoranda of—of the battles in which I have distinguished myself!"

"Plenty of blank leaves, I see!" the Tortoise cheerily remarked. "We shall need them *all*!" (Achilles shuddered.) "Now write as I dictate:

(*A*) Things that are equal to the same are equal to each other.

(*B*) The two sides of this triangle are things that are equal to the same.

(*C*) If *A* and *B* are true, *Z* must be true.

(*Z*) The two sides of this Triangle are equal to each other."

"You should call it *D*, not *Z*," said Achilles. "It comes *next* to the other three. If you accept *A* and *B* and *C*, you *must* accept *Z*."

"And why *must* I?"

"Because it follows *logically* from them. If *A* and *B* and

C are true, *Z must* be true. You don't dispute *that*, I imagine?"

"If *A* and *B* and *C* are true, *Z must* be true," the Tortoise thoughtfully repeated. "That's *another* Hypothetical, isn't it? And, if I failed to see its truth, I might accept *A* and *B* and *C*, and *still* not accept *Z*, mightn't I?"

"You might," the candid hero admitted; "though such obtuseness would certainly be phenomenal. Still, the event is *possible*. So I must ask you to grant one more Hypothetical."

"Very good. I'm quite willing to grant it, as soon as you've written it down. We will call it

(*D*) If *A* and *B* and *C* are true, *Z* must be true.

"Have you entered that in your note-book?"

"I *have*!" Achilles joyfully exclaimed, as he ran the pencil into its sheath. "And at last we've got to the end of this ideal race-course! Now that you accept *A* and *B* and *C* and *D*, *of course* you accept *Z*."

"Do I?" said the Tortoise innocently. "Let's make that quite clear. I accept *A* and *B* and *C* and *D*. Suppose I *still* refuse to accept *Z*?"

"Then Logic would take you by the throat, and *force* you to do it!" Achilles triumphantly replied. "Logic would tell you 'You ca'n't help yourself. Now that you've accepted *A* and *B* and *C* and *D*, you *must* accept *Z*!' So you've no choice, you see."

"Whatever *Logic* is good enough to tell me is worth *writing down*," said the Tortoise. "So enter it in your book, please. We will call it

(*E*) If *A* and *B* and *C* and *D* are true, *Z* must be true.

"Until I've granted *that*, of course, I needn't grant *Z*. So it's quite a *necessary* step, you see?"

"I see," said Achilles; and there was a touch of sadness in his tone.

Here the narrator, having pressing business at the Bank, was obliged to leave the happy pair, and did not again pass the spot until some months afterwards. When he did so, Achilles was still seated on the back of the much-enduring Tortoise, and was writing in his note-book, which appeared to be nearly full. The Tortoise was saying "Have you got that last step written down? Un-less I've lost count, that makes a thousand and one. There are several millions more to come. And *would* you mind, as a personal favour—considering what a lot of instruc-tion this colloquy of ours will provide for the Logicians of the Nineteenth Century—*would* you mind adopting a pun that my cousin the Mock-Turtle will then make, and allowing yourself to be re-named Taught-Us?"

"As you please!" replied the weary warrior, in the hollow tones of despair, as he buried his face in his hands. "Provided that *you*, for *your* part, will adopt a pun the Mock-Turtle never made, and allow yourself to be re-named A Kill-Ease!"

THE TWO CLOCKS

Which is better, a clock that is right only once a year, or a clock that is right twice every day? "The latter," you reply, "unquestionably." Very good, now attend.

I have two clocks: one doesn't go *at all*, and the other loses a minute a day: which would you prefer? "The losing one," you answer, "without a doubt." Now ob-serve: the one which loses a minute a day has to lose twelve hours, or seven hundred and twenty minutes be-fore it is right again, consequently it is only right once in two years, whereas the other is evidently right as often as the time it points to comes round, which happens twice a day.

So you've contradicted yourself *once*.

"Ah, but," you say, "what's the use of its being right twice a day, if I ca'n't tell when the time comes?"

Why, suppose the clock points to eight o'clock, don't

you see that the clock is right *at* eight o'clock? Consequently, when eight o'clock comes round your clock is right.

"Yes, I see *that*," you reply.

Very good, then you've contradicted yourself *twice*: now get out of the difficulty as best you can, and don't contradict yourself again if you can help it.

You *might* go on to ask, "How am I to know when eight o'clock *does* come? My clock will not tell me." Be patient: you know that when eight o'clock comes your clock is right, very good; then your rule is this: keep your eye fixed on your clock, and *the very moment it is right* it will be eight o'clock. "But——," you say. There, that'll do; the more you argue the farther you get from the point, so it will be as well to stop.

PHOTOGRAPHY EXTRAORDINARY

THE recent extraordinary discovery in Photography, as applied to the operations of the mind, has reduced the art of novel-writing to the merest mechanical labour. We have been kindly permitted by the artist to be present during one of his experiments; but as the invention has not yet been given to the world, we are only at liberty to relate the results, suppressing all details of chemicals and manipulation.

The operator began by stating that the ideas of the feeblest intellect, when once received on properly prepared paper, could be "developed" up to any required degree of intensity. On hearing our wish that he would begin with an extreme case, he obligingly summoned a young man from an adjoining room, who appeared to be of the very weakest possible physical and mental powers. On being asked what we thought of him we candidly confessed that he seemed incapable of anything but sleep; our friend cordially assented to this opinion.

The machine being in position, and a mesmeric rapport established between the mind of the patient and the object glass, the young man was asked whether he wished to say anything; he feebly replied "Nothing". He was then asked what he was thinking of, and the answer, as before, was "Nothing". The artist on this pronounced him to be in a most satisfactory state, and at once commenced the operation.

After the paper had been exposed for the requisite time, it was removed and submitted to our inspection; we found it to be covered with faint and almost illegible characters. A closer scrutiny revealed the following:

"The eve was soft and dewy mild; a zephyr whispered in the lofty glade, and a few light drops of rain cooled the thirsty soil. At a slow amble, along the primrose-bordered path rode a gentle-looking and amiable youth, holding a light cane in his delicate hand; the pony moved gracefully beneath him, inhaling as it went the fragrance of the roadside flowers; the calm smile, and languid eyes, so admirably harmonizing with the fair features of the rider, showed the even tenor of his thoughts. With a sweet though feeble voice, he plaintively murmured out the gentle regrets that clouded his breast:

> 'Alas! she would not hear my prayer!
> Yet it were rash to tear my hair;
> Disfigured, I should be less fair.
>
> 'She was unwise, I may say blind;
> Once she was lovingly inclined;
> Some circumstance has changed her mind.'

There was a moment's silence; the pony stumbled over a stone in the path, and unseated his rider. A crash was heard among the dried leaves; the youth arose; a slight bruise on his left shoulder, and a disarrangement of his cravat, were the only traces that remained of this trifling accident."

"This", we remarked, as we returned the paper, "belongs apparently to the milk-and-water School of Novels."

"You are quite right," our friend replied, "and, in its present state, it is, of course, utterly unsaleable in the present day: we shall find, however, that the next stage of development will remove it into the strong-minded or Matter-of-Fact School." After dipping it into various acids, he again submitted it to us; it had now become the following:

"The evening was of the ordinary character, barometer at 'change'; a wind was getting up in the wood, and some rain was beginning to fall; a bad look-out for the farmers. A gentleman approached along the bridle-road, carrying a stout knobbed stick in his hand, and mounted on a serviceable nag, possibly worth some £40 or so; there was a settled business-like expression on the rider's face, and he whistled as he rode; he seemed to be hunting for rhymes in his head, and at length repeated, in a satisfied tone, the following composition:

'Well! so my offer was no go!
She might do worse, I told her so;
She was a fool to answer "No".

'However, things are as they stood;
Nor would I have her if I could,
For there are plenty more as good.'

At this moment the horse set his foot in a hole, and rolled over; his rider rose with difficulty; he had sustained several severe bruises and fractured two ribs; it was some time before he forgot that unlucky day."

We returned this with the strongest expression of admiration, and requested that it might now be developed to the highest possible degree. Our friend readily consented, and shortly presented us with the result, which he informed us belonged to the Spasmodic or German School. We perused it with indescribable sensations of surprise and delight:

"The night was wildly tempestuous—a hurricane raved through the murky forest—furious torrents of rain lashed the groaning earth. With a headlong rush—down a precipitous mountain gorge—dashed a mounted horseman armed to the teeth—his horse bounded beneath him at a mad gallop, snorting fire from its distended nostrils as it flew. The rider's knotted brows—rolling eyeballs—and clenched teeth—expressed the intense agony of his mind—weird visions loomed upon his burning brain—while with a mad yell he poured forth the torrent of his boiling passion:

> 'Firebrands and daggers! hope hath fled!
> To atoms dash the doubly dead!
> My brain is fire—my heart is lead!
>
> 'Her soul is flint, and what am I?
> Scorch'd by her fierce, relentless eye.
> Nothingness is my destiny!'

There was a moment's pause. Horror! his path ended in a fathomless abyss. . . . A rush—a flash—a crash—all was over. Three drops of blood, two teeth, and a stirrup were all that remained to tell where the wild horseman met his doom."

The young man was now recalled to consciousness, and shown the result of the workings of his mind; he instantly fainted away.

In the present infancy of the art we forbear from further comment on this wonderful discovery; but the mind reels as it contemplates the stupendous addition thus made to the powers of science.

Our friend concluded with various minor experiments, such as working up a passage of Wordsworth into strong, sterling poetry: the same experiment was tried on a passage of Byron, at our request, but the paper came out scorched and blistered all over by the fiery epithets thus produced.

As a concluding remark: *could* this art be applied (we

put the question in the strictest confidence)—*could* it, we ask, be applied to the speeches in Parliament? It may be but a delusion of our heated imagination, but we will still cling fondly to the idea, and hope against hope.

~~~~~~~~~~~~~~~~~~~~~~~~~~~~~~~~~~~~~~

HINTS FOR ETIQUETTE; OR, DINING OUT MADE EASY

As caterers for the public taste, we can conscientiously recommend this book to all diners-out who are perfectly unacquainted with the usages of society. However we may regret that our author has confined himself to warning rather than advice, we are bound in justice to say that nothing here stated will be found to contradict the habits of the best circles. The following examples exhibit a depth of penetration and a fullness of experience rarely met with:

I

In proceeding to the dining-room, the gentleman gives one arm to the lady he escorts—it is unusual to offer both.

II

The practice of taking soup with the next gentleman but one is now wisely discontinued; but the custom of asking your host his opinion of the weather immediately on the removal of the first course still prevails.

III

To use a fork with your soup, intimating at the same time to your hostess that you are reserving the spoon for the beefsteaks, is a practice wholly exploded.

IV

On meat being placed before you, there is no possible objection to your eating it, if so disposed; still, in all such delicate cases, be guided entirely by the conduct of those around you.

V

It is always allowable to ask for artichoke jelly with your boiled venison; however, there are houses where this is not supplied.

VI

The method of helping roast turkey with two carving-forks is practicable, but deficient in grace.

VII

We do not recommend the practice of eating cheese with a knife and fork in one hand, and a spoon and wine-glass in the other; there is a kind of awkwardness in the action which no amount of practice can entirely dispel.

VIII

As a general rule, do not kick the shins of the opposite gentleman under the table, if personally unacquainted with him; your pleasantry is liable to be misunderstood —a circumstance at all times unpleasant.

IX

Proposing the health of the boy in buttons immediately on the removal of the cloth is a custom springing from regard to his tender years, rather than from a strict adherence to the rules of etiquette.

A HEMISPHERICAL PROBLEM

HALF of the world, or nearly so, is always in the light of the sun: as the world turns round, this hemisphere of light shifts round too, and passes over each part of it in succession.

Supposing on Tuesday, it is morning at London; in another hour it would be Tuesday morning at the west of England; if the whole world were land we might go on tracing[1] Tuesday morning, Tuesday morning all the way round, till in twenty-four hours we get to London again. But we *know* that at London twenty-four hours after Tuesday morning it is Wednesday morning. Where, then, in its passage round the earth, does the day change its name? Where does it lose its identity?

Practically there is no difficulty in it, because a great part of the journey is over water, and what it does out at sea no one can tell: and besides there are so many different languages that it would be hopeless to attempt to trace the name of any one day all the year round. But is the case inconceivable that the same land and the same language should continue all round the world? I cannot see that it is: in that case either[2] there would be no distinction at all between each successive day, and so week, month, etc., so that we should have to say, "The Battle of Waterloo happened to-day, about two million hours ago," or some line would have to be fixed where the change should take place, so that the inhabitants of one house would wake and say, "Heigh-ho,[3] Tuesday morning!" and the inhabitants of the next (over the line), a

---

[1] The best way is to imagine yourself walking round with the sun and asking the inhabitants as you go, "What morning is this?" If you suppose them living all the way around, and all speaking one language, the difficulty is obvious.

[2] This is clearly an impossible case, and is only put as an hypothesis.

[3] The usual exclamation at waking, generally said with a yawn.

few miles to the west would wake a few minutes afterwards and say, "Heigh-ho! Wednesday morning!" What hopeless confusion the people who happened to live *on* the line would be in, is not for me to say. There would be a quarrel every morning as to what the name of the day should be. I can imagine no third case, unless everybody was allowed to choose for themselves, which state of things would be rather worse than either of the other two.

I am aware that this idea has been started before—namely, by the unknown author of that beautiful poem beginning, "If all the world were apple pie," etc.[1] The particular result here discussed, however, does not appear to have occurred to him, as he confines himself to the difficulties in obtaining drink which would certainly ensue.

A SELECTION FROM SYMBOLIC LOGIC

(*Even in his most abstruse works on mathematics and logic, Lewis Carroll could not fully repress his instinct for nonsense. SYMBOLIC LOGIC, for instance, shows the mind of Charles Lutwidge Dodgson rather than the whimsical Lewis Carroll. There would be little logic in offering here the entire text of SYMBOLIC LOGIC. Accordingly, the editors have chosen a single example to represent Carroll as he appeared in a completely un-Carrollean book.*)

INTRODUCTION

TO LEARNERS

THE Learner, who wishes to try the question *fairly*, whether this little book does, or does not, supply the ma-

---

[1] "If all the world were apple pie,
 And all the sea were ink,
 And all the trees were bread and cheese,
 What *should* we have to drink?"

terials for a most interesting mental recreation, is *earnest-ly* advised to adopt the following Rules:

(1) Begin at the *beginning*, and do not allow yourself to gratify a mere idle curiosity by dipping into the book, here and there. This would very likely lead to your throwing it aside, with the remark "This is *much* too hard for me!", and thus losing the chance of adding a very *large* item to your stock of mental delights. This Rule (of not *dipping*) is very *desirable* with *other* kinds of books—such as novels, for instance, where you may easily spoil much of the enjoyment you would otherwise get from the story, by dipping into it further on, so that what the author meant to be a pleasant surprise comes to you as a matter of course. Some people, I know, make a practice of looking into Vol. III first, just to see how the story ends: and perhaps it *is* as well just to know that all ends *happily*—that the much-persecuted lovers *do* marry after all, that he is proved to be quite innocent of the murder, that the wicked cousin is completely foiled in his plot and gets the punishment he deserves, and that the rich uncle in India (*Qu.* Why in *India*? *Ans.* Because, somehow, uncles never *can* get rich anywhere else) dies at exactly the right moment—before taking the trouble to read Vol. I. This, I say, is *just* permissible with a *novel*, where Vol. III has a *meaning*, even for those who have not read the earlier part of the story; but, with a *scientific* book, it is sheer insanity: you will find the latter part *hopelessly* unintelligible, if you read it before reaching it in regular course.

(2) Don't begin any fresh Chapter, or Section, until you are certain that you *thoroughly* understand the whole book *up to that point*, and that you have worked, correctly, most if not all of the examples which have been set. So long as you are conscious that all the land you have passed through is absolutely *conquered*, and that you are leaving no unsolved difficulties *behind* you, which will be sure to turn up again later on, your triumphal progress will be easy and delightful. Otherwise, you will

find your state of puzzlement get worse and worse as you proceed, till you give up the whole thing in utter disgust.

(3) When you come to any passage you don't understand, *read it again*: if you *still* don't understand it, *read it again*: if you fail, even after *three* readings, very likely your brain is getting a little tired. In that case, put the book away, and take to other occupations, and next day, when you come to it fresh, you will very likely find that it is *quite* easy.

(4) If possible, find some genial friend, who will read the book along with you, and will talk over the difficulties with you. *Talking* is a wonderful smoother-over of difficulties. When *I* come upon anything—in Logic or in any other hard subject—that entirely puzzles me, I find it a capital plan to talk it over, *aloud*, even when I am all alone. One can explain things so *clearly* to one's self! And then, you know, one is so *patient* with one's self: one *never* gets irritated at one's own stupidity!

If, dear Reader, you will faithfully observe these Rules, and so give my little book a really *fair* trial, I promise you, most confidently, that you will find Symbolic Logic to be one of the most, if not *the* most, fascinating of mental recreations! In this First Part, I have carefully avoided all difficulties which seemed to me to be beyond the grasp of an intelligent child of (say) twelve or fourteen years of age. I have myself taught most of its contents, *vivâ voce*, to *many* children, and have found them take a real intelligent interest in the subject. For those, who succeed in mastering Part I, and who begin, like Oliver, "asking for more", I hope to provide, in Part II, some *tolerably* hard nuts to crack—nuts that will require all the nut-crackers they happen to possess!

Mental recreation is a thing that we all of us need for our mental health; and you may get much healthy enjoyment, no doubt, from Games, such as Backgammon, Chess, and the new Game "Halma". But, after all, when you have made yourself a first-rate player at any one of these Games, you have nothing real to *show* for it, as a *result*! You enjoyed the Game, and the victory, no doubt, *at the time*: but you have no *result* that you can treasure up and get real *good* out of. And, all the while, you have been leaving unexplored a perfect *mine* of wealth. Once master the machinery of Symbolic Logic, and you have a mental occupation always at hand, of absorbing interest, and one that will be of real *use* to you in *any* subject you may take up. It will give you clearness of thought—the ability to *see your way* through a puzzle—the habit of arranging your ideas in an orderly and get-at-able form—and, more valuable than all, the power to detect *fallacies*, and to tear to pieces the flimsy illogical arguments, which you will so continually encounter in books, in newspapers, in speeches, and even in sermons, and which so easily delude those who have never taken the trouble to master this fascinating Art. *Try it*. That is all I ask of you!   L.C.

29, BEDFORD STREET, STRAND.
February 21, 1896.

Sets of Concrete Propositions, proposed as Premisses for Sorites. Conclusions to be found.

I

(1) Babies are illogical;
(2) Nobody is despised who can manage a crocodile;
(3) Illogical persons are despised.

> Univ. "persons"; a = able to manage a crocodile; b = babies; c = despised; d = logical.

2

(1) My saucepans are the only things I have that are made of tin;
(2) I find all *your* presents very useful;
(3) None of my saucepans are of the slightest use.

> Univ. "things of mine"; a = made of tin; b = my saucepans; c = useful; d = your presents.

3

(1) No potatoes of mine, that are new, have been boiled;
(2) All my potatoes in this dish are fit to eat;
(3) No unboiled potatoes of mine are fit to eat.

Univ. "my potatoes"; a = boiled; b = eatable; c = in this dish; d = new.

4

(1) There are no Jews in the kitchen;
(2) No Gentiles say "shpoonj";
(3) My servants are all in the kitchen.

Univ. "persons"; a = in the kitchen; b = Jews; c = my servants; d = saying "shpoonj".

5

(1) No ducks waltz;
(2) No officers ever decline to waltz;
(3) All my poultry are ducks.

Univ. "creatures"; a = ducks; b = my poultry ; c = officers; d = willing to waltz.

6

(1) Every one who is sane can do Logic;
(2) No lunatics are fit to serve on a jury;
(3) None of *your* sons can do Logic.

Univ. "persons"; a = able to do Logic; b = fit to serve on a jury; c = sane; d = your sons.

7

(1) There are no pencils of mine in this box;
(2) No sugar-plums of mine are cigars;
(3) The whole of my property, that is not in this box, consists of cigars.

Univ. "things of mine"; a = cigars; b = in this box; c = pencils; d = sugar-plums.

8

(1) No experienced person is incompetent;
(2) Jenkins is always blundering;
(3) No competent person is always blundering.

    Univ. "persons"; a = always blundering; b = competent; c = experienced; d = Jenkins.

9

(1) No terriers wander among the signs of the zodiac;
(2) Nothing, that does not wander among the signs of the zodiac, is a comet;
(3) Nothing but a terrier has a curly tail.

    Univ. "things"; a = comets; b = curly-tailed; c = terriers; d = wandering among the signs of the zodiac.

10

(1) No one takes in the *Times*, unless he is well-educated;
(2) No hedge-hogs can read;
(3) Those who cannot read are not well-educated.

    Univ. "creatures"; a = able to read; b = hedge-hogs; c = taking in the *Times*; d = well-educated.

11

(1) All puddings are nice;
(2) This dish is a pudding;
(3) No nice things are wholesome.

    Univ. "things"; a = nice; b = puddings; c = this dish; d = wholesome.

12

(1) My gardener is well worth listening to on military subjects;
(2) No one can remember the battle of Waterloo, unless he is very old;
(3) Nobody is really worth listening to on military subjects, unless he can remember the battle of Waterloo.

Univ. "persons"; a = able to remember the battle of Waterloo; b = my gardener; c = worth listening to on military subjects; d = very old.

13

(1) All humming birds are richly coloured;
(2) No large birds live on honey;
(3) Birds that do not live on honey are dull in colour.

     Univ. "birds"; a = humming-birds; b = large; c = living on honey; d = richly coloured.

14

(1) No Gentiles have hooked noses;
(2) A man who is a good hand at a bargain always makes money;
(3) No Jew is ever a bad hand at a bargain.

     Univ. "persons"; a = good hands at a bargain; b = hook-nosed; c = Jews; d = making money.

15

(1) All ducks in this village that are branded "B", belong to Mrs. Bond;
(2) Ducks in this village never wear lace collars, unless they are branded "B";
(3) Mrs. Bond has no gray ducks in this village.

     Univ. "ducks in this village"; a = belonging to Mrs. Bond; b = branded "B"; c = gray; d = wearing lace collars.

16

(1) All the old articles in this cupboard are cracked;
(2) No jug in this cupboard is new;
(3) Nothing in this cupboard, that is cracked, will hold water.

Univ. "things in this cupboard"; a = able to hold water; b = cracked; c = jugs; d = old.

17

(1) All unripe fruit is unwholesome;
(2) All these apples are wholesome;
(3) No fruit, grown in the shade, is ripe.

Univ. "fruit"; a = grown in the shade; b = ripe;
c = these apples; d = wholesome.

18

(1) Puppies, that will not lie still, are always grateful for the loan of a skipping-rope;
(2) A lame puppy would not say "thank you" if you offered to lend it a skipping-rope;
(3) None but lame puppies ever care to do worsted-work.

Univ. "puppies"; a = caring to do worsted-work;
b = grateful for the loan of a skipping-rope;
c = lame; d = willing to lie still.

19

(1) No name in this list is unsuitable for the hero of a romance;
(2) Names beginning with a vowel are always melodious;
(3) No name is suitable for the hero of a romance, if it begins with a consonant.

Univ. "names"; a = beginning with a vowel; b = in this list; c = melodious; d = suitable for the hero of a romance.

20

(1) All members of the House of Commons have perfect self-command;
(2) No M.P., who wears a coronet, should ride in a donkey-race;
(3) All members of the House of Lords wear coronets.

Univ. "M.P.'s"; a = belonging to the House of Commons; b = having perfect self-command; c = one who may ride in a donkey-race; d = wearing a coronet.

21

(1) No goods in this shop, that have been bought and paid for, are still on sale;

(2) None of the goods may be carried away, unless labeled "sold";

(3) None of the goods are labeled "sold" unless they have been bought and paid for.

Univ. "goods in this shop"; a = allowed to be carried away; b = bought and paid for; c = labeled "sold"; d = on sale.

22

(1) No acrobatic feats, that are not announced in the bills of a circus, are ever attempted there;

(2) No acrobatic feat is possible, if it involves turning a quadruple somersault;

(3) No impossible acrobatic feat is ever announced in a circus bill.

Univ. "acrobatic feats"; a = announced in the bills of a circus; b = attempted in a circus; c = involving the turning of a quadruple somersault; d = possible.

23

(1) Nobody, who really appreciates Beethoven, fails to keep silence while the Moonlight-Sonata is being played;

(2) Guinea-pigs are hopelessly ignorant of music;

(3) No one, who is hopelessly ignorant of music, ever keeps silence while the Moonlight-Sonata is being played.

Univ. "creatures"; a = guinea-pigs; b = hopelessly ignorant of music; c = keeping silence while the Moonlight-Sonata is being played; d = really appreciating Beethoven.

24

(1) Coloured flowers are always scented;
(2) I dislike flowers that are not grown in the open air;
(3) No flowers grown in the open air are colourless.

Univ. "flowers"; a = coloured; b = grown in the open air; c = liked by me; d = scented.

25

(1) Showy talkers think too much of themselves;
(2) No really well-informed people are bad company;
(3) People who think too much of themselves are not good company.

Univ. "persons"; a = good company; b = really well-informed; c = showy talkers; d = thinking too much of one's self.

26

(1) No boys under 12 are admitted to this school as boarders;
(2) All the industrious boys have red hair;
(3) None of the day-boys learn Greek;
(4) None but those under 12 are idle.

Univ. "boys in this school"; a = boarders; b = industrious; c = learning Greek; d = red-haired; e = under 12.

27

(1) The only articles of food, that my doctor allows me, are such as are not very rich;
(2) Nothing that agrees with me is unsuitable for supper;
(3) Wedding-cake is always very rich;
(4) My doctor allows me all articles of food that are suitable for supper.

Univ. "articles of food"; a = agreeing with me; b = allowed by my doctor; c = suitable for supper; d = very rich; e = wedding-cake.

28

(1) No discussions in our Debating-Club are likely to rouse the British Lion, so long as they are checked when they become too noisy;

(2) Discussions, unwisely conducted, endanger the peacefulness of our Debating-Club;

(3) Discussions, that go on while Tomkins is in the Chair, are likely to rouse the British Lion;

(4) Discussions in our Debating-Club, when wisely conducted, are always checked when they become too noisy.

Univ. "discussions in our Debating-Club"; a = checked when too noisy; b = dangerous to the peacefulness of our Debating-Club; c = going on while Tomkins is in the Chair; d = likely to rouse the British Lion; e = wisely conducted.

29

(1) All my sons are slim;

(2) No child of mine is healthy who takes no exercise;

(3) All gluttons, who are children of mine, are fat;

(4) No daughter of mine takes any exercise.

Univ. "my children"; a = fat; b = gluttons; c = healthy; d = sons; e = taking exercise.

30

(1) Things sold in the street are of no great value;

(2) Nothing but rubbish can be had for a song;

(3) Eggs of the Great Auk are very valuable;

(4) It is only what is sold in the streets that is really *rubbish*.

Univ. "things"; a = able to be had for a song; b = eggs of the Great Auk; c = rubbish; d = sold in the street; e = very valuable.

31

(1) No books sold here have gilt edges, except what are in the front shop;
(2) All the *authorized* editions have red labels;
(3) All the books with red labels are priced at 5s. and upwards;
(4) None but *authorized* editions are ever placed in the front shop.

Univ. "books sold here"; a = authorized editions; b = gilt-edged; c = having red labels; d = in the front shop; e = priced as 5s. and upwards.

32

(1) Remedies for bleeding, which fail to check it, are a mockery;
(2) Tincture of Calendula is not to be despised;
(3) Remedies, which will check the bleeding when you cut your finger, are useful;
(4) All mock remedies for bleeding are despicable.

Univ. "remedies for bleeding"; a = able to check bleeding; b = despicable; c = mockeries; d = Tincture of Calendula; e = useful when you cut your finger.

33

(1) None of the unnoticed things, met with at sea, are mermaids;
(2) Things entered in the log, as met with at sea, are sure to be worth remembering;
(3) *I* have never met with anything worth remembering, when on a voyage;
(4) Things met with at sea, that are noticed, are sure to be recorded in the log.

Univ. "things met with at sea"; a = entered in log; b = mermaids; c = met with by me; d = noticed; e = worth remembering.

34

(1) The only books in this library, that I do *not* recommend for reading, are unhealthy in tone;

(2) The bound books are all well-written;

(3) All the romances are healthy in tone;

(4) I do not recommend you to read any of the unbound books.

Univ. "books in this library"; $a=$bound; $b=$healthy in tone; $c=$recommended by me; $d=$romances; $e=$well-written.

35

(1) No birds, except ostriches, are 9 feet high;

(2) There are no birds in this aviary that belong to any one but *me*;

(3) No ostrich lives on mince-pies;

(4) I have no birds less than 9 feet high.

Univ. "birds"; $a=$in this aviary; $b=$living on mince-pies; $c=$my; $d=$9 feet high; $e=$ostriches.

36

(1) A plum-pudding, that is not really solid, is mere porridge;

(2) Every plum-pudding, served at my table, has been boiled in a cloth;

(3) A plum-pudding that is mere porridge is indistinguishable from soup;

(4) No plum-puddings are really solid, except what are served at *my* table.

Univ. "plum-puddings"; $a=$boiled in a cloth; $b=$distinguishable from soup; $c=$mere porridge; $d=$really solid; $e=$served at my table.

37

(1) No interesting poems are unpopular among people of real taste;

(2) No modern poetry is free from affectation;
(3) All *your* poems are on the subject of soap-bubbles;
(4) No affected poetry is popular among people of real taste;
(5) No ancient poem is on the subject of soap-bubbles.

Univ. "poems"; a=affected; b=ancient; c=interesting; d=on the subject of soap-bubbles; e=popular among people of real taste; h=written by you.

38

(1) All the fruit at this Show, that fails to get a prize, is the property of the Committee;
(2) None of my peaches have got prizes;
(3) None of the fruit, sold off in the evening, is unripe;
(4) None of the ripe fruit has been grown in a hot-house;
(5) All fruit, that belongs to the Committee, is sold off in the evening.

Univ. "fruit at this Show"; a=belonging to the Committee; b=getting prizes; c=grown in a hot-house; d=my peaches; e=ripe; h=sold off in the evening.

39

(1) Promise-breakers are untrustworthy;
(2) Wine-drinkers are very communicative;
(3) A man who keeps his promises is honest;
(4) No teetotalers are pawnbrokers;
(5) One can always trust a very communicative person.

Univ. "persons"; a=honest; b=pawnbrokers; c=promise-breakers; d=trustworthy; e=very communicative; h=wine-drinkers.

40

(1) No kitten, that loves fish, is unteachable.
(2) No kitten without a tail will play with a gorilla;
(3) Kittens with whiskers always love fish;
(4) No teachable kitten has green eyes;

(5) No kittens have tails unless they have whiskers.

Univ. "kittens"; a = green-eyed; b = loving fish;
c = tailed; d = teachable; e = whiskered;
h = willing to play with a gorilla.

41

(1) All the Eton men in this College play cricket;
(2) None but the Scholars dine at the higher table;
(3) None of the cricketers row;
(4) *My* friends in this College all come from Eton;
(5) All the Scholars are rowing-men.

Univ. "men in this College"; a = cricketers; b = dining at
the higher table; c = Etonians; d = my friends;
e = rowing-men; h = Scholars.

42

(1) There is no box of mine here that I dare open;
(2) My writing-desk is made of rose-wood;
(3) All my boxes are painted, except what are here;
(4) There is no box of mine that I dare not open, unless
it is full of live scorpions;
(5) All my rose-wood boxes are unpainted.

Univ. "my boxes"; a = boxes that I dare open;
b = full of live scorpions; c = here; d = made of rose-wood;
e = painted; h = writing-desks.

43

(1) Gentiles have no objection to pork;
(2) Nobody who admires pigsties ever reads Hogg's
poems;
(3) No Mandarin knows Hebrew;
(4) Every one, who does not object to pork, admires pigsties;
(5) No Jew is ignorant of Hebrew.

Univ. "persons"; a = admiring pigsties; b = Jews;
c = knowing Hebrew; d = Mandarins; e = objecting to
pork; h = reading Hogg's poems.

44

(1) All writers, who understand human nature, are clever;
(2) No one is a true poet unless he can stir the hearts of men;
(3) Shakespeare wrote "Hamlet";
(4) No writer, who does not understand human nature, can stir the hearts of men;
(5) None but a true poet could have written "Hamlet".

Univ. "writers"; a = able to stir the hearts of men; b = clever; c = Shakespeare; d = true poets; e = understanding human nature; h = writer of "Hamlet".

45

(1) I despise anything that cannot be used as a bridge;
(2) Everything, that is worth writing an ode to, would be a welcome gift to me;
(3) A rainbow will not bear the weight of a wheel-barrow;
(4) Whatever can be used as a bridge will bear the weight of a wheel-barrow;
(5) I would not take, as a gift, a thing that I despise.

Univ. "things"; a = able to bear the weight of a wheel-barrow; b = acceptable to me; c = despised by me; d = rainbows; e = useful as a bridge; h = worth writing an ode to.

46

(1) When I work a Logic-example without grumbling, you may be sure it is one that I can understand;
(2) These Jorites are not arranged in regular order, like the examples I am used to;
(3) No easy example ever makes my head ache;
(4) I ca'n't understand examples that are not arranged in regular order, like those I am used to;
(5) I never grumble at an example, unless it gives me a headache.

Univ. "Logic-examples worked by me"; a =arranged in regular order, like the examples I am used to; b =easy; c =grumbled at by me; d =making my head ache; e =these Sorites; h =understood by me.

47

(1) Every idea of mine, that cannot be expressed as a Syllogism, is really ridiculous;

(2) None of my ideas about Bath-buns are worth writing down;

(3) No idea of mine, that fails to come true, can be expressed as a Syllogism;

(4) I never have any really ridiculous idea, that I do not at once refer to my solicitor;

(5) My dreams are all about Bath-buns;

(6) I never refer any idea of mine to my solicitor, unless it is worth writing down.

Univ. "my idea"; a =able to be expressed as a Syllogism; b =about Bath-buns; c =coming true; d =dreams; e =really ridiculous; h =referred to my solicitor; k =worth writing down.

48

(1) None of the pictures here, except the battle-pieces, are valuable;

(2) None of the unframed ones are varnished;

(3) All the battle-pieces are painted in oils;

(4) All those that have been sold are valuable;

(5) All the English ones are varnished;

(6) All those in frames have been sold.

Univ. "the pictures here"; a =battle-pieces; b =English; c =framed; d =oil-paintings; e =sold; h =valuable; k =varnished.

49

(1) Animals, that do not kick, are always unexcitable;

(2) Donkeys have no horns;

(3) A buffalo can always toss one over a gate;

(4) No animals that kick are easy to swallow;

(5) No hornless animal can toss one over a gate;

(6) All animals are excitable, except buffaloes.

Univ. "animals"; a = able to toss one over a gate;
b = buffaloes; c = donkeys; d = easy to swallow;
e = excitable; h = horned; k = kicking.

50

(1) No one, who is going to a party, ever fails to brush his hair;

(2) No one looks fascinating, if he is untidy;

(3) Opium-eaters have no self-command;

(4) Every one, who has brushed his hair, looks fascinating;

(5) No one wears white kid gloves, unless he is going to a party;

(6) A man is always untidy, if he has no self-command.

Univ. "persons"; a = going to a party; b = having brushed one's hair; c = having self-command; d = looking fascinating; e = opium-eaters; h = tidy; k = wearing white kid gloves.

51

(1) No husband, who is always giving his wife new dresses, can be a cross-grained man;

(2) A methodical husband always comes home for his tea;

(3) No one, who hangs up his hat on the gas-jet, can be a man that is kept in proper order by his wife;

(4) A good husband is always giving his wife new dresses;

(5) No husband can fail to be cross-grained, if his wife does not keep him in proper order;

(6) An unmethodical husband always hangs up his hat on the gas-jet.

Univ. "husbands"; a = always coming home for his tea; b = always giving his wife new dresses; c = cross-grained; d = good; e = hanging up his hat on the gas-jet; h = kept in proper order; k = methodical.

52

(1) Everything, not absolutely ugly, may be kept in a drawing-room;
(2) Nothing, that is encrusted with salt, is ever quite dry;
(3) Nothing should be kept in a drawing-room, unless it is free from damp;
(4) Bathing-machines are always kept near the sea;
(5) Nothing, that is made of mother-of-pearl, can be absolutely ugly;
(6) Whatever is kept near the sea gets encrusted with salt.

Univ. "things"; a = absolutely ugly; b = bathing machines; c = encrusted with salt; d = kept near the sea; e = made of mother-of-pearl; h = quite dry; k = things that may be kept in a drawing-room.

53

(1) I call no day "unlucky", when Robinson is civil to me;
(2) Wednesdays are always cloudy;
(3) When people take umbrellas, the day never turns out fine;
(4) The only days when Robinson is uncivil to me are Wednesdays;
(5) Everybody takes his umbrella with him when it is raining;
(6) My "lucky" days always turn out fine.

Univ. "days"; a = called by me "lucky"; b = cloudy; c = days when people take umbrellas; d = days when Robinson is civil to me; e = rainy; h = turning out fine; k = Wednesdays.

54

(1) No shark ever doubts that it is well fitted out;
(2) A fish, that cannot dance a minuet, is contemptible;
(3) No fish is quite certain that it is well fitted out, unless it has three rows of teeth;

(4) All fishes, except sharks, are kind to children;

(5) No heavy fish can dance a minuet;

(6) A fish with three rows of teeth is not to be despised.

Univ. "fishes"; a = able to dance a minuet; b = certain that he is well fitted out; c = contemptible; d = having 3 rows of teeth; e = heavy; h = kind to children; k = sharks.

55

(1) All the human race, except my footmen, have a certain amount of common sense;

(2) No one, who lives on barley-sugar, can be anything but a mere baby;

(3) None but a hop-scotch player knows what real happiness is;

(4) No mere baby has a grain of common sense;

(5) No engine-driver ever plays hop-scotch;

(6) No footman of mine is ignorant of what true happiness is.

Univ. "human beings"; a = engine-drivers; b = having common sense; c = hop-scotch players; d = knowing what real happiness is; e = living on barley-sugar; h = mere babies; k = my footmen.

56

(1) I trust every animal that belongs to me;

(2) Dogs gnaw bones;

(3) I admit no animals into my study, unless they will beg when told to do so;

(4) All the animals in the yard are mine;

(5) I admit every animal, that I trust, into my study;

(6) The only animals, that are really willing to beg when told to do so, are dogs.

Univ. "animals"; a = admitted to my study; b = animals that I trust; c = dogs; d = gnawing bones; e = in the yard; h = my; k = willing to beg when told.

57

(1) Animals are always mortally offended if I fail to notice them;

(2) The only animals that belong to *me* are in that field;

(3) No animal can guess a conundrum, unless it has been properly trained in a Board-School;

(4) None of the animals in that field are badgers;

(5) When an animal is mortally offended, it always rushes about wildly and howls;

(6) I never notice any animal, unless it belongs to me;

(7) No animal, that has been properly trained in a Board-School, ever rushes about wildly and howls.

Univ. "animals"; a = able to guess a conundrum; b = badgers; c = in that field; d = mortally offended if I fail to notice them; e = my; h = noticed by me; k = properly trained in a Board-School; l = rushing about wildly and howling.

58

(1) I never put a cheque, received by me, on that file, unless I am anxious about it;

(2) All the cheques received by me, that are not marked with a cross, are payable to bearer;

(3) None of them are ever brought back to me, unless they have been dishonoured at the Bank;

(4) All of them, that are marked with a cross, are for amounts of over £100;

(5) All of them, that are not on that file, are marked "not negotiable";

(6) No cheque of yours, received by me, has ever been dishonoured;

(7) I am never anxious about a cheque, received by me, unless it should happen to be brought back to me;

(8) None of the cheques received by me, that are marked "not negotiable", are for amounts of over £100.

Univ. "cheques received by me"; a = brought back to me; b = cheques that I am anxious about; c = honoured;

d = marked with a cross; e = marked "not negotiable"; h = on that file; k = over £100; l = payable to bearer; m = your.

59

(1) All the dated letters in this room are written on blue paper;
(2) None of them are in black ink, except those that are written in the third person;
(3) I have not filed any of them that I can read;
(4) None of them, that are written on one sheet, are undated;
(5) All of them, that are not crossed, are in black ink;
(6) All of them, written by Brown, begin with "Dear Sir";
(7) All of them, written on blue paper, are filed;
(8) None of them, written on more than one sheet, are crossed;
(9) None of them, that begin with "Dear Sir", are written in the third person.

Univ. "letters in this room"; a = beginning with "Dear Sir"; b = crossed; c = dated; d = filed; e = in black ink; h = in third person; k = letters that I can read; l = on blue paper; m = on one sheet; n = written by Brown.

60

(1) The only animals in this house are cats;
(2) Every animal is suitable for a pet, that loves to gaze at the moon;
(3) When I detest an animal, I avoid it;
(4) No animals are carnivorous, unless they prowl at night;
(5) No cat fails to kill mice;
(6) No animals ever take to me, except what are in this house;
(7) Kangaroos are not suitable for pets;
(8) None but carnivora kill mice;

(9) I detest animals that do not take to me;

(10) Animals, that prowl at night, always love to gaze at
the moon.

Univ. "animals"; *a*=avoided by me; *b*=carnivora;
c=cats; *d*=detested by me; *e*=in this house;
h=kangaroos; *k*=killing mice; *l*=loving to gaze
at the moon; *m*=prowling at night; *n*=suitable for pets;
r=taking to me.

Answers

1. Babies cannot manage crocodiles.
2. *Your* presents to me are not made of tin.
3. All my potatoes in this dish are old ones.
4. My servants never say "shpoonj".
5. My poultry are not officers.
6. None of *your* sons are fit to serve on a jury.
7. No pencils of mine are sugar-plums.
8. Jenkins is inexperienced.
9. No comet has a curly tail.
10. No hedge-hog takes in the *Times*.
11. This dish is unwholesome.
12. My gardener is very old.
13. All humming-birds are small.
14. No one with a hooked nose ever fails to make money.
15. No gray ducks in this village wear lace collars.
16. No jug in this cupboard will hold water.
17. These apples were grown in the sun.
18. Puppies, that will not lie still, never care to do worsted-work.
19. No name in this list is unmelodious.
20. No M.P. should ride in a donkey-race, unless he has
perfect self-command.
21. No goods in this shop, that are still on sale, may be
carried away.
22. No acrobatic feat, which involves turning a quadruple somersault, is ever attempted in a circus.

23. Guinea-pigs never really appreciate Beethoven.
24. No scentless flowers please me.
25. Showy talkers are not really well-informed.
26. None but red-haired boys learn Greek in this school.
27. Wedding-cake always disagrees with me.
28. Discussions, that go on while Tomkins is in the chair, endanger the peacefulness of our Debating-Club.
29. All gluttons, who are children of mine, are unhealthy.
30. An egg of the Great Auk is not to be had for a song.
31. No books sold here have gilt edges, unless they are priced at 5s. and upwards.
32. When you cut your finger, you will find Tincture of Calendula useful.
33. *I* have never come across a mermaid at sea.
34. All the romances in this library are well-written.
35. No bird in this aviary lives on mince-pies.
36. No plum-pudding, that has not been boiled in a cloth, can be distinguished from soup.
37. All *your* poems are uninteresting.
38. None of my peaches have been grown in a hot-house.
39. No pawnbroker is dishonest.
40. No kitten with green eyes will play with a gorilla.
41. All *my* friends dine at the lower table.
42. My writing-desk is full of live scorpions.
43. No Mandarin ever reads Hogg's poems.
44. Shakespeare was clever.
45. Rainbows are not worth writing odes to.
46. These Sorites-examples are difficult.
47. All my dreams come true.
48. All the English pictures here are painted in oils.
49. Donkeys are not easy to swallow.
50. Opium-eaters never wear white kid gloves.
51. A good husband always comes home for his tea.
52. Bathing-machines are never made of mother-of-pearl.
53. Rainy days are always cloudy.
54. No heavy fish is unkind to children.
55. No engine-driver lives on barley-sugar.

56. All the animals in the yard gnaw bones.
57. No badger can guess a conundrum.
58. No cheque of yours, received by me, is payable to order.
59. I cannot read any of Brown's letters.
60. I always avoid a kangaroo.

RULES FOR COURT CIRCULAR

(*A New Game of Cards for Two or More Players*)

SECTION I. (*For Two Players*)

I

C U T for precedence. Highest is "first-hand"; lowest "dealer". Dealer gives 6 cards to each, one by one, beginning with first-hand, and turns up the 13th, which is called the "Lead". It is convenient that the same player should be dealer for the whole of each game.

II

First-hand then plays a card; then the other player, and so on, until 6 cards have been played, when the trick is complete, and he who can make (out of the 3 cards he has played, with or without the Lead), the best "Line", wins it.

First hand.

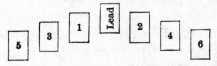

N.B. The cards in the figure are numbered in the order of playing.

III

A "Line" consists of 2, or all 3, of the cards put down by either player, with or without the Lead. In making a Line, it does not matter in what order the 3 cards have been put down. Lines rank as follows:

(1) 3, or 4, CARDS, (LEAD *included*)

Trio—i.e. 3 of a sort, (e.g. 3 Kings, or 3 Nines.)
Sequence—i.e. 3, or 4, in Sequence, (e.g. Eight, Nine, Ten, Knave.)
Sympathy—i.e. 3, or 4, Hearts.
Court—i.e. 3, or 4, Court-cards, (if 4, it is called Court Circular.)

N.B. In this Class a Line of 4 cards beats a *similar* Line of 3. The Lead must not be reckoned in the middle of a Sequence.

(2) 3 CARDS, (LEAD *excluded*)

Names as above.

N.B. In making a Sequence, the Ace may be reckoned either with King, Queen, or with Two, Three.

(3) 2 CARDS, (LEAD *excluded*)

Pair—i.e. 2 of a sort.
Valentine—i.e. 2 Hearts.
Etiquette—i.e. 2 Court-cards.

IV

If both have made Lines of the same kind, he whose Line contains the best card wins the trick; and if neither has made a Line, he who has played the best card wins it. Cards rank as follows:

(1) Hearts.
(2) The rest of the pack, in order Aces, Kings, &c.

N.B. If no Hearts have been played, and the highest cards on each side are equal, (e.g. if each have played an Ace,) they rank in the order Diamonds, Clubs, Spades.

V

The winner of a trick chooses, as Lead for the next trick, any one of the cards on the table, except the old Lead; he then takes the rest, turning them face upwards, if he be first-hand, but if not, face downwards; and he becomes first-hand for the next trick.

VI

The dealer then gives cards to each, one by one, beginning with first-hand, until each hand is made up again to 6 cards.

VII

At any time during a trick, after the first card of it has been played, and before either has played 3 cards, he whose turn it is to play may "resign" instead; in which case no more cards are played in that trick, and the other player wins it and proceeds as in Rule V. But when either has played 3 cards, the other must not resign.

VIII

When the pack is exhausted neither player may resign. The winner of the last trick clears the board. Each then reckons up the cards he has won, which count as follows:

Cards face upwards ..... 2 each.
             downwards ... 1
Hearts 1
Court-cards 1

(so that a Court-Heart, if face upwards, counts 4 altogether.) The winner scores the difference between his own and the loser's marks, the loser scoring nothing. Game is 20 or 50.

SECTION II. *(For Three or More Players)*

The same rules apply, with the following necessary changes. The Lead is placed in the middle; first-hand then plays a card; then the player on his left-hand, and so on all round, each putting down his 3 cards in a row from the Lead towards himself. He who makes the best Line wins the trick, and is first-hand for the next trick. At any time during a trick, after the first card of it has been played, and before any one has played 3 cards, he whose turn it is to play may "resign" instead; in which case he loses his chance of winning that trick, and the other players go on without him. But when any one has played 3 cards, no other player may resign. In the case where all players but one "resign", he who is left to the last wins the trick. At the end of each game all the players but the lowest score the difference between their own marks and those of the lowest, the lowest scoring nothing. Game is 50.

January, 1860.

CROQUET CASTLES

(For Five Players)

I

THIS Game requires the 10 arches, and 5 of the 8 balls used in the ordinary game, and, in addition to them, another set of 5 balls, (matching these in colour, but marked so as to be distinct from them), and 5 flags, also matching them. One set of balls is called "soldiers"; the other, "sentinels". The arches and flags are set up as in a figure, making 5 "castles", and each player has a castle, a soldier, and a sentinel; the sentinel's "post" is half-way between the "gate" and the "door" of the castle, and the soldier is placed, to begin the game, just within the gate.

(N.B. The distance from one gate to the next should be 6 or 8 yards, and from the gate of a castle to the door 4 yards; and the distance from the door to the flag should be equal to the width of the door.)

II

The soldiers are played in order, as marked above; then the sentinels, in the same order, and so on. Each soldier has to "invade" the other 4 castles, in order, (e.g. soldier No. 3 has to invade castles Nos. 4, 5, 1, 2,) then to re-enter his own, and touch the flag; and whoever does this first, wins. To "invade" a castle, he must enter the gate, go through the door, then between the door and the flag, then out at the gate again: but he cannot enter a castle, unless either the sentinel of that castle, or his own sentinel, be out of its castle.

(N.B. No ball can enter or leave a castle, except by passing through the gate.)

III

If a sentinel touch a soldier, both being in the sentinel's castle, the soldier is "prisoner"; he is replaced (if necessary) where he was when touched, the sentinel is placed in the gate, and the castle is "fortified". The prisoner cannot move, and nothing can go through the gate, till the castle is opened again, which is done either by the prisoner's comrade coming and touching the sentinel in the gate, or by the sentinel leaving the gate to go and rescue his own comrade: in the former case, both sentinels are replaced at their posts.

IV

When a prisoner is set free, he cannot be again taken prisoner until after his next turn.

V

If a ball touch another (except a prisoner, or a sentinel in his castle), the player may, if he likes, replace it where it was when touched, and use it to croquet his own with: in the excepted cases, he must replace it, but can do no more.

VI

If a soldier go through an arch, or between a door and flag, in his proper course, or if a sentinel go through the gate of his castle, the player has another turn.

VII

A player whose soldier is a prisoner, plays all his turns with his sentinel; and one, whose castle is fortified, with his soldier, unless it be taken prisoner, when he must play his sentinel to rescue it.

VIII

The sentinel of a fortified castle is considered to be in, or out of, the castle, as the owner chooses: that is, if he wishes to invade a castle, the sentinel of which is within it, he may consider his own sentinel as *out* of its castle (which gives him the right of invasion): or, if he wishes to go and rescue his soldier, he may consider it as *in* (so that he first plays it *through* the gate, and then has another turn).

CH.CH., OXFORD, *May 4, 1863.*

N.B. This game does not absolutely require more than *two* additional balls, beside those used in the ordinary game; these may be Light Blue and Light Green, and the 10 balls may be arranged as follows—

Soldiers	*Sentinels*
BLUE.	LIGHT BLUE.
BLACK.	BROWN.
ORANGE.	YELLOW.
GREEN.	LIGHT GREEN.
RED.	PINK.

MISCHMASCH

(A Word-Game for Two Players or Two Sets of Players)

"Pars pro toto."

THE essence of this game consists in one Player proposing a "nucleus" (i.e. a set of two or more letters, such as "gp", "emo", "imse"), and in the other trying to find a "lawful word" (i.e. a word known in ordinary society, and not a proper name), containing it. Thus, "magpie", "lemon", "himself", are lawful words containing the nuclei "gp", emo", "imse".

A nucleus must not contain a hyphen (e.g. for the nucleus "erga", "flower-garden" is not a lawful word).

Any word, that is always printed with a capital initial (e.g. "English"), counts as a proper name.

RULES

1. Each thinks of a nucleus, and says "ready" when he has done so. When both have spoken, the nuclei are named. A Player may set a nucleus without knowing of any word containing it.

2. When a Player has guessed a word containing the nucleus set to him (which need not be the word thought of by the Player who set it), or has made up his mind that there is no such word, he says "ready", or "no word", as the case may be: when he has decided to give up trying, he says "I resign". The other must then, within a stated time (e.g. 2 minutes), say "ready", or "no word", or "I resign", or "not ready". If he says nothing, he is assumed to be "not ready".

3. When both have spoken, if the first speaker said "ready", he now names the word he has guessed: if he said "no word", he, who set the nucleus, names, if he can, a word containing it. The other Player then proceeds in the same way.

4. The Players then score as follows—(N.B. When a Player is said to "lose" marks, it means that the other scores them,)

> Guessing a word, rightly,   scores 1.
>   ,,   ,, wrongly,   loses 1.
> Guessing "no word", rightly, scores 2.
>   ,,   ,, wrongly,   loses 2.
> Resigning   loses 1.

This ends the first move.

5. For every other move, the Players proceed as for the first move, except that when a Player is "not ready", or has guessed a word wrongly, he has not a new nucleus set to him, but goes on guessing the one in hand, having first, if necessary, set a new nucleus for the other Player.

6. A "resigned" nucleus cannot be set again during the same game. If, however, one or more letters be added or subtracted, it counts as a new one.

7. The move, in which either scores 10, is the final one; when it is completed, the game is over, and the highest score wins, or, if the scores be equal, the game is drawn.

November, 1882.

DOUBLETS

A Word-Puzzle

PREFACE

On the 29th of March, 1879, the following article appeared in *Vanity Fair*—

A NEW PUZZLE

The readers of *Vanity Fair* have during the last ten years shown so much interest in the Acrostics and Hard

Cases which were first made the object of sustained competition for prizes in this journal, that it has been sought to invent for them an entirely new kind of Puzzle, such as would interest them equally with those that have already been so successful. The subjoined letter from Mr. Lewis Carroll will explain itself, and will introduce a Puzzle so entirely novel and withal so interesting, that the transmutation of the original into the final word of the Doublets may be expected to become an occupation to the full as amusing as the guessing of the Double Acrostics has already proved.

In order to enable readers to become acquainted with the new Puzzle, preliminary Doublets will be given during the next three weeks—that is to say, in the present number of *Vanity Fair* and in those of the 5th and 12th April. A competition will then be opened—beginning with the Doublets published on the 19th April, and including all those published subsequently up to and including the number of the 26th July—for three prizes, consisting respectively of a Proof Album for the first and of Ordinary Albums for the second and third prizes.

The rule of scoring will be as follows—A number of marks will be apportioned to each Doublet equal to the number of letters in the two words given, For example, in the instance given below of "Head" and "Tail", the number of possible marks to be gained would be eight; and this maximum will be gained by each one of those who make the chain with the least possible number of changes. If it be assumed that in this instance the chain cannot be completed with less than the four links given, then those that complete it with four links only will receive eight marks, while a mark will be deducted for every extra link used beyond four. Any competitor, therefore, using five links would score seven marks, any competitor using eight links would score four, and any using twelve links or more would score nothing. The marks gained by each competitor will be published each week.

DEAR VANITY.—Just a year ago last Christmas, two young ladies—smarting under that secret scourge of feminine humanity, the having "nothing to do"—besought me to send them "some riddles". But riddles I had none at hand, and therefore set myself to devise some other form of verbal torture which should serve the same purpose. The result of my meditations was a new kind of Puzzle—new at least to me—which, now that it has been fairly tested by a year's experience and commended by many friends, I offer to you, as a newly-gathered nut, to be cracked by the omnivorous teeth which have already masticated so many of your Double Acrostics.

The rules of the Puzzle are simple enough. Two words are proposed, of the same length; and the puzzle consists in linking these together by interposing other words, each of which shall differ from the next word *in one letter only*. That is to say, one letter may be changed in one of the given words, then one letter in the word so obtained, and so on, till we arrive at the other given word. The letters must not be interchanged among themselves, but each must keep to his own place. As an example, the word "head" may be changed into "tail" by interposing the words "heal, teal, tell, tall". I call the two given words "a Doublet", the interposed words "Links", and the entire series "a Chain", of which I here append an example—

HEAD
heal
teal
tell
tall
TAIL

It is, perhaps, needless to state that it is *de rigueur* that the links should be English words, such as might be used in good society.

The easiest "Doublets" are those in which the consonants in one word answer to consonants in the other, and the vowels to vowels; "head" and "tail" constitute a

Doublet of this kind. Where this is not the case, as in "head" and "hare", the first thing to be done is to transform one member of the Doublet into a word whose consonants and vowels shall answer to those of the other member (e.g. "head, herd, here", after which there is seldom much difficulty in completing the "Chain".

I am told there is an American game involving a similar principle. I have never seen it, and can only say of its inventors, *"pereant qui ante nos nostra dixerunt!"*

LEWIS CARROLL

RULES

1. The words given to be linked together constitute a "Doublet"; the interposed words are the "Links"; and the entire series a "Chain". The object is to complete the Chain with the least possible number of Links.

2. Each word in the Chain must be formed from the preceding word by changing one letter in it, and one only. The substituted letter must occupy the same place, in the word so formed, which the discarded letter occupied in the preceding word, and all the other letters must retain their places.

3. When three or more words are given to be made into a Chain, the first and last constitute the "Doublet". The others are called "Set Links", and must be introduced into the Chain in the order in which they are given. A Chain of this kind must not contain any word twice over.

4. No word is admissible as a Link unless it (or, if it be an inflection, a word from which it comes) is to be found in the following Glossary.[1] Comparatives and superlatives of adjectives and adverbs, when regularly formed, are regarded as "inflections" of the positive form, and are not given separately: e.g. the word "new" being given, it is to be understood that "newer" and "newest" are also admissible. But nouns formed from verbs (as

[1] The glossary mentioned here is a list of common English words which appeared in the original edition of "Doublets". It has not been included in this volume. Ed.

"reader" from "read") are not so regarded, and may not be used as Links unless they are to be found in the Glossary.

METHOD OF SCORING
ADOPTED IN "VANITY FAIR"

1. The marks assigned to each Doublet are as follows— If it be given without any Set Links, so many marks are assigned to it as there are letters in the two words together (e.g., a four-letter Doublet would have eight marks assigned to it). If it be given with Set Links, so that the Chain is made up of two or more portions, so many marks are assigned to it as would have been assigned if each portion had been a separate Chain (e.g., a four-letter Doublet which has two Set Links, so that the Chain is made up of three portions, would have twenty-four marks assigned to it).

2. Each competitor, who completes the Chain with the least possible number of Links, will receive the full number of marks assigned; and each who uses more than the least possible number of Links will lose a mark for every additional Link.

3. Each competitor is required to send his three Chains, with his signature attached, written on *one* piece of paper.

4. The Editor of *Vanity Fair* will be glad to receive any suggestions, both as to words which it seems desirable to omit, and as to omitted words which it seems desirable to insert: but any words proposed for insertion or for omission *should be exhibited as a Link between two other words*.

5. Alterations will not be made in this Glossary during any competition, but will be duly announced before the commencement of a new competition, so that those who already possess copies will be able to correct them, and will not be obliged to buy a new edition.

"Vanity Fair" Office,
13, Tavistock Street,
Covent Garden,
LONDON.

DOUBLETS ALREADY SET
IN "VANITY FAIR"

March 29: Drive PIG into STY.
              Raise FOUR to FIVE.
              Make WHEAT into BREAD.

April 5:   Dip PEN into INK.
              Touch CHIN with NOSE.
              Change TEARS into SMILE.

April 12: Change WET to DRY.
              Make HARE into SOUP.
              PITCH TENTS.

April 19: Cover EYE with LID.
              Prove PITY to be GOOD.
              STEAL COINS.

April 26: Make EEL into PIE.
              Turn POOR into RICH.
              Prove RAVEN to be MISER.

May 3:   Change OAT to RYE.
              Get WOOD from TREE.
              Prove GRASS to be GREEN.

May 10:   Evolve MAN from APE.
              Change CAIN into ABEL.
              Make FLOUR into BREAD.

May 17:   Make TEA HOT.
              Run COMB into HAIR.
              Prove a ROGUE to be a BEAST.

May 24:   Change ELM into OAK.
              Combine ARMY and NAVY.
              Place BEARS on SHELF.

May 31:   HOOK FISH.
              QUELL a BRAVO.
              Stow FURIES in BARREL.

June 7:   BUY an ASS.
          Get COAL from MINE.
          Pay COSTS in PENCE.

June 14: Raise ONE to TWO.
          Change BLUE to PINK.
          Change BLACK to WHITE.

June 21: Change FISH to BIRD.
          Sell SHOES for CRUST.
          Make KETTLE HOLDER.

A POSTAL PROBLEM

(*June*, 1891)

THE Rule, for Commissions chargeable on overdue Postal Orders, is given in the "Post Office Guide" in these words, (it is here divided, for convenience of reference, into 3 clauses)—

(a) After the expiration of 3 months from the last day of the month of issue, a Postal Order will be payable only on payment of a Commission, equal to the amount of the original poundage;

(b) with the addition (if more than 3 months have elapsed since the said expiration) of the amount of the original poundage for every further period of 3 months which has so elapsed;

(c) and for every portion of any such period of 3 months over and above every complete period.

You are requested to answer the following questions, in reference to a Postal Order for 10/-. (on which the "original poundage" would be 1d.) issued during the month of January, so that the 1st "period" would consist of the months February, March, April; the 2nd would consist of the months May, June, July; and the 3rd would consist of the months August, September, October.

(1) Supposing the Rule to consist of clause (a) only, on what day would a "Commission" begin to be chargeable? (   )

(2) What would be its amount? (   )

(3) Supposing the Rule to consist of clauses (a) and (b), on what day would the lowest "Commission" begin to be chargeable? (   )

(4) What would be its amount? (   )

(5) On what day would a larger "Commission" (being the sum of 2 "Commissions") begin to be chargeable? (   )

(6) What would be its amount? (   )

(7) On what day would a yet larger "Commission" begin to be chargeable? (   )

(8) What would be its amount? (   )

(9) Taking the Rule as consisting of all 3 clauses, in *which* of the above-named 3 "periods" does clause (c) first begin to take effect? (   )

(10) *Which* day, of any "period", is the earliest on which it can be said that a "portion" of the "period" has elapsed? (   )

(11) On what day would the lowest "Commission" begin to be chargeable? (   )

(12) What would be its amount? (   )

(13) On what day would a larger "Commission" begin to be chargeable? (   )

(14) What would be its amount? (   )

(15) On what day would a yet larger "Commission" begin to be chargeable? (   )

(16) What would be its amount? (   )

Signature...............................

Date...............................

THE Rule is given, below, in a form which exhibits its grammatical construction—

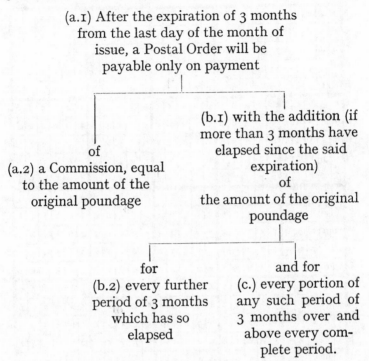

(a.1) After the expiration of 3 months from the last day of the month of issue, a Postal Order will be payable only on payment

of
(a.2) a Commission, equal to the amount of the original poundage

(b.1) with the addition (if more than 3 months have elapsed since the said expiration) of the amount of the original poundage

for
(b.2) every further period of 3 months which has so elapsed

and for
(c.) every portion of any such period of 3 months over and above every complete period.

THE ALPHABET-CIPHER

	A	B	C	D	E	F	G	H	I	J	K	L	M	N	O	P	Q	R	S	T	U	V	W	X	Y	Z	
A	a	b	c	d	e	f	g	h	i	j	k	l	m	n	o	p	q	r	s	t	u	v	w	x	y	z	A
B	b	c	d	e	f	g	h	i	j	k	l	m	n	o	p	q	r	s	t	u	v	w	x	y	z	a	B
C	c	d	e	f	g	h	i	j	k	l	m	n	o	p	q	r	s	t	u	v	w	x	y	z	a	b	C
D	d	e	f	g	h	i	j	k	l	m	n	o	p	q	r	s	t	u	v	w	x	y	z	a	b	c	D
E	e	f	g	h	i	j	k	l	m	n	o	p	q	r	s	t	u	v	w	x	y	z	a	b	c	d	E
F	f	g	h	i	j	k	l	m	n	o	p	q	r	s	t	u	v	w	x	y	z	a	b	c	d	e	F
G	g	h	i	j	k	l	m	n	o	p	q	r	s	t	u	v	w	x	y	z	a	b	c	d	e	f	G
H	h	i	j	k	l	m	n	o	p	q	r	s	t	u	v	w	x	y	z	a	b	c	d	e	f	g	H
I	i	j	k	l	m	n	o	p	q	r	s	t	u	v	w	x	y	z	a	b	c	d	e	f	g	h	I
J	j	k	l	m	n	o	p	q	r	s	t	u	v	w	x	y	z	a	b	c	d	e	f	g	h	i	J
K	k	l	m	n	o	p	q	r	s	t	u	v	w	x	y	z	a	b	c	d	e	f	g	h	i	j	K
L	l	m	n	o	p	q	r	s	t	u	v	w	x	y	z	a	b	c	d	e	f	g	h	i	j	k	L
M	m	n	o	p	q	r	s	t	u	v	w	x	y	z	a	b	c	d	e	f	g	h	i	j	k	l	M
N	n	o	p	q	r	s	t	u	v	w	x	y	z	a	b	c	d	e	f	g	h	i	j	k	l	m	N
O	o	p	q	r	s	t	u	v	w	x	y	z	a	b	c	d	e	f	g	h	i	j	k	l	m	n	O
P	p	q	r	s	t	u	v	w	x	y	z	a	b	c	d	e	f	g	h	i	j	k	l	m	n	o	P
Q	q	r	s	t	u	v	w	x	y	z	a	b	c	d	e	f	g	h	i	j	k	l	m	n	o	p	Q
R	r	s	t	u	v	w	x	y	z	a	b	c	d	e	f	g	h	i	j	k	l	m	n	o	p	q	R
S	s	t	u	v	w	x	y	z	a	b	c	d	e	f	g	h	i	j	k	l	m	n	o	p	q	r	S
T	t	u	v	w	x	y	z	a	b	c	d	e	f	g	h	i	j	k	l	m	n	o	p	q	r	s	T
U	u	v	w	x	y	z	a	b	c	d	e	f	g	h	i	j	k	l	m	n	o	p	q	r	s	t	U
V	v	w	x	y	z	a	b	c	d	e	f	g	h	i	j	k	l	m	n	o	p	q	r	s	t	u	V
W	w	x	y	z	a	b	c	d	e	f	g	h	i	j	k	l	m	n	o	p	q	r	s	t	u	v	W
X	x	y	z	a	b	c	d	e	f	g	h	i	j	k	l	m	n	o	p	q	r	s	t	u	v	w	X
Y	y	z	a	b	c	d	e	f	g	h	i	j	k	l	m	n	o	p	q	r	s	t	u	v	w	x	Y
Z	z	a	b	c	d	e	f	g	h	i	j	k	l	m	n	o	p	q	r	s	t	u	v	w	x	y	Z
	A	B	C	D	E	F	G	H	I	J	K	L	M	N	O	P	Q	R	S	T	U	V	W	X	Y	Z	

EXPLANATION

EACH column of this table forms a dictionary of symbols
representing the alphabet: thus, in the A column, the

symbol is the same as the letter represented; in the B column, A is represented by B, B by C, and so on.

To use the table, some word or sentence should be agreed on by two correspondents. This may be called the "key-word", or "key-sentence", and should be carried in the memory only.

In sending a message, write the key-word over it, letter for letter, repeating it as often as may be necessary: the letters of the key-word will indicate which column is to be used in translating each letter of the message, the symbols for which should be written underneath: then copy out the symbols only, and destroy the first paper. It will now be impossible for any one, ignorant of the key-word, to decipher the message, even with the help of the table.

For example, let the key-word be *vigilance*, and the message "meet me on Tuesday evening at seven", the first paper will read as follows—

v i g i l a n c e v i g i l a n c e v i g i l a n c e v i
m e e t m e o n t u e s d a y e v e n i n g a t s e v e n
h m k b x e b p x p m y l l y r x i i q t o l t f g z z v

The second will contain only "h m k b x e b p x p m y l
l y r x i i q t o l t f g z z v".

The receiver of the message can, by the same process, retranslate it into English.

N.B.—If this table be lost, it can easily be written out from memory, by observing that the first symbol in each column is the same as the letter naming the column, and that they are continued downwards in alphabetical order. Of course it would only be necessary to write out the particular columns required by the key-word: such a paper, however, should not be preserved, as it would afford means for discovering the key-word.

INTRODUCTION TO
"THE LOST PLUM CAKE"

(In 1897 Lewis Carroll wrote an introduction to "The Lost Plum Cake", a "tale for tiny boys" by E. G. Wilcox. It is completely in character: in its devotion to children, its advice to mothers, its engaging whimsicality, and its childlike preoccupation with the cover. It is a fitting piece for the end of this book because it is the last thing he ever wrote for his beloved children. He died soon afterwards.)

THE writer of the Introduction to a book, who is not himself the author of the book, enjoys one singular privilege —he can discuss its merits with a freedom that very few authors would venture to use: since, however sweet the "blowing one's own trumpet" may sound to the enraptured trumpeter, it is apt to pall on other ears. Let me, then, avail myself of this privilege by saying that I believe Mrs. Egerton Allen has a very special talent for writing books for very young children. Her dialogues have all the vividness of a photograph; and I feel sure that all *real* children—children who have not been spoiled by too much notice, and thus taught to give themselves the airs of little men and women—will like to read the story of tiny "Joey", and will enjoy the clever and sympathetic sketches with which Mrs. Shute has adorned it. It is, I think, a real loss to the thousands of child-readers, for whom so many charming books have been written, that Mrs. Allen's first little book—"Little Humphrey's Adventure"—has been allowed by the Publishers, who hold the copyright of it, to go out of print. It is a *thorough* child's book, and I trust the S.P.C.K. may ere long see their way to issuing another edition of it.

But the writer of this Introduction is not alone in his good fortune: the *reader* of this little book has *also* a singular privilege at his command, in connection with the *cover*, which was designed for it by Miss E. Gertrude

Thomson. Holding the book at the middle point of each side, and turn it about till the light (which should come from *behind* him) causes what look like little hills on the red cover to glitter, he can then fidget it about—he will soon catch the knack—till the gold ornamentation seems to lift itself a good half-inch off the cover; and he can easily persuade his *eye*, if not his intellect, to believe that, in turning the book about, he is causing the gold to cover now one part of the red and now another. It is a really curious optical illusion.

Let me seize this opportunity of saying one earnest word to the mothers into whose hands this little book may chance to come, who are in the habit of taking their children to church with them. However well and reverently those dear little ones have been taught to behave, there is no doubt that so long a period of enforced quietude is a severe tax on their patience. The hymns, perhaps, tax it least: and what a pathetic beauty there is in the sweet fresh voices of the children, and how earnestly they sing! I took a little girl of six to church with me one day: they had told me she could hardly read at all—but she made me find all her places for her! And afterwards I said to her elder sister, "What made you say Barbara couldn't read? Why, I heard her joining in, all through the hymn!" And the little sister gravely replied, "She knows the *tunes*, but not the *words*." Well, to return to my subject—children in church. The lessons and the prayers, are not wholly beyond them: often they can catch little bits that come within the range of their small minds. But the sermons! It goes to one's heart to see, as I so often do, little darlings of five or six years old, forced to sit still through a weary half-hour, with nothing to do, and not one word of sermon that they can understand. Most heartily can I sympathize with the little charity-girl, who is said to have written to some friend, "I thinks, when I grows up, I'll never go to church no more. I thinks I'se getting sermons enough to last me all my life!" But need it be so? Would it be so *very* irreverent to let your child have a story-book to read during the sermon, to while away that tedious half-hour, and to make church-going a bright and happy memory, instead of rousing the thought "I'll never go to church no more?" I think not. For my part, I should love to see the experiment tried. I am quite sure it would be a success. My advice would be to *keep* some books for that special purpose—I would call such books "Sunday-treats"—and your little boy or girl would soon learn to look forward with eager hope to that half-hour, once so tedious. If I were the preacher, dealing with some subject too hard for the little ones, I should love to see them all enjoying their picture-books. And if *this* little book should ever come to be used as a "Sunday-treat" for some sweet baby-reader, I don't think it could serve a better purpose.

LEWIS CARROLL

Christmas, 1897.

INDEX OF FIRST LINES
OF VERSE

A boat, beneath a sunny sky, 250
A is for [Acland], who'd physic the Masses, 826
Alas! she would not hear my prayer! 724, 1110
All in the golden afternoon, 11
A Mother's breast, 843
And cannot pleasures, while they last, 775
"And did you really walk," said I, 748
Around my lonely hearth to-night, 840
"Are you deaf, Father William?" the young man said, 834
As curly-headed Jemmy was sleeping in bed, 735
A short direction, 704
As I was sitting on the hearth, 707
As one who strives a hill to climb, 760
A stick I found that weighed two pound, 733
Ay, 'twas here, on this spot, 795

Beautiful Soup, so rich and green, 103
Beloved Pupil! Tamed by thee, 881
Beneath the waters of the sea, 727
Blow, blow your trumpets till they crack, 807

Child of the pure unclouded brow, 123

"Don't they consult the 'Victims', though?" 756
Dreaming of apples on a wall, 733
Dreams, that elude the Maker's frenzied grasp—, 459

Empress of Art, for thee I twine, 804

Fair stands the ancient Rectory, 712
"First, the fish must be caught," 242
Five fathom square the Belfry frowns, 1034
Five little girls, of Five, Four, Three, Two, One, 789
Five seeing, and seven blind, 736

From his shoulder Hiawatha, 768
From sackcloth couch the Monk arose, 293

Girt with a boyish garb for boyish task, 679

Hark, said the dying man, and sighed, 856
"Heard ye the arrow hurtle in the sky?" 816
He looked again, and found it was, 631
"Here I bee, and here I byde," 1004
Here's to the Freshman of bashful eighteen! 1053
He saw her once, and in the glance, 849
He shouts amain, he shouts again, 837
He steps so lightly to the land, 404
He thought he saw a Banker's Clerk, 306
He thought he saw a Buffalo, 301
He thought he saw a Coach-and-Four, 318
He thought he saw a Garden-Door, 344
He thought he saw a Kangaroo, 314
He thought he saw an Albatross, 342
He thought he saw an Argument, 632
He thought he saw an Elephant, 294
He thought he saw a Rattlesnake, 303
He trilled a carol fresh and free, 776
His barque had perished in the storm, 996
"How shall I be a poet?" 790
Hush-a-by lady, in Alice's lap! 236

I charm in vain: for never again, 842
I dreamt I dwelt in marble halls, 725
If such a thing had been my thought, 706
I have a fairy by my side, 700
I have a horse—a ryghte goode horse—, 768
I'll tell thee everything I can, 225
I love the stillness of the wood, 860
"I'm EMInent in RHYME!" she said, 843
I met an aged, aged man, 727
I never loved a dear Gazelle—, 788
In her eyes is the living light, 861
In Shylock's bargain for the flesh was found, 735
In stature the Manlet was dwarfish—, 605
In the dark silence of an ancient room, 852
"In these degenerate days," we oft hear said, 736

In winter, when the fields are white, 200
I painted her a gushing thing, 811
Is all our Life, then, but a dream, 253
I sing a place wherein agree, 828
Is it the glow of conscious pride—, 1031
I stood within the gate, 872
"It is the lawyer's daughter," 839

John gave his brother James a box, 733
"Just the place for a Snark!" the Bellman cried, 680

King Fisher courted Lady Bird—, 479

"Ladies and Gentlemen" seems stiff and cold, 737
Lady Clara Vere de Vere, 765
Lady dear, if Fairies may, 13
Let craft, ambition, spite, 316
Little Birds are dining, 653
Little maidens, when you look, 827
"Look on the Quadrangle of Christ Church, squarely, for is it
    not a Square?" 1035
Lorenzo dwelt at Heighington, 1002
Love-lighted eyes, that will not start, 835

Maidens, if a maid you meet, 833
"Maidens! if you love the tale," 834
Maiden, though thy heart may quail, 836
Man naturally loves delay, 701
Matilda Jane, you never look, 509
Methought I walked a dismal place, 705
Museum! loveliest building of the plain, 823
"My First—but don't suppose," he said, 745
My First is singular at best, 806
My first lends his aid when I plunge into trade, 842
"My mother bids me bind my hair," 811

Oh, dear beyond our dearest dreams, 384
"Oh, do not forget the day when we met," 809
"Oh pudgy podgy pup!" 838
"Oh, when I was a little Ghost," 752
"One thousand pounds per annum," 569
One winter night, at half-past nine, 741

"Only a woman's hair!" Fling it aside! 868
Our Latin books, in motley row, 876
Our Willie had been sae lang awa', 1041

"Peter is poor," said noble Paul, 331
Puck has fled the haunts of men, 877

Rise, oh, rise! The daylight dies, 367
Round the wondrous globe I wander wild, 832

Said the Moon to the Sun, 734
Say, what is the spell, when her fledgelings are cheeping, 624
See! There are tears upon her face—, 870
"Seek ye Love, ye fairy-sprites?" 837
Seven blind of both eyes, 734
Shall soldiers tread the murderous path of war, 737
"She is gone by the Hilda," 722
She's all my fancy painted him, 723
"Sister, sister, go to bed!" 702
Speak roughly to your little boy, 62

That salmon and sole Puss should think very grand, 735
The air is bright with hues of light, 805
The day was wet, the rain fell souse, 709
The elder and the younger knight, 925
The ladye she stood at her lattice high, 797
The light was faint, and soft the air, 863
The morn was bright, the steeds were light, 867
The night creeps onward, sad and slow, 875
There are certain things—as, a spider, a ghost, 766
There be three Badgers on a mossy stone, 383
There was an old farmer of Readall, 702
There was an ancient City, stricken down, 802
There was a Pig, that sat alone, 329
There was a young lady of station, 843
There were two brothers at Twyford school, 716
The royal MAB, dethroned, discrowned, 836
The sun was shining on the sea, 168
The Youth at Eve had drunk his fill, 721
They passed beneath the College gate, 812
They told me you had been to her, 115
Three children (their names were so fearful, 831

Three little maidens weary of the rail, 828
Three little maids, one winter day, 830
Three sisters at breakfast were feeding the cat, 734
'Tis a melancholy song, and it will not keep you long, 730
'Tis the voice of the Lobster: I heard him declare, 101
To the Looking-Glass world it was Alice that said, 239
'Twas brillig, and the slithy toves, 140
Tweedledum and Tweedledee, 166
Twinkle, twinkle, little bat! 72
'Twixt "Perhaps" and "May Be", 735
Two little girls near London dwell, 833
Two thieves went out to steal one day, 832

Were I to take an iron gun, 703
What hand may wreathe thy natal crown, 838
What is most like a bee in May? 733
"What's this?" I pondered. "Have I slept?" 764
"What though the world be cross and crooky? 995
When . a . y and I . a told . a . . ie they'd seen a, 830
When Maggie once to Oxford came, 844
When midnight mists are creeping, 841
When on the sandy shore I sit, 793
"Wiffie! I'm *sure* that something *is* the matter," 739
With saddest music all day long, 772
"Will you walk a little faster?" said a whiting to a snail, 98
Written by Maggie B——, 848

"You are old, Father William," the young man said, 50
Ytte wes a mirke an dreiry cave, 707